The Criminalization of Mental Illness

The Criminalization of Mental Illness

Crisis and Opportunity for the Justice System

THIRD EDITION

Risdon N. Slate

Kelly Frailing

W. Wesley Johnson

Jacqueline K. Buffington

CAROLINA ACADEMIC PRESS

Durham, North Carolina

LIBRARY OF CONGRESS CATALOGING-IN-PUBLICATION DATA
Names: Slate, Risdon N., author. | Frailing, Kelly, author. |
Johnson, W. Wesley, author. | Buffington, Jacqueline K., author.
Title: The criminalization of mental illness : crisis and opportunity for
the justice system / Risdon N. Slate, Kelly Frailing, W. Wesley Johnson,
Jacqueline K. Buffington.
Description: Third edition. | Durham, North Carolina : Carolina Academic
Press, 2021. | Includes bibliographical references and index.
Identifiers: LCCN 2021017700 (print) | LCCN 2021017701 (ebook) |
ISBN 9781531004422 (paperback) | ISBN 9781531004439 (ebook)
Subjects: LCSH: Insanity (Law)--United States. | Mentally ill--Commitment
and detention--United States. | Mentally ill offenders--United States.
Classification: LCC KF9242 .S59 2021 (print) | LCC KF9242 (ebook) |
DDC 364.3/80973--dc23
LC record available at https://lccn.loc.gov/2021017700
LC ebook record available at https://lccn.loc.gov/2021017701

Carolina Academic Press
700 Kent Street
Durham, North Carolina 27701
(919) 489-7486
www.cap-press.com

Printed in the United States of America

To Claudia and Virginia Slate for your love and support, to Dean Shoe for helping me find my voice, and to Ron Vogel for assisting me in finding the confidence to use it. Martin Luther King, Jr. (1963) said in his book Strength to Love: "The ultimate measure of a man is not where he stands in moments of comfort and convenience but where he stands at times of challenge and controversy. The true neighbor will risk his position, his prestige and even his life for the welfare of others. In dangerous valleys and hazardous pathways, he will lift some bruised and beaten brother to a higher and more noble life" (p. 35). I, Risdon Slate, am that brother, and Ron Hudson is that neighbor. Without Ron's courageous, selfless, and innovative actions this book would likely never have been written. — RNS

To Jay and Matilda Reese for their love, to my colleagues at Loyola University New Orleans for their encouragement and for their enthusiastic embrace of the criminalization of mental illness as a topic worthy of inclusion in our curriculum, and to the women and men who work tirelessly, often with little respite or recognition, to support people with mental illness. — KF

To my family and friends who have ridden with me on the roller coaster of life, to the many caring professionals in the mental health and criminal justice systems that are dedicated to people that are troubled by their own thoughts, to members of the National Alliance of Mental Illness for decades of hard work and advocacy, and to my wife, Jennifer Ingram Johnson, who has helped me address issues surrounding my own mental health and help me advocate for the rights of all. — WWJ

To the men and women at the state hospitals and jails who allowed me into their lives, enabled me to see through their eyes the problems with the system, and motivated me to change it. — JKB

Contents

Foreword

*H. Richard Lamb, MD**

The enormously increased presence of persons with serious mental illness in the criminal justice system is one of the great problems of our time. Estimates place the number at 360,000 or more incarcerated in the U.S. at any given time. As a result, mental health professionals and society generally have become much more concerned about the number of persons with serious mental illness in jails and prisons, as well as the treatment provided to these persons, both while incarcerated and after release. These issues are relatively recent. Reports of large numbers of persons with mental illness in U.S. jails and prisons began appearing in the 1970s, a phenomenon that had not been reported since the nineteenth century.

Criminalization of persons with serious mental illness is a subject of enormous complexity in terms of understanding how it came about, the problems that these mentally ill persons face in our jails and prisons and how to confront these problems, how to reverse criminalization and how to treat these persons in the community, either after release or, if possible, before they have been criminalized. Drs. Slate, Buffington-Vollum, and Johnson have chosen to present a comprehensive summary of these issues so that our understanding is deepened and our knowledge of what needs to be done is clarified.

One of the major concerns in present-day psychiatry is that placement in the criminal justice system poses a number of important problems and obstacles for the treatment and rehabilitation of persons with serious mental illness. Even when quality psychiatric care is provided in jails and prisons, the inmate/patient still has been doubly stigmatized as both a mentally ill person and a criminal. Furthermore, jails and prisons have been established to mete out punishment and to protect society, their primary mission and goals are not to provide treatment. The correctional facility's overriding need to maintain order and security, as well as its mandate to implement

---

* Dr. Lamb was Professor Emeritus of Psychiatry, Keck School of Medicine, University of Southern California, and authored the foreword for the second edition of *The Criminalization of Mental Illness: Crisis and Opportunity for the Justice System*. Since the publication of the second edition, Dr. Lamb passed away. He was a pioneer in terms of research regarding the criminalization of mental illness. Though some things have changed (e.g., estimates place the number of those incarcerated with a mental illness higher now, near 500,000, and Dr. Kelly Frailing has stepped in as second author of this book and Dr. Johnson as third), Dr. Lamb's words still ring true and are arguably even more consequential today, and we have included them again.

society's priorities of punishment and social control, greatly restrict the facility's ability to establish a therapeutic milieu and provide all the necessary interventions to treat mental illness successfully.

After giving an exceptionally clear picture of how we have reached the sorry state of the present-day criminalization of persons with serious mental illness, the authors of this book present a detailed description of what needs to be done by law enforcement, by custody staff in jails and prisons, by the courts, by probation and parole, by mental health professionals, by families, and by society generally. Important subjects in the efforts to decrease criminalization, such as the police as first responders and police Crisis Intervention Teams, Mental Health Courts, Assertive Community Treatment, Assisted Outpatient Treatment, the role of substance abuse and how to deal with it, and reentry strategies for persons with serious mental illness are described with clarity and in detail.

This book is a very important contribution to the literature and to the understanding of a problem which should never have been allowed to happen in a Country like ours. The authors are to be highly commended for the immense amount of work that went into writing it.

Acknowledgments

We offer a special thank you to Dick Lamb, posthumously, for writing the foreword that we are including to this edition of the book. Hank Steadman wrote the foreword to the first edition, and he is now retired. Between these two gentlemen, we cannot think of any more admirable contributors to the study of the criminalization of mental illness. These men have devoted their professional lives to researching and seeking reasoned solutions to the intractable problems surrounding the interface of the mental health and criminal justice systems. We applaud their efforts.

We would like to thank our friends and colleagues who have provided understanding and/or levity during this project. On the home front, Claudia Slate provided comfort and expert editing skills. Jay and Matilda Reese provided delightfully random breaks from the work, mostly in the form of humor, but alas also in the form of emergent homeschool issues that were less fun, to put it mildly. Also, we are indebted to the Carolina Academic Press team, especially Beth Hall, Steve Oliva, and TJ Smithers for expert handling and guidance during this process.

We appreciate Paul Gormley's contribution to the chapter on competency and insanity. In addition, various professionals submitted significant input regarding their personal experiences with the interface of the mental health and criminal justice systems. We are pleased to include these offerings from Scott Anders, Steven Bacallao, Sam Cochran, Lee Cohen, Angela Cowden, Doug Dretke, Steve Feinstein, Howard Finkelstein, Susan Flood, Brian Garrett, Brian Haas, Mark Heath, Marcia Hirsch, Stephen Hudak, Chris Jordan, Ginger Lerner-Wren, Barbara Lewis, Jose Lopez, Janeice Martin, Paul Michaud, Joseph Mucenski, Stephanie Rhoades, Jack Richards, Jim Rice, Tony Rolón, Denise Spratt, Jon Stanley, Arlene Stoltz, Mike Thompson, L. Wall, George Welch, Anne Marie Wendel, Joyce Wilde, Kendall Wiley, Michael Zabarsky, and Derek Zimmerman.

Thanks also to Grady Judd for his commitment to CIT training and willingness to explore alternatives to the incarceration of persons with mental illnesses. Stephen Bacallao and Peggy Symons are to be commended for their tenacity and sharing their bureaucratic battle with us. In addition, Kristie Blevins and Irina Soderstrom demonstrated professional collegiality by sharing their cutting-edge research with us for inclusion in the book, and we appreciate them and their work. We also appreciate the statements of support reflected on the back cover of our book offered by Ginger Lerner-Wren and Michael Perlin.

Last but not least, we appreciate the efforts of all of our students who have assisted in editing this book. Elia Mattke did a superb job of conducting research to update this edition of the book. Kaitlyn Manning and Whitney McBay did a superlative job of double and in many cases triple checking citation and references for accuracy and for appropriateness for inclusion.

The Criminalization of
Mental Illness

Chapter 1

Introduction

"The world breaks everyone and afterward many are strong at the broken places."

— Ernest Hemingway[1]

According to the most recent, comprehensive epidemiological study of mental illness in the United States, nearly one in five individuals has a diagnosable mental illness over the span of a year (NIMH, 2021). Approximately 5.2% have a serious mental illness (Kessler et al., 2005; NIMH, 2012, NIMH, 2021). Think about this the next time that you are on a commercial airline flight: as you look at the individuals sitting on your row, the probability is that one of you has a mental disorder, possibly even a serious mental illness. Of course, unless it is you, you will probably never know which of the people you encounter in your daily life is mentally ill. Indeed, people with mental illnesses are not physically different, and most people with mental illnesses do not exhibit noticeable abnormal behavior. Many are highly successful people — among them, psychiatrists and psychologists, lawyers and judges, businessmen and women, and even professors. Yet, the stigma imposed by our society upon persons with mental illnesses often prevents them from publicly acknowledging their diagnosis.

From the perspective of the criminal justice system, the substantial (and rising) prevalence of mental illness is noteworthy, given that those with mental illnesses are significantly more likely to come into contact with the criminal justice system (Council of State Governments, 2002). Indeed, as Stone (1997, p. 286) articulated,

> There is no more complicated or intractable a problem within criminal justice than that posed by the needs of persons with severe mental disorders, and ... the failure to rationally respond to the issues raised by the incarceration of persons with severe mental disorders results in the unfair and disproportionate criminalization of persons with severe disorders.

This complicated problem, along with possible solutions, is the primary focal point of this book.

---

1. Hemingway (1929, p. 249).

Defining Serious Mental Illness

Before proceeding, it is important to clarify what is meant by "serious mental illnesses." This is imperative not only because there is a great deal of misinformation that contributes to misunderstanding of, misconception about, and ultimately, to stigma regarding these illnesses, but also because it is these illnesses that form the focus of this book. In the coming chapters, unless otherwise indicated, the focus is on people with serious mental illnesses — often referred to as "severe" or "serious and persistent" mental illness — in contrast to those with mental illnesses that are less severe.[2]

The disorders that typically fall within this category are schizophrenia, schizoaffective disorder, bipolar disorder, and major depression with psychotic features,[3] as defined by the American Psychiatric Association's Diagnostic and Statistical Manual (DSM).[4] Each of these disorders will be defined below. The categories of symptoms within the disorders are differentiated here because some studies in the book will make reference to these categories.

Schizophrenia

Schizophrenia is a severe disorder of thought and perception, with accompanying disturbance in mood and behavior. Schizophrenia affects approximately 0.25% to 0.64% of adults in the U.S. general population,[5] where schizophrenia is estimated to affect 0.33% to 0.75% of individuals internationally (NIMH, 2018). Schizophrenia is characterized by psychosis or a loss of touch with reality, comprising the following symptoms:

- *Hallucinations* — False sensory perceptions. Although the most common type of hallucination is auditory (e.g., "hearing voices" that are not reality-

---

2. Certainly, individuals with almost any mental illness subjectively experience distress, discomfort, and, at least, a disruption in functioning. In this sense, the descriptor "serious" primarily refers to the severity and distance from "normal" experience of symptoms.

3. The DSM is currently in the fifth edition.

4. In some classifications, "uncomplicated" major depression (i.e., without psychosis), post-traumatic stress disorder (PTSD), and even panic disorder, obsessive-compulsive disorder (OCD), and borderline personality disorder are included (National Alliance on Mental Illness, n.d.). However, these will not be discussed here, as we are primarily focusing on the four mentioned above. Moreover, contrary to popular perception, despite receiving widespread attention from the media, disorders such as psychopathy (a personality disorder characterized by impulsivity, irresponsibility, callousness, remorselessness, and in most cases, criminal behavior) and, recently, Asperger's Disorder (a neurodevelopmental disorder that falls on the autism spectrum and is characterized by relatively high functioning but impaired interpersonal understanding and responsiveness) do *not* constitute serious mental illness.

5. Although prevalence estimates vary by study, those included here are judged by NIMH (2018) to be the "best" statistics available in the literature at this time.

based), hallucinations can affect any of the senses: vision, touch, and even smell and taste.

- *Delusions* — Fixed, false beliefs that are held despite impossibility. They are very strongly held and are resistant to reason or attempts at persuasion from others. The most common type of delusion — and the one most involved in cases in which a person with mental illness commits an act of violence (Elbogen & Johnson, 2009) — is paranoid/persecutory, which can manifest itself in the belief that one is in danger or threatened. Paranoid delusions frequently have a specific focus or an object (e.g., a particular person, group [e.g., the FBI], or entity [e.g., the devil]) that one perceives to be threatening him/her. Other common themes of delusions are grandiose, such as the belief that one is a special person or has special abilities, acquaintances, etc.; control delusions, the belief that one's thoughts, feelings, or actions are being controlled by another; and religious delusions.

- *Cognitive disorganization* — A cluster of symptoms regarded by experts as the crux of schizophrenia, thought disorder. These symptoms reflect internal cognitive dysfunction and confusion. Although not as well-known as hallucinations or delusions, cognitive disorganization symptoms tend to be the most overtly noticeable to others, particularly in the individual's speech. Most commonly, an individual's ideas tend to be unrelated or slip "off track." In its most extreme form, a person with schizophrenia may produce *word salad*, in which he/she unintentionally combines unrelated words — and in some cases, words that do not appear in the individual's language (*neologisms*) — that when strung together, are incoherent. There are many different symptoms of thought disorganization, which tend to fall at either end of a continuum in the degree of focus of one's thoughts.

- *"Negative" symptoms* — Labeled as such because they represent an absence of experiences that most people without schizophrenia have and/or the individual experienced prior to the onset of his/her illness. These symptoms often resemble depression (and/or substance abuse). They include, among others, social withdrawal or inappropriate social behavior, inability to find the motivation to perform even basic life activities (e.g., attend to one's hygiene), and flat emotions. These symptoms are significant because they are the first to emerge.

- *Anosognosia* — Lack of insight into one's illness or inability to recognize one's symptoms, even when pointed out. It is particularly problematic because it is responsible for failure to obtain or comply with treatment (Amador, 2007). Although commonly perceived to be a psychological defense mechanism or conscious choice to deny one's illness, it actually appears to be related to the disrupted brain chemistry of psychosis (Amador, 2007).

Bipolar Disorder

Bipolar disorder is a mood disorder characterized by extreme highs (mania) and lows (depression) in emotion over time. It is estimated that approximately 4.4% of adults in the general U.S. population will be diagnosed with bipolar disorder at some time in their lives, with 82.9% of these cases being severe (NIMH, 2017).

- *Mania* — Consists of extreme happiness, excitement, and/or irritability; excessive energy, less need for sleep, and restlessness; and inability (or, in some cases, inordinate ability) to concentrate with racing thoughts. Individuals in manic phases tend to engage in excessive goal-directed behavior (e.g., acting on unattainable goals) and, most problematically, pleasurable (e.g., hypersexual) and dangerous activities that are out of character for them.

- *Depression* — Consists of extreme sadness, anxiety, and/or irritability; loss of energy and changes in appetite or sleep; difficulty concentrating and making decisions; and/or having thoughts of suicide.

- *Psychotic symptoms* — Either severe mania or severe depression can involve psychotic features, such as hallucinations and delusions. Individuals in manic episodes tend to have grandiose or euphoric delusions and hallucinations, whereas those in depressed episodes tend to have negative delusions and hallucinations.

Major Depressive Disorder

Major depressive disorder (MDD) is a mood disorder characterized by extended, extreme lows in emotion discussed previously (under *bipolar disorder*); there is no manic component. Individuals with severe MDD may also experience episodes of psychosis. Approximately 7% of adults in the U.S. population will be diagnosed with MDD; 30% of these cases are considered severe (Kessler et al., 2005; NIMH, 2012).

Understanding the types, symptoms and dynamics of mental illness is critical to developing responses that help ameliorate rather than aggravate mental illness. For too long the shroud of shame that veils mental illness has complicated life in our communities. That shroud perpetuates stigma. Stigma kills. It kills those with mental illness, police officers, citizens, families, and communities. It is past time for change.

Prevalence of Mental Illness in the Criminal Justice System

Persons with mental illness are disproportionately represented in the criminal justice system. Compared to U.S. adults with no serious mental illness, a significantly higher proportion of people with a serious mental illness reported recent criminal justice involvement or being arrested at some point in their lives (Kennedy-Hendricks, Huskamp, Rutkow, & Barry, 2016). Persons with mental illnesses have been found to be almost twice as likely as individuals without any known mental illnesses to be arrested for behavior in similar situations (Teplin, 1984). Approximately half of all persons with mental illnesses have been arrested at least once (Solomon & Draine, 1995a; Walsh & Bricourt, 1997; Kennedy-Hendricks, et al., 2016). Indeed, some of these individuals recycle dozens and even hundreds of times in and out of custody within the criminal justice system (Osher, Steadman, & Barr, 2003). However, contrary to media sensationalism, persons with mental illnesses, when arrested, are usually arrested on minor charges (Cuellar, Snowden, & Ewing, 2007).

Individuals with mental illnesses also make up an exceedingly large proportion of the criminal justice population.[6] Although the rates vary slightly, some researchers have assessed the percentage of persons with mental illnesses who are incarcerated in the United States to be from five to eight times greater than the percentage of persons with mental illnesses in free society (Panzer, Broner, & McQuistion, 2001; Stone, 1997; Watson, Hanrahan, Luchins, & Lurigio, 2001) Individuals living in neighborhoods with high prison admission rates were more likely to meet the criteria for a current and lifetime generalized anxiety disorder than those from a neighborhood with a low prison admission rate (Hatzenbuehler, Keyes, Hamilton, Udden, & Galea, 2015). The most commonly cited estimate of the prevalence of mental illness in jails and prisons comes from Ditton's 1999 Bureau of Justice Statistics (BJS) report, which indicated that 7% of federal inmates, 16% of state inmates, and 16% of jail inmates had a mental illness. A study by Steadman, Osher, Robbins, Case, and Samuels (2009), considered by many to be the most methodologically rigorous study in recent years, found results similar to Ditton's findings, with 14.5% of males and 31% of females in jails exhibiting serious mental illness (TAC, 2016). Wilper et al. (2009) obtained slightly higher rates than Ditton (1999) and Steadman et al. (2009), with 15% of federal inmates, 26% of state inmates, and 25% of jail inmates suffering from a mental health condition prior to their arrest. While criticized on methodological grounds that limit its generalizability, a 2006 BJS report by James and Glaze suggested that rates of mental illness soar as high as 45% of federal prisoners, 56% of state prison inmates, and 64% of those housed in jail, with illness rates higher among women than men (Al-Rousan, Rubenstein, Sieleni, Deol, & Wallace, 2017). With that said, these rates are consistent with research in the juvenile justice system, which finds that between 50% and 75% of youthful offenders have mental health problems (Hicks, 2011; Usher, 2012; TAC, 2016).

These heightened rates of serious mental illness are primarily a result of a backlog effect of individuals with mental illnesses entering jails and prisons yet not being released as quickly as those without mental illness. Indeed, research verifies that individuals with mental illnesses have a tendency to remain in custody for longer periods

---

6. As mental illness is most likely to be routinely assessed in jails and prisons, this is the most common setting in which the prevalence of mental illness in the criminal justice system is researched.

of time than those persons brought in on similar charges who are not mentally ill (Solomon & Draine, 1995b; Baron, Draine, & Salzer, 2013).

Overall, more persons with mental illnesses are residing in prisons and jails today than in public psychiatric hospitals (Lamb & Bachrach, 2001; TAC, 2016). There are about 10 times more individuals with serious mental illness are in jails and state prisons than in the remaining state mental hospitals (TAC, 2016). Indeed, this is the greatest reflection of the brokenness of the system and the history underlying it. At this time, the three largest inpatient psychiatric facilities in the country are jails, with the Los Angeles County Jail, Rikers Island Jail in New York City, and the Cook County Jail in Chicago, each individually housing more persons with mental illnesses than any psychiatric institution in the United States (National Public Radio, 2011). Specifically, jails and prisons in the U.S. hold approximately three to five times more individuals with mental illnesses than state psychiatric hospitals do across the country (Leifman, 2001; Lerner-Wren, 2000). As you read this, the largest inpatient psychiatric institution in your home state is very likely a jail or a prison.

Due to lack of access and linkages to treatment in the community, the reality is that for many persons with mental illnesses — especially those who are homeless or uninsured — the only avenue to mental health services is via the criminal justice system (Osher et al., 2003). Gilligan (2001) contends that jails, prisons, and the prison mental hospitals are the last mental hospitals in operation. Thus, treatment of persons with mental illnesses by the criminal justice system reflects both constructive and destructive trends. A constructive trend, if it can be so labeled, is that many jails and prisons are providing at least a modicum of mental health treatment. However, as in Dorothea Dix's time, which will be described in Chapter 2, it is more of a destructive trend: Large numbers of individuals with major mental illnesses are being sent to jails and prisons, an environment that tends to create rather than alleviate the signs and symptoms of mental illness.

Mental Illness and the Criminal Justice System: Defining the Issues

Criminals and/or people with mental illness have been perceived to be toxic waste (see Simon & Feeley, 1995), and law enforcement and jails have traditionally served a cleansing, social sanitation role. Consistent with "broken windows"/order maintenance policing (Wilson & Kelling, 1982), law enforcement sweeps the unsightly rabble off the streets and disposes of it in jails (Austin & Irwin, 2001; Rothman, 1971). The jails, in turn, ensure that the rabble is out of sight and out of mind.

Historically, researchers have tried to differentiate criminals from law-abiding citizens by physical characteristics. They have proposed phrenology, or the study of bumps on the head to identify malformations of the brain that might be linked to crime and aberrant behavior; physiognomy, judging character by facial features; and body type theories, suggesting that certain physical types were more prone to certain types of criminality (Vold, Bernard, & Snipes, 1998). Likewise, persons with mental illnesses have been portrayed as physically different, atavistic (i.e., throwbacks to an earlier evolutionary stage) in nature (see Wahl, 2003).

How comforting it is for the lay public to be able to feel a sense of superiority, by believing that they are physically and mentally more evolved than those maladaptive beings institutionalized in prisons, jails, and asylums. Such a perspective is also palatable to the powers that be, the lawmakers and the policymakers. For the very same reason that Cesare Lombroso is considered the Father of the Positive School of Criminology — as opposed to Guerry and Quetelet, statisticians who blamed social problems on those in power (see Vold et al., 1998) — biological explanations for aberrant behavior resonate more with lawmakers and policymakers than the idea that they need to re-examine how their own social policies may be contributing to the mental health crisis in America. If the problem with mental illness is an inherently biological, genetic, hereditary malady, how can lawmakers and policymakers be considered responsible or blamed?

Certainly, it would also simplify criminal justice professionals' jobs if there were a set of genetic characteristics that facilitated the identification of criminals. At the current time, however, there is no conclusive evidence that people with mental illness are physically different than those without mental illness (Wahl, 2003) or that physical type theories have any substantive relationship to crime causation (Vold et al., 1998). In the absence of such an "easy" approach to criminal justice, we are left with determining how best to treat, manage, and supervise the heterogeneous population of offenders with whom we are faced. Among the most challenging groups of offenders are individuals with mental illness. Such is the focus of the rest of the book.

In Chapter 2, we address the historical handling of persons with mental illnesses, including religious exorcisms, up to today's remaining contributions to stigma. The closing of state hospitals (or deinstitutionalization), seemingly performed with the best of intentions and for the right reasons, is considered in light of the abysmal failure to establish a cohesive network of community mental health treatment and to link persons with mental illnesses to treatment in the community. In turn, trans-institutionalization has occurred, as persons with mental illnesses have fallen through the cracks and had their health-induced aberrant behaviors criminalized, resulting in encounters with criminal justice authorities and often incarceration in the nation's jails and prisons. The traditional criminal justice system, however, tends to look backward, finding fault, assessing blame, and meting out punishment, with little if any thought about the future consequences wrought by the imposition of a sanction on the perpetrator or society (Slate, 2003). One needs to look no further than our system's high recidivism rates to witness this approach. In most instances we could merely flip a coin and do just as well, if not better, at preventing recidivism.

In Chapter 3, the unmet needs and challenges of people with serious mental illness are addressed. Considered by the U.S. Surgeon General (U.S. Department of Health and Human Services, 1999) to be the greatest obstacle for people with mental illness, stigma is discussed in detail. In fact, most of the challenges faced by people with mental illness can be conceptualized within a framework of mental illness stigma, ranging from the macro-level (e.g., structural stigma, public stigma) to the micro-, individual level (e.g., self-stigma, label avoidance). Certainly, stigma — either self-imposed or as a result of structural hindrances — is responsible for many people with mental illness going without treatment, which in turn sets them up to be propelled into the criminal justice system. While most people with mental illness are not violent, this negative stereotype abounds in the minds of the lay public. In Chapter 3, we consider the effect of this stereotype and the media's effect on stigma; but mainly we focus on the difficulties experienced by persons with mental illnesses who do not come to the attention of the media, who often suffer in silence. Those who never make the headlines comprise the bulk of where the work is done with persons with mental illnesses who encounter the criminal justice system but is an area that is seldom illuminated.

The gates to the criminal justice system are open 24 hours a day and the police are its gatekeepers. Law enforcement officers are faced with the daunting task of responding to all disruptions of public order. As such, they are often the first point of contact for persons with mental illnesses in crisis. There are a myriad of reasons that will be explored in this book as to why this is the case. The reality is that police officers are equipped with a vast amount of discretion: They can either escort an individual with mental illness to treatment (either voluntarily or involuntarily) or transport the individual to jail.

In an ideal world, people with mental illness would willingly seek and appreciatively accept treatment. However, in reality, many do not recognize their illness, let alone their need for treatment, leaving some to necessitate involuntary civil commitment. Civil commitment, as part of a notoriously underfunded mental health system, is fraught with issues. Most problematically, inpatient civil commitment deprives people with mental illness — at no fault of their own — of their right to freedom and, many would argue, due process. Alternatives that are intended to be more palatable, such as outpatient commitment have been implemented. However, outpatient commitment, too, has revealed a host of problems. Such is the focus of Chapter 4.

Frequently untrained to work with people with mental illness, law enforcement officers oftentimes find themselves with a lack of alternatives, or a lack of awareness of those alternatives, for resolving situations involving persons with mental illnesses in crisis. Officers are all too aware of the futility of seeking civil commitment and/or arresting people with mental illness and putting them in jail. In both instances, people with mental illness usually return quickly to the community, where they do not receive treatment, and begin the cycle again.

In response, law enforcement agencies across the country have developed and implemented programs in an attempt to divert persons with mental illnesses from the criminal justice system and instead to directly link them to treatment in the community. Regardless of whether these programs involve specialized police training or pairing mental health professionals with police to assist them in responding to crisis calls, the primary goals are ensuring officer, individual, and community safety and preventing persons with mental illnesses from recycling over and over through the criminal justice system. Chapter 5 includes a description of these challenges and these efforts.

Typically, defense attorneys are guided by their clients' wishes — however irrational and short-sighted those desires may be — when embroiled in the adversarial process (Miller, 1997). Usually, the long-range consequences for their clients and society are not considered (Finkelman & Grisso, 1994). This criticism is not limited to defense attorneys, however. Indeed, the entire traditional criminal court system, as it pertains to individuals with mental illness, tends to operate under the same principles. Although ostensibly in the best interests of defendants with mental illness, merely recognizing competency to stand trial and sanity at the time of the offense, without considering long-term mental health needs, fails not only the individual but society. These issues will be considered in Chapter 7.

Winick (1997) has maintained that the traditional criminal defense model does not promote the effective assessment of treatment needs for persons with mental illnesses and is, in fact, anti-therapeutic. As such, Winick (1997, p. 187) proposed a new form of jurisprudence:

> Therapeutic jurisprudence seeks to apply social science to examine law's impact on the mental and physical health of the people it affects. It recognizes that, whether we realize it or not, law functions as a therapeutic agent, bringing about therapeutic or nontherapeutic consequences.

Therapeutic jurisprudence decisions are rendered with concern for the future impact on individuals, relationships, and the community at large long after an individual's contact with the criminal justice system has ended (Slate, 2003).

Specialty courts, such as mental health courts and drug courts, operate with the therapeutic jurisprudence philosophy, as well as the use of "therapeutic leverage" (Lichtenberg, 2012, p. 50) and "caring coercion" (Sharfstein, 2005, p. 3). Armed with these tools, specialty court professionals can link persons with mental illnesses to treatment in the community in an attempt to divert them from further involvement with the criminal justice system. The unique approach of these courts is discussed in Chapter 8.

Challenges posed by the inordinate number of inmates in jails and prisons are addressed in Chapters 6 and 9. Individuals with mental illness frequently enter jail in crisis, after months or even years without community treatment. Moreover, jail and prison inmates with mental illness do not cope well with the stress and conditions of confinement. They are often victimized while in custody, and many times mental health treatment is either unavailable or inadequate. Indeed, many of the case studies referenced in this book are the result of absent or ineffective treatment, either within the community or in the institution. It has long-term ripple effects for individuals, family members, communities and the criminal justice system. While the primary focus of correctional administrators is security, and health care has frequently taken a "back seat" to management and control, there is a growing appreciation for the role of effective treatment in maintaining security and order in institutional settings. These issues and protocols for better handling incarcerated persons with mental illnesses in jail and prison systems will be delineated.

All too often justice-involved persons with mental illnesses return to society without adequate links to treatment in the community. Time and again, persons with mental illnesses are set up to fail upon their release from custody. As a result, these individuals perpetually recycle through the system, to the point that they are often known as "frequent flyers" due to their repeated contact with the criminal justice system. Issues of reentry, discharge planning, and diversion as an alternative to incarceration comprise the core of Chapter 10.

Addressing Persons with Mental Illness in the Criminal Justice System: Successes and Goals for the Future

While the overrepresentation and needs of people with mental illness in the criminal justice system are immense, the optimistic news is that the issues are no longer hidden from view. Indeed, in the past decade, significant strides have been made by professionals at the intersection of the criminal justice and mental health systems. These successful initiatives will be discussed here and highlighted throughout this book.

One of the earliest, and arguably the most significant and concerted, efforts to highlight the challenges and suggest solutions with regard to persons with mental illness in the criminal justice system is known as the Criminal Justice/Mental Health Consensus Project (Abreu & Griffin, 2015). The Council of State Governments partnered with the Association of State Correctional Administrators, the Bazelon Center on Mental Health Law, the Center for Behavioral Health, Justice and Public Policy, the National Association of State Mental Health Program Directors, the Police Research Forum, and the Pretrial Services Resource Center to convene experts and citizens who recognized the importance of addressing this issue. Professionals — including sheriffs, police chiefs, judges, prosecutors, public defenders, court administrators, mental health advocates, mental health providers, county executives, state legislators, consumers of mental health services, families, victim advocates, crime victims, parole officials, parole board members, probation officials, pretrial service administrators, researchers, jail administrators, state corrections directors, correctional mental health providers, substance abuse providers, and state mental health directors — and interested citizens offered input into recommended strategies for both the mental health and criminal justice systems in working with persons with mental illnesses (Wilson & Draine, 2006). Four advisory boards, representing law enforcement,[7] courts, corrections, and mental health, were established to synthesize infor-

---

7. One of the authors of the textbook, Risdon N. Slate, served on the Law Enforcement Advisory Board for the Consensus Project.

mation that resulted in policy statements, exemplary programs, and strategies for implementation targeting various intervention points in the criminal justice system. In 2002, a 430-page report was generated and made available to the public to assist any locality that seeks to develop a program to better serve people with mental illness in the criminal justice system in their area (Wilson & Draine, 2006).[8]

The Criminal Justice/Mental Health Consensus Project continues to this day, with the Justice Center of the Council of State Governments leading the way to seek reform of the mental health and criminal justice systems (see http://consensusproject.org/). Other clearinghouses on the interface between the criminal justice and mental health systems include:

- Substance Abuse and Mental Health Services Administration (see http://www.samhsa.gov/)

- SAMHSA's GAINS Center for Behavioral Health and Justice Transformation (see http://gainscenter.samhsa.gov/)

- Bazelon Center for Mental Health Law (see http://www.bazelon.org/)

- Treatment Advocacy Center (see http://www.treatmentadvocacycenter.org/)

- National Alliance on Mental Illness (see http://www.nami.org/)

- University of Memphis Crisis Intervention Team (CIT) Center (see http://cit.memphis.edu/)

- CIT International (see http://www.citinternational.org/)

Navigating the criminal justice and mental health systems can be a seemingly impossible task. The ability to assist an arrested family member or friend whose current mental state is decompensating through this maze is daunting. The ability of the person with mental illness to do so presents even greater challenges. From the Consensus Project report (Council of State Governments et al., 2002, p. 25), Figure 1 depicts the complexity of processing that persons with mental illnesses face when they encounter these systems.

An off-shoot of the Consensus Project, which has received increasing attention by localities seeking to identify ways to better serve individuals with mental illness in the criminal justice system, is Cross-Systems Mapping based on the Sequential Intercept Model (SIM) (Munetz & Griffin, 2006). The SIM[9] is a visual-conceptual framework of intercept points — similar to the Consensus Project's diagram on the next page — at which communities can organize targeted strategies to strengthen

---

8. This report is available on the Consensus Project website at consensusproject.org/the_report.
9. A graphic illustration of the SIM can be obtained at Munetz and Griffin (2006, p. 545).

Figure 1. A Person with Mental Illness in the Criminal Justice System: A Flowchart of Select Events

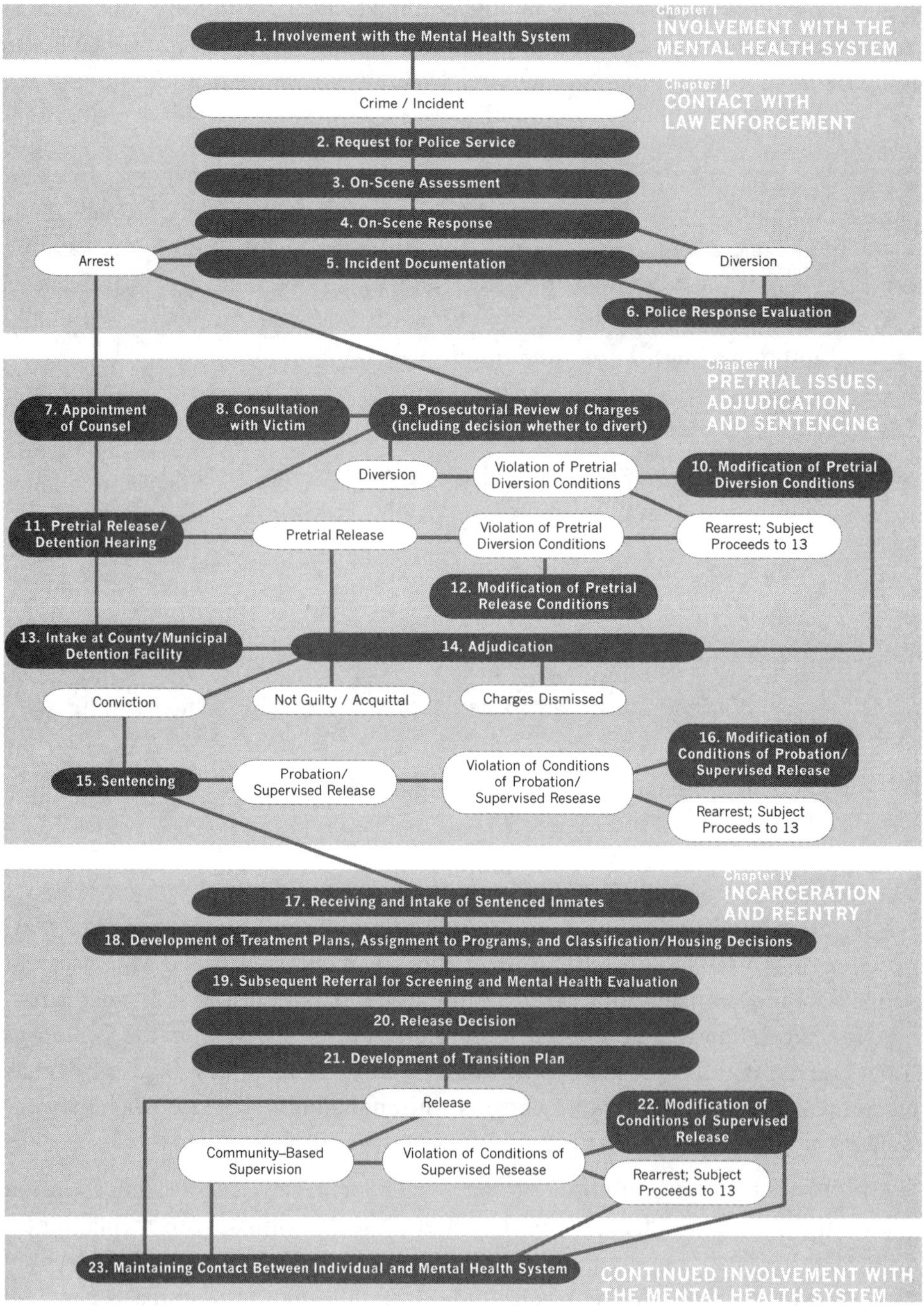

linkages between the criminal justice and mental health systems for the benefit of justice-involved individuals with serious mental illness (Abreu & Griffin, 2015). The purposes of the SIM, in general — and of Cross-Systems Mapping of a particular region — are to help communities understand the big picture of interactions between the criminal justice and mental health systems, identify points in the systems at which to intervene with individuals with mental illness, suggest which populations might be targeted at each point of interception, highlight the likely decision-makers who can authorize movement from the criminal justice system, and identify who needs to be at the table to develop interventions at each point of interception (Abreu & Griffin, 2015). By addressing the problem at the level of each sequential intercept, a community can develop targeted strategies to enhance effectiveness that can evolve over time (Munetz & Griffin, 2006). The Sequential Intercept Model as utilized in Cross Systems Mapping has become a focal point for states and communities to assess available resources, to determine gaps in services, and to strategize a specific plan for community change (Pennsylvania Mental Health and Justice Center for Excellence, 2012). As with the Consensus Project, it is asserted that these activities are best accomplished by a team of stakeholders with local expertise that cross over multiple systems, including mental health, substance abuse, law enforcement, pre-trial services, courts, jails, community corrections, housing, health, social services, and many others (Munetz & Griffin, 2006).

Of course, all the intercept points in the world for diverting persons from the criminal justice system are of little value if practitioners lack insight into the signs and symptoms of mental illness, services are inadequate or nonexistent for referral, and/or practitioners in both the mental health and criminal justice systems are unable or unwilling to collaborate. These are issues that will be discussed throughout the book.

There is much that can be done to help alleviate the burden placed on criminal justice practitioners. There is much that they can learn from mental health professionals and vice versa. However, too often avenues of communication are blocked, and one group blames the other for problems without knowing the other side's perspective. While the criminal justice system receives a significant brunt of the criticism, many of the factors that contribute to persons with mental illnesses being in crises are simply not the fault of the criminal justice system, but rather the result of an inadequate mental health system. Likewise, the mental health system is blamed, but it is notoriously overextended and underfunded by the government, which operates under the hand of a stigmatizing society. Certainly, there is enough blame to go around. However, collaborations between criminal justice and mental health professionals, plus consumers of mental health services and their family members, can be instrumental in influencing reasonable decisions to correct this trend. As will be discussed, among other strategies, cross-training between mental health and criminal justice professionals can serve to knock down barriers to communication and establish common ground as well.

Likewise, a crucial consideration in navigating the handling of persons with mental illnesses is striking the balance between public safety and individual civil liberties. Trying to ensure a harmonious balance between the two can be like trying to maneuver on a quagmire. For example, with limited state hospital beds, *parens patriae*, i.e., the responsibility of the state to protect those who cannot protect themselves, is increasingly implicated. At the same time, the civil liberties of those subjected to compulsory treatment must be considered. All the while, law enforcement struggles to uphold its police power responsibilities. It has been said that it is all right for one to perceive oneself as Napoleon, as long as the individual does not declare war (Levine, 2007). What boundaries can one's behavior cross during crisis before intervention — in either the form of involuntary civil commitment or of arrest and incarceration — is warranted? Ultimately, the challenge to establishing solid public policy is that the answer to this question varies from person to person, depending on one's demographics, political affiliation, and profession, among other attitudinal determinants.

Chinese character wēi
danger

Chinese character jī
(in simplified form)
opportunity

According to modern interpretation, two characters, one symbolizing danger and the other opportunity, represent the word crisis in Mandarin Chinese (Mair, 2007). Indeed, in any crisis there is danger, but there is also, often unrealized, the opportunity for positive change. Many persons with mental illnesses who reach the breaking point, if given the chance, may come to realize what Ernest Hemingway (1929, p. 249) meant when he said, "The world breaks everyone and afterward many are strong at the broken places." Just as individuals can recover from crises, the criminal justice system can also get better.

As Samuel Walker (2006) has noted, sensationalized, celebrated cases often drive policy within the criminal justice system. These cases tend to be the exception rather than the rule. Nevertheless, these aberrations tend to drive policy. In other words, crisis drives policy.

This has certainly been the case — tragedies involving persons with mental illnesses have been instrumental in initiating outpatient commitment statutes, in establishing and implementing police responses to persons in crises with mental illnesses, in creating mental health courts, and in instituting reentry procedures for persons with mental illnesses returning to the community after being in the custody of the criminal justice system. As noted by Borum (2000), such tragedies can result in opportunities for the criminal justice system to develop meaningful solutions. By and large, the influential criminal justice system has stepped to the forefront in capitalizing on crises involving persons with mental illnesses to drive policy. Hopefully, this can be done for the good of all — for the community, in the reduction of future tragedies, as well as for persons with mental illness, in recognizing their civil liberties and connecting them to treatment.

The information in this book is designed to provide the reader with an understanding of the impact that the "criminalization of mental illness" has had on our society. Since the first edition of this book in 2008, there has been a substantial investment in diverting those with mental illness who come into contact with the police into treatment rather than imprisoning them. Those diversions are only possible with the collaboration of law enforcement, hospitals, clinicians, and treatment facilities and staff. For the first time in the lives of these authors, treatment and law enforcement personnel are getting "on the same page." As both prisons and mental hospitals "downsize," greater pressure will be placed on local communities to provide a network of care for individuals experiencing mental illness. The effectiveness (and in some instances, the ineffectiveness) of such collaborations will be a primary focus of the information in the following chapters.

The experiences of our past provide us with clear evidence that it is much cheaper to treat mental illness than to "pay" for the direct and indirect costs of crises. Crises like the shooting of President Reagan and, more recently, Columbine, Virginia Tech, the shooting of former U.S. Representative Gabrielle Giffords, the theater shooting in Aurora, Colorado, and the elementary school shootings in Newtown, Connecticut, will forever be etched in U.S. history. Crisis will always drive policy. However, only effective, proactive policy can improve life for all in our individual communities. While there is much work that has been done, there is still a long way to go to correct the many injustices of our past and present concerning the intersection of criminal justice and mental health.

References

Abreu, D., & Griffin, P. (2015). *Bridging the gaps between criminal justice and mental health summit*. New York, NY: Policy Research Associates.

Al-Rousan, T., Rubenstein, L., Sieleni, B., Deol, H. & Wallace. R. (2017). Inside the nation's largest mental health institution: A prevalence study in a state prison system. *BMC Public Health, 17*, 342–351.

Amador, X. (2007). *I am not sick. I don't need help! How to help someone with a mental illness accept treatment* (2nd ed.) Peconic, NY: Vida Press.

American Psychiatric Association. (2013). *Diagnostic and statistical manual of mental disorders — Fifth edition*. Washington, DC: Author.

Austin, J., & Irwin, J. (2001). *It's about time: America's imprisonment binge* (3rd ed.) Belmont, CA: Wadsworth.

Baron, R., Draine, J., & Salzer, M. (2013). "I'm not sure that I can figure out how to do that": Pursuit of work among people with mental illnesses leaving jail. *American Journal of Psychiatric Rehabilitation, 16*, 115–135.

Borum, R. (2000). Improving high-risk encounters between people with mental illness and the police. *The Journal of the American Academy of Psychiatry and the Law, 28*, 332–337.

Council of State Governments. (2002). *Fact sheet: Mental illness and jails*. New York, NY: Author. Retrieved from http://consensusproject.org/downloads/fact_jails.pdf.

Council of State Governments, Police Executive Research Forum, Pretrial Services Resource Center, Association of State Correctional Administrators, Bazelon Center for Mental Health Law, & the Center for Behavioral Health, Justice, and Public Policy. (2002). *Criminal Justice/Mental Health Consensus Project*. New York, NY: Council of State Governments. Retrieved from consensusproject.org/the_report.

Cuellar, A. E., Snowden, L. M., & Ewing, T. (2007). Criminal records of persons served in the public mental health system. *Psychiatric Services, 58*(1), 114–120.

Ditton, P. M. (1999, July). *Special report: Mental health treatment of inmates and probationers* (NCJ 174463). Washington, D.C.: U.S. Department of Justice, Bureau of Justice Statistics. Retrieved from http://bjs.ojp.usdoj.gov/index.cfm?ty=pbdetail&iid=787.

Elbogen, E. B., & Johnson, S. C. (2009). The intricate link between violence and mental disorder: Results from the National Epidemiologic Survey on Alcohol and Related Conditions. *Archives of General Psychiatry, 66*(2), 152–161.

Finkelman, D., & Grisso, T. (1994). Therapeutic jurisprudence: From idea to application. *New England Journal on Criminal and Civil Confinement, 20*, 243–257.

Gilligan, J. (2001). The last mental hospital, *Psychiatric Quarterly, 2*, 45–77.

Hatzenbuehler, M., Keyes, K., Hamilton, A., Udden, M., & Galea, S. (2015). The collateral damage of mass incarceration: Risk of psychiatric morbidity among non-incarcerated residents of high-incarceration neighborhoods. *American Journal of Public Health, 105*, 138–143.

Hemingway, E. (1929). *A farewell to arms*. New York, NY: Scribner.

Hicks, S. S. (2011). Behind prison walls: The failing treatment choice for mentally ill minority youth. *Hofstra Law Review, 39*, 979–1010.

James, D. J., & Glaze, L. E. (2006, September). *Special report: Mental health problems of prison and jail inmates* (NCJ 213600). Washington, D.C.: U.S. Department of Justice, Bureau of Justice Statistics. Retrieved from http://bjs.ojp.usdoj.gov/content/pub/pdf/mhppji.pdf.

Kennedy-Hendricks, A., Huskamp, H., Rutkow, L., & Barry, C. (2016). Improving access to care and reducing involvement in the criminal justice system for people with mental illness. *Health Affairs, 35*, 1076–1083.

Kessler, R. C., Chiu, W. T., Demler, O., & Walters, E. E. (2005). Prevalence, severity, and comorbidity of twelve-month DSM-IV disorders in the National Comorbidity Survey Replication (NCS-R). *Archives of General Psychiatry, 62*(6), 617–27.

Lamb, H. R., & Bachrach, L. L. (2001). Some perspectives on deinstitutionalization. *Psychiatric Services, 52*(8), 1039–1043.

Leifman, S. (2001, August 16). Mentally ill and in jail. *The Washington Post*, p. A25.

Lerner-Wren, G. (2000). Broward's mental health court: An innovative approach to the mentally disabled in the criminal justice system. *Community Mental Health Report, 1*(1), 5–6, 16.

Levine, A. (2007). *Institutional madness: As South Florida's mental health system spirals out of control, troubled minds are meeting tragic, preventable ends.* Retrieved from http://artlevine.blogspot.com/articles/Institutional%20Madness.htm.

Lichtenberg, J. D. (2012). Therapeutic action: Old and new explanations of therapeutic leverage. *Psychoanalytic Inquiry: A Topical Journal for Mental Health Professionals, 32*(1), 50–59.

Mair, V. H. (2007). danger + opportunity crisis: How a misunderstanding about Chinese characters has led many astray. A guide to the writing of Mandarin Chinese in Romanization. Retrieved from http://www.pinyin.info/chinese/crisis.html.

Miller, R. D. (1997). Symposium on coercion: An interdisciplinary examination of coercion, exploitation, and the law: III. Coerced confinement and treatment: The continuum of coercion: Constitutional and clinical considerations in the treatment of mentally disordered persons. *Denver University Law Review, 74,* 1169–1214.

Munetz, M. R., & Griffin, P. A. (2006). Use of the Sequential Intercept Model as an approach to decriminalization of people with serious mental illness. *Psychiatric Services, 57*(4), 544–549.

NIMH (2017). National Institutes of Mental Health Mental Health Information: Bipolar Disorder. Retrieved from: https://www.nimh.nih.gov/health/statistics/bipolar-disorder.shtml.

NIMH. (2018). National Institutes of Mental Health Mental Health Information: Schizophrenia. Retrieved from: https://www.nimh.nih.gov/health/statistics/schizophrenia.shtml.

NIMH. (2021). National Institutes of Mental Health Mental Illness Statistics. Retrieved from: https://www.nimh.nih.gov/health/statistics/mental-illness.shtml.

National Institute of Mental Health. (n.d.). *Statistics.* Rockville, MD: Author. Retrieved from http://www.nimh.nih.gov/statistics/index.shtml.

National Institute of Mental Health. (2012, September 12). *The numbers count: Mental disorders in America.* Rockville, MD: Author. Retrieved from http://www.nimh.nih.gov/health/publications/the-numbers-count-mental-disorders-in-america/index.shtml#Intro.

National Public Radio. (2011, September 4). *Nation's jails struggle with mentally ill prisoners*. Washington, D.C.: Author. Retrieved from http://www.npr.org/2011/ 09/04/140167676/nations-jails-struggle-with-mentally-ill-prisoners.

Osher, F., Steadman, H. J., & Barr, H. (2003). A best practice approach to community reentry from jails for inmates with co-occurring disorders: The APIC model. *Crime & Delinquency, 49*(1), 79–96.

Panzer, P. G., Broner, N., & McQuistion, H. L. (2001). Mentally ill populations in jails and prisons: A misuse of resources. *Psychiatric Quarterly, 72*(1), 41–43.

Pennsylvania Mental Health and Justice Center for Excellence. (2012). *Cross Systems Mapping training*. Pittsburgh, PA: Author. Retrieved from http://www.pacenterof excellence.pitt.edu/cross_system.html.

Rothman, D. J. (1971). *The discovery of the asylum: Social order and disorder in the new republic*. Boston, MA: Little Brown.

Sharfstein, S. (2005, September 2). Individual rights must be balanced with 'caring coercion.' *Psychiatric News, 40*(17), 3.

Simon, J., & Feeley, M. (1995). True crime: The new penology and public discourse on crime. In T. Blomberg & S. Cohen (Eds.), *Punishment and social control*. New York, NY: Aldine de Gruyter.

Slate, R. N. (2003). From the jailhouse to Capitol Hill: Impacting mental health court legislation and defining what constitutes a mental health court. *Crime & Delinquency, 49*(1), 6–29.

Solomon, P., & Draine, J. (1995a). Issues in serving the forensic client. *Social Work, 40*(1), 25–33.

Solomon, P., & Draine, J. (1995b). Jail recidivism in a forensic case management program. *Health and Social Work, 20*(3), 167–173.

Stone, T. H. (1997). Therapeutic implications of incarceration for persons with severe mental disorders: Searching for rational health policy. *American Journal of Criminal Law, 24*, 283–358.

Steadman, H. J., Osher, F. C., Robbins, P. C., Case, B., & Samuels, S. (2009). Prevalence of serious mental illness among jail inmates. *Psychiatric Services, 60*(6), 761–765.

TAC. (2016). Serious mental illness (SMI) prevalence in jails and prisons. Treatment Advocacy Center. Retrieved from: https://www.treatmentadvocacycenter.org/ evidence-and-research/learn-more-about/3695.

Teplin, L. A. (1984). Criminalizing mental disorder: The comparative arrest rate of the mentally ill. *American Psychologist, 39*(7), 794–803.

U.S. Department of Health and Human Services. (1999). *Mental health: A report of the Surgeon General*. Rockville, MD: U.S. Department of Health and Human Services, Substance Abuse and Mental Health Services Administration, Center for Mental Health Services.

Usher, L. (2012). Unlikely allies in the fight for mental health services: Criminal justice leaders speak out. *NAMI Advocate, 10*(3), 20–21.

Vold, G. B., Bernard, T. J., & Snipes, J. B. (1998). *Theoretical criminology* (4th ed.). New York, NY: Oxford University Press.

Wahl, O. F. (2003). *Media madness: Public images of mental illness.* New Brunswick, NJ: Rutgers University Press.

Walker, S. (2006). *Sense and non-sense about crime and drugs: A policy guide* (6th ed.). Belmont, CA: Thomson-Wadsworth.

Walsh, J., & Bricourt, J. (1997, July–August). Services for persons with mental illness in jail: Implications for family involvement. *Families in Society: The Journal of Contemporary Human Services, 78*(4), 420–428.

Watson, A., Hanrahan, P., Luchins, D., & Lurigio, A. (2001). Mental health courts and the complex issue of mentally ill offenders. *Psychiatric Services, 52*(4), 477–481.

Wilper, A. P., Woolhandler, S., Boyd, J. W., Lasser, K. E., McCormick, M. D., Bor, D. H., & Himmelstein, D. U. (2009). The health and health care of U.S. prisoners: Results of a nationwide survey. *American Journal of Public Health, 99*, 666–672.

Wilson, A. B., & Draine, J. (2006). Collaborations between mental health and criminal justice systems for prisoner reentry. *Psychiatric Services, 57*, 875–878.

Wilson, J. Q., & Kelling, G. L. (1982). Broken windows. *Atlantic Monthly, 249*(3), 29–38.

Winick, B. J. (1997). The jurisprudence of therapeutic jurisprudence. *Psychology, Public Policy and Law, 3*, 184–206.

World Health Organization. (2012). Schizophrenia. *Mental health.* Geneva, Switzerland: Author. Retrieved from http://www.who.int/mental_health/management/schizophrenia/en/.

Chapter 2

The History of Criminalization of Persons with Mental Illnesses

"If I am cold, they are cold; if I am weary, they are distressed; if I am alone, they are abandoned and cast out."

— Dorothea Dix[1]

The maintenance of order in society is a dynamic, yet tenuous, process that involves an infinite number of social, cultural, political, and economic factors. It also involves the morale, vitality, and mental health of communities and of the individuals within communities. Reciprocally, the manner in which order is maintained impacts the morale, vitality, and mental health of individuals and communities. Less privileged classes, in particular — women, racial minorities, children, immigrants, criminals, and persons with mental illnesses — suffer severe mental and emotional distress from repressive justice practices.

Perceptions of people with mental illness and attitudes about their care, treatment, and/or control have vacillated since the beginning of recorded history (Stavis, 1995). During some periods of time, the public has believed that people suffer from mental illness at no fault of their own and deserve humane and empathetic treatment; alternately, society has blamed, punished, and dehumanized those with mental illness.[2] Likewise, there have been alternating periods of institutionalization — the most intrusive form of state intervention, second only to capital punishment — and deinstitutionalization of persons with mental illness (Johnson, 2011).

The struggle to find the "right" balance between care and control has been exacerbated by the difficulty in discerning who "has" a "mental illness," who "is" a "criminal," and who is a combination of the two. These judgments have not only been shaped by sociocultural, political, and economic factors but also by advancements in the fields of science, medicine, and psychology. This chapter examines the evolution of these factors on the care, treatment, and/or control of persons with mental illnesses.

---

1. As cited in Ghareeb (n.d., p. 1).
2. Even within a single time period, members of the general population differ in their beliefs about these issues.

Early World History of Mental Illness

Pre-Civilization

The perceived causes and appropriate treatment/management of mental illness have been matters of debate since the earliest human societies. Dating back to the Stone Age, early tribal groups attributed disturbed behavior to evil spirits,[3] and the management of those with mental illness fell to the family or clan (Ebert, 1999). Archeological findings from 7,000 to 8,000 years ago suggest that one form of treatment included trephination, or removing parts of an individual's skull, in order to expose the brain to release the spirits (Prioreschi, 1991).

Prior to the development of formal governments, the management of people with mental illness was solely a family/clan responsibility (Ebert, 1999). The management of clans was usually the responsibility of elder relatives. Individuals who threatened the well-being of the clan who could not be managed by the family were ultimately banished. Considering the importance of the group for the purposes of eating and defense, this equated with death (Ebert, 1999).

The Ancient Civilizations

Philosophers in ancient Greece were the first to document their perspectives on the mind and mental illness. Plato (429–347 BC) proposed that the body and soul were distinct, yet interdependent, entities (Kraut, 2012); and he believed that the brain was the center of mental processes (Timeline of psychology, 2003). Hippocrates (460–377 BC), who is regarded as the father of modern medicine, argued that malfunctioning physiology — specifically, imbalances in the body's fluids, such as phlegm and bile — was the basis of mental illness, despite concurring with Plato's conceptualization of the brain as the core of mental processes. Hippocrates wrote a cogent description of behavior as a result of mental disturbance: "Those who are mad from phlegm are quiet, and do not cry out nor make a noise; but those from bile are vociferous, malignant, and will not be quiet, but are always doing something improper. If the madness be constant, these are the causes of it" (Hippocrates, Adams, & Sydenham Society, 1849, p. 344). He was the first to identify conditions that are now regarded as mental illnesses, such as phobias, anxiety, depression, and mania. Given his conceptualization of mental illness as being centered in the body, rather than the brain, he argued the conditions were best treated with laxatives and surgery to cleanse the body of impurities. Overall, unlike those in the pre-civilization era and even in later time periods, the Greeks and Romans believed that the mentally ill were people with an illness, who should be humanely cared for in a comfortable, sanitary, well-lighted place (Brakel & Rock, 1971).

Formal governing bodies began to develop, initially along blood lines. While families were still the first line of care, treatment, and control for people with mental ill-

---

3. Interestingly, this perspective would show a resurgence millennia later, when religions became powerful institutions in society, as will be discussed below.

ness, governments became more involved. These trends were evident in the early Greek and Roman civilizations. The Romans, for example, appointed a "curator" or guardian to a person with mental illness in order to safeguard the person's property. The guardian's decisions were to be guided by the wishes of the individual with mental illness during lucid moments; legal proceedings were held as necessary to debate the individual's true intentions (Brakel & Rock, 1971).

The Middle Ages

During the Middle Ages, religious institutions became entwined with governments. Most relevant to Western civilization was the teaming of the Catholic Church and ruling monarchies. Undoubtedly due to the church's influence, demonology predominated as an explanation for abnormal behavior and mental illness (Suich, 2005). The belief in demonology affected both the "diagnosis" and "treatment" of those identified to be possessed (Suich, 2005). For example, the Egyptians looked for spots on the skin, *stigmata diablo* (devil spots), to identify individuals who were possessed by demonic spirits, and magical charms and incantations were used to exorcise them (Suich, 2005).[4] In Judaic folklore, it was believed that a *dybbuk,* an evil or doomed spirit, possesses a victim and brings about mental illness; and they must be expelled and either redeemed or sent to hell (Suich, 2005). Hindus, too, historically practiced exorcism rituals through such means as blowing cow dung smoke, burning pig excreta, reciting prayers or mantras, pulling the victim's hair, or otherwise beating the individual (Suich, 2005).[5]

Both the teaming monarchies and church amassed great amounts of wealth, at the expense of the poor masses (White, 1888). Such an imbalance of economic power enabled the monarchy and church to impose their will on the populace, which, in turn, enabled them to accumulate even more wealth, creating a self-perpetuating cycle. Laws set out to regulate human behavior clearly reflected and reinforced notions of salvation, spiritual conversion, and allegiance to the rituals of the church; and they were often enforced through violent means. Specifically, when individuals refused or were incapable of comporting their behavior to the prevailing moral code of the church, governments quickly used torture and/or execution (Ebert, 1999). Such acts

---

4. As will be discussed in Chapter 3, the eventual derivative concept, stigma, is a critically relevant concept with regard to the treatment of those with mental illness today.

5. As outdated as these practices may seem, the use of exorcisms to remove demons is not completely a treatment of the past. In 2000, a Reverend envisioned that six inhabitants of the Kingsboro Psychiatric Center were possessed by demons and offered a discount rate for the expulsion of the demons (Cohen, 2000). However, when challenged, the court concluded that no responsible jury could perceive the hiring of the Reverend as an exorcist as reasonable medical care (*Lambert v. New York State Office of Mental Health,* 2000). In another example, the mother of Seung Hui Cho (the perpetrator of the Virginia Tech University massacre in 2007), in realizing her son had problems, sought out the assistance of Presbyterian church members to heal him of "demonic power" (Gardner & Cho, 2007) Before the intervention could take place, however, Cho had to return for his senior year of school, just months prior to the mass murder.

of torture and execution were often displayed in a public venue, intended as a deterrent to others who might choose to disregard the church-state's power.

Perhaps the most well-known example of the power wielded by the church in regulating deviant human behavior, as institutionalized through the government, was the *Malleus Maleficarum*. Latin for *The Hammer of Witches*, the *Malleus Maleficarum* was a treatise of the Catholic Church drafted to identify, interrogate, and punish those believed to be witches in the late 1400s. Over the course of nearly 250 years, anywhere from 600,000 to 9 million innocent outcasts — including people with mental illness — were tortured and murdered (e.g., burned at the stake, drowned) (Nyland, n.d.). Anyone who questioned these practices was considered a heretic and often faced the same fate. Fear of being labeled a witch and suffering torture and/or execution motivated citizens to express allegiance to the State and the Church, thereby reaffirming the power of government and religion and maintaining social order (Suich, 2005).

The first successful challenge to the *Malleus Maleficarum* was posed by Johann Weyer (1515–1588), a Dutch physician who many consider to be the first psychiatrist (Norman, n.d.). He asserted that many of the persecuted witches were actually suffering from mental illness, which he argued was not the work of demon forces but was instead a condition that was scientifically verifiable and treatable (Zilboorg, 1935). He backed his claims with comparisons to a number of case histories from his own clinical experience (Norman, n.d.). Weyer's successful criticism of the Catholic Church was possible only with protection from Dutch royalty (Zilboorg, 1935).

The Renaissance

During the Renaissance movement, ending the Middle Ages, a new philosophy of humanism emerged with an emphasis on life in the present, individual expression, personal development, and concern for others (Israel, 2006). As such, in an attempt to eradicate the previous practices of torture and execution, institutions devoted to confinement of the mentally ill emerged. Bethlem Royal Hospital (or Bedlam, as it came to be infamously known), in England, became the first institution in the Western world for the confinement of "lunatics" (Gado, n.d.). However, the conditions at the "hospital" were far from healing. It quickly gained the reputation of being a place of suffering and misery: With no sanitation measures in place, patients were chained to walls, tortured, and left screaming in the darkness and squalor under the premise that it was therapeutic (Gado, n.d.).[6] Adding insult to injury, philanthropists in the London upper class were invited to tour the hospital and donate to the charity, but instead "lewd and disorderly" casual visitors came in droves to catch a glimpse of the "picturesque delusions" (Stevenson, 1996, p. 254).[7] Moreover, the hospital became

---

6. As a result of this association, the word "bedlam" became synonymous with "chaos and confusion" in the English language (Gado, n.d.).

7. At the height of its popularity, Bethlem attracted more tourists than Westminster Abbey and the Tower of London (Gado, n.d.).

a further subject of scrutiny following allegations that some patients had been hospitalized for no other reason but to be silenced or discredited by their political enemies (Bethlem Royal Hospital, n.d.).

The Age of Enlightenment

Although the Age of Enlightenment (also known as the Age of Reason, generally regarded as comprising the 18th century) was relatively short in duration, it involved significant changes in thought and social response to mental illness and other forms of deviance, such as criminality. With a premium on logic, reason, criticism, and freedom of thought, a worldview emerged with the belief that empirical observation and examination of human life could reveal the truth about the self (Wilde, n.d.). Thought about mental processes and, by extension, mental illness was led by, among others, the mathematician René Descartes (1596–1650)[8] (Toch, 1979). Descartes reframed the early Greeks' conceptualization of the soul as the "mind" in his mind-body dualism; this theory marks the beginning of modern psychology and psychiatry (Custance & Travis, 1979). According to his now famous proof, *cogito ergo sum*, "I reflect, therefore I am," man could not doubt the existence of his/her own self (mind/soul) unless there was a self to do the doubting (Custance & Travis, 1979). Moreover, the writings of Descartes and others spawned a new enlightened way of thinking about the relationship between man and society and man and government. Specifically, it called into question the arbitrariness of decision making in monarchial systems and argued for more democratic forms of government (McLynn, 1989).

However, by the 1700s, punishment — including imprisonment and broad use of the death penalty, became the primary form of social control (McLynn, 1989). Cesare Bonesana, the Marquis of Beccaria (1738–1794), proposed that laws should be based upon the notion that man has free will, is rational, and thus crime can be deterred through punishment (Staples, 1977). The move during this time period to confine a wide range of "undesirables" — the mentally ill, criminals, drunkards, the homeless, even those guilty of idleness — has since been called The Great Confinement (Foucault, 1965). Confinement, as the "new solution," entailed provision of food, shelter, and at some level, security, which was not only responsive to moral and philosophical thought, but also to the economic insecurity of the time (Foucault, 1965).

At approximately the same time, there was a call by some in the psychiatric field to treat people with mental illness with more humane, psychological therapies. For example, Franz Mesmer (1734–1815) proposed mesmerism (now referred to as hypnosis) as a treatment for some mental illnesses. Most notably, Phillipe Pinel (1745–1826), who is considered by some to be the father of modern psychiatry, developed a new approach to the understanding and care of psychiatric hospital patients that diverged greatly from the practices of the time (Weiner, 2010). Pinel was appointed

---

8. Although Descartes technically preceded the Age of Reason, given his divergence of thought from his contemporaries and the impact that it had on the development of thought during the Enlightenment, he is considered to have been an Enlightenment thinker.

medical director of Bicetre Hospital in France in 1793 and quickly became interested in the patients on the mental health ward. Although he also developed an authoritative classification of mental disorders, his primary contribution was his approach to working with individuals with mental illness, what came to be known as moral therapy (Weiner, 2010). Pinel eliminated the use of painful practices of the day (e.g., bleeding), and instead visited each patient several times a day, carefully observing and engaging them in conversations with the purpose of compiling a detailed case history of the patient's illness (Weiner, 2010). Through his attention to detailed history, Pinel was among the first to recognize that mental illnesses are dynamic conditions that fluctuate over time, with periods of improvement and decline, in response to psychosocial stressors (Weiner, 1992). In terms of treatment for mental illness, he believed the interventions must be tailored to each individual and informed by the person's own perspective; contrary to most physicians, he regarded medication and other medical treatment as secondary to psychological techniques (Gerard, 1997). Pinel was also concerned with recognizing individuals' liberties when exerting control and authority in their treatment and custodial care. He asserted that even those patients considered to be most mentally disordered and/or dangerous were often made so by irresponsible treatment and that their behavior could be changed by providing space, kindness, humor, respect, and hope. As such, he forbade all punishments aside from use of the straitjacket and seclusion in his facility (Gerard, 1997). Ultimately, Pinel is considered to be responsible for the release of the first group of patients from confinement in mental institutions, characterized as the first deinstitutionalization movement (Weiner, 2010).[9]

American History of Mental Illness Prior to Deinstitutionalization

Pre-Civil War

In colonial America, mental illness was viewed as immorality. As such, people with mental illness were subject to ridicule, harassment, and at times punishment, such as whipping (Brakel & Rock, 1971). There were few community provisions for the treatment or management of persons with mental illnesses. Thus, people with mental illness who did not have family to care for them wandered the countryside in bands (Brakel & Rock, 1971).

Eventually, in 1773, the first organized societal initiative to manage the mentally ill in the colonies was implemented, construction of the Eastern Lunatic Asylum in

---

9. Although Pinel is usually credited with releasing the patients from their chains, evidence has emerged that his former patient and later prized apprentice and colleague, Jean-Baptiste Pussin, was actually responsible (Weiner, 2010).

Williamsburg, Virginia.[10] Having a single institution that housed mentally disordered people also enabled the introduction of the idea of treatment, rather than outright punishment, for mental illness. Benjamin Rush (1746–1813) — considered by many to be the father of American Psychiatry (Benjamin Rush, 2011)[11] — introduced the radical idea of moral therapies, particularly recreational and occupational therapies (Brodsky, 2004), to the United States. He was also among the first to propose that addictions, like mental illness, are a medical disease that must be treated with a therapeutic, rather than a punitive, approach (Durrant & Thakker, 2003). Furthermore, after witnessing horrifying conditions at the Pennsylvania Hospital where he worked, he successfully fought for more humane conditions in the state's hospitals (Deutsch, 2007). However, Rush's legacy was not completely positive. Adhering to the incorrect belief that mental illness was caused by irritation of the blood vessels in the brain, he continued to use what are considered by many to be inhumane practices, such as bleeding, purging, and immersion in hot and cold baths; he even invented such crude treatment devices as a restraining chair, involving a box to be placed over the patient's head, and a board that spun the patient at high speeds (Benjamin Rush, 2011).

The few American asylums gradually lost their narrow purpose of confining only violent persons with mental illness, instead, becoming warehouses for non-violent persons with mental illness and persons without mental illness as well (Brakel & Rock, 1971). Moreover, many were confined with few or no procedural safeguards (Brakel & Rock, 1971). An 1842 New York statute, for example, called for the confinement of all "lunatics" in the community, not just those who were dangerous, and dispatched "assessors" to actively search for such people (Dershowitz, 1974). This was akin to policemen seeking out law breakers. The individuals presented by the assessors received little to no procedural justice prior to being committed to the asylum and often endured this blight on their civil liberties this for the rest of their lives.

Arguably more problematically, the persons with mental illness were more likely to be incarcerated in jails, intended for criminals, than in asylums. Dorothea Dix (1802–1887), a socially active teacher and nurse, was and always will be a significant figure in having effected changes for persons with mental illness criminalized in the United States (Ghareeb, n.d.). Beginning as a religious devotional hour for inmates in March of 1841, Dix's visit to the East Cambridge Jail in Massachusetts became a personal mission to change the conditions of the persons with mental illness who were imprisoned (Ghareeb, n.d.). During her tour of the jail, she witnessed the horrific conditions experienced by persons with mental illness: no heat, no light, no sanitation,

---

10. Although initially designed to incarcerate violent people, many of whom happened to have mental illness (Brakel & Rock, 1971), it is widely considered to be the first psychiatric institution in America.

11. Rush was also one of the founding fathers of the U.S., a signer of the Declaration of Independence.

little to no clothing, rendered beatings with rods by staff, and confined alongside criminals, irrespective of their age and sex (Ghareeb, n.d.), leaving persons with mental illness at risk of physical and sexual abuse by their fellow prisoners. She was told that persons with mental illness did not need heat because they were unable to feel discomfort or pain (Ghareeb, n.d.). Upon touring every facility in Massachusetts, and later hundreds of facilities throughout the U.S. and Europe, Dix found that her observations in Cambridge were the norm rather than the exception (Ghareeb, n.d.). Arguing that punishment should be replaced with healing that focused on the root cause of the mental illness (Gilligan, 2001), she informed state legislatures and the U.S. Congress about the plight of the mentally ill in jails (Ghareeb, n.d.). By the end of her 40-year career, in which she traveled over 30,000 miles, she had convinced 14 states to build 32 hospitals and train hospital staff (Gollaher, 1995). Moreover, in 1854, she persuaded both houses of the U.S. Congress to sign bills to set aside over 5 million acres of land to build psychiatric institutions (Ghareeb, n.d.). Ultimately, however — reflecting the thought of many at the time and what continues to stymie change for the criminalized mentally ill — President Franklin Pierce vetoed the bill, arguing that states, not the federal government, should be responsible for social welfare (Herstek, 2001). Nevertheless, the era of hospital confinement for persons with mental illness had begun and would last for over a century (Torrey, 1997).[12]

Biological Determinism

Societal thought in the 19th and early 20th centuries was influenced by biological determinism (Burke & Embrick, 2008). At its extreme, biological determinists subscribe to the position that all human behavior is innate, dictated by biological factors (e.g., genes, brain size), to the neglect of recognizing social factors, culture, or free will (Burke & Embrick, 2008). Such beliefs were reflected, for example, in the racial supremacy of the time, manifested in the use of slavery in the U.S. until the Civil War. It is not surprising, then, that theories on the causes of mental illness and criminal behavior during the 19th and early 20th centuries were also heavily focused on biology and physiology. In 1808, Franz Gall (1758–1828) popularized phrenology, the notion that a person's skull shape and placement of bumps on the head can reveal personality traits and determine one's propensity for deviant behavior (Wilson & Hernstein, 1985). Likewise, Cesare Lombroso (1835–1909) proposed a theory of atavism in 1876, asserting that criminality is an inherited trait that could be predicted by body shape (Wilson & Hernstein, 1985). While these theories were refuted, they were important because they challenged popular theories of the time that espoused rationality, self-determination, and deterrence (Wilson & Hernstein, 1985). Furthermore, they presaged the research and practice that would soon follow.

Approaches to managing deviants also reflected the biological determinism discussed previously. In essence, such a viewpoint — "He was (or they were) born that

---

12. Although several psychiatric hospitals had opened during the late 1700s and early 1800s in the U.S., the majority of them opened in the late 1800s and early 1900s.

way" — leads to the conclusion that a person (or group of people) cannot be changed (e.g., treated, rehabilitated, reformed). Thus, a call began for the elimination of deviants, such as persons with mental illness and criminals, from society in the form of forced sterilization, eugenics (i.e., "better breeding" by disallowing persons with mental illness from reproducing), and even euthanasia.[13] Well-respected academics such as Harvard anthropologist E. A. Hooton advocated for use of these practices with persons with mental illness (Vold & Bernard, 1986). More dangerously, the movement spread to policymakers. Surprisingly to some, the United States has a sordid history of forced sterilization of persons considered mentally defective, justified on the basis that they were a burden to society. In fact, the United States was the first country to systematically undertake compulsory sterilization programs for the purpose of eugenics (Iredale, 2000), and when scrutinized, the practice was upheld as Constitutional by the United States Supreme Court in the case of *Buck v. Bell* (1927). Justice Oliver Wendell Holmes, in his majority opinion, stated emphatically, "Three generations of imbeciles is enough" (*Buck v. Bell*, 1927, p. 207). More well-known is the Nazis' handling of millions of persons with mental illness and other groups of people considered inferior by the regime — whom they referred to as "life unworthy of life" and "useless eaters" — with systematic sterilization and even "euthanasia" via lethal injection or gas by a 1939 order from Adolf Hitler (Nazi Persecution of the Disabled, 2007).

Advances in Understanding the Brain

The 1800s and 1900s were also a time of great advances in the scientific understanding of the link between the human brain and behavior, marking the genesis of biological psychiatry and neuropsychology. The famous case of Phineas Gage (1848) — a victim of a construction accident, in which an explosion sent a steel rod through his skull, disconnecting his frontal lobes from the rest of his brain — drew widespread public attention (Macmillan, 2000). Miraculously, Gage survived, but most accounts suggest that he suffered from significant changes in his personality that manifested in behavior such as fits of violence, irreverence, and profanity (Macmillan, 2000).[14]

Despite Gage's negative outcome related to his brain injury, some physicians and scientists concluded that surgery to intentionally sever the frontal lobes from the rest of the brain (what would later be termed frontal "leucotomies" or "lobotomies") might actually be beneficial for patients with mental illnesses (Peterson, 1999). As such, in 1892, Gottlieb Burkhardt, a Swiss physician and supervisor of an insane asylum, performed an operation to remove parts of the cortexes of six patients with

---

13. Biological determinism is often discussed alongside social Darwinism, or theories that seek to apply biological concepts, such as evolution and survival of the fittest, to social groups. Sterilization to prevent members of "unfit" groups from reproducing and euthanasia clearly represent applications of social Darwinism.

14. Macmillan (2000) noted, however, that there were wide-ranging accounts of Gage's post-accident behavior, none of which were firsthand.

schizophrenia (Sabbatini, 1997). While his operations calmed the behavior of the patients, two died soon after the surgery, quieting enthusiasm for these procedures, at least for the next 40 years (Sabbatini, 1997). By the 1930s, however, these procedures experienced a resurgence as a treatment of choice for severe mental illness.[15] In 1935, Dr. Antônio Egas Moniz, a Portuguese neuropsychiatrist, performed the first leucotomies with modest success: per his report, 35% of the patients improved greatly, 35% improved moderately, and 30% showed no change (Christmas, 2012). However, no patients died or suffered convulsions; thus, it was considered a success worthy of the Nobel Prize for Medicine and Physiology in 1949 (Christmas, 2012). As a result of this notoriety, more leucotomies were performed in the ensuing three years than in all previous years; this occurred despite Moniz's warnings that the procedure only be used as a last resort (Sabbatini, 1997). In the United States, the procedure was introduced in 1936 by Walter Freeman, a clinical neurologist and physician, after hearing Moniz speak the year before on his new psychosurgery (Christmas, 2012). Freeman's ascension to fame was his "refined" procedure that he termed the prefrontal "lobotomy," in which he used a local anesthetic, a common ice pick, and a hammer. Freeman claimed the procedure was less messy, could be performed in a matter of minutes, and could be conducted on an out-patient basis; he used this sales pitch to convince hospitals and institutions that the surgical procedure could solve their overpopulation and management problems (Sabbatini, 1997). By the end of his career, Freeman had performed approximately 3,500 lobotomies (Rowland, 2005).[16]

While there were over 18,000 lobotomies performed between 1939 and 1951, many veteran neurosurgeons were upset by the primitive nature of this new method and expressed ethical concerns regarding the potential misuses of the procedure (Sabbatini, 1997). Similar to compulsory sterilization, state governments often made decisions to lobotomize individuals for purposes of behavior management (e.g., to reduce externalizing, violent, or merely inconvenient behaviors) rather than for health interests (Sabbatini, 1997). Evidence of abuses of the procedure abounded throughout the world (Sabbatini, 1997): Amateur surgeons would often perform hundreds of lobotomies without even doing a systematic psychiatric evaluation. It was not uncommon for the criminally insane to be operated on without their, or their families', consent. Other families submitted difficult relatives to the procedure. In Japan, most lobotomies were performed on "problem" children; in Russia, rebels and political opponents were operated on for being ostensibly mentally deranged by authorities. Concern with lobotomies mounted until the Soviet Union finally took the first step to outlaw the procedure in the 1940s (Sabbatini, 1997). Opposition in the U.S. grew between

---

15. Insulin coma therapy, electric shock, and metrazol-convulsive shock were also introduced as treatments for mental illness in the 1930s, but they were never used as widely as lobotomies (Valenstein, 1986).

16. It is noteworthy that Freeman performed a failed lobotomy on President John F. Kennedy's sister, Rosemary, leaving her unable to move or speak more than a few words (National Public Radio, 2005). The effect on the president — and in turn, the nation — will be discussed below.

1950 and 1960, fueled by scientific research questioning the costs and benefits of the operation to the individual and to society and was translated into law in the 1970s (Sabbatini, 1997).

The World Wars

A combination of advances in industrialization and science enabled volatile global politics at the turn of the 20th century to spread into two World Wars. Within the United States, attitudes toward immigrants were particularly negative. Among other influences, fear of communism promoted xenophobia, i.e., fear or hatred of people from other countries (e.g., their politics, culture) (Collins English Dictionary, 2003). Moreover, American industrialists learned during World War I that the U.S. economy could be self-sufficient without immigrant labor. Thus, the American public called for restrictions on immigration. In 1924, Congress instituted immigration quotas, placing significant restrictions on the number of immigrants allowed into the country, particularly targeting those of "undesirable" nationalities (Immigration restriction, 2012).[17] In addition, following the Japanese attack of Pearl Harbor during World War II, the U.S. forcibly removed and detained over 100,000 Japanese American citizens in internment camps (Head, n.d.).

As war gave way to peace and great economic prosperity in the post-World War era, the strong drive to eliminate those who were different continued; but this time the focus was on elimination of our own. Funded by the post-war G.I. Bill, Americans settled into a remarkable level of conformity, and this was epitomized by the emergence of middle-class suburbia reflected in long rows of new, cookie-cutter homes, and the ideal conception of the traditional family (consisting of the businessman father, domestic housewife mother, and two to three children) happily huddled around their brand new television set (Years of Conformity, n.d.). The sense of national unity from World War II and the growing threat of communism contributed to a sense of togetherness. Media, corporations, and communities reinforced established norms; these checks on conformity, along with racial and economic segregation, stifled any semblance of social tumult (Years of Conformity, n.d.). Those who were different were kept out of sight and out of mind.

Nevertheless, in reality, the wars left behind innumerable physically and emotionally scarred victims of war and repression. The personal and social costs were enormous. Trauma symptoms from the war were so widespread that a new disorder, Post-Traumatic Stress Disorder (PTSD), was eventually created (Favaro, Tenconi, Colombo, & Santonastaso, 2006). Some soldiers returned home to families and communities with limited resources to cope. Many veterans with mental illnesses were left to work

---

17. As a result of these quotas, the proportion of foreign-born citizens to the total U.S. population ranged from a high of 15% in 1910 to 12% in 1930, down to 7% in 1950 (Gibson & Lennon, 1999). The quotas remained in effect until 1965, when the civil rights movement challenged them.

out their problems without professional assistance. Scores of individuals self-medicated with alcohol or street drugs. Many became homeless (Favaro et al., 2006).[18]

State Hospital Censuses Increased, Support Decreased

Admission to "state hospitals" or state-funded psychiatric facilities was touted as the boon for the mentally ill population following the Civil War and became the primary means of treating people with mental illness. Most of these hospitalizations were forced upon persons against their will (i.e., involuntary or civil commitment), as it was the prevailing belief in America that persons with mental illness were incapable of making decisions about their own well-being and that even involuntary commitment was in their best interests (Anfang & Appelbaum, 2006). Thus, it was considered acceptable — indeed, it was an obligation, under the doctrine of *parens patriae* (i.e., Latin for "parent of the country"; Testa & West, 2010, p. 31) — for the state to commit people with mental illness against their will. As such, standards for civilly committing people to these institutions were relaxed even further during the first two-thirds of the 20th century (Melton, Petrila, Poythress, & Slobogin, 2007). In general, all that was required was the presence of mental illness and a recommendation for treatment. In some localities, little evidence was necessary to establish the mental illness, mere endorsement for hospitalization by a family member was sufficient, and no legal proceeding before a judge or magistrate was necessary to procure indefinite commitment to an institution (Brakel & Rock, 1971). For example, in some states, a husband could legally commit his wife to a psychiatric institution without much evidence of mental disorder solely at the discretion of the superintendent of the facility (Anfang & Appelbaum, 2006). Such was the case of Elizabeth Packard, who, in 1860, was committed to an Illinois psychiatric asylum after arguing with her Calvinist minister husband about theology (Curtis, 2001).[19] She was diagnosed with "moral insanity," held involuntarily in the hospital for three years, and lost custody of her children and ownership of her property (Levison, 2003). Only after requesting a jury trial, in which she was able to present witnesses, was she declared legally sane (West & Friedman, 2009), but she never recovered custody of her children or her belongings.

Without any effective treatments for the cause of mental illness, most patients were warehoused in state hospitals for long periods of time. Indeed, the average length of stay per patient admitted to state hospitals in 1950 was 20 years (Gillon, 2000). As such, censuses at psychiatric institutions soared. At the beginning of the 20th century, there were approximately 145,000 persons hospitalized in state psychiatric institutions (Earley, 2006); by 1955, that number had quadrupled to 559,000 patients (Lamb & Weinberger, 2005). Half of all hospital beds nationally were occupied by persons with mental illness (Gorman, 1956). As admissions to publicly-funded

---

18. As will be discussed in Chapter 3, the personal and social costs of veterans have only increased over the decades since the World Wars.

19. There is some evidence to suggest that Ms. Packard did have a psychotic disorder, but her symptoms were not sufficient to be hospitalized according to modern standards (Curtis, 2001).

state psychiatric institutions proliferated, the number of patients surpassed the reasonable functioning of the facilities.

Accordingly, the fiscal burden of the state hospitals accelerated, as public support for state hospitals waned. Between 1939 and 1949, for example, the per patient cost for inpatient mental health treatment had increased by 150% and continued to climb throughout the 1950s and 1960s (Gillon, 2000). As economic prospects shrunk in post-war America, much of the public and, by extension, legislators argued that the elaborate social protections of the 1930s welfare state were no longer feasible (Farland, 2002). Similarly, reflecting the biological determinism and xenophobia of the time, White Anglo-Saxon Protestants (WASPs) lost interest in supporting public hospitals that included in their populations thousands of new immigrants and newly emancipated African American slaves (Gilligan, 2001). Those who had persons with mental illness in their families hospitalized did not want their relatives to be housed and treated alongside such undesirables. In total, the taxpaying American public had a growing distaste for state hospitals.

Negative Publicity

All of these dynamics — coupled with the fact that most state hospitals, due to "not in my backyard" (NIMBY) attitudes, had been built in the most remote locations, far away from the oversight of family members (Wright, 1997) — set the stage for serious deterioration of conditions at the hospitals and brutal abuses of patients. American state hospitals became a virtual reenactment of the horrors committed against persons with mental illness at numerous points throughout history, including those witnessed by Dorothea Dix a century before. The main differences from Dix's day were that instead of jails and prisons, this abuse was occurring in state hospitals, which were supposed to be places of healing. Moreover, instead of a philanthropic teacher and nurse informing and lobbying state legislators, the media assumed the responsibility to expose the brutality to the general public. *Life* magazine journalist, Albert Q. Maisel (1946), best articulated the indignities he witnessed in his tours of state hospitals in his twelve-page article entitled "Bedlam 1946: Most U.S. Hospitals are a Shame and a Disgrace." The following is an illustrative excerpt from the piece:

> ... Through public neglect and legislative penny-pinching, state after state has allowed its institutions for the care and cure of the mentally sick to degenerate into little more than concentration camps on the Belsen pattern.
>
> Court and grand-jury records document scores of deaths of patients following beatings by attendants. Hundreds of instances of abuse, falling just short of manslaughter, are similarly documented. And reliable evidence, from hospital after hospital, indicates that these are but a tiny fraction of the beatings that occur, day after day, only to be covered up by a tacit conspiracy of mutually protective silence and a code that ostracizes employees who sing too loud.

Yet beatings and murders are hardly the most significant of the indignities we have heaped upon most of the 400,000 guiltless patient-prisoners of over 180 state mental institutions.

We feed thousands a starvation diet, often dragged further below the low-budget standard by the withdrawal of the best food for the staff dining rooms. We jam-pack men, women and sometimes even children into hundred-year-old firetraps in wards so crowded that the floors cannot be seen between the rickety cots, while thousands more sleep on ticks, on blankets, or on the bare floors. We give them little and shoddy clothing at best. Hundreds — of my own knowledge and sight — spend twenty-four hours a day in stark and filthy nakedness. Those who are well enough to work slave away in many institutions for 12 hours a day, often without a day's rest for years on end. One man at Cleveland, Ohio — and he is no isolated exception — worked in this fashion for 19 solid years on a diet the poorest sharecropper would spurn.

Thousands spend their days — often for weeks at a stretch — locked in devices euphemistically called "restraints": thick leather handcuffs, great canvas camisoles, "muffs," "mitts," wristlets, locks and straps and restraining sheets. Hundreds are confined in "lodges" — bare, bedless rooms reeking with filth and feces — by day lit only through half-inch holes though steel-plated windows, by night merely black tombs in which the cries of the insane echo unheard from the peeling plaster of the walls.

Worst of all, for these wards of society we provide physicians, nurses and attendants in numbers far below even the minimum standards set by state rules. Institutions that would be seriously unmanned even if not overcrowded find themselves swamped with 30%, 50% and even 100% more patients than they were built to hold. These are not wartime conditions but have existed for decades. Restraints, seclusion and constant drugging of patients become essential in wards where one attendant must herd as many as 400 mentally deranged charges.

Paid wages insufficient to attract able personnel, even by prewar standards, and often working 10- and 12-hour days, these medical staffs have almost ceased (with some significant exceptions) to strive for cures. Many have resigned themselves, instead, to mere custodial care on a level that led one governor to admit that "our cows in the hospital barns get better care then the men and women in the wards."

The same year, Mary Jane Ward (1946) corroborated Maisel's expose' when she published the semi-autobiographical novel, *Snake Pit*.[20] This novel, best known for

---

20. The title stems from an ancient practice of dealing with persons with mental illness where they were thrown into a pit of snakes. The theory was that such a practice would make a normal person insane; therefore it must work in reverse. Of course, there is no evidence that this sort of strategy works.

its vivid description of living conditions in psychiatric hospitals at that time, became a best seller. It enjoyed such acclaim that it was subsequently produced into a movie by the same name starring Olivia de Havilland in 1948.

The atrocities long hidden behind the walls were now out in the open for the public to see. The publicity received caused an uproar in the public, to the point that the federal government became involved. Specifically, in late 1946, Congress forwarded and President Harry Truman signed a bill creating the National Institute of Mental Health (NIMH), calling for a "cure" for mental illness (National Institutes of Health, 2011).

Discovery of Thorazine

It would not be long before a purported cure would surface. In 1950, the drug chlorpromazine, which would later come to be known as Thorazine, was discovered in Paris (Earley, 2006). Initially used to treat allergies and nausea, doctors began to notice the sedating effect the drug had on patients, which prompted the idea that it could be used to treat symptoms of mental illness (Healy, 2004). In 1953, it was used for this purpose for the first time, with striking results: previously agitated, psychotic patients suddenly became calm and controllable (Healy, 2004).

Earley (2006) described the history of Thorazine in the United States and its producer's capitalistic gains: Despite the discovery of sedating effects for psychotic patients, Thorazine was not readily accepted by the psychiatric community, who at the time believed that Freudian psychoanalysis and other talk therapies were the most promising treatment approaches (Earley, 2006). Thus, Smith Kline, the pharmaceutical company who produced the drug, bypassed the psychiatric profession and marketed the drug to state legislators. Touted as a "wonder drug," Smith Kline promised legislators millions of tax dollars in savings by providing a means by which the half-million institutionalized persons with mental illness could be "cured" and released into the community.

In its first eight months of release, Thorazine was administered to more than two million individuals; in the next ten years, over 50 million patients worldwide would receive the drug (Earley, 2006). However, as the continued existence of mental illness attests, Thorazine was not a cure for mental illness. It was, however, a wonder drug for Smith Kline, whose revenues doubled three times in 15 years (Earley, 2006). In the end, just as in various shifts in correctional policy over the years, it was money—not some great concern and compassion for persons with mental illness—that motivated the flooding of the drug Thorazine into the market (Earley, 2006).

Anti-Psychiatry Movement

This reality was not lost on the anti-psychiatry movement. Led by Michel Foucault (France), R.D. Laing (Great Britain), and Thomas Szasz (America), the anti-psychiatry movement of the 1960s consisted of psychiatrists and academics critical of the profession of psychiatry; many were skeptical of the very concept of mental illness. Laing (1960), a psychiatrist, inaugurated the movement when he wrote the book, *The Divided Self: An Existential Study in Sanity and Madness*, which became a college bestseller in Great Britain and the United States. In it, Laing contended that mental illness was due purely to social causes and, in so doing, implied that mental illness could be eradicated through social remedies. Likewise, Foucault (1965), in his book, *Madness and Civilization: A History of Insanity in the Age of Reason*, argued that economic factors and cultural interests have always defined mental illness, and he maintained that the concepts of sanity and insanity are merely social constructs indicative of the power of the "sane" over the "insane." He opined that psychiatry had become "a third order of repression" (p. 37), a tool of the state's law enforcement and judiciary.

Foucault's assertions echoed in part the claims of American psychiatrist and psychoanalyst, Thomas Szasz, in his article (1960) and eventual best-selling book (1961) by the same name, *The Myth of Mental Illness*. In it, Szasz claimed that the American state, similar to Nazi Germany and the Soviet Union, uses psychiatric coercion to fulfill its need to silence nonconformists, the rabble, and dissidents (Rissmiller & Rissmiller, 2006). He referred to this collusion between psychiatry and the government as the most destructive force to impact American society in the previous fifty years. Szasz went so far as to call for the prosecution and imprisonment of psychiatrists for crimes against humanity (Rissmiller & Rissmiller, 2006).[21]

In the same year that Szasz's book was published, Erving Goffman released his book *Asylums: Essays on the Social Situation of Mental Patients and Other Inmates* (1961). Weinstein (1982), 20 years after its original publication, reviewed the book and provided the following observations: Although slightly less vitriolic than Szasz, Goffman, too, compared the psychiatric hospital to prisons and even concentration camps, as he described what he perceived to be the subjective experience of state hospital patients and the insidious, detrimental effects of long-term hospitalization. He characterized the state hospital as a "total institution": Individual "inmates," as he referred to patients, were but members of a large group, who were all treated alike, in an impersonal manner, by the distant, hierarchically superior hospital staff. Meanwhile, all aspects of daily life were tightly scheduled and controlled (e.g., when to

---

21. Szasz's credibility is marred, however, by the professional company he kept and the circles in which his work became popularized. In particular, he co-founded the radical anti-psychiatry organization, Citizens Commission on Human Rights, with L. Ron Hubbard, science fiction writer and founder of Scientology, which is considered by many to be a cult and, at least, one of the most controversial new religious movements to have arisen in the 20th century. Among Hubbard's rhetoric, he insisted, "There is not one institutional psychiatrist alive who could not be arraigned and convicted of extortion, mayhem, and murder" (Rissmiller & Rissmiller, 2006, p. 864). Moreover, Timothy Leary, once Harvard professor turned counterculture legend and notorious proponent of mind-altering drugs, considered "the *Myth of Mental Illness* [to be] the most important book in the history of psychiatry ... perhaps ... the most important book published in the twentieth century" (Rissmiller & Rissmiller, 2006, p. 864).

sleep, eat, and excrete; if, when, and with whom they can have contact outside the institution; whether or not to accept medication), in the same place, by the same authority figures; information about the patients' fate was withheld. Patients were repeatedly assured that all deprivations of autonomy and humiliations were "for their own good." According to Goffman, these conditions stripped inmates of their pre-patient identities, and a new identity that supported the goals of the institution was formed. To the extent that inmates "successfully" adapted to the total institution, they became less capable to live in the outside world and, thus, were more likely to stay and/or return to the institution. Thereby, their status as inmates of the institution became a permanent part of who they were (Weinstein, 1982).[22]

A series of creative works, which surfaced in the early 1960s, were influential as they appealed to the masses.[23] Most notably, Ken Kesey's (1962) One Flew Over the Cuckoo's Nest attracted widespread attention, so much so that it was made into a Broadway play as well as an Academy Award-winning film featuring Jack Nicholson in 1975. As observed by Vargas (2011), the novel was ostensibly an overt illustration of a psychiatric institution, consistent with anti-psychiatry tenets, it further compared the institution figuratively to the expectations of conformity and the suppression of individual freedoms by society. Through the narration of Chief Bromden, the silent, half-Indian, long-term "chronic" patient, the audience witnessed the new patient, brash, defiant Randall McMurphy, disrupt the controlled, orderly institution maintained by Nurse Ratched. As punishment, Nurse Ratched had McMurphy lobotomized, the ultimate squelching of his self-expression (Vargas, 2011). In many respects,

22. Although it was not published until a decade after the anti-psychiatry movement began—and by this time, the circumstances of psychiatric hospitals had changed drastically—psychologist David Rosenhan captured further media attention with his 1973 Science article, "On Being Sane in Insane Places." In the study, Rosenhan's investigators posed as potential patients presenting to admissions departments at various psychiatric hospitals (e.g., 12 hospitals in 5 states). The researchers presented with vague complaints of auditory hallucinations that did not fit with any known disorder; all other behavior and self-reported experiences (of mood, thoughts) were "normal." Strikingly, all were admitted immediately to the hospital, and all but one were given a diagnosis of schizophrenia. Once on the ward, the researchers showed no further signs of mental illness, yet the researchers were held in the hospitals for periods ranging from 7 to 52 days. In fact, typically normal behavior—such as "writing behavior," occurring for the purposes of making observational notes for the study—was interpreted by staff as symptoms of their illness. Interestingly, however, nearly 30% of the genuine patients recognized the researchers as not actually being patients! Altogether, the 8 researchers/pseudo-patients were given an estimated 2100 pills of medication (for non-existent symptoms), which were either pocketed or flushed down the toilet (along with, according to the researchers, many other patients' medications). With regard to the treatment by staff on the ward, the researchers noted that nurses spent approximately 90% of their time in the office, shut away from the patients; each patient spent, on average, only 7 minutes per day with psychiatrists and psychologists; and orderlies would frequently be brutal to patients until another staff member appeared. Ultimately, all of the researchers were discharged with the diagnosis of "schizophrenia in remission," suggesting staff believed they legitimately had symptoms but that they had been treated such that they were not present at the time of discharge.

23. Sylvia Plath's The Bell Jar (1963) is one such creative work that attracted widespread attention from the public regarding the conditions of psychiatric hospitals and the experiences of former psychiatric patients (Farland, 2002).

One Flew Over the Cuckoo's Nest personifies Goffman's components and processes of the total institution: Nurse Ratched as the powerful authority figure of the bureaucratic psychiatric institution; Chief Bromden as the, initially, "good" passive inmate who conforms to the requirements of the institution; and McMurphy as the "bad," challenging inmate. Not only wide-reaching and influential in its time, the book has been recognized as one of the 100 best novels between 1923 and 2005 by Time magazine (Grossman & Lacayo, 2005).

Likewise, several legal experts of the time could be described as being part of the anti-psychiatry movement and were responsible for much of the mental health litigation that will be described below. Probably best known was U.S. Court of Appeals Judge David L. Bazelon. Bazelon was a champion of the rights of the poor and the powerless, which certainly included people with mental disabilities (Eisler, 1993). Opposed to what he perceived to be the authoritarian nature of the practice of psychiatry, he was responsible for several integral developments in the realm of mental health law, including patients' right to receive treatment in the least restrictive setting (e.g., in the community, rather than in a hospital, as appropriate).[24] Similarly, in order to ensure the highest level of integrity in this previously neglected area of law, American Civil Liberties Union (ACLU) attorney Bruce Ennis founded the "mental health bar," an informal organization of attorneys who practiced in the specialty of mental health law (e.g., defending individuals who faced being committed to a psychiatric hospital for treatment against their will,[25] suing psychiatric hospitals for their failure to meet a patient's right to adequate treatment). Ennis's personal goal in establishing the bar was to develop an arsenal of solid mental health attorneys who could abolish involuntary commitments entirely or, at least, could prevent them as much as possible by requiring the state to build strong cases prior to committing a person against his/her will.

The Civil Rights Movement and Right to Treatment Litigation

The civil rights movement of the 1960s in America went beyond striving for equality in race relations, hotel accommodations, public transit opportunities, restaurant accessibility, and access to restroom facilities. The wave of the movement also, among other things, led to the extension of broader civil and legal rights to groups traditionally considered to be in need of caretaking—e.g., juveniles, women, and individuals with disabilities, including persons with mental illness. Indeed, beginning in the 1940s

---

24. As a testament to his impact on the field, the Judge David L. Bazelon Center for Mental Health Law (2012a), a national legal advocacy organization for individuals with mental disabilities, was founded in his name. The Bazelon Center works to achieve the ideals of self-determination, human dignity, and civil rights for people with mental illness, as well as the practical outcomes of community integration, access to services, and equal access to the courts, by providing individual case legal assistance and promoting progressive mental health law legislation and policy.

25. Such forced psychiatric hospitalizations are referred to as "involuntary" and/or "civil commitments," the focus of Chapter 4.

and 50s, people with disabilities began to organize for political change; this culminated in the founding of the disability rights movement, which successfully fought for the enactment of anti-discrimination and civil rights laws as it pertains to federal programs, education, and employment for this population in the 1970s. Among other causes, this movement fought for the rights of people with mental illness. In particular, they sought to limit involuntary hospitalizations unless absolutely necessary and to ensure better conditions at state hospitals by getting the courts to recognize patients' Constitutional right to adequate treatment (National Council on Independent Living, 2013).

Morton Birnbaum, a physician and civil rights attorney, first articulated the idea of a Constitutional right to treatment in 1960. According to Birnbaum, if a person is going to be involuntarily hospitalized, then he/she has a right to adequate treatment. Although, in his initial article, he did not specifically define "adequate treatment," he alluded to "treatment so that he may regain his health, and therefore his liberty, as soon as possible" (p. 502), and he explicated institutional standards of care (e.g., staffing ratios, requirements for physical facilities to avoid overcrowding) that he considered to be part of adequate treatment. He asserted that without treatment, the institution constitutes a "mental prison" (p. 503), in which inmates have been deprived of liberty without due process. As such, he argued, without treatment, the patient should be released "in spite of the existence or severity of the mental illness" (p. 503), contradicting the *parens patriae* principle that had governed civil commitment for so long.

Birnbaum's right to treatment argument was highly controversial, both within the medical field and in much of the legal world. In fact, his initial article was rejected by more than 50 journals before the American Bar Association agreed to publish it, and angry judges were known to eject him from their courtrooms when he defended the rights of patients with mental illness (Birnbaum, 2012). This was because many interpreted Birnbaum's words to be calling for the release of patients from state hospitals. He had proposed the concept, however, to serve as a mechanism to improve hospital treatment — a laudable goal.

It was not long, though, before Birnbaum's thesis began to be used for the very purpose that he had not intended. The first right to treatment case, *Rouse v. Cameron* (1966), involved an individual who had been found not guilty by reason of insanity (NGRI) of a misdemeanor criminal charge (carrying a weapon), which, had he been found guilty rather than having been acquitted, carried a maximum one-year sentence. Instead, Rouse spent more than four years in a state hospital. His confinement was challenged on right to treatment grounds. After hearing the appeal, Judge Bazelon ruled that failure to provide adequate treatment during indefinite psychiatric commitment, even to a Not Guilty by Reason of Insanity (NGRI) acquittee, called into question Constitutional rights concerning due process of law, equal protection, and freedom from cruel and unusual punishment. In particular, Bazelon echoed Birnbaum's assertion that the purpose of involuntary hospitalization is "treatment, not punishment," and that "absent treatment, the hospital is transformed into a penitentiary." *Rouse* was also the first case in which an attempt to define "adequate psychiatric treatment" was presented. Specifically, Bazelon indicated that psychiatric care and treatment should include initial and periodic assessments of the needs and conditions of the patient, a treatment program suited to the patient's individual needs, contact with psychiatrists and other hospital staff, and efforts to provide treatment that is adequate in light of present knowledge. Although he acknowledged that a hospital cannot ensure that treatment will cure the patient, he asserted that there must be a bona fide effort to do so (*Rouse v. Cameron*, 1966).

Along with the right to treatment, Bazelon conceived that treatment should be provided in the least restrictive setting possible (e.g., in the community versus in an institution, whenever available and appropriate, given the circumstances of the case) (Judge David L. Bazelon Center for Mental Health Law, 2012b).[26] First conceptualized in *Rouse v. Cameron*, the standard was further developed in Bazelon's ruling of the civil commitment case, *Lake v. Cameron* (1966). Lake was a 60-year-old female with mental illness who was psychiatrically hospitalized after being found wandering the streets and was subsequently diagnosed with "senile brain disease" (i.e., what would now be labeled dementia). Bazelon ruled that, with the availability of family members who could care for her and/or nursing homes, Lake should not be kept in the hospital with the "complete deprivation of liberty" it entails (*Lake v. Cameron*, 1966).[27]

The next right to treatment case did not surface until nearly a decade later, but it turned out to be the landmark case on the issue. *Wyatt v. Stickney* (1972) was the first case in which the right to treatment argument was applied to civil, involuntary commitment (as opposed to not guilty by reason of insanity, a quasi-criminal commitment situation, as in *Rouse*). The basis for the class-action lawsuit was brought about by state funding cuts for mental health in the state of Alabama; as a result of the cuts, many mental health staff were laid off, resulting in a sharp blow to an already ailing system. Even prior to the cuts, there were horrific incidents recorded: a boy with profound mental retardation had a garden hose inserted into his rectum and filled with water by staff, rupturing his spleen and killing him; a patient had been scalded to death; another patient was kept in a strait jacket for nine years to prevent finger sucking (Carr, 2004). After the cuts, at one of the state hospitals, there was only one psychiatrist for every 5000 patients (Treatment Advocacy Center [TAC], 2011). With this extreme lack of oversight, one can only imagine the brutalities experienced by patients. Alabama attorney, George Dean, along with co-counsel, Morton Birnbaum, the founder of the right to treatment argument (discussed above), filed a federal lawsuit, arguing that the employee shortage was seriously harming the quality of treatment being provided at the hospital, thereby violating patients' right to treatment. The attorneys highlighted the case of Ricky Wyatt, a 15-year-old who had been

---

26. In current mental health law, this is commonly referred to as the "least restrictive alternative" or "least restrictive environment" standard.

27. The "least restrictive environment" standard later became national law by the enactment of the Americans with Disabilities Act of 1990.

hospitalized years earlier in an attempt to "make him behave. He did not have a mental illness." (Carr, 2004, p. 2). Ricky was locked in a cell with the only light coming through slats in the door, and he slept on the wet floors. He was heavily medicated and threatened with shock therapy so he would not act out.

Although Federal District Judge Frank M. Johnson in *Wyatt* overruled the attempt to get the employees reinstated, asserting that the state department of mental health had the ultimate authority to make decisions about hiring and firing, the judge did believe a federal question existed about the minimum standards for treatment in the facility. In particular, he ruled that patients "*unquestionably* have a constitutional right to receive such *individual* treatment as will give each of them a *realistic opportunity to be cured or to improve* his/her mental condition" (italics added) and that, in failing to provide such treatment, Alabama state hospitals were violating patients' due process rights. Judge Johnson interpreted the right to treatment very strictly, stipulating the required number of staff—not only mental health professionals, but all the way down to maintenance workers—as well as standards for the physical operation of the facilities (e.g., how often bed sheets should be changed, the type and amount of furniture in the dayroom, even the temperature of the dishwashing) (TAC, 2011). He gave the hospitals six months to develop and implement standards of care that met his ruling.

While the conditions of the Alabama hospitals were clearly deplorable, *Wyatt* has been criticized as paving the way for massive deinstitutionalization and, thereby, a loss of *any* treatment for a substantial segment of the severely mentally ill population (TAC, 2011). By setting exceedingly costly, unreachable standards for hospitals that already were operating on miniscule budgets, many states chose instead to empty their hospitals. In Alabama, for example, the state hospital population dropped by almost two-thirds from 1970 to 1975, amidst a 327% increase in costs to run the facilities (TAC, 2011). It was also after *Wyatt* that Bruce Ennis founded the Mental Health Law Project, renamed the Bazelon Center for Mental Health Law, and ultimately established the mental health bar discussed previously, thereby further restricting involuntary treatment (TAC, 2011).[28]

---

28. Two other cases are considered to be right to treatment cases related to civil commitment; however, they are not as pivotal as the preceding cases on this topic and, thus, will not be discussed fully. In *O'Connor v. Donaldson* (1975), for example, while the circuit court recognized a constitutional right to treatment, upon appeal, the U.S. Supreme Court elected not to rule on that aspect of the case. And, in *Youngberg v. Romeo* (1982), regarding a patient with mental retardation, the U.S. Supreme Court seemed to backtrack somewhat on the right to treatment, ruling that involuntarily committed patients are only entitled to treatment to the extent that it assures their freedom from restraint and preventable assault inside the institution. Furthermore, *Estelle v. Gamble* (1976) could also be considered a right to treatment case, in the context of corrections. Specifically, the U.S. Supreme Court determined in this case that deliberate indifference to an inmate's medical needs could constitute a violation of the 8th Amendment's prohibition against cruel and unusual punishment.

A Federal Call for Community Mental Health Care

Although Harry Truman was the first U.S. President to show interest in the plight of persons with mental illness, signing into law the National Mental Health Act of 1946, it was not until 1955, under the Eisenhower administration, that Congress called for a thorough, systematic examination of the issue on a national level. The Mental Health Study Act led to the formation of the Joint Commission on Mental Illness and Health, which issued its final report, *Action for Mental Health*, in 1961 (National Institutes of Health, 2011). The primary recommendation of the Commission report was a national program to treat people with mental illness in community-based clinics, with a focus on prevention and early intervention. Secondary goals were to significantly improve hospitals, which were to be reserved for those most impaired by mental illness, and to increase training for mental health professionals in order to ensure a necessary workforce that had been lacking previously for serving this population. The Commission called for spending on mental health to double in five years and triple in ten years (Koyanagi, 2007).

In 1963, President John F. Kennedy became the first president to address Congress on mental health issues. Unbeknownst to many, Kennedy had a special interest in the issue of mental illness, having had a sister who was institutionalized for much of her life and eventually lobotomized (Stroman, 2003); he had committed to making mental illness a focus of his New Frontier agenda. Consistent with the Joint Commission's recommendations, Kennedy called for a "strengthening of non-institutional services" and a downsizing of the "massive subsidizing of existing, anachronistic state public health institutions" (Gillon, 2000, p. 93). The short-term goal was to reduce the number of patients in state hospitals by 50% (Gillon, 2000), with the intention of eventually replacing most institutions with comprehensive community health care agencies. Kennedy, too, called for a tripling of funds, which would be directed to communities rather than to states; localities would be expected to develop community hospitals and community mental health centers, while states would remain responsible for long-term institutional services (Koyanagi, 2007). Of the hold-outs in Congress, Kennedy appealed to their pocketbooks, stressing, "Here [e.g., the topic of mental health] more than in any other area, an ounce of prevention is worth more than a pound of cure. For prevention is ... far more economical and far more likely to be successful" (Isaac & Armat, 1990, p. 77). On October 31, 1963, the Mental Retardation Facilities and Community Mental Health Centers Construction Act (or the Community Mental Health Centers (CMHC) Act, as it came to be called) was signed into law.

The Beginning of Deinstitutionalization

In its original conceptualization, "deinstitutionalization" consisted of three sequential processes: (1) the establishment of specialized community treatment services for persons with mental illnesses; (2) the movement of psychiatric hospital patients out of state hospitals into community treatment facilities and services; (3) the diversion of individuals who would have previously been hospitalized to alternative community facilities and treatment (Lamb & Bachrach, 2001). It was a great plan, in theory. Minimizing institutionalization was best for everyone: for patients as it allowed them to be (re)integrated into their communities and for the public because community mental health care cost less than institutionalization. It also placed accountability for the care of the mentally ill back in the hands of local authorities rather than states or the federal government. Plus, the CMHC Act appropriated money for the development of community treatment programs.

The problem arose, however, in that the funding was never fully allocated. With the assassination of President Kennedy a month after the act was signed into law, coupled with the need to finance the Vietnam War, attention — and resources — were diverted elsewhere. Without pressure from the executive branch, community resistance to placement of the CMHCs in their neighborhood (e.g., due to a "not in my backyard" (NIMBY) mentality) won the battle (Gilligan, 2001). According to Rabkin (1979), "Such resistance [was] vocal, effective, and widespread, leading to the passage of municipal ordinances and legal barriers to the establishment of local facilities" (p. 1). As such, plans for the establishment of a network of half-way houses, community residences, outpatient clinics, and other alternatives to mental hospitals never cohesively materialized. Even the centers that were built went largely under-funded. Indeed, CMHCs received less federal funding from 1963 to 1981 than the total disbursement of Supplemental Security Income and Social Security Disability Insurance payments to persons with mental illness in 1981 alone (Cournos & Le Melle, 2000). Although the Joint Commission had outlined a comprehensive approach, with a major focus on persons with mental illness at risk of institutionalization, by the time the act was implemented, the original intent was forgotten. Instead, the centers prioritized their services, focusing their funding on higher-functioning clientele (e.g., those with less severe, and potentially more treatable, disorders), ignoring the needs of the severely and persistently mentally ill who were or were about to be released by state hospitals (Koyanagi, 2007). Furthermore, with no instruments in place to measure an agency's fidelity to the intended purpose of the funding and/or the effectiveness of the services, there was no accountability and, thus, no opportunity for recourse.

Despite the failure to implement the first phase of the deinstitutionalization process, the second phase began in earnest. Thousands of patients were released from mental hospitals with the plan for them to be connected with community care. From a high of 559,000 state hospital patients in 1955 (Lamb & Weinberger, 2005), the number plummeted. In the decade between 1965 and 1975, total state hospital censuses plunged from just over 500,000 patients to approximately 200,000 (Torrey, 1997). By 1980, this number reached fewer than 100,000 (Earley, 2006).[29]

---

29. Although the deinstitutionalization movement of the 1960s, '70s, and '80s is well-known, a little recognized fact is that more state psychiatric hospitals closed in the 1990s than in the 1970s and '80s combined (NASMHPD, 2000). With data from NASMHPD, Torrey, Fuller, Geller, Jacobs, and

Without community care available, thousands of people with serious mental illness — many of whom lacked the wherewithal or resources to care for themselves after decades of hospitalization — flooded the streets. Untreated, many quickly decompensated into active mental illness, now with nowhere to turn. Many — the "social junk" (Spitzer, 1976) or "toxic waste" (Feeley & Simon, 1992), as they have been called — became homeless, were arrested and incarcerated, and/or died (Gilligan, 2001).

Restricting Civil Commitment

Ironically, at the same time that increasing numbers of people with untreated mental illness were filling the communities, civil commitment statutes by which they could be provided treatment when they needed it were being modified, making it more difficult for the state to treat people against their will. The modifications were brought about by the civil rights movement's success in securing patients' right to treatment, including treatment in the least restrictive environment, discussed previously. Likewise, states revised their statutes to conform to several cases that changed the standards and proceedings: *O'Connor v. Donaldson* (1975) and *Lessard v. Schmidt* (1976). All of these cases significantly altered the legal landscape of civil commitment as it had previously been known.

O'Connor v. Donaldson (1975) for the first time directly addressed the requirements and limitations that due process put on the state's traditional *parens patriae* power to civilly commit a person, which had governed involuntary hospitalizations up to that point (Stavis, 1995). Donaldson was civilly committed after voicing concerns to his father that his neighbors were poisoning him. Although the case was obviously relevant to the right to treatment — Donaldson was hospitalized without treatment for 15 years, on a 1000-patient ward that was staffed by a single doctor (an obstetrician, not even a psychiatrist) and a nurse — the U.S. Supreme Court avoided making a judgment on the issue. The Court did consider the case, however, on grounds of the standard by which Donaldson was committed. First, he was committed without the benefit of counsel at his commitment hearing. Moreover, he maintained throughout his stay that he did not have a mental illness and consistently sought his release.

Upon hearing the case, the U.S. Supreme Court ruled that "[a] State cannot constitutionally confine, without more, a *non-dangerous* individual who is *capable of surviving safely in freedom* by himself or with the help of willing and responsible family members or friends" (*O'Connor v. Donaldson*, 1975, p. 576; italics added). This was a radical ruling as the Court had never before contradicted the *parens patriae* power of the state to care for those who are incompetent to make their own treatment

---

Ragosta (2012) report that, as of 2010, the number of persons with mental illnesses housed in state psychiatric hospitals had been reduced to approximately 43,000, 92% less than the number of state hospital beds in 1955 (Lamb, Weinberger, & Gross, 2004), possibly as low as 40,000 persons (Florida Supreme Court, 2007). Whichever number is correct, this represents more than a 90% decrease since the heyday of state institutionalization.

decisions; rather, it had always verified this important power of government. As such, many legal experts argued that the Court did not intend to eliminate or hinder the state's power. Other mental health law attorneys (such as Ennis's mental health bar) and even lower courts, however, interpreted the ruling to mean that patients must be proven to be "dangerous" (i.e., a danger to themselves or others) before they could be involuntarily civilly committed. Regardless of the true intent of the Court, it caused a great deal of debate and, thus, set into motion substantial limiting of the state's ability to act swiftly in its *parens patriae* capacity (Stavis, 1995).

Lessard v. Schmidt (1976), in turn, narrowed civil commitment standards even further. The case began with an involuntary commitment in a manner that was fairly routine during that time period: Alberta Lessard was taken into custody by police after a reported suicide attempt and was taken to a mental health facility. She was hospitalized for an extended period of time for evaluation, during which she was diagnosed with schizophrenia, and then the hospital requested her permanent commitment; she was ultimately committed for nearly a year (Erickson, Vitacco, & Van Rybroek, 2005). She was not notified of any of these proceedings and, thus, was neither at the proceedings nor able to present her own evidence. The point at which Lessard's case differed from a typical civil commitment is that, on her own initiative, she retained an attorney and pursued a class action lawsuit. In the lawsuit, Lessard claimed that the Wisconsin civil commitment statute violated her (and others subsumed under the class action) due process rights.

Ultimately, the federal district court ruled in favor of Lessard. First, the court addressed the standard for involuntary commitment. Following *O'Connor*, the court vacated the *parens patriae* basis for civil commitment and more clearly defined the "dangerousness standard" that governs involuntary civil commitment to this day. Specifically, the court stipulated that involuntary hospitalization was only permissible when there is an "*extreme likelihood* that if the person is not confined he will do *immediate* harm *to himself or others*" (*Lessard v. Schmidt*, 1976, p. 1093; italics added). The *Lessard* court also asserted for the first time that subjects of civil commitment proceedings should be afforded all the constitutional protections of a criminal suspect (e.g., right to counsel, standard of proof beyond a reasonable doubt[30]), recognizing that the repercussions of civil commitment are at least as serious as those of criminal incarceration. Specifically, the court noted that the difficulty of obtaining release, the stigma, the loss of civil rights, and even the mortality rate faced by civilly committed patients are greater than that of criminal inmates (Erickson et al., 2005; TAC, 2011). In many spheres, *Lessard* is considered to be the most revolutionary case in mental health law, bringing an end to broad commitment standards and the view that involuntary commitment is first and foremost a medical decision; instead, the case

---

30. *Addington v. Texas* (1978) revised the standard of proof in civil commitment proceedings to the moderate "clear and convincing evidence" level of certainty (i.e., between the most stringent, "beyond a reasonable doubt" standard of criminal proceedings and the least stringent, "preponderance of the evidence" [i.e., comparatively more evidence is in favor of requiring civil commitment than is not] used in most civil proceedings).

drew civil commitment firmly into the realm of police power and quasi-criminal court proceedings (TAC, 2011).

States began to revise their civil commitment standards in accordance with these cases. California presaged the reform movement in 1967 — when the first right to treatment cases (discussed previously) were decided, before *O'Connor v. Donaldson* and *Lessard v. Schmidt* were ruled on — when it implemented the Lanterman-Petris-Short Act. The Lanterman-Petris-Short Act, dubbed by some as the "Magna Carta of the mentally ill" (Abramson, 1972), placed strict legal limits on involuntary psychiatric hospitalizations in California. It was a highly popular bill, passing both the House of Representatives and the Senate without a single dissenting vote from either civil liberties-oriented Democrats or fiscally conservative Republicans (Farland, 2002). Other states followed suit shortly thereafter with enactments, most coming into effect in the 1970s. The exact standards varied somewhat from state to state, but most restricted grounds for commitment to dangerousness to self or others and/or grave disability (generally defined as the inability to provide for one's basic needs, such as food, clothing, and/or shelter; Lenell, 1977), along with adopting more rigorous legal procedures (Fisher & Grisso, 2010). Overall, involuntary civil commitment statutes made commitment to and retention in psychiatric hospitals more difficult. Although many — mental health professionals, judges, and family members alike — were concerned with the impact such changes would have, having removed the primary means by which persons with mental illness could be treated when they lacked the insight to recognize their illness, politicians capitalized on the changes as a cost-saving mechanism.

Governmental Cost Shifting

Seemingly in the best interests of persons with mental illness, Congress — with the various representatives serving their own state's interests — began to pass various laws that made persons with mental illnesses eligible for federal assistance programs. In 1965, Medicaid and Medicare began to cover persons with mental illness (Koyanagi, 2007). Housing assistance, disability insurance, supplemental income, and food stamps soon followed (Earley, 2006; Goldman, Adams, & Taube, 1983; Torrey, 1997). Upon closer examination, however, such actions were merely evidence of money driving public policy. Indeed, these decisions were made in the face of the mounting class-action lawsuits and increasing public scrutiny of state hospitals; thus, state legislators seized upon these federal programs as an opportunity to unload the costs of caring for persons with mental illnesses from the states to the federal government (Earley, 2006; Goldman et al., 1983).

One such example of transferring responsibility from the state to the federal system was the advent of the practice of treating persons with mental illnesses in homes for the aged and dependent instead of state hospitals (Cournos & Le Melle, 2000). Specifically, between 1950 and 1980, as states used federal matching money for nursing homes, the percentage of institutionalized persons in psychiatric hospitals decreased from 40% to 10%, while the percentage of institutionalized persons in nursing homes increased from 20% to more than 50% (Koyanagi, 2007). By 1980, people with serious mental illness represented 44% of the nursing home population (Solomon, Gordon, & Davis, 1984). In total, all of these cost shifting mechanisms from states to the federal government effectively obscured the need for intensive, residential services, thereby further propelling the deinstitutionalization movement.

Federal support for social assistance and services to the mentally ill has been fickle throughout U.S. history, fluctuating with the agendas of the political party in power at any given time. This was particularly true in the period of (and following) deinstitutionalization (Farland, 2002). Set into motion with Kennedy's Community Mental Health Centers Act and continued by Lyndon Johnson, Richard Nixon quickly rescinded funding for the centers after he took office in 1969. President Jimmy Carter took a renewed interest in fixing the federal community mental health centers program by expanding services beyond clinical care alone, but his Mental Health Systems Act was repealed and funds were cut by 25% during President Ronald Reagan's administration (Koyanagi, 2007; Thomas, 1998). Hundreds of thousands of people with mental illness were left without income and became homeless as federal disability rules were changed and federal support for low-income housing was slashed.[31] As noted by Koyanagi (2007, p. 8), "With no money, nowhere to live and an underfunded mental health service system, many were in dire straits."

Greater Visibility, Fear, and Punitiveness toward Persons with Mental Illness

With state hospitals closing, many former patients were being released into communities. With limited treatment available in the communities, many became acutely ill and homeless. The general public began to be exposed to people with serious mental illness more than ever before. No longer were persons with mental illness out of sight and out of mind. No longer did the streets feel safe. For the first time, the general public began to witness bizarre, seemingly inexplicable behavior from persons with untreated, serious mental illness (e.g., the homeless man on the street yelling obscenities at the aliens following him); people tend to be afraid of that with which they are not familiar or do not understand. Furthermore, in fear, they generalized this seemingly threatening behavior to all people with mental illness, even though research showed that most persons with mental illness never acted violently.[32] As such, the mentally ill became more visible and more feared. Although mental illness had always been stigmatized, fear of individuals with mental illness grew after the 1950s. In fact, research documented that the proportion of U.S. society who believed people with mental illness are dangerous, violent, and/or frightening increased by 250% between 1950 and 2000, with 75% of the public currently holding such beliefs (Phelan, Link, Stueve, & Pescosolido, 2000).

---

31. It is noteworthy — and ironic — that Ronald Reagan, who had then been governor of California, had been one of several key politicians responsible for the Lanterman-Petris-Short Act, considered to be a mark of the liberation of institutionalized mentally ill, in 1967.

32. The research on the relationship between mental illness and violence will be discussed in more detail in Chapter 3.

Undoubtedly, this tendency to fear persons with mental illness was due in part to shifts in the media's depictions. Whereas in previous decades, when the media focused on the inhumane and degrading treatment in state hospitals (i.e., the injustices *against* persons with mental illness), the media began to shift its focus to sensationalizing the rare, but seemingly random and threatening, acts of violence committed by the deinstitutionalized persons with mental illness. The public is drawn to these depictions, partially because it validates their fears, partially because it feeds their fears, and the media is happy to accommodate (Stossel, 2007).

In the 1980s, U.S. society also shifted its attitudes about what it considered crime and its response to deviance. In particular, the public moved away from its rehabilitative ideals to a more retributive, punitive stance. This was evident in criminal justice policies such as three strikes laws, tougher drug control laws, and zero tolerance policies (Tonry, 2004). As a result, U.S. jail and prison populations soared. Between 1978 and 2000 — i.e., in half the time period as the 90% decline in state hospital censuses — the number of jail and prison inmates increased approximately 400%, from just under 475,000 to nearly 2 million (Lamb & Weinberger, 2005).

These punitive attitudes extended to people with mental illness. Those who were just liberated from the indignities of the state hospitals were now seen as worthy of arrest and unworthy of treatment in the criminal justice system (Lamb & Weinberger, 1998). By the 1980s, persons with mental illness began arriving in jails and prisons in such numbers that the term "transinstitutionalization" replaced "deinstitutionalization" in some spheres (Barr, 2003; Lurigio & Swartz, 2000). Indeed, between 1980 and 1992 alone, the number of individuals with mental illness in jails increased by 154% (Watson, Hanrahan, Luchins, & Lurigio, 2001).

Criminalization of Persons with Mental Illness

This phenomenon has also come to be known as the "criminalization of mental illness" (or "criminalization of the mentally ill"). Abramson first coined the phrase "criminalization of mentally disordered behavior" in 1972 after passage of the Lanterman-Petris-Short Act of 1967 (Abramson, 1972; Lamb & Weinberger, 1998; Miller, 1992). He had found that in the year following implementation of the act, the number of persons with mental illness entering the criminal justice system had doubled. Predicting more of the same, he remarked on restricting civil commitment in the name of civil liberties, "It would indeed be ironic if the Magna Carta of the mentally ill ... led to their criminal stigmatization and incarceration in jails and prisons, where little or no mental health treatment is provided" (Abramson, 1972, p. 105). And indeed, this irony was clearly revealed by several research studies examining the California act. One study, comparing arrests in San Mateo County from three and one-half years before to four and one-half years after passage of the act, found that the arrest rate for persons with mental illnesses had increased four and one-half times over this time period (Sosowsky, 1978).

This was not the first time, nor the last time, that someone had found evidence for the theory that the more difficult it is to civilly commit people with mental illness, the more likely the criminal justice system will become involved, both on an aggregate level and on an individual level. As early as 1939, Penrose found that as psychiatric hospital populations decreased, prison populations increased, and vice versa (Lamb & Weinberger, 1998). And studies have documented this phenomenon since deinstitutionalization of state hospital patients during the latter half of the 20th century. Raphael (2000), for example, recently maintained that a strong inverse, causal relationship exists between deinstitutionalization and incarceration rates. While there is some debate about whether deinstitutionalization *caused* the criminalization of persons with mental illnesses (Fisher, 2003; Hogan, 2000),[33] there is evidence that deinstitutionalization at least contributed to it (Lamb et al., 2004; Lamb & Weinberger, 1998).

As state hospitals were downsized or closed, more and more individuals with mental illnesses drifted into the streets and encountered the criminal justice system — a system that was ill-quipped to deal with their needs (Butterfield, 1998; Kerle, 1998). This phenomenon is captured in the editorial cartoon by Englehart (2000) below. A great deal of research has been conducted since the advent of deinstitutionalization comparing arrest rates of those with mental illness and prevalence rates of mental illness in jails and prisons with those in the general public. The research has consistently illustrated a criminalization effect.[34]

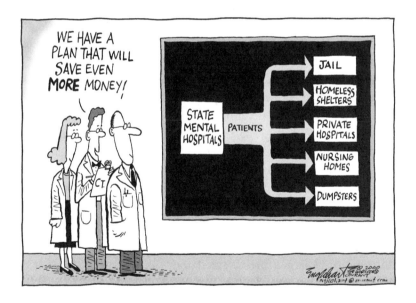

© Bob Englehart, Hartford (CT) Courant

---

33. Some have expressed concern that the belief that deinstitutionalization caused the criminalization of persons with mental illnesses may wrongly imply that reinstitutionalization is the answer (Hogan, 2000). Lamb and Bachrach (2001) believe that most persons with mental illnesses, including those who are homeless or inappropriately incarcerated, can realize their potential and function within society with the provision and implementation of adequate community resources.

34. It should be noted, however, that without studies of the same events conducted prior to the 1960s, one cannot definitively conclude that the high rates of criminal justice involvement of people with mental illness are a result of deinstitutionalization.

Given the increased numbers of people with mental illness in the streets following deinstitutionalization and the role of police officers as first responders, police came to be recognized as "street-corner psychiatrists" (Teplin & Pruett, 1992, p. 139), providers of "psychiatric first aid" (Bittner, 1967, p. 288), "de facto mental health providers" (Patch & Arrigo, 1999, p. 23), and the "primary gatekeepers" of both the criminal justice and mental health systems. In this role, police had the discretion to resolve encounters with persons with mental illness either informally, through referral to community mental health agencies, or formally, through arrest. However, with the lack of community treatment resources, it made it difficult to handle mental illness calls informally. This was consistently borne out in research: In the decades since deinstitutionalization began, police arrested persons with mental illness at a significantly higher rate than those without mental illness. In the seminal study on this issue, Teplin (1984) found that police arrested 47% of suspects exhibiting signs of mental illness, compared to only 28% of suspects under similar circumstances who did not exhibit such signs. Likewise, a number of studies revealed that, of persons with mental illness, 40% to 50% have been arrested at least once (Frankle et al., 2001; Solomon & Draine, 1995; Walsh & Bricourt, 1997). The most direct examinations of the effect of deinstitutionalization on arrest rates, though, were conducted by Rabkin (1979) and Sosowsky (1980). Rabkin critically analyzed eight American studies on the arrest rates of discharged psychiatric patients conducted between 1965 and 1978 (deinstitutionalization era) and compared them to the arrest rate of patients prior to 1950 (pre-deinstitutionalization). She discovered that, compared to the pre-deinstitutionalization era when arrest rates for those with mental illness were lower than those reported for the general population, each study during the deinstitution-alization era found arrest and/or conviction rates of former state hospital patients to equal or exceed those of the general public. Likewise, Sosowsky (1980) found, that in California between 1972 and 1975, discharged patients with no prior arrest history were arrested three times more frequently than the general public; discharged patients with a history of prior arrests were approximately eight times more likely to be arrested than the general population. Overall, this body of research was important as contact with law enforcement is the first, pivotal point in the path of criminal justice involvement.

Contrary to popular perceptions, people with mental illness were not usually being arrested for serious, violent crimes; instead, they were being detained primarily on minor, misdemeanor charges (Clark, Ricketts, & McHugo, 1999; Cuellar, Snowden, & Ewing, 2007; Torrey, 1997). Indeed, persons with mental illness were four times as likely to be charged with minor crimes as those without mental illness (Valdiserri, Carroll, & Hartl, 1986). With pressure to "clean up the streets," police charged persons with mental illness — especially the homeless mentally ill — with minor-nuisance crimes, such as loitering and trespassing (Clark et al., 1999). A person with mental illness who, for example, talked too loudly to the voices in his/her head or to a fearful passerby was prone to be charged with disorderly conduct. Many were charged with subsistence crimes, such as misdemeanor shoplifting of food or hygiene products. In other cases, well-intentioned police — who accurately perceived there to be no suitable treatment alternatives — charged individuals with mental illness on bogus charges in an attempt to save them from the dangers of the street (e.g., sexual assault, exposure to the elements), in what have come to be referred to as "mercy bookings" (Lamb, Weinberger, & DeCuir, 2002). Likewise, police sometimes agreed to charge a person with mental illness with a crime in order to "help" a family get treatment for their loved one, albeit in the criminal justice system, after the person had been turned away repeatedly by the mental health system.

Research on U.S. jails and prisons following the advent of deinstitutionalization also confirmed a heightened rate of serious mental illness (including psychotic disorders, such as schizophrenia, and serious mood disorders, such as bipolar disorder) as compared to the rate of mental illness in the general public. One of the first such studies, conducted by Swank and Winer (1976), found that 22% of more than 500 inmates were diagnosed as psychotic,[35] and 23% had a history of long-term (more than one month) and/or multiple hospitalizations. Many had been state hospital patients. This was a fact not lost on the jail personnel, who noted a marked increase in those with severe mental illness entering the jail. Similarly, Whitmer (1980) found that only 6% of his study population was receiving treatment at the time of their arrests, leading him to conclude that deinstitutionalization had forced a large number of patients into the criminal justice system. Although the rates of serious mental illness in jails in most studies in the 1980s were not as pronounced as those of Swank and Winer (1976), the rates were consistently several times higher than rates of mental illness in the general public, hovering around 5% to 7% (Guy, Platt, Zwerling, & Bullock, 1985; Teplin, 1990).[36] Likewise, studies of prisons revealed similar, if not slightly higher, rates of serious mental illness among inmates (ranging from approximately 7% to 10%) when compared to the general, non-institutionalized population (James, Gregory, Jones, & Rundell, 1980; Jemelka, Trupin, Chiles, 1989; Steadman, Fabisiak, Dvoskin, & Holohean, 1987).

As the above body of research accumulated, it was hard to refute that many former state hospital patients were being propelled into the criminal justice system. Not only were people with serious mental illness being arrested at a disproportionately high rate, they were being convicted, jailed, and imprisoned at a disproportionate level. The criminalization of persons with mental illness was well underway.

Conclusion

There have been marked societal shifts throughout history in the perceived need to care for versus control people with mental illness. Most salient to the contemporary criminalization effect is the changing beliefs in the appropriateness of institutional-

---

35. Schizophrenia is generally estimated to affect approximately 1% of the general population, as does bipolar disorder.

36. As discussed in Chapter 1, this rate has increased, with the most commonly cited statistic to be 16% of the jail population (Ditton, 1999; Steadman, Osher, Robbins, Case, & Samuels, 2009).

ization, on the one hand, and deinstitutionalization on the other (Johnson, 2011). Such judgments are formed by the prevailing sociocultural, political, and economic forces of the time, as was delineated throughout this chapter.

In particular, the deinstitutionalization movement initiated in the 1960s was prompted by a unique convergence of factors, including media exposure and popular culture critiques of state psychiatric hospitals, made accessible by new technologies (e.g., TV) and a push for liberty and freedom by the civil rights movement. A sort of power vacuum within the psychiatric community occurred as moral, talk therapies declined and new medications were marketed as a cost-saving mechanism to politicians, including a president who had a strong personal interest in the treatment of mental illness. These factors set into motion a mass exodus of individuals with serious mental illness from state-run psychiatric institutions into the community. Despite the federal government's plan to establish community mental health services, the intense conformity and "not in my backyard" mentality in the community, coupled with distraction of attention and resources to President Kennedy's assassination and the Vietnam War, prevented its successful implementation. This left the former patients without the community mental health network — or, more aptly, safety net — that they so desperately needed. With no money, no place to live, and no treatment, people with mental illness ended up homeless, in the criminal justice system, or dead.

The criminalization of persons with mental illness resulting from, at least partially, the deinstitutionalization movement of the 20th century forms the basis for this book. In particular, the following chapter focuses on the needs and challenges of those with mental illness within the criminal justice system at the current time. As the pendulum of deinstitutionalization continues to swing, it remains to be seen how the correctional trend of imprisonment of the 1990s and the current trend of managed care and privatization will affect forensic mental health care.

References

Abramson, M. F. (1972). The criminalization of mentally disordered behavior: Possible side-effect of a new mental health law. *Hospital & Community Psychiatry, 23*(4), 101–105.

Addington v. Texas, 441 U.S. 418 (1979).

Anfang, S. A., & Appelbaum, P. S. (2006). Civil commitment — The American experience. *Israel Journal of Psychiatry and Related Sciences, 43*(3), 219–228.

Barr, H. (2003). Transinstitutionalization in the courts: *Brad H. v. City of New York*, and the fight for discharge planning for people with psychiatric disabilities leaving Rikers Island. *Crime & Delinquency, 49*(1), 97–123.

Benjamin Rush, M.D. (1749–1813): "The Father of American Psychiatry." (2011, September 13). *Diseases of the Mind: Highlights of American Psychiatry through 1900.* Bethesda, MD: National Institutes of Health, U.S. National Library of Medicine. Retrieved from http://www.nlm.nih.gov/hmd/diseases/benjamin.html.

Bethlem Royal Hospital. (n.d.). *Science Museum: Brought to life: Exploring the history of medicine.* Retrieved from http://www.sciencemuseum.org.uk/broughttolife/techniques/bethlemroyalhospital.aspx.

Birnbaum, M. (1960). The right to treatment. *American Bar Association Journal, 46,* 499–505.

Birnbaum, R. (2012). Remembering the "right to treatment." *American Journal of Psychiatry, 169,* 358–359.

Bittner, E. (1967). Police discretion in emergency apprehension of mentally ill persons. *Social Problems, 14,* 278–292.

Brakel, S. J., & Rock, R. S. (1971). *The mentally disabled and the law.* Chicago, IL: University of Chicago Press.

Brodsky, A. (2004). *Benjamin Rush: Patriot and physician.* New York, NY: Truman Talley Books.

Buck v. Bell, 274 U.S. 200. (1927).

Burke, M. A., & Embrick, D. G. (2008). Biological determinism. *International Encyclopedia of the Social Sciences.* Retrieved from http://www.encyclopedia.com/topic/Biological_determinism.aspx.

Butterfield, F. (1998, March 5). Prisons replace hospitals for the nation's mentally ill. *New York Times,* pp. 1A, 18A.

Carr, L. W. (2004, July). Wyatt v. Stickney: A landmark decision. *Alabama Disabilities Advocacy Program Newsletter,* 1–3.

Christmas, D. (2012, September 10). *A brief history of neurosurgery for mental disorder.* Edinburgh, Scotland: National Services of Scotland, Advanced Interventions Service. Retrieved from http://www.advancedinterventions.org.uk/NMD_history_3_5.htm.

Clark, R. E., Ricketts, S. K., & McHugo, G. J. (1999). Legal system involvement and costs for persons in treatment for severe mental illness and substance use disorders. *Psychiatric Services, 50,* 641–647.

Cohen, F. (2000, September/October). Hiring discount exorcist to treat delusional forensic patient leads to executive's dismissal. *Correctional Mental Health Report, 2*(3), 1.

Collins English Dictionary. (2003). *Xenophobia.* Retrieved from http://www.thefreedictionary.com/xenophobia.

Cournos, F., & Le Melle, S. (2000). The young adult chronic patient: A look back. *Psychiatric Services, 51,* 996–1000.

Cuellar A. E., Snowden, L. M., & Ewing T. (2007). Criminal records of persons served in the public mental health system. *Psychiatric Services, 58*(1), 114–120.

Curtis, A. (2001, December). Involuntary commitment. *Bad Subjects: Political Education for Everyday Life, 58.* Retrieved from http://psychrights.org/states/Maine/InvoluntaryCommitmentbyAliciaCurtis.htm.

Custance, A. C., & Travis, L. E. (1979). *The mysterious matter of mind*. New York, N.Y.: Zondervan. Retrieved from http://custance.org/old/mind/ch2m.html.

Dershowitz, A. (1974). The origin of preventive confinement in Anglo-American Law, Part II. *University of Cincinnati Law Review, 43*, 781–846.

Deutsch, A. (2007). *The mentally ill in America: A history of their care and treatment from colonial times*. Stamford, CT: Holley Press.

Ditton, P. M. (1999, July). *Special report: Mental health treatment of inmates and probationers* (NCJ 174463). Washington, D.C.: U.S. Department of Justice, Bureau of Justice Statistics. Retrieved from http://bjs.ojp.usdoj.gov/index.cfm?ty=pbdetail&iid=787.

Dorothea Dix. (n.d.). *United States History*. Retrieved from http://www.u-s-history.com/pages/h1092.html.

Durrant, R., & Thakker, J. (2003). *Substance use and abuse: Cultural and historical perspectives*. Thousand Oaks, CA: Sage.

Earley, P. (2006). *Crazy: A father's search through America's mental health madness*. New York, NY: G. P. Putnam and Sons.

Ebert, T. G. (1999). *Mental illness and its treatment in the late 19th and early 20th century*. Lima, OH: Wyndham Hall Press.

Eisler, K. I. (1993). *A justice for all: William J. Brennan, Jr., and the decisions that transformed America*. New York, NY: Simon & Schuster

Erickson, S. K., Vitacco, M. J., & Van Rybroek, G. J. (2005). Beyond overt violence: Wisconsin's progressive civil commitment statute as a marker of a new era in mental health law. Marquette Law Review, 89, 359–405.

Estelle v. Gamble, 429 U.S. 97 (1976).

Farland, M. (2002). Sylvia Plath's anti-psychiatry. *The Minnesota Review, n.s.* 55–57. Retrieved from http://www.theminnesotareview.org/journal/ns55/farland.htm.

Favaro, A., Tenconi E., Colombo, G., & Santonastaso, P. (2006). Full and partial Post-Traumatic Stress Disorder among World War II prisoners of war. *Psychopathology, 39*, 187–191.

Feeley, M. M., & Simon, J. (1992). The new penology: Notes on the emerging strategy of corrections and its implications. Criminology, 30, 449–474.

Fisher, W. H. (2003). *Community based interventions for criminal offenders with severe mental illness*. Oxford, England: Elsevier.

Fisher, W. H., & Grisso, T. (2010). Civil commitment statues-40 years of circumvention. *Journal of the American Academy of Psychiatry and Law, 38*(3), 365–368.

Foucault, M. (1965). *Madness and civilization: A history of insanity in the age of reason* (R. Howard. Trans.). New York, NY: Pantheon.

Frankle, W. G., Shera, D., Berger-Hershkowitz, H., Evins, A. E., Connolly, C., Goff, D. C., & Henderson, D. C. (2001). Clozapine-associated reduction in arrest rates of psychotic patients with criminal histories. *American Journal of Psychiatry, 158*, 270–274.

Gado, M. (n.d.). *The insanity defense.* Retrieved from http://www.trutv.com/library/crime/criminal_mind/psychology/insanity/2.html.

Gardner, A., & Cho, D. (2007, May 6). Isolation defined Cho's senior year. *Washington Post*, p. A01.

Gerard, D. L. (1997). Chiarugi and Pinel considered: Soul's brain/person's mind. *Journal of the History of the Behavioral Sciences, 33*(4), 381.

Ghareeb, L. (n.d.). *Dorothea Dix.* Retrieved from http://learningtogive.org/papers/paper89.html.

Gibson, C. J., & Lennon, E. (1999, February). *Historical census statistics on the foreign-born population of the United States: 1850 to 1990* (Population Division Working Paper No. 29). Washington, D.C.: U.S. Bureau of the Census. Retrieved from http://www.census.gov/population/www/documentation/twps0029/twps0029.html.

Gilligan, J. (2001). The last mental hospital, *Psychiatric Quarterly, 72*(1), 45–77.

Gillon, S. (2000). *That's not what we meant to do: Reform and its unintended consequences in Twentieth-century America.* New York, NY: Norton.

Goffman, E. (1961). *Asylums: Essays on the social situation of mental patients and other inmates.* New York, NY: Penguin.

Goldman, H. H., Adams, N. H., & Taube, C. A. (1983). Deinstitutionalization: The data demythologized. *Psychiatric Services, 34*, 129–134.

Gollaher, D. (1995). *Voice for the mad: The life of Dorothea Dix.* New York, NY: Free Press.

Gorman, M. (1956). *Every other bed.* Cleveland, OH: World Publishing Co.

Grossman, L., & Lacayo, R. (2005, October 16). All-time 100 novels. *Time.* Retrieved from http://entertainment.time.com/2005/10/16/all-time-100-novels/#how-we-picked-the-list.

Guy, E., Platt, J. J., Zwerling, I., & Bullock, S. (1985). Mental health status of prisoners in an urban jail. *Criminal Justice and Behavior, 12*, 29–53.

Head, T. (n.d.). *American xenophobia: A short illustrated history of xenophobia in the United States.* Retrieved from http://civilliberty.about.com/od/immigrants rights/tp/Xenophobia-in-United-States.htm.

Healy, D. (2004). *The creation of psychopharmacology.* Cambridge, MA: Harvard University Press.

Herstek, A. P. (2001). *Dorothea Dix: Crusader for the mentally ill.* New Jersey: Enslow Publishers.

Hippocrates., Adams, F., & Sydenham Society. (1849). *The genuine works of Hippocrates.* London: Printed for the Sydenham Society.

Hogan, M. F. (2000, September 21). *Testimony before the Subcommittee on Crime of the Committee on the Judiciary, U.S. House of Representatives.* Retrieved from www.house.gov/judiciary/hoga0921.htm.

Immigration restriction. (2012, June 8). *Digital History: The Jazz Age — The American 1920s.* Retrieved from http://www.digitalhistory.uh.edu/database/article_display. cfm?HHID=446.

Iredale, R. (2000). Eugenics and its relevance to contemporary health care. *Nursing Ethics, 7*(3), 205–214.

Isaac, R. J., & Armat, V. (1990). *Madness in the streets: How psychiatry and the law abandoned the mentally ill.* New York, NY: Free Press.

Israel, J. I. (2006). *Enlightenment contested: Philosophy, modernity, and the emancipation of man 1670–1752.* Oxford, England: Oxford University Press.

James, J. F., Gregory, D., Jones, R. K., & Rundell, O. H. (1980). Psychiatric morbidity in prisons. *Hospital & Community Psychiatry, 11*, 674–677.

Jemelka, R., Trupin, E., & Chiles, J. A. (1989). The mentally ill in prisons: A review. *Hospital & Community Psychiatry, 40*, 481–485.

Johnson, W. W. (2011). Rethinking the interface between mental illness, criminal justice and academia. *Justice Quarterly, 28,* 15–22.

Judge David L. Bazelon Center for Mental Health Law. (2012a). *Judge David L. Bazelon: The jurist.* Washington, D.C.: Author. Retrieved from http://www. bazelon.org/Who-We-Are/History/Judge-David-L.-Bazelon.aspx.

Judge David L. Bazelon Center for Mental Health Law. (2012b). *Who we are.* Washington, D.C.: Author. Retrieved from http://www.bazelon.org/Who-We-Are. aspx.

Kerle, K. E. (1998). *American jails: Looking to the future.* Boston, MA: Butterworth-Heinemann.

Kesey, K. (1962). *One flew over the cuckoo's nest.* New York, NY: Viking Press.

Koyanagi, C. (2007). *Learning from history: Deinstitutionalization of people with mental illness as precursor to long-term care reform.* Washington, D.C.: Kaiser Family Foundation, Kaiser Commission on Medicaid and the Uninsured. Retrieved from http://www.nami.org/Template.cfm?Section=About_the_Issue& Template=/ContentManagement/ContentDisplay.cfm&ContentID=137545.

Kraut, R. (2012, Summer). Plato. In E. N. Zalta (Ed.), The Stanford Encyclopedia of Philosophy. Retrieved from http://plato.stanford.edu/archives/sum2012/entries/ plato/.

Laing, R. D. (1960). *The divided self: An existential study in sanity and madness.* London, England: Tavistock.

Lake v. Cameron, 364 F.2d 657 (D.C. Cir. 1967).

Lamb, H. R., & Bachrach, L. L. (2001). Some perspectives on deinstitutionalization. *Psychiatric Services, 52*(8), 1039–1045.

Lamb, H. R., & Weinberger, L. E. (1998). Persons with severe mental illness in jails and prisons: A review. *Psychiatric Services, 49*(4), 483–492.

Lamb, H. R., & Weinberger, L. E. (2005). The shift of psychiatric inpatient care from hospitals to jails and prisons. *Journal of the American Academy of Psychiatry and the Law, 33*, 529–534.

Lamb, H. R., Weinberger, L. E., & DeCuir, W. J., Jr. (2002). The police and mental health. *Psychiatric Services, 53*, 1266–1271.

Lamb, H. R., Weinberger, L. E., & Gross, B. H. (2004). Mentally ill persons in the criminal justice system: Some perspectives. *Psychiatric Quarterly, 75* (2), 107–126.

Lambert v. New York State Office of Mental Health, 2000 WL 863461 (E.D.N.Y., June 2000).

Lenell, M. (1977). The Lanterman-Petris-Short Act: A review after ten years. *Golden Gate University Law Review, 7*(3), 733–764.

Lessard v. Schmidt, 349 F. Supp. 1078 (E.D. Wis. 972), vacated and remanded, 414 U.S. 473, on remand, 379 F. Supp. 1376 (E.D. Wis. 1974), vacated and remanded, 421 U.S. 957 (1975), reinstated, 413 F. Supp. 1318 (E.D. Wis. 1976).

Levison, J. R. (2003). Elizabeth Parsons Ware Packard: An advocate for cultural, religious, and legal change. *Alabama Law Review, 54*(3), 987–1077.

Lurigio, A. J., & Swartz, J. A. (2000). Changing the contours of the criminal justice system to meet the needs of persons with serious mental illness. In J. Horney (Ed.), *Policies, processes, and decisions of the criminal justice system* (pp. 45–108). Washington, D.C.: U.S. Department of Justice, National Institute of Justice.

Macmillan, M. (2000). *An odd kind of fame: Stories of Phineas Gage.* Cambridge, MA: MIT Press.

Maisel, A. Q. (1946, May 4). Bedlam 1946: Most U.S. hospitals are a shame and a disgrace. *Life Magazine,* 102–118. Retrieved from http://www.pbs.org/wgbh/americanexperience/features/primary-resources/lobotomist-bedlam-1946/.

McLynn, F. L. (1989). *Crime and punishment in eighteenth century England.* London, England: Routledge.

Melton, G. B., Petrila, J., Poythress, N., & Slobogin, C. (2007). *Psychological evaluations for the courts: A handbook for mental health professionals and lawyers* (3rd ed.). New York, NY: Guilford Press.

Miller, R. D. (1992). Economic factors leading to diversion of the mentally disordered from the civil to the criminal commitment systems. *International Journal of Law and Psychiatry, 15*, 1–12.

National Association of State Mental Health Program Directors Research Institute. (2000, August 10). Closing and refinancing state psychiatric hospitals, 2000. *NASMHPD State Profile Highlights, 1*, 1–2. Retrieved from http://www.nri-inc.org/projects/profiles/SH_RPT.pdf.

National Council on Independent Living. (2013). *About NCIL*. Washington, DC: Author. Retrieved from http://www.ncil.org/about/.

National Institutes of Health. (2011, October 12). National Institute of Mental Health: Important events in NIMH history. *NIH Almanac*. Retrieved from http://www.nih.gov/about/almanac/organization/NIMH.htm.

National Public Radio. (2005, November 16). *Frequently asked questions about lobotomies*. Retrieved from http://www.npr.org/templates/story/story.php?storyId=5014565.

Nazi Persecution of the Disabled. (2007, October 19). *Murder of the "unfit"*. Washington, D.C.: United States Holocaust Memorial Museum. Retrieved from http://www.ushmm.org/museum/exhibit/focus/disabilities_02/.

Norman, J. (n.d.). "In an Expose of the Witchcraft Delusion, One of the First Scientific Approaches to the Study of Mental Illness" (1563). *From Cave Paintings to the Internet: Chronological and Thematic Studies on the History of Information and Media*. Retrieved from http://www.historyofinformation.com/index.php?id=2271.

Nyland, E. (n.d.). *Summation of the Malleus Maleficarum*. Retrieved from http://www.bibliotecapleyades.net/cienciareal/cienciareal12.htm.

O'Connor v. Donaldson, 422 U.S. 563 (1975).

Patch, P. C., & Arrigo, B. A. (1999). Police officer attitudes and use of discretion in situations involving the mentally ill: The need to narrow the focus. *International Journal of Law and Psychiatry, 22*, 23–35.

Penrose, L. (1939). Mental disease and crime: Outline of a comparative study of European statistics. *British Journal of Medical Psychology, 18*, 1–15.

Peterson, G. (1999). The humanizing brain: Where religion and neuroscience meet. Retrieved from http://www.gpc.edu/~bbrown/psyc1501/brain/psychosurg.htm.

Phelan, J. C., Link, B. G., Stueve, A., & Pescosolido, B. A. (2000). Public concepts of mental illness in 1950 and 1996: What is mental illness and is it to be feared? *Journal of Health & Social Behavior, 41*, 188–207.

Plath, S. (1963). *The bell jar*. New York, NY: Harper.

Prioreschi, P. (1991). Possible reasons for Neolithic trephining, *Perspectives in Biology and Medicine, 34*, 296–303.

Rabkin, J. (1979). Criminal behavior of discharged mental patients: A critical appraisal of the research. *Psychological Bulletin, 86*, 1–27.

Raphael, S. (2000, September). *The deinstitutionalization of the mentally ill and growth in the U.S. prison populations 1971 to 1996.* Retrieved from http://socrates.berkeley.edu/~raphael/raphael2000.pdf.

Rissmiller, D. J., & Rissmiller, J. H. (2006). Evolution of the antipsychiatry movement into mental health consumerism. *Psychiatric Services, 57*(6), 863–866.

Rosenhan, D. L. (1973). On being sane in insane places. *Science, 179*(4070), 250–258.

Rouse v. Cameron, 373 F.2d 451 (D.C. Cir., 1966).

Rowland, L. (2005). Walter Freeman's psychosurgery and biological psychiatry: A cautionary tale. *Neurology Today, 5*(4), 70–72.

Sabbatini, R. M. E. (1997, June). The history of psychosurgery. *Brain & Mind Magazine.* Retrieved from http://www.cerebromente.org.br/n02/historia/lobotomy.htm.

Solomon, P., & Draine, J. (1995). Issues in serving the forensic client. *Social Work, 40*(1), 25–33.

Solomon, P. L., Gordon, B. H., & Davis, J. M. (1984). *Community services to discharged psychiatric patients.* Springfield, IL: Charles C. Thomas.

Sosowsky, L. (1978). Crime and violence among mental patients reconsidered in view of the new legal relationship between the state and the mentally ill. *American Journal of Psychiatry, 135,* 33–42.

Sosowsky, L. (1980). Explaining the increased arrest rate among mental patients: A cautionary note. *American Journal of Psychiatry, 137,* 1602–1605.

Spitzer, S. (1976). Toward a Marxian theory of deviance. *Social Problems, 22,* 638–651.

Staples, W. (1977). *Culture of surveillance.* New York, NY: St. Martin's Press.

Stavis, P. F. (1995, July 21). *Civil commitment: Past, present, and future.* Address at the Annual Conference of the National Alliance for Mental Illness, Washington, D.C. Retrieved from http://www.treatmentadvocacycenter.org/component/content/article/360.

Steadman, H. J., Fabisiak, S., Dvoskin, J., & Holohean, E. J. (1987). A survey of mental disability among state prison inmates. *Hospital & Community Psychiatry, 38,* 1086–1090.

Steadman, H. J., Osher, F. C., Robbins, P. C., Case, B., & Samuels, S. (2009). Prevalence of serious mental illness among jail inmates. *Psychiatric Services, 60,*761–765.

Stevenson, C. (1996). Robert Hooke's Bethlem. *Journal of the Society of Architectural Historians, 55*(3), 254–275.

Stossel, J. (2007, March 21). The media likes scaring us, and we like it. *Real Clear Politics.* Retrieved from http://www.realclearpolitics.com/articles/2007/03/the_media_likes_scaring_us_and.html.

Stroman, D. (2003). *The disability rights movement: From deinstitutionalization to self-determination.* University Press of America.

Suich, P. (2006, September 27). *Mental illness: The role of the faith community.* Lakeland, FL: Florida Center for Science and Religion.

Swank, G. & Winer, D. (1976). Occurrence of psychiatric disorder in a county jail population. *American Journal of Psychiatry, 133,* 1331–1333.

Szasz, T. (1960). The myth of mental illness. *American Psychologist, 15,* 113–118.

Szasz, T. (1961). The myth of mental illness: Foundations of a theory of personal conduct. New York, NY: Hoeber-Harper & Row.

Teplin, L. A. (1984). Criminalizing mental disorder: The comparative arrest rate of the mentally ill. *American Psychologist, 39,* 794–803.

Teplin, L. A. (1990). The prevalence of severe mental disorder among male urban jail detainees: Comparison with Epidemiologic Catchment Area program. *American Journal of Public Health, 80,* 663–669.

Teplin, L. A. & Pruett, N. S. (1992). Police as street-corner psychiatrist: Managing the mentally ill. *International Journal of Law and Psychiatry, 15*(2), 139–156.

Testa, M., & West, S. G. (2010). Civil commitment in the United States. *Psychiatry, 7*(10), 30–40.

Timeline of Psychology. (2003). *History of psychology (387 BC to present).* Retrieved from http://allpsych.com/timeline.html.

Thomas, A. R. (1998). Ronald Reagan and the commitment of the mentally ill: Capital, interests groups, and the eclipse of social policy. *Electronic Journal of Sociology.* Retrieved from http://www.sociology.org/content/vol003.004/thomas.html.

Toch, H. (1979). *The psychology of crime and criminal justice.* Prospect Heights, IL: Waveland Press.

Tonry, M. (2004). *Thinking about crime: Sense and sensibility in American penal culture.* NY: Oxford University Press.

Torrey, E. F. (1997). *Out of the shadows: Confronting America's mental illness crisis.* New York, NY: John Wiley & Sons.

Torrey, E. F., Fuller, D. A., Geller, J., Jacobs, C., & Ragosta, K. (2012, July 19). *No room at the inn: Trends and consequences of closing public psychiatric hospitals.* Arlington, VA: Treatment Advocacy Center.

Treatment Advocacy Center. (2011). *Wyatt v. Stickney.* Arlington, VA: Author. Retrieved from http://www.treatmentadvocacycenter.org/get-help/know-the-options/345.

Valdisseri, E. Y, Carroll, K. R., & Hartl, A. J. (1986). A study of offenses committed by psychotic inmates in a county jail. *Hospital and Community Psychiatry, 37,* 163–165.

Valenstein, E. S. (1986). *Great and desperate cures: The rise and decline of psychosurgery and other radical treatments for mental illness.* New York, NY: Basic Books.

Vargas, H. P. (2011, July 17). One Flew Over The Cuckoo's Nest: Provisions of the normal. *Politics and Film.* Retrieved from http://polsci167.blogspot.com/2011/07/one-flew-over-cuckoos-nest-provisions.html.

Vold, G. B., & Bernard, T. J. (1986). *Theoretical criminology* (3rd ed.) New York: Oxford University Press.

Walsh, J., & Bricourt, J. (1997). Services for persons with mental illness in jail: Implications for family involvement. *Families in Society: The Journal of Contemporary Human Services, 78*(4), 420–428.

Ward, M. J. (1946). *The snake pit.* New York: Random House.

Watson, A. C., Hanrahan, P., Luchins, D., & Lurigio, A. (2001). Mental health courts and the complex issue of mentally ill offenders. *Psychiatric Services, 52,* 477–481.

Weiner, D. B. (1992). Philippe Pinel's "Memoir on Madness" of December 11, 1794: A fundamental text of modern psychiatry. *American Journal of Psychiatry, 149*(6), 725–732.

Weiner, D. B. (2010). The madmen in the light of reason. Enlightenment psychiatry: Part II. Alienists, treatises, and the psychologic approach in the era of Pinel. In E. R. Wallace & J. Gach (Eds.), *History of Psychiatry and Medical Psychology: With an Epilogue on Psychiatry and the Mind-Body Relation* (pp. 281–304). New York, NY: Springer.

Weinstein R. (1982). Goffman's Asylums and the Social Situation of Mental Patients. *Orthomolecular Psychiatry, 11*(4), 267–274.

West, S. G., & Friedman, S. H. (2009). Civil commitment. In C. Edwards (Ed)., *Wiley Encyclopedia of Forensic Sciences.* Hoboken, N.J.: John Wiley & Sons.

White, E. (1888). *The great controversy between Christ and Satan: The conflict of the ages in the Christian disposition.* Mountain View, CA: Pacific Press.

Whitmer, C. (1980). From hospitals to jails: The fate of California's deinstitutionalized mentally ill. *American Journal of Orthopsychiatry, 50,* 65–75.

Wilde, R. (n.d.). The Enlightenment: Introduction to the Enlightenment. *European History.* Retrieved from http://europeanhistory.about.com/od/thenineteenth century/a/enlightenment.htm.

Wilson, J. Q., & Hernstein, R. (1985). *Crime and human nature: The definitive study of the causes of crime.* New York, NY: Simon & Schuster.

Wright, D. (1997). Getting out of the asylum: Understanding the confinement of the insane in the nineteenth century. *Social History of Medicine, 10*(1), 137–155.

Wyatt v. Stickney, 325 F. Supp. 781(M.D. Ala., 1971), 334 F. Supp. 1341 (M.D. Ala., 1971), 344 F. Supp. 373 (M.D. Ala., 1972), sub nom Wyatt v. Aderholt, 503 F.2d 1305 (5th Cir. 1974).

Years of conformity: 1943–1954. (n.d.). Retrieved from http://www.duke.edu/~ajc6/7up/Conformity.htm.

Youngberg v. Romeo, 457 U.S. 307 (1982).

Zilboorg, G. (1935). *The medical man and the witch during the Renaissance.* Baltimore, MD: Johns Hopkins Press.

Chapter 3

Challenges and Needs of Persons with Mental Illness in the Criminal Justice System

"If you are to punish a man, you must injure him. If you are to reform a man, you must improve him, and men are not improved by injuries."

— George Bernard Shaw[1]

Often, in an effort to do the right thing, we end up doing more harm than good. This is the best way to characterize what followed the attempt to revamp the mental health system beginning in the 1960s. In particular, as discussed in Chapter 2, ostensibly in an attempt to do the "right" thing (not to mention to save money), the deinstitutionalization movement brought about the release of thousands of individuals with severe and persistent mental illness into the community. However, as the majority of the envisioned community mental health centers were never constructed, many went without treatment and quickly decompensated. Furthermore, seemingly in the best interests of those with mental illness, the civil rights movement brought about a tightening of civil commitment requirements, but this resulted in many individuals with severe mental illness being unable to obtain acute care when they decompensated. Record numbers of persons ended up homeless, self-medicating with illegal substances, and/or entangled in the criminal justice system—the phenomenon widely referred to as the criminalization of the mentally ill. It is these challenges and/or needs of those with mental illness that this chapter is about.

To this day—or maybe it should be said, *especially* today—individuals with serious mental illnesses face many challenges to functioning successfully in society, not the least of which is stigma that occurs at both the micro- and macro-levels. Most agree that stigma contributes to a host of challenges for people with mental illness, including those mentioned above that were initially brought about by legal and policy changes

---

1. As cited in Kittrie (1978, pp. 1–2).

65

enacted in the 1960s and 1970s. Additional challenges include poverty, unemployment, housing, actions and inactions by treatment providers, and individuals themselves refusing to seek mental health care. Each of these challenges, or needs, will be discussed in this chapter, within the framework of levels of stigma. If such needs are not met, the likelihood of a person being propelled into the criminal justice system increases dramatically.

Stigma

Mental illness has always carried a stigma, as is clear by the cyclical periods of maltreatment and ineffective care of persons with mental illness. The term "stigma" has roots in ancient Greece, when it was used to refer to physical signs on the body, such as brands or tattoos, that indicated something negative about the moral character of the bearer. Erving Goffman (1961) was the first to apply the term to those with mental illness. In particular, Goffman used stigma to refer to an attribute, behavior, or reputation that is socially discrediting; because individuals bearing the stigma are not able to adhere to standards that society has deemed to be normal, they are unable to gain full social acceptance. The "normals" in society cast off the stigma-bearers as outsiders and generate undesirable, rejecting stereotypes about the group of stigmatized individuals (Becker, 1963).

Federal funds were appropriated for community mental health centers following the deinstitutionalization movement, but stigma and the associated "not in my backyard" (NIMBY) mentality, as well as other reasons discussed in Chapter 2, were responsible for the failure to allocate them. And this relationship proved to be bidirectional: As the lay public (and, by extension, law enforcement) began to be exposed in the streets to this previously hidden segment of the population, the stigma that rendered deinstitutionalization a failure was reinforced and magnified. Rather than question what may be propelling persons with mental illnesses into the streets and jails — i.e., a broken mental health system — the public instead blamed them, the victims of the broken system, and further criminalized them.

According to the U.S. Surgeon General (U.S. Department of Health and Human Services [U.S. DHHS], 1999), and reiterated by the World Health Organization (2001), stigma currently is "the most formidable obstacle to future progress in the arena of mental illness and health" (U.S. DHHS, 1999, p. 3). There is a general consensus among experts that the majority of Americans endorse stigmas about people with mental illness, more so than those related to other conditions, such as physical illnesses (Corrigan & Watson, 2002; Parcesepe & Cabassa, 2013). As the World Health Organization [WHO] (2013) notes, stigma is a barrier to accessing mental health care and even has a negative impact on resource allocation for mental health services. Components and types of mental illness stigma will be outlined below.

Components of Mental Illness Stigma

Link and Phelan (2001), two of the primary contemporary researchers of stigma related to mental illness, have developed a model of how stigma develops. In particular, mental illness stigma exists when the following components converge.

Labeling Differences

First, mainstream society identifies and labels as "deviant" any individuals who are different in ways that are considered to be socially important. All individuals with these characteristics are clustered into a group and are reduced to caricatures of the labels placed on them (Corrigan, 2007). For example, members of the group labeled "mentally ill" are identified by society with diagnostic labels applied by the mental health field and/or with being seen in certain settings (e.g., leaving a psychiatrist's office), as well as with behavioral manifestations of psychiatric symptoms, social skills deficits, and appearance, e.g., unkempt and/or poor hygiene (Corrigan, 2000; Penn & Martin, 1998). Clearly, this process involves gross oversimplification and lack of appreciation of human diversity and the fact that other explanations for these characteristics could be responsible (Link & Phelan, 2001). In addition, social judgments of these characteristics vary by time and place. For instance, Lombroso in the 19th century (1876) in Italy argued that criminals could be identified with distinguishing physical characteristics, such as skull size and facial asymmetry. Of course, research has not supported this theory, and, thus, we no longer believe these propositions. It is noteworthy that Lombroso even used the term "stigmata" to refer to these characteristics, and he identified the "insane" criminal who, despite bearing few physical stigmata, committed criminal acts as a result "of an alteration of the brain, which completely upset their moral nature."[2] It is this culture of discrimination and the complicity in stigmatization that creates a barrier in labeling oneself as mentally ill (Stolzenburg, Frietag, Evans-Lacko, Muehlan, Schmidt, & Schomerus, 2017).

Linking Differences with Stereotypes

Those labeled quickly become coupled with negative stereotypes, or knowledge structures of collectively agreed upon notions about a particular group of people (Corrigan, 2007), based on prevailing cultural beliefs (Link & Phelan, 2001). This aspect of the process of stigmatizing others was emphasized by Goffman (1961) and is included as a key component in Link and Phelan's (2001) model. In particular, with regard to

---

2. Historically, in an effort to set criminals apart and to shame them, we branded them with stigmata (e.g. a "T" branded on the forehead of a thief). A similar approach was to lock a criminal's head and hands in the pillory and nail his ears to the wood so that the earlobes would have to be ripped at the cessation of the publicly displayed punishment, leaving a permanent mark that upstanding citizens would readily recognize as that of a criminal (see Welch, 2004).

the group of "the mentally ill," the most common stereotype, with vast implications, is that they are violent or dangerous (Corrigan, Edwards, Green, Diwan, & Penn, 2001; Crisp, Gelder, Rix, Meltzer, & Rowlands, 2000; Link, Phelan, Bresnahan, Stueve, & Pescosolido, 1999; Rueve & Welton, 2008). Indeed, despite a general increase in knowledge about mental illness, 75 percent of the general population believed that people with mental illness were violent, a rate that represents a 250 percent *increase* in this belief since the 1950s (Phelan, Link, Stueve, & Pescosolido, 2000). This is a critical finding, as viewing people with mental illness as violent leads to fear, which, in turn, precipitates social avoidance (Angermeyer & Matschinger, 1996), not only by members of the lay public but by mental health professionals (Covarrubias & Han, 2011; Link, Yang, Phelan, & Collins, 2004) and criminal justice professionals (Kropp, Cox, Roesch, & Eaves, 1989; for a summary of findings of perceptions of people with mental illness, see Frailing & Slate, 2016). Ultimately, this results in either a lack of or poor quality of treatment, a tendency to arrest and incarcerate rather than to divert, and other dire consequences for people with mental illness. Because of the centrality and pervasiveness of this stereotype, the myths, realities, and effects of the dangerousness stereotype will be discussed in detail later in this chapter.

Other widely accepted stereotypes about people with mental illness include that they are incapable, incompetent, or even childlike in nature (Caputo & Rouner, 2011; Link et al., 1999; Penn, Chamberlin, & Mueser, 2003) and/or that they are at fault for their mental illness (Corrigan et al., 2000; Link et al., 1999; Wahl, Wood, Zaveri, Drapalski, & Mann, 2003) due to perceived weak character (Corrigan, 2004). In a collaborative project of the Substance Abuse and Mental Health Services Administration (SAMHSA) and the Centers for Disease Control (CDC), via the 2006 Health-Styles survey,[3] several enlightening findings about the current status of these stereotypes in the general American public emerged (U.S. Department of Health and Human Services [DHHS], 2007): Even though 85 percent of Americans indicated that they did not explicitly blame people with mental illness for their condition, only 26 percent expected that others would be caring and sympathetic toward those with mental illness. Further, when assessing their own personal attitudes, only 25 percent of the respondents believed that a person with mental illness can eventually recover and live a normal life, including 54 percent who know someone with a mental illness; only 42 percent believed that a person with mental illness could be as successful at work as others without mental illness. All of these beliefs contradict what is actually found in the research, e.g., most people with mental illness do improve and many recover completely; there are no differences in productivity when people with mental illness are compared to other employees (U.S. DHHS, 2007).

---

3. The HealthStyles Survey is conducted annually by Porter Novelli to assess attitudes and beliefs about chronic and infectious disease and behaviors, exposure to health information, health communication campaigns, and self-reported symptoms, risk factors, diseases and disorders. In 2006, CDC and SAMHSA collaborated to suggest a series of questions to assess the public's attitudes about mental illness. The survey was based on a stratified random sample of 20,000 potential respondents in the U.S., weighted to match population estimates of age, sex, marital status, race/ethnicity, income, and region.

Separating "Us" from "Them"

Integral to the process of stigmatization, labeled individuals are relegated to merely group status; the group is considered fundamentally different, characterized only by its perceived negative features. The emotional responses and evaluations of mainstream society that correspond to endorsed cognitive stereotypes (i.e., prejudices) allow the public to morally disengage from individual members within the group and to act accordingly (i.e., discriminate). For instance, those who view people with mental illness to be at fault for their illness (particularly as a result of choice or poor moral character) are more likely to respond to offenders with mental illness with anger, denial of help, and a call for punishment (Weiner, Perry, & Magnusson, 1988). By developing an "us" and "them" mentality, the "other" group comes to be regarded as less than human in nature (Corrigan & Ben-Zeev, 2011; Thoits, 2016). Such beliefs are clearly at the base of the inhumane treatment inflicted upon people with mental illness throughout the centuries, as described in Chapter 2, and, too often, in jails and prisons of today (Earley, 2006).

Status Loss

By differentiating the stigmatized group from the rest of society, unequal conditions are created (or often already existed), and members of the stigmatized group experience further status loss. The ultimate status degradation ceremony is the humiliation of being "processed" through the criminal justice system, beginning with arrest (Vold, Bernard, & Snipes, 1998).[4] For persons with mental illnesses in the criminal justice system, a double stigma occurs: they are stigmatized for their mental illnesses, and they are stigmatized for being processed by the criminal justice system. However, persons with mental illnesses are not only stigmatized when their own actions are illegal; they are also branded when *others* who are believed to be mentally ill act out, particularly when those actions are of a violent nature.[5]

Status loss requires differential access of groups to social, economic, and political power; by definition, there must be a more powerful societal group that disapproves, rejects, excludes, and/or discriminates against the stigmatized group (Link & Phelan, 2001). The would-be stigmatizing group must have sufficient power over the stigmatized group in order for discrimination to be impactful. For example, although inmates might have stereotypes (negative beliefs) and prejudices (negative emotions and judgments) about correctional officers who imprison them, the inmates do not enjoy the social, economic, or political power to act upon those thoughts in the form of discriminatory actions that impact the officers. Although not all definitions of

---

4. It is striking that the same terminology is used for leading an animal to slaughter.

5. Gusfield, as cited in Williams and McShane (2004), maintains that we as a society have a tendency to push the actions of individuals who commit such unconventional acts as mass murder into the sick deviant category because law-abiding citizens cannot fathom the possibility of a rational person engaging in such reprehensible behavior, and it helps conventional society to better cope with such atrocities.

stigma include the status loss aspect, Link and Phelan (2001) argue that it occurs naturally as individuals are labeled, set apart, and linked to derogatory characteristics.

Discrimination forms a vicious, self-perpetuating cycle, with discrimination begetting further discrimination. Members of already disadvantaged stigmatized groups are disadvantaged even further when they face discrimination in employment, education, housing, and medical and mental health care. They face further discrimination still when their functioning declines as a result of discrimination in their daily lives.

Types of Mental Illness Stigma

Corrigan and colleagues have identified several types of mental illness stigma, ranging from the macro- to the micro-level: structural stigma, public stigma, self-stigma, and label avoidance (Corrigan, Markowitz, & Watson, 2004; Corrigan & Watson, 2002; see also Shah, Tooley, & Corrigan, 2018). These types of stigma interact and exacerbate each other. Most models of stigma assume that stigmatization primarily occurs at an individual level, but stigma can quite quickly become institutionalized in the form of structural and/or public stigma. When this happens, it arguably has farther-reaching impact than stigmatization by individuals alone.

The rest of the chapter will outline the various challenges experienced by people with mental illness, particularly those within the criminal justice system, discussed within the categories or levels of stigma involving mental illness. Some of the challenges or needs are caused by stigma; in other cases, stigma is caused by these challenges and/or needs, and in many cases, these factors relate bidirectionally to stigma. All of these difficulties fall within the continuum from the macro- (i.e., structural, public) to the micro-level (i.e., some of the public stigmas, self-stigma, and label avoidance).

Structural Stigma and Its Challenges

At the broadest, macro level, there are *structural* stigmas brought about by rules, policies, or procedures of private or governmental institutions that restrict the opportunities of people with mental illness (Corrigan, et al., 2004; Corrigan & Watson, 2002). These stigmas can be intentional (or actions taken deliberately by institutions with the explicit purpose of restricting the rights of people with mental illness) or unintentional (Pincus, 1996; Pincus & Ehrlich, 1998). Many of the governmental actions discussed in Chapter 2 inadvertently became mechanisms of structural stigma. The longstanding, massive underfunding of the mental health system reveals the undervaluing of the mentally ill population. Other contemporary policies, such as the shift to managed care in the U.S., reforms to Medicare, and states' abridgements of rights of people with mental illness, can also be characterized as structural stigmas. Structural stigma is also seen in the limitations on public funding for mental health research, which limits progress in this area (see World Health Organization, 2013).[6] Beginning with deinstitutionalization, funding has continually decreased after false promises of allocating money to community psychiatry, in turn creating dangerously low resources for those with a genuine need (Frances & Ruffalo, 2018).

Limited Civil Rights

People with mental illness are among the most marginalized groups in society, and this stigma is institutionalized within American law. In an examination of state statutes with regard to civil liberties held by those with mental illness, Hemmens, Miller, Burton, and Milner (2002) found that one-third of states limited political rights: Specifically, 44 states restricted the right of an individual with mental illness to serve on a jury, 37 restricted the right to vote, and 24 restricted the right to hold elective office. Personal, familial rights are also significantly restricted, with 33 states restricting the right of an individual with mental illness to remain married; 27 restricted parental rights.

What is most concerning is that there is a trend toward states becoming more, rather than less, restrictive of civil rights for persons with mental illness over time. Since the baseline study performed by Burton (1990) in the late 1980s, more states have enacted restrictions on each of the previously discussed political and familial rights. Every state has restricted at least one right; 28 restricted at least four rights, and 13 states added a total of 18 additional restrictions between 1989 and 1999 alone (Hemmens, et al., 2002). No state *removed* a restriction that was in place as of 1989. Strikingly, as noted by Burton (1990), people with mental illness even suffer more legal restrictions on their civil rights those previously incarcerated for felony crimes.

Unfortunately, such restriction of rights is not entirely surprising, given that persons with mental illness, as a group, lack the capital to influence the political system.[7] Thereby, their rights can be rescinded with relatively little consequence to legislators or the public. However, limiting rights does hold serious consequences for people with mental illness. As noted by Hemmens et al. (2002, p. 130), "Restrictions on the ability of an individual to exercise their civil rights have an impact not only on the ability of that person to fully exercise their citizenship and participate in a free society, but on the social status of the individual." As such, it becomes a cruel, self-perpetuating cycle — i.e., those with mental illness lack social status, so they cannot protect their civil rights; then as their civil rights are revoked, they further lose social status.

---

6. As outlined by Gallagher (2012), in 1989, only $11 per person with mental illness was spent on researching mental illness, compared to $161 spent for every person with multiple sclerosis (MS) and $1,000 per person with muscular dystrophy. This is particularly noteworthy given the relative prevalence of these disorders in the general population: as of 2006, schizophrenia — which is only one type of mental illness — was 5 times more common than MS and 60 times more common than muscular dystrophy. Furthermore, research expenditures have decreased in the past decade, from $1,825 per person to $1,591 per person currently (Gallagher, 2012).

7. It is surprising, however, that people with mental illness have fewer rights than felons, who also lack political capital.

Socio-Economics of Mental Health Care: A Lesson in Cost Shifting

Economics permeates virtually every aspect of life, including medical care and mental health care in particular. As was illustrated by the deinstitutionalization of state hospitals, in an attempt to influence the economy, politicians dictate health care. After President Kennedy's Community Mental Health Centers Act was signed into law, states began closing state hospitals. Congress began passing laws that made people with mental illness eligible for federal assistance programs (Earley, 2006; Goldman, Adams, & Taube, 1983; Torrey, 1997), ostensibly in the best interests of persons with mental illness. However, these actions were merely further evidence of economics driving public policy. In the face of mounting class-action litigation, state legislators seized upon these federal programs as an opportunity to shift the costs of caring for persons with mental illnesses from their states to the federal government (Earley, 2006; Goldman et al., 1983; Montague, 2014; Torrey, 2014).

People with mental illness, as a group, are stricken by poverty (to be discussed below) and therefore lack the capital to influence the political system.[8] As such, people with mental illness face increasingly fragmented services (if services are provided at all), inadequate access to care, and poor quality of care (Parks, Svendsen, Singer, & Foti, 2006). Indeed, one's lot in life, including socioeconomic status and the availability of potential caregivers, affect what options, if any, are available when crises emerge.

A Fragmented and Underfunded Mental Health Care System

In many parts of the country, the mental health system is a fragmented, complicated mess. Compton and Kotwicki (2007) outlines these services, ranging from least to most intensive: *non-crisis outpatient care*, in which patients are seen by a case manager approximately every two weeks and by a psychiatrist every two to three months; *intensive outpatient treatment*, in which psychotherapeutic services are provided, typically, at least three days a week for a few hours each day; *intensive non-residential services*, such as day treatment programs (patients go to an agency for treatment during the day, but live at their home) and assertive community treatment teams (a mental health team provides services to the patient at his/her place of residence), with services typically provided at least five days a week; *non-secure residential treatment*, such as group homes and residential rehabilitation programs, where nursing, medication administration, and direct care supervision are provided 24 hours per day, seven days per week; and *secure residential inpatient care*, or psychiatric hospitalization. Even if one understands the differences between these services, which most do not, services and facilities are not necessarily so labeled in most communities. For example, in Virginia, community mental health services are referred to as "Community

---

8. As noted by Piers Anthony, the rich are considered eccentric, while the poor are viewed as crazy (An Interview with Piers Anthony, 2004).

Services Boards," a seemingly arbitrary (and for many unfamiliar with the system, unknown) name. To further complicate matters, given the high rate of co-occurrence between serious mental illness and substance abuse, many need both types of services; it is often unclear whether these services are provided separately by different agencies or in an integrated manner by a single agency. Finally, many people have other non-mental health needs, such as medical health conditions and housing needs, that are sometimes provided within a comprehensive community mental health system; in other areas, they are not. Clearly, mental health systems are complicated, and they differ widely from state to state, even from county to county or city to city.

Difficult for even those without the cognitive dysfunction of some mental illnesses, it can be virtually impossible for a person with serious mental illness to navigate the mental health system. As a result of this confusion, many wait to seek help, if they do at all, until they are in crisis. It is no wonder that the 2003 President's New Freedom Commission on Mental Health identified the fragmented mental health care system as one of the main barriers to treatment in the country.

As discussed in Chapter 2, the mental health system has a long history of being notoriously underfunded. This occurs at the local, state, and federal levels. It cannot be denied that this is a reflection of structural mental health stigma, institutionalizing the general public's lack of regard, or at least disinterest, in vulnerable populations such as persons with mental illness. Many lack access to these interventions due to an egregious lack of funding and the failure to carry out the promise of deinstitutionalization (Osher, 2016).

Although always problematic, this lack of funding holds grave implications for people with mental illness during economic downturns, such as that directly resulting from the COVID-19 pandemic, not only in the U.S. but worldwide. In what has been described as "the worst recession in the U.S. since the Great Depression" (National Alliance on Mental Illness [NAMI], 2011b, p. 1), many Americans have lost health insurance due to unemployment; a similar situation was observed during the aforementioned pandemic. Those were especially difficult times for these outcomes, as many have begun to experience mental health issues or their mental illness has become exacerbated due to stressors related to their situation since the recession in 2008 and since the pandemic of 2020 (Wamsley, 2020). In total, more people have turned to the public system for mental health care, placing additional burden on an already underfunded and overextended mental health system (Lutterman, 2010).

At the same time, state budgets have been drastically cut as a result of the recession[9] and are suffering again as a result of the pandemic. A 2008 survey of the National Association of State Mental Health Program Directors (NASMHPD) found that 32 state mental health agencies experienced budget cuts on average of 5 percent for fiscal year 2009; one state reported a cut as high as 17.5 percent (NASMHPD Research

---

9. This does not have to be the case. While this is the practice within the United States, some countries experiencing similar recessions are actually putting additional funding into the mental health system in anticipation of increased mental health problems (Hodgkin & Karpman, 2010).

Institute, 2008). Since 2008, approximately $2.1 billion was cut from state mental health budgets (Lacey, Sack, & Sulzberger, 2011).[10] Furthermore, as an increasing share of mental health spending is routed through Medicaid (Mark, Levit, Buck, Coffey, & Vandivort-Warren, 2007), the policies of states lowering Medicaid payments to providers and eliminating coverage for certain programs that are not federally required have significant implications for the mental health system and, thus, mental health services available to consumers (Vu, 2009).

Among the most commonly affected programs of the recession and of the pandemic have been adult community mental health services. As will be discussed throughout this book, community mental health services were already notoriously limited. With the recession and again with the pandemic, the hardest hit are crisis stabilization programs, intensive case management services, and intensive treatment programs (NAMI, 2011b). Important financial assistance for housing and medication assistance for people with mental illness has also taken drastic cuts (NAMI, 2011b). Elimination or cutbacks on all of these services will undoubtedly have grave implications for people with mental illness and, quite possibly, the general public.

Lack of Access to Long-Term Care

The other most drastic cut to mental health care as a result of the recession is adult inpatient services (Torrey, Geller, Jacobs, & Ragosta, 2012); similar cuts are again observable as a result of the pandemic. Of course, this was by no means the first blow to the provision of long-term care. Rather, it was just one more stage of the deinstitutionalization that began in the 1960s. From 1992 to 2002, the number of state psychiatric hospitals, which are most likely to treat individuals with severe, chronic mental illness who require long-term care, declined by 35 percent (McCann, 2005). Between 2005 and 2010, the number of state psychiatric beds decreased by another 14 percent, and another 3 percent was predicted by state mental health program directors in 2011 and 2012. Five states closed 40 percent of their hospitals (Torrey et al., 2012). In total, between 1955 and 2010, the U.S. has closed 92 percent of its state hospital beds (Lamb & Weinberger, 2005; Torrey et al., 2012). To put things in perspective, the U.S. has reached the lowest number of psychiatric beds per capita since Dorothea Dix began her crusade in the mid-1800s.

Even in areas in which mental hospitals remain in operation, stays are significantly reduced. Indeed, the average length of hospital stay in the 1950s was 20 years. Today, the length-of-stays range from 18 days (Texas Department of State Health Services, 2012) to 140 days (Utah Division of Substance Abuse and Mental Health, 2004).[11]

---

10. One judge in Sacramento County, California, in 2010 blocked the county from cutting mental health services despite budget issues, citing the practice as a violation of the Americans with Disabilities Act and stating that the "catastrophic harm" to thousands of people with mental illness would potentially result in high litigation costs for the county (Hubert & Walsh, 2010).

11. This was based on readily available websites of states' mental health departments, not a comprehensive compilation of states' official statistics. Thus, these numbers are anecdotal; it is unclear

Moreover, the quality of care at state hospitals is declining. During the recession, states had to lay off hospital staff. And of course, during the pandemic, the main focus of hospitals was on treating (and in many, many instances, providing end of life care) to COVID-19 patients. States are also beginning to "privatize" state hospital services to contain costs. With privatization, services (e.g., medical and physician services, direct patient care services), in whole or in part, are contracted out to private companies (NASMHPD, 2000). These companies, motivated by profit margins, limit services that are provided; when provided, the services tend to be of poor quality (Veysey, 2011). As of 2000, 10 states had moved toward "privatizing" their hospitals (NASMHPD, 2000). Although no numbers are available on the current status, given the economic recession and the pandemic, it is likely that this trend has only increased, as state governments are doing whatever they can to cut costs.

Despite the theory behind deinstitutionalization, even if the quality of community mental health care were to be optimized, there will always be a need for intermediate and long-term twenty-four hour structured care for a minority of chronically, seriously ill patients (Fisher et al., 2001; Hogan, 1995; Lamb & Shaner, 1993). Emery (2006) argues that communities must have access to twenty-four hour acute psychiatric care with the possibility of median stays of thirty days or less. Lamb and Weinberger (2005), too, recognize that there needs to be opportunities for twenty-four hour hospitalization, including lock-up facilities, for some individuals with mental illness. Likewise, Trudel and Lesage (2006) indicate that long-term residential services, ranging from 10 to 40 beds per 100,000 in the population (depending upon the number of citizens, population density, and degree of social deprivation of the area) should be available in the community. And Torrey (2014) advocates for 40 to 60 hospital beds per 100,000 residents. Yet, before long, if the trends identified above continue, such facilities will be a thing of the past. As these services dwindle, people with serious mental illness are swept into the criminal justice system (Greenberg, Shah, & Seide, 1993). Research supports this thesis, finding that across countries and time periods, there is a consistent, inverse relationship between psychiatric hospital populations and prison populations (Lamb & Weinberger, 1998; Penrose, 1939; Raphael, 2000).

The Shift to Managed Care

Health care, including mental health care, in the United States is primarily covered by some form of managed care. Although this is primarily true of the private system of health care, in which people have health insurance, the practice is increasing in the public system as well. Managed care typically refers to a health care delivery system that has replaced traditional fees-for-service payment schemas with negotiated, capitated payment plans for enrollees. In order for the managed care company to minimize expenditures, services are closely monitored, and many must be authorized prior to the services being performed (Mowbray, Grazier, &

---

to what extent they generalize to all states. Moreover, it should be noted that the length-of-stay at Utah state hospitals was based on a somewhat dated 2004 report.

Holter, 2002). The goal of managed care agencies is to produce profits, not nec-essarily to provide quality services (Xiang, Owen, Langi, Yamaki, Mitchell, Heller, Karmarkar, French, & Jordan, 2019). This can be seen when comparing countries that have universal single payer systems (e.g., Canada) or multi-payer systems that are by law non-profit (e.g., Germany) with the managed care system of the United States: In Canada and Germany, 95 cents on the dollar goes to patient care, as op-posed to only 50 cents on the dollar going to patient care among managed care agencies in the United States.[12]

Toward this end, psychiatric managed care corporations can and do deny needed care to reduce expenditures and thereby ensure huge profits (Sodaro & Ball, 1999). Specific incidences of such cost cutting by managed care companies abound: A large insurer in Rhode Island was fined for paying incentives to the company's psychiatrist to deny treatment coverage for mental illness and maximize profits. In Iowa, each denial of hospital admission for inpatient psychiatric care was awarded with an $880.00 commission to the responsible party who ensured the denial of the coverage (Sodaro & Ball, 1999). Given the potentially grave consequences of untreated mental illness (e.g., suicide), managed behavioral health care is not the right model of health-care coverage for individuals with mental illness. Due to its profit motive, managed care tends to result in limited choice for consumers, decreased access to care, and deficiencies in quality, appropriateness, and outcomes (Mowbray et al., 2002).[13]

Kane (1995) cautioned that the alleged offerings of managed care and health main-tenance organizations (HMOs) sound very similar to the false promises of deinsti-tutionalization — e.g., a system with efficient provision of prevention services, coupled with early intervention and continuity of care. Likewise, the structure of managed care parallels the restrictions placed on civil commitment laws during the 1970s; pre-certification and close service review of managed care produce the same results as restricted admission procedures and limited involuntary commitment stays (SAMHSA, 1996). As such, results similar to that of deinstitutionalization of the 1960s might reasonably be predicted. With more restricted opportunities for treat-ment, police will increasingly utilize the criminal code for less serious offenses com-mitted by persons with mental illnesses to remove them from the community (Bonovitz & Bonovitz, 1981; Veysey, 2011). Thereby, the cost-saving measures of managed care result in mere cost shifting, rather than cost saving, to the government (Veysey, 2011).

Medicaid and Medicaid Reform

For those in the United States who do not have private health care (mostly through managed care corporations, as discussed above), services rendered are

---

12. Brink (1998) actually reports on a managed mental health care company where 67% of the money went to profits and overhead, a fact that employers are often not aware of.
13. NAMI (n.d.-b) outlines their stance on managed care as a form of financing mental health treatment in their Public Policy Forum online.

covered by governmental programs such as Medicaid.[14] In fact, today, Medicaid is the main provider of funding for persons with severe and persistent mental illness in the U.S., covering approximately 50 percent of all public mental health allocations (NAMI, 2005; Xiang, et al., 2019). With Medicaid, both the state and federal governments cover a portion of the cost. With Medicare, the government assumes the entire cost As such, states often shift costs to the federal government by switching patients who are eligible for both programs entirely to Medicare (Bubolz, Emerson, & Skinner, 2012).

In a further attempt to contain costs, many states have followed the lead of private insurance companies and have implemented some form of managed care to oversee Medicaid benefits for persons seeking mental health services. In fact, by 2002, two-thirds of U.S. state governments had done so (Kaye, 2005). This practice was institutionalized at the federal level via President George W. Bush's Deficit Reduction Act of 2006, which provided a mechanism that would allow Medicaid to become more like privately managed plans; Medicaid recipients would only be able to see providers in their plans' network. The act was predicted to provide an estimated savings of 6.9 billion dollars to the federal government. In reality, though, these costs were merely shifted back to the states.

Ultimately, as expected by many, privately managed care through Medicaid has not fulfilled the promises to improve care while limiting costs (Galewitz, 2010). There is a shortage of medical doctors who are willing to participate in Medicaid's managed care networks because they are being paid the same low rates as in traditional Medicaid (Ostrow, Steinwachs, Leaf, & Naeger, 2017). This leaves patients with long waiting lists and long distances to travel to visit a covered specialist. Often, the managed care companies are refusing to reimburse, sometimes after the patient has already received the services. Moreover, when profits do not comport with predicted earnings, the companies further cut benefits. Furthermore, problems are heightened as state and federal agencies face obstacles in overseeing the private companies managing Medicaid (Bloom, Williams, Land, McFarland, & Reichlin, 1998).

Managed Medicaid care holds potentially horrendous consequences not only for the most vulnerable (Koyanagi, 2006) but also for the public. As noted in NAMI's (2006, p. 9) Grading the States report, in which the average grade for state public adult mental health care systems was a D and in which no state received an A,[15] "The long-run costs of Medicaid 'reforms' often run higher than short-term savings. Costs

---

14. Medicaid is a program of health coverage administered by the states in partnership with the federal government whereby federal matching funds can be provided to states for specific persons with extremely high medical expenses or low incomes. The availability and amount of coverage depends on age, disability, or family status and on an individual's or family's ability to pay based on income and available resources. Benefits are paid directly to providers, not to consumers (Center for Medicare Advocacy, 2006).

15. The grading distribution remained relatively unchanged in the 2009 updated survey of the states, with the average grade remaining a D and no state receiving an A (NAMI, 2009). Twenty-three states' grades remained unchanged, 14 improved, and 12 declined.

are only shifted elsewhere. Cuts shift costs to hospital emergency departments.... Inadequate treatment leads to relapses. Relapses lead to hospitalizations. Medicaid 'reforms' come with a price. Inadequate treatment can also lead to jail or prison."

Even prior to the above-mentioned Medicaid reforms, Medicaid recipients who became involved with the criminal justice system experienced loss of access to Medicaid benefits upon entry into jail. Upon release from jail, the application for reinstatement of benefits can take as long as three months (Moses & Potter, 2007); meanwhile, these individuals often have to go without needed treatment. As will be discussed further in Chapter 10, this is despite the fact that, contrary to popular belief, federal law does not dictate such termination of benefits (GAINS Center, 2002). Nevertheless, this practice continues in most areas throughout the United States. Obviously, it holds grave implications for individuals' continuity of mental health care and, thus, for their successful reentry into the community.

While many of these issues still linger, President Obama's Patient Protection and Affordable Care Act (ACA) has rectified some of these issues. As outlined by NAMI (2011a), under the ACA, coverage for Medicaid was expanded to people with a slightly higher income level, and states are required to perform outreach to enroll vulnerable and underserved populations, including persons with mental illness. In addition, primary care providers are reimbursed a at higher rate, encouraging them to accept more Medicaid patients; thereby, individuals with mental illness will no longer have to travel long distances for care. Preventive care is emphasized, and additional funds are put toward developing innovative treatments for such mental illnesses as depression. Finally, a new demonstration program allowed eight states to permit Medicaid coverage of acute inpatient care in private psychiatric hospitals (NAMI, 2011a; see also Baumgartner, Aboulafia, & McIntosh, 2020). Mercifully, the Supreme Court has rejected attempts to dismantle the ACA three times, in 2012, in 2015, and in 2021, but it is important to note that the persistence of programs like this are always subject to who is in power in Congress and the White House.

Preferred Drug Lists/Restricted Formularies

Cost shifting from states to counties also can be seen today as states increasingly enforce preferred drug lists/restricted formularies. Preferred drug lists have been imposed by state legislatures, whereby Medicaid recipients face restricted access to medications in exchange for projected savings into the millions of dollars for states (Gudrais, 2006). Likewise, many individuals with private insurance are also subjected to these formularies, being covered at a much lower rate for brand-name prescription medications. With preferred drug lists or formularies, individuals are required (or for those with private insurance, strongly encouraged) to obtain generic drugs in lieu of brand-name medications. This poses additional difficulties when considering the wait time for generic approvals from the FDA (Young & Garfield, 2018). If no generic drugs for a particular condition are in existence, the least expensive brand-name medication is made available as an alternative. In situations where two or more brand-name alternative drugs are comparable in expense, states can negotiate a quantity discount for one of the drugs with the pharmaceutical company. Unfortunately, unlike many prescribed drugs, there are not many reliable, effective substitutes for psychotropic medications, and there is an extreme danger that without the treatment of choice, individuals will decompensate and relapse with potentially horrific consequences (Levine, 2006). See Rich (2009) for an example of how a reliance on a formulary can prove detrimental to one's health.

Clearly, the therapeutic jurisprudence ideal discussed in Chapter 1, of looking to the future ramifications of lawmakers' decisions on the individuals compelled to abide by them, is not considered with such restrictions in operation. While appeal processes are often in place for physicians to request that their patients be maintained on medications that have proven to be effective in the past, appeals are often denied; instead, fail-first policies are implemented — meaning that a patient will have to fail first on the cheaper medication before possibly being returned to the medication that has worked previously (Adams, 2006). The effects of failure can be irreversible and result in permanent damage and even death for persons with mental illnesses.

The following is an example of a letter written by Steven Bacallao, an advocate for people with psychiatric disabilities and CIT trainer for law enforcement officers in Florida (S. Bacallao, personal communication, October 3, 2007). Mr. Bacallao wrote this letter to the regional Medicare Office on behalf of Peggy Symons, a woman with schizophrenia who had been denied the only medications that had been found to be effective for her, after dozens of failed medication trials, several suicide attempts, and 16 hospitalizations. The letter demonstrates just how impersonal, unaccountable, and frustrating the bureaucratic appeals process can be, as evidenced by the inability to even locate a name of an individual to whom to address the correspondence. This matter was ultimately referred to U.S. Senator Bill Nelson's office, and only after inquiries from his office did the private corporate provider agree to allow coverage for this dosage of medication for one year.

October 3, 2007

Medicare Region 4
61 Forsythe St. S.W.
Suite 4T20
Atlanta, Ga. 30303

RE: Peggy Symons

Dear Region 4 Medicare Office,

I am an advocate for people with psychiatric disabilities. My wife and I are past co-presidents of The National Alliance on Mental Illness of Greater Orlando. In addition, I am also serving as the Chair of the Area 7 Florida Medicaid Behavioral Health Managed Care Advisory Group.

Peggy Symons has authorized me to act as her representative.

Peggy was auto enrolled by the State of Florida as a dual eligible in Company X[16] Medicare Part D Prescription Plan.

Since the very beginning Company X has been denying her prescription for Seroquel, 100 milligram tablets, the only antipsychotic medicine at the only dosing schedule that has ever worked for her. In addition, from the very first day coverage began Company X even refused to authorize a 30 day supply as required by law.

In 20 months of coverage by Company X Part D, Peggy's prescription has been denied more often than honored.

In 1998, after months of balancing multiple medicines at multiple doses, her psychiatrist of 25 years, Dr. Walter J. Muller finally found the medicines that have saved her life and kept her out of hospitals.

Florida Medicaid Medically Needy Catastrophic Costs coverage never dishonored, denied or overrode Dr. Muller's clinical judgment or long term experience with Peggy's illness.

Throughout 20 months of denials, the Group for Psychiatry and Peggy have filed numerous expedited appeals, multiple Prior Authorizations, severe adverse reaction reports, plea after desperate plea for her life and her medicine.

The following information has been provided to Company X's Clinical Pharmacy Review Committee and Grievance and Appeals Department in nearly every one of these appeals and contacts.

Peggy Symons:

1) Has been stabilized on this medicine at this dose since 1998.

2) Prior to this medication regime she was hospitalized 16 times.

3) She has failed on over 30 medicines and alternative doses.

4) She failed to improve even after a series of shock treatments.

5) She survived several serious suicide attempts even with a gun and slashed wrists.

6) She lives with a chronic disease of the brain that requires daily doses of her medication taken on time.

For months Company X has received urgent warnings and red flags warning that the denial of this critically necessary medicine has created a huge risk of relapse, re hospitalization and suicide. These warnings came from the Group for Psychiatry, Medicare, and from Peggy. For 20 months Company X has turned deaf ears and blind eyes to these desperate pleas for life and justifiably prescribed medication.

---

16. The name of the private provider has been removed from the letter since no response was obtained from him/her. As such, his/her name has been replaced with "Company X."

On August 14, 2007, in a call referenced telephone communication, Company X denied that Medicare had sent red flags and warnings on August 7, 2007, that Peggy was out of medication, and that there were life threatening consequences. Company X stated that prior to receiving a "life threatening" message from Medicare on August 14, 2007 (second complaint filed), "they never knew there was an issue of suicide relevant to their denials" of Peggy's medication.

On August 15, 2007, Peggy's illness blew up in her face; she began to hear voices, started to engage in behaviors to outrun the devil, and made suicide threats. This was a previously stable psychotic illness. The Group for Psychiatry saw her in an emergency appointment, gave her more sample medicine and had to make the decision of whether or not to re-hospitalize her. The denials continued.

On September 24, 2007, Peggy brought a new prescription to the pharmacy. Once again she was turned away by Company X without her medicine. The Group for Psychiatry finally threw up their hands and told Peggy that after 20 months and hours of fruitless paperwork, appeals and Prior Authorizations, there was nothing more they could do to help her access her prescription. This was treatment time being taken from Peggy and other patients.

Over the years that I have been an advocate for the mentally ill, I have trained police officers, taught advocacy to college students and guided many families through severe mental illnesses. I have never seen an appropriately prescribed antipsychotic medicine denial go this far.

Although Peggy speaks and writes with a fair fluency she cannot follow even the most basic sequence of directions or instructions. Peggy Symons doesn't know the difference between left and right. This is the very nature of psychiatric disabilities.

A review of Company X's denials and appeals processes reveals that they are so complicated and time consuming even a PhD would have endless trouble complying with all the terms and conditions.

A 20 month and very well documented paper trail shows that Peggy has put up a good fight, but as of the last denial of her prescription on October 2, 2007 it is very clear that she is completely and totally unable to navigate this company's procedures for her prescription, (we have copies of all denials, appeals, certified letters, Prior Authorizations; call reference numbers, appeal file numbers, detailed records from the Group for Psychiatry, pharmacy denial printouts, records of sample medications, we have names, dates, call center locations etc.).

In addition to these unjust and dangerous denials of a life sustaining medicine Company X has:

1) Refused to comply with three requests sent by certified mail to provide a history of complaints, grievances and appeals filed against
Company X by other members in the past." Company X is required
by law to provide this information on request.

2) Failed to respond to expedited appeals within the 24 to 72 hour
required time frame.

3) Company X refused three requests sent by certified mail to provide
information in numbered appeal files that contain the clinical criteria and rationale that were relied on to deny appeals for Peggy's
medicine. By law Company X must comply with this request.

Peggy continues to live with significant deficits caused by a lifelong
battle with schizophrenia and bipolar disorder, but with the constant
support of the Group for Psychiatry and the love of her family she has
tried very hard to build up a life of meaning and purpose.

This company has had 20 months to make choices between honoring
a profound responsibility to their weakest and sickest customers or to
dishonor it in pursuit of profit and profit alone. Company X has withheld
an expensive antipsychotic medicine to their cost advantage, leaving a
customer who has no ability to fight back as good as dead. At the very
least, Company X Medicare Part D Prescription Plan would have left
Medicare holding the bag for numerous hospitalizations at $1,300 a day.
Without the intensive assistance of the Group for Psychiatry, her family
and sample medication Peggy would have died.

Peggy and her family survived 25 years of a daily fight with severe
mental illness and potential suicide. Every single denial issued to her by
Company X Medicare Part D Prescription Plan has been a potential
death sentence. For the corporate equivalent of a pocketful of change a
very fragile individual is being forced to return to a chronic and severe
mental illness, hospitals and a daily battle against suicide.

If this is happening to Peggy it is also happening to other Medicare
Part D customers with schizophrenia and bipolar disorder (Peggy has
both). No doubt, like Peggy, they are being turned away from pharmacies
without appropriately prescribed and critically necessary antipsychotic
medicines. With no medicine and no hope of help, some may be falling
ill or dying with the first denials.

These are invisible Medicare Part D customers who have the very least
ability to stand up. They are being taken advantage of by a globally wealthy
corporation. They are losing their lives behind a corporate curtain of privacy laws and no accountability. These abuses will remain hidden and entrenched unless they are shaken out, investigated and made visible.

Hopefully, Medicare will act to protect these powerless and profoundly ill people with specific laws and regulations that will allow them access to their medications without having to navigate impossible "cost containment" strategies that are potentially costing lives.

In addition, a close look reveals that there may be even wider civil rights issues involving discrimination against people with severe mental illnesses.

A review of Peggy Symons pharmacy records show that in 20 months of Company X coverage, prescriptions have been filled for 11 medical conditions as well as for an anticonvulsant drug. None of them were in any way restricted or denied. The only medicine Company X Medicare Part D Prescription Plan has consistently refused to cover is her prescription for Seroquel, at the 100mg per dosing level prescribed by her doctor, a modern antipsychotic medicine used to treat her schizophrenia and bipolar disorder.

In closing, I appreciate any assistance you can provide me in resolving this on-going and despicable situation. Peggy Symons has turned to me as her last hope of accessing her medicine. Please respond to this request, in writing, in as timely a manner as possible.

Sincerely,

Stephen Bacallao,
CC: Peggy Symons

Shortly after her medication was finally approved, the provider contacted Ms. Symons, offering to switch her to a small co-pay for future provision of medication. Ms. Symons agreed, but the provider never sent a representative to sign her up. This provider has since ended its relationship with Medicare in Florida, and Ms. Symons has been automatically transferred to another provider with no problems so far (S. Bacallao, personal communication, April 24, 2008). How many others without such resilience, contacts, and networking ability would have succumbed to the corporate beast and given up?

Admissions to Emergency Rooms

With troubled community mental health centers, dwindling psychiatric hospitals,[17] and limited options by which to afford services and medication, individuals with mental illness are increasingly receiving services in non-specialty medical settings,

---

17. Private psychiatric hospitals, which are more inclined to treat those in imminent psychiatric crisis, have also declined precipitously. Between 1992 and 2002, the number of these hospitals was reduced by 52 percent (McCann, 2005).

especially emergency rooms (ERs). With the average length-of-stay of all mental health hospitalizations nationwide, including longer-term state hospitals, being only 7.5 days (Centers for Disease Control and Prevention, 2012), it is not substantially longer than an emergency room visit. And patients are less likely to be turned away by ERs.

Indeed, ERs have become inundated with patients with serious mental illness in the past decade. Between 1992 and 2003, there was a 56 percent increase (from 2,381,000 to 3,718,000) in the number of persons with mental illness visiting emergency room departments across the country (McCann, 2005). A 2017 study revealed a 44 percent increase in visits related to mental health and substance abuse (Novotney, 2018). And one North Dakota hospital's ER reported that the number of patients with psychosis as their primary diagnosis, not even including those in which psychosis is secondary, has doubled (San Miguel, 2012). In terms of prevalence, a 2007 survey found that one in eight patients seen in ERs had a psychiatric and/or substance abuse condition (Owens, Mutter, & Stocks, 2010). Moreover, Glover, Miller, and Sadowski, in a March 2012 briefing to Congress, reported that 70 percent of 6,000 ERs surveyed across the U.S. "boarded" patients with mental illness for "hours or days," with some even reporting holding them for several weeks (Torrey, et al., 2012). ERs in Maryland have reported a dozen patients being boarded for days (Colarossi, 2016).

However, emergency rooms are known to be frequently underfunded, as well as overcrowded, shorthanded, and lacking connections for referrals to more adequate mental health services. To say the least, provision of mental health care in general medical care facilities to indigent patients who cannot afford private treatment is less than optimal — not only for these people with mental illness, but for the hospitals. In an attempt to contain costs and bolster their profit margins, private community hospitals have devised ways to avoid treating indigent patients with mental illness, some of them inhumane. One such strategy is to literally dump them on the streets (Coleman, 1997):

Anderson Cooper opened his *60 Minutes* segment, entitled "Dumped on Skid Row" on May 17, 2007, by noting, "The first rule in medicine is do no harm" (Klatell, Flaum, & Klug, 2007). Yet, he revealed a videotape of a homeless woman being dropped off at Los Angeles' Skid Row upon release from the hospital. In another instance, a paraplegic man was dropped off on the street, without a wheelchair, via a van from the Hollywood Presbyterian Hospital four blocks from the Midnight Mission on Skid Row. When Cooper asked one of the Skid Row regulars about the dumping, the man replied, "It's nothing new ... It just got noticed because they [sic] been bringing 'em [sic] down in their hospital gowns." Chief of Hollywood Presbyterian Hospital, Kaylor Shemberger, deflected blame, pointing out that hospital care for the homeless is only part of a much larger problem. In Los Angeles County alone, about 88,000 people do not have a roof over their heads on any given day. He says there simply are not enough shelters and clinics to care for them. "When these people are discharged from a medical facility, they need a place to go, and we need a place to take them to that can accommodate their needs. Those resources are, you know, just lacking in this community," Shemberger says. Asked if he thinks the hospitals are just an easy target, Shemberger says, "I think we're being unfairly pursued in these particular cases. After all, you know, we're here to take care of their medical needs, not their housing needs."

Just as crises often drive policies within the criminal justice system (Walker, 2006), so do policies drive crises. Most clearly, the imposition of cost-saving tactics to behavioral healthcare — both by governments and by private companies — is detrimental in terms of the human suffering caused for persons with mental illness. Indeed, some argue that there is a causal relationship between restrictive insurance regulations and the manifestation of serious, persistent mental illness (Stone, 1997). Specifically, fewer persons with mental illnesses are able to access psychotropic medication and other treatment because it is too expensive for them to afford, which leads to exacerbation of mental illness.

In turn, untreated persons with serious mental illness frequently end up arrested and in jail as a result of aberrant behavior. Without opportunities for proper services, more and more persons with mental illness have become ensnared in the criminal justice system (Emery, 2006). Between 1980 and 1992 alone, there was a 154 percent increase in the reported number of persons with mental illnesses in jails (Watson, Hanrahan, Luchins, & Lurigio, 2001). Likewise, police-accompanied visits of persons with mental illness to psychiatric emergency departments increased from 32 to 56 percent of calls since the advent of managed care (Claassen, Kashner, Gilfillan, Larkin, & Rush, 2005). Furthermore, cities with a predominance of private psychiatric hospital beds have significantly higher official crime and arrest rates (Markowitz, 2006). This suggests that when mental health treatment is limited by privatization and managed care, police have fewer referral options and, thus, are more likely to make an arrest. Ultimately, these cost-saving tactics do not save money; they merely shift costs to cities and counties, who are responsible for law enforcement and jail. Is it any wonder that Linda Teplin, professor of psychiatry at Northwestern University, lamented that "jails have become the poor person's mental hospitals" (Butterfield, 1999, p. A10)?

Not only are these cost-saving strategies costly for individuals with mental illness, they are costly for the community, in the form of sometimes tragic consequences.[18] Such crises will be addressed in the discussion of civil commitment in Chapter 4, in the cases of Seung-Hui Cho, Jared Loughner, and Andrew Goldstein. Problems brought about by the decisions made by treatment providers will be addressed in Chapter 8's analysis of mental health courts, as well as in congressional testimony contained in the final chapter. For many reasons, allowing profit motive to take priority over societal and treatment interests is reprehensible (Cordner, 2006). These barriers also apply to those with private insurance coverage. The introduction of managed care placed more power in insurers' hands, as they are the entities approving the aid a person was eligible to receive (Cohn, 2015).

Public Stigma and Its Challenges

Public stigma falls at the nexus between the macro and micro levels. It occurs when members of the general public take negative action against individuals with mental illness (Corrigan, Markowitz et al., 2004; Corrigan & Watson, 2002). There are countless effects of public stigma, particularly related to the fear generated by the dangerousness stereotype, transmitted far and wide by the media (Stout, Villegas, & Jennings, 2004). The misconception that a mental illness is synonymous with danger has aided society's isolation of those suffering. This can be highly attributed to high-profile cases in which a person with mental illness engages in violence (Batastini, Lester, & Thompson, 2018). Mental illness stigma leads members of the public to avoid employing and/or working with, as well as to avoid renting to and/or living near people with mental illness, particularly those with severe disorders such as schizophrenia (Corrigan & Penn, 1999; Penn & Martin, 1998). Moreover, it prevents people from being willing to socialize with those with mental illness, contributing to the mainstream public's social distance from people with mental illness and the isolation of individuals with mental illness from society. In total, stigma limits patients' access to opportunities and resources, which contributes to economic poverty, lack of interpersonal connection, and less than full participation in society (SAMHSA, 2006; U.S. DHHS, 1999; but see Frailing & Slate, 2016 for practices that can help reduce public stigma against people with mental illness).

The Dangerousness Stereotype

One of the most powerful social misperceptions that contributes to the stigma of mental illness — and, accordingly, various negative outcomes for people with mental illness — is that they are inherently violent. Many come to the conclusion that if a person commits an act of violence, he/she must be mentally ill. As such, much of the

---

18. In testimony before the Florida Senate Committee on Health Care, Slate (2005) forewarned lawmakers that implementation of such policies would indeed lead to crises.

general public regards those with mental illness, and serious mental illness in particular, as unpredictable, dangerous, and to be avoided (Angermeyer, Cooper, & Link, 1998; Link et al., 1999; Pescosolido, Monahan, Link, Stueve, & Kikuzawa, 1999; Van Dorn, Swanson, Elbogen, & Swartz, 2005).

Certainly, there are highly publicized incidents of individuals with mental illness becoming violent, even infamously so. One must only look to recent history to find such accounts: the Virginia Tech shootings in 2007, the attempted assassination of Arizona Congresswoman Gabrielle Giffords and murders of several innocent bystanders in 2011, the shootings in the movie theater in Colorado in July 2012, and the deaths by gunfire at an elementary school in Newtown, Connecticut in December 2012. The instinct to blame mental illness for horrific events such as these spills over into those in which the shooter was not known to have a history of mental illness, including the mass shooting at a country music festival in Las Vegas in 2017, the mass shooting at a high school in Parkland, Florida in 2018, and the mass shooting at a Wal-Mart in El Paso, Texas in 2019. Yet, these incidents are incredibly rare, and even when they do occur, mental illness is rarely a factor. Research has consistently shown that mental illness does not coincide with higher risk of violence (Shipley & Borynski, 2013). Indeed, among 41 school shooters responsible for 37 shooting incidents in the United States, very few had been determined to suffer from a mental illness (Dedman, 2000). Similarly, Fein and Vossekuil (1998, 1999) studied 83 individuals who assassinated or attempted to assassinate public figures in the United States from 1949 to 1996 and concluded that, while mental health histories may be relevant when conducting threat assessments, rarely does mental illness play a role in the assassinations. However, when bombarded by these horrific images in the media, with its very purpose to evoke strong emotions, the lay public tends to overestimate the likelihood of such events.

Media Effects

Few would deny that we are in an age of media sensationalism, in which it is the tendency of the media to report on the planes that crash and burn, the aberrant exceptions. We don't hear about all the planes that successfully land day after day, nor do we hear about all the persons with mental illnesses (psychiatrists, psychologists, judges, lawyers, legislators, and even professors) who get up each and every day and go to work, perform exceptionally, and return home safely.[19] And violence committed by people with mental illness is a topic of choice in much of the media. Wahl (1995), reporting on seventeen years of research monitoring television content, found that 72 percent of all mentally ill characters in prime-time dramas were depicted as violent, with 21 percent of these characters portrayed as murderers. This same study analyzed daytime soap operas and concluded that approximately 66 percent of mentally ill

---

19. NAMI (n.d.-a) offers a list of highly successful people who functioned with mental illnesses, such as Abraham Lincoln, Lionel Aldridge, Ludwig Beethoven, Leo Tolstoy, Tennessee Williams, Vincent Van Gogh, Issac Newton, Ernest Hemingway, Michelangelo, Winston Churchill, Patty Duke, and Charles Dickens.

characters in this medium were depicted as criminal and violent. Although the percentages are not as striking as the research on TV, studies have found similar over-representation of individuals with mental illness as dangerous in other types of media. Dietrich, Heider, Matschinger, and Angermeyer (2006) found that the majority of newspaper articles on mental illness selectively and almost exclusively focus on violence and dangerousness. Likewise, Levin (2005), in a study of over three thousand articles in seventy major outlets, determined that approximately 40 percent of the newspaper stories associated mental illness with crime and dangerousness. Many of these stories end up in the front sections of newspapers (Corrigan, Watson, Gracia, et al., 2005).

What's more, not only are there a significant *number* of misrepresentations of violence committed by people with mental illness, but research suggests that these misrepresentations are actually purposeful (Wahl, 1995). For example, casting for the movie, *One Flew Over the Cuckoo's Nest*, a darling of the anti-psychiatry counterculture movement (Rissmiller & Rissmiller, 2006), was reportedly suspended until the producers could locate actors who looked distinctively unusual enough to portray the perceived image of mental patients. Although the movie was filmed at the Oregon State Hospital and actual hospital patients were considered for parts in the movie, the producers declined because the actual patients did not look bizarre enough to play such a role on the big screen.

Of grave concern is that the media forms the citizenry's primary source of information on mental illness (Edney, 2004). In 2003, newspapers were the fundamental source of information about psychiatric disorders for 74 percent of 1,300 survey respondents (Wahl, 2003). More recently, Caputo and Rouner (2011) found that most of their sample received information about mental illness from television news programs (70 percent), newspapers (58 percent), television (51 percent), and news magazines (34 percent). Moreover, we know that media sensationalism has a significant impact on public perceptions and opinion regarding mental illness.[20] Granello and Pauley (2000), for example, revealed that people who engage in moderate to heavy

---

20. NAMI (n.d.-c) has established a StigmaBusters network, which has advocates throughout the country and around the world who fight against electronic and print media misrepresentations and hurtful messages regarding mental illnesses. Vickers (2006), a mental health advocate and trained attorney with bipolar disorder, believes that education is the key to overcoming the stigma of mental illnesses. In particular, she advocates for educating the legal profession. She is aware of other attorneys with mental illnesses who will not come to the aid of other colleagues for fear that by such associations they themselves might be outed; she tells of a judge who may be exhibiting signs and symptoms of mental illness but is afraid to see a psychologist or psychiatrist for an evaluation that might negatively impact his judicial career, as he would be required to report the contact to the judicial qualifying commission; there is the judge that believes that mental illnesses are the result of being possessed by the devil, and an exorcism by the church would more readily cast out the demon than anything doctors and drugs could do; and she describes an attorney that stated that all persons with mental illnesses should be sterilized or put behind bars. In the same vein, it is hoped that media coverage of celebrities with mental illness who have received treatment, such as Britney Spears and Catherine Zeta-Jones, can prove to be educable moments that reduce the stigma surrounding mental illness and encourage those in the public to seek treatment (see Blankstein, Gold, & Winton, 2008).

viewing of television tend to have more negative beliefs and greater intolerance for people with mental illness. Ultimately, media teaches social conventions of how to treat individuals with mental illness (Stout et al., 2004).

Even some mental health advocacy organizations, such as the Treatment Advocacy Center (TAC) — major proponents of involuntary outpatient commitment, which will be discussed in Chapter 4 — capitalize on the public's fear of violence to drive their agenda with lawmakers across the country. The TAC defends their tactic, arguing essentially that it does more good than harm. For example, D.J. Jaffee, one of the individuals affiliated with TAC, has indicated, "Laws change for a single reason, in reaction to highly publicized incidences of violence. People care about public safety. I am not saying it is right. I am saying this is the reality ... So, if you're changing your laws in your state, you have to understand that" (Corrigan, Watson, Warpinski, & Gracia, 2004, p. 577). Jaffee reasoned, "Once you understand that it means that you have to take the debate out of the mental health arena and put it in the criminal justice/public safety arena[;] ... [i]t may be necessary to capitalize on the fear of violence" (Vine, 2001).[21]

Critics of this approach, such as Corrigan, Watson, et al. (2004) and Perlick and Rosenheck (2002), argue that inculcating individuals with stories of linkages between mental illness and violence only contributes to stigma. As a result of these media misrepresentations, roughly half of all U.S. citizens perceive persons who have mental illnesses to be more violent than individuals who do not have mental illness (Mental Health Association of Pennsylvania, 2007). This clearly reveals that public perceptions of people with mental illness as dangerous are "greatly exaggerated" (Stuart & Arboleda-Florez, 2001, p. 654). And as has been mentioned previously, these misperceptions among the lay public are only increasing over time (Phelan, et al., 2000). In turn, despite the TAC's intention, Corrigan, Watson, et al. (2004) argue that the strategy of instilling fear is not likely to result in urges for increased funding for mental health treatment programs. Instead, it is likely to generate attitudes that result in the withholding of such help and further segregation of persons with mental illnesses from society.[22]

Empirical Evidence about Mental Illness and Violence

Because of the salience of the issue, a substantial body of research over multiple decades has accrued on violence and mental illness. Overwhelmingly, the research has demonstrated that most violent acts are not committed by persons with mental

---

21. Jonathan Stanley (2004) of TAC, in defense of allegedly playing the violence card, indicated that a search of a database of leading newspapers only produced 71 items with the keywords "violence" and "Treatment Advocacy Center" in the past five years, and a search with the keywords "violence" and "mental illness" revealed 536 pieces in the past month. Stanley (2004) retorted, "People can't see what doesn't happen and newspapers can't print it" (p. 834).

22. E. Fuller Torrey (2002), founder of the TAC, however, maintains that the primary cause of stigma is fear of violence, and unless violence is addressed and fear of violence allayed, stigma will continue in an unabashed fashion.

illness, but by those who are not mentally ill; the vast majority of persons with mental illnesses will never commit an act of violence (Appelbaum, Robbins, & Monahan, 2000; Shipley & Borynski, 2013; Steadman et al., 1998; Swanson et al., 1997; Swanson et al., 2006; Swartz et al., 1998; U.S. DHHS, 1999; Van Dorn, Volavka, & Johnson, 2012). While rates of violence among individuals with severe mental illness vary depending on the definition of mental illness and the methodology of the study, a review article found that across studies rates of violence ranged from 2 percent to 13 percent of patients receiving outpatient care and from 17 percent to 50 percent among those receiving inpatient care (Choe, Teplin, & Abram, 2008). Some studies report that less than one percent of persons with mental illnesses will ever become violent (McCampbell, 2001).

Others have put the risk of violence by people with mental illness in the perspective of other rare events. According to Szmukler (2000), the probability of being murdered by a psychotic stranger is about the odds of being struck by lightning and dying from the strike, about a one in a million chance. The chance of dying by influenza is four hundred times more likely than dying at the hands of a patient with mental illness (Dobson, 1998; Mental Health Association of Pennsylvania, 2007). Overall, the attributable risk for a person in the lay public to be victimized by someone with serious mental illness is somewhere between three to five percent, versus a seven times greater risk of being violently assaulted by someone who is not mentally ill but is abusing substances (Friedman, 2006).

Following the heightened risk of violence among substance abusers, most of the research on violence committed by individuals with mental illness reveals that only a small subset of persons with mental illnesses have an increased risk for violence and only when certain factors are present — primarily substance abuse. Indeed, Elbogen and Johnson (2009) conducted a study, in which 34,653 cases between 2001 and 2005 collected in a national survey were analyzed. In it, the researchers found that serious mental illness was unrelated to violence in the community unless co-occurring substance abuse or dependence was involved. In addition, co-occurring disorders were not even the strongest predictors of violence. Instead, historical, demographic, and contextual factors were more important. Specifically, Elbogen and Johnson (2009) found the following variables, from most to least, to be related to violence: age, history of any violent acts, gender, history of juvenile detention, divorce or separation in the past year, history of physical abuse, parental criminal history, unemployment for the past year, co-occurring severe mental illness and substance use, and personal victimization in the past year. Thus, general criminality (e.g., history of violence, having been in juvenile detention), trauma (e.g., a history of abuse, recent victimization) and other psychosocial stressors (e.g., recent divorce or unemployment) appeared to be more strongly related to violence than serious mental illness.[23] These

---

23. Van Dorn et al. (2012), however, re-examined Elbogen and Johnson's (2009) findings in order to rectify several methodological issues. Specifically, in their re-analysis, they used causal modeling, a recent past year diagnosis (rather than lifetime diagnosis) of mental illness, disaggregated serious mental illnesses into various diagnostic categories (schizophrenia, bipolar disorder, and major de-

latter factors were confirmed by Van Dorn et al (2012), who found that, when serious mental illness as a broad category was examined, adverse childhood events (e.g., physical abuse and/or neglect during childhood, having an antisocial household member during childhood) were the most robust factors, doubling the risk of violence in adulthood. They also confirmed the role of young age and current stressful life events as significant predictors of violence.

A substantial limitation of much of the research on violence among the mentally ill is that it examines "serious mental illness" as a broad category, rather than examining individual symptoms. In an effort to address this limitation, Swanson et al. (2006) studied specific symptoms of schizophrenia and their relationship to violence. They found that violence was more likely to occur when individuals experience positive symptoms[24] (e.g., persecutory delusions), while negative symptoms[25] (e.g., social withdrawal) tended to decrease the risk.[26] Likewise, various studies have found that lack of treatment and/or non-compliance with treatment (e.g., medication) is related to violence among persons with mental illness, if they commit any such crimes (Borum, Swanson, Swartz, & Hiday, 1997; Honberg, 2007; Monahan & Arnold, 1996; Steadman, et al., 1998; Swanson et al., 1997, 2008). Taken together, these findings suggest that any valid conclusions about violence among persons with mental illness must consider individual symptoms, treatment compliance, and substance abuse, rather than making blanket statements about "serious mental illness" or even about broad diagnostic categories (e.g., people with schizophrenia).

Even when an individual with mental illness does become violent, contrary to the popular image propagated by the media, most do not target strangers. Instead, in the vast majority of cases, the targets are people most involved in the person's care, such as family members (Steadman, et al., 1998), and the incidents do not usually result in serious injury. Ultimately, the United States Secret Service, involved in threat assessments at the highest levels in this country, has concluded that "mental illness is not critical to determining dangerousness; the ability and capacity to develop and

---

pression), a more homogeneous comparison group (e.g., without *any* less severe psychiatric issues or substance abuse), and other relevant variables that they perceived to have been missing in Elbogen and Johnson's study. In Van Dorn et al.'s re-analysis (2012), recent serious mental illness was in fact more related to violence than those without mental illness. However, their findings corroborated that those with co-occurring substance abuse was at the highest risk of violence. *When substance abuse was involved* and the individual serious mental illnesses were disaggregated, schizophrenia was the strongest predictor of violence, and bipolar disorder was closely behind. Perceiving hidden threats into others, ostensibly measured as a specific symptom of psychosis, was also significantly related to violence. Furthermore, binge drinking was a significant predictor.

24. "Positive" symptoms are so named because they represent an addition of an experience or behavior that individuals with mental illness did not experience prior to the onset of their illness and/or that others without mental illness do not experience.

25. "Negative" symptoms are those that represent a reduction in normal functioning, compared to an individual's functioning prior to developing the mental illness and/or to those without the illness.

26. They also found signs of depression, childhood conduct problems, and victimization to be related to violence, corroborating the research above.

execute a plan is much more significant" (United States Secret Service, 2006). As Baumann and Teasdale (2017) found, access to firearms among people with mental illness is associated with increased suicidality, but not with increased violence against others.

Victimization of Persons with Mental Illness

A reality that often goes unnoticed — even in the research literature — due to the media's inflammatory misrepresentations, is that persons with severe mental illnesses are significantly more likely to be victims of crime, including violent crime, than those without mental illness. Of the U.S. studies on the topic (Brekke, Prindle, Bae, & Long, 2001; Goodman et al., 2001; Hiday, Swartz, Swanson, Borum, & Wagner, 1999; Teasdale, 2009; Teplin, McClelland, Abram, & Weiner, 2005; White, Chafetz, Collins-Bride, & Nickens, 2006), rates of violent victimization within the mentally ill samples ranged from 8 percent (Hiday et al., 1999) to 34 percent (Brekke et al., 2001). Likewise, rates of non-violent criminal victimization ranged from 21 percent (Teplin et al., 2005) to 38 percent (Brekke et al., 2001). Taken together, this suggests that people with mental illness are approximately 14 times more likely to be the victim of violent crime than a perpetrator (Brekke et al., 2001).

Additionally, persons with severe mental illnesses are significantly more likely to be victimized than the general population. This is especially true for those that exhibit behaviors that make their illness readily observable (Policastro, Teasdale, & Daigle, 2015). Individuals with serious mental illness in Teplin et al.'s (2005) study were 11 times more likely to be victims of violent crime. This included being 8 times more likely to be robbed, 15 times more likely to be victims of assault, 23 times more likely to be victims of rape, and 140 times more likely to have property stolen from their person (Teplin et al., 2005). Overall, the studies found that victimization among persons with mental illness is closely related to substance abuse, having more severe symptomatology, and being homeless (Hiday et al., 1999; Maniglio, 2009; Teasdale, 2009). Maniglio (2009) also found a relationship between victimization and criminal activity among the mentally ill. Among men, the experience of stress also predicted one's own victimization (Maniglio, 2009).

Unemployment and Underemployment

Various symptoms of mental illness — e.g., the social withdrawal, avolition (lack of motivation), anhedonia (inability to experience pleasure in most activities) and cognitive dysfunction, to name a few — can interfere with an individual's ability to work effectively or at all. Much of the public perceives such symptoms to be mere laziness, but they are in fact reflections of the individual's illness. Indeed, research shows that people with mental illness want to work (Mueser, Salyers, & Mueser, 2001), and most can work in at least some capacity (Russinova, Wewiorski, Lyass, Rogers, & Massaro, 2002). However, they are more likely than their non-mentally ill counterparts to be unemployed (Anthony, Buell, Sharratt, & Althoff, 1972; Bond &

McDonel, 1991). Specifically, among people with a recognized serious mental health disability, only approximately 25 percent are employed (Draine, Salzer, Culhane, & Hadley, 2002), and this rate has remained fairly stable over the past several decades (Trupin, Sebesta, Yelin, & LaPlante, 1997). Even with supported employment, in which people are placed in positions according to their needs and receive extra supports at work, the highest rate of employment across studies was 34 percent, with an average of 16.5 weeks on the job (Drake, Becker, Clark, & Mueser, 1999). Overall, the median length of time on a job among employed persons with a serious psychiatric diagnosis is approximately seven months (McCrohan, Mowbray, Bybee, & Harris, 1994), with most having worked a total of 19 months on average across their lifespan (Baron & Salzer, 2000).

Most have explained unemployment and/or underemployment among those with serious mental illness to be related to inability to cope with the stresses of work, poor social skills, and diminished cognitive abilities (Draine et al., 2002). However, it appears that many may be turned down for employment before they can even start. As noted in the 1999 U.S. Surgeon General's report (U.S. DHHS, 1999), mental health stigma reduces patients' access to resources and opportunities pertaining to jobs and housing. Indeed, of a sample of stabilized outpatients with schizophrenia, 50 percent had not been hired after it was learned they had received psychiatric treatment (Dickerson, Sommerville, Origoni, Ringel, & Parente, 2002). This relationship might be further explained by the moderating effect of education (Draine et al., 2002). It is well-established that early onset of a mental illness may limit a person's educational achievement (Kessler, Foster, Saunders, & Stang, 1995), which then in turn reduces one's employment prospects, which then in turn heightens stress (Lo & Cheng, 2013).

Poverty

People with mental illness are among the most marginalized and, thus, impoverished groups in society. In the U.S., approximately 33 percent of persons with mental illness live at or below the poverty line, compared to 10 percent of people without mental illness (Cook, 2006); note that these data precede both the recession of the early 2000s and the pandemic of 2020; those two events have undoubtedly increased both of these percentages. Moreover, families with a household member with a severe mental illness have on average a total income that is 38 percent lower than other families (Vick, Jones, & Mitra, 2012). This represents a three times greater risk of being poor and a 52 percent increase in depth of poverty than families without a mentally ill member. Looking at it from a slightly different angle, people living in poverty have the poorest overall health, as well as the poorest mental health specifically (Adler et al., 1994). In particular, individuals living in poverty are four times more likely to experience serious levels of psychological distress than those living over twice above the poverty line (CDC, 2009), and they are two to three times more likely to have a diagnosable mental disorder (Holzer et al., 1986; Muntaner, Eaton, Diala, Kessler, & Sorlie, 1998; Regier et al., 1993).

The relationship between mental illness and poverty can be explored in two broad ways. Simply put, poverty causes mental illness or mental illness causes poverty. On the one hand, it is argued that living in poverty renders an individual more likely to be exposed to stressful social environments (e.g., residing in high crime areas, exposure to violence, victimization) and less likely to be cushioned by social/material resources (McLeod & Kessler, 1990), thereby rendering a person more likely to develop a mental illness. And as noted above, those with access to benefits often lose these lose them if they become incarcerated, but this is a less a matter of law than it is a matter of practice. Conversely, the alternative explanation, known as the selective social drift hypothesis (Goldberg & Morrison, 1963), is that having a mental illness leads to declined functioning and economic productivity, which in turn results in poverty. Each of these explanations is likely accurate in different cases.

Substandard Housing

As noted by Uehara (1994, p. 309), "It is widely acknowledged that persons with severe and persistent mental illness face formidable obstacles in securing permanent, safe housing." In capitalist American society, housing is not considered a fundamental right, as evidenced by alarming rates of homelessness. Between a shortage of decent, affordable housing, which decreases the supply side of the supply-demand business equation, and negative mental illness stigma, which prevents property owners from renting to individuals with mental illness, people with mental illness frequently find themselves in low quality or substandard housing (Uehara, 1994). In Dickerson et al's (2002) sample, 39 percent of respondents had difficulty finding housing when their psychiatric disorder was known.

The problem of finding acceptable housing is particularly applicable to men, especially African American men, with mental illness living in urban areas with a history of jail admissions, substance abuse issues, and aggression (Uehara, 1994). Yet, this also occurs in small towns where alternative housing options are unavailable.

In Staunton, Virginia, a 106-year-old dilapidated hotel, well-known for housing the area's mentally ill population upon release from the local state hospital, was condemned due to repeated and extensive violations of life safety measures (e.g., lack of exit lights, broken handrails on stairs, water and sewage leaks, a pest infestation, and structural issues) (Davis, 2011). With one week's notice, all tenants were evicted. But for Building Official and Zoning Administrator, John Glover, it was not soon enough, he reported that he "lost sleep each night residents continued to occupy the building after the final eviction notice was given." Staunton City Manager, Steve Owen, stated that he had "never seen such a situation in three decades in local government" (Davis, 2011). A year later, he still lamented the situation, "It was appalling. It was unfit for human living" (Dennis, 2012). One former tenant said he preferred living on the street after being evicted, recalling how filthy the hotel had been. "There were roaches and everything else. A sewer line burst and flooded the basement. So you can imagine how that stunk" (Dennis, 2012). The owner lives in Florida and refused to comment (Davis, 2011).

Acting Assistant City Manager, Jim Gallaher, saw the situation for what it was: "It's really unusual to have a building in that kind of condition that can keep its tenants. I think that really speaks to the difficulty in finding housing these residents had. They were really between a rock and a hard place."

The conditions of designated "assisted living facilities" (ALFs) — intended to care for individuals who cannot care for themselves but are not in need of inpatient hospitalization — are frequently just as miserable. Earley (2006), in his expose of the mental health and criminal justice systems in Miami, paints a tragic picture. Of 647 boarding homes in Miami, only 250 are licensed by the state. The other 397 consistently fail to meet minimum standards. Yet these facilities continued to cut costs, in order to maximize profits, by hiring newly arrived immigrants and paying them less than minimum wage to run the homes. The workers, many of them unable to speak English and none with specialized training for working with people with mental illness, dispense medications. Patients are often given the wrong medications and are physically abused. Despite this knowledge, the state continued to issue the ALFs "limited licenses" and pay them to care for patients with mental illness, while reportedly having no other alternatives for the patients.

Homelessness

Many individuals with mental illness end up homeless. Indeed, as noted by Folsom et al. (2005), "[h]omeless persons with serious mental illness represent one of the most vulnerable and disadvantaged segments of the society" (p. 375). Not only do they face the struggles involved with having a mental illness and of being homeless — and in many cases, the struggles of being mentally ill, homeless, and African American — they experience multiple stigmas related to being part of these marginalized groups. These experiences form a reciprocal, often cyclical, relationship: having a mental illness places an individual at heightened risk of becoming homeless, and being homeless contributes to and exacerbates one's mental illness. Moreover, if one then becomes involved in the criminal justice system, he/she faces a triple (or quadruple) stigma and all the challenges that come with it.

Determining the exact prevalence of homelessness is an inherently difficult task, as homeless individuals are, by the nature of their circumstances, elusive. The only nationwide, standardized assessment of the scope of homelessness is the point-in-time counts performed by the U.S. Department of Housing and Urban Development (HUD).[27] According to these counts, there were over 636,000 homeless people in

---

27. These point-in-time counts are performed to provide a snapshot of the state of homelessness across the country. Conducted biennially, they enable tracking of changes in homeless rates over

America on a single night in January, 2011 (U.S. DHUD, 2011). Of these, 38 percent literally lived on the streets, whereas 62 percent lived in homeless shelters. Thirty-seven percent were members of homeless families, and 14 percent were veterans.[28] In terms of prevalence over a given year, it is conservatively estimated that twice these numbers — with some sources estimating as many as 3.5 million — are likely to experience homelessness (National Law Center on Homelessness and Poverty, 2004). This translates into approximately 1 percent of the general population being homeless each year (Burt & Aron, 2000).

Compared to the general population, individuals with mental illness are at particularly high risk for homelessness. Specifically, approximately 15 percent of people with serious mental illness are homeless over the course of a year (Folsom et al., 2005), compared to 1 percent of the general population, as cited above. Not only are people with mental illness more likely to be homeless, but those with mental illness form a notable percentage of the homeless population, particularly when compared to the rate of serious mental illness in the general population. Although rates have varied widely over the years and depending on methodology (Draine et al., 2002), 20 to 33 percent of homeless persons in the U.S. have a current serious mental illness (Fischer & Breakey, 1991; Folsom & Jeste, 2002; Paquette, 2010; Sullivan, Burnam, Koegel, & Hollenberg, 2000; U.S. DHUD, 2010; Wong, 2002). Some reports, such as in Colorado, however, suggest that this rate is actually closer to 66 percent, with one-third of homeless men and two-thirds of homeless women experiencing mental illness (Newsome & Bencel, 2009). When broadening the scope to a *history* of mental illness, it is estimated that approximately 50 percent of homeless persons have a history of mental illness (Caton et al., 2005).

---

time. The counts must be interpreted with caution, however, due to the methodology by which they are performed. First, point-in-time counts, which assess homelessness on a single day (versus period prevalence counts, which measure homelessness over a designated period of time), tend to underestimate those who are temporarily homeless. Moreover, HUD carries out the study by enlisting the assistance of each geographic region's Continuum of Care (CoC), the area's local planning agency responsible for coordinating housing and homeless services, who are required to share their information in order to receive federal funding from HUD. As such, these estimates may be understated or overstated, depending on the locality. On the one hand, many CoCs serve exceedingly large geographic areas and, thus, their resources (e.g., funding for shelters, staff to perform the counts) are spread thin. If shelters are unavailable or filled to capacity, a segment of the homeless population may go undetected (and uncounted), resulting in an underestimation of the true prevalence. Likewise, if there are not enough staff to conduct adequate counts, underestimation is more likely to occur. On the other hand, given that the CoCs are applying for funding to provide homeless services in their communities, they may be motivated to overestimate the true extent of the problem in their region.

28. Contrary to expectations, given the economic recession since 2008, the U.S. DHUD (2011) counts indicate that homelessness (at least, according to official statistics) has declined by 5% since 2007. Likewise, the longer the military's presence in Iraq and Afghanistan and the more soldiers involved, the greater one would expect the rate of homelessness among returned veterans to be; however, the rate of homelessness among veterans has reportedly declined by nearly 11% since HUD started tracking this population in 2009. These decreases are hypothesized to be related to increased funding and coordination from the federal government to reduce homelessness, especially among veterans (Sullivan, 2011).

There are several reasons for the relationship between mental illness and homelessness (National Coalition for the Homeless, 2009b). First, mental illness can disrupt one's ability to manage activities of daily living, such as self-care. Likewise, individuals with mental illness may have difficulty with relationships, including with family, friends, and other potential sources of support; thereby, many lack a safety net when they experience economic difficulties and other crises (Nishio, Horita, Sado, Mizutani, Watanabe, Uehara & Yamamoto, 2017). Moreover, such struggles with self-care and relationships are exacerbated by the frequent co-occurrence of substance abuse among persons with mental illness.[29] (This co-occurrence will be discussed in greater detail later in this chapter.)

Furthermore, aberrant behavior of homeless persons with mental illnesses is more likely to come to the attention of the authorities and result in criminal justice sanctions. As such, increased homelessness is related to higher crime rates in an area (Markowitz, 2006). On an individual level, inmates with mental illness in jails and prisons have higher rates of homelessness. In particular, between 19 percent and 30 percent of inmates with mental illness had been homeless at some point in the previous year, compared to only 3 percent to 17 percent of inmates without mental illness (Ditton, 1999). Likewise, 4 percent to 7 percent of inmates with mental illness were homeless at the time of arrest, compared to 0.3 percent to 3 percent of non-mentally ill inmates (Ditton, 1999).[30] Of a host of demographic, historical, and clinical factors, homelessness had the strongest association with misdemeanor arrests and additional days in jail for individuals with mental illness (Constantine et al., 2010).[31] The evidence on the relationship between mental illness, homelessness, and serious crime, however, is less consistent, with some finding an increased risk of violence (Markowitz, 2006) and others finding a decreased risk of any felony arrests (Constantine et al., 2010).

The following describes some agencies' treatment of and "solutions" for homelessness in their areas:

Daytona Beach, Florida, a beachside city, renowned for its tourism, expansive beaches, enticing year-round climate, and the Daytona 500 NASCAR race, has also attracted a sizeable homeless population. In 2006, Daytona Beach Police Chief Michael Chitwood proposed to "help" the homeless by offering each

---

29. Studies have found rates of co-occurring drug and alcohol abuse among the homeless mentally ill population ranging from 35% (U.S. DHUD, 2010) to 65% (Wong, 2002); 53% had a lifetime diagnosis of a substance use disorder (Caton et al., 2005).

30. Jail inmates consistently showed the highest rates of homelessness, followed by state prison inmates. Federal prison inmates had the lowest rates of homelessness.

31. Despite this apparent relationship, some experts caution that the apparent relationship between mental illness, homelessness, and criminal justice involvement is actually related to an extraneous variable, such as poverty, rather than mental illness causing these problems (Draine et al., 2002).

homeless person a one-way Greyhound bus ticket to anywhere but Daytona. He claimed that this would give them an opportunity to reconnect with family and friends. However, experts contended that these are ties that have likely been severed long ago and are no longer existent (Ma, 2006; Orlando Sentinel Editorial Board, 2006). Steve Feinstein (personal communication, January 1, 2007) maintains similar practices of "Greyhound therapy" — busing people out of catchment areas with a few dollars for food so that services would be obtained on someone else's dime — have been tried by state hospital providers in the past, with little success.[32]

Other Florida law enforcement agencies have also been covered in press accounts for encounters with the homeless. In 2007, St. Petersburg police received negative press attention about the slashing of tents by their police officers caught on videotape during a raid at a homeless camp (Raghunathan, 2007) that led to the unveiling of a strategy for alleviating immediate needs of the homeless and plans for a shelter (Sharockman, 2007).

Not all press depicts negative law enforcement officer encounters with homeless individuals, however. For example, a Bradenton police officer, Nicolas Evans, was heralded by advocates for the homeless after pulling a shopping cart containing a homeless woman's belongings alongside his police car as he took her to jail to book her for violating a court order (Anderson, 2007). However, a second encounter the following night, in which he provided the same shopping cart transportation service, resulted in a recommendation by Evans' supervisor that he be terminated; instead, the police chief imposed a thirty-day suspension.

Veterans, Mental Illness, and Homelessness

One group that is particularly relevant to a discussion of mental illness and homelessness is veterans, as they represent a disproportionate subset of the homeless population. While only 8 percent of the general population of the United States can claim veteran status (Martinez & Bingham, 2011; National Coalition for Homeless Veterans, n.d.), veterans constitute anywhere from 14 percent (U.S. DHUD, 2011) to 33 percent (U.S. Department of Veterans Affairs, n.d.) of the homeless population. Indeed, the Veterans Administration (VA) estimates that veterans are 50 percent more likely than others in the general population to fall into homelessness (New York Times Editorial Desk, 2011). In particular, veterans represent roughly 40 percent of homeless males (National Coalition for the Homeless, 2009a). Additionally, homeless veterans

---

32. Greyhound therapy was employed with Russell Weston, who was hospitalized in Montana after making a threat against then President Clinton. Upon release, Weston was provided with a one way ticket to Illinois. He decompensated and ultimately ended up in a hallway of the Capitol, shooting and killing two law enforcement officers before being detained (Butterfield, 1998; *Los Angeles Times* Editorial, 1998).

are disproportionately represented among minority racial and ethnic groups; 56 percent of homeless veterans are African American or Hispanic, despite these racial/ethnic groups accounting for only 13 percent and 15 percent of the U.S. population, respectively (National Coalition for Homeless Veterans, n.d.). In sheer numbers, approximately 67,500 veterans were homeless on a single night in 2011 (U.S. DHUD, 2011); however, conservatively, twice that number is homeless over the course of a year (National Coalition for Homeless Veterans, n.d.). In fact, McClam (2008) estimated that in 2006, 336,000 U.S. veterans were homeless, with 1,500 of these homeless veterans having emerged from the conflicts in Iraq and Afghanistan. Undoubtedly, these numbers are much higher now, with many more servicemen and women having served in these conflicts.

The primary causes of homelessness among veterans are mental illness, substance abuse, and medical issues, coupled with lack of services and social support, and the economic challenges associated with all of the above (Veterans, Inc., 2010; Tsai, Hoff, & Harpaz-Rotem, 2017). Upon their return, veterans often find themselves unable to function in civilian society related to, among other things, mental illness developed as a result of their service to the country. Particularly in the recent conflicts in Iraq and Afghanistan (Operation Iraqi Freedom [OIF] and Operation Enduring Freedom [OEF]), the majority of servicemen and women have experienced high intensity guerilla warfare and faced the constant threat of danger from improvised explosive devices (IEDs) (National Center for Post-Traumatic Stress Disorder and the Walter Reed Army Medical Center, 2004; Seal, Bertenthal, Miner, Sen, & Marmar, 2007). Many have experienced traumatic injury, including significant traumatic brain injuries, and more of the wounded survive than in any previous war (U.S. Army Surgeon General, 2005). Furthermore, they spend extended periods of time away from their social support networks in the U.S. and frequently must return to Iraq and Afghanistan for multiple tours of duty (Gawande, 2004; U.S. Army Surgeon General, 2005). All of these factors place veterans at high risk of developing a mental illness, especially post-traumatic stress disorder (PTSD) and depression, both of which are complicated by traumatic brain injuries (McClam, 2008). Seal and colleagues (2007, 2009) conducted the most comprehensive study of OIF and OEF veterans, finding that 25 percent of nearly 104,000 veterans (between 2001 to 2005) and 37 percent of nearly 290,000 veterans (between 2002 to 2008) receiving services at VA health care facilities have been diagnosed with mental illnesses. Specifically, 22 percent were diagnosed with PTSD, a rate which increased 4 to 7 times after the invasion of Iraq. More than 17 percent were diagnosed with depression (Seal et al., 2009), and nearly half of all OIF/OEF veterans diagnosed with depression had also experienced traumatic brain injury (Seal et al., 2007). Significantly, a majority of veterans (56 percent) were diagnosed with two or more distinct mental health diagnoses (Seal et al., 2007).[33] Decline

---

33. A few caveats are in order in interpreting these findings, however. On the one hand, these may be somewhat of an overestimate, as there is a significant degree of overlap between the samples in the two articles. Conversely, and most importantly, these estimates are based only on veterans who have sought and received services through the VA; thus, they fail to account for the myriad of ser-

in functioning as a result of mental illness leaves many veterans struggling to maintain housing, thereby placing them at risk for becoming homeless.

A variety of factors prevent veterans with mental illness from obtaining needed mental health treatment, which leads to further deterioration and in many cases homelessness. First, the stigma of mental illness and of receiving mental health treatment in the military precludes many troops from seeking treatment at all. In a Department of Defense study, for example, approximately 17 percent of servicemen and women reported experiencing symptoms of mental illness, such as PTSD, yet 60 percent of these respondents admitted they would be reluctant to reveal such symptoms to superiors or peers because they believed that they would be treated differently (Welch, 2008). Second, the VA system is having difficulty keeping up with the added mental health needs of the returning cohorts of veterans (Trivedi, et al., 2015). According to Abramson and Gordemer (2012), although any veteran asking for help is supposed to be evaluated within 24 hours and start treatment within two weeks, an investigation by the VA's Inspector General revealed that the average waiting time in some areas is three months. In response, then President Obama issued an executive order on August 31, 2012, authorizing the VA to hire 1,600 new mental health personnel and to expand crisis services to veterans (Horsley, 2012). Nevertheless, former vice chief of staff of the Army, retired General Peter Chiarelli, argues that merely hiring more mental health professionals is not the answer, as there have not been enough qualified mental health professionals seeking employment within the VA to even fill job openings (Abramson & Gordemer, 2012). Finally, and arguably most importantly, clinical and scientific understanding of PTSD and traumatic brain injury lags behind the demand for expertise required to treat today's veterans (Abramson & Gordemer, 2012). Heightened rates of mental illness, coupled with stigma about mental illness and lack of adequate mental health treatment in the military, combine to result in a large mentally ill, homeless veteran population. Indeed, overall, it is estimated that 45 percent of homeless veterans have a mental illness, and 70 percent have an alcohol or drug abuse problem (Center for American Progress, 2008).

Self-Stigma and Its Challenges

Lack of opportunities and social isolation is not solely related to public stigma and discrimination. Individuals with mental illness fail to pursue opportunities and resources as a result of internalized structural and public stigma, or as Corrigan refers to it, *self-stigma* (Corrigan, Markowitz, et al., 2004; Corrigan & Watson, 2002). After

---

vicemen and women who have not sought help. Lastly, this study was conducted by employees of a VA medical center, who may have a vested interest to either overestimate mental illness (e.g., to support requests for additional staff, to highlight the amount of work they do) or underestimate (e.g., to counter attacks from outsiders that adequate services are not being provided by the VA system).

years of indoctrination to the same mental illness stereotypes to which the rest of society is exposed, individuals with mental illness commonly feel unworthy, incapable, and/or hopeless about pursuing life goals (Corrigan, Larson, & Rusch, 2009). Individuals with mental illness are keenly aware of the stereotypes applied to them. Dickerson et al. (2002) found that 87 percent of stabilized outpatients with schizophrenia worried at least occasionally that others would view them unfavorably because they have received psychiatric treatment. Of these outpatients, 83 percent had been exposed to media accounts about people with mental illness that they found hurtful or offensive; 81 percent had been in situations in which they personally heard others say unfavorable or otherwise offensive things about people with mental illness; 77 percent had been shunned or avoided by others when they learned of the person's mental illness; and 76 percent had been treated as less competent by others who have learned of the person's mental illness. Indeed, many say that the stigma and prejudice associated with their illness is as distressing as the symptoms themselves (Hocking, 2003). The enduring but often erroneous connection the media makes between mass shootings and mental illness also contributes to self-stigma (Park, MinHwa, & Seo, 2019). Undoubtedly, these experiences and the associated internalized stigma are largely responsible for self-destructive acts, such as co-occurring substance abuse and heightened rates of suicide.

Co-Occurring Substance Abuse

As will be discussed throughout this book, many people with serious mental illness also abuse substances. In fact, this happens with such regularity that the pairing has come to be called "co-occurring disorders" or "dual diagnosis" (Harnish, Corrigan, Byrne, Pinals, Rodrigues & Smelson, 2016). While approximately 35 percent of Americans will be diagnosed with a substance use disorder at some point in their lives (Kessler et al., 2005), up to 70 percent of those with serious mental illnesses exhibit substance abuse and/or dependence (Parks et al., 2006). Research suggests that having a psychiatric disorder triples the risk of having problems related to alcohol and/or drugs (Lehman, Myers, Corty, & Thompson, 1994). Looking at dual diagnosis from a slightly different perspective, 39 percent of alcoholics and 53 percent of drug abusers had a co-occurring mental illness (Regier et al., 1990). These rates climb sharply among the jail and prison population, where up to 85 percent of all inmates have a substance abuse disorder (National Center on Addiction and Substance Abuse, 2010). Moreover, of jail inmates with mental illness, approximately 75 percent have a comorbid substance abuse disorder at intake (Abram & Teplin, 1991; James & Glaze, 2006; Teplin, Abram, & McClelland, 1996) and 90 percent have a *lifetime* co-occurrence of mental illness and substance abuse (Roskes, Cooksey, Feldman, Lipford, & Tambree, 2005). These rates are significantly higher than among inmates without mental illness (Teplin et al., 1996). Such individuals face more barriers in receiving treatment while incarcerated. In some cases, individuals who had co-occurring substance abuse were not properly documented as having a severe mental illness (Wood, 2017).

Serious mental illness and substance abuse disorders are closely related for a number of reasons. It is certainly true that people with mental illness are drawn to alcohol and drugs for many of the same reasons that those without mental illness are drawn to them: due to peer pressure, the experience of sedation, extra energy, cognitive experiences, and other effects of drugs. However, given the higher prevalence rates, people with mental illness must abuse substances for other reasons as well. To determine these, one must first ask the classic question, "Does substance abuse cause mental illness or does mental illness cause substance abuse?" The answer to that is resoundingly, "It depends." There are people who never abused alcohol or drugs until they were in the early stages of their mental illness and/or in the throes of an acute psychiatric episode. Conversely, many people with substance abuse issues, as a result of the constant chemical imbalances to which they submit their body and/ or the psychosocial stressors that follow, eventually develop a mental illness. For example, in one sample of people with substance abuse issues, 54 percent had no history of an independent mental illness, only psychiatric disorders following from their substance use (Lehman et al., 1994).

In light of these trajectories, there are several possible, non-exclusive reasons for the high rates of co-occurring mental illness and substance abuse. First, many use alcohol and/or drugs to self-medicate — to numb themselves, distract themselves, make themselves less aware of, or lead them to care less about their symptoms. Likewise, they may abuse alcohol and drugs to numb themselves from the psychosocial stressors caused by their symptoms. Indeed, drugs of abuse do a "better" job of meeting these needs than do psychotropic medications, which are merely intended to return the individual's brain chemistry and experiences to "normal," not to give them a necessarily pleasurable experience per se. In fact, some would prefer not to be returned to normal or reality, in which they must come to terms with their illness and/or life situation. Nevertheless, in the long run, substances of abuse tend to exacerbate people's mental illnesses, make treatment less effective, and aggravate their life circumstances even more. Of course, poor judgment as a result of the cognitive symptoms of people's mental illnesses may render them unable to appreciate these considerations, both prior to starting to use substances and/or while using them.

People with dual diagnoses present particular challenges for both the mental health and criminal justice systems. Co-occurring substance disorders are associated with a wide range of negative outcomes, including a greater number of psychotic symptoms and psychotic relapses, poorer treatment compliance, greater use of more expensive crisis services and inpatient care, and increased risk of violence toward self and others (Dixon, 1999; Parks et al., 2006). Indeed, rates of non-compliance with medication are eight times higher for people with both mental illness and substance abuse disorders than for those who do not abuse substances (Owen, Fischer, Booth, & Cuffel, 1996; Parks et al., 2006). Additionally, these individuals are more likely to demonstrate poor money management and to experience issues with housing and homelessness (Dixon et al., 1999). Finally, they suffer more accidents (Parks et al., 2006) and medical problems, including infectious diseases such as HIV (Dixon et al., 1999).

Given these wide-ranging problems, people with co-occurring mental illness and substance abuse receive surprisingly little treatment. In 2002, only 39 percent of males and 54 percent of females with co-occurring disorders received specialized care for either or both disorders (SAMHSA, 2004). This is likely related not only to refusal to seek care but to poor past experiences with treatment and/or being turned away from treatment. Certainly, this population and disorder constellation is exceedingly challenging. It is difficult to tease apart the effects of mental illness versus the effects of substances, to determine which disorder is primary, and to safely manage patients' medications when they continue to abuse substances, leaving the potential for dangerous interactions and even death. Indeed, research in the past two decades has found that treatment for these disorders can only be effective if approached from an integrated perspective, addressing both disorders simultaneously (Osher, 2006). This requires special expertise that not all clinicians have. Likewise, it can be taxing to work with individuals with such high rates of relapse and crisis behaviors (e.g., suicide, self-injury, overdose).

Medical Issues

A final challenge for people with mental illness—which does not fall neatly into any single category of mental illness stigma, but rather is a result of combined structural stigma, public stigma, and self-stigma—revolves around health and medical issues. According to a review of the topic, compiled by the National Association of State Mental Health Program Directors (NASMHPD) (Parks et al., 2006), persons with serious mental illness are currently dying 25 years earlier than the general population (see also Colton & Manderscheid, 2006).[34] While most who hear this statistic postulate that this is due to heightened rates of suicide, injury and suicide only account for 30 percent to 40 percent of premature deaths (Parks et al., 2006). Instead, the research suggests that the remainder, 60 percent, of the excess mortality among people with serious mental illness is due to medical conditions caused, or at least exacerbated, by their mental illness (Parks et al., 2006). What's more, this rate of death has accelerated over time (Parks et al., 2006).

The majority of the NASMHPD report focused on the reasons why people with mental illness are dying so much earlier than those without it. Of course, there is no single reason (Parks et al., 2006). First, there is the impact of particular symptoms of mental illness interfering with accessing and/or remaining compliant with care. For example, paranoid delusions can cause an individual to distrust the health care system, both initially and over the course of treatment. Second, medical health issues can be hidden behind psychiatric symptoms (e.g., hypothyroidism presenting as depression). Likewise, strong psychotropic medications can contribute to but mask symptoms of medical illness (e.g., an antidepressant treating the seemingly depressed

---

34. Actually, when factoring out the outlier (Virginia) from the seven states considered in Colton and Manderscheid's (2006) analysis of premature mortality, people with serious mental illness die closer to 28 years earlier than those without mental illness.

symptoms reflecting an underlying brain tumor), and being on multiple medications at once can in the long run be damaging to an individual's body. Additionally, as discussed above, medications such as antipsychotics can cause a dangerous and potentially fatal metabolic syndrome which can lead to, among other conditions, obesity and ultimately cardiovascular disease. Furthermore, there is the inherent vulnerability to medical complications involved in higher rates of poverty and lack of health care, as well as unemployment, homelessness, trauma, victimization, and involvement with the criminal justice system.

Perhaps most encouragingly — from the perspective that something can be done to reverse, or at least stop, this trend of heightened mortality among the mentally ill — people with mental illnesses primarily have treatable medical conditions with modifiable risk factors (Parks et al., 2006).[35] These conditions include obesity, cardiovascular disease, respiratory diseases caused by smoking, substance abuse, and infectious diseases, to name a few (Janssen, McGinty, Azrin, Juliano-Bult, & Daumit, 2015). Each of these will be discussed briefly below.

Obesity

Research suggests obesity is more common in those with a mental illness than those without (Jonikas, Cook, Razzano, Steigman, Hamilton, Swarbrick, & Santos, 2016). Obesity among individuals with mental illness occurs for a variety of reasons, including poor nutrition, lack of exercise, and alcohol consumption (Parks et al., 2006). However, obesity is largely caused by the very thing intended to help people with mental illness — psychotropic medications (Jonikas et al., 2016). In particular, the newer antipsychotic medications have been found to have notable effects on metabolism. This change in a person's body chemistry alone can cause an individual to gain 25 pounds, 50 pounds, or even more; but it also further depletes an individual's energy, contributing to an inability to engage in activities of daily living, much less to exercise, which in turn leads to further weight gain. Residence in group homes and homeless shelters, which is common among people with mental illness, renders such persons less able to regulate (i.e., improve) their own nutritional and/or exercise practices (Parks et al., 2006).

As has been well-established, obesity can have significant effects on an individual's health, including heightened rates of cardiovascular disease, diabetes, and the like. In fact, cardiovascular disease is associated with the largest number of deaths in the mentally ill population, at a rate two to three times greater than in the general population (Parks et al., 2006). The weight gain also has effects on self-esteem (i.e., self-stigma) and label avoidance, particularly given society's stigma regarding obesity.

---

35. Jail and prison inmates, too, have higher rates of medical health conditions than the general population (Wilper et al., 2009). For example, inmates have a rate of diabetes ranging from 8% to 11%, versus 6.5% in the general U.S. population. Likewise, rates of hypertension range from 27% to 31%, compared to 26% of the U.S. population; 2% to 6% of inmates have had a prior heart attack, compared to 3% of the general population. Rates of cirrhosis hover around 2%, and hepatitis rates range from 5% to 6% among inmate populations. (No comparable rates of cirrhosis and hepatitis are available for the U.S. population.)

Smoking

A disproportionate number of people with mental illness smoke cigarettes: 41 percent of persons with mental illness smoke (National Institute of Drug Abuse [NIDA], 2010) versus only 23 percent of the general population (Parks et al., 2006). Among clinical samples of patients with schizophrenia, this rate has ranged as high as 90 percent (NIDA, 2010). Research suggests that this heightened rate of nicotine abuse may be explained by effects the drug has on an individual's symptoms of mental illness, which reinforce its use (NIDA, 2010). In particular, the stimulating effect of nicotine may compensate for some of the cognitive impairments involved in the disorder, and it may ameliorate psychotic symptoms and/or the negative side effects of antipsychotic medications. Furthermore, research has identified certain circuits of the brain that not only predispose individuals to schizophrenia, but also increase the experience of positive effects of drugs like nicotine and/or reduce their ability to quit smoking (NIDA, 2010). This effect is evident by the fact that certain antipsychotic medications can be used for treating schizophrenia and/or reducing a person's desire to smoke. Cigarette use, however, obviously increases the risk of dangerous respiratory diseases which contribute to premature death (Parks et al., 2006).

Infectious Diseases

People with serious mental illness are also at increased risk of infectious diseases (Parks et al., 2006). For example, placement in group care facilities and homeless shelters place people with mental illness at heightened exposure to tuberculosis and other infectious diseases; this list certainly includes COVID-19. Additionally, as a result of intravenous drug use and unsafe sexual behavior, individuals with mental illness have a higher prevalence of hepatitis and HIV (Rosenberg et al., 2004; Hughes, Bassi, Gilbody, Bland, & Martin, 2016). These are but a few examples of the risk for infectious diseases among persons with mental illness.

Inadequate Medical Care

Although inadequate access to medical care has been discussed previously, it was in the context of structural, systemic factors. However, people with mental illness may fail to seek treatment and thus receive inadequate care due to symptoms of fearfulness and/or paranoia about medical providers, general lack of motivation, and social withdrawal (Parks et al., 2006). Furthermore, and most relevant in the context of self-stigma and label avoidance, many people with mental illness avoid medical care due to the stigma involved (Parks et al., 2006).

Label Avoidance and Its Challenges

The final level of mental illness stigma, according to Corrigan's model, is label avoidance (Corrigan, Markowitz, et al., 2004; Corrigan & Watson, 2002). Label avoidance is a variant of self-stigma in which individuals with mental illness explicitly choose not to engage socially in order to avoid detection, labeling, and/or the prejudice and discrimination involved in being part of the group. Of Dickerson et al.'s (2002) sample of outpatients with schizophrenia, described above, 83 percent acknowledged at least occasionally avoiding telling others that they have received psychiatric treatment. In fact, many would rather tell an employer that they had been incarcerated for a petty crime than to admit they had been psychiatrically hospitalized (U.S. DHHS, 2003). Label avoidance is one of the primary reasons why people underutilize (or completely forego) mental health services (Link & Phelan, 2006; Nieweglowski & Corrigan, 2017). Indeed, of the known population with mental illness in the U.S., almost half refuse to seek treatment (U.S. DHHS, 2003), largely for this reason. As is discussed throughout this book, untreated mental illness is a significant risk factor for propelling people into the criminal justice system.

Failure to Seek Treatment

Another negative repercussion of the stigma surrounding mental illness is that it prevents many from seeking mental health treatment when they need it (U.S. DHHS, 1999). As described by Corrigan and Watson (2002), this is referred to as label avoidance. As has been discussed previously, as a result of mental illness stigma and its accompanying misconceptions about the people who have mental illness, the majority of the public seeks to avoid such persons (Link et al., 1999). In particular, people who hold these attitudes, who blame others for their mental illness, for example, are least likely to seek mental health care themselves when the need arises (Cooper, Corrigan, & Watson, 2003; Leaf, Bruce, Tischler, & Holzer, 1987). Those who do seek treatment often do so years after the illness began, often resulting in progression into comorbid disorders and other complicating factors (Wang, Berglund, Olfson, & Kessler, 2004).

Unfortunately, a substantial proportion of people who begin treatment terminate prematurely (i.e., prior to the treatment taking effect), or they ostensibly continue treatment (e.g., continue to visit their treatment professional) but stop taking the medication, for example. This is known as "treatment non-compliance." People who endorse mental illness stereotypes, in particular, are likely to become non-compliant with their treatment (Sirey et al., 2001).

People refuse to seek treatment and/or become non-compliant with their treatment (especially medications) for a number of reasons. These reasons include, among others, the symptom of anosognosia and negative side effects of medications. Each of these is discussed below.

Anosognosia

Many individuals with severe and persistent mental illness lack insight into their symptoms (Amador, 2006). Although historically believed to be mere denial (a psychological defense to avoid the reality that one has a chronic mental illness), increasing evidence suggests that this accounts for only a small portion of lack of insight (Kasapis, Amador, Yale, Strauss, & Gorman, 1995). Recent research suggests that, instead, this is a condition reflecting a neuropsychological deficit related to brain damage to specific parts of the brain (Flashman, 2001; Amador & David, 2004). It is believed that it is caused by the deterioration of the brain related to unstable brain chemistry, which results in symptoms of mental illness. This condition, labeled "anosognosia," parallels the symptom sometimes found in stroke victims, who may wrongly sense that they are moving their extremities when in actuality they are not. Yet with mental illness, anosognosia manifests as a *severe* lack of awareness of their illness and symptoms, the belief persisting despite evidence of their symptoms, and compulsively generating explanations to refute the evidence and defend their belief (Amador & Paul-Odouard, 2000). Although everyone around the person with mental illness is blatantly aware of the individual's erratic behavior, the individual with mental illness does not recognize a problem with his/her behavior and/or that it is related to an illness rather than to choice. As such, anosognosia is a *symptom* of mental illness. Indeed, what a cruel disease. Mental illness affects the very part of our bodies that enables us to recognize we have an illness — our brains.

Research suggests that anosognosia affects a significant proportion of people with serious mental illness. Specifically, studies suggest that anywhere from 40 percent (Torrey & Zdanowicz, 2001) to nearly 90 percent (Wilson, Ban, & Guy, 1986) of all individuals with serious mental illness experience this symptom. Anosognosia is most likely found among individuals with psychosis (e.g., hallucinations, delusions) (Amador et al., 1994; Fennig, Everett, Bromet, & Jandorf, 1996). With regard to specific diagnosis, this includes approximately 50 percent of people with schizophrenia[36] and 40 percent of people with bipolar disorder are also believed to have anosognosia (NAMI, 2005; TAC, 2016).

Anosognosia is problematic because it is associated with failure to seek treatment, non-compliance with treatment, a greater number of involuntary commitments, and poorer course of illness (Amador & Gorman, 1998; Amador, Strauss, Yale, & Gorman, 1991; Heinrichs, Cohen, & Carpenter, 1985; McEvoy et al., 1989; McGlashan & Carpenter, 1981). Indeed, approximately half of all people with severe mental illnesses have not received treatment in the past year; it is estimated that for 55 percent of them it is because of anosognosia (Kessler et al., 2001). Similarly, anosognosia is the single largest reason why people with schizophrenia and bipolar disorder are non-compliant with medication (TAC, 2005). Nevertheless, if such individuals can somehow be persuaded to take antipsychotic medication, one-third of individuals with schizophrenia and even more of those with bipolar disorder improve in their insight (Jorgensen, 1995).

Negative Side Effects of Medications

Some individuals refuse or discontinue taking their medication(s) for mental illness due to the adverse side effects associated with the medications. These side effects vary from person to person but can include dry mouth, weight gain, tiredness, and depression (NIMH, 2016). The older antipsychotics, such as Thorazine and Haldol,

---

36. Amador et al. (1994) found 60% and the World Health Organization (1973) found as many as 81% of individuals with schizophrenia in their samples suffered anosognosia.

began to be formulated in the 1950s. Some of the more extreme side effects associated with these medications,[37] include the following (New York State Office of Mental Health, 2006):

Akathisia: subjective feelings of distress and discomfort, agitation, restlessness, frequent arm and leg movements, and non-localized pain.

Dystonia: sudden involuntary muscle contractions, bizarre and uncontrolled movements of face, neck, tongue and back, oculogyric crisis. These side effects are often mistaken as seizure activity.

Parkinsonism: slowed movement, expressionless face, shuffling gait, tremors.

Tardive dyskinesia: a movement disorder characterized by jerking muscle movements, body rocking, and tic-like movements of face and tongue. Symptoms range in severity, with some experiencing mild, isolated movements; whereas for others, effects can progress to the entire body and become irreversible. Side effects tend to increase with age and duration of drug use, but they can appear and persist long after the medication has been discontinued.

Some of these side effects, if not promptly addressed, can become permanent. Nevertheless, at the time, this is all that was available for the treatment of psychosis. Currently, although the older antipsychotics continue to be used, because of their side effects, they have fallen into disfavor. Moreover, as patents have expired for these medications, they have become less expensive.

As a result of these factors, pharmaceutical companies began to develop new, "atypical" antipsychotics. Common examples of the new antipsychotics are Risperdal, Seroquel, Abilify, and Clozaril. Although having fewer of the motor side effects, these medications can have equally inconvenient and, in some cases, dangerous — indeed, life-threatening — effects. As discussed above, these drugs have significant effects on metabolism and, accordingly, on one's energy level, weight, and ultimately health. Likewise, these medications — especially the most aggressive antipsychotic, Clozaril — can lead to agranulocytosis, a severe adverse side effect involving the loss of white blood cells that fight infection (New York State Office of Mental Health, 2006). The life-threatening implications of this side effect require that individuals taking the drug be monitored with blood tests every one to two weeks. As such, such medications tend to be reserved for the most treatment-resistant cases.

Conclusion

People with mental illness face powerful stigma, from the lay public, from system-level institutionalized forces, and even internalized stigma learned from being part of society. This stigma has far-reaching consequences, placing before persons with mental illnesses a wide range of challenges. In particular, structural stigma is

---

37. Most of these affect motor and muscular behavior, as the medications target the part of the brain responsible for motor movement.

woven into the stance of legislators toward the mental health system. Socioeconomics has plagued the mental health care system for the last half-century, leading to fragmented services with little in the way of critical long-term care. In an attempt to cut costs, state governments have turned to managed care and Medicaid reform, with little success. As a result of these factors, as well as self-stigma, label avoidance, anosognosia, and poor experiences with prior treatment (e.g., disrespectful providers, negative side effects of medication), people with mental illness frequently go without treatment. Many prefer to suffer alone rather than to face the public stigma and misperceptions that they might be dangerous, a message promulgated by the media.

Those that can no longer suffer quietly are propelled into emergency rooms and the criminal justice system (Lamb & Weinberger, 1998; Lamb, Weinberger, Marsh, & Gross, 2007; Lee-Griffin, 2001; Sigurdson, 2000). This is not entirely surprising, given the striking similarities in experiences between those with mental illness and those in the criminal justice system (Scheyett, Vaughn, & Taylor, 2009). As has been discussed in this chapter, people with mental illnesses — like offenders — face vast challenges and unmet needs, including restricted civil rights, greater rates of victimization, unemployment, poverty, housing issues, and co-occurring substance abuse and medical issues. As noted by Veysey (2011, p. 2):

> The intersection of poverty, poor health and justice involvement is not accidental. The three factors go hand in hand. Poor people are more likely than their more affluent counterparts to be arrested; they are less likely to have health insurance of any kind, including Medicaid, and to have received regular health care; and they have high rates of mental health and substance use disorders and consequently other medical concerns.

Like indigent offenders, people with mental illness as a group lack the capital — both literally and figuratively — to influence their politicians and to avoid the criminal justice system. Indeed, there is a great deal of cross-over between these two groups, the very basis for this book.

On June 11, 2002, the U.S. Senate Judiciary Committee held hearings to discuss the "criminalization of mental illness." They listened to police and prosecutors, local officials and mental health professionals, and advocates for people with mental illnesses. It is very rare for representatives from groups with such wide-ranging points of view to agree on an issue. But on this day, everyone was in agreement. All those who spoke echoed the sentiments of Chris Koyanagi from the Bazelon Center for Mental Health Law who said:

> Our country is punishing people with mental illnesses for the failure of the mental health system. We used to warehouse people with mental disorders in large state institutions. Today, increasingly, we simply incarcerate them in jail. We must reverse this trend. This means forging new and continuing coordination between criminal justice and mental health agencies. It will also require improved training of law enforcement officials to recognize and respond appropriately to people with mental illnesses, expanded options for

jail diversion and adequate planning and community support for inmates with mental illnesses when they are released. In the long term, we must slow the tide of people with mental illnesses who end up in the criminal justice system. We can do this only if we ensure access to mental health treatment, adequate housing, vocational help and the other forms of social support necessary for someone with a mental illness to lead an independent and dignified life (Jordan, 2002).

In order to ensure adequate access to treatment and to begin to ameliorate some of the challenges people with mental illness face, public and structural stigma must be addressed. These types of stigma, coupled with the economic situation in the country, have important implications for public allocation of funding for mental health services and research. People who endorse myths about individuals with mental illness (e.g., people with mental illness are responsible for their disease, people with mental illness are dangerous) tend to respond to individuals with mental illness with greater avoidance, as well as endorsement of coercive treatment (Corrigan, Markowitz, Watson, Rowan, & Kubiak, 2003). Politicians, too, who subscribe to these stigmas are influenced by their constituents who endorse these attitudes, and these notions are ultimately institutionalized in law and policy. Thus, reducing stigma is key.

As will be discussed in the final chapter, it is believed that true parity in financial coverage of mental health treatment (i.e., covering treatment for mental illness on par with that of physical illness) is a crucial step toward educating the general public on the fact that mental illnesses are no different from physical illnesses. We do not treat someone with diabetes, caused by a chemical imbalance, as if they are to blame for their illness, nor should we blame someone with a mental illness. Parity can go a long way towards tearing down the walls of stigma that have been built up and surround mental illness in America today. This would in turn enable greater access to mental health treatment and would ensure that more individuals, with stigma diminished, would more readily seek treatment.

President Obama's Affordable Care Act (ACA) has been the basis for better mental health care for people in the criminal justice system. In general, the ACA promised to improve the health of all Americans through prevention and early intervention, including jail and prison inmates. In particular, expanding Medicaid coverage to a wider cross-section of the low-income bracket makes more justice-involved individuals eligible for care (NAMI, 2011a). Even more importantly, there is a provision in the Act that allows pre-trial inmates who are eligible for Medicaid to enroll and/or maintain their coverage, at least until they are convicted (National Association of Counties, 2012). Other specific benefits for those at the intersection of the mental health and criminal justice systems include parity for mental health and substance use disorders and increased access to medications (Veysey, 2011). Furthermore, where federal reimbursement of health care for detainees is approved, it allows jails and prisons to contract with local community providers for services, rather than privatizing with distant companies and decreasing quality of services. Such reimbursement encourages community practitioners to treat inmates upon their release, ensuring continuity of care.

The ACA also faciliates communication between systems by using electronic medical records. Indeed, multi-system collaboration is a key to solving the problems facing the mental health and criminal justice systems today. In the chapters that follow, we will explore innovative strategies for bolstering the mental health system and alleviating the criminal justice system from further becoming a dumping ground for persons with mental illnesses.

References

Abram, K. M., & Teplin, L. A. (1991). Co-occurring disorders among mentally ill jail detainees: Implications for public policy. *American Psychologist 46,* 1036–1045.

Abramson, L. (Writer) & Gordemer, B. (Director). (2012, April 25). VA struggles to provide vets with mental health care [Radio news program episode]. In M. Sikka (Executive Producer), *Morning edition.* Washington, D.C.: National Public Radio. Retrieved from http://www.npr.org/2012/04/25/151319599/va-struggles-to-provide-vets-with-mental-health-care.

Adams, R. W. (2006, July 12). Depression takes financial toll in Florida. *The Ledger.* Retrieved from http://www.theledger.com/apps/pbcs.dll/article?Date=20060712&Category=NEWS&ArtNo=607120355&SectionCat=&Template=printart.

Adler, N. E., Boyce, T., Chesney, M. A., Cohen, S., Folkman, S., Kahn, R. L., & Syme, S. L. (1994). Socioeconomic status and health: The challenge of the gradient. *American Psychologist, 49,* 15–24.

Amador, X. F. (2006). *I am not sick. I don't need help! How to help someone with mental illness accept treatment.* Peconic, NY: Vida Press.

Amador, X. F., Andreasen, N. C., Flaum, M., Strauss, D. H., Yale, S. A., Clark, S., & Gorman, J. M. (1994). Awareness of illness in schizophrenia, schizoaffective and mood disorders. *Archives of General Psychiatry, 51*(10), 826–836.

Amador, X. F., & David, A. S. (Eds.). (2004). *Insight and psychosis.* New York: Oxford University Press.

Amador, X. F., & Gorman, J. M. (1998). Psychopathologic domains and insight in schizophrenia. *Psychiatric Clinics of North America, 20,* 27–42.

Amador, X. F., & Paul-Odouard, R. (2000). Defending the Unabomber: Anosognosia in schizophrenia. *Psychiatric Quarterly, 71*(4), 363–371.

Amador, X. F., Strauss, D. H., Yale, S. A., & Gorman, J. M. (1991). Awareness of illness in schizophrenia. *Schizophrenia Bulletin, 17,* 113–132.

Anderson, J. (2007, February 5). Bradenton officer punished for insubordination. *Bay News 9.* Retrieved from http://www.baynews9.com/content/36/2007/2/1/220206.html.

Angermeyer, M. C., Cooper, B., & Link, B. G. (1998). Mental disorder and violence: Results of epidemiological studies in the era of de-institutionalization. *Social Psychiatry and Psychiatric Epidemiology, 33,* S1–S6.

Angermeyer, M. C., & Matschinger, H. (1996). The effect of violent attacks by schiz-ophrenic persons on the attitude of the public towards the mentally ill. *Social Science and Medicine, 43*, 1721–1728.

An interview with Piers Anthony. (2004, June 26). Retrieved from http://www.angel fire.com/film/rings/interviews/piers.html.

Anthony, W. A., Buell, G. J., Sharatt, S., & Althoff, M. E. (1972). Efficacy of psychiatric rehabilitation. *Psychological Bulletin, 78*(6), 447–456.

Appelbaum, P. S., Robbins, P. C., & Monahan, J. (2000). Violence and delusions: Data from the MacArthur Violence Risk Assessment Study. *American Journal of Psychiatry, 157*(4), 566–572.

Baron, R. C., & Salzer, M. S. (2000). Career patterns of persons with serious mental illness: Generating a new vision of lifetime careers for those in recovery. *Psychiatric Rehabilitation Skills, 4*, 136–156.

Batastini, A., Lester, M., & Thompson, R. A. (2018). Mental illness in the eyes of the law: Examining perceptions of stigma among judges and attorneys. *Psychology, Crime & Law, 24*, 673–686.

Baumann, M., & Teasdale, B. (2018). Severe mental illness and firearm access: Is violence really the danger? *International Journal of Law and Psychiatry 56*, 44–49.

Baumgartner, J., Aboulafia, G., & McIntosh, A. (2020). The ACA at 10: How has it impacted mental health care? *The Commonwealth Fund.* Retrieved from: https://www.commonwealthfund.org/blog/2020/aca-10-how-has-it-impacted-mental-health-care.

Becker, H. (1963). *Outsiders: Studies in the sociology of deviance.* New York, NY: Free Press.

Blankstein, A., Gold, S., & Winton, R. (2008, February 1). Precision teamwork in Spears operation. *Los Angeles Times.* Retrieved from articles.latimes/2008/feb/01/local/.

Bloom, J. D., Williams, M. H., Land, C., McFarland, B., & Reichlin, S. (1998). Changes in public psychiatric hospitalization in Oregon over the past two decades. *Psychiatric Services, 49*(3), 366–369.

Bond, G. R., & McDonel, E. C. (1991). Vocational rehabilitation outcomes for persons with psychiatric disabilities: An update. *Journal of Vocational Rehabilitation, 1*(3), 9–20.

Bonovitz, J. C., & Bonovitz, J. S. (1981). Diversion of the mentally ill into the criminal justice system: The police intervention perspective. *American Journal of Psychiatry, 138*(7), 973–976.

Borum, R., Swanson, J., Swartz, M., & Hiday, V. (1997). Substance abuse, violent behavior and police encounters among persons with severe mental disorder. *Journal of Contemporary Criminal Justice, 13*(3), 236–250.

Brekke, J. S., Prindle, C., Bae, S. W., & Long, J. D. (2001). Risks for individuals with schizophrenia who are living in the community. *Psychiatric Services, 52*(10), 1358–1365.

Brink, S. (1998, January 19). I'll say I'm suicidal: The mentally ill struggle through the maze of managed care. *U.S. News Online.* Retrieved from http://www.redand green.org/Medical/Suicidal/19mana.htm.

Bubolz, T., Emerson, C., & Skinner, J. (2012). State spending on dual eligible under age 65 shows variations, evidence of cost shifting from Medicaid to Medicare. *Health Affairs, 31*, 939–947.

Burt, M., & Aron, L. (2000, February 1). *America's homeless II — Populations and services.* Washington, D.C.: Urban Institute. Retrieved from http://www.urban.org/Presentations/AmericasHomelessII/index.htm.

Burton, V. S. (1990). The consequences of official labels: A research note on rights lost by the mentally ill, mentally incompetent, and convicted felons. *Community Mental Health Journal, 26*, 267–276.

Butterfield, F. (1998, July 28). Treatment can be illusion for violent mentally ill. *The New York Times.* Retrieved from the World Wide Web on June 16, 2007: http://query.nytimes.com/gst/fullpage.html?res=950CEFDA1638F93BA15754C0A96 E958260&sec=health&spon=&pagewanted=print.

Butterfield, F. (1999, July 12). Prisons brim with mentally ill, study finds. *New York Times*, p. A10.

Caputo, N. M., & Rouner, D. (2011). Narrative processing of entertainment media and mental illness stigma. *Health Communication, 26(7)*, 595–604.

Caton, C. L. M., Dominguez, B., Schanzer, B., Hasin, D. S., Shrout, P. E., Felix, A., … Hsu, E. (2005). Risk factors for long-term homelessness: Findings from a longitudinal study of first-time homeless single adults. *American Journal of Public Health, 95*(10), 1753–1759.

Center for American Progress. (2008, April 9). *Homeless veterans by the numbers.* Washington, D.C.: Author. Retrieved from http://www.americanprogress.org/issues/military/news/2008/04/09/4249/homeless-veterans-by-the-numbers/.

Centers for Disease Control and Prevention. (2009). *Health United States, 2008. Table 61.* Retrieved from http://www.cdc.gov/nchs/data/hus/hus08.pdf.

Centers for Disease Control and Prevention (2012, August 20). *Mental health.* Retrieved from http://www.cdc.gov/nchs/fastats/mental.htm.

Center for Medicare Advocacy. (2006). *What's the difference between Medicare and Medicaid?* Willimantic, CT: Author. Retrieved from http://www.medicare advocacy.org/Medicaid_Diff.Vs.Medicare.htm.

Choe, J. Y., Teplin, L. A., & Abram, K. M. (2008). Perpetration of violence, violent victimization, and severe mental illness: Balancing public health concerns. *Psychiatric Services, 59*, 153–164.

Claassen, C. A., Kashner, T. M., Gilfillan, S. K., Larkin, G. L., & Rush, A. J. (2005), Psychiatric emergency service use after implementation of managed care in a public mental health system. *Psychiatric Services, 56*(6), 691–698.

Cohn, J. (2015). The long and winding road of mental illness stigma. *Milbank Quarterly*. Retrieved from: https://www.milbank.org/quarterly/articles/the-long-and-winding-road-of-mental-illness-stigma/.

Colarossi, T. (2016). Let's take our national mental-health crisis out of the emergency room. *MarketWatch*. Retrieved from: https://www.marketwatch.com/story/lets-take-our-national-mental-health-crisis-out-of-the-emergency-room-2016-07-19.

Coleman, B. C. (1997, December 10). Study: Most hospitals dump mental patients. *The Ledger*, p. A4.

Colton, C. W., & Manderscheid, R. W. (2006). Congruencies in increased mortality rates, years of potential life lost, and causes of death among mental health clients in eight states. *Preventing Chronic Disease: Public Health Research, Practice, and Policy, 3*(2), 1–14.

Compton, M. T., & Kotwicki, R. J. (2007). *Responding to individuals with mental illnesses*. Boston, MA: Jones & Bartlett.

Constantine, R., Andel, R., Petrila, J., Becker, M., Robst, J., Teague, G., … Howe, A. (2010). Characteristics and experiences of adults with a serious mental illness who were involved in the criminal justice system. *Psychiatric Services, 61*(5), 451–457.

Cook, J. (2006). Employment barriers for persons with psychiatric disabilities: Update of a report for the President's Commission. *Psychiatric Services, 57*, 1391–405.

Cooper, A., Corrigan, P. W., & Watson, A. C. (2003). Mental illness stigma and care seeking. *Journal of Nervous and Mental Disease, 191*, 339–341.

Cordner, G. (2006). *People with mental illness. Problem-oriented guides for police, guide no. 40*. Washington, D.C.: Office of Community Oriented Policing Services, U.S. Department of Justice.

Corrigan, P. W. (2000). Mental health stigma as social attribution: Implications for research methods and attitude change. *Clinical Psychology: Science and Practice, 7*, 48–67.

Corrigan, P. W. (2004). Target-specific stigma change: a strategy for impacting mental illness stigma. *Psychiatric Rehabilitation Journal, 28*(2), 113–121.

Corrigan, P. W. (2007). How clinical diagnosis might exacerbate the stigma of mental illness. *Social Work, 52*, 31–39.

Corrigan, P. W. & Ben-Zeev, D. (2011). The particular role of stigma. In N. L. Cohen & S. Galea (Eds.), *Population Mental Health: Evidence, Policy, and Public Health Practice* (pp. 92–116). New York: Routledge.

Corrigan, P. W., Edwards, A. B., Green, A., Diwan, S. L., & Penn, D. L. (2001). Prejudice, social distance, and familiarity with mental illness. *Schizophrenia Bulletin, 27*(2), 219–225.

Corrigan, P. W., Larson, J. E., & Rusch, N. (2009). Self-stigma and the "why try" effect: impact on life goals and evidence-based practices. *World Psychiatry, 8*(2), 75–81.

Corrigan, P. W., Markowitz, F. E., & Watson, A. C. (2004). Structural levels of mental illness stigma and discrimination. *Schizophrenia Bulletin, 30*, 481–492.

Corrigan, P., Markowitz, F. E., Watson, A., Rowan, D., & Kubiak, M. A. (2003). An attribution model of public discrimination towards persons with mental illness. *Journal of Health and Social Behavior, 44*(2), 162–179.

Corrigan, P. W. & Penn, D. L. (1999). Lessons from social psychology on discrediting psychiatric stigma. *American Psychologist, 54,* 765–776.

Corrigan, P. W., River, L. P., Lundin, R. K., Wasowski, K. U., Campion, J., Mathisen, J., ... & Kubiak, M. A. (2000). Stigmatizing attributions about mental illness. *Journal of Community Psychology, 28*, 91–103.

Corrigan, P. W., & Watson, A. C. (2002). The paradox of self-stigma and mental illness. *Clinical Psychology: Science and Practice, 9*, 35–53.

Corrigan, P. W., Watson, A. C., Gracia, G., Slopen, N., Rasinski, K., & Hall, L. L. (2005). Newspaper stories as measures of structural stigma. *Psychiatric Services, 56*(5), 551–556.

Corrigan, P. W., Watson, A. C., Warpinski, A. C., & Gracia, G. (2004). Implications of educating the public on mental illness, violence, and stigma. *Psychiatric Services, 55*(5), 577–580.

Covarrubias, I. & Han, M. (2011). Impact of social contact and beliefs about serious mental illness (SMI) on two mental health stigma: social distance and restrictions. *Social Work, 56*(4), 317–325.

Crisp, A. H., Gelder, M. G., Rix, S., Meltzer, H. I., & Rowlands, O. J. (2000). Stigmatisation of people with mental illnesses. *British Journal of Psychiatry, 177*, 4–7.

Davis, M. (2011, September 30). Building condemnation leaves tenants homeless. *The News Virginian.* Retrieved from http://www2.newsvirginian.com/news/2011/sep/30/building-condemnation-leaves-tenants-homeless-ar-1347745/.

Dedman, B. (2000, October 15). School shooters: Secret service findings. *Chicago Sun-Times.* Retrieved from http://www.secretservice.gov/ntac/chicago_sun/find15.htm.

Dennis, S. (2012, August 4). Some former residents of the Beverley Hotel struggle to find housing. *News Leaders-Staunton, Virginia.* Retrieved from http://www.newsleader.com/article/20120804/NEWS01/308040031/Some-former-residents-Beverley-Hotel-struggle-find-housing.

Dickerson, F. B., Sommerville, J., Origoni, F., Ringel, N. B., & Parente, F. (2002). Experiences of stigma among outpatients with schizophrenia. *Schizophrenia Bulletin, 28*(1), 143–154.

Dietrich, S., Heider, D., Matschinger, H., & Angermeyer, M. C. (2006). Influence of newspaper reporting on adolescents' attitudes toward people with mental illness. *Social Psychology and Psychiatric Epidemiology, 41*, 318–322.

Ditton, P. M. (1999, July). *Special report: mental health treatment of inmates and probationers* (NCJ 174463). Washington, D.C.: U.S. Department of Justice, Bureau of Justice Statistics. Retrieved from http://bjs.ojp.usdoj.gov/index.cfm?ty=pb detail&id=787.

Dixon, L. (1999). Dual diagnosis of substance abuse in schizophrenia: Prevalence and impact on outcomes. *Schizophrenia Research, 35,* S93–S100.

Dixon, L., Lyles, A., Scott, J., Lehman, A., Postrado, L., Goldman, H. & McGlynn, E. (1999). Services to adults with schizophrenia: From treatment recommendations to dissemination. *Psychiatric Services, 50,* 233–238.

Dobson, R. (1998, July). Are schizophrenics the lepers of our time? *Independent Review, 21,* 11.

Draine, J., Salzer, M., Culhane, D. P., & Hadley, T. R. (2002). Role of social disadvantage in crime, joblessness, and homelessness among persons with a serious mental illness. *Psychiatric Services, 53*(5), 565–573.

Drake, R. E., Becker, D. R., Clark R. E., & Mueser, K. T. (1999). Research on the individual placement and support model of supported employment. *Psychiatric Quarterly, 70,* 289–301.

Earley, P. (2006). *Crazy: A father's search through America's mental health madness.* New York, NY: G.P. Putnam and Sons.

Edney, D. R. (2004, January). *Mass media and mental illness: A literature review.* Ontario, Canada: Canadian Mental Health Association. Retrieved from www.ontario.cmha.ca/content/about_mental_illness/mass_media.asp.

Elbogen, E. B., & Johnson, S. C. (2009). The intricate link between violence and mental disorder: Results from the National Epidemiologic Survey on Alcohol and Related Conditions. *Archives of General Psychiatry, 66*(2), 152–161.

Emery, B. D. (2006, November). *The crisis in acute psychiatric care: Report of a focus group meeting held on June 19–20.* Washington, D.C.: National Association of State Mental Health Program Directors.

Fein, R. A., & Vossekuil, B. (1998). Protective intelligence and threat assessment investigations: A guide for state and local law enforcement officials. Washington, D.C.: U.S. Department of Justice, Office of Justice Programs, National Institute of Justice.

Fein, R. A., & Vossekuil, B. (1999). Assassination in the United States: An operational study of recent assassins, attackers, and near-lethal approachers. *Journal of Forensic Sciences, 44*(2), 321–333.

Fennig, S., Everett, E., Bromet, E. J., & Jandorf, L. (1996). Insight in first-admission psychotic patients. *Schizophrenia Research, 22*(3), 257–263.

Fischer, P. J., & Breakey, W. R. (1991). The epidemiology of alcohol, drug, and mental disorders among homeless persons. *American Psychologist, 46,* 1115–1128.

Fisher, W. H., Barreira, P. J., Geller, J. L., White, A. W., Lincoln, A. K., & Sudders, M. (2001). Long-stay patients in state psychiatric hospitals at the end of the 20th century. *Psychiatric Services, 52*(8), 1051–1056.

Flashman, L. A. (2001). Specific frontal lobe subregions correlated with unawareness of illness in schizophrenia. *Journal of Neuropsychiatry and Clinical Neuroscience, 13*, 255–257.

Folsom, D. P., Hawthorne, W., Lindamer, L., Gilmer, T., Bailey, A., Golsham, S., ... Jeste, D. V. (2005). Prevalence and risk factors for homelessness and utilization of mental health services among 10,340 patients with serious mental illness in a large public mental health system. *American Journal of Psychiatry, 162*, 370–376.

Folsom, D., & Jeste, D. V. (2002). Schizophrenia in homeless persons: a systematic review of the literature. *Acta Psychiatrica Scandinavica, 104*, 1–10.

Frailing, K., & Slate, R. (2016). Changing students' perceptions of people with mental illness. *Applied Psychology in Criminal Justice, 12*: 54–70.

Frances, A., & Ruffalo, M. L. (2018). Mental illness, civil liberty, and common sense. *Psychiatric Times, 35*(7). Retrieved from: https://www.psychiatrictimes.com/view/mental-illness-civil-liberty-and-common-sense.

Friedman, R. A. (2006). Violence and mental illness — How strong is the link? *New England Journal of Medicine, 355*, 2064–2066.

GAINS Center. (2002). *Fact sheet: Maintaining Medicaid benefits for jail detainees with co-occurring mental health and substance use disorders.* Delmar, NY: Author.

Galewitz, P. (2010, November 12). Medicaid managed care programs grow; so do issues. *USA Today.* Retrieved from http://www.usatoday.com/money/industries/health/2010-11-12-medicaid12_CV_N.htm.

Gallagher, B. J., III. (2012). *The sociology of mental illness* (5th ed.). Cornwall-on-Hudson, NY: Sloan.

Gawande, A. (2004). Casualties of war: Military care for the wounded from Iraq and Afghanistan. *New England Journal of Medicine, 351*, 2471–2475.

Glover, R. W., Miller, J. E., & Sadowski, S. R. (2012, March 22). *Proceedings on the state budget crisis and the behavioral health treatment gap: The impact on public substance abuse and mental health systems.* Washington, D.C.: National Association of State Mental Health Program Directors.

Goffman, E. (1968). *Asylums: Essays on the social situation of mental patients and other inmates.* Harmondsworth, England: Penguin.

Goldberg, E. M., & Morrison, S. L. (1963). Schizophrenia and social class. *British Journal of Psychiatry, 109*(463), 785–802.

Goldman, H. H., Adams, N. H., & Taube, C. A. (1983). Deinstitutionalization: The data demythologized. *Psychiatric Services, 34*, 129–134.

Goodman, L. A., Salyers, M. P., Mueser, K. T., Rosenberg, S. D., Swartz, M., Essock, S. M., ... Swanson, J. (2001). Recent victimization in women and men with severe mental illness: Prevalence and correlates. *Journal of Traumatic Stress, 14*, 615–632.

Granello, D., & Pauley, P. S. (2000). Television viewing habits and their relationship to tolerance toward people with mental illness. *Journal of Mental Health Counseling, 22*(2), 162.

Greenberg, W. M., Shah, P. J., & Seide, M. (1993). Recidivism on an acute psychiatric forensic service. *Hospital and Community Psychiatry, 44*(6), 583–585.

Gudrais, E. (2006, July 27). New Medicaid law on generic drugs draws criticism. *The Providence Journal*. Retrieved from http://www.projo.com/news/content/projo_20060727_drugs24.3541833.html.

Harnish, A., Corrigan, P., Byrne, T., Pinals, D. A., Rodrigues, S., & Smelson, D. (2016). Substance use and mental health stigma in veterans with co-occurring disorders. *Journal of Dual Diagnosis, 12*, 238–243.

Heinrichs, D. W., Cohen, B. P., & Carpenter, W. T., Jr. (1985). Early insight and the management of schizophrenic decompensation. *Journal of Nervous and Mental Disease, 173*, 133–138.

Hemmens, C., Miller, M., Burton, V. S., & Milner, S. (2002). The consequences of official labels: An examination of the rights lost by the mentally ill and the mentally incompetent ten years later. *Community Mental Health Journal, 38*, 129–140.

Hiday, V. A., Swartz, M. S., Swanson, J. W., Borum, R., & Wagner, H. R. (1999). Criminal victimization of persons with severe mental illness. *Psychiatric Services, 50*(1), 62–68.

Hocking, B. (2003). Reducing mental illness stigma and discrimination: Everybody's business. *Medical Journal of Australia, 178*(9), 47–48.

Hodgkin, D., & Karpman, H. E. (2010). Economic crises and public spending on mental health care. *International Journal of Mental Health, 39*(2), 91–106.

Hogan, M. F. (1995). Letters: Deinstitutionalization. *Psychiatric Services, 46*(10), 1078–1079.

Holzer, C., Shea, B., Swanson, J., Leaf, P., Myers, J., George, L., … Bednarski, P. (1986). The increased risk for specific psychiatric disorders among persons of low socioeconomic status. *American Journal of Social Psychiatry, 6*, 259–271.

Honberg, R. S. (2007, May 10). *Federal gun reporting requirements and their application to people with mental illness*. Testimony before the Domestic Policy Subcommittee of the House Oversight and Government Reform Committee.

Horsley, S. (2012, September 1). Obama Campaigns for Veterans' Mental Health. *National Public Radio*. Retrieved from http://m.npr.org/news/font/160421139?page#1.

Hughes, E., Bassi, S., Gilbody, S., Bland, M., & Martin, F. (2016). Prevalence of HIV, hepatitis B, and hepatitis C in people with severe mental illness: a systematic review and meta-analysis. *The Lancet Psychiatry, 3*, 40–48.

Hubert, C., & Walsh, D. (2010, July 22). Sacramento County Mental Health cuts blocked by federal judge. *Sacramento Bee*.

James, D. J., & Glaze, L. E. (2006, September). Special report: Mental health problems of prison and jail inmates (NCJ 213600). Washington, D.C.: U.S. Department of Justice, Bureau of Justice Statistics. Retrieved from http://bjs.ojp.usdoj.gov/content/pub/pdf/mhppji.pdf.

Janssen, E. M., McGinty, E. E., Azrin, S. T., Juliano-Bult, D., & Daumit, G. L. (2015). Review of the evidence: prevalence of medical conditions in the United States population with serious mental illness. *General Hospital Psychiatry, 37*, 199–222.

Jonikas, J. A., Cook, J. A., Razzano, L. A., Steigman, P. J., Hamilton, M. M., Swarbrick, M. A., & Santos, A. (2016). Associations between gender and obesity among adults with mental illnesses in a community health screening study. *Community Mental Health Journal, 52*, 406–415.

Jordan, P. (2002). *Jailing people with mental illness*. Retrieved from http://www.wpas-rights.org/Envoy percent20Archives/jailing_people_with_medical_illness.htm.

Jorgensen, P. (1995). Recovery and insight in schizophrenia. *Acta Psychiatrica Scandinavica, 92*, 436–440.

Kane, C. F. (1995). Deinstitutionalization and managed care: Deja vu? *Psychiatric Services, 46*, 883–884.

Kasapis, C., Amador, X. F., Yale, S. A., Strauss, D. H., & Gorman, J. M. (1995). Poor insight in schizophrenia: Neuropsychological and defensive aspects. *Schizophrenia Research, 15*, 123.

Kaye, N. (2005, June). *Medicaid managed care: Looking forward, looking back*. Washington, D.C.: National Academy for State Health Policy, Association of Community Affiliated Plans. Retrieved from http://209.85.165.104/search?q=cache:gRclmiesA58J:www.nashp.org/Files/mmc_guide_final_draft_6-6.pdf+managed+care+and+medicaid&hl=en&ct=clnk&cd=3&gl=us.

Kessler, R. C., Berglund, P. A., Bruce, M. L, Koch, R., Laska, E. M., Leaf, P. J., … Wang, P. S. (2001). The prevalence and correlates of untreated serious mental illness. Health Services Research, 36, 987–1007.

Kessler, R. C., Berglund, P., Demler, O., Jin, R., Merikangas, K. R., & Walters, E. E. (2005). Lifetime prevalence and age-of-onset distributions of *DSM-IV* disorders in the National Comorbidity Survey Replication. *Archives of General Psychiatry, 62*, 593–602.

Kessler, R. C., Foster, C. L., Saunders, W. B., & Stang, P. E. (1995). Social consequences of psychiatric disorders: I. Educational attainment. *American Journal of Psychiatry, 152*(7), 1026–1032.

Kittrie, N. N. (1978). *The right to be different: Deviance and enforced treatment*. Baltimore: John Hopkins University Press.

Klatell, J. M. (Writer), Flaum, A. T. (Director), & Klug, R. (Director). (2007, May 17). Dumped on skid row [Television series episode]. In J. Fager (Executive Producer), *60 Minutes*. New York, NY: Central Broadcasting Service. Retrieved from http://www.cbsnews.com/stories/2007/05/17/60minutes/main2823079.shtml.

Koyanagi, C. (2006). Economic grand rounds: The Deficit Reduction Act: Should we love it or hate it? *Psychiatric Services, 57*(12), 1711–1712.

Kropp, P. R., Cox, D. N., Roesch, R., & Eaves, D. (1989). The perceptions of correctional officers toward mentally disordered offenders. *International Journal of Law and Psychiatry, 12*, 181–189.

Lacey, M., Sack, K., & Sulzberger, A. G. (2011, January 20). States' budget crises cut deeply into financing for mental health programs. *New York Times*. Retrieved from http://www.nytimes.com/2011/01/21/us/21mental.html.

Lamb H. R., & Shaner, R. (1993). When there are almost no state hospitals left. *Hospital and Community Psychiatry, 44*(10), 973–976.

Lamb, H. R., & Weinberger, L. E. (1998). Persons with severe mental illness in jails and prisons: A review. *Psychiatric Services, 49*(4), 483–492.

Lamb, H. R., & Weinberger, L. E. (2005). The shift of psychiatric inpatient care from hospitals to jails and prisons. *Journal of the American Academy of Psychiatry and the Law, 33*(4), 529–534.

Lamb, H. R., Weinberger, L. E., Marsh, J. S., & Gross, B. H. (2007). Treatment prospects for persons with severe mental illness in an urban county jail. *Psychiatric Services, 58*(6), 782–786.

Lee-Griffin, P. A. (2001). The criminalization of individuals suffering from symptoms of mental illness: An exploratory study. *Dissertation Abstracts International: Section B: The Sciences & Engineering, 62*(1-B), 156.

Leaf, P. J., Bruce, M. L., Tischler, G. L., & Holzer, C. E. (1987). The relationship between demographic factors and attitudes towards mental health services. *Journal of Community Psychology, 15*, 275–284.

Lehman, A. F., Myers, C. P., Corty, E., & Thompson, J. W. (1994). Prevalence and patterns of "dual diagnosis" among psychiatric inpatients. *Comprehensive Psychiatry, 35*(2), 106–112.

Levin, A. (2005). When mental illness makes news, facts often missing in action. *Psychiatric News, 40*(12), 18.

Levine, S. (2006, February 6). Stability of mentally ill shaken by Medicare drug plan problems. *Washington Post*, p. A01.

Link, B. G., & Phelan, J. C. (2001). Conceptualizing stigma. *Annual Review of Sociology, 27*, 363–385.

Link, B. G., & Phelan, J. C. (2006). Stigma and its public health implications. *The Lancet, 367*, 528–529.

Link, B. G., Phelan, J. C., Bresnahan, M., Stueve, A., & Pescosolido, B. A. (1999). Public conceptions of mental illness: labels, causes, dangerousness, and social distance. *American Journal of Public Health, 89*(9), 1328–1333.

Link, B. G., Yang, L. H., Phelan, J. C., & Collins, P. Y. (2004). Measuring mental illness stigma. *Schizophrenia Bulletin, 30*, 511–541.

Lo, C., & Cheng, T. (2014). Race, unemployment rate, and chronic mental illness: A 15-year trend analysis. *Social Psychology and Psychiatric Epidemiology, 49*, 1119–1128.

Lombroso, C. (1876). *Criminal man*. Milan, Italy: Torin.

Los Angeles Times Editorial. (1998, August 3). From tragedy, new hope. *Los Angeles Times*. Retrieved from the World Wide Web on June 16, 2007: http://www.desert pacific.mirecc.va.gov/news/lps-reform/LATimes-8-3-98.html.

Lutterman, T. (2010, October 12). *The impact of the state fiscal crisis on state mental health systems: Fall 2010 update*. Washington, D.C.: NASMHPD Research Institute. Retrieved from http://www.nri-inc.org/reports_pubs/2010/ImpactOfStateFiscalCrisisOnMentalHealthSytems_Fall_2010_NRI_Study.pdf.

Ma, K. (2006, December 28). Daytona chief: Bus homeless out of city. *Orlando Sentinel*. Retrieved from http://lists.co.alachua.fl.us/cgi-bin/wa.exe?A2=ind0612e&L=rodney-j-long&P=660.

Maniglio, R. (2009). Severe mental illness and criminal victimization: A systematic review. *Acta Psychiatrica Scandinavica, 119*(3), 180–191.

Mark, T. L., Levit, K. R., Buck, J. A., Coffey, R. M., & Vandivort-Warren, R. (2007). Mental health treatment expenditure trends, 1986–2003. *Psychiatric Services, 58*(8), 1041–1048.

Markowitz, F. E. (2006). Psychiatric hospital capacity, homelessness, and crime and arrest rates. *Criminology, 44*(1), 45–72.

Martinez, L., & Bingham, A. (2011, November 11). U.S. veterans: By the numbers. *ABC News*. Retrieved from http://abcnews.go.com/Politics/us-veterans-numbers/story?id=14928136.

McCampbell, S. W. (2001). Mental health courts: What sheriffs need to know. *Sheriff, 53*(2), 40–43.

McCann, K. (2005, June 15–16). *Testimony before the Medicare Program Emergency Medical treatment and Labor Act (EMTALA) Technical Advisory Group (Tag) meeting*. Washington, D.C.: National Association of Psychiatric Health Systems. Retrieved from http://www.naphs.org/whatsnew/documents/TestimonyEMTALATAG61505REV3.pdf.

McClam, E. (2008, January 20). New generation of homeless vets emerges. *Washington Post*. Retrieved from http://www.washingtonpost.com/wp-dyn/content/article/2008/01/20/AR2008012000568_p.

McCrohan, N. M., Mowbray, C. T., Bybee, D., & Harris, S. N. (1994). Employment histories and expectations of persons with psychiatric disorders. *Rehabilitation Counseling Bulletin, 38*(1), 59–71.

McEvoy, J. P., Freter, S., Everett, G., Geller, J. L., Appelbaum, P., Apperson, L. J., & Roth, L. (1989). Insight and the clinical outcome of schizophrenics. *Journal of Nervous and Mental Disorders, 177*, 48–51.

McGlashan, T. H., & Carpenter, W. T., Jr. (1981). Does attitude toward psychosis relate to outcome? *American Journal of Psychiatry, 138*, 797–801.

McLeod, J. D., & Kessler, R. C. (1990). Socioeconomic status differences in vulnerability to undesirable life events. *Journal of Health and Social Behavior, 31*, 162–172.

Mental Health Association of Pennsylvania. (2007). *Open minds open doors fact sheet: Violence and mental illness: The facts.* Harrisburg, PA: Author. Retrieved from http://www.openmindsopendoors.com/documents/FACTSHEETViolenceMyth_000.doc.

Monahan, J., & Arnold, J. (1996). Violence by people with mental illness: A consensus statement by advocates and researchers. *Psychiatric Rehabilitation Journal, 19*(4), 67–70.

Montague, B. (2017). Mental healthcare: Underappreciated and underfunded. *Institute for Policy Studies.* Retrieved from: https://ips-dc.org/mental_healthcare_under appreciated_and_underfunded/.

Moses, M., & Potter, R. H. (2007, June). Obtaining federal benefits for disabled offenders: Part 2 — Medicaid benefits. *Corrections Today,* 76–78. Retrieved from https://www.ncjrs.gov/pdffiles1/nij/220104.pdf.

Mowbray, C. T., Grazier, K. L., & Holter, M. (2002). Managed behavioral health care in the public sector: Will it become the third shame of the states? *Psychiatric Services, 53*(2), 157–170.

Mueser, K. T., Salyers, M. P., & Mueser, P. R. (2001). A prospective analysis of work in schizophrenia. *Schizophrenia Bulletin, 27*(2), 281–296.

Muntaner, C., Eaton, W. W., Diala, C., Kessler, R. C., & Sorlie, P. D. (1998). Social class, assets, organizational control and the prevalence of common groups of psychiatric disorders. *Social Science and Medicine, 47*, 2043–2053.

National Alliance on Mental Illness. (2005, January). *Medicaid funding of mental illness treatment.* Arlington, VA: Author. Retrieved from http://www.nami.org/Template.cfm?Section=Issue_Spotlights&template=/ContentManagement/ContentDisplay.cfm&ContentID=43405.

National Alliance on Mental Illness. (2006). *Grading the states: A report on America's health care system for serious mental illness.* Arlington, VA: Author.

National Alliance on Mental Illness. (2009). *Grading the states 2009: A report on America's health care system for adults with serious mental illness.* Arlington, VA: Author.

National Alliance on Mental Illness. (2011a, January). The Affordable Care Act: How it helps individuals and families living with mental illness. Alexandria, VA: Author. Retrieved from http://www.nami.org/Content/NavigationMenu/State_Advocacy/About_the_Issue/Affordable_Care_Act_Fact_Sheet_2011.pdf.

National Alliance on Mental Illness. (2011b, March). *State mental health cuts: A national crisis.* Arlington, VA: Author.

National Alliance on Mental Illness. (n.d.-a). *People with mental illness enrich our lives,* Retrieved from http://www.nami.org/Template.cfm?Section=Helpline1& template=/ContentManagement/ContentDisplay.cfm&ContentID=4858.

National Alliance on Mental Illness. (n.d.-b). *Public Policy Forum: 6. Financing of treatment and services: 6.5 Managed care.* Arlington, VA: Author. Retrieved from http://www.nami.org/Template.cfm?Section=NAMI_Policy_Platform& Template=/ContentManagement/ContentDisplay.cfm&ContentID=38250.

National Alliance on Mental Illness. (n.d.-c). *Fight stigma: Become a StigmaBuster.* Arlington, VA: Author. Retrieved from http://www.nami.org/Template.cfm? Section=Fight_Stigma.

National Association of Counties. (2012, March). *County jails and the Affordable Care Act: Enrolling eligible individuals in health coverage.* Washington, D.C.: Author. Retrieved from http://www.naco.org/research/pubs/Documents/Health, percent20Humanpercent20Servicespercent20and percent20Justice/Community percent20Servicespercent20Docs/WebVersion_PWFIssueBrief.pdf.

National Association of State Mental Health Program Directors Research Institute. (2000, August 10). Closing and refinancing state psychiatric hospitals, 2000. *NASMHPD State Profile Highlights, 1,* 1–2. Retrieved from http://www.nri-inc.org/ projects/profiles/SH_RPT.pdf.

National Association of State Mental Health Program Directors Research Institute. (2008, December 5). *SMHA budget shortfalls: FY 2009, 2010, & 2011.* Retrieved from http://www.nri-inc.org/reports_pubs/2009/BudgetShortfalls.pdf.

National Center for Post-Traumatic Stress Disorder and the Walter Reed Army Medical Center. (2004). *Iraq War clinician guide.* Washington, D.C.: Department of Veterans Affairs.

National Center on Addiction and Substance Abuse at Columbia University. (2010, February). *Behind bars II: Substance abuse and America's prison population.* New York, NY: Author. Retrieved from http://www.casacolumbia.org/articlefiles/575-report2010behindbars2.pdf.

National Coalition for Homeless Veterans. (n.d.). *Background & Statistics.* Washington, D.C.: Author. Retrieved from http://nchv.org/index.php/news/media/ background_and_statistics/.

National Coalition for the Homeless. (2009a). *NCH fact sheet: Homeless veterans.* Washington, D.C.: Author. Retrieved from http://www.nationalhomeless.org/ factsheets/veterans.pdf.

National Coalition for the Homeless. (2009b). *NCH fact sheet: Mental illness and homelessness.* Washington, D.C.: Author. Retrieved from http://www.national homeless.org/factsheets/mental_illness.pdf.

National Institute on Drug Abuse. (2010, September). *Research report series: Comorbidity: Addiction and other mental illness* (NIH Publication #10-5771). Washington, D.C.: U.S. Department of Health and Human Services, National Institutes of Health, NIDA.

National Law Center on Homelessness and Poverty. (2004, January 14). *Homelessness in the United States and the human right to housing.* Washington, D.C.: Author. Retrieved from http://www.nlchp.org/content/pubs/HomelessnessintheUSand RightstoHousing.pdf.

Newsome, B., & Bencel, L. (2009, January 9). Mental health troubles dog the chronically homeless. *Colorado Springs Gazette.*

New York State Office of Mental Health. (2006, January 20). *Medication: What types of antipsychotic medications are there?* Albany, NY: Author. Retrieved from http://www.omh.state.ny.us/omhweb/ebp/adult_medication.htm#Healthcenter website.

New York Times Editorial Desk. (2011, December 19). Help for homeless veterans. *New York Times.* Retrieved from http://web.ebscohost.com/ehost/detail?vid= 9&hid=11&sid=e182d35a-955e-4746-8fa3a9e81000c900percent40sessionmgr 10&bdata=JnNpdGU9ZWhvc3QtbGl2ZSZzY29wZT1zaXRl#db=n5h&AN= 69728456.

Nieweglowski, K., & Corrigan, P. W. (2017). Stigma and health. In *Oxford Research Encyclopedia of Psychology*. New York, NY: Oxford University Press.

NIMH. (2016). Mental health medications. *National Institutes of Mental Health.* Retrieved from: https://www.nimh.nih.gov/health/topics/mental-health-medications/index. shtml.

Nishio, A., Horita, R., Sado, T., Mizutani, S., Watanabe, T., Uehara, R., & Yamamoto, M. (2017). Causes of homelessness prevalence: Relationship between homelessness and disability. *Psychiatry and Clinical Neurosciences, 71,* 180–188.

Novoteny, A. (2018). Guarding mental health in the emergency room. *Monitor on Psychology.* Retrieved from: https://www.apa.org/monitor/2018/06/mental-health-emergency.

Orlando Sentinel Editorial Board. (2006, December 30). No solution. *Orlando Sentinel.* Retrieved from http://www.highbeam.com/doc/1G1-156509865.html.

Osher, F. (2006, May). *Integrating mental health and substance abuse services for justice-involved persons with co-occurring disorders.* Delmar, NY: National GAINS Center.

Osher, F. (2016). We need better funding for mental health services. *The New York Times.*

Ostrow, L., Steinwachs, D., Leaf, P., & Naeger, S. (2017). Medicaid reimbursement of mental health peer-run organizations: Results of a national survey. *Administrative Policy and Mental Health, 44,* 501–511.

Owen, R. R., Fischer, E. P., Booth, B. M., & Cuffel, B. J. (1996). Medication noncompliance and substance abuse among patients with schizophrenia. *Psychiatric Services, 47* (8), 853–858.

Owens, P., Mutter, R., & Stocks, C. (2010, July). *Mental health and substance abuse-related emergency department visits among adults,* 2007 (HCUP Statistical Brief #92). Rockville, MD: Agency for Healthcare Research and Quality.

Paquette, K. (2010). *Individuals experiencing homelessness.* Rockville, MD: SAMHSA Homelessness Resource Center. Retrieved from http://homeless.samhsa.gov/Resource/View.aspx?id=48800.

Parcesepe, A. & Cabassa, L. (2013). Public stigma of mental illness in the United States: A systematic literature review. *Administrative Policy in Mental Health and Mental Health Services, 40,* 384–399.

Park, K., MinHwa, L., & Seo, M. (2019). The impact of self-stigma on self-esteem among persons with different mental disorders. *International Journal of Social Psychiatry, 65,* 558–565.

Parks, J., Svendsen, D., Singer, P., & Foti, M.E. (2006). *Morbidity and mortality in people with serious mental illness.* Alexandria, VA: National Association of State Mental Health Program Directors.

Penn, D. L., Chamberlin, C., & Mueser, K. T. (2003). The effects of a documentary film about schizophrenia on psychiatric stigma. *Schizophrenia Bulletin, 29*(2), 383–391.

Penn, D. L. & Martin, J. (1998) The stigma of severe mental illness: Some potential solutions for a recalcitrant problem. *Psychiatric Quarterly, 69,* 235–247.

Penrose, L. (1939). Mental disease and crime: Outline of a comparative study of European statistics. *British Journal of Medical Psychology, 18,* 1–15.

Perlick, D. A., & Rosenheck, R. R. (2002). Stigma and violence: In reply. *Psychiatric Services, 53*(9), 1179.

Pescosolido, B. A., Monahan, J., Link, B. G., Stueve, A., & Kikuzawa, S. (1999). The public's view of the competence, dangerousness, and need for legal coercion of persons with mental health problems. *American Journal of Public Health, 89*(9), 1339–1345.

Phelan, J. C., Link, B. G., Stueve, A., & Pescosolido, B. A. (2000). Public conceptions of mental illness in 1950 and 1996: What is mental illness and is it to be feared? *Journal of Health and Social Behavior, 41,* 188–207.

Pincus, F. L. (1996). Discrimination comes in many forms: Individual, institutional, and structural. *American Behavioral Scientist, 40*(2), 186–194.

Pincus, F. L., & Ehrlich, H. J. (1998). *Race and ethnic conflict: Contending views on prejudice, discrimination, and ethnoviolence* (2nd ed.). Boulder, CO: Westview Press.

Policastro, C., Teasdale, B., & Daigle, L. E. (2016). The recurring victimization of individuals with mental illness: A comparison of trajectories for two racial groups. *Journal of Quantitative Criminology, 32*(4), 675–693.

President's New Freedom Commission on Mental Health. (2003). *Achieving the promise: Transforming mental health care in America. Final report* (DHHS Publication No. SMA-03-3832). Rockville, MD: U.S. Government Printing Office.

Raghunathan, A. (2007, February 2). Homeless fight back with high tech. *St. Petersburg Times.* Retrieved from http://www.sptimes.com/2007/02/02/Southpinellas/ Homeless_fight_back_w.shtml.

Raphael, S. (2000, September). *The deinstitutionalization of the mentally ill and growth in the U.S. prison populations 1971 to 1996.* Retrieved from http://socrates.berkeley. edu/~raphael/raphael2000.pdf.

Regier, D. A., Farmer, M. E., Rae, D. S., Locke, B. Z., Keith, S. J., Judd, L. L., & Goodwin, F. K. (1990). Comorbidity of mental disorders with alcohol and other drug abuse. Results from the Epidemiologic Catchment Area (ECA) Study. *Journal of the American Medical Association, 264*(19), 2511–2518.

Regier, D. A., Narrow, W. E., Rae, D. S., Manderscheid, R. W., Locke, B. Z., & Goodwin, F. K. (1993). The de facto U.S. mental and addictive disorders service system. Epidemiologic Catchment Area prospective 1-year prevalence rates of disorders and services. *Archives of General Psychiatry, 50,* 85–94.

Rich, W. J. (2009). The path of mentally ill offenders. *Fordham Urban Law Journal, 36,* 89–119.

Rissmiller, D. J., & Rissmiller, J. H. (2006). Evolution of the antipsychiatry movement into mental health consumerism. *Psychiatric Services, 57*(6), 863–866.

Rosenberg, S., Brunette, M., Oxman, T., Marsh, B., Dietrich, A., Mueser, K., ... Vidayer, R. (2004). The STIRR model of best practices for blood-borne diseases among clients with serious mental illness. *Psychiatric Services, 55*(6), 660–664.

Roskes, E., Cooksey, C., Feldman, R., Lipford, S., & Tambree, J. (2005). Management of offenders with mental illnesses in outpatient settings. In E. Roskes, C. Cooksey, R. Feldman, S. Lipford, & J. Tambree (Eds.), *Handbook of correctional mental health* (pp. 229–257). Arlington, VA, American Psychiatric Publishing.

Rueve, M. & Welton, R. (2008). Violence and mental illness. *Psychiatry, 5,* 34–48.

Russinova, Z., Wewiorski, N. J., Lyass, A., Rogers, E. S., & Massaro, J. M. (2002). Correlates of vocational recovery for persons with schizophrenia. *International Review of Psychiatry, 14*(4), 303–311.

San Miguel, M. (2012, June 15). *More mental health patients.* Retrieved from http:// www.kfyrtv.com/News_Stories.asp?news=57677.

Scheyett, A., Vaughn, J., & Taylor, M. F. (2009). Screening and access to services for individuals with serious mental illnesses in jails. *Community Mental Health Journal, 45,* 439–446.

Seal, K. H., Bertenthal, D., Miner, C. R., Sen, S., & Marmar, C. (2007). Bringing the war back home: Mental health disorders among 103,788 U.S. veterans returning from Iraq and Afghanistan seen at Department of Veterans Affairs facilities. *Archives of Internal Medicine, 167*(5), 476–482.

Seal, K. H., Metzler, T. J., Gima, K. S., Bertenthal, D., Maguen, S., & Marmar, C. R. (2009). Trends and risk factors for mental health diagnoses among Iraq and Afghanistan veterans using Department of Veterans Affairs health care, 2002–2008. *American Journal of Public Health, 99*(9), 1651–1658.

Sharockman, A. (2007, February 1). St. Pete unveils plan to help the homeless. *The Ledger*. Retrieved from http://www.theledger.com/apps/pbcs.dll/article?AID=/20070201/NEWS/702010447/1004.

Shah, B. Tooley, A., & Corrigan, P. (2018). Stigma in mental illness. In K. Frailing and R. Slate (Eds.), *The criminalization of mental illness: A reader* (pp. 45–62). Durham, NC: Carolina Academic Press.

Shipley, S. L., & Borynski, M. L. (2013). Mental illness and violence: A misunderstood relationship. In J. B. Helfgott (Ed.), *Criminal psychology volume 2: Typologies, mental disorders, and profiles* (pp. 63–96). Santa Barbara, CA: Praeger.

Sigurdson, C. (2000). The mad, the bad and the abandoned: The mentally ill in prisons and jails. *Corrections Today, 62*(7), 70–78.

Sirey, J. A., Bruce, M. L., Alexopoulos, G. S., Perlick, D. A., Friedman, S. J., & Meyers, B. S. (2001). Stigma as a barrier to recovery: Perceived stigma and patient-rated severity of illness as predictors of antidepressant drug adherence. *Psychiatric Services, 52*(12), 1615–1620.

Slate, R. N. (2005, April 12). *Medicaid reform, preferred drug lists, and allowing open access to psychotropic medications.* Testimony before the Florida Senate Committee on Health Care, Tallahassee, FL.

Sodaro, E. R., & Ball, J. (1999, January). *Neglected adolescent mental illness: Managed care at its worst.* Commack, NY: National Coalition of Mental Health Professionals and Consumers. Retrieved http://www.thenationalcoalition.org/neglect.html.

Stanley, J. (2004). Stigma and public education about mental illness: To the editor. *Psychiatric Services, 55*(7), 833–834.

Steadman, H. J., Mulvey, E. P., Monahan, J., Robbins, P. C., Appelbaum, P. S., Grisso, T., ... Silver, E. (1998). Violence by people discharged from acute psychiatric in-patient facilities and by others in the same neighborhoods. *Archives of General Psychiatry, 55*(5), 393–401.

Stolzenburg, S., Freitag, S., Evans-Lacko, S., Muehlan, H., Schmidt, S., & Schomerus, G. (2017). The stigma of mental illness as a barrier to self labeling as having a mental illness. *Journal of Nervous and Mental Disease, 205*(12), 903–909.

Stone, T. H. (1997). Therapeutic implications of incarceration for persons with severe mental disorders: Searching for rational health policy. *American Journal of Criminal Law, 24*, 283–358.

Stout, P. A., Villegas, J., & Jennings, N. A. (2004). Images of mental illness in the media: identifying gaps in the research. *Schizophrenia Bulletin, 30*(3), 543–61.

Stuart, H. L., & Arboleda-Florez, J. E. (2001). A public health perspective on violent offenses among persons with mental illness. *Psychiatric Services, 52*, 654–659.

Substance Abuse and Mental Health Services Administration. (1996, December). *Community support: An overview of evaluations of the Massachusetts Medicaid Managed Behavioral Health Care Program.* Washington, D.C.: U.S. Department of Health and Human Services. Retrieved from http://mentalhealth.samhsa.gov/cmhs/communitysupport/research/publications/pn23ch7.asp.

Substance Abuse and Mental Health Services Administration. (2006). *Developing a stigma reduction initiative* (SAMHSA Pub No. SMA-4176). Rockville, MD: Substance Abuse and Mental Health Services Administration, Center for Mental Health Services.

Substance Abuse and Mental Health Services Administration Office of Applied Studies. (2004, June 23). *Results from the 2002 National Survey on Drug Use and Health: Summary of national findings* (DHHS Publication No. SMA 03-3836, NSDUH series H-22). Rockville, MD: Author.

Sullivan, B. (2011, December 13). *Press release: Obama administration announces decline in homelessness in 2011: More than 3,000 communities report number of homeless individuals, families and veterans* (HUD No. 11-288). Washington, D.C.: U.S. Department of Housing and Urban Development. Retrieved from http://portal.hud.gov/hudportal/HUD?src=/press/press_releases_media_advisories/2011/HUDNo.11-288.

Sullivan, G., Burnam, A., Koegel, P., & Hollenberg, J. (2000). Quality of life of homeless persons with mental illness: results from the Course-of-Homelessness Study. *Psychiatric Services, 51*, 1135–1141.

Swanson, J. W., Estroff, S. E., Swartz, M. S., Borum R., Lachicotte, W., Zimmer, C., & Wagner, H. R. (1997). Violence and severe mental disorder in clinical and community populations: The effects of psychotic symptoms, comorbidity, and lack of treatment. *Psychiatry, 60*, 1–22.

Swanson, J. W., Swartz, M. S., Van Dorn, R. A., Elbogen, E. B., Wagner, H. R., Rosenheck, R. A., ... Lieberman, J. A. (2006). A national study of violent behavior in persons with schizophrenia. *Archives of General Psychiatry, 63*, 490–499.

Swanson, J. W., Swartz, M. S., Van Dorn, R. A., Volavka, J., Monahan, J., Stroup, T. S., ... Lieberman, J. (2008). A comparison of antipsychotic drugs for reducing violence in persons with schizophrenia. *British Journal of Psychiatry, 193*, 37–43.

Swartz, M. S., Swanson, J. W., Hiday, V. A., Borum, R., Wagner, H. R., & Burns, B. J. (1998). Violence and severe mental illness: The effects of substance abuse and nonadherence to medication. *American Journal of Psychiatry, 155*(2), 226–231.

Szmukler, G. (2000). Homicide enquiries: What sense do they make? *Psychiatric Bulletin, 24*, 6–10.

TAC. (2005). Briefing Paper: Anosognosia (impaired awareness of illness): A major problem for individuals with schizophrenia and bipolar disorder. *Treatment Ad-*

vocacy Center. Retrieved from http://www.nami.org/Content/Microsites86/NAMI_Albuquerque/Home82/Current_Activities/NAMIWalks6/Briefing-anosognosia_(05).pdf.

TAC. (2016). Serious mental illness and anosognosia. *Treatment Advocacy Center.* Retrieved from: https://www.treatmentadvocacycenter.org/key-issues/anosognosia/3628-serious-mental-illness-and-anosognosia.

Teasdale, B. (2009). Mental disorder and violent victimization. *Criminal Justice and Behavior, 36*(5), 513–535.

Teplin, L. A., Abram, K., & McClelland, G. M. (1996). Prevalence of psychiatric disorders among incarcerated women, I: pretrial jail detainees. *Archives of General Psychiatry, 53*(6), 505–512.

Teplin, L. A., McClelland, G. M., Abram, K. M., & Weiner, D. A. (2005). Crime victimization in adults with severe mental illness: Comparison with the national crime victimization survey. *Archives of General Psychiatry, 62*, 911–921.

Texas Department of State Health Services. (2012, May 24). *Welcome to Austin State Hospital — Over 150 years of continued excellence.* Retrieved from http://www.dshs.state.tx.us/mhhospitals/austinsh/default.shtm.

Thoits, P. (2016). "I'm not mentally ill:" Identity reflection as a form of stigma resistance. *Journal of Health and Social Behavior, 57*, 135–151.

Torrey, E. F. (1997). *Out of the shadows: Confronting America's mental illness crisis.* New York, NY: John Wiley & Sons.

Torrey, E. F. (2002). Stigma and violence. *Psychiatric Services, 53*(9), 1179.

Torrey, E. F. (2014). *American psychosis: How the federal government destroyed the mental illness treatment system.* New York, NY: Oxford University Press.

Torrey, E. F., Fuller, D. A., Geller, J., Jacobs, C., & Ragosta, K. (2012, July 19). *No room at the inn: Trends and consequences of closing public psychiatric hospitals.* Arlington, VA: Treatment Advocacy Center.

Torrey, E. F., & Zdanowicz, M. (2001). Outpatient commitment: What, why, and for whom. *Psychiatric Services, 52*(3), 337–341.

Trivedi, R. B., Post, E. P., Sun, H., Pomerantz, A., Saxon, A. J., Piette, J. D., … & Nelson, K. (2015). Prevalence, comorbidity, and prognosis of mental health among US veterans. *American Journal of Public Health, 105*, 2564–2569.

Trudel, J. F., & Lesage, A. (2006). Care of patients with the most severe and persistent mental illness in an area without a psychiatric hospital. *Psychiatric Services, 57*(12), 1765–1770.

Trupin, L., Sebesta, D. S., Yelin, E., & LaPlante, M. E. (1997). Trends in labor force participation among persons with disabilities, 1983–1994. *Disability Statistics Report, 10.* Washington, D.C.: U.S. Department of Education, National Institute on Disability and Rehabilitation Research.

Tsai, J., Hoff, R. A., & Harpaz-Rotem, I. (2017). One-year incidence and predictors of homelessness among 300,000 US Veterans seen in specialty mental health care. *Psychological Services, 14,* 203.

Uehara, E. S. (1994). Race, gender, and housing inequality: An exploration of correlates of low-quality housing among clients diagnosed with severe and persistent mental illness. *Journal of Health and Social Behavior, 35*(4), 309–321.

United States Secret Service. (2006). *National Threat Assessment Center.* Washington, D.C.: Author. Retrieved from http://www.secretservice.gov/ntac.shtml.

U.S. Army Surgeon General. (2005). *Mental Health Advisory Team (MHAT-II): Report.* Washington, D.C.: Department of the Army, Office of the Surgeon General.

U.S. Department of Health and Human Services. (1999). *Mental health: A report of the Surgeon General* (DHHS Publication No. 0167-024-01653-5). Rockville, MD: U.S. Department of Health and Human Services, Substance Abuse and Mental Health Services Administration, Center for Mental Health Services, National Institutes of Health, National Institute of Mental Health.

U.S. Department of Health and Human Services. (2003, February). *Fact sheet: Antistigma: Do you know the facts?* Washington, D.C.: U.S. Department of Health and Human Services, Substance Abuse and Mental Health Services Administration, Center for Mental Health Services, National Mental Health Information Center. Retrieved from http://www.nkhs.org/documents/Anti-Stigma_DoYou KnowtheFacts.pdf.

U.S. Department of Health and Human Services. (2007). *National Mental Health Anti-Stigma Campaign: What a difference a friend makes: Social acceptance is key to mental health recovery.* Rockville, MD: U.S. Department of Health and Human Services, Substance Abuse and Mental Health Services Administration. Retrieved from http://www.whatadifference.samhsa.gov/docs/SAMHSA_CDC_ Report.pdf.

U.S. Department of Housing and Urban Development. (2010). *The 2010 Annual Homeless Assessment Report to Congress.* Washington, D.C.: Author.

U.S. Department of Housing and Urban Development. (2011, December). *The 2011 point-in-time estimates of homelessness: Supplement to the Annual Homeless Assessment Report.* Washington, D.C.: Author. Retrieved from http://www.hudhre. info/documents/PIT-HIC_SupplementalAHARReport.pdf.

U.S. Department of Veterans Affairs. (n.d.) *Homelessness.* Washington, D.C.: Author. Retrieved from http://www.mentalhealth.va.gov/homelessness.asp.

Utah Division of Substance Abuse and Mental Health. (2004). *Utah State Hospital: FY2004 fact sheet.* Retrieved from http://www.dsamh.utah.gov/docs/04_ush_fact. pdf.

Van Dorn, R. A., Swanson, J. W., Elbogen, E. B., & Swartz, M. S. (2005). A comparison of stigmatizing attitudes toward persons with schizophrenia in four stakeholder groups: Perceived likelihood of violence and desire for social distance. *Psychiatry: Interpersonal and Biological Processes, 68*(2), 152–163.

Van Dorn, R., Volavka, J., & Johnson, N. (2012). Mental disorder and violence: Is there a relationship beyond substance use? *Social Psychiatry and Psychiatric Epidemiology, 47*(3), 487–503.

Veterans, Inc. (2010). *Statistics*. Worcester, MA: Author. Retrieved from http://www.veteransinc.org/about-us/statistics/.

Veysey, B. M. (2011, January). Issue paper: The intersection of public health and public safety in U.S. jails: Implications and opportunities of federal health care reform. *Exploring Health Reform and Criminal Justice: Rethinking the Connection between Jails and Community Health*. Oakland, CA: Community Oriented Correctional Health Services. Retrieved from http://www.cochs.org/files/Rutgers percent20Final.pdf.

Vick, B., Jones, K., & Mitra, S. (2012). Poverty and severe psychiatric disorder in the U.S.: Evidence from the Medical Expenditure Panel Survey. *Journal of Mental Health Policy and Economics, 15*(2), 83–96.

Vickers, A. D. (2006). *Brain bondage: The delay in mental illness recovery*. Jacksonville, Florida: The Hartley Press, Inc.

Vine, P. (2001, May/June). *Mindless and deadly: Media hype on mental illness and violence*. Retrieved from http://www.narpa.org/media.hype.htm.

Vold, G. B., Bernard, T. J., & Snipes, J. B. (1998). *Theoretical criminology* (4th ed.). New York, NY: Oxford University Press.

Vu, P. (2009, February 6). *Medicaid programs feel weight of recession*. Washington, D.C.: Pew Center on the States. Available at www.stateline.org/live/details/story?contentId=374699, accessed April 10, 2010.

Wahl, O. F. (1995). *Media madness: Public images of mental illness*. New Brunswick, NJ: Rutgers University Press.

Wahl, O. F. (2003). News media portrayal of mental illness: implications for public policy. *American Behavioral Scientist, 46*(12), 1594–1600.

Wahl, O. F., Wood, A., Zaveri, P., Drapalski, A. & Mann, B. (2003). Mental illness depiction in children's films. *Journal of Community Psychology, 31*(6), 553–560.

Walker, S. (2006). *Sense and nonsense about crime and drugs: A policy guide* (6th ed.). Belmont, CA: Wadsworth.

Wamsley, L. (2020). After COVID-19 diagnosis, nearly 1 In 5 are diagnosed with mental disorder. *National Public Radio*. Retrieved from: https://www.npr.org/sections/coronavirus-live-updates/2020/11/11/933964994/after-covid-diagnosis-nearly-1-in-5-are-diagnosed-with-mental-disorder.

Wang, P., Berglund, P., Olfson, M., & Kessler, R. (2004). Delays in treatment contact after first onset of a mental disorder. *Health Services Research, 39*, 393–416.

Watson, A., Hanrahan, P., Luchins, D., & Lurigio, A. (2001). Mental health courts and the complex issue of mentally ill offenders. *Psychiatric Services, 52*(4), 477–481.

Weiner, B., Perry, R. P., & Magnusson, J. (1988). An attributional analysis of reactions to stigmas. *Journal of Personality and Social Psychology, 55*, 738–748.

Welch, M. (2004). *Corrections: A critical approach* (2nd ed.). New York, NY: Mc-Graw-Hill.

Welch, W. M. (2008). Trauma of Iraq war haunting thousands returning home. *USA Today.* Retrieved from http://usatoday.printthis.clickability.com/pt/cpt?action=cpt&title=USATODAY.com+-+Trauma+of+Iraq+war+haunting+thousands+returning+home&expire=&urlID=13378250&fb=Y&url=httppercent3Apercent2Fpercent2Fwww.usatoday.compercent2Fnewspercent2Fworld percent2Firaq percent2F2005-02-28-cover-iraq-injuries_x.htm&partnerID=1660.

White, M. C., Chafetz, L., Collins-Bride, G., & Nickens, J. (2006). History of arrest, incarceration and victimization in community-based severely mentally ill. *Journal of Community Health, 31*, 123–135.

Williams, F. P. & McShane, M. D. (2004). *Criminological theory* (4th ed.). Upper Saddle River, NJ: Prentice Hall.

Wilper, A. P., Woolhandler, S., Boyd, J. W., Lasser, K. E., McCormick, D., Bor, D. H., & Himmelstein, D. U. (2009). The health and health care of US prisoners: Results of a nationwide survey. *American Journal of Public Health, 99*, 666–672.

Wilson, W. H., Ban, T. A., & Guy, W. (1986). Flexible system criteria in chronic schizophrenia. *Comprehensive Psychiatry, 27*, 259–265.

Wood, S. R. (2018). Co-occurring serious mental illnesses and substance use disorders as predictors of assaultive infraction charges among adult male jail inmates. *The Journal of Forensic Psychiatry & Psychology, 29*, 189–210.

World Health Organization. (2013). *Investing in mental health: Evidence for action.* Retrieved from: https://www.who.int/mental_health/publications/financing/investing_in_mh_2013/en/.

Wong, Y. I. (2002). Tracking change in psychological distress among homeless adults: An examination of the effect of housing status. *Health & Social Work, 27*(4), 262–273.

World Health Organization. (1973). *Report of the International Pilot Study of Schizophrenia.* Geneva, Switzerland: World Health Organization Press.

World Health Organization. (2001). *The world health report 2001-Mental health: New understanding, new hope.* Geneva, CH: WHO. Retrieved from www.who.int/whr/2001/en.

Xiang, X., Owen, R., Langi, F. L. F. G., Yamaki, K., Mitchell, D., Heller, T., Karmarkar, A., French, D., & Jordan, N. (2019). Impacts of an integrated Medicaid managed care program for adults with behavioral health conditions: The experience of Illinois. *Administrative Policy and Mental Health, 46*, 44–53.

Young, K., & Garfield, R. (2018). Snapshot of recent state initiatives in Medicaid prescription drug cost control. *Kaiser Family Foundation*. Retrieved from: https://www.kff.org/medicaid/issue-brief/snapshots-of-recent-state-initiatives-in-medicaid-prescription-drug-cost-control/.

Chapter 4

Civil Commitment

"In a free society you have to take some risks. If you lock everybody up, or even if you lock up everybody you think might commit a crime, you'll be pretty safe, but you won't be free."

— Former United States Senator Sam Ervin[1]

"The opposition to involuntary committal and treatment betrays a profound misunderstanding of the principle of civil liberties. Medication can free victims from their illness — free them from the Bastille of their psychoses — and restore their dignity, their free will, and the meaningful exercise of their liberties."

— Herschel Hardin[2]

"Of all tyrannies a tyranny sincerely exercised for the good of its victims may be the most oppressive."

— C. S. Lewis[3]

A young man with treatment for depression and emotional detachment since early childhood becomes a college student. A university professor expresses concerns about the violent content of his writing, and he makes his classmates uncomfortable with his angry detachment, to the point that he is removed from class to receive one-on-one tutoring. Campus police advise him to stay away from several female students who have felt harassed by his "annoying" instant messages, after which he indicates that he "might as well kill [him]self." Other professors report their concerns, too, about the content of his writing — one depicting the protagonist killing his classmates and then himself — and with his reactions to his grades. One professor goes so far as to offer to attend counseling with him. The student receives treatment but stops going (Virginia Tech Review Panel, 2007).

---

1. As cited in Cook (2002, p. 2).
2. Hardin (1993, p. A15).
3. As cited in Seitler (2008, p. 31).

Another young man, despite academic and musical talent, begins to abuse alcohol and smoke marijuana and drops out of high school. Slowly, his "passionate opinions about government" and his "fascination with dreams" — appreciated by friends — become increasingly nonsensical and obsessive. He, too, comes to the attention of campus police for repeated disruptions and angry reactions to professors. He withdraws from family and friends and instead rants on the internet — eventually posting an "unsettling video" about his "scam" education, the "need for a new money system, and the government's mind-manipulation of the masses through language." He is so disturbing of a presence, tellers at a local bank "feel for the alarm button when he walk[s] in" (Barry, 2011).

A third young man, with schizophrenia, in his late twenties, has been hospitalized 13 times. He frequently reports to the emergency room, complaining of hearing relentless voices and describing bizarre — but seemingly innocuous, non-dangerous — delusions that he had lost his neck, his brain had been removed, and he had been inhabited by people (Winerip, 1999).

What is the commonality between these cases? Readers who pay attention to the media know that the first two cases describe Seung-Hui Cho and Jared Loughner, two of the most infamous mass murderers in recent history. You might have thought that this was the commonality or that the similarity was coming to the attention of university authorities, merely being a male in one's twenties, and/or slowly unraveling, failing at school and withdrawing from family and friends. However, the third case violates this seeming pattern.

There are factors that connect all three of the cases described above. First, each of the individuals described has a mental illness. What's more, each of them had an untreated mental illness. Third, each of them committed a horrific act of murder. Cho killed 32 people and wounded 17 others, before killing himself, in two separate but related incidents on the campus of Virginia Polytechnic Institute and State University (commonly known as "Virginia Tech") on April 16, 2007. He had previously been diagnosed with depression, and post-mortem, it has been suspected that he had begun to decline into delusional psychosis. Loughner killed 6 and wounded 13 others at a public meeting with Congresswoman Gabrielle Giffords on January 8, 2011, in Tucson, Arizona. He has since been diagnosed with schizophrenia, yet he has pled guilty to all counts (Spagat & Christie, 2012).[4] The last case describes Andrew Goldstein, a man with chronic schizophrenia, who pushed an unsuspecting stranger,

---

4. It is suspected that James Holmes, who allegedly killed 12 people and wounded 58 others in a movie theater in Aurora, Colorado, on July 20, 2012, was also mentally ill. Previously a talented doctoral student in neuroscience, James Holmes' academic performance began to decline in the spring of 2012 (Leonnig & Achenbach, 2012). He started seeing a university psychiatrist, and by June, she became concerned enough about his potential dangerousness that she called campus police and alerted the university's threat assessment team (Bazelon, 2012). In the meantime, Holmes failed his oral exams, and he dropped out three days later, before the team had a chance to convene (Harris, 2012). What information has been made available since suggests he received no further mental health treatment prior to July 20, 2012. As with Cho and Loughner, Holmes' case certainly holds implications for college and university policies regarding dangerousness and gun control for individuals with mental illness.

Kendra Webdale, from a subway platform into an oncoming train in New York City on January 3, 1999.

Sadly, it isn't until horrific tragedies are committed by people like Cho, Loughner, and Goldstein that the issue of mental illness captures the public's attention and, hopefully, brings about positive change. Sadly, it is also cases like these that fuel the stigma and fear of people with mental illnesses.

Knowing what we know now about the acts they would commit, their behavior leading up to the offenses is haunting. Yet, despite concerns by their treating mental health professionals, not even these clinicians could have predicted the havoc their clients would wreak. We only have this luxury in hindsight. This leads us to the final commonality between Cho, Loughner, and Goldstein — the similarity least likely to be recognized by the lay public: None of them, despite their behavior leading up to the acts, would have been civilly committed — forced by the state — into treatment in the mental health system.

What Is Civil Commitment?

"Involuntary" or "civil commitment" are the terms used when the state intervenes civilly and treats, without one's consent, individuals with mental illness who require care and/or incapacitation because of self-harming or dangerous tendencies (Melton, Petrila, Poythress, & Slobogin, 2007). Historically, civil commitment has occurred in inpatient settings (e.g., hospitals). In recent years, particularly in the past three decades, however, involuntary treatment has been increasingly ordered in the community (i.e., outpatient commitment).

Involuntary, or civil, commitment entails split goals of treatment for those who need it, on the one hand, and public safety, on the other. As such, there is an inherent tension, which forms the basis for the intense debate surrounding civil commitment. This chapter will examine this controversy at length. Indeed, some consider civil commitment statutes "the most important forensic mental health laws ... [because t]hey affect the largest number of people of any of the law — mental health interactions ... [and they] provide a buffer between the voluntary mental health and criminal justice systems" (Bloom, 2004, p. 430). Others call for the wholesale abolition of civil commitment laws on grounds that they are coercive and unconstitutional.

Similarities and Differences between Civil and Criminal Commitment

The courts must consider the differences between criminal justice commitment (e.g., incarceration, probation/parole), which implicates public safety, first and foremost, and the dual-purposed civil commitment. Essentially, both civil and criminal commitment allow institutionalization of an individual because of behavior that society deems unacceptable (Melton et al., 2007). The key, most fundamental difference between the two types of institutionalization is that civil commitment is based in civil law, whereas criminal commitment (i.e., incarceration) is rooted in criminal law. Related to the different philosophies of these two systems of law, the enforcement of criminal law is based in the state's police power, propelled by the need of society to protect its citizens from harm inflicted by others (Hiday & Wales, 2013). As such, the primary function of criminal incarceration is punishment for the purposes of retribution (i.e., receiving "just desserts" for acts one has committed against others/ society) and deterrence (i.e., showing the state's force so as to prevent the person and others from committing similar future acts); due to its punitive orientation, criminal commitment occurs in a jail or prison (Melton et al., 2007).

Civil commitment, on the other hand, is grounded in the state's power of *parens patriae* — i.e., Latin for "parent of the country" (Testa & West, 2010, p. 31). With this authority, the state has the paternalistic duty to assist those who are unable to care for themselves, whether that is due to age, immaturity, or, in the case of mental disorder, illness and irrationality (Hiday & Wales, 2013). The focus of *parens patriae* is on the needs of the individual and less about (although not entirely unrelated to) the needs of society; with the addition of the dangerousness criterion of civil commitment, however, the jurisprudential basis of civil commitment has blurred into the domain of police power as well. Related to the paternalistic duty to assist those impaired by mental illness, the primary purpose of civil commitment is treatment, rather than punishment, and, therefore, is implemented within a psychiatric institution (Melton et al., 2007).

Next, although the same behavior (e.g., dangerousness) can trigger both civil and criminal commitment, the two processes differ in the specificity by which the proscribed behavior is defined (Melton et al., 2007). Due to the punitive nature of incarceration, the foundation of our government requires that criminal law give sufficient notice about what it considers "illegal" actions and, thus, delineates in no uncertain terms what is meant by the different crimes. Given that civil commitment is ostensibly non-punitive, courts have upheld the position that the same level of specificity about its guiding criteria (e.g., "mental disorder," "need for treatment," and "dangerousness") is unnecessary. In fact, this may be by design: whereas criminal law punishes for conduct that has already occurred, civil commitment seeks to prevent future behavior. However, aside from generally "needing treatment" or being "dangerous," the specific behavior to be prevented in any given individual is a legal (and, in many cases, clinical) judgment that must be made in context. For example, the state may seek to prevent suicide in one person, prevent harm to another in a second person, and prevent failure to care for one's basic life needs in a third; these are three different acts, and each of these behaviors can be accomplished in any number of ways. Thus, it would severely limit the state's ability to help if it were forced to define each and every act in which authorities could intervene. Finally, in order to prevent the behavior, it must be predicted (or at least, anticipated). However, because of the combination of an infinite number of biological, psychological, and social factors, prediction of human behavior is exceedingly difficult — if not impossible (at least, with 100 percent accuracy). Therefore, by leaving the behavior to be predicted up to some level of interpretation, it again keeps open the state's ability to assist.

Also related to the purposes of criminal versus civil commitment, the legal process by which the state can intervene is somewhat formalized (Melton et al., 2007). Again, since criminal incarceration is intended to punish an individual for his/her wrong-doings, the Constitution requires the state to prove its case with a high degree of proof (e.g., "beyond a reasonable doubt") and to guarantee the defendant a host of due process safeguards. For civil commitment, on the other hand, given its purported intention to help, it has been decided that only "clear and convincing evidence" is necessary to establish the need for treatment. Moreover, although the process has become increasingly formalized since the 1960s, it is still relatively lax with regard to ensuring a potential committed person's rights.

Consistent with the extent of notice regarding proscribed acts and the legal due process believed to be deserved by individuals within the criminal justice system versus the civil commitment system, the duration of confinement also varies (Melton et al., 2007). At least during the current time, in which there has been a move away from indeterminate sentencing, criminal offenders know at the point of sentencing what their maximum sentence will be; in most cases, they will get out sooner than the original sentence imposed. Civilly committed patients, on the other hand, enjoy no such "luxury." Most jurisdictions impose no limits on the duration of civil commitment, albeit under the parameters that the individual continues to meet requirements for commitment and is provided regular hearings to establish this fact.

Implied in the distinctions described above is that, as a society, we are not as troubled by unjustified, extended civil commitment than by false criminal convictions and sentencing (Melton et al., 2007). What, then, does it communicate about society's thoughts about persons with mental illness, as compared to offenders?

A final note is warranted to explain the location of this discussion of civil commitment before the chapter on law enforcement. Despite its distinction from the criminal justice system, civil commitment can be used by law enforcement as a mechanism for executing its duty to protect society—including protecting individuals within society, even from themselves. Law enforcement officers, when responding to the scene of a call, have a great amount of discretion in the way they resolve the incident. Specifically, they can formally arrest a suspect or transport the individual for evaluation of civil commitment, or they can informally provide a verbal warning of future arrest and/or referral to treatment services (Cooper, McLearen, & Zapf, 2004; Sellers, Sullivan, Veysey, & Shane, 2005). What's more, these options are available for almost any call, whether a crime has been committed or not (e.g., a call for responding to a person with mental illness who has not committed a crime). Clearly, law enforcement officers are entrusted with a great amount of power; what they do with that power depends not only on their professional experience, but on systemic and situational factors, as well as their personal experiences, attitudes, and fears of people with mental illness (Patch & Arrigo, 1999). This body of literature will be discussed in detail in Chapter 5. From this point forward, we divide this chapter into the two main types of civil commitment, inpatient civil commitment and outpatient civil commitment.

Inpatient Civil Commitment: History and Reform

For some people with mental illnesses, hospitalization is "a critical first step in initiation of psychiatric care" (Testa & West, 2010, p. 31), particularly for those who lack insight into their illness and/or seek to avoid the stigma of mental illness by refusing to accept treatment in the community. By avoiding treatment, individuals with serious mental illnesses may decline to such a point that they can no longer function effectively and/or become a danger to themselves or others. At such a time, they may be offered the opportunity to voluntarily enter the hospital; if they continue to refuse treatment, and they meet certain statutory criteria, discussed below, they may be civilly committed against their will.

Decisions to civilly commit are, although ostensibly to benefit the individual with mental illness, largely for the benefit of society. Stone (1975) identified four social goals of inpatient civil commitment, which are as true now as they were after the building of the first state hospital. Through hospitalization, involuntary inpatient commitment provides care and treatment for those who require it. By removing individuals from the community and placing them in an institution with 24-hour care and supervision, it prevents those who are considered irrational and irresponsible by virtue of mental illness from harming themselves. Likewise, when individuals are removed from the community, society is protected from their potentially dangerous actions. Similarly, according to Stone (1975), inpatient commitment relieves society, and especially families, from accommodating those who are bothersome, by placing individuals in an institution that provides care for all of the patients' basic needs, in a setting isolated from everyone else. In this way — e.g., removal from society of those considered troublesome — it becomes evident how controversial civil commitment can become (Melton et al., 2007).

History of Inpatient Civil Commitment

Before proceeding to a discussion of the concerns of inpatient civil commitment, a brief recap of the contemporary history of involuntary hospitalization within the United States from Chapter 2 is in order. Prior to the 1960s, virtually anyone could be admitted to a psychiatric hospital on the words of a disgruntled family member or, at best, a few psychiatrists convincing a judge. As noted by Geller and Stanley (2005b), "This lax standard resulted in many commitments deemed, in retrospect, to be arbitrary, discriminatory, and clinically unnecessary" (p. 129). This recognition arose at the same time that the civil rights movement gained momentum, and treatment of persons with mental illness became a target of reform. With *Lessard v. Schmidt* (1976), the U.S. Supreme Court tightened the criteria for involuntary hospitalization to the now universal "dangerousness to self or others" standard and asserted that people facing civil commitment proceedings should receive many of the same constitutional protections of a criminal suspect.

Simultaneously, related to a convergence of factors — not the least of which were deplorable conditions at the state hospitals and the belief that the pharmaceutical profession had found in Thorazine the cure for mental illness — deinstitutionalization of state hospitals began in earnest. Hundreds of thousands of former psychiatric patients were released into the communities without treatment, many of them set up to fail and to need treatment in an intensive hospital setting that was no longer there.

Civil Commitment Reform

Beginning with California's Lanterman-Petris-Short Act in 1967, states throughout the country revised their civil commitment statutes. In particular, legislatures revised their standards for civil commitment, the procedures by which determinations of civil commitment occurred, and the due process guarantees of those potentially committed. Each will be discussed.

Post-Reform Involuntary Commitment Criteria

Although varying slightly from state to state, certain commonalities exist across statutes in their civil commitment criteria. All restricted grounds for commitment to dangerousness to self or others, and most included grave disability (Fisher & Grisso, 2010). Some also adopted other elements, such as need for treatment, as part of their civil commitment standard (Melton et al., 2007). No matter the specific grounds for civil commitment, all required that such findings be based in mental illness (Melton et al., 2007).

Mental Illness

First and foremost, all states require that a *mental illness* exists. Although this seems to be a given, the point of its inclusion is to emphasize that a person cannot be committed for dangerousness to others, for example, without the person also suffering mental illness.[5] Indeed, contrary to popular belief, the vast majority of people who commit violent crimes are not mentally ill (Choe, Teplin, & Abram, 2008) and, thus, are not committable.

---

5. It is, in part, for this reason that "civil commitment" of sexually violent predators (SVPs) is so controversial. The mechanism of civil commitment was initially intended to provide involuntary treatment to those who, due to serious mental illness, could not appreciate their need for treatment (Melton et al., 2007). This typically involved individuals with serious mental illness who, in the past half century at least, could be relatively quickly stabilized on medication(s) and released after a brief period of time. However, the vast majority of sex offenders — violent and predatory or not — do not suffer from a serious mental illness. Rather, they have a personality disorder, which is not readily amenable to psychiatric treatment. By definition, characterological disorders comprise long-standing patterns of psychosocial dysfunction, not temporary symptoms of serious mental illness that can be

Most states employ a broad definition of mental illness, similar to Virginia's current standard (Virginia Code § 37.2-100, emphasis added): "A disorder of thought, mood, emotion, perception, or orientation that significantly impairs judgment, behavior, [or] capacity to recognize reality ..."[6] Embedded within this definition are several components. First, virtually any major mental illness can qualify as long as cognition (e.g., thought, perception, orientation) and/or mood is affected. Second, the disorder must significantly affect the individual to the point of impairment; mild or slight effects are insufficient for civil commitment. Thus, between the locus of symptoms (mood or thought) and the focus of impairment (in judgment, behavior, or capacity to recognize reality), it becomes evident that these statutes are intended for psychotic disorders (e.g., schizophrenia, mood disorders with psychosis). Moreover, the individual must be experiencing current symptoms. A mere history of mental illness is generally insufficient for civil commitment.

Dangerousness to Self or Others

All states include the dangerousness criterion in their civil commitment statutes, as it is firmly established in case law (Melton et al., 2007). In addition, almost all states include dangerousness of a physical nature. Beyond that, however, there is wide variation in if and how dangerousness is defined. If dangerousness is defined further, do emotional harm, danger to property, and other lesser forms of aggression qualify? Is some sort of overt act, proving dangerousness, required? And what severity, probability/likelihood, frequency, and/or imminence of harm are required to warrant involuntary commitment? Furthermore, individual dangerousness determinations rely on a combination of these factors and are largely contextual. For example, an individual who has an estimated 10 percent chance of committing murder is more likely to be civilly committed than someone who has an estimated 90 percent chance of verbally abusing another due to mental illness. Moreover, an assessment of the planning and feasibility of one's intention to do harm bears on the determination of dangerousness.

"stabilized" with medication. Moreover, many state statutes employ the term "mental" or "behavioral abnormality" (*Kansas v. Hendricks*, 1997, p. 358), which has no basis in psychiatry or psychology, but is rather a legal term (Fisher & Grisso, 2010; Group for the Advancement of Psychiatry [GAP], 1977). Despite these criticisms, the U.S. Supreme Court asserted the state's right to define "mental illness" in whatever manner it chooses (*Kansas v. Hendricks*, 1997).

6. The remainder of the impairment clause (Virginia Code § 37.2-100, emphasis added) is essentially a prelude to the dangerousness criterion ("that failure to provide care and treatment would jeopardize the *health, safety, or recovery of the individual* or the *safety of others*") and grave disability criterion ("the ability to *address basic life necessities*").

Grave Disability

The grave disability standard of involuntary commitment relates to an individual's inability to care for his/her basic needs due to treatable mental illness (Melton et al., 2007). In most states, these typically include survival needs, such as food, clothing, shelter, medical care, and personal safety. Furthermore, in order to be committed against one's will, the failure to meet needs must be severe enough that it could cause harm to the individual.

Although the Lanterman-Petris-Short Act (1967) included grave disability, not all states followed suit at the time of the initial reforms. However, over the years, approximately 75 percent of states have come to include this criterion explicitly, and the rest encompass the inability to meet survival needs under the dangerousness to self criteria (Melton et al., 2007).

Need for and/or Incompetency to Consent to Treatment

Although not all states include the need for and/or incompetency to consent to treatment as a main tenet of their civil commitment statutes, the majority incorporate some variant of this as a clause (Melton et al., 2007). The need for treatment, for example, is usually embedded into the definition of mental illness or in the grave disability criterion, although a few states include it explicitly as a ground for commitment. Likewise, a few states require that the disorder causes a lack of recognition of the need for treatment, one component of incompetency to consent to treatment (e.g., informed consent). Despite its relative lack of emphasis in statutes, some legal commentators argue that it should be a primary focus of any decision to force someone into treatment against their will (Melton et al., 2007). However, including this requirement complicates matters of dangerousness (Bloom, 2004); should an individual who is otherwise committable by virtue of dangerousness not be committed if they are competent to make treatment decisions? This could be the reason why most states elect to ignore this clause.

Least Restrictive Alternative

Some states also include a clause in their civil commitment statutes requiring that hospitalization can be authorized only if no less restrictive alternative is available (Melton et al., 2007). However, some argue that explicit inclusion of this requirement — even though a hallmark of Judge Bazelon's vision[7] — can render involuntary commitment less effective and, potentially, harmful. For example, sometimes a short hospitalization is more effective, such as in the case of stabilizing medication, than treatment in the least restrictive environment. Moreover, as described vividly by

---

7. As discussed in Chapter 2, Judge David L. Bazelon was a federal appeals court judge and champion of individuals with mental disabilities.

Earley (2006), some unregulated assisted living facilities (ALFs) can involve unsanitary, constrained, and even abusive conditions, despite being ostensibly "less restrictive" than hospitals. Ultimately, the question of whether the statute is intended to refer to the least restrictive environment in an ideal world or in the particular community in which the commitment is being considered, which is limited by resources available and the quality of such facilities, is left to the interpretation of the court (Melton et al., 2007).

Post-Reform Civil Commitment Procedures

Most states adopted a multi-stage process for evaluating eligibility for and ultimately determining whether an individual should be civilly committed (Bloom, 2004), although the specifics of the process — e.g., the exact number of steps, the specific issues to be addressed at each step, the professionals involved and at which step, whether the procedures occur in the community or in the hospital, the amount of time allowed to elapse at each stage — vary by state. Almost all states include an initial screening, one or more pre-commitment evaluation(s) (Bloom, 2004), and a commitment hearing. At screening, the key determination is whether the individual should be petitioned for commitment at all. The screener, typically an employee of the state (e.g., a psychologist, psychiatrist, or social worker employed by the community mental health agency or state hospital), conducts an interview of the individual and, depending on the state's specific practices, collects collateral information. Treating physicians, psychologists, mental health case managers, law enforcement officers, and family members are among the key informants regarding the individual's behavior that precipitated the petition, although when exactly their testimony is sought depends on the state.

If, after the screening, it is concluded that there is sufficient evidence to proceed with the petition, one or more "independent" evaluators become involved. The question of how "independent" the evaluator(s) are also varies by state: in many states, investigators are yet more employees of the state; in others, investigators are clinicians in private practice. At a minimum, the evaluator(s) reviews the initial petition. In many states, they also perform an interview and review of collateral sources.

The purpose of the pre-commitment evaluation is to provide information at the commitment hearing to the judge, by which he/she can make an informed determination of whether probable cause exists that the potentially committed person meets the statutory definition of mental illness. The formality of the hearing, again, varies widely by state. In some states, it is an obligatory, pro forma hearing at which the decision is announced. In other states, and in Washington, D.C., the hearing can become a full-fledged adversarial trial, with both the defense attorney and the prosecution presenting evidence, witnesses testifying, and a jury of peers making the ultimate decision.

Post-Reform Due Process

Further, reforms ensured potential civilly committed people due process rights on par with criminal law. These rights include the typical criminal law rights to notice, to a hearing, to counsel, and to cross-examination. In addition, committed persons were also guaranteed safeguards specific to civil commitment, such as the right to regular review, to determinate periods of commitment, and to treatment in the least restrictive alternative. Many areas even heightened the state's burden to prove by "clear and convincing evidence"[8] that the individual was in need of inpatient treatment (Hiday, 1988).

Overall, these reforms made involuntary commitment to psychiatric hospitals more difficult, in an effort to rescind psychiatry's previously unlimited power. Almost everyone — including many psychiatrists — agreed that these reforms were long overdue (Fisher & Grisso, 2010). However, some treating professionals expressed concerns about the dangerousness criteria. Primarily, they argued that the criteria were too stringent and would, thereby, leave too many people who needed help without services (Anfang & Appelbaum, 2006). Others feared that it would change the psychiatric hospital population — and thus, any ability for the environment to be therapeutic — to wards of dangerous miscreants. Moreover, skepticism was not entirely unwarranted as many of these changes — although ostensibly made in the "best interests" of those who might have previously been committed — were largely motivated by financial and political constituents' pressure. This is clear in the business approach many states took in artificially adjusting supply and demand of state hospital beds: as the availability of hospital beds fell, the "solution" was to interpret already strict, newly revised civil commitment standards even more narrowly, admit only those patients most seriously in need of commitment, and apply pressure to discharge patients (Anfang & Appelbaum, 2006).

Effects of Civil Commitment Reform

Ultimately, however, research suggested that not much had changed, at least in the number of admissions or in the characteristics of committed patients from before to after the statutory changes (Anfang & Appelbaum, 2006; Hiday, 1988). First, although, as predicted, some states found substantial declines in involuntary commitments, at least in the short-term, most states showed little to no permanent effect on commitment rates due to the statutory changes (Anfang & Appelbaum, 2006). Most detected initial drop-offs, followed by a gradual return to pre-reform numbers. Moreover, the demographic breakdown of the civilly committed population remained the same (Hiday, 1988):[9] Committed people were overwhelmingly from the lowest rung of the social structure — poor/indigent, of low education, and un- or under-employed — as they lacked the resources to procure services outside the public system. The population tended to be young males and older females, and between 30 percent and 60 percent had never been married. In rural areas, individuals were primarily

---

8. The "clear and convincing" burden of proof is the moderate standard, falling between the most rigorous "beyond a reasonable doubt" level of certainty required in criminal cases and the "preponderance of the evidence" standard (i.e., more evidence supportive of a finding than not) previously used in civil commitment.

9. By and large, these characteristics remain unchanged even today.

petitioned for commitment by family members; whereas the state was more likely to pursue commitment in urban areas. Early research on race was mixed, with slightly more studies suggesting that black males were disproportionately represented in the involuntarily committed population (Hiday, 1988).

As with demographic variables, the clinical and criminogenic characteristics of civilly committed patients remained largely unchanged (Hiday, 1988). The majority of patients carried a diagnosis of serious mental illness, particularly psychosis, and their histories of mental illness tended to be chronic with numerous hospitalizations, both prior to the immediate involuntary hospitalization and after. Upon discharge, rates of rehospitalization surpassed 55 percent in some studies (Hiday, 1988). Probably most surprisingly, the research suggested that the residual population of committed people were not as dangerous as expected (Hiday, 1988). Instead, a substantial proportion of patients were committed on "grave disability" grounds (Anfang & Appelbaum, 2006). In most cases in which an individual was certified as "dangerous to self or others," the judgments were primarily based on clinical predictions rather than on objective acts (Hiday, 1988). Research on bona fide violence by Californians committed under the Lanterman-Petris-Short Act found no significant increase from before to after its implementation (McNiel & Binder, 1986). It was even possible for family members to still obtain hospitalization for unruly "loved ones" (Hiday, 1988).

What did change in the characteristics of civil commitment patients from the pre- to post-reform eras suggests that a criminalization effect had emerged. Following the changes to the statutes, involuntary patients were more likely to have an arrest history and to be arrested upon discharge from the hospital. Some interpreted this to mean that the population was, in fact, more dangerous. However, the arrests were primarily for non-violent misdemeanors (e.g., larceny, disorderly conduct, trespassing, drunkenness) (Hiday, 1988). As such, it was actually more likely that individuals with mental illness who would otherwise have been hospitalized were getting arrested and charged with minor crimes as a result of not being able to find treatment — or as an effort by law enforcement to get them treatment — in the community. In total, more former psychiatric patients ended up involved in the criminal justice system, manifesting in more arrests, a decline in the severity of charges and number of prior convictions among the inmate population, and a rise in the number of requests for psychiatric services within jails and prisons (Hiday, 1988).

Early research also examined system-level changes following the civil commitment reform that began in the 1960s. In this regard, too, it appeared that some things had changed. First, mental health professionals' practices differed, primarily in that both evaluating and treating clinicians paid attention to dangerousness in making their assessments (Hiday, 1988). In turn, although it was not a global finding, most studies found substantial improvement in the quality of civil commitment legal hearings. Candidates were more likely to be present, hearings lasted longer than previously, attorneys were more active in presenting evidence related to the statutory criteria, and both attorneys and judges were less deferential to the opinions of psychiatrists (Hiday, 1988). However, research suggested that local financial, administrative, and logistical factors had greater bearing on civil commitment decisions in the post-reform era than any statutory changes (Anfang & Appelbaum, 2006).

Ultimately, though, conclusions based on the research had to be made cautiously as many of the studies were inherently flawed (Hiday, 1988). First, many "studies" were grounded in mere observation or anecdotal evidence by psychiatrists (Anfang & Appelbaum, 2006). Moreover, most of the empirical studies had serious methodological flaws. For example, research on dangerousness was of questionable generalizability to states' actual experiences because the laws and the research used vastly different definitions of dangerousness (Hiday, 1988). Laws tended to use vague language, but by the nature of research, specific operational definitions had to be adopted for purposes of reliability. Even between researchers, there was wide variability in operational definitions, sources of data (e.g., official records versus patients' self-reports), and time frames (e.g., 2 weeks after release to 3 years). And even among the quality empirical studies, establishing actual causality and non-spuriousness (e.g., that findings were related to changes in commitment statutes, rather than to some other variable(s)) was not possible as random assignment was infeasible or, at least, was not used (Hiday & Wales, 2013). Finally, the findings of studies of the increased criminal justice outcomes (e.g., arrests) following civil commitment reform might have been overstated, with most studies making conclusions based on the number of persons with mental illness, in general, who were arrested, rather than specifically following those who had been released from state hospitals.

Controversies Surrounding Inpatient Civil Commitment

Neither the aforementioned social goals of civil commitment nor many of the characteristics of civilly committed patients have changed much over the years. Likewise, concerns about civil commitment remain largely the same. The discussion below outlines these controversies.

Inpatient Civil Commitment Is Coercive

The biggest concern is, and always has been, that inpatient civil commitment is coercive. By definition, civil commitment involves removal — or as labeled by the U.S. Supreme Court, "a massive curtailment" (*Humphrey v. Cady*, 1972, p. 509) — of freedom against an individual's will (i.e., involuntarily). As such, committed individuals commonly feel they are deprived of any control or choice over their treatment decisions (Zervakis et al., 2007). In particular, respondents perceived numerous aspects of the civil commitment process as coercive, including using the law as a tool to force treatment, being excluded from the admission process, and being verbally ordered to do something either by "show of force" or by threats (Zervakis et al., 2007). It is no wonder that these patients would feel coerced, however, as in actuality, 30 percent were placed in seclusion, 27 percent were placed in physical restraints,

18 percent were forcibly medicated, and 28 percent were denied their medications of choice (Zervakis et al., 2007). If not applied carefully and respectfully by treating professionals, coercion has great potential to infringe upon individuals' legal rights.[10] In fact, the Bazelon Center for Mental Health Law (2000), consistent with its founder's ideals,[11] cites opposing unnecessary coercion as a key focus of its work to protect the rights of people with mental illness.

Perceptions of coercion do not seem to dissipate much over time but instead hinder patients' future encounters with treatment providers. Katsakou and Priebe (2006) reviewed studies of civil commitment worldwide, 28 percent of which were performed in the U.S.; and they found that, in retrospect, most patients had largely positive opinions about their hospitalizations. In particular, they tended to rate their admission as correct or necessary and that the hospitalization forced upon them was justified, and these views tended to become increasingly positive over time. Yet, a sizeable proportion still did not feel that their treatment was justified or that they benefited from treatment up to three years later (Katsakou & Priebe, 2006). Specifically, in some of the studies reviewed, nearly 50 percent of respondents continued to believe that they did not need hospital admission, an equal percent explicitly stated that their involuntary admission was unjustified, and up to one-third perceived no benefits or even felt harmed by their treatment years after their discharge (Katsakou & Priebe, 2006). Furthermore, individuals who have previously been involuntary hospitalized are more likely to perceive coercion in later, even voluntary, admissions (Zervakis et al., 2007).

Inpatient Civil Commitment Is Anti-Therapeutic

Another major criticism of involuntary civil commitment is that it is ultimately anti-therapeutic. Research suggests that feelings of coercion frequently damage the patient-provider relationship (Swartz et al., 2003), and, thus, involuntary treatment is found to be associated with poorer clinical outcomes (Bonsack & Borgeat, 2005). As noted by Campbell (2002) about involuntary inpatient commitment in particular, "People with mental illness are often skeptical of the system to begin with, and when the state starts invoking its police power to take away their liberties, they are less likely to seek treatment voluntarily in a community mental health setting" (p. 203). Thus, past involuntary hospitalizations make people more likely to require involuntary

---

10. Or worse, if not implemented properly, restraints can lead to death. Sadly, this was the outcome for Gloria Huntley in Virginia in June, 1996. Huntley died of breathing-related complications after having been strapped to a bed for nearly 300 hours in the month of her death, twice for more than 4 days (Baskerville, 1997). Following Gloria's death, which was reminiscent of a similar death in May, 1993, the U.S. Department of Justice initiated an investigation of, among other things, the hospital's use of restraints (Baskerville, 1997).

11. As mentioned previously, Judge Bazelon was responsible for the "least restrictive alternative" standard of civil commitment.

hospitalization again in the future (Fennig, Rabinowitz, & Fennig, 1999; Munk-Jorgensen, Mortensen, & Machon, 1991). Arguably, this defeats the purpose of treatment.

Inpatient Civil Commitment Is Stigmatizing

Not only is civil commitment coercive and anti-therapeutic, it is argued that it contributes significantly to and perpetuates the stigma associated with mental illness, particularly the stigma that people with mental illness are violent. Notably, since the adoption of the "dangerous to self or others" criteria of civil commitment in the 1960s, as will be discussed further below, perceptions that people with mental illness are violent or frightening has increased by 250 percent (Phelan, Link, Stueve, & Pescosolido, 2000), despite the public knowing more about the biological causes of mental illness. Probably most clearly suggesting a link between the language of civil commitment laws and the violence stigma, Phelan and Link (1998) found that among survey respondents who mentioned violence in their description of a person with mental illness, 44 percent used "danger to self or others" phrasing, as compared to only 4 percent of respondents in 1950. And the belief that people with mental illness are violent seems to have a bidirectional relationship with stigma: The greater the belief that people with mental illness are violent, the greater the stigmatizing treatment of persons with mental illness; likewise, the greater the stigma, the more likely the public is to believe that people with mental illness are violent.

Inpatient Civil Commitment Is Discriminatory

Related to stigma, the contention is that involuntary hospitalization is racially discriminatory. In particular, research over the past 50 years — although somewhat mixed — suggests that blacks, and black males specifically, are involuntarily hospitalized at a higher rate than other men and women (Adebimpe, 1994; Gibbs, 1962; Lawson, Hepler, Holladay, & Cuffel, 1994; Rosenfield, 1984; Snowden & Cheung, 1990; Wanchek & Bonnie, 2012). While hospitalized, research shows that blacks tend to receive more severe diagnoses (Adebimpe, 1994; Lawson et al., 1994). Although some might argue that severe mental illness is merely more common among blacks (Swanson et al., 2009), this is a matter of debate. For example, some of the largest epidemiological studies, intended to examine patterns and causes of disease (including mental illness), have found wide differences between the reported prevalence of severe mental illness among blacks in treated populations versus in the general community population (Adebimpe, 1994). One could interpret these findings as being due to a greater inclination of mental health professionals to diagnose, and thus treat, blacks; this could be related to, among other factors, subtle cultural differences that manifest in each groups' presentations, which clinicians then interpret as symptoms of mental illness among blacks (Adebimpe, 1994).

Not only do committed blacks receive more severe diagnoses, they are more likely to be treated with coercion while hospitalized. For instance, in both adolescent and adult populations, blacks were more often placed in restraint and seclusion — sometimes, four times more often (Bond, DiCandia, & MacKinnon, 1988) — even though no racial differences in psychopathology or behavior were apparent (Flaherty & Meagher, 1980). Likewise, black inpatients were given more emergency medications (i.e., administered on an "as needed" basis, which involves interpretation and discretion), were less likely to receive privileges as part of behavioral reinforcement/ incentive plans, and received less recreational or occupational therapy (which is generally considered more positive, enjoyable treatments that build on individuals' strengths) than whites (Flaherty & Meagher, 1980).

Rosenfield (1984) performed the most comprehensive analysis of other possible explanations for the greater rates of inpatient hospitalization among blacks to date. She found that the effect remains, even after controlling for severity of psychiatric condition, disorders that were defined to be more closely related to violence, negative attitudes toward treatment, and the race of the physician. The only variable that explained the finding was the higher degree of police involvement in black males' hospitalizations.

The main limitation of much of this body of literature, however, was that the researchers did not factor out the effects of socioeconomic status. Moreover, there are some studies that suggest there are no racial differences in civil commitment rates (Hiday, 1988). Regardless, Swanson et al. (2009) encourages consideration of several factors in the treatment of the issue of racial difference versus disparity in involuntary commitment:

> We should see these differences against the historical backdrop of long-term institutional confinement of people with mental illnesses — blacks in greater proportions than whites — and the subsequent "revolving door" syndrome of involuntary hospital readmissions. We should also consider the segregating effects of a de facto two-tier system of care: a private system of care for people with employer based insurance and a public system of care for people who are poor, unemployed, and uninsured or who have public, entitlement-based insurance (p. 819).

Inpatient Civil Commitment Is Driven by Money

A final criticism is that civil commitment — and all the accompanying misery — is driven completely by money as opposed to benevolent treatment for those who need it. This was certainly true at the time of deinstitutionalization, and it is no less true today. Indeed, given the cost savings to the state, it is not surprising that legislators continue to close state hospitals, as will be discussed in the next section. Specifically, according to the Substance Abuse and Mental Health Services Administration (SAMHSA, 2011), the state must foot approximately 79 percent of an individual's treatment in a state hospital, in comparison to an average of only 55 percent — and in some states, as low as 20 percent — of community mental health treatment. Thereby, the cost is shifted from the state to the local county. From this perspective, if those with mental illness are subsumed by the criminal justice system, all the better; this, too, shift the costs from the state to the county.

Dwindling Hospital Beds

The Treatment Advocacy Center (TAC), the flagship organization of well-known psychiatrist and advocate, E. Fuller Torrey, posted a report on recent trends and consequences of the continued closing of public psychiatric hospitals (Torrey, Fuller, Geller, Jacobs, & Ragosta, 2012). As was mentioned in Chapter 2, in an analysis of data collected through 2010, obtained from the National Association of State Mental Health Program Directors (NASMHPD), Torrey et al. (2012) found that the number of state psychiatric beds decreased by 14 percent between 2005 and 2010 alone, from 50,509 to 43,318 beds.[12] Thirteen states closed 25 percent or more of their beds, including five states that closed 40 percent. Moreover, according to Torrey et al. (2012), NASMHPD reports that an additional 1,249 beds were planned to be eliminated, representing a cumulative 17 percent reduction since 2005. Most strikingly, relative to the size of the general population, per capita state psychiatric bed populations declined to 1850 levels (14 beds per 100,000 persons in the general population). Compared to the "minimally adequate" figure of 50 beds per 100,000,[13] an estimate derived from 15 experts published previously, the current level is nearly two-thirds below this estimate (Torrey et al., 2012).

As has been discussed, despite the theory behind deinstitutionalization, there remains a small subset of persons with serious, chronic mental illness who need inpatient hospitalization. As noted by Torrey et al. (2012), many of these people are incapable of seeking treatment voluntarily or paying for it privately and tend to only receive treatment when they decompensate to a point at which they can be civilly committed. Unfortunately, due to the criminalization effect of the civil commitment reforms of the 1960s, discussed earlier in this chapter and throughout this book, more and more hospital beds are being used by forensic patients. In 2010, 33 percent of all public psychiatric beds (SAMSHA, 2011) — and in some states, up to 92 percent (Romney, 2012) — went to forensic patients. Accordingly, this takes away beds from non-forensic patients who desperately need inpatient hospitalization (Torrey et al., 2012).[14]

The effects of state hospital downsizing are immense. Thousands of seriously mentally ill individuals who meet criteria for civil commitment are "streeted" — i.e., released from custody because there are no state psychiatric beds available and/or the emergency custody order expires before an order for a full evaluation can be obtained

---

12. At the height of psychiatric institutionalization in 1955, there were 559,000 patients in state hospitals nationwide (Lamb & Weinberger, 2005). In comparison, the 2010 figures represent a 92 percent decrease in the number of state hospital beds since 1955.

13. By way of comparison, England had 63.2 beds/100,000 in 2008 (Torrey et al., 2012).

14. Of course, it could be argued that these now forensic patients are those who would previously have needed hospitalization as a non-forensic patient.

from the court (Huffman, 2011). Indeed, the burden on emergency rooms, law enforcement, and jails has reached a point of crisis.[15]

In emergency rooms (ERs), one in eight patients had a mental health or substance abuse condition, a number that has been increasing for over a decade (Owens, Mutter, & Stocks, 2010). In Arizona, for example, "emergency room psychiatric consultations [in 2011] ha[d] spiked by 40 percent since [the previous] spring" (Reinhart, 2011). Not only are greater numbers of persons with mental illness arriving at emergency rooms, more ERs are "boarding" these patients and for longer and longer periods of time. In a briefing before Congress, NASMHPD reported that 70 percent of more than 6,000 emergency departments nationwide indicated they boarded individuals in psychiatric crisis for "hours or days," and 10 percent boarded such patients for several weeks (Glover, Miller, & Sadowski, 2012).

Many law enforcement officials hypothesize a direct relationship between the closing of public psychiatric beds and an increase in persons with mental illness involved with the criminal justice system (Torrey et al., 2012). Not only is it stressful for law enforcement, many of whom are not trained to intervene with people with mental illness, but it is a huge drain on limited financial resources. As noted by the TAC (2012), "Police and sheriffs in every state have been overwhelmed by an increasing number of mental illness-related calls" (p. 12). For example, in a 2011 survey of more than 2,400 law enforcement officials, as reported by the TAC (2012), mental illness-related calls outnumbered calls for larceny, traffic accidents, and domestic disputes combined. Moreover, various studies have found an inverse relationship between the number of public psychiatric beds and the prevalence of violent crimes necessitating arrest (Torrey et al., 2012; Markowitz, 2006), even though the strength of the relationship was relatively weak.[16] Finally, there is a statistically significant increase in the number of individuals with mental illness killed during an arrest in states with a decreased capacity for public psychiatric beds (Torrey et al., 2012).

Jails and prisons, too, are deluged with inmates with serious mental illness. Research has demonstrated that this is negatively related to the number of state hospital beds, a trend witnessed since the initiation of deinstitutionalization (Torrey et al., 2012; Lamb & Weinberger, 1998; Raphael, 2000). As discussed in Chapter 1, approximately 16 percent of jail and prison inmates (Ditton, 1999) — and as many as 80 percent, according to one Montana sheriff (Stukey, 2012) — reportedly have a serious mental illness (Ditton, 1999).[17] As noted by Torrey, Kennard, Eslinger, Lamb, and Pavle (2010), there are three times as many individuals with serious mental illness in jails and prison than in hospitals.

---

15. It must be noted that most research has not been able to *directly* connect these statistics to the decrease in hospital beds. Torrey et al. (2012) imply that they are related, and, undoubtedly, there is a good degree of truth to this; but most of the research has not explicitly investigated this link.

16. Torrey et al. (2012) also noted, "When individuals with severe mental illness receive appropriate and effective treatment, their risk of committing violent acts is no greater than that of the general population" (p. 15).

17. More on this topic can be found in Chapters 6 (Jails) and 9 (Prisons).

Statutory Changes to Inpatient Civil Commitment Laws

Currently, opinions about the state of civil commitment law fall along polar opposites, with many arguing that standards for involuntary treatment are currently too strict and others arguing that they are too lax and permissive. This dialectic is not inaccurate, however, as the practice of civil commitment has taken unusual twists and turns in its application. Moreover, not only do commitments vary by circumstance, they vary by time and place.

Inpatient Civil Commitment Has Become Too Permissive

In some ways, involuntary treatment has become increasingly permissive. This is most argued with regard to use of the grave disability criterion. Practically immediately after the civil commitment reforms went into effect, psychiatrists, judges, and even attorneys began to "bend" the law to fit individual cases (Fisher & Grisso, 2010). Although most commitments fit within the parameters of the standards, there were a minority of cases that did not. In these cases, a "beneficent" collaboration sought the most practical result (Anfang & Appelbaum, 2006, p. 214). Psychiatrists increasingly pursued hospitalization on grounds of grave disability for those who they deemed to need care but who did not meet the dangerousness criteria; attorneys tended to look past these clients' expressed desire for release to think of their clients' "best interests," advocating for treatment even if that meant a more restrictive environment; and judges approved these decisions. This happened with such frequency that within the last 20 years several legislatures officially changed their statutes to broaden the definition of "grave disability" to include the possibility of severe deterioration or inability to care for self (Anfang & Appelbaum, 2006). Indeed, the grave disability standard has come to serve as a catch-all for individuals with serious mental illness who need treatment on clinical grounds but would otherwise be unable to get it under the literal interpretation of the civil commitment criteria (Anfang & Appelbaum, 2006). Of course, this approach has its critics, who argue for preservation of patients' rights (Mickle, 2012) and for the obligations of mental health to support patient recovery and patient empowerment principles (Henwood, 2008).

The trend toward greater permissiveness can also be seen in several applications to which involuntary treatment and commitment were not intended. Traditional civil commitment is reserved for individuals with severe mental illness (e.g., psychosis) who need treatment to stabilize their illness. However, as mentioned previously, legislators have exploited this mechanism of civil law to indefinitely remove from society "sexually violent predators" (SVPs) (Fisher & Grisso, 2010). Specifically, with SVP civil commitment, upon completion of the sexual offender's criminal sentence, he/she is then civilly committed, not to a typical psychiatric hospital, but to a maximum-security facility. These facilities are usually run by the state mental health department, but they resemble prisons. One of the greatest criticisms is that SVP laws are a "bastardization" of civil commitment, using mental health professionals to control criminals. As previously discussed, most sex offenders do not suffer from a serious mental illness, but from a personality disorder, which is not readily amenable to psychiatric treatment (e.g., medication or even, in many cases, psychotherapeutic interventions). Furthermore, some fear that such an expansion of the civil commitment process will have a reciprocal effect, providing a slippery slope to the infringement upon the civil liberties of persons with mental illnesses. Notwithstanding these concerns, this does not deter states from using SVP laws, and the U.S. Supreme Court have supported them (*Kansas v. Hendricks*, 1997).

Inpatient Civil Commitment Has Become Too Restrictive

At the opposite end of the controversy, civil commitment has become more restrictive, not so much in the standards set forth by state law but in the shift to managed care. Although seemingly unrelated to the civil commitment reform of the 1960s, which limited unnecessary involuntary commitment to state hospitals, most of the acute psychiatric admissions in the U.S. today are to psychiatric units in general hospitals (Fisher & Grisso, 2010). The care provided in these facilities are governed by managed care, in which admissions must be pre-certified, hospital stays are closely monitored, and discharge is urged — indeed, often forced — before the patient is clinically ready. This sounds very similar to the stringent admission and discharge standards in the wake of dwindling state hospital beds following civil commitment reform: both seek to severely limit psychiatric hospitalizations (Fisher & Grisso, 2010).

There is another type of civil commitment, with perhaps even wider ranging implications for people with mental illness and surrounded by perhaps even greater controversies, and it is to this second type that we now turn.

Outpatient Commitment

Outpatient commitment (OC) — otherwise known as "assisted outpatient treatment" or "involuntary outpatient commitment" — is the community treatment version of traditional inpatient civil commitment. Like inpatient civil commitment, outpatient commitment is a civil law mandate ordering an individual to obtain treatment against one's will. Most states even use identical criteria for involuntary outpatient commitment as they do for civil inpatient commitment, at least for certain types of OC (Swartz & Swanson, 2008). Similarly, the profile of a "typical" subject of outpatient commitment is similar to that of inpatient commitment: a young man with schizophrenia, several hospital admissions, a history of noncompliance with community treatment, and often a history of incarceration or other forensic care (Dawson, 2005). The main difference is that with outpatient commitment, individuals retain the freedom to continue their "normal" lives in the community (Hiday & Wales, 2013).

With the failures of deinstitutionalization, on the one hand, and involuntary hospitalization, on the other, outpatient commitment has been touted as a panacea. Typically, when an individual is not an *imminent* danger to him- or herself or to others, outpatient commitment has been more readily accepted. Moreover, it is better received when it is utilized in a limited role with patients who can competently choose between outpatient commitment with involuntary medication or involuntary hospitalization. Ultimately, the goal is that involvement in such a choice would bind them to the treatment should future need arise (Saks, 2003).

Outpatient commitment orders may compel an individual with mental illness to submit to any combination of conditions: attending full-day treatment programs; participating in psychotherapy with a therapist, and/or, depending on the state, taking psychotropic medications; undergoing routine urine and blood tests; attending substance abuse groups or self-help meetings; maintaining employment and/or residence in a supervised living facility (Allen & Smith, 2001; Torrey & Zdanowicz, 2001; Wagner, Swartz, Swanson, & Burns, 2003) — or risk sanctions for noncompliance. The ultimate consequence for not following involuntary outpatient commitment strictures is not criminal in nature but is instead a civil sanction — i.e., more intensive community treatment and/or forced hospitalization. If an outpatient commitment patient fails to comply with treatment, most statutes allow the presiding clinician to ask the police to bring the non-compliant patient to an outpatient facility, where efforts will be undertaken to encourage the patient to comply with the treatment regimen or be evaluated for inpatient hospitalization (Swartz, Swanson, Kim, & Petrila, 2006).

The use of outpatient commitment has been "fueled by several factors, including limited inpatient resources and brief hospital stays, insufficient community-based resources, a growing homeless persons with mental illness population, highly publicized cases of untreated mentally ill persons, and substance abusers causing havoc or harm" (Anfang & Appelbaum, 2006, p. 212). Depending on the type of outpatient commitment, it is intended, among other things, to prevent relapse, hospital readmission, homelessness, and incarceration (Swartz et al., 2006).

Types of Outpatient Commitment

Generally in the research literature, three types of outpatient commitment (OC) are discussed. The first is *conditional release* from the hospital, whereby individuals are prescribed community mental health treatment under threat that they can be returned to hospital care if they are non-compliant with treatment protocols or otherwise deteriorate (Hiday & Wales, 2013). Conditional release is the earliest type of outpatient commitment, having emerged at the beginning of the twentieth century with the primary purpose of reintegrating persons back into society (Cornwell, 2003). Specifically, it is used to "test" a patient's ability to function in the community while still under supervision before the state has to completely relinquish control. About 80% of states have conditional release provisions in their statutes (Melton et al., 2007). It appears, of all of these types of outpatient commitment, the conditional release form is used most frequently (Melton et al., 2007).

The second type of outpatient commitment is the traditional conception, or "front-end" version, of OC. In this format, outpatient commitment is intended to allow mandated community treatment *instead of* involuntary hospitalization in the first place, i.e., a less restrictive alternative (LRA) (Wales & Hiday, 2006). Approximately two-thirds of states have this type of outpatient commitment by statute (Melton et al., 2007). "Front-end" outpatient commitment tends to use the same criteria for outpatient commitment as it does for inpatient civil commitment.

The final, and most controversial, type of outpatient commitment is what has come to be labeled *preventive outpatient commitment.* As the name suggests, preventive OC orders community treatment for those who do not yet meet civil commitment criteria, with the purpose of preventing deterioration to the point that civil commitment criteria are met and involuntary hospitalization is needed. It is generally intended for those who are unwilling and/or unable to accept treatment voluntarily, who have a history demonstrating the need for treatment to prevent deterioration that might lead to multiple hospitalizations or dangerousness to self/others, and/or to prevent the revolving door between the mental health and criminal justice systems (Wales & Hiday, 2006). Preventive outpatient commitment can involve forced medication in the community based on a lesser standard than is necessary for involuntary hospitalization (see O'Connor, 2002; Saks, 2003; Schopp, 2003). It is for this reason — e.g., it involves the greatest reach of state authority into an individual's liberty on the least grounds — that preventive OC has received the most attention, and criticism. Almost all states have laws that permit some form of outpatient commitment, with 32 states having a preventive type of outpatient commitment law (SAMHSA, 2019).

The most well-known and researched of all outpatient commitment laws is New York's preventive OC statute, colloquially referred to as Kendra's Law. Kendra's Law, more formally known as the New York Mental Hygiene Law (2004), defines eligibility for assisted outpatient treatment (AOT) within the following framework (Treatment Advocacy Center, 2008, p. 3):

- Eighteen years of age or older
- Suffers from a mental illness
- Unlikely to survive safely in the community without supervision, based on a clinical determination
- History of non-adherence with treatment that has:
  - Been a significant factor in one being in a hospital, prison or jail at least twice within the last thirty-six months, or
  - Resulted in one or more acts, attempts or threats of serious violent behavior toward self or others within the last forty-eight months

- Unlikely to voluntarily participate in treatment
- Based on treatment history and current behavior, in need of AOT in order to prevent a relapse or deterioration which would be likely to result in the following:
  - A substantial risk of physical harm to the individual as manifested by threats of or attempts at suicide or serious bodily harm or conduct demonstrating that the individual is dangerous to himself or herself, or
  - A substantial risk of physical harm to other persons as manifested by homicidal or other violent behavior by which others are placed in reasonable fear of serious physical harm
- Likely to benefit from AOT

As outlined by Perlin (2003), petitioners — who can include "parents, spouses, persons with whom the subject resides, children, siblings, a qualified treating psychiatrist, or a probation or parole officer charged with supervising the individual" (p. 195) — must present a supporting affidavit from a doctor in order to initiate court proceedings for outpatient commitment. The doctor must establish in the affidavit that he/she has seen the patient in the last ten days and deems that the patient is in need of outpatient commitment, or, if an examination of the patient has not been possible, the doctor is to state why he/she believes outpatient commitment is necessary. The doctor submitting the affidavit is required to testify at a hearing before the patient/respondent who is given notice and is authorized to have legal counsel present. The treatment plan provided by the doctor must demonstrate that the recommended intervention is the least restrictive alternative under the circumstances. The court may also order an involuntary examination of the patient/respondent at this stage. Upon satisfaction that the least restrictive alternative for intervention is in place and that clear and convincing evidence proves that outpatient commitment is needed, the court may direct the patient to initially be placed in outpatient commitment status for up to six months (Perlin, 2003).

Controversies Surrounding Outpatient Commitment

Few topics within mental health law spark as much debate as outpatient commitment. Indeed, it is controversial the world over (Dawson, 2005). As such, there is little consensus on its effectiveness. "In the United States," however, according to Geller (2006, p. 235), "it has been characterized by considerably more opinion than fact." Indeed, historically there has been a paucity of solid research on the topic, although there have been several large-scale projects in recent years attempting to fill this gap. Both opinion and "fact" (i.e., research) will be considered below.

The "Facts" about Outpatient Commitment: Critique of the Research

Before proceeding, it is necessary to provide a few caveats about the body of research on outpatient commitment. First, as has been noted by various authors, it is difficult to study the effectiveness of OC because it is rarely used (Honig & Stefan, 2005; O'Connor, 2002); when it is used, it is limited to a few states, and even a few counties within the states. Because of this, some have concluded that there is "little evidence" to support the effectiveness of outpatient commitment (Honig & Stefan, 2005). This statement is not inaccurate: there has been little research to test the effectiveness of OC. However, some interpret this to mean that OC is *ineffective*, which is not necessarily accurate. Given the tendency for OC to be used in only certain areas, there is the potential for selection bias in any research samples from these locales. Thereby, research findings derived from these samples may unduly inflate or deflate the true effectiveness of the intervention.

The second caveat about outpatient commitment research is a broader issue beyond concerns about sample quality: that is, the existing research available on outpatient commitment has been limited by methodological inadequacies in general (Hiday & Wales, 2013; Leone, 2000). While most studies on outpatient commitment prior to the late 1990s suggested that the intervention was effective, these studies were contaminated with selection bias (e.g., only those patients who were most likely to succeed were chosen for outpatient commitment) (Hiday & Wales, 2013), thereby artificially inflating findings of effectiveness. After inpatient civil commitment was largely eliminated, studies were plagued by selection bias in the opposite direction: Outpatient commitment, as the only remaining alternative, was reserved for those individuals at highest risk of treatment noncompliance and/or dangerousness (i.e., those who would have otherwise been civilly committed to a hospital). Thereby, results about effectiveness (or lack thereof) in these studies were unduly deflated due to the sample (Hiday & Wales, 2013).

Thus, in the mid-1990s, two teams of researchers set out to overcome these problems by performing randomized controlled studies — the optimal design for research to study treatment effectiveness. The first team of researchers in North Carolina, consisting of premier experts on the topic of civil commitment such as Swartz, Swanson, Hiday, and Borum, among others, conducted what has come to be referred to as the "Duke Mental Health Study." Between 1993 and 1996, they randomly assigned individuals with serious mental illness who were being discharged from involuntary inpatient treatment to one of four groups: (1) an experimental group undergoing court-ordered outpatient treatment (i.e., outpatient commitment) and community mental health services, (2) an experimental group undergoing court-ordered OC only, (3) a control group receiving only community mental health services, with no

OC, and (4) a control group receiving no community mental health services or OC. The researchers examined all participants' history in the three years preceding the study and compared it to various outcomes while under outpatient commitment. Numerous articles examining different aspects of this project were published and will be discussed below. Overall, the researchers uncovered numerous positive outcomes, but primarily only when the outpatient commitment was intensive and extended (Hiday & Wales, 2013).[18]

The second team of researchers to conduct a randomized controlled study of outpatient commitment was led by Steadman and was based on a pilot study examining the OC program at Bellevue Hospital in New York between 1996 and 1998 (Steadman et al., 2001).[19] In this project, researchers randomly assigned patients to one of two groups — e.g., one receiving intensive treatment under court-ordered outpatient commitment, the other receiving intensive treatment without being under court order — and compared various outcome measures (e.g., re-hospitalizations, lengths of hospitalizations, arrests) in the year before and the year following assignment to the treatment condition. Overall, the study found no significant differences in the outcomes between the groups. However, due to several critical methodological issues, their results do not necessarily generalize to actual practice.[20]

While employing a stronger research design than most studies, both of these research projects were limited by the fact that they both examined only the "back-end" type of outpatient commitment, or conditional release from inpatient hospitalization, rather than preventive OC. Of course, this was out of the control of the researchers, as preventive OC had not been "discovered" yet; it would not be until 1999 that New York would enact its new law. Nevertheless, this is a critical consideration when critiquing the applicability of this research to current practice. Given that most of the current, controversial statutes are of the preventive type of OC, it is unclear the degree to which these earlier studies are generalizable to contemporary outcomes.

The next "best," most methodologically rigorous type of study is a pre-post design, without random assignment but, ideally, with at least one experimental and a control group (Hiday & Wales, 2013). This is the method adopted by what could be considered

---

18. Despite being the most rigorous research study available on the topic, the Duke Mental Health Study did have a few limitations, as outlined by Hiday and Wales (2013). In particular, there was still selection bias involved because the length and intensity of outpatient commitment ordered were up to the treatment team coordinating services and, ultimately, to the judge. Understandably, researchers were not allowed to randomly assign patients to different lengths of OC; rather, courts assigned conditions of OC based on patients' needs.

19. It is important to note that this program preceded the enactment of Kendra's Law. The Bellevue program is not the same or even comparable to the current outpatient commitment program of "assisted outpatient treatment" (AOT), which is the focus of most research on OC in New York.

20. In particular, the Steadman et al. (2001) study employed a small sample size. Second, persons with a history of violence were excluded from the program, thereby rendering the sample qualitatively different than most individuals under OC. Furthermore, and most importantly, there were huge logistical problems, ranging from control subjects (non-OC) thinking they were actually under outpatient commitment, to there being no consequences for non-adherence to the OC plan, to there being significantly more substance abusers in the OC group than in the non-OC group.

the third generation of outpatient commitment research (Leone, 2000). The best project, performed by the above research teams (combined), has been conducted on approximately 3500 individuals subjected to New York's current assisted outpatient treatment (i.e., outpatient commitment) program between 1999 and 2007 (Swartz, 2010). It has resulted in numerous publications between 2008 and 2011, which — along with the research leading up to that time — are discussed below.

Although arguably considered the strongest and most relevant research to a discussion of contemporary preventive outpatient commitment laws, these studies are limited to a single state, whose experience is not very representative. For one, New York has invested a great amount of money to fund its outpatient commitment. As a result, in many parts of the state, relatively cohesive networks of community mental health services that are able to offer services that are intensive and of an extended duration.

Opponents' Opinions about Outpatient Commitment

The main protagonists in the debate about outpatient commitment within the United States are the Treatment Advocacy Center (TAC), led by E. Fuller Torrey, which supports OC, and the Bazelon Center for Mental Health Law (Bazelon Center), which opposes it (Kahan, Braman, Monahan, Callahan, & Peters, 2010).[21] Their differences are evident down to the terms they use for this form of civil commitment. The TAC calls it "assisted outpatient treatment," invoking the image of beneficence; whereas the Bazelon Center refers to it as "involuntary outpatient commitment," emphasizing the forced nature of the intervention (Geller & Stanley, 2005b).[22] It is striking how the two advocacy centers can interpret the very same research results in completely opposite manners (see Kahan et al., 2010).

Likewise, as noted by Kisely, Campbell, Scott, Preston, and Xiao (2007, p. 12, emphasis added), "It is striking how *reviews* of the same studies can come to markedly different conclusions." It is not *surprising*, however, as research suggests that individual members of the public — and thus, even experts — differ widely in their opinions about outpatient commitment. First, attitudes differ depending on the side of the practical implementation of OC one is on. Specifically, research has found that psychiatrists (Dawson, 2005; Mullen, Dawson, & Gibbs, 2006) and patients' family members (Mullen, Gibbs, & Dawson, 2006) tend to favor the use of outpatient commitment

---

21. By way of background, the Treatment Advocacy Center's crusade appears to be driven by personal experiences. E. Fuller Torrey, its founder, is a psychiatrist who has a sister with schizophrenia; Mary Zdanowicz, former executive director of the TAC, has a sister and a brother with schizophrenia; and Jonathan Stanley, an attorney working for the TAC, has bipolar disorder (Fritz, 2006). As such, the TAC's perspective about outpatient commitment is generally consistent with that of the psychiatric field and/or family members of individuals with mental illness. The Bazelon Center operates under the tradition of Judge David L. Bazelon, the federal appeals court judge who decided several key cases in mental health law; and as such, the Center's focus is on the legal rights of those with mental illness.

22. Some opponents go so far as to categorize them as "leash laws" (Dawson, 2005), the more pejorative term used.

and to view it as beneficial, whereas those actually committed by OC and due process advocates dislike the intervention (Dawson, 2005). Further, support for outpatient commitment is related to individuals' cultural cognitive perspectives (Kahan et al., 2010). In particular, those with a worldview that endorses communitarianism (belief that individuals' interests are less important than the interests of the collective) and hierarchical ideals (belief that individuals' rights and duties are justifiably distributed based on salient, unchanging characteristics) tend to support outpatient commitment laws (Kahan et al., 2010). Conversely, those who believe in individualism (that individuals are responsible for their own success) and egalitarianism (that rights, duties, and goods should be split evenly between members) are more likely to oppose OC laws (Kahan et al., 2010).[23]

Tragedy Drives Policy

One of the biggest concerns with outpatient commitment as with changes to Virginia's civil commitment statute following the Virginia Tech massacre — is that laws often only emerge following a tragedy. As is discussed throughout this book, crisis drives policy, and this proves to be no exception with outpatient commitment. The implementation of Kendra's Law in New York — the first well-known, widely-used outpatient commitment statute — resulted from the tragic death of Kendra Webdale, who was pushed in front of a subway train by a man with schizophrenia in 1999 (Campbell, 2002; Huggins, 2004; Watnik, 2001). Just prior to Webdale's death, New York had witnessed other awful events involving people with mental illness, including the pushing of Edgar Rivera in front of a subway train, resulting in the severing of both of his legs, by a person with untreated schizophrenia, as well as the shooting of a person with mental illness swinging a sword on a passenger train by police (Watnik, 2001).

Likewise, tragedy was the impetus for court-ordered outpatient commitment reform in numerous other states. Below are just a few examples:

- In Florida, a man with schizophrenia shot and killed Seminole County Deputy Sheriff Gene Gregory and wounded two deputies, before he was shot and killed himself by law enforcement after a 13-hour standoff. The man's sister, Alice Petree, and Deputy Sheriff Gregory's widow, Linda Gregory, joined forces with Seminole County Sheriff Donald Eslinger and the Florida Sheriffs' Association to push the state legislature to develop an outpatient commitment law (Fritz, 2006; TAC, 2005).

- California established outpatient commitment through Laura's Law, named after Laura Wilcox, who, along with two other individuals, was shot and killed by a man with mental illness in Nevada County, California (Moller, 2006).

---

23. Linda Gregory and Alice Petree also provide quite a powerful tandem as crisis intervention team trainers for law enforcement officers as well, as they join together to share their compelling story.

- Michigan established Kevin's Law after 24-year-old Kevin Heisinger was beaten to death at a Kalamazoo bus station by a Vietnam veteran with a history of schizophrenia (Fritz, 2006).
- New Mexico attempted to invoke a form of Kendra's Law, after a person with mental illness was charged with killing two law enforcement officers and two other individuals (Jadrnak, 2006).

Because OC reforms so consistently follow in the wake of such heartbreaks, Kendra's Law and other similar statutes have been called "knee-jerk response[s] to a political and media-driven problem" (Campbell, 2002, p. 202). This strong emotion does not lend itself to — and usually hinders or prevents — wise decision-making. In similar fashion to Walker's (2006) admonition about crisis driving policy, Appelbaum (2001) noted, "Here, as in most circumstances, a handful of highly visible cases constitute a dubious basis for social policy" (p. 347). Indeed, as noted by Bonnie et al. (2009) following the Virginia Tech massacre, "tragedy-driven policy making is often misguided and counterproductive" (p. 793). Moreover, not only does it lead to the development of hasty policies, such events — and emotion — also enable the public and policymakers to overlook outright injustices against the entire sociocultural group to which the immediate perpetrator(s) belongs, such as in the treatment of Arab Americans following 9/11 (Slevin, 2004).

Outpatient Commitment Statutes Are Unconstitutional

Among the most blatant and concerning injustices with regard to outpatient commitment that the public is willing to overlook are allegations that OC statutes are unconstitutional (Cornwell, 2003). Petrila (2002) noted that there has been considerable debate about whether legal rights are sufficiently protected in civil commitment proceedings in general. Outpatient commitment — and particularly, preventive outpatient commitment — draw the most vehement criticisms on these grounds. Broadly speaking, some contend that outpatient commitment "appears to violate the constitutional rights to travel, to privacy, to personal dignity, to freedom from restraint and bodily integrity, to freedom of association, and to the free communication of ideas" (Allen & Smith, 2001, p. 343). More specifically, although most will concede that liberty can be justifiably limited when an individual poses an imminent danger to others or to self, civil commitment for anything less holds dangerous implications in terms of infringement of civil liberties. For example, after analyzing the 1987 American Psychiatric Association's position in endorsing outpatient commitment even in cases not exclusively limited to imminent danger, Hoge and Grottole (2000) concluded that the APA's standard supported individual liberty violations. Indeed, Campbell (2002) put it best when he concluded:

> Kendra's Law is a failure … because it ultimately places the nonviolent mentally ill in a position in which they must submit to the will of the State for fear of losing fundamental constitutional liberties. Unless Kendra's Law is reformed to address the due process concerns inherent in forcing the mentally ill to receive treatment, it will remain a prime example of how

good intentions can easily become not only bad policy, but oppressive law (p. 205).

Those who support outpatient commitment, however, have ready retorts to such assertions of illegality. First, Torrey and Zdanowicz (2001) support outpatient commitment on both humanitarian and public safety grounds, contending that "medically needed treatment should be provided in the best interest of both the individual and society" (p. 340). Torrey and Zdanowicz quoted a statement made by even a civil liberties advocate, Herschel Hardin (1993), to prove their point:

> The opposition to involuntary committal and treatment betrays a profound misunderstanding of the principle of civil liberties. Medication can free victims from their illness — free them from the Bastille of their psychoses — and restore their dignity, their free will, and the meaningful exercise of their liberties (p. 340).

In particular, since outpatient commitment standards typically require a documented history of violence or prior inpatient hospitalization to justify commitment, many argue that OC statutes stand on solid ground, even rendering forced medication for outpatients constitutional (Cornwell, 2003).

Additionally, most advocates of OC argue that commitment on mere grounds of past *history* of dangerousness (or even less) as a result of non-compliance with treatment — not even current, imminent danger — is constitutionally defensible (Geller & Stanley, 2005b). They maintain that this is based in both the state's powers of *parens patriae*, to aid those incapable of maintaining needed treatment in the community, and police power, to contain those who have previously been dangerous as a result of non-compliance with treatment (Geller & Stanley, 2005b). In fact, when an individual is so impaired that he/she cannot recognize his/her own illness, some states go so far as to characterize the individual as being a danger to him or herself (Geller & Stanley, 2005b). In such cases, Straticzuk (2000) asserted, it is *our societal duty* to intervene. Treffert (1973) noted, "In our zeal to protect basic, human freedoms ... we have created a legal climate in which mentally ill patients, and sometimes the people around them, are dying with their rights on" (p. 1041). To rectify this, as was recognized by the court in *In re Urcuyo* (2000), "Kendra's Law provides the means by which society does not have to sit idly by and watch the cycle of decompensation, dangerousness and hospitalization continually repeat itself" (Geller & Stanley, 2005b, p. 137).

Likewise, various jurisdictions have supported outpatient commitment on grounds of grave disability as well. The Washington Supreme Court, for example, determined that outpatient commitment criteria conditioned "on whether a person with mental illness 'manifests severe deterioration in routine functioning ... and is not receiving such care as is essential for his health or safety'" is constitutional (Geller & Stanley, 2005b, p. 134). The "court approved the continued hospitalization of one of the petitioners because, although his 'condition was in the process of stabilizing,' he was likely to become medication non-compliant and consequently deteriorate if released"

(Geller & Stanley, 2005b, p. 134). Overall, outpatient commitment statutes — even preventive OC statutes such as Kendra's Law — have repeatedly, successfully withstood due process and equal protection challenges in the courts (O'Connor, 2002).

Outpatient Commitment Is Coercive

Another aspect of outpatient commitment that is overlooked in the wake of tragedy is its coercive nature. As with inpatient civil commitment, outpatient commitment has been criticized for its coerciveness (Cornwell, 2003). The most controversial aspect, in many people's opinion, is the connection between commitment and forced medication. This forced drugging is viewed as a core element of outpatient commitment; it is feared that OC will merely become equivalent with forced medication in the community, if it is not already (Perlin, 2003). In contrast to inpatient commitment, OC is considered coercive primarily because of the extension of the state's power beyond the hospital into the community (Wales & Hiday, 2006). This is because outpatient commitment has primarily been implemented as a "back-end" procedure — as conditional release, i.e., as an outlet for those discharged from inpatient care to become re-acclimated to society — rather than the front-end alternative for persons in the community to ascertain treatment, as it is often touted (Petrila, Ridgely, & Borum, 2003). Thereby, it is also misleading a misinformed public. Furthermore, outpatient commitment has been criticized as coercive on grounds that it does not provide clear guidelines for the individual as to when the order ceases to exist — in this case, misleading an *un*informed *patient*.

Several articles from the Duke Mental Health Study considered patients' experiences of coercion. Swartz, Wagner, Swanson, Hiday, and Burns (2002) found that several characteristics of patients under outpatient commitment and the conditions of outpatient commitment were related to increased perceptions of coercion. In particular, they found that feelings of being coerced were more likely to be expressed by African Americans, those with substance abuse problems, those with anosognosia (lack of insight), and those with more severe symptoms. Furthermore, perceptions of coercion in outpatient commitment arrangements increased the more case managers actively attended to non-compliance issues and the longer the individual was subjected to outpatient commitment.

Persons who have been court ordered to outpatient commitment are also more likely to subjectively experience it as coercive and to report dissatisfaction with treatment. In particular, Swartz, Swanson, and Monahan (2003) found that most persons exposed to outpatient commitment did not feel it was beneficial because either they did not think they needed it or it had not made them more compliant with treatment. Likewise, Swartz et al. (2006) found that individuals exposed to outpatient commitment were more likely to have had encounters with the criminal justice system, to have perceived their experiences across multiple systems as coercive, and to have reported little satisfaction with the treatment received. Thus, many persons view outpatient commitment as ineffective, show little appreciation for its value, and/or are ambivalent towards it, at best (Swartz, Swanson, & Monahan, 2003).

Retorts to the claims of coercion begin, simply, by emphasizing that the leading case on outpatient commitment, *In re K.L.* (2004), upheld outpatient commitment because very little coercion was determined to be involved in the process (Monahan et al., 2005). Nevertheless, as noted by Appelbaum (2005), just because something is legal does not necessarily indicate that it constitutes sound policy.

Advocates of outpatient commitment also note that, despite reporting ambivalence and disdain for coercion, patients tend to appreciate, at least in retrospect, the help, structure, safety, and security that results from the intervention (Hiday & Wales, 2013). With regard to forced medication, for example, Torrey and Zdanowicz (2001) found that almost three-fourths of people who were coerced in this manner acknowledged in retrospect that it had been in their best interest. Similarly, Gardner et al. (1999) found that the majority of patients who initially believed that they did not require hospitalization modified their assessment after hospital discharge and indicated that they had actually been in need of hospital care. Nevertheless, coerced patients did not appear to be grateful for the experience of hospitalization, even if they later concluded that they had needed it (Gardner et al., 1999).

At a minimum, at least in order to preserve some semblance of patient dignity, patients should be given the opportunity to participate in the planning of their treatment, at least in some capacity. Research has shown that whether treatment is voluntary or forced, if patients perceive they had a voice in the matter they are significantly less likely to view the process as coercive (Cornwell, 2003). In turn, those who feel they have been treated fairly and given the opportunity to voice concerns are more likely to report better qualities of life and may potentially be more apt to comply with treatment regimens in the long term (O'Connor, 2002; Watson & Angell, 2007).[24] Ideally, all less coercive means would be exhausted and shown totally ineffective before resorting to such a compulsory mechanism as outpatient commitment (Appelbaum, 2001).

Deception and Coercion

Some states (e.g., New York) avoid constitutional challenges about forced medication by not formally including it in statutory language but still including it in the OC treatment plan, implying that accepting forced medication is required, even though no actions will be taken if the patient does not comply (Winick, 2003). Of course, the patient does not realize this sleight of hand. This is revealed by a North Carolina study in which most of the participants felt coerced to take psychotropic medication erroneously, believing that if they did not it would be forcibly administered

---

24. Cornwell (2003) lauds Kendra's Law as an exemplary model for giving a voice to patients in developing their treatment plans. This is despite concerns that Kendra's Law may too easily authorize use of involuntary civil commitment and that treatment orders can be enacted with the outpatient in absentia. If this is giving someone the opportunity to voice their opinion about treatment options, one can only imagine how other states' outpatient commitment programs operate (Perlin, 2003).

(Cornwell, 2003).[25] This apparent deception raises questions on ethical grounds. Some allege that OC statutes that mislead patients into mistakenly believing the false implications that they will be forced to take medications if they are noncompliant "devalues the individuals being served, and undermines the physician-patient relationship ... A strategy that relies on patient misinformation to foster its success violates ethics principles, the integrity of the physician-patient relationship, and the notion of informed consent" (Hoge & Grottole, 2000, p. 167). Thus, deception can prove to be coercive when there are implications that medication is required, and this in turn can undermine trust and interfere with treatment goals (Winick, 2003).

Enforcement

Another criticism of outpatient commitment that seems to be the opposite of coercion is that OC treatment plans cannot be enforced. As a civil law mechanism of forced treatment, "[T]he law's only 'teeth' should patients fail to comply with a judicial order for outpatient treatment [is] to permit them to be picked up and detained for up to 72 hours to determine whether they me[e]t inpatient commitment criteria" (Appelbaum, 2005, p. 791).[26] However, even this aspect of OC has become increasingly coercive. Although it was true historically that OC laws lacked "teeth," some courts have begun to utilize criminal contempt of court citations to keep outpatients compliant with treatment regimens (Perlin, 2003) — including compliance with medication, which is not always included in the formal statute and, thus, some argue should be off limits to court scrutiny.[27]

Coercion Is Anti-Therapeutic and Disempowering

In its coerciveness and deceptiveness, outpatient commitment also appears to be becoming increasingly anti-therapeutic and disempowering of patients. Again, Allen and Smith (2001) articulate it best when they note:

> At its core, outpatient commitment requires a person, on pain of entering police custody and undergoing rehospitalization, to comply with the treatment decisions of another person, undermining the fundamental right of a competent, nondangerous person to determine the course of his/her treatment (p. 343).

In so doing, they argue that it may actually push persons with mental illness away from turning to mental health treatment providers for help (Allen & Smith, 2001).

---

25. Cornwell (2003), however, does not suggest that outpatient commitment is anti-therapeutic because even those involuntarily hospitalized believe their treatment has helped them and are satisfied, and, at discharge, those who have been medicated against their will report that they believe the decision to do so was the right one.

26. This is despite the fact that some OC statutes like Kendra's Law explicitly stipulate "that an order of assisted outpatient treatment shall not be grounds for involuntary civil commitment" (Perlin, 2003, p. 196).

27. Higher courts have not always upheld such tactics.

Its Coerciveness Is Not Balanced by Its Benefits

It is also argued that, while outpatient commitment appears to be becoming increasingly coercive, and in many cases, deceptive, it is not doing much to improve patients' lives to justify this level of state control. Campbell (2002, p. 203) cogently articulated this tension:

> In places like the District of Columbia, where U.S. Marshals will arrest individuals who do not comply with their outpatient commitment programs and civilly commit them as inpatients, the mentally ill live in fear of being confined in the district mental hospital.... 'There is a kind of terror' among the mentally ill, who often do not understand the law well enough to realize that seeking mental health treatment does not automatically mean involuntary inpatient commitment or the forced administration of drugs. Thus, the punitive threat of statutes like Kendra's Law hang over the heads of the mentally ill and coerce them into submitting to a treatment plan that they may not believe is in their best interest ... Aside from forcibly medicating the mentally ill, what else is being done to better their lives? In particular, what is being done to help the most vulnerable and desperately ill individuals?[28]

However, even some critics acknowledge that OC can do more good than harm, both at the aggregate and individual levels. For example, Perlin (2003), who disagrees with some components of outpatient commitment, does believe that there are redeeming aspects, such as the publicity surrounding the law potentially enticing more persons with mental illnesses to seek treatment. He also concedes that utilization of a judicial process with representation by legal counsel can ensure procedural protections, due process, and fairness.

Because it is on the topic of OC's coercion that supporters and opponents most strongly disagree, we now detail supporters' responses to that claim.

Supporters' Responses to Outpatient Commitment Being Coercive

Coerced Treatment Is Better Than No Treatment

Proponents of outpatient commitment, however, are adamant that coerced care is less damaging than being left untreated. For example, past president of the American Psychiatric Association, Sharfstein (2005) argues that there is such a thing as "caring coercion" (p. 3) — that at times, sufficient coercion must be applied in order to provide treatment in the best interests of the patient. Indeed, "the consequences of non-treat-

---

28. Campbell (2002) indicates that under then New York Governor George Pataki, funding for supportive housing for persons with mental illnesses was not replenished, and Pataki's administration commenced to close down hospitals, resulting in persons such as Andrew Goldstein being forced into the streets homeless and psychotic. Campbell (2002) contends that anywhere from 33% to 50% of homeless persons are mentally ill. "However, Kendra's Law fails to address the greater problem of the homeless mentally ill[;] [i]f we are to seriously address the issue of violence among the mentally ill, it is necessary to do more than simply drug them and put them back on the streets without any resources and support to help them get well" (Campbell, 2002, p. 204).

ment are all too well documented: relapse symptoms, re-hospitalization, homelessness, arrests, victimization, suicide, and episodes of violence" (Zdanowicz, 2003–2004, p. 1). The effects of outpatient commitment on each of these will be discussed below. Ultimately, Geller and Stanley (2005b, p. 138) noted, "The abrogation of the opportunity for treatment is a much greater impediment to autonomy and self-determination than is the denial of treatment in the name of sustaining the faux liberty of a psychotic state" (p. 138).

Outpatient Commitment Increases Treatment Exposure

Supporters of OC also argue that outpatient commitment, despite being coercive, does increase service engagement and medication compliance. In Ohio, outpatient commitment more than doubled the average attendance at outpatient psychiatric appointments (from 5.7 to 13.0 appointments per year) and day treatment sessions (from 23 to 60 sessions per year) (Munetz, Grande, Kleist, & Peterson, 1996). Likewise, in an Iowa study in the late 1990s, OC was related to heightened rates of treatment compliance (up to 80 percent) by patients (Rohland, 1998). More recently, in New York, the percent of patients in the group who demonstrated "good" service engagement increased by 50 percent (from 41 percent before to 62 percent after implementation of Kendra's Law) (New York State Office of Mental Health, 2005). Furthermore, among assisted outpatient treatment (ROT) recipients (i.e., those subjected to OC), there was an 89 percent increase in participation in case management services from three years prior to AOT compared to the time period while in AOT (Pataki & Carpinello, 2005). In the largest study to date, involving more than 3500 individuals receiving court-ordered outpatient treatment between 1999 and 2007, outpatient commitment increased the likelihood of receiving and engaging in any form of case management services — as rated by case managers — both in the initial six months and in the subsequent six-month renewal of the court order (Swartz et al., 2010).

In terms of medication compliance, application of outpatient commitment has had similar effects across multiple decades. In North Carolina, in the late 1980s, 70 percent of patients receiving assisted outpatient treatment accepted medication, compared to only one-third of patients not under AOT (Hiday & Scheid-Cook, 1987). In a second Duke study in the late 1990s and early 2000s, patients who received OC plus consistent community services for more than six months were more likely to be compliant with psychiatric treatment compared to those who did not receive such services. Similarly, in New York, commitment to AOT resulted in a doubling of "good" adherence to medication (from 34 percent before to 69 percent after enactment of Kendra's Law) (New York State Office of Mental Health, 2005). Further, among those committed to AOT, the likelihood of possessing medication for 80 percent or more of the days in any month increased by 50 percent from prior to OC to the initial six-month period of commitment and by 90 percent by the time they reached the end of the six-month renewal (Swartz et al., 2010). Additionally, when comparing rates of recommended medication possession between those in New York who were involuntarily committed via an outpatient commitment order, those who received voluntary "enhanced" services, and those who received neither such intervention, the greatest increase in medication compliance was among the involuntarily committed group (Busch, Wilder, Van Dorn, Swartz, & Swanson, 2010). In particular, the percent of those in AOT who showed 80 percent or better medication compliance increased by 31 percent to 40 percent over time, followed by only a 15 percent to 22 percent increase in voluntarily treated patients (Busch et al., 2010).

Outpatient commitment even appears to increase the likelihood of engaging in continued treatment after OC ends. In Arizona, for example, 71 percent of OC patients voluntarily maintained treatment up to six months after their orders expired, whereas virtually none of those who were not court-ordered to treatment did so (Van Putten, Santiago, & Berren, 1988). Approximately the same percentage, about 75 percent, remained in treatment on a voluntary basis in Iowa upon expiration of the OC order (Rohland, 1998). Assisted outpatient treatment in New York, however, exhibited a slightly more complex relationship to long-term voluntary compliance with treatment. Specifically, individuals who continued with intensive case management services even after their AOT term *of six months or less* expired maintained medication compliance and reduction in hospitalization; those who did not continue these services after their AOT order expired did not (Van Dorn et al., 2010). Conversely, those who were court-ordered to *longer than six months* of AOT maintained medication compliance and reductions in hospitalization, whether or not they continued intensive services (Van Dorn et al., 2010).

Treatment, Even By Outpatient Commitment, Leads to Better Quality of Life

Several studies have found that individuals with severe psychiatric illness who are committed to treatment as outpatients enjoy a better quality of life as evidenced by several rough indicators. For example, per case managers' reports, at least 10 percent more patients under Kendra's Law were able to manage their own personal finances and medications, as well as to effectively handle conflict, participate in social activities, and ask for help when needed after being court-ordered to outpatient commitment compared to before OC (Swartz, Swanson, Steadman, Robbins, & Monahan, 2009). Rates of self-harm have substantially and consistently declined by 55 percent there as well (New York State Office of Mental Health, 2005; Pataki & Carpinello, 2005; Swartz et al., 2009).

Furthermore, several studies have reported a decline in homelessness among those under OC. The Duke Mental Health Study, for example, found that committed outpatients who received consistent, frequent community services for longer than six months experienced a decline in homelessness (Compton et al., 2003), compared to those who did not receive this combination of services.[29] In New York, too, in a study conducted in 2005, individuals subjected to Kendra's Law experienced a 74 percent decline in homelessness as compared to before AOT (New York State Office of Mental

---

29. Interestingly, this effect vanished if frequent community services were not provided and/or if OC combined with consistent community services was only provided for a shorter period of time (Compton et al., 2003).

Health, 2005). Follow-up research on the same patients in 2009 still found a decrease in homelessness (between a 33 percent to 42 percent decline) compared to before being placed on AOT (Swartz et al., 2009). However, it is noteworthy that the rate of improvement had declined.

Likewise, criminal victimization has been reported to have declined as a result of being under outpatient commitment in multiple studies. In the Duke Mental Health Study of the late 1990s, individuals with severe psychiatric illnesses who were not on outpatient commitment were almost twice as likely to be victimized (42 percent) as were outpatient commitment subjects (24 percent). The authors suggested that "outpatient commitment reduces criminal victimization through improving treatment adherence, decreasing substance abuse, and diminishing violent incidents" that may evoke retaliation (Hiday, Swartz, Swanson, Borum, & Wagner, 2002, p. 1409).

Outpatient Commitment Is Better Than Inpatient Commitment or Criminal Justice Confinement

The argument that outpatient commitment is preferable to inpatient civil commitment or criminal justice confinement is grounded in two factors: economics and degree of coercion. First, policymakers and the public tend to prefer outpatient commitment due to the fact that it is more economical than either form of institutional confinement, especially when criminal justice incarceration involves attempting to handle persons with serious mental illness who are decompensating (Esposito, Westhead, & Berko, 2008). Torrey and Zdanowicz (2001) and their colleague Jon Stanley (J. Stanley, personal communication, June 23, 2007) contend that outpatient commitment should actually lower expenses overall by resulting in fewer costly hospitalizations and less incarcerations, thereby benefiting all patients.

Outpatient commitment is also "better" than either form of institutional confinement in that it is less intrusive by definition (e.g., outpatient versus inpatient, community treatment versus institutional confinement). Although Saks (2003) maintains that coercion and infringement on freedom certainly accompany outpatient commitment, it is much less so than with involuntary hospitalization (see also Pandya [2007] and Perlin [2003]). Furthermore, Pandya (2007) adds that the reality is that doctors and judges are much more willing to release an individual who meets the criteria for civil commitment into the community if there is some legal mechanism in place to assist in ensuring compliance with treatment plans. Otherwise, without the option for outpatient commitment, all people qualifying for civil commitment would be committed to the hospital, and as already stated, outpatient commitment is preferable to hospital commitment.[30]

---

30. According to Geller and Stanley (2005b), "As judges are understandably hesitant to find individuals to be an imminent danger to themselves or others and then order their release to the community at the same hearing, an effective outpatient commitment statute must include a non-danger

Outpatient Commitment Results in Less Inpatient Commitment or Criminal Justice Confinement

A sizeable body of research has accrued over several decades on the effects of out-patient commitment on later hospitalizations, arrests, and criminal justice involve-ment. Overall, this research suggests that use of outpatient commitment results in less of these outcomes for an individual over the long-run. For example, according to eight studies across nearly 25 years, the average number of hospital admissions, per patient, per year, decreased by between 25 percent (in New York; Swartz et al., 2010) to 77 percent (in Iowa; Rohland, 1998) from before to during outpatient com-mitment. Likewise, when hospitalized, the length of hospitalizations in New York tended to decrease by 39 percent at six months and 44 percent at 12 months into outpatient commitment (Swartz et al., 2009; Swartz et al., 2010).

With regard to arrest, outpatient commitment (OC) also appears to reduce the arrest rate, both between groups (e.g., OC patients versus non-OC patients) and within individuals (e.g., rates of OC patients' arrests prior to OC versus during/after OC). In North Carolina, among high-risk individuals with a history of multiple hos-pital admissions, arrests, and/or violence in the preceding year, those exposed to long-term, intensive outpatient commitment had a 12 percent arrest rate; whereas those who received services without a court order had a 47 percent arrest rate (Swan-son et al., 2001). This represents a 74 percent lower arrest rate for those with a court order than those without a court order. Likewise, in New York, OC patients had nearly two-thirds lower arrest rates than those not under an OC court order (Gilbert et al., 2010), and the risk of arrest for those never having received assisted outpatient treatment was double that of the AOT group during and shortly after being ordered to outpatient commitment (Link, Epperson, Perron, Castille, & Yang, 2011). Fur-thermore, following those in AOT from three years prior to outpatient commitment through their performance while on OC, their arrest rate fell from 30 percent to only 5 percent, constituting an 82 percent decline in overall arrests for this population (New York State Office of Mental Health, 2005; Pataki & Carpinello, 2005). A fol-low-up study found that those receiving AOT were nearly three times less likely to be arrested, and nearly nine times less likely to be arrested for a violent offense specifi-cally, in the period during and after AOT as compared to prior to AOT (Link et al., 2011).

Finally, since incarceration can result from arrest, it follows that those exposed to outpatient commitment also experienced a reduction in incarcerations. In particular, New York OC patients realized an 87 percent decrease in the rate of any incarceration from three years prior to OC (23 percent) to during OC (3 percent) (New York State Office of Mental Health, 2005; Pataki & Carpinello, 2005). Further, when incarcerated, the number of days spent jailed declined by 72 percent for those persons committed via OC in Florida (Esposito et al., 2008).

---

based eligibility standard, or at least a dangerous standard more broadly defined than the inpatient standard" (p. 128).

It is important to note, however, that outpatient commitment alone (i.e., without additional intensive case management services) is not always sufficient to bring about the aforementioned changes in hospitalization and/or criminal justice involvement. Particularly in the New York and North Carolina studies, researchers tended to find that these differences were only evident when intensive services were received for an extended period of time. Thus, these positive changes discussed above — such as fewer subsequent psychiatric hospitalizations and arrests (Pollack, McFarland, Mahler, & Kovas, 2005) — were not found in every study.

Outpatient Commitment Reduces Violence

Research on outpatient commitment recipients has found a reduction in violence in general regardless of whether it is the violence itself or the media coverage of violence that is the actual cause of mental illness stigma, and regardless of whether outpatient commitment could prevent isolated acts of serious violence. In the Duke mental health study, individuals in long-term (i.e., longer than six months), court-ordered assisted outpatient treatment had a significantly lower rate of violence than individuals in the same intensity of treatment without the court order (Swanson et al., 2001). This was true even of a group categorized as "seriously violent": 37.5 percent of those in long-term AOT committed a violent act, compared to 63.3 percent of those who were not in long-term AOT.[31] Similarly, those in the long-term, court-ordered AOT group showed a 36 percent lower rate of violence than the group in court-ordered AOT for less than six months. More recently, a study of New York City committed outpatients found that, despite having a more violent history than the control group of other outpatients, were four times less likely to commit serious violence (Phelan et al., 2010).

Likewise, New York outpatient committed persons showed a 44 percent decrease in harmful behaviors from three years prior to their court order to at least six months into their OC (New York State Office of Mental Health, 2005; Pataki & Carpinello, 2005). In particular, these outpatients demonstrated a 47 percent decrease in physical harm to another person, 43 percent decrease in threats of physical harm to another person, as well as a 55 percent decrease in violence to self (i.e., suicide attempt) and 46 percent decrease in violence to property, respectively.

With OC supporters' responses to OC being coercive now covered, we return to opponents' other opinions about OC.

Outpatient Commitment Is Stigmatizing

Once again, similar to inpatient commitment, outpatient commitment has been criticized as contributing to the belief among the public in the false causal link between mental illness and dangerousness (Cornwell, 2003). In fact, Allen and Smith (2001) contented champions of outpatient commitment, like Torrey and Zdanowicz at the Treatment Advocacy Center, capitalize on public fears about mental illness and violence, selling books and building national campaigns for interventions of their

---

31. Even among this high risk group, the acts committed were relatively minor acts of violence.

choice. By design, exposure to these campaigns captures the public's attention, but it also serves to intensify fears and exacerbate stigma. As a result of fear-inducing publicity, the general population and politicians may rise to action against "the mentally ill" — in this case, by enacting outpatient commitment statutes — even though the very basis of involuntary commitment, the notion that society can predict who may become a danger in the future, is faulty (Couch & Finlayson, 2007); the vast majority of individuals with mental illness will never commit an act of violence (Appelbaum, 2001). Meanwhile, the public continues to be apathetic toward and neglects the non-violent people with mental illness (Karasch, 2003), as evidenced by the paucity of public funds allocated to the mental health system.

Furthermore, outpatient commitment is expected to have a potentially larger contribution to stigma than inpatient commitment (Perlin, 2003) for two reasons. First, by being an economical alternative to inpatient commitment, more people may be drawn into the public mental health arena — and stigmatized — than would otherwise be, if OC statutes did not exist (Perlin, 2003). And, by being in the community, OC patients are more visible to the public than are inpatients.

Torrey and Zdanowicz (2001) counter that the greatest cause of mental illness stigma is not the media but the violent outbursts committed by persons with mental illnesses; they contend that outpatient commitment provides a mechanism for reducing such violent episodes. Cornwell (2003) falls somewhere between these two perspectives. While he agrees that persons with mental illnesses, as long as compliant with medication and treatment regimens, are no more violent than persons without mental illnesses, he is concerned about that small percentage who are not compliant who might commit an act of violence; he believes outpatient commitment can allow for intervention to prevent decompensation, thus serving to thwart the violence that leads to worsening stigma for persons with mental illnesses. Ultimately, however, it is not clear, even if Loughner, Holmes, or Goldstein met outpatient commitment requirements, that OC would have prevented their acts (Appelbaum, 2001).

Outpatient Commitment Is Discriminatory

Another controversial aspect of outpatient commitment — similar to inpatient commitment — is whether or not it is discriminatory based on race. Swanson et al. (2009) examined this issue with regard to outpatient commitment in New York. Specifically, between 1999 and 2008, 35 percent of individuals with outpatient commitment orders in New York were African Americans, while making up only 17 percent of the state population (Swanson et al., 2009). Conversely, whites make up 61 percent of the New York population but only 33 percent of outpatient commitments. Even after controlling for racial breakdown in the population, an African American is about five times more likely to be ordered to OC than is a white; in counties and years with particularly high overrepresentation of black service recipients, this rate increased to nine times beyond whites (Swanson et al., 2009).

However, Swanson et al. (2009) concluded that this difference did not represent a racial "disparity" (i.e., due to systemic, structural, or clinician bias) per se. First, when factors such as poverty, prevalence of mental illness in the community, and rates of treatment were controlled, the differential rate of outpatient commitment became insignificant. Moreover, the researchers reasoned that individuals who are considered for outpatient commitment tend to be drawn from a population in which blacks are "naturally" overrepresented (e.g., psychiatric patients with multiple civil commitments in public hospitals).[32] Finally, while acknowledging that such differences must be considered in the context of the history of oppression, institutional confinement, and relegation of blacks to the public system of care, Swanson et al. (2009) argued that one's opinion of fairness depends on one's view about treatment: if one focuses on the coercive nature and other negative aspects of outpatient commitment, then African Americans may be considered disadvantaged because they are disproportionately exposed to this intervention. On the other hand, if one's perspective is that "more treatment is better," then it could be argued that whites are at a disadvantage.

Outpatient Commitment Depends on the Availability of Services

While court mandates may serve as leverage to push some toward treatment, a court order alone, without adequate services, is insufficient to ensure positive results. In fact, it is likely to ultimately fail, as clinical stability has little to do with the wording of new statutes, no matter how politically expedient they seem at the time (Perlin, 2003; Ridgely, Borum, & Petrila, 2001). In an evidence-based assessment of existing research, Ridgely et al. (2001) observed that merely making a statutory modification in criteria for involuntary outpatient commitment without substantial investment in the treatment services' infrastructure is futile (see also Perlin, 2003; Swartz et al., 2001). Moreover, involuntary outpatient commitment "statutes must require *access* to treatment to have the desired effect" (Petrila et al., 2003, p.165, emphasis added). Laws alone do not guarantee that adequate mental health services will be available or accessible (Flug, 2003).

Among the most consistent research findings is that the keys to the effectiveness of outpatient commitment are the availability of intensive treatment services and supervision for a prolonged period of time (Borum, 1999; Swanson et al., 1997, 2000, 2001; Wagner et al., 2003). This is largely a function of case managers' abilities to identify those at greatest risk and, most importantly, to access and leverage resources, including inpatient hospitalization (Swanson et al., 1997). And all of this "requires a substantial commitment of treatment resources to be effective" (Swartz, et al., 1999, p. 1968).

However, most communities do not enjoy such expansive mental health treatment services. Most community mental health services are not adequately funded, even when they are inundated with clients (McKinney, 2006; Petrila et al., 2003). Indeed,

---

32. The authors attributed this overrepresentation to greater rates of mental illness among African Americans. They did not note that blacks may be over-diagnosed and/or that there may be a lower threshold for blacks to be exposed to coercive measures than whites.

this is such a truism that even the Bazelon Center and the Treatment Advocacy Center agree on this point. The Bazelon Center estimates that state spending on treatment for individuals with serious mental illness is a third less today than it was in the 1950s, once numbers are adjusted for inflation and population growth (Winerip, 1999); Torrey and Zdanowicz (2001) acknowledge that public mental health treatment resources are inadequate in almost every state (see National Alliance on Mental Illness *Grading the States report*, 2009).

Without a doubt, mental health treatment services are overextended and underfunded. Add to this the wider net cast by outpatient commitment, i.e., the tendency to commit more individuals to treatment in the community than would have been committed to a more restrictive, more expensive state hospital (Saks, 2003). This was evident in New York, as the overall service volume for community mental health agencies increased by 400 percent between 1999 and 2007, and there were indicators suggesting that patients were shifted from voluntary services before to involuntary outpatient commitment after enactment of Kendra's Law (Swanson et al., 2010).[33]

Aside from the concern about financial expenditures, many are troubled by the likelihood of having to "rob Peter to pay Paul" (Swanson et al., 2010).[34] Specifically, the fear is that, with only so many resources to go around, others who have not come to the attention of authorities due to problematic behavior may have their treatment delayed or do without, potentially resulting in them decompensating (Torrey & Zdanowicz, 2001). Although some argue that the funds merely follow the greatest need (Wagner et al., 2003) — and some suggest that opposing this redistribution of funds implies that involuntary patients are less deserving and voluntary patients are more deserving recipients (Torrey & Zdanowicz, 2001) — there is an inherent justice issue raised by this dynamic.

Again, New York's experience is informative in this regard. In the first three years of the implementation of outpatient commitment, despite a doubling of services available, most of these resources were directed toward individuals under outpatient commitment, to the detriment of voluntary care seekers (e.g., not receiving desired services, having services they had been receiving discontinued) (Swanson et al., 2010). However, beyond the first three years, services expanded for both involuntary and voluntary patients, suggesting that the extra funding earmarked for outpatient commitment actually benefited all patients in the long run.

They Asked for Help But Did Not Receive It

By definition, a discussion of involuntary commitment — whether inpatient or outpatient — tends to focus on coercion. However, sadly, many individuals

---

33. Other studies do not support the net-widening hypothesis (Wales & Hiday, 2006).

34. A slightly more optimistic euphemism is queue jumping (Rosenheck, 2000), or that giving priority access to one targeted population may simply displace others who also need services, rather than completely taking the resources intended for another.

who we, as a society, in retrospect angrily conclude should have been "committed" actually asked for help but did not receive it.

Andrew Goldstein on January 3, 1999, killed Kendra Webdale by pushing her in front of a subway train in New York. Afterwards, he became the impetus for involuntary treatment. The irony is that Goldstein had *asked* repeatedly for treatment and support services. Yet, the state repeatedly turned him away (Flug, 2003; Appelbaum, 2001). "Goldstein had *begged* for help," Campbell (2002, p. 204, emphasis added) noted. "In all 13 of his hospitalizations, he had voluntarily checked himself into psychiatric hospitals and asked to be given psychotropic drugs" (Campbell, 2002, p. 204).

Indeed, the details of the weeks leading up to Kendra Webdale's death — and the extent to which Goldstein was failed by the system — are haunting (Winerip, 1999):

- On November 20, 1998, a month and a half before the events of January 3, Goldstein entered the emergency room, requesting hospitalization. He reported he was hearing voices, his brain had been removed and he had been inhabited by people. Goldstein was unable to explain why his brain had been removed, but he said the voices were warning him that something would happen; he was unable to cope. He had a history of psychosis when off his medication.

- He was hospitalized from November 24 to December 15. Ostensibly upon admission, his bizarre delusions were clearly documented:

  At various times, he had told psychiatrists that he was turning purple, that he had shrunk six to eight inches, that he had lost his neck, had developed an oversized penis because of contaminated food and that a homosexual man named Larry was stealing his excrement from the toilet "through interpolation" then eating it with a knife and fork. The voices seemed so real, so relentless, that on Nov. 24 a psychiatrist wrote, "He requested eyeglasses so that he will find the people talking to him" (pp. 43–44).

- Records reflect that two weeks into his three-week hospitalization, he was considered to be "disorganized, thought-disordered ... talking to himself ... very delusional" (p. 45). However, under intense financial pressure of managed care to discharge psychiatric patients, Goldstein was only one week later released with a seven days' supply of medication and a piece of paper informing him to seek counseling at a community mental health center.

- As had been the case in the past, by late December, he began to miss appointments, and shortly thereafter, he ceased his medication entirely.

- On December 26, a mental health worker mailed a form letter requesting that Goldstein phone the clinic by January 6, 1999, or else his case would be closed.

- On January 3, 1999, at 5:06 P.M., the N train pulled into the station at 23rd Street and Broadway. As Goldstein later wrote in his confession: "I felt a sensation, like something was entering me.... I got the urge to push, shove or sidekick. As the train was coming, the feeling disappeared and came back.... I pushed the woman who had blond hair" (p. 45).[35]

Likewise, in the days leading up to Julio Perez pushing Edgar Rivera in front of an oncoming subway train, Perez expressed desires to be hospitalized, but his recommended hospitalization by caseworkers was passed over by psychiatrists, and his attempts to re-continue his medication were thwarted by a canceled Medicaid card. On the very day of the tragic incident, Perez, an Army veteran, even made a last ditch effort to seek help at the emergency room of a Veteran's Administration Hospital but to no avail. Some five hours later, Rivera would be pushed into the path of the oncoming train (Bernstein, 1999).

Heung-Sui Cho and James Holmes,[36] too, voluntarily sought treatment initially. Cho was ultimately ordered to undergo outpatient commitment less than a year and a half before the Virginia Tech tragedy, but because of lack of clear policy in the state statute, there was no mechanism to make sure he complied with treatment. He, like Goldstein, stopped attending his sessions and eventually deteriorated, culminating in the events of April 16, 2007 (Virginia Tech Review Panel, 2007).

The secondary "safety net" of their respective universities' threat assessment teams also failed Cho, Holmes, and Loughner. All came to the attention of university administration as potential dangers, but to no avail.

- Numerous professors and students expressed concern about Cho's behavior, and his case was even referred to the school's Care Team, consisting of, among others, top administrators for various student services, which reviews cases of students with behavioral problems. However, they took no substantive action (Virginia Tech Review Panel, 2007).

- Loughner had frequent contacts with campus police in the year prior to the Arizona mass murder in January 2011 (Barry, 2011). Less than six months prior to the events, a school administrator held a meeting with Loughner and his mother. Not long after this meeting, he was informed by campus police that he had been suspended, and he was sent a letter indicating that he must present documentation from a mental health professional that he was not a threat before he could be readmitted. No further action—by the university or by Loughner—was taken.

---

35. In October 2006, after several attempts at justice, Andrew Goldstein entered into a plea bargain that would send him to prison for 23 years to be followed by five years of supervised release (*New York Post* Editorial Board, 2006).

36. Based on currently available information, it appears that Holmes' psychiatric treatment was insufficient to overcome barriers in order to *keep* him in treatment (e.g., to find another psychiatrist in the community after he dropped out of his doctoral program).

- Holmes' psychiatrist contacted the campus threat assessment team, indicating she believed him to be a danger, in June 2012. However, he dropped out before the team had a chance to convene (Harris, 2012). The team did not call local police, despite procedural recommendations to develop an active risk management plan and "possibl[y] liaison with local police to compare red flags" (Kane, Landrock, & Ferrugia, 2012).

It is easy for us — as a society and as individuals — to demonize, to hate, people who could commit such acts. It is understandable to be frightened by the idea that someone could harm us, or one of our loved ones, so unexpectedly and without provocation. We are angered that Goldstein and Cho would stop treatment. Although, this was undoubtedly due to cognitive disorganization and anosognosia of untreated mental illness for which they had previously asked for help. It was likely also related to a sense of resignation and learned helplessness from having been turned away — for Goldstein, at least, many times — due to an underfunded and overextended mental health system. As Winerip (1999) characterized Goldstein's situation, "This was like a bad joke — that a man so sick, with his history, would be sent into the community with so little support" (p. 45). But these events were no jokes. They were tragedies.

It is easy for us to blame — and even be angry at — the mental health system and/or the mental health professionals who "should have seen this coming." However, as stated cogently by David Kaczynski (2012) — the brother of Theodore Kaczynski, otherwise known as "The Unabomber," who also suffers from mental illness — who has frequently asked what he, as Ted's brother, could have done to "see it coming":

> Hindsight is always 20/20. It's easy to say, in the aftermath of a horrific tragedy, that someone should have done something to help these troubled men before they turned violent. But … there are no easy answers that jump out from these tragedies. Most people with mental illness are not at all dangerous. Most people who indulge violent fantasies or who make veiled threats at some point in their lives never act on them. So how do we distinguish between the merely troubled person and someone who is likely to carry out violence?

The task of prediction is not easy or even possible with any degree of accuracy (Couch & Finlayson, 2007). What is also not easy is looking at our own role — as a public, who is responsible for voicing our concerns and to force the hand of legislators to put money where it is needed, in the mental health system — in situations such as this. Again, Kaczynski (2012) notes in response to the Holmes' Colorado massacre:

> [B]y ignoring the reality of mental illness — by assuming as a matter of ideology that just about everyone is a free, autonomous actor entirely responsible for their own actions — we effectively absolve ourselves from

any responsibility to the next group of victims. And that is being irresponsible ... We need to embark on a conversation that doesn't immediately default to ideology but rather one that takes serious measure of
the human costs of untreated mental illness.

We are left with millions of unanswered questions in the wake of these incidents.
Could coercing these individuals to "take their medication" via an outpatient
commitment law have prevented these unnecessary deaths? Probably not. This
was proven by Cho and Virginia Tech. Outpatient commitment without intensive
mental health treatment and specially trained case managers — whose jobs it is
to locate their clients, determine the reason for their noncompliance, and assist
them to their appointments — would be ineffective. Could stricter gun control
for individuals with mental illness have thwarted these tragedies? This is often
the first solution people turn to (Hammack, 2011). With an issue this complex,
there is no single answer. These are questions that can only be adequately addressed in an open community dialogue.

Conclusion

Inpatient Commitment

America has long demonstrated a desire to banish from its view the "social rabble"
and undesirables, including persons with mental illnesses (Austin & Irwin, 2001;
Rothman, 1971). For centuries, such exclusion came in the form of geographic displacement and institutionalization in asylums (Gilligan, 2001). Traditional, restrictive,
inpatient civil commitment statutes, such as the Lanterman-Petris-Short Act in California, were enacted with the intention of protecting civil liberties. However, ironically, they actually have ended up depriving individuals of their freedom (Karasch,
2003). Although a mechanism of civil law by nature, with the focus of statutes over
the last fifty years focusing on dangerousness, it increasingly blurs the line between
the civil and criminal justice systems, between the state's — and in particular, law enforcement's — police power and duty of *parens patriae*.

Due to restricted access to treatment, more and more individuals with mental illnesses find themselves propelled into the criminal justice system (Lamb & Weinberger,
2005). Such criminalization of persons with mental illness is doubly stigmatizing;
their status is damaged not only because of mental illness but due to the criminal
record as well. Such inherent contradictions lie at the very heart of the controversy
surrounding involuntary, civil commitment.

The criticisms of civil commitment are many, as outlined in this chapter. Primary
among them is that it is a coercive and, thus, anti-therapeutic mechanism that actually
discourages individuals from seeking treatment voluntarily in the future. Others
argue that it is discriminatory and stigmatizing, contributing to the inaccurate belief
that people with mental illness are violent and unpredictable. What's more, civil com-

mitment is based on the false premise that mental health professionals — and, by extension, the courts — can predict who may become a danger in the future (Couch & Finlayson, 2007).

One proposed alternative is the use of outpatient commitment, instead of inpatient commitment. Certainly, it is less invasive than hospitalization and, as such, it does not involve the same level of coercion. But could outpatient commitment have prevented the tragedies in Arizona and New York? From Cho, we know a poorly managed outpatient commitment system could not.

Outpatient Commitment

Outpatient commitment has been proposed as a "better" alternative to the more invasive form of civil commitment, involuntary hospitalization. However, outpatient commitment shares many of the same criticisms as inpatient civil commitment: it is a coercive, anti-therapeutic, discriminatory, stigmatizing, and it based on the false premise that we can predict who will act out in the future. Others focus on the fact that, at least with outpatient commitment, its success hinges upon the availability and quality of mental health services in the community, while these services are notorious for being fragmented, overextended, and underfunded (Sirica, 2000).[37]

Advocates of outpatient commitment maintain that coerced treatment is better than its alternative: no treatment, inpatient commitment, and/or criminal justice confinement. As noted by the Treatment Advocacy Center:

> They live on the streets and eat out of garbage cans. They are periodically jailed. Some are a clear danger to themselves or others. We believe that the public should not have to wait for services to improve while vulnerable persons and the public are at risk (Torrey & Zdanowicz, 2001, p. 339).

Those advocates point to the research literature which, although criticized for its flaws, finds that outpatient commitment is related to a variety of positive outcomes. These benefits include heightened compliance with treatment (both medication and case management services), reduced hospitalization, better quality of life (e.g., less self-harm, homelessness, and victimization) and reduced rates of involvement with the criminal justice system (e.g., arrest and/or incarceration).

Even if one concedes that these positive outcomes are "fact" — which, as discussed while critiquing the research literature, is far from certain, given the inherent selection bias and other methodological issues involved — there is still a need to consider the humanistic issues of patients' sense of empowerment and self-determination. To ensure effectiveness, Sirica (2000) argues, "The policies must ... mak[e] sure that the people who are subject to these actions believe that they have been treated fairly and with concern for their well-being" (p. 10). As such, evaluation research should not only consider utilization of services and reductions in violence, arrests, incarcerations,

---

37. Of course, if there were sufficient resources in place to begin with, the need for such legal mechanisms as outpatient commitment would be minimal.

and the like; it is also important to assess satisfaction with treatment, quality of life, and risk management (Geller & Stanley, 2005a).

Philosopher John Rawls' (1971) concept of "veil of ignorance" is illustrative in this context. In delineating his theory of justice, Rawls posits that someone engaged in trying to design the optimal social contract would not know where he/she stood in society (Jedicke, 1997). They would not know "their class position or social status, their natural talents, abilities, intelligence or strength, and what their plan for a good life" (Jedicke, 1997) might be in designing such a contract, nor would they know their disabilities. Indeed, if those involved in planning and implementing civil commitment — e.g., legislators, judges, mental health professionals — would heed Rawls' warning and recognize the fact that they, too, could be vulnerable to mental illness and even come under the control of the state, civil commitment in policy and practice might be much more empathic and humane. Of course, if you yourself did not know your status within society, how would you want such policies and practices carried out? Would you be more concerned about possible infringements on civil liberties or public safety? Would you be more concerned about being able to freely express yourself or engaging in embarrassing and frightening behaviors? What system would you design?

Outpatient commitment has been advanced as a means to avoid criminalization of individuals with mental illness. Though civil in nature, it has been touted as a means to divert persons with mental illnesses from the criminal justice system altogether and link them to treatment in the community. As such,

> Whether outpatient commitment is adopted matters not just to those interested in public mental health, but to those in the criminal justice system as well. If outpatient commitment succeeds in the policy goals it espouses, then that should be of great interest to those in the criminal justice system who share the goals of reducing risk and obtaining treatment for individuals with serious mental illnesses. If outpatient commitment does not reach its goals then that should be of interest as well (Petrila et al., 2003, p. 169).

Although Torrey and Zdanowicz (2001) do not view outpatient commitment as a panacea, they argue that it is a commonsensical and compassionate approach in a world that is plagued with increasing homelessness, suicide, violence, and incarceration among persons with mental illnesses (see also Allen & Smith, 2001).

Due to the scarcity of mental health funding, concerns about the possible coerciveness of outpatient commitment, and distaste for working with "criminals," community mental health agencies are sometimes content to have criminal justice professionals assume the responsibility for handling the mentally ill in criminal justice facilities (Zdanowicz, 2001). If not an active choice by the mental health system to "pass the buck," it is at least a passive paralysis, an inability to treat everyone that comes to its doors. Jails, on the other hand, cannot say no (Lamb, Weinberger, & Gross, 2004).

If the criminal justice system is going to have to absorb this population of "offenders," Petrila et al. (2003) recommended that criminal justice professionals lobby for additional funds for mental health services. As is discussed throughout this book, the criminal justice system — and particularly, law enforcement — is leading the way in obtaining funding for innovative programs addressing the interface of the mental health and criminal justice systems. Indeed, with the clout that the criminal justice system commands in today's world, the attention of criminal justice professionals to the matter might benefit everyone involved. Zdanowicz (2001), for example, encouraged sheriffs to champion the cause for changes in commitment laws that make it easier to get a person with mental illness into treatment. The National Sheriffs' Association must have heard this call, as they are increasingly vocal in supporting statutes that allow courts to order involuntary outpatient treatment in the community (Faust, 2003). Now there needs to be more influence from criminologists and research in this area reflected in the criminal justice literature.

Other criminal justice agencies are trying to reverse the roles — and in some cases, funding — so as to shift responsibility back to the "rightful" owners of the problem. In Texas, for example, increased funding for the mental health system was attained in the legislature based on the reasoning that this would lessen the number of persons with mental illnesses who are incarcerated and could thereby thwart the need to construct a prison (Lamb & Weinberger, 2005). Certainly, criminal justice diversion programs, such as police-based diversion programs or mental health courts, are destined for failure, so long as no concerted effort to augment mental health services in the community is made to provide for those singled out by such programs for diversion and linkage to treatment. Even if community services such as outpatient commitment, intensive case management, and assertive community treatment can work for most persons with mental illnesses, there is still a need for an increase in the number of psychiatric inpatient beds for a subset of the population (Lamb & Weinberger, 2005). This is the only way to keep some out of jails and prisons.

Ultimately, it cannot be an "either-or" solution. The mental health and criminal justice systems, for better or for worse, are inextricably linked; what happens in the mental health system affects what occurs in the criminal justice system and vice versa (Petrila et al., 2003). Indeed, even prior to deinstitutionalization, research demonstrated that as opportunities for civil commitment decrease, involvement with the criminal justice system increases (Lamb and Weinberger, 1998). Certainly, the better that mental health providers can treat persons with mental illness, the more likely arrests and jail admissions will be reduced and positive results will occur for persons with mental illness and the criminal justice system (Dvoskin & Steadman, 1994). However, the revolving door between the criminal justice and mental health systems currently has too much momentum to be halted in the near future.

It is fair to say that everyone agrees: something is terribly wrong with the process when the only means to acquire involuntary treatment for some families is to have

their loved one with mental illness arrested. One should not have to commit a crime—
or, in some cases, merely be accused of one—to get help (Faust, 2003). Regardless
of the process chosen for intervention, whether civil or criminal, the solution is the
provision of sufficient mental health treatment services. The responsibility for providing sufficient mental health treatment resources lies squarely with the legislature.
In the absence of such resources and mental health services, more and more persons
with mental illnesses are coming into contact with law enforcement, the focus of the
next chapter.

References

Adebimpe, V. R. (1994). Race, racism, and epidemiological surveys. *Hospital and Community Psychiatry, 45*(1), 27–31.

Allen, M., & Smith, V. F. (2001). Opening Pandora's Box: The practical and legal dangers of involuntary outpatient commitment. *Psychiatric Services, 52*(3), 342–346.

Anfang, S. A., & Appelbaum, P. S. (2006). Civil commitment—The American experience. *Israel Journal of Psychiatry and Related Sciences, 43*(3), 209–218.

Appelbaum, P. S. (2001). Thinking carefully about outpatient commitment. *Psychiatric Services, 52*(3), 347–350.

Appelbaum, P. S. (2005). Assessing Kendra's Law: Five years of outpatient commitment in New York. Psychiatric Services, 56(7), 791–792.

Austin, J., & Irwin, J. (2001). *It's about time: America's imprisonment binge* (3rd ed.). Belmont, CA: Wadsworth.

Barry, D. (2011, January 15). Looking behind the mug-shot grin. *New York Times.* Retrieved from http://www.nytimes.com/2011/01/16/us/16loughner.html?page wanted=all.

Baskerville, B. (1997, July 13). A psychiatric patient spends final month in solitary torment. *Los Angeles Times.* Retrieved from http://articles.latimes.com/1997/jul/ 13/news/mn-12216.

Bazelon, E. (2012, August 10). How do we stop the next Aurora? We need a mental health system that helps men like James Holmes—and Jared Loughner, and Seung-Hui Cho—before it's too late. *Slate.* Retrieved from http://www.slate.com/ articles/news_and_politics/crime/2012/08/aurora_shooting_how_to_prevent_ men_like_james_holmes_from_striking_again.html.

Bazelon Center for Mental Health Law. (2000, April). *Position statement on invol-
untary commitment.* Washington, D.C.: Author. Retrieved from http://www. bazelon.org/issues/commitment/position statement.html.

Bloom, J. D. (2004). Thirty-five years of working with civil commitment statutes. *Journal of the American Academy of Psychiatry and the Law, 32*(4), 430–439.

Bond, C. F., DiCandia, C. G., MacKinnon, J. R. (1988). Responses to violence in a psychiatric setting: The role of patient's race. *Personality and Social Psychology Bulletin, 14*, 448–458.

Bonnie, R. J., Reinhard, J. S., Hamilton, P., & McGarvey, L. (2009). Mental health system transformation after the Virginia Tech tragedy. *Health Affairs, 28*(3), 793–804.

Bonsack, C., & Borgeat, F. (2005). Perceived coercion and need for hospitalization related to psychiatric admission. *International Journal of Law and Psychiatry, 28*(4), 342–347.

Borum, R. (1999). *Increasing court jurisdiction and supervision over misdemeanor offenders with mental illness.* Tampa, FL: Department of Mental Health Law & Policy, Louis de la Parte Florida Mental Health Institute, University of South Florida.

Busch, A. B., Wilder, C. M., Van Dorn, R. A., Swartz, M. S., & Swanson, J. W. (2010). Changes in guideline-recommended medication possession after implementing Kendra's Law in New York. *Psychiatric Services, 61*(10), 1000–1005.

Campbell, K. M. (2002). Blurring the lines of the danger zone: The impact of Kendra's Law on the rights of the nonviolent mentally ill. *Notre Dame Journal of Law, Ethics, & Public Policy, 16*, 173–205.

Churchill, R., Owen, G., Singh, S., & Hotopf, M. (2007). *International experiences of using community treatment orders.* London, UK: Department of Health. Retrieved from http://www.dh.gov.uk/en/Publicationsandstatistics/Publications/Publications PolicyAndGuidance.

Choe, J. Y., Teplin, L. A., & Abram, K. M. (2008). Perpetration of violence, violent victimization, and severe mental illness: Balancing public health concerns. *Psychiatric Services, 59*, 153–164.

Compton, S. N., Swanson, J. W., Wagner, H. R., Swartz, M. S., Burns, B. J., & Elbogen, E. B. (2003). Involuntary outpatient commitment and homelessness in persons with severe mental illness. *Mental Health Services Research, 5*(1), 27–38.

Cook, B. L. (2002, September–October). Protecting our country while preserving liberty and freedom. *The Champion.* Retrieved from http://www.nacdl.org/Champion.aspx?id=22491.

Cooper, V. G., McLearen, A. M., & Zapf, P. A. (2004). Dispositional decisions with the mentally ill: Police perceptions and characteristics. *Police Quarterly, 7*, 295–310.

Cornwell, J. K. (2003). Preventive outpatient commitment for persons with serious mental illness: Exposing the myths surrounding preventive outpatient commitment for individuals with chronic mental illness. *Psychology, Public Policy, and Law, 9*, 209–232.

Couch, S., & Finlayson, G. (2007, February 22). Investment in mental health pays off. *The Albuquerque Journal.* Retrieved from http://www.abqjournal.com/opinion/guest_columns/540223opinion02-22-07.htm.

Dawson, J. (2005). *Community treatment orders: International comparisons.* Otago, NZ: The Law Foundation New Zealand.

Ditton, P. M. (1999, July). *Special report: Mental health treatment of inmates and probationers* (NCJ 174463). Washington, D.C.: U.S. Department of Justice, Bureau of Justice Statistics.

Dvoskin, J. A., & Steadman, H. J. (1994). Reducing the risk of living with mental illness: Managing violence in the community. *Hospital and Community Psychiatry, 45*, 679–684.

Earley, P. (2006). *Crazy: A father's search through America's mental health madness.* New York, NY: Berkley Trade.

Esposito, R., Westhead, V., & Berko, J. (2008). Florida's outpatient commitment law: Effective but underused. *Psychiatric Services, 59*, 328.

Faust, T. N. (2003). Shift the responsibility of untreated mental illness out of the criminal justice system, *Sheriff, 65*(2), 6–7.

Fennig, S., Rabinowitz, J., & Fennig, S. (1999). Involuntary first admission of patients with schizophrenia as a predictor of future admissions. *Psychiatric Services, 50*(8), 1049–1052.

Fisher, W. H., & Grisso, T. (2010). Civil commitment statutes — 40 years of circumvention. *Journal of the American Academy of Psychiatry and the Law, 38*(3), 365–368.

Flaherty, J. A., & Meagher, R. (1980). Measuring racial bias in inpatient treatment. *American Journal of Psychiatry, 137*(6), 679–682.

Flug, M. (2003). No commitment: Kendra's Law makes no promise of adequate mental health treatment. *Georgetown Journal on Poverty Law & Policy, 10*, 105–129.

Fritz, M. (2006, February 1). Strong medicine: A doctor's fight: More forced care for the mentally ill. *The Wall Street Journal*, p. A1.

Gardner, W., Lidz, C. W., Hoge, S. K., Monahan, J., Eisenberg, M. M., Bennett, N. S., ... Roth, L. H. (1999). Patients' revisions of their beliefs about the need for hospitalization. *American Journal of Psychiatry, 156*, 1385–1391.

Geller, J. L. (2006). The evolution of outpatient commitment in the USA: From conundrum to quagmire. *International Journal of Law and Psychiatry, 29*(3), 234–248.

Geller, J. L., Grudzinskas, A. J., McDermeit, M., Fisher, W. H., & Lawlor, T. (1998). The efficacy of involuntary outpatient treatment in Massachusetts. *Administration and Policy in Mental Health, 25*(3), 271–285.

Geller, J. L., & Stanley, J. (2005a). Outpatient commitment debate: Response. *New England Journal on Criminal and Civil Confinement, 31*, 123–126.

Geller, J. L., & Stanley, J. (2005b). Outpatient commitment debate: Settling the doubts about the constitutionality of outpatient commitment. *New England Journal on Criminal and Civil Confinement, 31*, 127–138.

Gibbs, J. P. (1962). Rates of mental hospitalization: A study of societal reaction to deviant behavior. *American Sociological Review, 27,* 782–792.

Gilbert, A. R., Moser, L. L., Van Dorn, R. A., Swanson, J. W., Wilder, C. M., Robbins, P. C., … Swartz, M. S. (2010). Reductions in arrest under assisted outpatient treatment in New York. *Psychiatric Services, 61*(10), 996–999.

Gilligan, J. (2001). The last mental hospital. *Psychiatric Quarterly, 72*(1), 45–77.

Glover, R. W., Miller, J. E., & Sadowski, S. R. (2012, March 22). *Proceedings on the state budget crisis and the behavioral health treatment gap: The impact on public substance abuse and mental health systems.* Washington, D.C.: National Association of State Mental Health Program Directors.

Hammack, L. (2011, April 16). Virginia Tech tragedy prompts positive changes. *The Roanoke Times.* Retrieved from http://www.roanoke.com/news/roanoke/wb/283 546.

Hardin, H. (1993, July 22). Uncivil liberties. *Vancouver Sun,* p. A15.

Harris, D. (2012, July 25). James Holmes bought rifle after failing oral exam at University of Colorado. *ABC News.* Retrieved from http://abcnews.go.com/US/james-holmes-bought-rifle-failing-oral-exam-university/story?id=16850268#.UBDFcD G3CFc.

Henwood, B. (2008). Involuntary inpatient commitment in the context of mental health recovery. *American Journal of Psychiatric Rehabilitation, 11*(3), 253–266.

Hiday, V. A. (1988). Civil commitment: A review of empirical research. *Behavioral Sciences & the Law, 6*(1), 15–43.

Hiday, V. A., & Scheid-Cook, T. L. (1987). The North Carolina experience with outpatient commitment: A critical appraisal. *International Journal of Law and Psychiatry, 10,* 215–232.

Hiday, V. A., Swartz, M. S., Swanson, J. W., Borum, R., & Wagner, H. R. (2002). Impact of outpatient commitment on victimization of people with severe mental illness. *American Journal of Psychiatry, 159*(8), 1403–1411.

Hiday, V. A., & Wales, H. W. (2013). Mental illness and the law. In C. S. Aneshensel, J. C. Phelan, & A. Bierman (Eds.), *Handbook of the sociology of mental illness* (2nd edition, pp. 563–582). New York, NY: Springer.

Hoge, M. A., & Grottole, E. (2000). The case against outpatient commitment. *Journal of the American Academy of Psychiatry and the Law, 28*(2), 165–170.

Honig, J., & Stefan, S. (2005). Outpatient commitment debate: New research continues to challenge need for outpatient commitment. *New England Journal on Criminal and Civil Confinement, 31,* 109–122.

Huffman, M. (2011, December). Legal and ethical challenges in mental health care law: A primer for Virginia lawyers. *Virginia Lawyer,* 60, 32–35.

Huggins, E. S. (2004). Assisted outpatient treatment: An unconstitutional invasion of protected rights or a necessary government safeguard? *Journal of Legislation, 30,* 305–325.

Humphrey v. Cady, 405 U.S. 504 (1972).

In re K.L., 1 N.Y. 3d 362 (2004).

In re Urcuyo, 714 N.Y.S.2nd 862 (Sup. Ct. 2000).

Jadrnak, J. (2006, February 7). Not everyone backs Kendra's Law. *Albuquerque Journal.* Retrieved from http://www. nyaprs.org/pages/View_ENews.cfm?ENewsID=5217.

Jedicke, P. (1997, November 12). Notes on John Rawls. Retrieved from http://infotech. fanshawec.on.ca/faculty/jedicke/rawls.htm.

Kaczynski, D. (2012, August 3). Unabomber's brother on violence and treating mental health. *Houston Chronicle.* Retrieved from http://www.chron.com/news/article/Unabomber-s-brother-on-violence-and-treating-3760714.php.

Kahan, D. M., Braman, D., Monahan, J., Callahan, L., & Peters, E. (2010). Cultural cognition and public policy: The case of outpatient commitment laws. *Law and Human Behavior, 34*(2), 118–140.

Kane, A., Landrock, T., & Ferrugia, J. (2012, August 22). *James Holmes court case: Did university officials consider Aurora suspect 'high risk' for violence?* Retrieved from http://www.wptv.com/dpp/news/national/james-holmes-court-case-did-university-officials-consider-aurora-suspect-high-risk-for-violence.

Kansas v. Hendricks, 521 U.S. 346 (1997).

Karasch, M. (2003). Where involuntary commitment, civil liberties, and the right to mental health care collide: An overview of California's mental illness system. *Hastings Law Journal, 54,* 493–523.

Katsakou, C., & Priebe, S. (2006). Outcomes of involuntary hospital admission — A review. *Acta Psychiatrica Scandinavica, 114,* 232–241.

Kisely, S., Campbell, L., Scott, A., Preston, N., & Xiao, J. (2007). Randomized and non-randomized evidence for the effect of compulsory community and involuntary out-patient treatment on health service use: Systematic review and meta-analysis. *Psychological Medicine, 37,* 3–14.

Lamb, H. R., & Weinberger, L. E. (1998). Persons with severe mental illness in jails and prisons: A review. *Psychiatric Services, 49*(4), 483–492.

Lamb, H. R., & Weinberger, L. E. (2005). The shift of psychiatric inpatient care from hospitals to jails and prisons. *Journal of the American Academy of Psychiatry and the Law, 33*(4), 529–534.

Lamb, H. R., Weinberger, L. E., & Gross, B. H. (2004). Mentally ill persons in the criminal justice system: Some perspectives. *Psychiatric Quarterly, 75*(2), 107–126.

Lanterman-Petris-Short Act. (1967). Cal. Welf & Inst. Code, sec. 5000 et seq.

Lawson, W. B., Hepler, N., Holladay, J., & Cuffel, B. (1994). Race as a factor in in-patient and outpatient admissions and diagnosis. *Hospital and Community Psychiatry, 45*(1), 72–74.

Leone, T. (2000, December). *Policy brief: Misdemeanor offenders with mental illness in Florida.* Tampa, FL: Department of Mental Health Law & Policy, Louis de la Parte Florida Mental Health Institute, University of South Florida.

Leonnig, C. D., & Achenbach, J. (2012, July 20). James Holmes, held in Colorado shooting, had academic promise but was struggling. *The Washington Post.* Retrieved from http://www.washingtonpost.com/national/health-science/james-eagan-holmes-held-in-colorado-shooting/2012/07/20/gJQA213UyW_print.html.

Lessard v. Schmidt, 349 F. Supp. 1078 (E.D. Wis. 972), vacated and remanded, 414 U.S. 473, on remand, 379 F. Supp. 1376 (E.D. Wis. 1974), vacated and remanded, 421 U.S. 957 (1975), reinstated, 413 F. Supp. 1318 (E.D. Wis. 1976).

Lewis, C. S. (2002). *God in the dock.* Grand Rapids, MI: W.B. Eerdmans.

Link, B. G., Epperson, M. W., Perron, B. E., Castille, D. M., & Yang, L. H. (2011). Arrest outcomes associated with outpatient commitment in New York State. *Psychiatric Services, 62*, 504–508.

Markowitz, F. E. (2006). Psychiatric hospital capacity, homelessness, and crime and arrest rates. *Criminology, 44*, 45–72.

McKinney, R. Jr. (2006). Involuntary commitment: A delicate balance. *The Quinnipiac Probate Law Journal, 20*, 36–46.

McNiel, D. E., & Binder, R. L. (1986). Violence, civil commitment, and hospitalization. *Journal of Nervous and Mental Disease, 174*(2), 107–111.

Melton, G. B., Petrila, J., Poythress, N., & Slobogin, C. (2007). *Psychological evaluations for the courts: A handbook for mental health professionals and lawyers* (3rd ed.). New York, NY: Guilford Press.

Mickle, C. (2012). Safety or freedom: Permissiveness vs. paternalism in involuntary commitment law. *Law & Psychology Review, 36*, 297–310.

Moller, D. (2006, March 2). Second try for Laura's law. *TheUnion.com.* Retrieved from http://www.theunion.com/apps/pbcs.dll/article?AID=/20060302/NEWS/103020136&template=printart.

Monahan, J., Redlich, A. D., Swanson, J., Robbins, P.C., Appelbaum, P. S., Petrila, J., ... McNiel, D. E. (2005). Use of leverage to improve adherence to psychiatric treatment in the community. *Psychiatric Services, 56*(1), 37–44.

Mullen, R., Dawson, J., & Gibbs, A. (2006) Dilemmas for clinicians in use of community treatment orders. *International Journal of Law and Psychiatry, 29*, 535–550.

Mullen, R., Gibbs, A., & Dawson, J. (2006). Family perspective on community treatment orders: a New Zealand study. *International Journal of Social Psychiatry, 52*, 469–478.

Munetz, M. R., Grande, T., Kleist, J., & Peterson, G. A. (1996). The effectiveness of outpatient civil commitment. *Psychiatric Services, 47*(11), 1251–1253.

Munk-Jorgensen, P., Mortensen, P. B., & Machon, R. A. (1991). Hospitalization patterns in schizophrenia: A 13-year follow-up. *Schizophrenia Research, 4*(1), 1–9.

National Alliance on Mental Illness. (2009, March). *Grading the states: A report on America's health care system for serious mental illness.* Arlington, VA: Author.

New York Mental Hygiene Law 9.60(C)–(D) (2004).

New York Post Editorial Board. (2006). Imperfect justice. *New York Post.* Retrieved from http://www.nypost.com/seven/10152006/postopinion/editorials/imperfect_justice_editorials_htm.

New York State Office of Mental Health. (2005, March). *Kendra's Law: Final report on the status of assisted outpatient treatment.* Albany, NY: Author. Retrieved from www.omh.state.ny.us/omhweb/kendra_web/finalreport.

O'Connor, E. (2002). Is Kendra's Law a keeper? How Kendra's Law erodes fundamental rights of the mentally ill. *Journal of Law and Policy, 11,* 313–367.

Owens, P., Mutter, R., & Stocks, C. (2010, July). *Mental health and substance abuse-related emergency department visits among adults, 2007. HCUP Statistical Brief #92.* Rockville, MD: Agency for Healthcare Research and Quality.

Pandya, A. (2007). *Outpatient civil commitment: A family perspective.* New York: NY: National Alliance on Mental Illness, A Consumer Journal for Mental Health Advocacy, New York City Voices. Retrieved from http://www.nycvoices.org/article_67.php.

Pataki, G. E., & Carpinello, S. E. (2005). *Kendra's Law: Final report on the status of assisted outpatient treatment.* Albany, NY: New York State Office of Mental Health.

Patch, P. C., & Arrigo, B. A. (1999). Police officer attitudes and use of discretion in situations involving the mentally ill: The need to narrow the focus. *International Journal of Law and Psychiatry, 22*(1), 23–35.

Perlin, M. L. (2003). Preventive outpatient commitment for persons with serious mental illness: Therapeutic jurisprudence and outpatient commitment law: Kendra's Law as a case study. *Psychology, Public Policy, and Law, 9,* 183–208.

Petrila, J. (2002, November). *Policy brief: The effectiveness of the Broward mental health court: An evaluation.* Tampa, FL: Department of Mental Health Law & Policy, Louis de la Parte Florida Mental Health Institute, University of South Florida.

Petrila, J., Ridgely, M. S., & Borum, R. (2003). Debating outpatient commitment: Controversy, trends and empirical data. *Crime & Delinquency, 49*(1), 157–172.

Phelan, J. C., & Link, B. G. (1998). The growing belief that people with mental illnesses are violent: The role of the dangerousness criterion for civil commitment. *Social Psychiatry and Psychiatric Epidemiology, 33*(S1), S7–S12.

Phelan, J. C., Link, B. G., Stueve, A., & Pescosolido, B. A. (2000). Public concepts of mental illness in 1950 and 1996: What is mental illness and is it to be feared? *Journal of Health & Social Behavior, 41,* 188–207.

Phelan, J. C., Sinkewicz, M., Castille, D. M., Huz, S., Muenzenmaier, K., & Link, B. G. (2010). Effectiveness and outcomes of assisted outpatient treatment in New York State. *Psychiatric Services, 61*(2), 137–143.

Pollack, D. A., McFarland, B. H., Mahler, J. M., & Kovas, A. E. (2005). Outcomes of patients in a low-intensity, short duration involuntary outpatient commitment program. *Psychiatric Services, 56*(7), 863–866.

Raphael, S. (2000, September). *The deinstitutionalization of the mentally ill and growth in the U.S. prison populations: 1971 to 1996.* Retrieved from http://ist-socrates. berkeley.edu/~raphael/raphael2000.pdf.

Reinhart, M. (2011, September 21). Mental health cuts' toll debated. *The Arizona Republic.*

Ridgely, M. S., Borum, R., & Petrila, J. (2001). *The effectiveness of involuntary outpatient treatment: Empirical evidence and the experience of eight states.* Santa Monica, CA: RAND Institute for Civil Justice.

Rohland, B. M. (1998). *The role of outpatient commitment in the management of persons with schizophrenia.* Iowa City: Iowa Consortium for Mental Health, Services, Training, and Research.

Romney, L. (2012, July 19). Report calls for more inpatient treatment for the mentally ill. *Los Angeles Times.* Retrieved from http://www.latimes.com/news/local/la-me-state-psychiatric-beds-20120719,0,7173400.story.

Rosenheck, R. (2000). Cost-effectiveness of services for mentally ill homeless people: The application of research to policy and practice. *American Journal of Psychiatry, 157,* 1563–1570.

Rosenfield, S. (1984). Race differences in involuntary hospitalization: Psychiatric vs. labeling perspectives. *Journal of Health and Social Behavior, 25,* 14–23.

Rothman, D. J. (1971). *The discovery of the asylum: Social order and disorder in the new republic.* Boston, MA: Little Brown.

Saks, E. R. (2003). Preventive outpatient commitment for persons with serious mental illness: Involuntary outpatient commitment. *Psychology, Public Policy, and Law, 9,* 94–104.

SAMHSA. (2011). *Funding and characteristics of state mental health agencies, 2010.* Rockville, MD: Author.

SAMHSA. (2019). *Civil commitment and the mental health care continuum: Historical trends and principles for law and practice.* Rockville, MD: Substance Abuse and Mental Health Services Administration. Retrieved from: https://www.samhsa.gov/sites/default/files/civil-commitment-continuum-of-care.pdf.

Schopp, R. F. (2003). Preventive outpatient commitment for persons with serious mental illness: Outpatient civil commitment: A dangerous charade or a component of a comprehensive institution of civil commitment. *Psychology, Public Policy, and Law, 9,* 33–69.

Seitler, B. (2008). Once the wheels are in motion: Involuntary hospitalization and forced medicating. *Ethical Human Psychology & Psychiatry, 10*(1), 31–42.

Sellers, C. L., Sullivan, C. J., Veysey, B. M., & Shane, J. M. (2005). Responding to persons with mental illnesses: Police perspectives on specialized and traditional practices. *Behavioral Sciences and the Law, 23,* 647–657.

Sharfstein, S. (2005, September 2). Individual rights must be balanced with 'caring coercion.' *Psychiatric News, 40*(17), 3.

Sirica, C. (2000, July 11). *Outpatient commitment in mental health (Issue brief no. 757).* Washington, D.C.: National Health Policy Forum, George Washington University.

Slevin, P. (2004, July 29). Arab Americans report abuse: U.Mich. study finds nearly 60 percent fear for families. *Washington Post,* p. A05. Retrieved from http://www.washingtonpost.com/wp-dyn/articles/A21888-2004Jul28.html.

Snowden, L. R., & Cheung, F. K. (1990). Use of inpatient mental health services by members of ethnic minority groups. *American Psychologist, 45,* 347–355.

Steadman, H. J., Gounis, K., Dennis, D., Hopper, K., Roche, B., Swartz, M., & Robbins, P. C. (2001). Assessing the New York City involuntary outpatient commitment pilot program. *Psychiatric Services, 52*(3), 330–336.

Stone, A. (1975). *Mental health and the law: A system in transition.* Rockville, MD: National Institute of Mental Health.

Straticzuk, A. (2000, October 2). *Thoughts on assisted treatment: Personal communication from adjunct professor of Philosophy.* Daytona Beach, FL: Daytona Beach Community College.

Stukey, K. (2012, May 19). *Mental illness takes toll on law enforcement system.* Retrieved from http://www.krtv.com/news/mental-illness-takes-toll-on-law-enforcement-system/.

Swanson, J., Swartz, M., Van Dorn, R. A., Monahan, J., McGuire, T. G., Steadman, H. J., & Robbins, P. C. (2009). Racial disparities in involuntary outpatient commitment: Are they real? *Health Affairs, 28*(3), 816–826.

Swanson, J. W., Borum, R. Swartz, M. S., Hiday, V. A., Wagner, H. R., & Burns, B. J. (2001). Can involuntary outpatient commitment reduce arrests among persons with severe mental illness? *Criminal Justice and Behavior, 28*(2), 156–189.

Swanson, J. W., Swartz, M. S., Borum, R., Hiday, V. A., Wagner, H. R., & Burns, B. J. (2000). Involuntary out-patient commitment and reduction of violent behaviour in persons with severe mental illness. *British Journal of Psychiatry, 176,* 324–331.

Swanson, J. W., Swartz, M. S., George, L. K., Burns, B. J., Hiday, V. A., Borum, R., & Wagner, H. R. (1997). Interpreting the effectiveness of involuntary outpatient commitment: A conceptual model. *Journal of the American Academy of Psychiatry and Law, 25*(1), 5–16.

Swanson, J., Swartz, M., Van Dorn, R. A., Monahan, J., McGuire, T. G., Steadman, H. J., & Robbins, P. C. (2009). Racial disparities in involuntary outpatient commitment: Are they real? *Health Affairs, 28*(3), 816–826.

Swanson, J. W., Van Dorn, R. A., Swartz, M. S., Cislo, A. M., Wilder, C. M., Moser, L. L., … McGuire, T. G. (2010). Robbing Peter to pay Paul: Did New York State's outpatient commitment program crowd out voluntary service recipients? *Psychiatric Services, 61*(10), 988–995.

Swartz, M. S. (2010). Introduction to the special section on assisted outpatient treatment in New York State. *Psychiatric Services, 61*(10), 967–969.

Swartz, M. S., Swanson, J. W., Hiday, V. A., Wagner, H. R., Burns, B. J., & Borum, R. (2001). A randomized controlled trial of outpatient commitment in North Carolina. *Psychiatric Services, 52*(3), 325–329.

Swartz, M. S., Swanson, J. W., Kim, M., & Petrila, J. (2006). Use of outpatient commitment or related civil court treatment orders in five U.S. communities. *Psychiatric Services, 57*(3), 343–349.

Swartz, M. S., Swanson, J. W., & Monahan, J. (2003). Preventive outpatient commitment for persons with serious mental illness: Endorsement of personal benefit of outpatient commitment among persons with severe mental illness. *Psychology, Public Policy, and Law, 9*, 70–90.

Swartz, M. S., Swanson, J. W., Steadman, H. J., Robbins, P. C., & Monahan, J. (2009, June 30). *New York State Assisted Outpatient Treatment Program evaluation.* Durham, N.C.: Duke University School of Medicine. Retrieved from http://www. macarthur.virginia.edu/aot_finalreport.pdf.

Swartz, M. S., Swanson, J. W., Wagner, H. R., Hannon, M. J., Burns, B. J., & Shumway, M. (2003). Assessment of four stakeholder groups' preferences concerning outpatient commitment for persons with schizophrenia. *American Journal of Psychiatry, 160*(6), 1139–1146.

Swartz, M. S., Swanson, J. W., Wagner, H. R., Burns, B. J., Hiday, V. A., & Borum, R. (1999). Can involuntary outpatient commitment reduce hospital recidivism? Findings from a randomized trial with severely mentally ill individuals. *American Journal of Psychiatry, 156*(12), 1968–1975.

Swartz, M. S., Wagner, H. R., Swanson, J. W., Hiday, V. A., & Burns, B. J. (2002). The perceived coerciveness of involuntary outpatient commitment: Findings from an experimental study. *Journal of the American Academy of Psychiatry and Law, 30*(2), 207–217.

Swartz, M. S., Wilder, C. M., Swanson, J. W., Van Dorn, R. A., Robbins, P. C., Steadman, H. J., … Monahan, J. (2010). Assessing outcomes for consumers in New York's assisted outpatient treatment program. *Psychiatric Services, 61*(10), 976–981.

Testa, M., & West, S. G. (2010). Civil commitment in the United States. *Psychiatry, 7*(10), 30–40.

Torrey, E. F., Fuller, D. A., Geller, J., Jacobs, C., & Ragosta, K. (2012, July 19). *No room at the inn: Trends and consequences of closing public psychiatric hospitals.* Arlington, VA: Treatment Advocacy Center.

Torrey, E. F, Kennard A. D., Eslinger D., Lamb, R., & Pavle, J. (2010). *More mentally ill persons are in jails and prisons than hospitals: A survey of the states.* Arlington, VA: Treatment Advocacy Center.

Torrey, E. F., & Zdanowicz, M. (2001). Outpatient commitment: What, why, and for whom. *Psychiatric Services, 52*(3), 337–341.

Treatment Advocacy Center. (2008, October 10). *A guide to Kendra's Law* (3rd edition). Arlington, VA: Author.

Treffert, D. A. (1973). Letter: "Dying with their rights on." *American Journal of Psychiatry, 130,* 1041.

Van Dorn, R. A., Swanson, J. W., Swartz, M. S., Wilder, C. M., Moser, L. L., Gilbert, A. R., … Robbins, P. C. (2010). Continuing medication and hospitalization outcomes after assisted outpatient treatment in New York. *Psychiatric Services, 61*(10), 982–987.

Van Putten, R. A., Santiago, J. M., & Berren, M. R. (1988). Involuntary outpatient commitment in Arizona: A retrospective study. *Hospital and Community Psychiatry, 39,* 953–958.

Virginia Tech Review Panel. (2007, August). *Mass shootings at Virginia Tech — April 16, 2007: Report of the Review Panel presented to Governor Kaine, Commonwealth of Virginia.* Retrieved from http://www.governor.virginia.gov/TempContent/ techPanelReport-docs/FullReport.pdf.

Wagner, H. R., Swartz, M. S., Swanson, J. W., & Burns, B. J. (2003). Preventive outpatient commitment for persons with serious mental illness: Does involuntary outpatient commitment lead to more intensive treatment? *Psychology, Public Policy, and Law, 9,* 145–157.

Wales, H. W., & Hiday, V. A. (2006). PLC or TLC: Is outpatient commitment the/ an answer? *International Journal of Psychiatry and Law, 29,* 451–468.

Walker, S. (2006). *Sense and nonsense about crime and drugs: A policy guide* (6th ed.). Belmont, CA: Wadsworth.

Wanchek, T.N., & Bonnie, R.J. (2012). Use of longer periods of temporary detention to reduce mental health civil commitments. *Psychiatric Services, 63,* 643–648.

Watnik, I. L. (2001). A constitutional analysis of Kendra's Law: New York's solution for treatment of the chronically ill. *University of Pennsylvania Law Review, 149,* 1181–1228.

Watson, A. C., & Angell, B. A. (2007). Applying procedural justice theory to law enforcement's response to persons with mental illness. *Psychiatric Services, 58*(6), 787–793.

Winerip, M. (1999, May 23). Bedlam on the streets. *New York Times Magazine, 56*, 42–49, 65–66, 70.

Winick, B. J. (2003). Preventive outpatient commitment for persons with serious mental illness: Outpatient commitment: A therapeutic jurisprudence analysis. *Psychology, Public Policy, and Law, 9*, 107–135.

Zdanowicz, M. T. (2001, May/June). A sheriff's role in arresting the mental illness crisis. *Sheriff, 62*, 38–40.

Zdanowicz, M. T. (2003, Winter–2004, Spring). Coerced care vs. no care. *Catalyst: Newsletter of The Treatment Advocacy Center*. Arlington, VA: Treatment Advocacy Center.

Zervakis, J., Stechuchak, K. M., Olson, M. K., Swanson, J. W., Oddone, E. Z., Weinberger, M., ... Strauss, J. L. (2007). Previous involuntary commitment is associated with current perceptions of coercion in voluntarily hospitalized patients. *International Journal of Forensic Mental Health, 6*(2), 105–112.

Chapter 5

The Law Enforcement Response to Persons with Mental Illnesses in Crises

"Mental Illness is a disorder, not a decision."

— S.M. Francis 2020[1]

By the nature of their roles, law enforcement officers are accustomed to issuing directives, expecting cooperation with their commands. Often, they adopt a "good guys" versus "bad guys" mindset and implement techniques involving force to gain the cooperation of reluctant, recalcitrant, or defiant suspects. However, what happens when subjects disobey officers' demands—not because they are bad guys with a disdain and disrespect for authority, attempting to elude capture, but because they are ill, confused, and unable to comport their behavior to the officers' and society's expectations?

We all come to each encounter as a culmination of our past experiences, which serve to influence our expectations about how to resolve problems that we are confronted with on a daily basis. Unfortunately, the traditional tactics utilized by law enforcement officers to quell disturbances and subdue bad guys may instead escalate police encounters with persons with mental illnesses, sometimes resulting in tragedy.[2] Furthermore, the implementation of specialized police training in handling encounters with persons with mental illnesses has often been precipitated by nearly tragic or deadly events in the past.[3] Even so, contrary to media sensationalism, as

---

1. Shatel M. Francis, (2020).

2. The Treatment Advocacy Center in Arlington, Virginia, maintains a "Preventable Tragedies" database, which can be found at: https://www.treatmentadvocacycenter.org/evidence-and-research/preventable-tragedies. Included in these tragedies are what has been referred to as "suicide by cop" (SBC) or "victim-precipitated homicide" (VPH). Lord (2004) offers definitions of SBC, "Incidents in which individuals bent on self-destruction, engage in life-threatening and criminal behavior to force the police to kill them," (p. 4), and VPH, "The suicidal person confront[s] an assailant, with a real or perceived lethal weapon, forcing the assailant to respond with deadly force" (p. 5).

3. CIT was implemented in 1988 in Memphis following a police shooting of a person with mental illness (Cochran, 2004; Dupont & Cochran, 2000). Two incidents, one resulting in death of a person with mental illness and another that took too long to resolve and inconvenienced the citizenry, which would have preferred a quicker resolution by police, led to the establishment of CIT in Seattle based

previously demonstrated, most persons with mental illnesses are not violent individuals. Unfortunately, as discussed in Chapter 1 and will be elaborated on in the final chapter, it often seems to take crises to influence policy within the criminal justice system.

Of course, the resolution of a law enforcement encounter with a person with mental illness in crisis can vary from agency to agency, individual to individual, and situation to situation. Fear from both sides can certainly be a factor in this equation, especially for the person who is to be subdued, which can contribute to the potential escalation of violence (Ruiz & Miller, 2004; Watson, Corrigan, & Ottati, 2004).

In deaths caused by law enforcement, Fowler et al. (2014) found that 21.6% of these tragedies involved a subject with a diagnosis of mental illness — typically related to a co-occurring substance abuse problem. Similarly, Saleh et al. (2018) found that 23% of persons killed by police in 2015 were exhibiting signs of mental illness. The National Alliance on Mental Illness reports that half of the people killed by police have a mental disability, and the Treatment Advocacy Center indicates that 25 to 50 percent of fatal police shootings involve persons with unmet mental health needs (Uyeda, 2020). As for school shooters, the U.S. Secret Service has concluded that there is no student shooter profile, though half had obtained at least one contact with a mental health provider prior to their illegal activity, and almost every shooter had been subject to a negative home atmosphere — characterized by domestic abuse, parental separation, divorce, substance abuse, and/or criminals among family members (Alathari, 2019).

The public nature of an event may often serve to influence officer discretion (Cooper, McLearen, & Zapf, 2004). Patch and Arrigo (1999) note that when calls to

---

on the Memphis model (Jamieson & Wilson, 2000). The Louisville Metropolitan Police Department implemented CIT training after officers were involved in the fatal shooting of a man with mental illness (D. Spratt, personal communication, May 8, 2007), as did the Polk County Sheriff's Office in Bartow, Florida (B. Garrett, personal communication, June 8, 2007). A modified version of CIT was implemented at the St. Petersburg Police Department, in St. Petersburg, Florida after an officer shot a man with mental illness in 1997 (T. Rolón, personal communication, February 22, 2007). NAMI Board Member Dave Lushbaugh (personal communication, June 19, 2007) indicates what could have been a tragic encounter with a loved one of his and the police has led to CIT training in Georgia and the support of Director Vernon M. Keenan of the Georgia Bureau of Investigation in implementing that training statewide. Joyce Wilde, CIT Program Administrator, of the Ventura County Sheriff's Office informs us that in the summer of 1997, Camarillo State Hospital closed its doors. The state hospital was a fixture in Ventura County, California, for decades — serving thousands of severely mentally ill individuals. Ventura County is a beach community; over time, many of the individuals from the state hospital were released to the community and continued to live in the local area. In 1998, Ventura County law enforcement experienced seven lethal use-of-force incidents; five of the individuals were considered mentally ill. Local law enforcement experienced another higher than usual lethal use-of-force year in 2001, with seven incidents; four of the individuals were considered mentally ill. In 2001, Ventura Police Department (VPD) began to research a way to increase safe encounters with emotionally disturbed individuals. In December 2001, the first 40-hour CIT Academy was conducted in Ventura County and included countywide training for five police agencies and a sheriff's department. (J. Wilde, J. Frank, & M. Zabarsky, personal communication, May 1, 2007).

such crises are made by the citizenry, officers feel less leeway in their decision-making ability and will often proceed with an arrest. Thus, the more public an event, the more likely an arrest will follow in a law enforcement officer's encounter with a person with mental illness.[4] With the public's influence on the behavior of police officers in mind, the need for public education and de-stigmatization regarding mental illness is of paramount concern. A community generally receives the type of law enforcement it desires (Wilson, 1978), even if those desires are misguided. A misinformed public can in turn influence self-serving and self-aggrandizing policymakers to enact misguided policies.

Police Encounters with and Perceptions of Persons with Mental Illnesses

Approximately 60% of adults and almost 50% of kids who experienced mental illness maladies in the past year did not obtain treatment (Good Therapy, 2016). This contributes to people with serious and persistent mental illnesses being three times more likely to be confined in jail or prison as opposed to being hospitalized (Taheri, 2016).

The police are often the first responders when dealing with persons with mental illnesses in crises and serve as gatekeepers[5] to either the mental health or the criminal justice system, a role they are typically neither trained for nor prepared to deliver (Borum, Deane, Steadman, & Morrissey, 1998; Lamb, Weinberger, & DeCuir, 2002; Lamb, Weinberger, & Gross, 2004; Panzarella & Alicea, 1997; Patch & Arrigo, 1999; Price, 2005; Vermette, Pinals, & Appelbaum, 2005). It has been estimated that somewhere between 7 to 10% of police contacts involve encounters with persons with mental illnesses (Deane, Steadman, Borum, Veysey, & Morrissey, 1999; Kalinich, 2010; Watson et al., 2010). These encounters historically have tended to result disproportionately in arrests of persons with mental illnesses for minor offenses (Franz & Borum, 2011).

As noted by Cordner (2006), there is a tendency to blame persons with mental illnesses for their behavior. However, as discussed in the previous chapters, there are a myriad of factors that serve to make the behavior of persons with mental illnesses not truly volitional.[6] Lamb et al. (2002) maintain that inadequate training of law

---

4. Slate, Johnson, and Colbert (2007) found that the number one stressor for law enforcement officers is concern about negative press accounts of police actions.

5. In this role as gatekeeper in dealing with persons with mental illnesses, the police have been referred to as "amateur social workers," "forensic gatekeepers," "psychiatric medics" and "streetcorner psychiatrists" (see Green, 1997; Sellers, Sullivan, Veysey, & Shane, 2005; Teplin, 2000).

6. An example provided by Lt. Brian Garrett (personal communication, June 8, 2007), of the Polk County Sheriff's Office in Bartow, Florida, is illustrative of an individual not freely choosing mental illness:

A CIT deputy who finished training less than two weeks before responds to a call of a woman hearing voices from under her front porch. Upon arrival he makes contact with the woman who has previously been diagnosed with schizophrenia but is not currently taking her medications because she cannot afford them. She recognizes she is in crisis and

enforcement officers can contribute to the criminalization of persons with mental illnesses. Many officers have difficulty recognizing the signs and symptoms of mental illnesses, as they are essentially laypersons without proper training (Lamb et al., 2004). Unless officers have experienced interactions with family members or friends with mental illnesses and/or are equipped with adequate specialized training for such encounters, such escalations can result in unnecessary injury and even death to both persons with mental illnesses and officers. According to Borum (2000), encounters with persons with mental illnesses are more likely to escalate to uses of force when officers' stress levels are heightened, such as when officers lack training and self-confidence and are unable to control the situation; situations are least likely to escalate to uses of force when officers are able to communicate and utilize negotiation tactics, maintain a positive attitude and employ anger management skills.

Citizens rarely kill police officers, and "[l]ess than 1/20 of 1% of all police-citizen encounters result in a fatal shooting by a police officer" (Borum, 2000, p. 334). However, when a fatal shooting does happen involving a person with mental illness, heightened scrutiny and sensationalism occurs. As noted by Kerr, Morabito, and Watson (2011), focusing solely on media coverage results in injuries to persons with mental illness in encounters with police being exaggerated. According to Randy DuPont of the University of Memphis, people with mental illness are more likely to be victims of violence than perpetrators of violence (Pauly, 2013). In actuality, it is more likely for persons with mental illnesses to be harmed by the police than for the police to be injured by persons with mental illnesses. In fact, those with untreatable mental illnesses are 16 times more likely than others in the broader population to be killed by the police (Morris, 2018). Also, persons with mental illnesses are four times more likely to be killed by the police than the reverse (Cordner, 2006).

Previous research has reported that on average officers have six encounters per month with a person with mental illness in crisis. Borum et al. (1998) found 92% of officers in their study had encountered a person with mental illness in crisis in the past month, with 84% having had more than one such encounter during this time. Cooper et al. (2004) reported that arrest rates did not differ on the basis of race when

---

is worried about her two young children because she has no local support system. The CIT deputy involuntarily commits her for mental health stabilization and is forced to place the children in the custody of the state child welfare agency because there are no family members or friends available to care for them. The CIT deputy later re-contacted her to determine her wellbeing and learns she is still not medicine compliant because she was released from the mental health treatment facility with a prescription for her medicine that she could not afford and still be able to care for her two children. She was even further depressed after having to battle the welfare agency to get her children back home. The deputy then spent most of his next day off researching sources for low or no cost medicines for indigent persons in need. He was able to find a local pharmacy participating in the program and then paid for the two prescriptions out of his own pocket and delivered them to the subject who willingly accepted them. She stayed medicine compliant and had no further involuntary commitments until she moved from our service area due to her transitory nature. She has since been committed several times for not being medicine compliant.

encounters with persons with mental illnesses transpired, but officers were more likely to civilly commit whites for treatment rather than blacks.

The police generally do not have negative views of persons with mental illnesses (Watson & Angell, 2007); in fact, the police have actually been found to be more empathetic toward persons with mental illnesses than the general public (Price, 2005). However, Panzarella and Alicea (1997), in a study of Special Weapons and Tactics (SWAT) team members in a large metropolitan police department, did find that officers stereotypically believed that it was not possible to have a meaningful conversation with a mentally disturbed person. As noted by Ruiz and Miller (2004), the two most common misperceptions held by the police about persons with mental illnesses are that they are all incapable of reasoning and are violent. Of course, having preconceived notions about someone being violent increases the likelihood that more aggressive approaches will be taken by law enforcement when encounters with persons with mental illnesses in crises occur, increasing the potential for ratcheting up a situation. What is needed is education and training to increase opportunities for officer interactions with persons with mental illnesses in an attempt to debunk stereotypes and seek positive solutions.

Police Training and Preparedness for Dealing with Persons with Mental Illnesses in Crises

In a survey of Massachusetts law enforcement officers, Vermette et al. (2005) found that 90% of respondents indicated that training on the topic of mental illness was either fairly or very important to their jobs. However, Ruiz and Miller (2004) and Cooper et al. (2004) report that a common theme among officers is that they do not feel properly trained or qualified when dispatched to crisis calls involving persons with mental illnesses.

In a 1975 literature review, Teese and Van Wormer (1975) found no references to mental health consultation with the police. Lamb et al. (2004) indicate that some level of training regarding interactions with persons with mental illnesses in crises is needed for all sworn law enforcement officers, not just for those officers assigned to specialized response teams or units. They maintain that types of training topics recommended for all officers include recognition of mental illness, how to handle and de-escalate violence, identification of suicide warning signs and handling of suicidal persons, when to bring in a specialized response team, available community resources and how to access them, how to determine who to divert to the mental health system and who to process through the criminal justice system. Being first responders it is important that the police can recognize suicidal ideations, as Fowler et al. (2014) found that 43 percent of persons who committed suicide in their study had been diagnosed with a mental illness. As such Tartaro (2019) acknowledges the importance of crisis intervention team training by the police as a means for identifying suicidal ideations and linking persons with mental illness to treatment via pre-booking diversion.

Communication

Effective communication skills are key to successfully resolving police encounters with persons who have mental illnesses. Mastery of both verbal communication and nonverbal cues is extremely important to ensure the de-escalation of situations. As Curtis (1975) noted, a lack of verbal skills can be a precursor to violence. When people run out of things to say in a heated confrontation that may be the emotional tipping point at which they resort to a knife, a gun, a bat, or other implement that is handy to express themselves. This can be particularly true when a subject is irrational and paranoid during an encounter with police. Being willing and able to take the time to establish rapport with persons who are mentally ill and in crisis is critical to successful resolutions of such police interactions.

The first few seconds of a police encounter with a person with mental illness is considered to be the most critical (Reuland, 2004). A sizeable minority of law enforcement officers have a tendency to believe that it is best to resolve mental health calls quickly (Ruiz & Miller, 2004); however, if there is a rush to force compliance early on in an encounter, escalation into violence may very well result. If an officer spends the first few moments talking with the person in crisis, establishing rapport, and utilizing de-escalation skills, the chances of resolving the interaction successfully without violence are greatly improved (Watson & Angell, 2007).

Police Options

Police options when encountering a person with mental illness in crisis include handling the matter informally, making an arrest, civilly committing or involuntarily hospitalizing someone, or doing nothing (Cooper et al., 2004; Sellers et al., 2005). The availability or feasibility of some of these options may often be limited or at least perceived as limited by officers. Cooper et al. (2004), for example, in a survey of police officers' attitudes regarding the interface of the mental health and criminal justice systems, found the lowest rated item to be the supportiveness of local mental health facilities. Likewise, Husted, Charter, and Perrou (1995) state that the majority of law enforcement agencies report being dissatisfied with their interactions with mental health agency personnel. Borum et al. (1998) and Cooper et al. (2004) indicate that the mental health system is often viewed as unavailable or less than helpful when contacted by the police for assistance in resolving conflicts with persons with mental illnesses. Due to the rigidity of time-consuming civil commitment requirements and practices, with prior referrals by police to the mental health system viewed as botched and the futility of persons with mental illnesses rapidly re-emerging in the same or worse condition on the street after police referral to mental health clinicians, arrest and utilization of the criminal justice process is oftentimes perceived as a more expedient option than referral to the mental health system (Borum et al., 1998; Borum, Swanson, Swartz, & Hiday, 1997; Dempsey & Forst, 2008; Greenberg, 2001; Panzarella & Alicea, 1997; Price, 2005; Sellers et al., 2005).

The constriction of available mental health options due to civil commitment restrictions, among other things, results in service delivery for the mental health system coming from the criminal justice system. As social sanitation is still the rule, it is just easier to unlock the gates to the criminal justice system and herd persons with mental illnesses in. This has prompted some to refer to jails as "that part of the criminal justice system 'that can't say no'" (Lamb et al., 2002, p. 1267).

Arrest may even be perceived as a more beneficial alternative than the mental health system, with law enforcement officers engaging in what are termed mercy bookings (Greenberg, 2001; Lamb et al., 2002; Sargeant, 1992). The use of a mercy booking implies that the officer feels that by getting a person with mental illness booked into jail that individual will at least have basic needs met with the provision of food, shelter, a bed, and the opportunity to bathe. Therein, at least, persons with mental illnesses won't return immediately to the community to cause more unrest, and officers can get on with the crime fighting roles for which they have been trained. Since 1965, the trend has been toward a higher rate of arrest for former mental health patients (Patch & Arrigo, 1999). Bernstein and Seltzer (2003) report that persons with mental illnesses are almost twice as likely to be arrested by police during encounters on the street as opposed to police contacts with persons without mental illnesses; Teplin (2000) in one study found the likelihood of arrest of persons exhibiting signs and symptoms of mental illnesses to be 67% greater than those who did not appear to be mentally ill.

Evidence of law enforcement's frustration with the provision, or lack thereof, of mental health services is seen in the declaration of one police chief in a small town in Florida. As reported by Saenz (2002), Avon Park Chief Frank Mercurio put workers at a crisis stabilization unit (CSU) in Bartow, Florida, on notice that he would arrest them for obstructing justice the next time one of his officers made a medically necessary long haul transport to their CSU facility only to be turned away. Furthermore, provided persons with mental illnesses are accepted for treatment, complaints were registered against mental health personnel due to quick releases from the unit. The mental health provider, on the other hand, maintains that they are handcuffed by budget cuts and different protocols for handling persons abusing substances versus persons who have mental illnesses. Plus, policymakers continue to close state hospitals, creating greater burdens on both the mental health and criminal justice systems (Saenz, 2002).

To ensure clear delineation of and adherence to responsibilities in partnerships between the mental health and criminal justice systems, entities should enter into interagency agreements specified in memorandums of understanding [MOUs] (Sellers et al., 2005). Teplin (2000) has also discussed the importance of negotiated "no-decline" agreements between law enforcement agencies and treatment providers, specifying responsibilities so that providers do not, as is sometimes the case, skirt their duties by refusing to treat individuals because of a history of violence, frequent hospitalizations, abuse of substances, and/or inability to pay for services. Realizing the relative impact of substances, Watson et al. (2014) argue that Crisis Intervention Team (CIT) training should focus on co-occurring disorders and resistance management.

This dilemma regarding societal protection and civil liberties is often present when police encounter persons with mental illnesses in crises. Police decisions about whether, when, and how to intervene in such situations is not an exact science and can be very subjective while trying to balance public safety and civil liberties. A number of factors can enter into the resolution of such encounters.

As stated by Miller (1997),

> The state has a legitimate interest under its *parens patriae* powers in providing care to its citizens who are unable because of emotional disorders to care for themselves; the state also has authority under its police power to protect the community from the dangerous tendencies of some who are mentally ill (p. 1173).

Wood, Watson, and Fulambarker (2017) refer to this matter as the "gray zone" of police work. Sometimes the lines between this paternalistic protection by the state on the one hand and the awesome power to protect the citizenry on the other may become so blurred and murky that it is difficult to discern which function is of primary concern to the authorities. Roughly two million grownups with severe mental illness go to jail annually and have longer jail stays on average than other inmates (Lyons, 2015; Rogers, 2015).

Wood and Watson (2017) contend that officers who encounter people with mental illness in crisis should approach such matters as guardians, not warriors. Adams (2006), for example, in an article on law enforcement officers in Lakeland, Florida, following up after previous contact with persons with mental illnesses to check on their welfare and ensure that they are compliant with their medications, refers to these officers as "compassionate enforcers" (p. A1). Likewise, police in Ithaca, New York, have been featured for their efforts at prevention and revisits to persons with mental illnesses while accompanied by mental health personnel (Goodstein, 2000). More recently, the Ithaca Police Department, in compliance with an executive order issued by Governor Andrew Cuomo for submission of police reform plans from all New York municipal police agencies, have considered several proposals. One of the options is moving operation of the SWAT mobile command vehicle under the direction of a civilian controlled emergency response team, and another recommendation is creating an alternative system for law enforcement, using unarmed officers responding to crisis intervention calls and making referrals to wraparound human and health services delivery (Pierre, 2020; Tolve, 2021). However, it is not always readily discernable whose interests are primarily being considered. As indicated by Goodstein (2000),

> Henry J. Steadman, the president of Policy Research Associates, "There is a potential invasiveness there for individuals who would feel coerced into mental health services because the police are still checking up on them in the role of police officers.... If the person is simply seen as in need of treatment, then why should the police be hanging around forcing the person into treatment?" Ron Honberg, director of legal affairs at [the National Alliance on Mental Illness (NAMI)], said, "I think it's great that Ithaca cares enough to

do something creative. I just worry that if it's done the wrong way it conjures
up images of Big Brother at its worst."

There are those who do not believe that the police should be involved in the treatment
of persons with mental illnesses (Boyd, 2006; Florida Times-Union, 2006). The police
would agree (Borum, 2000), but they have no choice in the matter. Although there
have been a great deal of practices and programs to deal with persons with mental
illnesses implemented in the past 15 to 20 years, there has been reluctance by law
enforcement agencies to intervene in this area. This is partially due to a mentality
that if they intervene, it will become their problem; however, the reality is that it is
already their problem (Reuland, 2005).

According to Panzarella and Alicea (1997), "American police function least well
in paramilitary situations. To the extent that situations involving mentally disordered
persons are approached as paramilitary operations, they are likely to remain the bane
of police work" (p. 337). They suggest that a specialized unit designed to specifically
handle crises with persons with mental illnesses would likely work better than a paramilitary SWAT unit in successfully resolving such situations and avoiding escalation.

Police, even with current emphases on community-oriented policing and problem-oriented policing, prefer their role as crime fighters to that of service providers
(Perrott & Taylor, 1995). However, although specialized programs to divert persons
with mental illnesses from the criminal justice system are positive in theory (i.e., to
link individuals with mental illness to treatment, rather than incessantly recycling
through the system), some have cautioned that it may actually result in net widening
(Sellers et al., 2005). Thereby, this would bring more people — not less — into contact
with law enforcement and under control of the system. Thus, providing law enforcement officers with the knowledge, skills, and training to more efficiently resolve encounters with persons with mental illnesses in crises is necessary and, ultimately, can
serve to free officers up to spend more of their time as crime fighters. Commander
Barbara Lewis (personal communication, July 13, 2007) of the Orange County Sheriff's
Office in Orlando, Florida, provides an example of freeing an officer's time so he can
devote himself to crime fighting:

> I have a deputy that responded almost every shift to a residence of a single
> mother who had a very difficult son approximately eight years old. He would
> not listen to her, wouldn't go to school, do his homework, go to bed, etc.
> Sometimes the call would be that the child was fighting her. She would call
> 911 requesting a deputy for a family disturbance. Upon arrival the deputy
> would tell the child to do whatever it was the mother wanted and the boy
> would comply. This was very frustrating for the deputy as it was not really
> a law enforcement function to parent the child for the mother. However, he
> still had to respond to the disturbance. After CIT training, the deputy re-
> sponded again to this residence. During his assessment of the situation, using
> his newly required skills from CIT, he saw possible signs of mania in the
> child. After resolving the issue he was called there for, the deputy gave the
> mom a NAMI brochure. He explained the Family-to-Family program and

that she might be eligible to attend and that they might be able to teach her how to better handle her son. He also told her that there were services through NAMI to help identify if there was more going on with her son other than just bad behavior. The deputy said within a month he was no longer responding to the house. He believes the referral to NAMI (which he had no knowledge of previous to CIT) assisted the mother and connected her to services for her son. He believes the boy was likely bipolar and with proper diagnosis by a mental health professional, he was able to get help, thereby reducing interaction with law enforcement and preventing a negative contact (arrest or injury) for the child. The reduction of calls to this residence allowed the deputy to handle true law enforcement duties instead of parental duties of the mother. This was a major benefit to the agency.[7]

Specialized Police/Mental Health Responses to Persons with Mental Illnesses in Crises

One ostensible solution for addressing the conflicting police roles mentioned previously is to develop specialized responses — both within the police department and in cooperation with the mental health system — for dealing with persons with mental illnesses in crisis. Numerous models of specialized law enforcement responses for dealing with persons with mental illnesses in crises, often referred to as "pre-booking" diversion programs, have been proposed in the past decade. Overall, Deane et al. (1999) identified three broad categories of such specialized responses: (1) *police-based specialized police responses*, with 3% of the departments reporting this model, which fits in with the community policing concept; (2) *police-based specialized mental health responses*, with 12% of the departments reporting this approach; and (3) *mental health-based specialized mental health responses*, with 30% of the departments reporting this method (see also Martinez, 2010). Schwarzfeld, Reuland, and Plotkin (2008) maintain that there are ten essential components of the two specialized police-based responses discussed below for improving service to persons with mental illnesses. These elements are identified as follows: collaborative planning and implementation, program design, specialized training, call-taker and dispatcher protocols, stabilization, observation, and disposition, transportation and custodial transfer, information exchange and confidentiality, treatment supports and services, organizational support, and program evaluation and sustainability (see also, Reuland, 2010).

In the spirit of therapeutic jurisprudence, as discussed in Chapter 1, the goal of each of these specialized responses is to take a problem-solving approach that links

---

7. Law enforcement officers often establish strong relationships with NAMI affiliates, and NAMI can serve as a great resource for officer referrals. Deputy Sharon Clark of the Orange County Sheriff's Office was recently cited as CIT Deputy of the Year for her agency, and she raised more money for NAMI Walks [see http://www.nami.org/template.cfm?section=namiwalks] in 2005 than all other officers combined for her agency (B. Lewis, personal communication, July 13, 2007). Lt. Brian Garrett of the Polk County Sheriff's Office was recently elected president of his local NAMI affiliate.

individuals to treatment for the purpose of preventing future recycling through the system instead of merely incapacitating them temporarily (Borum et al., 1997). Of course, varying community characteristics may influence which type of specialized response is best for a particular community (Borum et al., 1998). Examples of each specialized response follow.

Mobile Crisis Team — Mental Health-Based Specialized Mental Health Response

A mobile crisis team (MCT) is a group of mental health professionals who respond in conjunction with police to persons with mental illnesses in crises. These teams are interdisciplinary in nature and can be comprised of various treatment personnel, including case managers, social workers, psychiatrists, psychologists, nurses, mental health technicians, addiction specialists, and peer counselors. MCTs typically operate under the supervision of community mental health facilities and hospitals and are usually housed separately from law enforcement agencies (Mobile Crisis Team, 2004). Currently, MCTs exist in Knoxville, Tennessee; Middletown, Connecticut (Reuland, 2005); and Anne Arundel County (Council of State Governments, 2002) and Montgomery County, Maryland (Crisis Center, 2007).

As with the other specialized response models, there are relative advantages to MCTs. Some experts (Lamb et al., 2004) favor the mobile crisis team approach because the presence of law enforcement provides safety to and reduces fears of mental health professionals. Likewise, the mental health team offers information and expertise to law enforcement officers in crisis situations with persons with mental illnesses, in which the officers might not have training or feel entirely comfortable or confident. Another significant advantage of mobile crisis teams is that mental health professionals can legally obtain the complete mental health history of a person in crisis, which is invaluable in such situations; whereas law enforcement officers acting on their own may have access only to available information from previous police contacts (Lamb et al., 2002).

Police-Based Specialized Mental Health Responses: PERT, MET, SMART, CIRT, HOT, & CSOs

This genre of responses have been acknowledged for lessening pressure on the criminal justice system and strengthening access to community services (Shapiro, et al., 2015). There are a number of variations of police-based specialized mental health response programs across the country. The following is one such example:

> [I]n San Diego County, Psychiatric Emergency Response Team (PERT) officers receive 40 hours of training as well as 7 hours of ongoing training on a monthly basis. The training includes modules on assessment of mental illnesses, resource networks, and the role of the clinician. The training team includes mental health professionals and police personnel (Reuland, 2005, p. 11).

In the PERT program, police and clinicians respond jointly to mental health crisis situations, with police typically being the first responders to the scene (Reuland, 2005).

As noted by Reuland (2005), the Long Beach, California, Police Department employs a Mental Evaluation Team (MET) that couples an officer with a graduate education with a mental health professional as co-responders to mental health crisis calls. Los Angeles has crisis intervention teams (see *Police-Based Specialized Police Response* below) and also utilizes a Systemwide Mental Assessment Response Team (SMART) that pairs a law enforcement officer with a clinician from the Los Angeles County Department of Mental Health as a secondary co-responder/evaluator. Officers are to have around-the-clock access via hotline to clinicians (Reuland, 2005).

The Crisis Intervention Response Team (CIRT) is a collaborative effort between the Houston Police Department, the Harris County Sheriff's Office, and the Mental Health Mental Retardation Authority of Harris County, which provides clinicians to ride with law enforcement officers and respond to CIT calls (Mental Health Unit, 2011). Since CIRT's inception in 2008, this one and only team in Texas has responded to over 14,000 situations with less than 1% of these crisis calls resulting in arrest. The Houston Police Department's Mental Health Unit also partners with a number of agencies under the auspices of its Homeless Outreach Team (HOT) in an attempt to link homeless persons with community services and investigates crimes against the homeless (Mental Health Unit, 2011).

Burnett et al. (2000) describe the role and responsibilities of Community Service Officers (CSOs) in Birmingham, Alabama. Although employed by the police department, CSOs are not sworn officers. Instead, they provide a social service component — including networking, brokering services and acting as an advocate — for persons with mental illnesses; individuals do not have to be in psychiatric crises to receive services. These officers work regular shifts but are also available on call to respond as needed to assist and advise officers. If circumstances permit, police can leave them at a scene to resolve non-criminal matters. They can also make follow-up visits with or without an officer's presence. CSOs must have at least a bachelor's degree in social work and usually at least a year of work experience as a social worker (or some other equivalent combination of education and experience).

Following the highly publicized death of George Floyd and other blacks via police encounters, cries to defund the police emerged. As a reported alternative to defunding the police, President Trump on June 16, 2020 signed an executive order to provide federal funding to law enforcement agencies to create co-responder programs to pair social workers with police officers to handle crises involving persons with mental illness and substance abusers; Pinellas County Sheriff Bob Gualtieri was present for the Rose Garden signing ceremony (Associated Press, 2020; Cochrane & Crowley, June 16, 2020). After the executive order was in place, both the Pinellas County and Hillsborough County Sheriffs' Offices in Florida, with CIT (previously mentioned and discussed in detail in the next section) already in place (Holton, 2020; NAMI Hillsborough), expanded their response to mental health crises and follow-up with co-responding clinicians partnered with the police (Rosales & Lopez, 2020; Varn, 2020).

As discussed previously, recent recommendations from the Ithaca Police Department reflect a similar evolution (Pierre, 2021).

Plans have been set forth to shift funds from the City Of Berkeley Police Department in California to a third-party to oversee a Specialized Care Unit, with police being replaced by medical personnel and licensed clinical social workers to respond to mental health crises and conduct wellness checks (Ruggiero, 2021; Uyeda, 2020). The Berkeley plan is is modeled after an approach from Eugene, Oregon, and San Francisco authorities voted in a similar approach recently (Uyeda, 2020). Knowing that traffic stops represent the most likely interaction a citizen will have with the police and that such stops can result in horrific consequences exposed by the media and individual citizens, the Berkeley City Council has proposed prohibiting minor traffic stops (such as those for having an expired license and not wearing a seat belt) and the creation of an unarmed enforcement body under the auspices of the Department of Transportation (Ruggiero, 2021; Ruiz-Grossman, 2021). Without weapons, it is hoped the police will be more focused on and reliant upon deescalation skills to control situations and less on uses of force.

In Albuquerque, New Mexico, a psychiatrist is employed by the police department, even though this can be costly, as psychiatrists earn on average more than $200,000 a year, while police officers average $60,000 a year (Morris, 2018). While the pay for such health care professionals up front can be expensive, there can be cost savings over time. For example, the city of Louisville's implementation of crisis intervention team (CIT) training resulted in excess of a million dollars saving (Morris, 2018). The full-time psychiatrist in Albuquerque, in addition to conducting CIT training, can also conduct psychiatric assessments of officers and serve as a liaison from the police force to behavioral health in the community.

CIT — A Police-Based Specialized Police Response

The Crisis Intervention Team (CIT) is the specialized response to persons in mental health crises most widely adopted by law enforcement agencies (Watson, 2010). The CIT concept is modeled after the prototypical program developed by the Memphis Police Department.[8] Extensive training (e.g., 40 hours of initial specialized training, including officer interaction with consumers of mental health services, along with regular updates) is the cornerstone to CIT. However, the Memphis model also emphasizes strong collaboration with the local mental health system. It requires the availability of a centralized, around-the-clock, "drop-off" treatment facility with a no-refusal policy, where officers can easily and safely transfer custody of the individual in crisis to mental health professionals.

Other police agencies have developed modified CIT approaches. One example of a police-based specialized police response hybrid is that of the Florence, Alabama,

---

8. As CIT will be described in detail in the last half of this chapter, the main components only will be summarized here.

Police Department, which employs an officer as a Community Mental Health Officer (CMHO) (Reuland, 2005). The CMHO has approximately 100 hours of mental health training and is available for responses to mental health crises around the clock. The officer is also involved in monitoring logs for and conducting follow-ups on individuals with mental illnesses in crises who encounter the criminal justice system, as well as maintaining outcome data (Council of State Governments, 2003). These CMHOs in Florence are different from the CSOs previously discussed in Birmingham, as the CMHOs are sworn police officers who have arrest powers. Also, the CMHOs undergo more training than CIT officers and are not considered CIT officers by the CIT Center (2012).

Comparisons of the Law Enforcement Response Models

There have been several studies comparing the aforementioned models of law enforcement specialized responses to crises involving persons with mental illnesses. The initial studies focused on officers' perceptions of the effectiveness of their department's specialized response to mental health crises. The first of its kind, by Borum et al. (1998), compared officers' opinions about a police-based specialized police response (Memphis, CIT), a police-based specialized mental health response (Birmingham, CSOs), and a mental health-based specialized mental health response (Knoxville, mobile crisis unit). Memphis officers — whether part of the specialized CIT team or not — were found to be more likely to perceive their agency as more effective in each of the following areas than were Birmingham or Knoxville officers: minimizing the amount of time spent on mental health-related crisis calls, fulfilling the needs of persons with mental illnesses in crisis situations, avoiding jail for persons with mental illnesses in crises, and providing safety for the community. Particularly the first two points were likely due to Memphis's program consisting of a collaborative drop-off treatment center. Overall, Memphis CIT officers felt better prepared to handle mental disturbance calls. Borum et al. (1998) predicted that, by increasing officers' confidence in mental health crisis situations and reducing the turnaround time for officers, CIT would increase the probability that some action will be taken and that the mental health system will be relied upon, while lessening the likelihood of arrest. In addition to these results, Hanafi, Bahora, Demir, and Compton (2008) noted that CIT training results in increased recognition of mental illnesses by officers, greater empathy, more patience, and better responsiveness to persons with mental illnesses in crises. Bahora, Hanafi, Chien, and Compton (2007) report that CIT-trained officers exhibit enhanced self-efficacy — self-confidence in one's ability to act in a specific situation such as a mental health crisis — while non-CIT-trained officers indicate feelings of being unprepared in such encounters (Ralph, 2010).

Deane et al. (1999) also examined law enforcement officers' perceptions of their department's specialized responses to mental health crisis calls. In this study, though limited by police officer self-perceptions, the authors found that the mobile crisis team approach (mental health-based specialized mental health response) was rated by officers as higher in terms of effectiveness (82%) than either of the police-involved responses: CIT (police-based specialized police response, 67%) or CSOs (police-based specialized mental health response, 70%). Perhaps this was due at the time to a perception on the part of law enforcement that persons with mental illnesses in crises should be the responsibility of the mental health system, with officers resenting involvement in the process. Indeed, reducing turnaround time for officers was pivotal in enhancing the perceived effectiveness of the program.

Steadman, Deane, Borum, and Morrissey (2000) found that the various specialized response models differ in terms of actual outcomes as well. Memphis CIT officers, for example, were more quickly on the scene and were much more likely to link individuals to treatment via transport than the other two sites. Accordingly, they also had the lowest arrest rate. Birmingham's police-based mental health response was much more likely to resolve matters on the scene than other models, yet they simultaneously had the highest arrest rates.[9] Lastly, in Knoxville, their mental health-based mental health response, the Mobile Crisis Team, had long response times and, thus, officers frequently opted for jail. Officers from all programs indicated that police diversion programs are a good way to avoid the inappropriate use of jails to house persons with mental illnesses.[10] Regardless of the model in place, essential ingredients that heighten the success rate in encounters with persons with mental illnesses have been identified. The CIT International (2012) organization maintains an updated list of success stories highlighting positive CIT interventions.

Steadman et al. (2001) examined police-based diversion programs in Memphis, Tennessee; Multnomah County, Oregon, which is modeled after the Memphis police crisis intervention team concept; and Montgomery County, Pennsylvania, where the program provides for the dispatch of psychiatric crisis counselors into the field. As noted in previous studies, the researchers found the crucial element that contributed to the success of each of these programs was the availability of a single, centralized, no-refusal, crisis-receiving facility that operated around the clock. It functioned with a single point of entry and a streamlined intake process to minimize confusion and officer downtime, enabling officers to get back on the street and tend to crime fighting duties. In this study, "the arrest rate in mental health crisis situations in cities with specialized police responses has been found to be only 6.7%. This rate is a third of

---

9. This finding could be an artifact of the staffing problems in Birmingham that were noted in the article. Specifically, the authors explained that there was limited availability of the CSO on nights and weekends. Thus, it is possible that during these periods of limited availability, officers elected to arrest instead, inflating the arrest rate above the other locations that had specialized responses at all times.

10. Unfortunately, recidivism rates for those handled on scene or arrested versus those referred for treatment were not monitored or compared.

that reported [in another study] for non-specialized police responses" (Steadman et al., 2001, p. 222).[11]

Reuland (2005) examined law enforcement agencies using either police-based police responses (75% of agencies) or police-based mental health responses (25% of agencies). Most of the police-based police response programs were modeled after the Memphis CIT model. Moreover, Reuland (2005) chose to include police-based responses that were combined with a mobile crisis team, but excluded mobile crisis teams alone because modifications in law enforcement training and protocol are not as pronounced. She concluded that CIT has emerged as the most popular specialized program among the police because officers are typically the first on the scene; in those first few crucial moments, whether a crisis escalates or de-escalates tends to revolve around the officers' actions. Thus, officers think the most effective approach is to intensively prepare officers, rather than relying on mental health professionals to co-respond.

In conclusion, of the three specialized responses, the Memphis Police Department's CIT program is the most well-known of all police diversion programs in the country (Steadman et al., 2000). It is also the most often replicated specialized response model (Adelman, 2003; Ritter, Teller, Munetz, & Bonfine, 2010), and it is considered to be the most effective in successfully resolving mental health crises (Sellers et al., 2005). The sections below discuss CIT in more detail, including the training involved, descriptions of successful CIT encounters, the plusses (e.g., procedural fairness, reduced agency costs, community benefits), and the results of outcome studies focusing exclusively on this model.

Understanding CIT

In a survey of experts, McGuire and Bond (2011) identified thirty-six essential elements of CIT programs considered to be very important by a majority of those surveyed. The most important components, identified by 80% or more of the respondents, in descending order were: intensive training, mental health services available 24/7, de-escalation by officers, rapid transfer of responsibility to mental health services, de-escalation training, involvement in program development to ensure buy-in, no-refusal policy of mental health receiving facility, and command staff commitment to CIT to demonstrate that the CIT program is a priority.

Professor Sam Cochran, formerly a major with the Memphis Police Department, is one of the founders of CIT and is considered the foremost expert on CIT training. He has assisted numerous jurisdictions in initiating their own CIT programs. In his own words, Cochran outlines the essence of CIT (personal communication, January 4, 2007):

---

11. It should be noted that Geller (2008) points to the uniqueness of having a streamlined single point of entry crisis receiving facility as perhaps making all the difference in police outcomes in encounters with persons with mental illnesses, not the CIT training of the officers. Likewise, Lord, Bjerregaard, Blevins, & Whisman, (2011) acknowledge that changes in leadership at a crisis stabilization center can affect the success of police CIT outcomes. Watson (2010) maintains that a multi-city study should be undertaken to assess the impact of different mental health systems on CIT outcomes.

The Essence of CIT: *The Crisis Intervention Team*

The Crisis Intervention Team is about uniting community partnerships, such as law enforcement, advocacy groups (NAMI), mental health providers, family members, and consumers of mental health services. CIT is committed to quality of services that are directed to those who struggle and cope with mental illnesses and other co-occurring disorders. CIT offers leadership to encourage and promote the accomplishments of community goals: safety, understanding and compassion. In promoting CIT, it is important to acknowledge and visualize the "CIT model as more than just training." Yes, CIT training is important, but the framing of CIT should be in collaboration with community partnerships/relationships. It is these attributes (necessary components) that manifest a change of "hearts" within people. [It is] a chance to accommodate quality of life issues and the building of hope [through]:

- Community collaboration/partnerships to the model
- Developing and maintaining community ownership and advocacy to the model
- Selecting, building and nurturing community anchors (leaders, team members and services)
- Creating and infusing of systems/infrastructures to accommodate appropriate and workable solutions/services
- Uncompromising and relentless approach to defeating stigma (mental illnesses)

The people of whom I speak are **not** just law enforcement officers. A more inclusive understanding of the word "people" should be considered within terms of **all people**—within communities, counties and states. It is important to bring forth a mindset of fairness and openness by which to understand and to acknowledge that we must not embrace nor deny the encroachment by which **"stigma"** has harmed us all. This may sound as if I am speaking only in terms of training. Not so, CIT is the "flagship" by which people of communities, counties and states work together within partnerships to better address and accommodate appropriate crisis services.

CIT has been proclaimed and noted as a model which is "more than just training." Again, training is important and indeed brings about attributes of stability and structure within the overall intent and purpose of community crisis services. The pursuit of the CIT model should be undertaken with honorable attributes of passion and service and should be viewed carefully within the context of the following points:

(1) Some law enforcement officers are not ready, nor suited for the role as a CIT Officer (leadership). Please understand that this concept holds true in consideration of individual placement within any "specialized" program/service.

(2) Communities that are careless by minimizing efforts of not advocating or seeking the implementation of other appropriate systems and infrastructures so as NOT to inappropriately/unnecessarily criminalize people with mental illnesses are in effect, performing on a fragile stage exhibiting little or no leadership standards by which to promote community safety, services and hope.

(3) Training is essential, but utilizing a training only approach will significantly adversely impact and marginalize the overall intent and purpose of the CIT model. Failing to consider or act on the fragmentation of systems and services undermines the CIT potential, projecting instead a quick-fix or "band-aid" or cosmetic approach in addressing very real and very complex community crisis issues. By default the intended paradigm becomes the truism: stigma of mental illnesses harms us all. CIT is about changing the hearts of America. The Crisis Intervention Team, it's more than just training.

Cochran (2004) states, ultimately, "The family members and the consumers: they're the people who inspire us. They're the people we need to address our attention and service to. With passion, we ask, 'Who are the mentally ill?' They're our fathers, our mothers, our sons and daughters, our cousins, aunts and uncles. They're us.... Persons with mental illnesses are deserving of special care and services."

CIT Training

As noted previously, intensive training of law enforcement officers is essential to CIT. First and foremost, the goal of CIT training is to ensure officer safety (Cochran, Deane, & Borum, 2000). Successful resolutions of crises with persons with mental illnesses cannot be achieved without maintaining officer security. Additional goals of CIT training are to reduce unnecessary arrests of persons with mental illnesses, improve understanding of the signs and symptoms of mental illnesses, improve officers' ability to identify community resources and alternative dispositions to increase referrals to and access to mental health services, bring diverse systems together, and enhance crisis communication skills so de-escalation can take place without physical confrontations, thereby enhancing safety of all concerned and reducing uses of force (Borum, 2000; Compton, Demir, Neubert, Broussard, et al., 2009; Kalinich, 2010; Watson, Ottati, Draine, & Morabito, 2011). CIT officers are specially trained to respond to mental health crises but perform the general duties of any other patrol officer when not on those calls (Reuland, 2005). In describing what he learned from CIT training, Officer Chris Jordan of the Collier County, Florida, Sheriff's Office indicated (personal communication, July 6, 2012), "The Golden Rule comes into play more often than not — simply treat others (sick, mentally ill, terminally ill) as you would like to be treated and all will be well. I stop and ask, 'How would I like my 81-year-old mother treated by law enforcement?' The answer is simple, with respect and due care."

Typical CIT training curriculum components include a history of how the criminal justice system became the de facto mental health system; why the actions of persons with mental illnesses who have encounters with law enforcement are not always volitional; signs and symptoms of mental illnesses; types of mental illnesses;[12] varieties of psychotropic medications; civil commitment process; pertinent laws and regulations; co-occurring disorders; suicide; departmental policies; identification of community resources, such as site visits of emergency rooms, mental health facilities, receiving facilities, drop-in centers, clubhouses, assisted living facilities, and the like; discussion of special programs, such as assertive community treatment;[13] interaction with consumers of mental health services and family members; and role-playing, videos, and training in de-escalation techniques. Other CIT training components may address cultural differences, developmental disabilities, substance abuse, and dementia/Alzheimer's disease.

---

12. Compton and Kotwicki (2007) recommend that the following disorders be covered in CIT training: schizophrenia and other psychotic disorders, mood disorders, anxiety disorders, personality disorders, childhood and emotional disorders, posttraumatic stress disorder, and neurological disorders (p. 37). However, it should be cautioned that the goal in CIT training is not to turn law enforcement officers into quasi-psychiatrists. Instead, the goal is for them to have enough knowledge about the disorders to recognize that a mental health problem exists and to safely get the person in crisis to a mental health clinician for evaluation and diagnosis. Officers in CIT training should be instructed that all they need to be able to do is to realize there is a problem in need of attention. While it may help to articulate some of the symptoms they have observed to a clinician, they do not have to know specifically what the problem is; they just need to link the individual to a professional for assessment and treatment. Judge Janeice Martin, who presides over the Collier County Mental Health Court (MHC) in Naples, Florida (mental health courts will be discussed in subsequent chapters), indicates,

> The MHC Team has a presence at *every* CIT training, during the final day in the Community Resources Segment. There, we do our best to let those officers know (1) exactly what MHC is, and what it isn't; (2) how MHC works, and (3) how they can help make sure someone comes to our attention when they think it might be appropriate. With regard to this last element, we spend a few minutes specifically addressing the importance of report writing — how they can quickly clue us in to what it is they are seeing at the scene, so that we can (hopefully) identify that person as being appropriate, and expedite them onto a therapeutic pathway. This effort has paid huge dividends, and we've been able to save some of our most appropriate participants many extra days or weeks in jail this way" (personal communication, July 22, 2012).

13. Knowing what community resources are available to assist persons with mental illnesses in crises is extremely beneficial for law enforcement officers. Lt. Anne-Marie Wendel of the Lakeland Police Department (LPD) in Lakeland, Florida (personal communication, April 30, 2007) describes engagement of an assertive community treatment (ACT) team counselor in the treatment process. (The ACT concept will be discussed in the chapter on diversion and reentry.) Lt. Wendel relates the following story:

> An ACT client came to LPD to try and check out computer equipment to stop the people stalking him through the television set. A CIT officer made contact with him in the lobby and worked with him for over an hour to include contacting his ACT counselor. The CIT officer did civilly commit him but had everything coordinated with the ACT counselor. The officer even took the extra step to take his bicycle (only mode of transportation) back to his apartment and lock it inside and then take the keys back to the hospital. Follow-up contacts have been successful. The individual continues to contact the CIT Officer to talk with the officer when things are not going too well, thus receiving more assistance.

Some CIT training formats, such as Polk County and Sarasota County, Florida, have also incorporated a simulation experience entitled "Hearing Disturbing Voices." This involves utilization of an audio recording of simulated auditory hallucinations developed by Dr. Patricia Deegan, who has schizophrenia (Fasshauer & Garrett, 2006). CIT trainees are asked to complete a number of tasks while hearing voices via their headsets. Audio/visual simulators have also been devised based on input from persons with schizophrenia and have been used in police CIT training in Brown County, Ohio (Lee, 2007), for example.

With an emphasis on officer safety, policies on use of force should be clearly delineated for CIT officers. Watson and Angell (2007) maintain that law enforcement officers need to know when to use force, and guidelines should be developed on how much force is necessary under specified circumstances. Compton and Kotwicki (2007) devote a chapter in their book to de-escalation techniques that include the stages of the escalation of a crisis as devised by the Memphis Police Department. Those officers who do well in de-escalating situations are empathetic, demonstrate good listening skills, remain calm, show patience, exercise flexibility, possess the ability to think on their feet, and exhibit assertiveness and control (Compton & Kotwicki, 2007). Good verbal and non-verbal communication skills, where simple requests are issued using a non-threatening approach (e.g., the officer may introduce him/herself by first name) and stance (e.g., calmly assessing an encounter with a person with mental illness), can serve to facilitate a successful resolution.

CIT-trained officers should also have access to less than lethal munitions. Cordner (2006) recommends use of less lethal weapons, such as pepper sprays, stun guns, and beanbag rounds, to employ the least amount of force necessary. Munetz, Fitzgerald, and Woody (2006) suggest that tasers might be issued to officers in communities that have established effective partnerships between the police and mental health providers. For example, in Akron, Ohio, they reported use of the taser 35 times — 27 of those incidents involved a person with mental illness — with no serious injuries in the first 18 months of utilization.

Cooper et al. (2004) contend that the mental health system owes it to the criminal justice system to familiarize criminal justice practitioners on the roles and responsibilities of mental health workers. Typically, CIT training engages clinicians from the local community as instructors to discuss their areas of expertise, such as signs and symptoms of mental illnesses and psychotropic medications, with law enforcement officers. This provides a good starting place for beginning and fostering a professional dialogue between the mental health and criminal justice systems. Healthy partnerships and alliances can be formed; CIT training can help identify viable options and link names and faces from one system to the other, thereby facilitating the expedient and efficient resolution of future conflicts between the two systems. Individuals who previously failed to communicate and pointed fingers of blame at each other can now work together collaboratively.

Memphis CIT training includes eight hours of police consumer interaction (Cochran, 2004). By 2005, the majority of CIT programs (61%) reflected some aspect of consumer and family member involvement (Honberg, 2005). Family members of persons with mental illnesses can also prove to be a valuable resource for police when crises occur, and family members should be engaged as CIT trainers. Since more and more responsibility for persons with mental illnesses is shifted from mental health authorities to families, as noted by Dempsey and Forst (2008), frequently it is family members who make the initial call to police for assistance with their loved one with mental illness in crisis.

Crisis intervention team training is a way of breaking down barriers by bringing together law enforcement officers, persons with mental illnesses, and their family members in order to establish rapport and enhance future interactions. It is important to get a buy-in from consumers and family members for mental health/criminal justice partnerships, and this lends credibility to programs and training. Consumers and family members should be engaged in the planning stages of specialized programs and involved as trainers, evaluators, and ambassadors of such programs as well. Typically, the best and most influential presenters are those that have had previous contact with the police while in crisis. The key is that both family members and consumers of mental health services involved in such training and collaborations need to be emotionally past the critical incidents and over any resentment from these prior contacts to be able to make a significant and meaningful contribution. Oftentimes officers, unless they have a friend or family member with mental illness, have never — to their knowledge — had an encounter with a person with mental illness who was not in crisis. It is amazing to watch the transformations that take place for all involved as consumers and family members share their compelling stories with law enforcement officers. Relationships are fostered that go beyond a training classroom.[14]

There are a number of places where agencies that want to engage consumers and family members in these kinds of productive partnerships can go in order to identify those willing to participate. These resources can be found at the local, state, and national levels. The headquarters for NAMI (n.d.) in Arlington, Virginia, for example, coordinates numerous programs through their Education, Training, and Peer Support Programs (ETP) Support Center, including Peer-to-Peer and In our Own Voice. In Our Own Voice (IOOV), for example, is a program that originated in 1996 to empower persons with mental illnesses to speak publicly about their illnesses and journeys

---

14. It is not uncommon to see police officers drop by assisted living facilities and drop-in centers to check in with persons with mental illnesses with whom they have worked, persons that they would have never taken time out for before except in a crisis. This type of behavior prompted one person at a drop-in center to remark, "In the past we used to duck under tables here anytime the police showed up, as there was always a crisis when they pulled up. Now, we sit down across the table and have a cup of coffee and chat with them." Just as the media can sensationalize and negatively portray persons with mental illnesses, it can also do the same to police officers. However, supposedly hardened, calloused, law enforcement officers have been seen taking up offerings to pay a speeding ticket for one CIT presenter who received a ticket while running late for a CIT presentation and to provide funds to purchase medication for a consumer presenter with schizophrenia who had lost his benefits because he was earning too much money from his service station job, leaving him unable to afford his psychotropic medication.

to recovery to a vast array of community and professional groups (Sultan, O'Brien, Farinholt, & Talley, 2006). It has been found to promote the concept of recovery and contribute to the de-stigmatization of persons with mental illnesses among attendees (Wood & Wahl, 2006).[15] Each NAMI state chapter also maintains a Consumer Council and a Speakers Bureau. Other national organizations that can assist criminal justice agencies that seek to engage consumers and family members in trainings include SAMHSA's GAINS Center (http://gainscenter.samhsa.gov/html/) and diagnosis-specific organizations, such as the Depression and Bipolar Support Alliance (http://www.ndmda.org/). Finally, local clinicians, advocacy centers for person with disabilities, agencies that train and utilize peer counselors, drop-in centers, clubhouses, student disability services, and counseling centers are valuable resources.

NAMI has also established a CIT Technical Assistance Resource Center to act as a clearinghouse for policymakers, law enforcement agents, mental health personnel, consumers of mental health services and family members to provide up-to-date information on CIT and related jail diversion initiatives (Dailey et al., 2006). The Center is engaged in the expansion of CIT via national networking and is able to provide assistance to advocates interested in implementing CIT programs adaptable to their particular jurisdictions. The critical role of involving consumers of mental health services and family members is also addressed by the Center.

NAMI has endorsed the 40-hour CIT training standard of the Memphis Model and encourages and supports the implementation of this model to the degree practicable nationwide (Honberg, 2005). In addition to training state, university, and local sworn law enforcement personnel, others reportedly trained in various jurisdictions include dispatchers, emergency medical technicians, fire personnel, paramedics, hospital/emergency room staff, probation officers, security officers, judges, detention/correctional officers (Honberg, 2005), and school resource officers (James, Logan, & Davis, 2011).

Types of CIT Encounters

As revealed by research and corroborated by actual officers in the field, suicidal ideations appear to be a common reason for dispatching CIT-trained officers to encounters with persons with mental illnesses (B. Lewis, personal communication, July 13, 2007; T. Rolón, personal communication, February 22, 2007; Skeem & Bibeau, 2008; D. Spratt, personal communication, May 8, 2007). CIT-trained officers have been found more likely to transport suicidal persons to treatment than others encountered on mental disturbance calls according to one study in Akron, Ohio (Ritter, Teller, Marcussen, Munetz, & Teasdale, 2011). Commander Barbara Lewis (personal communication, July 13, 2007) of the Orange County Sheriff's Office in Orlando,

---

15. The previously mentioned Montgomery County Emergency Service (MCES, 2005) in Pennsylvania offers a provider-run police school that emerged in 1974 and is considered to be the first systematic attempt to familiarize law enforcement with issues pertaining to mental illnesses in the nation. In provider training of police officers in Pennsylvania, MCES has engaged NAMI's IOOV presenters to share their personal struggles with mental illnesses and their recovery with officers.

Florida, relays the following story of Officer Peter Hernandez that was shared with her by Lt. James A. Como of the Ocoee Police Department in Ocoee, Florida. This story is indicative of how CIT training can thwart suicide attempts and save lives:

On April 5, 2006, a young gentleman approached Officer Hernandez outside the Ocoee Police Department. The gentleman related to Officer Hernandez his worry about his former girlfriend and mother of their children because of unsettling behavior she exhibited. The gentleman indicated how he attempted to speak with the woman, but because of their inability to resolve anything without arguing, he left. Although the gentleman had second thoughts about his concern and told Officer Hernandez not to worry about it after all, Officer Hernandez asked him where the woman lived and said he would like to go by and check on her anyway.

Officer Hernandez then went to the address he had been given and met with the woman, Jane Doe. Though Ms. Doe tried to assure Officer Hernandez that all was well and there was nothing to worry about, Officer Hernandez detected in her voice an uneasy calm that suggested otherwise. He felt something just wasn't right.

Officer Hernandez spent quite a while speaking with Ms. Doe, studying her body language and voice stress and was gradually able to break down emotional barriers that Ms. Doe had erected. Finally, Ms. Doe began to open up and confess to Officer Hernandez that on this evening she planned to take the lives of her daughter, age 4, and son, age 3, by suffocating them and then take her own life by an overdose of medication that she had already called into the pharmacy but did not have the chance to pick up because of the arrival of Officer Hernandez at her door. Officer Hernandez earned Ms. Doe's trust and was able to bring her to the Crisis Center, where she was admitted. The two children were placed with their grandparents.

Officer Hernandez had insisted on checking on Ms. Doe, even after her former boyfriend recanted. His intuition and instincts as a Crisis Intervention Team Officer enabled him to intervene before Ms. Doe had the chance to carry out the unspeakable act of taking the lives of her innocent young children and herself. Because of Officer Hernandez, these three lives were saved. Officer Hernandez received a commendation from the Ocoee Police Department and an award from the American Society for Industrial Security for his compassionate intervention.

Lt. Denise Spratt (personal communication, May 8, 2007) of the Louisville Metro Police Department, in Louisville, Kentucky, describes some of the encounters her department has had with persons with mental illnesses. Most of her related experiences are illustrative of severe symptoms of psychosis and/or mood disorders. The last is a success story:

- A female called stating her cat was "demonized." On arrival, the woman appeared quite calm and was looking down at the cat. However, she had stabbed herself in the throat and was bleeding profusely. The woman seemed almost unaware and stated that would stop the demons. She was in and out of reality during the dialogue.

- A man whose brother worked at the sanitation plant walked in and tried to jump in the incinerator.

- Several CIT runs involve patients being nude in public. One man was naked on the sidewalk walking around "preaching" incoherently with his hand in his anus.

- We have several bridges that go over the Ohio River between Kentucky and Indiana. We get several bridge jumpers or attempted jumpers.

- A man put his head on the railroad tracks to commit suicide but changed his mind at the last second and pushed himself off with his hands. Both of his arms were severed.

- A man stabbed himself in the heart with an ink pen. The pen was approximately 1/2 inch deep in his chest.

- A homeless female living in a viaduct, after multiple encounters with a CIT officer, is now living in government subsidized housing. She is compliant with her treatment.

Delusions are fixed, false beliefs; and religious delusions are common among persons with mental illnesses when symptomatic (Torrey, 2006). Perceiving oneself as Jesus, for example, is not an uncommon theme for persons who are delusional (see Buchanan, 2007; Staik, 2007). Officer Tony Rolón (personal communication, February 22, 2007) of the St. Petersburg Police Department relates the following encounter replete with religious overtones.

I was called to a first floor condo in a nice neighborhood to check the welfare of the man who lived there. I was surprised to find a smallish 30-something, meek-looking, soft-spoken man. We spoke at the door and I told him of my call. He assured me that there was nothing wrong. I learned that he had lived in the complex for several years. After I left, I checked and found that there were no prior police reports for this man.

I was called back to the apartment several weeks later. The caller advised that there were loud noises coming from within the apartment. I spoke with the meek man again. Just from looking at him and hearing him speak one would never think he would be capable of violence. He allowed me into the apartment on this day, but only the entry hallway.

The apartment was dark and I could see that a light fixture was pulled out of the hallway wall and hanging from the wires. I told the man that I had a number of hobbies and asked about his. He told me that he liked to shoot his hand gun. I asked to see it but he declined. He told me that everything was okay.

I was called out again to the condo a couple of weeks later. I spoke with the man, and he allowed me into the apartment again. I stepped inside a little further than I had the first time. I saw that the rear sliding glass doors had been shattered and glass was outside on the patio. Also on the patio was a loveseat. I asked what had happened. The man said that he had thrown the loveseat through the door. He said he had lost his job in the past months and was running out of money. I was able to see the handgun and convinced him to allow me to "hold onto it" for safekeeping.

I was called out several days later. The caller said the man was burning something. We had a good rapport and he allowed me into the apartment. He allowed me to take a tour of the condo on this occasion. I found that every light fixture had been pulled from the wall or ceiling and was hanging. The stereo was in the middle of the living room floor and was tuned to a local Christian talk radio show. In the kitchen I found that there were burn marks on the counters.

I got the man to explain the state of his home. He told me that everything was alright since he lost his job. He told me that God had begun to talk to him through the radio; that's why it had a prominent place in the living room. He needed to pull the light fixtures from the drywall to ensure that no evil spirits were behind them. The burn marks were burnt offerings to God. He was only doing as commanded.

I realized the potential for violence and began to inquire more about the commands and what God was telling him. He told me that his task on this world was to cleanse the lesbians. He believed that lesbians were evil and had to be cleansed. He would not tell me what the cleansing was.

I was able to get some help for the man. He was without funds so he was appointed a counselor to assist him. He got back on his medication, which stopped when he was fired. And he began to see a mental health professional on an outpatient basis. I was terribly afraid of his potential for violence, so I visited him almost daily. I enlisted the aid of another officer so we did not miss seeing him on any day. We both made sure the man took his medications while we were present.

Regardless of the assistance the man was getting, he fell into crisis. One evening he turned the radio up very loud and left his unit. He walked to the second floor where two college girls lived. He hacked at the door violently with a large knife. He then took a fire extinguisher and attempted to break the door open. Officers arrived on scene while he was still beating on the door and yelling unintelligibly. When the man saw the officers, he calmed down and obeyed all of their commands.

Generally, officers are advised in training not to reinforce a delusion that someone is experiencing unless it is necessary to resolve the situation. Commander Barbara Lewis (personal communication, July 13, 2007) of the Orange County Sheriff's Office in Orlando, Florida, shares the following story of an individual with Post-Traumatic Stress Disorder (PTSD):

> An encounter with an intoxicated heavily armed [with access to four loaded weapons] veteran suffering from Post-Traumatic Stress Disorder and believing that he was back in Vietnam was successfully resolved by using Navy jargon. The deputy even got the compliant subject to march into the crisis receiving center by chanting in cadence, "left, right, left ..."

Of course, as discussed, most persons with mental illnesses are not violent — even when compared to persons within the general population (Ellis, 2011). CIT programs have been touted for providing appropriate interventions to further de-escalate violence in law enforcement encounters with persons with mental illnesses (Hanafi et al., 2008; Morabito et al., 2012). As we shall see, a number of those programs and CIT-trained officers are emerging across the country.

CIT has been adapted for different communities and/or settings. Although initially developed in more urban areas, CIT has been adapted to meet the needs of rural areas as well. Lord et al. (2011) reported finding no differences in consumer outcomes regarding decisions made by rural (less than 50 officers on the force) and urban (more than 50 officers) law enforcement personnel in their study, with most encounters resulting in involuntary commitment or being resolved at the scene. Involuntary commitments were more likely to occur when consumers were believed to be using illegal drugs as opposed to alcohol, according to the researchers. They did find that officer decisions could be influenced by the availability of mental health services, even down to the detail of who was in charge of the local crisis stabilization facility. Likewise, in a study of police in Chicago, it was determined that the ability of CIT-trained law enforcement to link persons to mental health treatment was largely contingent upon the availability of mental health services in the surrounding community (Watson et al., 2011). Further, Lord et al., (2011) indicated that rural officers tended to be more inclined than urban officers to press for voluntary commitment or resolution of the matter at the scene of an encounter with a person with mental illness, as rural officers were often short-handed without sufficient back-up to endure a longer involuntary commitment process. CIT-trained officers in both rural and urban communities were found to be more likely than traditionally trained law enforcement officers to voluntarily commit persons with mental illnesses that they encountered in crises who were female and/or white, and these officers were more likely to arrest as the demeanor of consumers became increasingly agitated and the severity of the offense (such as a felony) was heightened (Lord et al., 2011).

The Procedural Fairness of CIT

Cooperation is more likely to be garnered when persons view the interaction with authorities as fair as opposed to coercive (Watson & Angell, 2007). Regardless of the outcome, individuals want to feel that they were treated with respect. If one's status has been eroded and diminished by the stigma of mental illness, a person's self-worth and self-respect may be further diminished — or bolstered — depending on their interaction with police. Moreover, contrary to popular belief that mental illness renders people globally incompetent, persons with mental illnesses are able to accurately judge when a police encounter is coercive, and they usually remember their encounters and the outcomes of those interactions with the police (Watson & Angell, 2007). Therefore, the quality of police interactions with individuals with mental illness will have repercussions for future encounters with authorities. How law enforcement officers treat individuals that they encounter has both immediate and long range effects.

According to Watson and Angell (2007), the CIT model clearly incorporates key elements of procedural justice. These include, from the perspective of the individual with mental illness: having a voice, participation and input into decisions that impact oneself, being listened to by the decider, being treated with dignity, respect and politeness, acknowledging one's rights, and trusting that the arbiter is concerned with one's well being. Such an example of treating a person with procedural justice is seen in the following example involving St. Petersburg, Florida, police officer Tony Rolón (personal communication, February 22, 2007):

I met Stella at Publix supermarket. She had been caught shoplifting again. The manager wanted me to arrest her and give her a trespass warning. I looked with a heavy heart upon the little old lady who could be my grandmother. I took the time to talk with her before I did anything. I saw she was paying for some items and stealing others, bread, oranges. I detected something in Stella. I gave her a little cognitive test, you know, "who is the president …?" She didn't do so well. I spoke to the manager and asked if I could take Stella. I pled her case. I told him that I believed that she was suffering from the infirmities of aging as well as a social security check which was way too small. He relented, and I took Stella home. Stella thanked me and unlocked her door. I walked in with her. She got mad. I went to the cupboards and fridge. Stella had next to nothing in food or belongings. She had notes everywhere to remind her to do this and do that. I knew what was going on. I told her I had to leave but would be back. It was check off. My sergeant asked about the little old lady and what I had done with her. I explained the circumstances to him. He gave me $5. I went to Publix Supermarket and bought the things Stella had tried to boost. I called the Department of Children and Families (the agency in Florida entrusted to look out for the public welfare of its citizens), blah, blah … not a risk … have to be in the criminal justice system to help ... blah. I was now on a crusade! I contacted the Little Old Lady League, an informal group of retired ladies who help other little old ladies out. Imagine that! I got some real clothes for Stella. One of the lady's sons is a podiatrist. Stella got her hammertoes fixed and got real shoes, and now she would not have to cut the sides out. I got her some real cookware. And, I finally found her daughter in Chicago. Gina wanted nothing to do with her mom. Stella was too much trouble, that's why she sent her to Florida. I tried to charge Gina criminally ... I couldn't find a crime which fit. We watched over Stella for several years until her health got to such a point that she needed a supported living environment. Stella went to a nursing home. After Stella met me she was never arrested for shoplifting again.

With that said, caution must be exercised, as procedural justice can be misused:

[O]veremphasizing procedural justice concerns ... could, if unchecked, lead to substantively unjust outcomes being obscured by seemingly fair procedures. Absent genuine concern, procedural justice techniques are simply a form of manipulation in the moment, which may backfire on officers in subsequent contacts with the individuals.... [I]n training police officers, the importance of substantively fair treatment, not simply the appearance of fair treatment [must be emphasized] (Watson & Angell, 2007, p. 792).

Confidentiality

There appear to be a lot of misconceptions and utter confusion about federal confidentiality laws, which serve to inhibit communications regarding persons with mental illnesses. According to Husted et al. (1995), confidentiality laws may prohibit mental health clinicians from sharing information with law enforcement personnel about specific persons with mental illnesses. The federal Health Insurance Portability and Accountability Act (HIPAA), which went into effect in 2001, does in fact govern some—but not all—communications regarding treatment of persons with mental illnesses:

Contrary to myth, HIPAA-covered entities do not include the courts, court personnel, ... law enforcement officials such as police or probation officers; [t]here are special rules for correctional facilities.... HIPAA ... permits [some] disclosures without the individual's consent. Those relevant here include disclosures for public health activities; judicial and administrative proceedings; law enforcement purposes; disclosures necessary to avert a serious threat to health or safety; and disclosures mandated under state abuse and neglect laws.... HIPAA incorporates the principle that in general disclosures should be limited to the 'minimal necessary' to accomplish the purpose for which disclosure is permitted (Petrila, 2007, pp. 2–3).

For example, protected health information, such as the release date of an arrestee, could be shared by a treating agency with police, as "HIPAA ... permits a covered entity to disclose protected health information to a law enforcement official's request for information for the purpose of identifying or locating a suspect, fugitive, material witness, or missing person" (Petrila, 2007, p. 2). Petrila offers the caveat that state confidentiality laws may be more stringent than the HIPAA federal law, and he suggests that uniform consent/waiver forms should be developed for release of information to ensure multi-agency cooperation.[16]

Another means for law enforcement to reasonably circumvent confidentiality requirements is to have consumers of mental health services voluntarily identify themselves to law enforcement. Residents of Orange, Seminole, Lake, Osceola, and Brevard counties in central Florida with mental health disabilities may register with the "Medical Security Program." Registrants will be issued a picture identification card and an identifiable bracelet recognizable to law enforcement personnel indicating that one is a voluntary enrollee in the program. This program is touted as a means of ensuring ready identification of persons with mental illnesses should crises occur and the initiation of a different tactic in safely handling these individuals in such situations (Beary, 2005). However, such a practice raises questions related to stigmatization.

Cordner (2006) also maintains that HIPAA does not apply to police personnel and communications amongst themselves; therefore, tracking repeat calls, counting incidents, mapping locations, days/times of calls and hot spots are perfectly acceptable by law enforcement officers. Certainly, specialized training to properly address the avoidance of labeling and stigmatization by the police should be undertaken, and Cordner cites an example in Charlotte, North Carolina where officers were summoned to the same residence over 100 times on mental disturbance calls before actually communicating amongst themselves and resolving the situation successfully.

Law enforcement personnel are certainly at liberty to discuss a person's mental health status with family members of a person with mental illness without being concerned about violating HIPAA. Lt. George Welch (personal communication, July 3, 2012) of the Collier County, Florida Sheriff's Office relates the following success story regarding a CIT intervention, with familial assistance, after multiple contacts:

> In 2008, shortly after I was appointed as the CIT coordinator for our agency, I was contacted by the sister of a consumer (Karen) who lived in our North Naples District. She was very concerned on the wellbeing of Karen and told me that she had contacted the Sheriff's Office numerous times to have her

---

16. An example of a form for the disclosure of confidential information is available online at http://www.gainscenter.samhsa.gov/html/resources/presentation_materials/pdfs/UniformPermission.pdf.

checked and Baker Acted.[17] Her sister suffered from schizophrenia, and had attempted to end her life on several occasions through self-starvation. I researched Karen's address and identified five instances in which we had responded to the residence over a one month period. Three of those calls were for welfare checks and two others were for disturbances with neighbors. All of the calls were cleared after a very short period of time on scene, and all were cleared status Z (handled in routine manner). Since our agency had just started CIT training, we had a limited number of CIT-trained deputies in our districts. Fortunately, the North Naples District had deputies that had been trained and I was able to contact one of them directly to respond to Karen's residence for a welfare check. The deputy responded and after spending some time with Karen at the screen door was able to convince her to allow him into the residence to verify her wellbeing. Upon entering the door the deputy observed a waste bucket next to the door with water inside. The deputy asked Karen why water was in the bucket and she informed him that it was rain water. He asked why she would have rain water and she told him her water supply was poisoned. Investigating further the deputy observed numerous boxes of food items, in plain view in the pantry. Upon closer inspection he discovered that the boxes were in fact empty, merely props to give the image that she was caring for herself. The deputy opened the refrigerator and freezer doors and observed rotten, moldy food inside. Further signs of her illness included a busted TV, turned towards the wall. All of her air vents were covered to keep the voices out, holes punched through the walls and every item in the residence labeled in permanent magic maker with her initials to prevent theft. Karen had also plugged the toilets and the sewage was running over and leaking into the apartment below her. The only food item found in the residence was saltine crackers, which we learned Karen ate to take away the hunger pains. The deputy initiated the Baker Act and Karen was taken to the local Baker Act receiving facility.

While Karen was being evaluated I communicated several times with her sister. The family was desperately trying to find a more long-term treatment facility but did not have enough time due to the 72 hour window of the Baker Act. I was able to provide photographs and updated history on Karen to the facility and they were able to petition the court to hold her longer, which allowed the family the time to transfer her directly to a facility in north-central Florida. While Karen was being treated I spoke with several members of the family and identified that when Karen first stops taking her medications, she starts making rambling phone calls to family members. I provided my phone numbers to her family, including family members who lived in New York City, San Francisco, Colorado Springs and Cleveland.

17. This refers to involuntary civil commitment which was discussed in Chapter 4.

A few months later when Karen was released from the facility I had the CIT deputy check on her and let her know that we were there for her. Though she was being checked every few weeks Karen again stopped taking her meds and I was immediately contacted by her out-of-state relatives. The same CIT deputy responded immediately to her residence and was able to convince her to resume taking her meds and continue with her outpatient care. This repeated itself several times until Karen willingly continued taking her meds daily.

Since 2009 we have not received any more calls from the family to check on her well-being. Since that time she has continued to take her meds and participate in consumer activities, through her friends at the Sara Ann Drop-In Center. A CIT Deputy continues to check on her regularly when time permits and has been accepted as a friend by the family. Without CIT, I am afraid that Karen would have continued her pattern of self-neglect to the point where she may have taken her life. This was our first CIT-related call, and this story is shared in each CIT class, to show that with training and compassion you can make a difference and save a life.

Inter-agency collaborations can also be feasible and acceptable within the parameters of HIPAA. The Houston Police Department in conjunction with the Mental Health Mental Retardation Authority of Harris County, Texas, has developed a Chronic Consumer Stabilization Initiative (CCSI) in an effort to prevent persons with mental illnesses from repeatedly entering into crisis situations resulting in police contact and/or psychiatric hospitalizations. The CCSI consists of collaboration between law enforcement, a psychiatric technician, and a case manager and has resulted in a 47% reduction in such chronic encounters with the Houston police Department (Mental Health Unit, 2011). Sampson and Scott (2000) contend that problem-solving police tactics can be used for successful interventions in such situations. They cite the example of 2,000 calls for police service over a three-year period being made by the same person with mental illness. The woman initiating the calls was ultimately prescribed appropriate medication as the result of a collaborative effort.[18]

Another example of inter-agency cooperation and communication is evident in the Durham, North Carolina, Police Department (Durham Police Department, 2012). Chief Jose Lopez was a staunch supporter of several initiatives within the Durham Police Department for interventions with persons with mental illnesses in crises and ensuring that such persons are linked to treatment. Durham combines CIT-trained police officers who make referrals to mental health case managers for follow-up after crisis calls as part of their Mental Health Outreach Program (MHOP). The goals of

---

18. Scott and Goldstein (2005) offer a guide for collaborative shifting and sharing of responsibilities between various agencies for solving public safety problems.

MHOP include increases in the number of persons linked to mental health services and reduction of re-arrest rates and repeat 911 calls by persons with mental illnesses

Proper tracking and flagging of such calls and sharing of information could serve to reduce unnecessary utilization of law enforcement resources. Even so, many law enforcement agencies have been hesitant to maintain a record of calls for service involving persons with mental illnesses due to the misperception that such logs would be in violation of the rights of persons with disabilities (Greenberg, 2001). Although mentally ill individuals' rights should be observed as much as possible, some would argue that HIPAA violations are sometimes warranted. Historically, HIPAA penalties have been modest in nature, but punishments have increased under the Recovery Act (see Petrila & Fader-Towe, 2010). While providing several successful examples, as noted by Petrila and Fader-Towe (2010), sharing of medical information within and between agencies is not an insurmountable obstacle to overcome. For obvious reasons, discussions on the topics of confidentiality laws and regulations should be included in any specialized police training concerning interactions with persons with mental illnesses,[19] and memorandums of understanding (MOUs) should be entered into by both mental health and criminal justice agencies to clearly delineate agreements and responsibilities.

Liability

There is an increased likelihood of liability for law enforcement agencies and officers for police encounters with persons with mental illnesses. These types of encounters can result in misuse of force, civil rights violations, and wrongful death claims (Borum, 2000).

Sergeant Kendall Wiley (personal communication, May 21, 2007), CIT Coordinator of the Las Vegas Metropolitan Police Department, reports some major incidents with persons with mental illnesses that resulted in use of deadly force with serious injuries to officers and/or consumers. Some resulted in litigation for her department:

1. Le Menn died while in custody on three misdemeanor charges at the Clark County Detention Center. Police said Le Menn, a 33-year-old French citizen, yelled that he was Satan and Jesus Christ. When guards were removing Le Menn from his cell, a struggle ensued in which the inmate was pepper sprayed. The fight ended with the Frenchman collapsing and dying on the cell floor from asphyxiation, according to Coroner Ron Flud.

2. Gavigan, who has a history of mental illness, ran into the house after the officers tried to persuade her to drop the knife. Gavigan then apparently

---

19. For example, Lisa Yanku, Manager of Emergency Services, with the Kent Center in Warwick, Rhode Island, includes the topic of permitted disclosures to law enforcement under HIPAA in specialized training for police responding to persons with mental illnesses (A. Stoltz, personal communication, October 10, 2007).

hurt herself with the knife, then moved toward the officers, police said. The other officer backed up until hitting a wall in the house. The officer fired one shot when Gavigan continued to advance toward the officers, police said.

3. Police fatally shot Herrera, a 27-year-old schizophrenic man, outside his home after he threatened police. Five officers responded to the call and unsuccessfully tried to subdue the knife-wielding Herrera with pepper spray and beanbag rounds fired from a shotgun. When Herrera came within five feet of the officer with a knife, the officer fired his handgun five times, striking Herrera four times. According to the case ruling, the case presented a genuine issue of fact as to whether officers had been inadequately trained in dealing with mentally ill persons and in the use of impact projectiles. Most importantly, it raised the question of whether the alleged inadequate training caused his death. The department settled (*Herrera v. Las Vegas Metropolitan Police*, 2004).

As pointed out by del Carmen (1998), in the law, duty follows knowledge (*City of Canton v. Harris*, 1989). In this same case, Hill and Logan (2001) note that the U.S. Supreme Court established that deliberate indifference can result "where the need for additional training is 'so obvious' and the failure to provide the additional training is 'so likely' to result in a constitutional violation" (pp. 30–31).

Mental health providers and clinicians are also not immune from liability for their actions or failures to act in their dealings with persons with mental illnesses. For example, the family of a person with mental illness in New Haven, Connecticut, has filed a lawsuit against doctors and a hospital for negligently allowing their loved one to decompensate to the point that he was placed in a position to be shot and killed by police (Mills, 2006).

Saunders, Slate, Judd, and Brown (2006) maintain that CIT can reduce police liability and avoid media/community scrutiny with minimal expenditures on the part of the criminal justice system, as expertise in local communities can be tapped to support training initiatives. Thus, implementation of specialized police training for dealing with persons with mental illnesses in crises will not prevent lawsuits, but it may very well increase the possibility of the dismissal of such suits.

Agency Costs and Community Benefits

The primary agency allocation necessary to implement CIT training is simply allowing officers time to attend the training sessions. Other than that, the costs are minimal, as instructors from the local community often donate their time. Of course, photocopying costs can be anticipated for the production of training manuals and compilation of community resource guides which provide contact information for local mental health resources. Access to appropriate space for the training is also necessary.

Most agencies signify that an officer has been CIT-trained by wearing a special pin on the police uniform. Persons with mental illnesses and their family members often look for such pins and find them to symbolize a source of comfort in crises. Lt. Brian Garrett (personal communication, June 8, 2007) of the Polk County Sheriff's Office, Bartow, Florida, describes one family's attachment to one of Garrett's CIT-trained officers:

> A request came in for a CIT deputy to respond to a report of a 13-year-old child out of control in his home. Upon arrival the CIT deputy found the child barricaded in his room threatening to harm himself. The child had been diagnosed with bipolar disorder but was not medicine compliant. The subject then left the house through the bedroom window and attempted to flee the area. The deputy, concerned for the child's safety, gave chase and was able to take him into protective custody down the street after a brief physical struggle. The deputy recognized the child was in need of emergency mental health intervention and declined to charge him criminally for resisting a law enforcement officer. During the car ride to the local mental health receiving center, the young CIT deputy established a rapport with the child and, consistent with CIT protocol, told him he would come by the house to see him once he received treatment.
>
> The deputy did make re-contact once the child got home, and they had the time to discuss video games and other interests they had in common; the deputy used the encounter to urge the child to stay on his medicines and agree to go to counseling, something he had refused to do previously.
>
> The deputy then gave the child his cell phone number and told him he could call anytime he needed someone to talk to and said he would return after the child's first counseling session. The child stabilized and is much improved in school and at home due to the intervention of a caring CIT deputy. The mother and I had actually spoken about her son after I gave a CIT presentation at the local NAMI meeting about a month prior to this incident. I had told her to specifically request that a CIT deputy respond if she needed help with her son in the future, and she remembered to do so.
>
> The mother later called me, in my capacity as the CIT coordinator, to thank the deputy for his efforts and to tell me what a difference it made in her son's life. She told me she was so impressed with the CIT deputy and the program in general that for several months when the family went out to eat or to other social activities they would only go to places in the county because the nearby city did not have a CIT program and would not have anyone to respond if her son was in crisis. She was very relieved when I told her we would send a CIT deputy anywhere in the county if she called needing help. She told me that immediately after the deputy told her son he would come back after he had been to counseling, her son began wanting to know when he would be seeing the counselor. He continued to ask her to take him in spite of the fact it was spring break from school

and it took several days to get an appointment. She also related that the CIT deputy's work schedule was on her calendar and his cell phone number in her speed dial list. The mother told me living with her son's illness was not perfect, but it was one thousand percent better than before the CIT intervention. We recruited this mother to speak from the family perspective during the 40-hour CIT training class, and she has done so regularly, becoming a popular presenter.

Typically, agencies have CIT graduation ceremonies and sometimes have banquets where distinguished officers, mental health providers, consumers of mental health services, and their family members can be recognized. Financial support for these and other costs may be obtained from grants, pharmaceutical companies, community organizations, and law enforcement academies (Saunders et al., 2006).

Need for Outcome Data

A number of researchers have questioned the mainly qualitative data that have been accumulated, sparse amount of in-depth research data that have been collected, and limited long-term outcome data (e.g., what happens to the person with mental illness after CIT contact) on the effectiveness of CIT programs, particularly in the face of the proliferation of the existence of such programs, which will be discussed later (Broussard, Krishan, Hankerson-Dyson, Husbands, Stewart-Hutto, & Compton, 2011; Compton, Bahora, Watson, & Oliva, 2008; Compton, Demir, Oliva, & Boyce, 2009: Demir, Broussard, Goulding, & Compton, 2009; Ellis, 2011; Geller, 2008; Lord et al., 2011; Morabito et al., 2012; Tucker, Van Hasselt, & Russell, 2008; Watson, 2010; Watson, Morabito, Draine, & Ottati, 2008; Watson et al., 2011). More recently, Watson, Compton, and Draine (2017) contend that officer cognition and attitudinal outcomes constitute evidence based practices for CIT trained officers. Similarly, James and James (2017) have devised what they term CIT metrics as a means for measuring the effectiveness of CIT training.

The Number and Types of CIT Programs

Since its inception in Memphis in 1988, Sam Cochran estimated that roughly 50 to 80 jurisdictions had implemented CIT by 2004. In a survey of 251 respondent law enforcement agencies, NAMI determined that 168 (67%) of the agencies reported having a CIT program in their communities by 2005 (Honberg, 2005). Steadman, in 2007, stated that there were 500 to 600 jurisdictions with CIT programs in place across the country. By 2010, CIT programs reportedly had been implemented in more than 1,000 locations (Ritter et al., 2010). Most recently, there are reportedly 2,645 CIT programs nationwide, in the District of Columbia and forty-six states with only four states [Alabama, Arkansas, Rhode Island, and West Virginia] without CIT programs. (CIT Center, 2021). With an excess of 15,000 city (Bureau of Justice Statistics, 2016a) and county law enforcement agencies (Bureau of Justice Statistics,

2016b) in America, this means less than 10% of these organizations have CIT programs in place. However, while not included in these figures, departments of correction are utilizing modified CIT training for correctional agencies. For example, see Davidson (2014) as roughly 18% of these agencies have created CIT teams that continue to grow in popularity.

As noted by Thompson and Borum (2006), the Memphis CIT Model requires that at least 15% to 20% of the sworn patrol force be CIT-trained to ensure around-the-clock coverage for mental health crises. According to Cochran (2004), the purpose of being selective in allowing officers in to the program is because some officers can't write a traffic citation without getting into a confrontation, much less interacting with someone in a psychiatric crisis. Compton et al. (2017) found that volunteering for CIT is associated with better outcomes for those encountered in crisis. However, with the majority of law enforcement agencies across the country employing less than 10 full-time sworn officers, adjustments to the program would need to occur to facilitate implementation of CIT with small departments and in rural areas. Even the Houston Police Department, for example, with 1,870 CIT-trained officers fielding 25,568 CIT calls in 2011, was only able to respond with a CIT officer on the scene in 42% of these calls (Mental Health Unit, 2011).

Jamieson and Wilson (2000) state that the Seattle Police Department adopted the Memphis CIT model, but the Seattle department has fewer less lethal weapons than Memphis, whose officers have access only to pepper spray and batons. A Seattle firearms instructor, Ken Saucier, explains, "You don't take a bean bag gun to a gun-fight," and expresses concern that if officers lessen their guard when encountering persons with mental illnesses in crises, they may do so at their peril (Jamieson & Wilson, 2000). However, this exemplifies another program that lacks fidelity to the Memphis CIT model. Moreover, whereas in a true CIT program, a trained officer on the scene of a crisis with a person with mental illness is designated to take charge of a situation regardless of the rank of the other officers (Watson & Angell, 2007), this is not the case in Seattle. Seattle allows most, if not all, of its officers to participate in CIT training, while Memphis, as previously discussed, is much more selective, identifying only those officers that appear to be best suited for this innovative approach (Jamieson & Wilson, 2000).

Results of CIT

There are a number of reasons that have been articulated as to why CIT has been singled out as the premiere model for responding to persons with mental illnesses in crises. As discussed previously, CIT has been identified as the best of the three specialized responses for lowering arrest rates and generating a greater perception of effectiveness on the part of the police (Borum et al., 1998; Honberg, 2005; Martinez, 2010; Steadman et al., 2000). CIT has also been touted for its effectiveness in reducing uses of force, diminishing injuries to both persons with mental illnesses and police officers, reducing arrests, increasing transports and access to mental health treatment services, and reducing jail suicides (Bonfire, Ritter, and Munetz, 2014; Bunch, 2005; Compton et al., 2015; Compton et al., 2014A; Compton et al., 2014B; Dupont & Cochran, 2000; Demir, Broussard, Goulding, & Compton, 2009; Ellis, 2014; Hanafi et al., 2008; Honberg, 2005; Reuland & Cheney, 2005; Skeem & Bibeau, 2008; Thompson & Borum, 2006; Watson, 2010). Communication between law enforcement and treatment personnel is enhanced as collaborations between the two systems occur and is essential to positive CIT outcomes (Hanafi et al., 2008; Oliva & Compton, 2008; Ralph, 2010).

Steadman et al. (2000), for example, found an arrest rate of 6.7% in cases involving CIT police encounters with persons with mental illnesses, while the estimated national average non-CIT arrest rate for such confrontations is 20% (Strauss et al., 2005). Despite methodological problems, Franz and Borum (2011) reported that 3% of CIT-trained police encounters with persons with mental illnesses over a five-year period resulted in arrest, whereas it was estimated that before the implementation of CIT training 19% of these situations would have ended in arrest. Skeem and Bibeau (2008) found that CIT officers in Las Vegas were four times less likely than non-CIT officers to make arrests in crisis encounters. In Memphis, referrals to treatment by officers doubled within four years of implementing the CIT program; and within one year of the establishment of a CIT program in Louisville, Kentucky, the average number of referrals by police to mental health treatment increased from 500 to 600 persons a month (Strauss et al., 2005). However, in a quasi-replication of the Strauss study, researchers discovered no fundamental differences in the numbers of referrals by CIT-trained and non-CIT officers to psychiatric emergency services (Broussard et al., 2010).

CIT training has also been found to potentially reduce law enforcement officers' stigmatizing attitudes toward persons with mental illnesses (Broussard et al., 2011; Compton, Esterberg, McGee, Kotwicki, & Oliva, 2006; Kalinich, 2010; Hanafi et al., 2008). CIT-trained officers, when compared to non-CIT-trained officers, have been discovered to require less social distance, a form of stigma measured by how far one physically places one's self away from a subject one encounters (Bahora et al., 2007). Non-CIT-trained officers reportedly prefer to avoid contact with persons with mental illnesses in crises (Ralph, 2010). Honberg (2005) noted that CIT results in improved relationships between law enforcement and advocates. CIT has been found to also reduce use of force incidents (Thompson & Borum, 2006; Watson, 2010), and injuries to persons with mental illnesses decreased by 40% shortly after implementation of CIT in Memphis (Council of State Governments, 2007). In Chicago, while CIT training was only marginally effective in reducing police uses of force, Morabito et al. (2012) did find that those officers who had received CIT training responded with less force than non-CIT-trained officers as the demeanor of a person with mental illness escalated. CIT also translates into fewer shootings of persons with mental illnesses by police (Watson & Angell, 2007) and fewer deaths for persons with mental illnesses and police (Honberg, 2005). Furthermore, while deployment of SWAT teams have reportedly decreased by 50% in Memphis and by almost 60% in Albuquerque after implementation of CIT (Reuland, Schwarzfeld, & Draper, 2009), no significant reductions in SWAT call-outs were found in Atlanta (Compton, Demir, Oliva, & Boyce, 2009). Compton, Demir, Neubert, Broussard, et al. (2009) concluded that CIT-trained officers may be an effective approach for reducing uses of force by police in encounters with persons with mental illnesses in crises, and Compton and Chien (2008) report that continuing training on mental illnesses can also be beneficial for CIT officers.

Strauss et al. (2005) projects that, in addition to reducing officer injuries and uses of force, de-criminalization of persons with mental illnesses may result in long-term cost savings and reductions in psychiatric morbidity by linking persons with mental illnesses to appropriate treatment. If so, the expectation would be that over time CIT contacts and referrals to emergency treatment providers would diminish. In other words, if operated efficiently and with the necessary mental health infrastructure in place, CIT operations may ultimately put themselves out of business, as mental health treatment will eventually take place where it should have been taking place all along: within the mental health system.[20]

Conclusion

Individual jurisdictions should decide if a pre-booking diversion program such as those described above is suitable for their communities and identify key stakeholders to become involved in considering such options. Community stakeholders that might be considered along with law enforcement for planning and training purposes include mental health providers, jail administrators, prosecutors, public defenders/defense attorneys, judges, consumers of mental health services, family members of persons with mental illnesses, and community organizations such as NAMI. Locales may want to identify a model program and send representatives to observe the program and/or training in operation. The Memphis Police Department's CIT program has served as a model visited by a number of jurisdictions around the country (e.g., Orange County Sheriff's Office in Orlando, Florida [B. Lewis, personal communication, July 13, 2007], Fulton County Police Department in Atlanta, Georgia [P. Michaud, personal communication, May 6, 2007]).

Specialized law enforcement interventions (i.e., pre-booking diversion programs) are indeed promising. They can be even more effective when coupled with assistance from the courts, such as what occurs in mental health courts (i.e., a post-booking diversion strategy). This forms the focus of Chapter 8. Nevertheless, as noted by Sam Cochran (2004) — who reiterates a recurrent theme throughout this book — all the planning, coordination and training in the world may not be enough in the absence of a sufficient infrastructure of mental health services and care. CIT is more than a police program with officers acting alone and solely responsible for all outcomes. As

---

20. Even prosecutors have been impressed with the results rendered by CIT training. Commander Barbara Lewis (personal communication, July 13, 2007) reports that, for example, Vance Voyles of the Orange County Sheriff's Office received praise from an assistant intake prosecutor for his insight in diverting a person with mental illness to treatment instead of arresting her.

noted by Steadman and Morrissete (2016), means for establishing ways for police to integrate with behavioral health care providers are essential. Helfgett, Hickman, and Labossiere (2016); Steadman and Morrissette (2016) recommend that partnerships between CIT officers and mental health providers be solidified within communities. For CIT to be effective local and state mental health providers must integrate it into their protocols and operations. Support from other community organizations such as schools, churches, NAMI, civic organizations, city and county commissions, as well as mayors is critical to making CIT a community program. The police are all too aware that they can't do this alone.

Beyond CIT and other police-involved methods for handling mental health crises, with continued societal unrest, lack of community mental health services, and calls for defunding the police, there is likely to be an increase in interventions outside law enforcement. As Beck, Reuland, and Pope (2020) determined in their analysis of alternative community responses to mental health crises, model innovative programs are in place in Eugene, Oregon via Crisis Assistance Helping Out on the Streets (CA-HOOTS) and in Olympia, Washington, where clinicians respond to such calls. The authors maintain such alternative approaches to police involvement can better link persons to needed community mental health services, benefit the well-being of all, and decrease arrest rates and possible violent confrontations with police for this population. Funding sources for securing intervention outside the police realm will need to be secured for similar programs.

In the face of some resistance, a direct example of defunding the police in an attempt to enhance community services can be found in Austin, Texas. The City Council of Austin chose to slash the city police department's budget of $430+ million by one-third over time, with an initial cessation of hiring officers to fill vacancies, increasing community access to food and abortion programs and eventually reclassifying forensic services as a civilian responsibility, not law enforcement (Venkataramanan, 2020). More recently, $6.5 million of the Austin police budget was set aside to buy a hotel, renovate it, and provide housing for the homeless in the area (Schwartz, 2021). Beck et al. (2020) conclude we do not need more police to handle persons with mental illnesses in crises; instead, we need more mental health care. How are things being handled in your community?

The next chapter is on jail processing of persons with mental illnesses. We now turn there for those unfortunate ones who are not properly linked to treatment prior to jail.

References

Adams, R. W. (2006, May 1). Compassionate enforcers — Police's new role. *The Ledger*, pp. A1, 8–9.

Adelman, J. (2003). *Study in blue and grey, police interventions with people with mental illness: A review of challenges and responses.* Canadian Mental Health Association. Retrieved from https://cmha.bc.ca/wp-content/uploads/2016/07/police report.pdf.

Alathari, Lina et al. (2019). Protecting America's Schools, U.S. Secret Service. Retrieved from https://www.secretservice.gov/data/protection/ntac/usss-analysis-of-targeted-school-violence.pdf.

Associated Press (2020, June 16). Trump signs order on police reform, doesn't mention racism in *Tampa Bay Times*. Retrieved from https://www.tampabay.com/news/2020/06/16/trump-signs-order-on-police-reform-doesnt-mention-racism/.

Bahora, M., Hanafi, S., Chien, V. H., & Compton, M. T., (2007). Preliminary evidence of effects of crisis intervention team training on self-efficacy and social distance. *Administration and Policy in Mental Health, 35*, 159–167.

Beary, K. (2005). *Identification bracelet programs*. Orlando, FL: Orange County Sheriff's Office. Retrieved from http://www.ocso.com/LinkClick.aspx?link=ID+BRACELET+PROGRAMS.pdf&tabid=115&mid=510.

Beck, J., Reuland, M., Pope, L. (2020) *Behavioral Health Crisis Alternatives: Shifting from police to community solutions.* Vera. Retrieved from https://www.vera.org/behavioral-health-crisis-alternatives.

Bernstein, R., & Seltzer, T. (2003). The role of mental health courts in system reform. *University of the District of Columbia Law Review, 7*, 143–162.

Bonfine, N., Ritter, C., & Munetz, M.R. (2014). Police officer perceptions of the impact of crisis intervention team (CIT) programs. *International Journal of Law and Psychiatry, 37*, 341–350.

Borum, R. (2000). Improving high risk encounters between people with mental illness and the police. *Journal of the American Academy of Psychiatry and the Law, 28*, 332–337.

Borum, R., Deane, M. W., Steadman, H. J., & Morrissey, J. (1998). Police perspectives on responding to mentally ill people in crisis: Perceptions of program effectiveness. *Behavioral Sciences and the Law, 16*, 393–405.

Borum, R., Swanson, J., Swartz, M., & Hiday, V. (1997). Substance abuse, violent behavior and police encounters among persons with severe mental disorder. *Journal of Contemporary Criminal Justice, 13*(3), 236–250.

Boyd, E. (2006). Appropriate use of police officers? *Psychiatric Services, 57*(12), 1811.

Broussard, B., Krishan, S., Hankerson-Dyson, D., Husbands, L., D'Orio, B., Thompson, N. J., Watson, A. C., & Compton, M. T., (2011). *Psychiatric crisis from the perspective of police officers: Stigma, perceptions of dangerousness, and social distance. An update of the National Institute of Corrections & Mental Health.* Retrieved from http://community.nicic.gov/blogs/mentalhealth/archive/2011/08/04/psychiatric-crisis-from-the-perspective-of-police-officers-stigma-perceptions-of-dangerousness-and-social-distance.aspx.

Broussard, B., Krishan, S., Hankerson-Dyson, D., Husbands, L., Stewart-Hutto, T., & Compton, M.T. (2011). Development and initial reliability and validity of four self-report measures used in research on interactions between police officers and individuals with mental illnesses. *Psychiatry Research, 189,* 458–462.

Broussard, B., McGriff, J. A., Demir Neubert, B. N., D'Orio, B., & Compton, M. T. (2010). Characteristics of patients referred to psychiatric emergency services by crisis intervention team police officers. *Community Mental Health Journal, 46,* 579–584.

Buchanan, D. (2007). *Commitment to recovery.* Arlington, VA: Treatment Advocacy Center. Retrieved from http://www.psychlaws.org/GeneralResources/pa10.htm.

Bunch, K. (2005, January 30). *When cops confront mental illness: Policing mental illness.* Retrieved from http://www.medicinenet.com/script/main/art.asp?articlekey=51068.

Bureau of Justice Statistics (2016A). Local police departments 2016: Personnel. Retrieved from https://www.bjs.gov/index.cfm?ty=pbdetail&iid=6706.

Bureau of Justice Statistics (2016B). Sheriffs' offices, 2016: Personnel. Retrieved from https://www.bjs.gov/index.cfm?ty=pbdetail&iid=6707.

Burnett, V. B., Henderson, B. C., Nolan, S. D., Parham, C. M., Tucker, L. G., & Young, C. (2000). How Birmingham's community service officers unit works. *Community Mental Health Report, 1*(1), 1–2, 13.

CIT Center. (2021). *National directory.* Memphis, TN: University of Memphis. Retrieved from http://cit.memphis.edu/.

CIT International. (2012). *International Crisis Intervention Team.* Retrieved from http://www.citinternational.org/.

City of Canton v. Harris, 489 U.S. 378 (1989).

Cochran, S. (2004, Winter). *Fighting stigma in law enforcement: The message has to come from the heart.* Washington, D.C.: U.S. Department of Health and Human Services, Substance Abuse and Mental Health Services Administration, Center for Mental Health Services, Resource Center to Address Discrimination and Stigma. Retrieved from http://www.stopstigma.samhsa.gov/memoranda/index winter2004.htm.

Cochran, S., Deane, M. W., & Borum, R. (2000). Improving police response to mentally ill people. *Psychiatric Services, 51*(10), 1315.

Cochrane, E., & Crowley, M. (June 16, 2020). Republicans signal narrow policing overhaul as Trump signs limited order. *The New York Times.* Retrieved from https://www.nytimes.com/2020/06/16/us/politics/trump-republicans-police-overhaul.html.

Compton, M. T., & Chien, V. H. (2008). Factors related to knowledge retention after crisis intervention team training for police officers. *Psychiatric Services, 59*(9), 1049–1051.

Compton, M. T., Bahora, M., Watson, A. C., & Oliva, J. R. (2008). A comprehensive review of extant research on crisis intervention team (CIT) programs. *Journal of the American Academy of Psychiatry and the Law, 36*(1), 47–55.

Compton, M. T., Demir, B., Oliva, J. R., & Boyce, T. (2009). Crisis intervention team training and special weapons and tactics callouts in an urban police department. *Psychiatric Services, 60*(6), 831–833.

Compton, M. T., Demir Neubert, B. N., Broussard, B., McGriff, J. A., Morgan, R., & Oliva, J. R. (2009). Use of force preferences and perceived effectiveness of actions among Crisis Intervention Team (CIT) police officers and non-CIT officers in an escalating psychiatric crisis involving a subject with schizophrenia. *Schizophrenia Bulletin, 37*(4), 737–745.

Compton, M. T., Esterberg, M. L., McGee, R., Kotwicki, R. J., & Oliva, J. R. (2006). Crisis intervention team training: Changes in knowledge, attitudes, and stigma related to schizophrenia. *Psychiatric Services, 57*(8), 1199–1202.

Compton, M.T., et al. (2017). Police officers' volunteering for (rather than being assigned to) crisis intervention team (CIT) training: Evidence for a beneficial self-selection effect. *Behavioral Science Law, 35*, 470–479.

Compton, M.T., et al. (2015). Surveys of police chiefs and sheriffs and of police officers about CIT programs. *Psychiatric Services, 66*(7), 760–763.

Compton, M.T., et al. (2014A). The police-based crisis intervention team (CIT) Model: I. Effects on officers' knowledge, attitudes, and skills. *Psychiatric Services, 65*(4), 517–522.

Compton, M.T., et al. (2014B). The police-bas5ed crisis intervention team (CIT) Model: II. Effects on level of force and resolution, referral, and arrest. *Psychiatric Services, 65*(4), 523–529.

Compton, M. T., & Kotwicki, R. J. (2007). *Responding to individuals with mental illnesses*. Boston, MA: Jones & Bartlett.

Cooper, V. G., McLearen, A. M., & Zapf, P. A. (2004). Dispositional decisions with the mentally ill: Police perceptions and characteristics. *Police Quarterly, 7*(3), 295–310.

Cordner, G. (2006). *People with mental illness. Problem-oriented guides for police, guide no. 40*. Washington, D.C.: U.S. Department of Justice, Office of Community-Oriented Policing Services.

Council of State Governments. (2003). *Community mental health officer*. New York, NY: Author. Retrieved from http://consensusproject.org/programs/one?program_id=77&searchlink=%2fprograms%2fsearch%3f%26show_p%3dt%26consensus_op%3dge%26order_by%3dtitle%26dir%3dasc.

Council of State Governments. (2007). *Fact sheet: Law enforcement and people with mental illness*. New York, NY: Author. Retrieved from http://consensusproject.org/resources/fact-sheets/factsheet_law.

Council of State Governments, Police Executive Research Forum, Pretrial Services Resource Center, Association of State Correctional Administrators, Bazelon Center for Mental Health Law, and the Center for Behavioral Health, Justice, and

Public Policy. (2002). *Criminal Justice/Mental Health Consensus Project.* New York, NY: Council of State Governments. Retrieved from consensusproject.org/the_report.

Crisis center: Mobile crisis team. (MCT). (2007, June 16). Rockville, MD: Montgomery County, Maryland, Government. Retrieved from http://www.montgomerycount-ymd.gov/hhstmpl.asp?url=/content/hhs/crisis_center/mct.asp.

Curtis, L. A. (1975). *Violence, race, and culture.* Lexington, MA: D.C. Heath.

Dailey, J., Daley, G., Lushbaugh, D., White, E., Slate, R. N., & Sultan, B. (2006, September 26). *The critical role of consumers and families in advocating for CIT and jail diversion.* Paper presented at the 2nd Annual Crisis Intervention Team (CIT) Conference, Orlando, FL.

Davidson, M.L. (2014). A criminal justice system-wide response to mental illness: Evaluating the effectiveness of the Memphis crisis intervention team training curriculum among law enforcement and correctional officers. *Criminal Justice Policy Review, 27*(1), 46–75.

Deane, M. W., Steadman, H. J., Borum, R., Veysey, B. M., & Morrissey, J. P. (1999). Emerging partnerships between mental health and law enforcement. *Psychiatric Services, 50*(1), 99–101.

del Carmen, R. V. (1998). *Criminal procedure: Law and practice* (4th ed.). Belmont, CA: Wadsworth.

Demir, B., Broussard, B., Goulding, S. M., & Compton, M. T. (2009). Beliefs about causes of schizophrenia among police officers before and after crisis intervention team training. *Community Mental Health Journal, 45,* 385–392.

Dempsey, J. S., & Forst, L. S. (2008). *An introduction to policing* (4th ed.). Belmont, CA: Thomson Wadsworth.

Dupont, R., & Cochran, S. (2000). Police response to mental health emergencies — Barriers to change. *Journal of the American Academy of Psychiatry and Law, 28,* 338–344.

Durham Police Department. (2012). Mental Health Outreach Program. *MHOP Report.* Durham, NC: Author.

Ellis, H.A. (2014). Effects of crisis intervention team (CIT) training program upon police officers before and after crisis intervention team training. *Archives of Psychiatric Nursing, 28,* 10–16.

Ellis, H. A. (2011). The crisis intervention team — A revolutionary tool for law enforcement: The psychiatric-mental health nursing perspective. *Journal of Psychosocial Nursing & Mental Health Services, 49*(11), 37–43.

Fasshauer, K. D., & Garrett, B. (2006, September 27). *Hearing Disturbing Voices™ — A program developed by the National Empowerment Center.* Paper presented at the Florida Council for Community Mental Health, Hope and Recovery Conference, Orlando, FL. Retrieved from www.fccmh.org/docs/FCCMH_conf_program.pdf.

Florida Times-Union. (2006, February 20). *Treatment of mentally ill should not be police duty*. Retrieved from http://www.jacksonville.com/tu-online/stories/022006/new_21145923.shtml.

Francis, Shantel M. (2020). *Mental Illness is a Disorder, not a Decision*, Partnership Against Domestic Violence. Retrieved from https://padv.org/mental-illness-is-a-disorder-not-a-decision.

Fowler, Katherine et al. (2014) Surveillance for Violent Deaths. *Surveillance Summaries*, Violence Prevention, National Center for Injury Prevention and Control, CDC.

Franz, S., & Borum, R. (2011). Crisis intervention teams may prevent arrests of people with mental illnesses. *Police Practice and Research: An International Journal, 12*(3), 265–272.

Geller, J. L. (2008). Commentary: Is CIT today's lobotomy? *Journal of the American Academy of Psychiatry and Law, 36* (1), 56–58.

Good Therapy (2016). How Crisis Intervention Training Helps First Responders. Retrieved from http://www.crisisresponse.org/How-Crisis-Intervention-Training-Helps-First-Responders/.

Goodstein, L. (2000, September, 6). Trying to prevent the next killer rampage. *New York Times*. Retrieved from http://query.nytimes.com/gst/fullpage.html?res=9A00E3DF1739F935A3575AC0A9669C8B63&sec=health&spon=&pagewanted=2.

Green, T. M. (1997). Police as frontline mental health workers. *International Journal of Law and Psychiatry, 20*(4), 469–486.

Greenberg, S. F. (2001). Police response to people with mental illness. In M. Reuland, C.S. Brito, & L. Carroll (Eds.), *Solving crime and disorder problems: Current issues, police strategies and organizational tactics* (pp. 43–58). Washington, D.C.: Police Executive Research Forum.

Hails, J., & Borum, R. (2003). Police training and specialized approaches to respond to people with mental illnesses. *Crime & Delinquency, 49*(1), 52–61.

Hanafi, S., Bahora, M., Demir, B. N., & Compton, M. T. (2008). Incorporating crisis intervention team (CIT) knowledge and skills into the daily work of police officers: A focus group study. *Community Mental Health Journal, 44*, 427–432.

Helfgott, J.B., Hickman, M.J., & Labossiere, A.P. (2016). A descriptive evaluation of the Seattle Police Departments' crisis response team officer/mental health professional partnership pilot program. *International Journal of Law and Psychiatry, 44*, 109–122.

Herrera v. Las Vegas Metropolitan Police, 298 F. Supp. 2d 1043 (D. Nev. 2004).

Hill, R., & Logan, J. (2001, June). Civil liability and mental illness: A proactive model to mitigate claims. *The Police Chief*, 29–32.

Holton, J. (2020, September 23) Pinellas County Sheriff adding six crisis specialists to address mental health situations. *FOX 13 Pinellas County*. Retrieved from https://www.fox13news.com/news/pinellas-county-sheriff-adding-six-crisis-specialists-to-address-mental-health-situations.

Honberg, R. (2005, May 12). *A national snapshot of CIT programs*. Paper presented at the 1st National Crisis Intervention Team (CIT) Conference, Columbus, OH.

Husted, J. R., Charter, R. A., & Perrou, B. (1995). California law enforcement agencies and the mentally ill offender. *Bulletin of the Academy of Psychiatry and the Law, 23*(3), 315–329.

IACP 2018.

James, L., & James, S. (2017). Crisis intervention team (CIT) metrics: A novel method of measuring police performance during encounters with people in crisis. *Mental Health and Addiction Research, 2*(4), 1–4.

James, R. K., Logan, J., & Davis, S. A. (2011). Including school resource officers in school-based crisis intervention: Strengthening student support. *School Psychology International, 32*(2), 210–224.

Jamieson, Jr., R. L., & Wilson, K. A. C. (2000, May 25). Mental illness frequently deepens tragedy of police shootings. *Seattle Post-Intelligencer*. Retrieved from http://www.theppsc.org/Archives/Victim.Precipitated.Homocide/mental_illness_frequently_deepen.htm.

Kalinich, A. O. (2010). *Crisis Intervention Team (CIT): Perspectives from mental health professionals* (Unpublished doctoral dissertation). Azusa Pacific University, Azusa, California.

Kerr, Amy N., Morabito, Melissa, & Watson, Amy C. (2010). Police Encounters Mental Illness and Injury: An Exploratory Investigation. *Journal of Police Crisis Negotiation, 1*(10), 116–132.

Lamb, H. R., Weinberger, L. E., & DeCuir, Jr., W. J. (2002). The police and mental health. *Psychiatric Services, 53*(10), 1266–1271.

Lamb, H. R., Weinberger, L. E., & Gross, B. H. (2004). Mentally ill persons in the criminal justice system: Some perspectives. *Psychiatric Quarterly, 75*(2), 107–126.

Lee, R. (2007, July 5). *Sympathy through technology: Virtual reality experience mimics schizophrenia to teach health professionals about their patients*. New York, NY: ABC News. Retrieved from http://www.abcnews.go.com/WN/story?id=3348856.

Lord, V. B. (2004). *Suicide by cop: Inducing officers to shoot*. Flushing, NY: Looseleaf Law Publications, Inc.

Lord, V. B., Bjerregaard, B., Blevins, K. R., & Whisman, H. (2011). Factors influencing the responses of crisis intervention team-certified law enforcement officers. *Police Quarterly, 14*(4), 388–406.

Lyons, E. (2019). Imprisoning America's mentally ill. *Prison Legal News*. Retrieved from https://www.prisonlegalnews.org/news/2019/feb/4/imprisoning-americas-mentally-ill/#:~:text=According%20to%20federal%20data%2C%2040, National%20Alliance%20on%20Mental%20IllnessMartinez, L. E. (2010). Police departments' response in dealing with persons with mental illness. *Journal of Police Crisis Negotiations, 10,* 166–174.

McGuire, A. B., & Bond, G. R. (2011). Critical elements of the crisis intervention team model of jail diversion: An expert survey. *Behavioral Sciences and the Law, 29,* 81–94.

Mental Health Unit. (2011). *Success through collaboration: Poised to enter another year of innovation: 2011 annual report.* Houston, TX: Houston Police Department.

Miller, R. D. (1997). Symposium on coercion: An interdisciplinary examination of coercion, exploitation, and the law: III. Coerced confinement and treatment: The continuum of coercion: Constitutional and clinical considerations in the treatment of mentally disordered persons. *Denver University Law Review, 74,* 1169–1214.

Mills, J. (2006, November 21). *Lawsuit: Cop shooting was hospital's fault.* New Haven, CT: The Health Care Connecticut Online Journalism Project. Retrieved from http://www.newhavenindependent.org/index.php/archives/entry/lawsuit_cop_shooting_was_hospitals_fault2/.

Mobile crisis team. (2004, June). New York, NY: New York Department of Health and Mental Hygiene. Retrieved from http://www.nyc.gov/html/doh/html/cis/cis_mct.shtml.

Montgomery County Emergency Service, Inc., Quest. (2005, September). MCES crisis intervention specialist (CIS) training: Enhancing police effectiveness in the community. *MCES Quest, 5*(1), 1–8. Norristown, PA: Author.

Morabito, M. S., Kerr, A. N., Watson, A., Draine, J., Ottati, V., & Angell, B. (2012). Crisis intervention teams and people with mental illness: Exploring the factors that influence the use of force. *Crime & Delinquency, 58*(1), 57–77.

Morris, N. (2018). Police encounter many people with mental-health crises. Could psychiatrists help? *Washington Post.* Retrieved from https://www.washington post.com/national/health-science/police-encounter-many-people-with-mental-health-crises-could-psychiatrists-help/2018/07/20/20561c26-7484-11e8-b4b7-308400242c2e_story.html.

Munetz, M. R., Fitzgerald, A., & Woody, M. (2006). Police use of the taser with people with mental illness in crisis. *Psychiatric Services, 57*(6), 883.

NAMI. (n.d.). *National Alliance on Mental Illness Homepage.* Arlington, VA: Author. Retrieved from www.nami.org.

NAMI, Hillsborough County, Florida (2020) Crisis Intervention Training Program *National Alliance on Mental Illness.* Retrieved from https://namihillsborough.org/nami-advocacy-group/crisis-intervention-training-programs/.

Oliva, J. R., & Compton, M. T. (2008). A statewide crisis intervention team (CIT) initiative: Evolution of the Georgia CIT program. *The Journal of the American Academy of Psychiatry and the Law, 36,* 38–46.

Panzarella, R., & Alicea, J. O. (1997). Police tactics in incidents with mentally disturbed persons. *Policing: An International Journal of Police Strategies & Management, 20*(2), 326–338.

Patch, P. C., & Arrigo, B. A. (1999). Police officer attitudes and use of discretion in situations involving the mentally ill: The need to narrow the focus. *International Journal of Law and Psychiatry, 22*(1), 23–35.

Pauly, Megan (2013). How police officers are (or aren't) trained in mental health. *The Atlantic*, Retrieved from https://www.theatlantic.com/health/archive/2013/10/how-police-officers-are-or-aren-t-trained-in-mental-health/280485/.

Perrott, S. B., & Taylor, D. M. (1995). Crime fighting, law enforcement and service provider role orientations in community-based police officers. *American Journal of Police, 14*(3/4), 173–195.

Petrila, J. (2007, February). *Dispelling the myths about information sharing between the mental health and criminal justice systems*. Delmar, NY: GAINS Center. Retrieved from http://gainscenter.samhsa.gov/text/integrated/Dispelling_Myths. asp.

Petrila, J., & Fader-Towe, H. (2010). *Information sharing in criminal justice-mental health collaborations: Working with HIPAA and other privacy laws*. New York, NY: Council of State Governments. Retrieved from http://consensusproject.org/jc_publications/info-sharing/Information_Sharing_in_Criminal_Justice-Mental_Health_Collaborations.pdf.

Pierre, S. (2021). Ithaca community reacts to public safety reforms. *The Ithacan*. Retrieved from https://theithacan.org/news/ithaca-community-reacts-to-public-safety-reform/.

Price, M. (2005). Commentary: The challenge of training police officers. *Journal of the American Academy of Psychiatry and the Law, 33*, 50–54.

Ralph, M. (2010). The impact of crisis intervention team programs: Fostering collaborative relationships. *Journal of Emergency Nursing, 36*(1), 60–62.

Reuland, M. (2004, January). *A guide to implementing police-based diversion programs for people with mental illness*. Delmar, NY: GAINS Center, Technical Assistance and Policy Analysis Center for Jail Diversion.

Reuland, M. (2005). *A guide to implementing police-based diversion programs for people with mental illness* (Rev. ed.). Delmar, NY: GAINS Center, Technical Assistance and Policy Analysis Center for Jail Diversion.

Reuland, M. (2010). Tailoring the police response to people with mental illness to community characteristics in the USA. *Police Practice and Research, 11*(4), 315–329.

Reuland, M., & Cheney, J. (2005, May). *Enhancing success of police-based diversion programs for people with mental illness*. Delmar, NY: GAINS Center, Technical Assistance and Policy Analysis Center for Jail Diversion.

Reuland, M., Schwarzfeld, M., & Draper, L. (2009). *Law enforcement response to persons with mental illnesses: A guide to research-informed policy and practice.* New York, NY: Council of State Governments Justice Center. Retrieved from http://consensusproject.org/downloads/le-research.pdf.

Ritter, C., Teller, J. L. S., Marcussen, K., Munetz, M. R., & Teasdale, B. (2011). Crisis intervention officer dispatch, assessment, and disposition: Interactions with individuals with severe mental illness. *International Journal of Law and Psychiatry, 34,* 30–38.

Ritter, C., Teller, J. L. S., Munetz, M. R., & Bonfine, N. (2010). Crisis Intervention Team (CIT) training: Selection effects and long-term changes in perceptions of mental illness and community preparedness. *Journal of Police Crisis Negotiation, 10* (1–2), 133–152.

Rosales, I. & Lopez, L. (2020, October 26). Hillsborough County Sheriff's Office launches Behavioral Resources Unit. *ABC Action News Tampa.* Retrieved from https://www.abcactionnews.com/news/region-hillsborough/hillsborough-county-sheriffs-office-launches-behavioral-resources-unit.

Ruggiero, A. (2021). Berkeley passes major police reforms: No more minor traffic stops. *Bay Area News Group.* Retrieved from https://www.mercurynews.com/2021/02/23/berkeley-council-passes-significant-police-reform/.

Ruiz, J., & Miller, C. (2004). An exploratory study of Pennsylvania police officers' perceptions of dangerousness and their ability to manage persons with mental illness. *Police Quarterly, 7,* 359–371.

Ruiz-Grossman, S. (2021). Berkeley, California, to end traffic stops by cops for low-level offenses. *Huffington Post.* Retrieved from https://www.huffpost.com/entry/berkeley-reform-police-traffic-stops-racism_n_6037016dc5b6ec4b56275e5c.

Saenz, T. J. (2002, May 1). AP police chief threatens crisis unit with arrest. *Highlands Today,* pp. 1–2.

Saleh, A. Z., Appelbaum, P. S., Liu, X., Stroup, S., & Wall, M. (2018). Deaths of people with mental illness during interactions with law enforcement. *International Journal of Law and Psychiatry, 58,* 110–116.

Sampson, R., & Scott, M. S. (2000). *Tackling crime and other public-safety problems: Case-studies in problem-solving.* Washington, D.C.: U.S. Department of Justice, Office of Community Oriented Policing Services.

Sargeant, G. (1992, December). Back to Bedlam: Mentally ill often jailed without charges. *Trial,* 96–98.

Saunders, M., Slate, R. N., Judd, G., & Brown, G. (2006, June 20). *Law enforcement/ mental health: Partnerships and initiatives for change.* Paper presented at the National Sheriffs' Association Conference, Orlando, FL.

Schwartz, R. (2021, January, 28) Austin just took money from its police force to buy a hotel for homeless people instead. *MIC.* Retrieved from https://www.mic.com/

p/austin-just-took-money-from-its-police-force-to-buy-a-hotel-for-homeless-people-instead-59439776.

Schwarzfeld, M., Reuland, M., & Plotkin, M. (2008). *Improving responses to people with mental illnesses: The essential elements of a specialized law enforcement-based program.* New York, NY: Council of State Governments and Police Executive Research Forum for the Bureau of Justice Assistance. Retrieved from http://consensusproject.org/downloads/le-essentialelements.pdf.

Scott, M. S., & Goldstein, H. (2005). *Shifting and sharing responsibility for public safety problems.* Washington, D.C.: U.S. Department of Justice, Office of Community Oriented Policing Services.

Sellers, C. L., Sullivan, C. J., Veysey, B. M., & Shane, J. M. (2005). Responding to persons with mental illnesses: Police perspectives on specialized and traditional practices. *Behavioral Sciences and the Law, 23,* 647–657.

Shapiro et al. (2015). Co-responding police-mental health programs: A review. *Administration and Policy in Mental Health, 42,* 606–620.

Skeem, J., & Bibeau, L. (2008). How does violence potential relate to crisis intervention team responses to emergencies? *Psychiatric Services, 59*(2), 201–204.

Slate, R. N., Johnson, W. W., & Colbert, S. (2007). Police stress: A structural model. *Journal of Police and Criminal Psychology, 22,* 102–112.

Staik, T. (2007, June 27). Man claiming to be Jesus surrenders after five-hour standoff. *Charlotte Sun Herald.* Retrieved from http://www.sun-herald.com/Newsheadline.cfm?headline=8838.

Steadman, H. J. (2007, June 21). *Treatment not jails: New leadership and promising practices.* Paper presented at the National Alliance on Mental Illness (NAMI) Annual Convention, San Diego, CA.

Steadman, H. J., Deane, M. W., Borum, R., & Morrissey, J. P. (2000). Comparing outcomes of major models of police responses to mental health emergencies. *Psychiatric Services, 51*(5), 645–649.

Steadman & Morrissette, (2016). Police responses to persons with mental illness: Going beyond CIT training. *Law & Psychiatry, 67*(10), 1054–1056.

Steadman, H. J., Stainbrook, K. A., Griffin, P., Draine, J., Dupont, R., & Horey, C. (2001). A specialized crisis response site as a core element of police-based diversion programs. *Psychiatric Services, 52*(2), 219–222.

Strauss, G., Glenn, M., Reddi, P., Afaq, I., Podolskaya, A., Rybakova, T., … El-Mallakh, R. S. (2005). Psychiatric disposition of patients brought in by crisis intervention team police officers. *Community Mental Health Journal, 41*(2), 223–228.

Sultan, B., O'Brien, S., Farinholt, K. S., & Talley, S. (2006, September 26). *CIT and In Our Own Voice: A natural partnership.* Paper presented at the 2nd Annual Crisis Intervention Team (CIT) Conference, Orlando, FL.

Taheri, Sema A. (2016). Do Crisis Intervention Teams Reduce Arrests and Improve Officer Safety? A Systematic Review and meta-Analysis, *Criminal Justice Policy Review, 27*(1), 76–96.

Tartaro, Christine (2019). *Suicide and self-harm in prisons and jails* (2nd ed.). Lanham, Maryland: The Rowman & Littlefield Publishing Group.

Teese, C. F., & Van Wormer, J. (1975). Mental health training and consultation with suburban police. *Community Mental Health Journal, 11*(2), 115–121.

Teller, J. L. S., Munetz, M. R., Gil, K. M., & Ritter, C. (2006). Crisis intervention team training for police officers responding to mental disturbance calls. *Psychiatric Services, 57*(2), 232–237.

Teplin, L. A. (2000, July). Keeping the peace: Police discretion and mentally ill persons. *National Institute of Justice Journal,* 8–15.

Thompson, L., & Borum, R. (2006). Crisis intervention teams (CIT): Considerations for knowledge transfer. *Law Enforcement Executive Forum, 6*(3), 25–36.

Tolve, C. (2021). Tompkins County and Ithaca pass public safety reforms. *The Ithacan.* Retrieved from https://theithacan.org/news/tompkins-county-and-ithaca-pass-public-safety-reforms/#:~:text=One%20of%20the%20reforms%20adopted,Ithaca%20Police%20Department%20(IPD).

Torrey, E. F. (2006). *Surviving schizophrenia* (5th ed.). New York, NY: Harper Collins.

Tucker, A. S., Van Hasselt, V. B., & Russell, S. A. (2008). Law enforcement response to the mentally ill: An evaluative review. *Brief Treatment and Crisis Intervention, 8,* 236–250.

Uyeda, R. V. (2020). Berkeley California, has pledged to replace some police with social workers. Will it work? *Mic.* Retrieved from https://www.mic.com/p/berkeley-california-has-pledged-to-replace-some-police-with-social-workers-will-it-work-30052899.

Varn, K. (2020, September 23). Pinellas Sheriff to expand unit that handles mental health-related calls. *Tampa Bay Times.* Retrieved from https://www.tampabay.com/news/pinellas/2020/09/23/pinellas-sheriff-to-expand-unit-that-handles-mental-health-related-calls/.

Venkataramanan, M. (2020, August 13). Austin City Council cuts police department budget by one-third, mainly through reorganizing some duties out from law enforcement oversight. *Texas Tribune.* https://www.texastribune.org/2020/08/13/austin-city-council-cut-police-budget-defund/.

Vermette, H. S., Pinals, D. A., & Appelbaum, P. S. (2005). Mental health training for law enforcement professionals. *Journal of the American Academy of Psychiatry and the Law, 33,* 42–46.

Watson, A. C. (2010). Research in the real world: Studying Chicago police department's crisis intervention team program. *Research on Social Work Practice, 20*(5), 536–543.

Watson, A. C., & Angell, B. A. (2007). Applying procedural justice theory to law en-forcement's response to persons with mental illness. *Psychiatric Services, 58*(6), 787–792.

Watson, A.C., Compton, M.T. & Draine, J.N. (2017). The crisis intervention team (CIT) model: An evidence-based policing practice? *Behavioral Sciences and the Law, 35,* 431–441.

Watson, A. C., Corrigan, P. W., & Ottati, V. (2004). Police officers' attitudes toward and decisions about persons with mental illness. *Psychiatric Services, 55*(1), 49–53.

Watson A.C. et al. (2014). Understanding how police officers think about mental/emotional disturbance calls. *International Journal of Law & Psychiatry, 37*(4), 351–358.

Watson, A. C., Morabito, M. S., Draine, J., & Ottati, V. (2008). Improving police re-sponse to persons with mental illness: A multi-level conceptualization of CIT. *International Journal of Law and Psychiatry, 31,* 359–368.

Watson, A. C., Ottati, V. C., Draine, J., & Morabito, M. (2011). CIT in context: The impact of mental health resource availability and district saturation on call dis-positions. *International Journal of Law and Psychiatry, 34,* 287–294.

Watson, A. C., Ottati, V. C., Morabito, M., Draine, J., Kerr, A. N., & Angell, B. (2010). Outcomes of police contacts with persons with mental illness: The impact of CIT. *Administration and Policy in Mental Health, 37*(4), 302–317.

Wilson, J. Q. (1978). *Varieties of police behavior.* Cambridge, MA: Harvard University Press.

Wood, A. L., & Wahl, O. F. (2006). Evaluating the effectiveness of a consumer-pro-vided mental health recovery education presentation. *Psychiatric Rehabilitation Journal, 30*(1), 46–53.

Wood, J.D. & Watson, A.C. (2017). Improving police interventions during mental health-related encounters: Past, present and future. *Policing and Society, 27*(3), 289–299.

Wood, J.D., Watson, A.C., & Fulambarker, A.J. (2017). The "gray zone" of police work during mental health encounters: Findings from an observational study in Chicago. *Police Quarterly, 20*(1), 81–105.

Chapter 6

Jail Processing of Persons with Mental Illnesses

"Jail is not the proper place for those who suffer from a mental illness."

— Montana Sheriff Chuck O'Reilly

"It is incumbent on sheriffs and jail directors to expose the unfortunate reality to their constituents. Only jail administrators have the power to open the door and compel our society to come to terms with this crisis. This begins with humanizing the detainees in custody."

— Cook County Sheriff Thomas J. Dart[1]

Police are often called the first line of defense against social disorder. If that assertion is true then jails are the second line of defense. Jails are often the community resource of last resort. When other control structures — family, school, church, welfare, and medical and/or mental health care — prove to be inadequate or ineffective when behavioral problems arise, jails are often relied upon to confine the "social rabble." In communities where there are inadequate or limited mental health care facilities, jails are relied upon to house and provide security for and, in some cases, treat the mentally ill. Over the last three decades, jails have been increasingly called upon to serve as the last resort for the care and confinement of persons with severe mental illness (Sayers et al., 2016).

Like law enforcement, jails have an exceedingly challenging job in general, and in particular when it comes to detainees with mental illness. At least one in five of pretrial inmates is mentally ill (National Alliance of Mental Illness Georgia, 2017). As a result, jail staff often must contend with mentally ill individuals who are frequently at their "sickest" — e.g., individuals who have been off their psychotropic medications for days, weeks, or even years and who are frequently intoxicated on and/or withdrawing from one or more substances. Substance abuse alone can make an individual's behavior unpredictable and volatile, but it also serves to exacerbate

---

1. http://cookcountysheriff.org/MentalHealthTemplate.html.

the individual's symptoms of mental illness. Almost inevitably, the vast majority of detainees are in crisis — e.g., having just been arrested and having their freedom removed, they experience intense anger at authority, both law enforcement and jail staff, and often at family, friends, and victims; their acts in the community were usually committed after experiencing significant psychosocial and interpersonal stressors. Unlike law enforcement, who has some discretion about whether to handle calls formally (e.g., arrest) or informally (e.g., merely provide a warning), jails typically do not have the option of refusing admission to those detained by police.[2] Furthermore, jails are then expected to house and provide care to the detainee, as the reality of his/her situation sets in, the effects of the substances he/she consumed wears off, and the individual is hit by the full intensity of his/her symptoms. The totality of circumstances often result in suicidal, homicidal, or at least, aggressive behavior. Then, jails are expected to provide mental health treatment to these individuals, with limited staff and limited city or county funding, to many who have no interest in — and many who fight — treatment. Finally, amidst this chaos, jails are blamed and subjected to huge liability lawsuits for any injuries (or death) to its wards.

Just as it is helpful to compare the tasks of law enforcement and jails, it is important to clarify at the outset of this chapter the differences between jails and prisons. Both involve incarceration within a facility and carry all the challenges involved with that: e.g., the responsibilities of caring for inmates' needs of daily living; managing individuals under intense stress in small quarters; keeping individuals who cannot get along, such as members of warring gangs, separate. Given this similarity, they are often mistakenly considered one and the same by the uninformed onlooker. However, there are significant differences that make the tasks of jails and prisons vastly different. First, by definition, jails house people awaiting trial and those sentenced to less than one year, whereas prisons house those sentenced to more than a year of incarceration. As such, although prisons tend to house a more homogenous group of "hardened" inmates, which entails a whole host of its own challenges, jails confine — often in an exceedingly small space, compared to prisons — an incredibly heterogeneous population of both misdemeanants and felons. This makes classification and housing, and knowing which groups of inmates can be housed together, a daunting task. Moreover, given the nature of the differing populations, jails are short-term facilities that undergo rapid turnover, with many people released after a few hours or a few days.

It is an understatement, then, that jails are best characterized as "people-processing institutions" (Veysey, 2011, p. 2). Conversely, prisons tend to be more stable and less chaotic. Next, as described above, jails deal with people right off the street, when

---

2. Sheriff Drew Alexander of Summit County, Ohio, was the first to implement a policy of refusing to accept individuals with mental illness into his jail (Armon, 2012). He had long threatened to do so but never followed through until he was emboldened by a National Institute of Corrections consultant's recommendation that such defendants be sent to the emergency room or psychiatric crisis center prior to being accepted into jail. "We're not going to be a dumping ground anymore for those people," Sheriff Alexander said.

they are at their "sickest" (e.g., having been off medications, intoxicated and/or withdrawing, often in crisis and/or angry). By the time inmates reach prisons, on the other hand, they have been in jail for usually an extended period of time as their court case is processed and resolved and, thus, they tend to be stabilized psychiatrically and have come to cope, at least to some degree, with their predicament. Lastly, jails are funded by cities and counties, and, thus, are notoriously underfunded and understaffed, while prisons are funded by state correctional budgets, which have tended to enjoy great financial backing in recent decades.

Jails, too, vary widely in terms of size and funding. Some jail facilities consist of a single holding cell or lock-up in a small town or precinct; accordingly, staff size and funding is equally small. Other jails in urban areas are large complexes with rated capacities of over 22,000 (Los Angeles County, California) (Veysey, 2011). These "adult detention centers," as they are frequently called, tend to employ hundreds of staff; and budgets can reach millions of dollars. In the United States, although small county jails with capacities less than 50 constitute about 40% of jails nationwide (Sabol & Minton, 2008), those with rated capacities of more than 1000 hold nearly 50% of the overall jail population (Minton, 2012).

Overrepresentation of People with Mental Illness in Jails

The size of jail and prison populations in the United States quadrupled between 1984 and 2009 (Wilper et al., 2009). In sheer numbers, over 2.3 million people are incarcerated, with more than 744,600 in local jails (Minton & Zeng 2015) and over 1.5 million in state and federal prisons (Kaeble & Glaze, 2016). In 2009, 1 in every 100 Americans was in jail or prison (Pew Center on the States, 2008), more people per capita than any other nation (International Centre for Prison Studies [ICPS], 2012).[3] However, on a positive note, between 2008–2018 the jail incarceration rate decreased 12% and the jail incarceration rate for black residents was lower in 2018 than any time since 1990 (Zeng, 2020).

Meanwhile, as discussed in Chapters 2 and 4, over the last several decades the number of state hospital beds plunged. As of 2014, there were over 170,000 residents in inpatient and other 24-hour residential treatment beds on any given night, an average of 53.6 patients per 100,000 population. Although 170,000 residents in 24-hour treatment beds every day may seem like a large number, it reflects a 64 percent decrease in psychiatric residents from 1970. When data are adjusted for the growth in the population of the United States since 1970, the decline in beds is even greater at 77.4 percent (Lutterman et al., 2017).

---

3. The 1 in 100 rate translates into 1000 per 100,000 citizens. By comparison, according to the ICPS, this is nearly double the rate of the international power with the next largest prison population: Russia, with 508. Other points of comparison include Iran (333), United Kingdom (154), China (121), Germany (83), and India (30).

With limited mental health treatment in the community, and even less for those who need inpatient hospitalization, jails have become our country's largest psychiatric institutions. Los Angeles County Jail, Rikers Island Jail in New York City, and the Cook County Jail in Chicago each house more persons with mental illnesses than any psychiatric facility in the United States (Council of State Governments, 2007). In Seattle, one mother who tried in 2011 on numerous occasions to commit her mentally disturbed son was told there were no beds available — he killed himself days later (Kihmm, 2013).

Los Angeles County jails in 2016 had an average daily population of 17,382 inmates, of which an estimated 4,160 were seriously mentally ill (McDonnell, 2016). The Los Angeles County Twin Towers alone is both the largest jail and the largest single provider of mental health services in the United States. It covers over 10 acres, 1.5 million square feet, and holds approximately 4,000 maximum security inmates and/or mentally ill inmates. Despite its size, overcrowding remains an issue at the towers. The towers consist of a medical services building and the Los Angeles County Medical Center Jail Ward. The Medical Services Building provides inpatient housing for inmates with various levels of acute medical and mental health needs (Los Angeles County Sheriff's Office, 2007).

For the past several decades, there have been more offenders in American jail and prisons with mental illnesses than in all state mental hospitals in the U.S. combined (Sigurdson, 2000; Treatment Advocacy Center & National Sheriffs Association, 2014). Specifically, jails and prisons in the U.S. hold approximately three to five times (Fellner, 2006; Leifman, 2001; Lerner-Wren, 2000) — and in some states, such as Arizona and Nevada, almost 10 times (Torrey, Kennard, Eslinger, Lamb, & Pavle, 2010; Treatment Advocacy Center & National Sheriffs Association (2014) — more individuals with mental illnesses than do state psychiatric hospitals. In 2012, it was estimated that there are 356,000 inmates with serious mental illness in jails and state prisons. This is 10 times more than the approximately 35,000 individuals with serious mental illness remaining in state hospitals.

Estimating the Prevalence of Serious Mental Illness in Jails

Prevalence rates of mental illness among jail inmates vary widely — from 6% (Teplin, 1990) to 64% (James & Glaze, 2006). This is primarily as a result of differences in research design. In particular, studies utilize differing methods of assessment of mental illness, and some examine varying levels of mental illness. Additionally, results vary in terms of the time frame of examination (e.g., in the year preceding arrest versus at the time of incarceration), as well as by the decade in which the study was performed.

Structured Diagnostic Interviews of Jail Inmates

Studies employing established, structured diagnostic interviews of inmates, performed by trained clinicians, are generally considered to be most methodologically sound. As such, it is surprising that the two earliest studies on the topic, both of which utilized this methodology, are so rarely noted. In particular, Swank and Winer (1976) and Schuckit, Herrman, and Schuckit (1977) both found that 5% of jail inmates in Denver and San Diego, respectively, were afflicted by serious mental illness.

The next study utilizing diagnostic interviews, considered by various experts in the field to be the most methodologically rigorous assessment of serious mental illness (Steadman, Scott, Osher, Agnes, & Robbins, 2005; Torrey et al., 2010; Veysey, 2011), was performed by Teplin in 1983 and 1984 (Teplin, 1990). Utilizing an established, structured diagnostic interview schedule of serious mental illness (schizophrenia, bipolar disorder, and major depression), she evaluated nearly 730 jail inmates in Cook County, Illinois. She found a prevalence rate of 6.4% of serious mental illness at the time of admission to jail (Teplin, 1990), which was slightly higher than her predecessors (above), yet slightly lower than the nationwide Epidemiological Catchment Area study — 7% of inmates had a lifetime history of schizophrenia symptoms (Robins & Reiger, 1991) — to which she compared her rates.

Separating out analyses by gender (males [Teplin, 1994], females [Teplin, Abram, & McClelland, 1996]), Teplin identified that 6% of males and 15% of females had current symptoms of serious mental illness, with comparable rates of schizophrenia (3.0% males versus 1.8% females) and bipolar disorder (1.2% males versus 2.2% females). Major depression, however, was significantly more likely among women (14%) as compared to men (3.4%), as was Post-Traumatic Stress Disorder (PTSD, 22% of women). Teplin and colleagues, further, expanded the operational definition of mental illness to other, less serious mental illnesses (e.g., finding that more than 50% of jail detainees suffered low-level depression, anxiety disorders, and personality disorders) and to lifetime prevalence rates (9% rate of mental illness in one's lifetime among men, 19% among women).

The next major and most well-respected study of serious mental illness in jails did not emerge until 2009. In this research, Steadman, Osher, Robbins, Case, and Samuels (2009) interviewed 822 inmates in two Maryland and three New York jails using the most recent version of the Structured Clinical Interview for the DSM-IV. In total, they found that 15% of males and 31% of females, 17% of the total inmates, met the criteria for a serious mental illness such as schizophrenia, bipolar disorder, and major depression. They noted, further, that if their prevalence figures were applicable to the total national jail census, 2.1 million people with serious mental illness were actually booked into jails in 2007.

A study that should be applauded for its comprehensive triangulation of multiple sources of data, including but not limited to a clinical interview — but that has received very little attention, likely as a result of the more informal nature of the publication in which it appears — is Maloney, Ward, and Jackson (2003). Between September 1998 and April 1999, the authors collected data on 1000 inmates in L.A. County Jail to determine who was at "risk of mental disorder," which was defined as either *currently* suffering or being at high risk for developing "psychological problems that would necessitate fairly immediate further evaluation or treatment" (Maloney et al., 2003, p. 101). In particular, the authors considered an inmate at risk based on one or more of the following: "probable mental disorder" based on mental status examination and elevations on a self-report questionnaire of psychiatric symptoms; current suicidal ideation; history of suicide attempt(s) within the past five years; treatment with psychotropic medication(s); psychiatric hospitalization within the past five years; and intensive psychiatric hospitalization in a jail or prison within the past five years. Based on these sources, and primarily on current symptoms, approximately 28% of the male inmates and 31% of the female inmates were deemed at risk of mental illness.

Bronson and Berzofsky (2017) reported that 1 in 4 jail inmates reported experiencing serious psychological distress (SPD) in the 30 days prior to participating in the survey. Their report used the Kessler 6 (K6) nonspecific psychological distress scale to assess SPD among jail and prison inmates. Their analysis found that prevalence of SPD among jail inmates was 26% compared to 14% among prison inmates. They also found that prescription medicine was the most common type of treatment for inmates who met the threshold for SPD in the last 30 days.

Self-Reports of Jail Inmates

A similar methodology to diagnostic clinical interviews that has been used in estimating the prevalence of mental illness among jail inmates is non-diagnostic interviews of inmates performed by non-clinical researchers. Although avoiding the issues of using official data and enabling greater flexibility in one's research questions, such studies are limited by the fact that they are based on inmates' self-report, which must be interpreted with caution due to potential for malingering (i.e., fabrication or over-reporting of symptoms) or under-reporting of symptoms in efforts to avoid stigma. Several studies, including a pair of studies by the Bureau of Justice Statistics of the federal governmental office, the U.S. Department of Justice, have utilized this methodology.

The most widely cited study involving this approach is the BJS report by Ditton (1999), in which she found that 16% of inmates in jails were considered to have a serious mental illness based on a broad definition (e.g., self-reported symptoms and/or treatment by a mental health professional *within 12 months prior* to incarceration). Indeed, this rate has become the standard, most well-respected estimate of mental illness, and it has been corroborated by such rigorous studies as Steadman et al. (2009) described above. The follow-up study to this, however, the BJS report by James and Glaze (2006), suggested that as many as 63% of males and 75% of females in jail exhibit symptoms of mental disorder and that 24% of jail inmates reported at least one symptom of a psychotic disorder. While these findings have been interpreted by some to be a striking increase in the rate of mental illness in only seven years' time, which is a useful finding for advocates who support diversion of persons with mental illnesses from the criminal justice system and linking them to treatment, there are significant questions about the reliability and validity of the James and Glaze (2006) study.

Dr. Henry J. Steadman of Policy Research Associates (personal communication, May 22, 2007), one of the foremost experts on this topic, noted several serious flaws in the James and Glaze (2006) study that "radically overestimate the actual rates of serious mental illness and less serious forms of mental illness in jails and prisons." In particular, they measured an exceedingly broad construct, which they labeled "mental health problems," representing a wide range of mental illness symptoms. Instead of weighting the items and deriving a summary score for level of mental illness, they merely reported on the percent of inmates who endorsed each individual item and identified them to have a "mental health problem," suggesting to many that this represented "mental illness." However, individual symptoms do not in and of themselves constitute a mental illness per se; rather, a person must have multiple symptoms for an extended duration to be diagnosed. Furthermore, some of the individual items, such as "insomnia or hypersomnia," "thoughts of revenge," or "persistent anger or irritability," are extremely common — i.e., not "abnormal" — feelings or experiences of people in jails or prisons. As such, they are not necessarily indicative of a mental health "problem." Furthermore, James and Glaze did not factor out the possible effects of substance abuse on symptoms of mental illness, such as psychosis. In total, Steadman (personal communication, May 22, 2007) concluded that James and Glaze's (2006) approach to measuring mental illness "has no basis in research or clinical practice.... These exceedingly high figures are nearly worthless for purposes of estimating the need for mental health and substance abuse services for inmates in jails and prisons." Put otherwise, these estimates cannot be interpreted to represent the prevalence of serious mental illness in jails.

The advocacy organization, Human Rights Watch (2003), also utilized non-clinical interviews, and estimated that approximately 20% of inmates, both in jails and in prisons, are seriously mentally ill. Likewise, Wilper et al. (2009) analyzed self-report interview data from the 2002 Survey of Inmates in Local Jails collected by the Bureau of Justice Statistics, and found that 25% of jail inmates, compared to 15% of federal inmates and 26% of state inmates had at least one previously diagnosed mental health condition when arrested.[4] However, this definition of mental illness was broad, including anxiety disorders and personality disorders, which are quite common within the general population and, by extension, within jails.

---

4. This is an unusual finding, given that jail inmates tend to have higher rates of acute mental illness than do state or federal prison inmates.

Indirect Measures of Mental Illness in Jails

The remaining studies have used more indirect indicators of the prevalence of mental illness in jails. One common method is to survey jail administrators and ask them to estimate the number and/or percentages of inmates in their jails with serious mental illness. For example, Torrey et al. (1992), in an early study on this topic, asked jail personnel to estimate the percentage of their inmates with schizophrenia, bipolar disorder, and related conditions. Of the 3,353 jails nationwide in the United States to whom the survey was sent, a member of the staff at 1391 jails responded and, on average, estimated that 7% of inmates had a serious mental illness. Some states have also begun to compile information on mental illness and have adopted surveys of jail administrators (or their designees) as an efficient means of obtaining this information. The Commonwealth of Virginia, for instance, has prepared an annual report on mental illness in the state's jails each year since 2005 for the state legislature. Its most recent survey (Virginia State Compensation Board, 2011), to which 64 of 48 local and regional jails responded, found that 25% of the 25,593 jail inmates was known or suspected to have a mental illness. Consistent with most studies, female inmates had a significantly higher rate of mental illness (60%) than male inmates (21%). Of inmates with mental illness, nearly half suffered from serious mental illness, as defined by schizophrenia or other psychotic/delusional disorder, bipolar disorder, or major depressive disorder. Specifically, 3% of all inmates had a diagnosis of schizophrenia and 10% had a major mood disorder diagnosis (bipolar or major depression). Although obviously limited by the fact that most jail staff are not trained to detect mental illness, such a method provides jails with the least hassle in compiling their data, thereby encouraging a greater cross-section of jails to participate in such surveys. As is evident, however, such a method can yield vastly different rates of mental illness.

Another common method to estimate the prevalence of mental illness in a jail is to count the number and/or proportion of inmates who are taking psychotropic medications. This is a convenient proxy for mental illness, as the information is relatively easy to obtain and taking medications intended for psychiatric symptoms is a fairly straightforward, albeit rough, indicator. Yet, as with surveys of jail staff, this method can yield wide ranges of numbers — 19% in Polk County, Florida (D. Zimmerman, personal communication, April 18, 2008) versus 40% in some Oklahoma jails (Fields, 2006) — depending on which types of psychotropic medications are of interest and the prescribing practices in the jails. For example, in some jails, certain antipsychotic medications (Seroquel) are used as a sleep aid, rather than for the treatment of psychosis. Therefore, measuring use of this medication as a proxy for mental illness can overestimate the true prevalence.

Constantine and colleagues (Constantine, Andel, et al., 2010; Constantine, Petrila, et al., 2010; Constantine et al., 2012), in their series of articles on inmates with mental illness in Pinellas County Jail in Florida, estimated mental illness based on diagnoses from service utilization data. Specifically, they performed a cross-reference of data from the jail with service utilization data from the public mental health system and determined that 10% of the jail inmates in their sample had a serious mental illness (disorders involving psychosis and mood disorders) (Constantine, Andel, et al., 2010; Constantine, Petrila, et al., 2010; Constantine, Robst, Andel, & Teague, 2012; Robst, Constantine, Andel, Boaz, & Howe, 2011). Separated out by gender, 8% of males and 18% of females had a diagnosis of one of the serious mental illnesses.

Finally, professional organizations sometimes promulgate their "official" estimate of mental illness in jails, based on their reading of the research literature. For example, the American Psychiatric Association, in 2000, estimated that approximately 20% of inmates have serious mental illness. Further, they approximate that 5% are actively psychotic at any time.

In summary, rates of mental illness in jails vary widely, both between and within different study methodologies. Overall, the prevalence of mental illness in U.S. jails tends to hover around 16%, but some studies suggest the actual rate is much higher. In comparison to the general public, even conservative rates of mental illness in jails are 2.5 to 10 times higher, depending on the statistic (Kessler, Chiu, Demler, & Walters, 2005).

It is also important to note that rates of serious mental illness in jails have increased over the last 20 years (Lamb et al., 2004; Torrey et al., 2010). Research showed that there was a 154% increase between 1980 and 1992 (Watson, Hanrahan, Luchins, & Lurigio, 2001), and the trend appears to have continued. From 1983 to 2010, for example, the rate of mental illness nearly tripled, from 6.4% in Teplin's (1990) seminal study during 1983–1984 to at least 16% currently (Steadman et al., 2009). In states like Virginia, in fact, the rate of mental illness in jails has increased by more than 50% in six years, from its initial snapshot in 2005, at 16%, to more than 25% in 2011 (Morris, 2006; Virginia State Compensation Board, 2011). Why are so many people with mental illness in jails, and why is this number increasing? It is to this topic that we now turn.

Characteristics of a Jail Inmate with Mental Illness

Research shows remarkable consistency in many characteristics of jail inmates with mental illness. Demographically, they tend to be young, African American males. In particular, recent research found that over half of mentally ill inmates were between 21 and 39 years of age (Constantine, Andel, et al., 2011). In another study, 23% of mentally ill inmates were African American, compared to only 13% of their non-incarcerated counterparts (Swanson et al., 2011). Furthermore, 67% were males, whereas males constituted only 46% of non-incarcerated mentally ill (Swanson et al., 2011).

Jail inmates with mental illness also tend to experience the same psychosocial and psychiatric characteristics. First, mentally ill jail inmates are more likely to have been homeless in the prior year (30%) than are non-mentally ill inmates (17%) (Ditton, 1999). Next, although substance abuse is common to all inmates, those with mental illness have an even higher rate of substance abuse (75% of females, 72% of males) than those without mental illness (70% of females, 61% of males) (Teplin et al., 1996). From a slightly different perspective, a recent study showed an even starker contrast in substance abuse rates among the mentally ill based on whether they are (65%) or are not criminal justice (CJ)-involved (28%).

Different types of mental health treatment received also appear to show fairly consistent patterns among jail detainees with serious mental illness. Specifically, those who have been arrested and detained are less likely to have used outpatient mental health services and more likely to have had an emergency room visit and/or inpatient psychiatric hospitalization. With regard to outpatient treatment, 24% of Constantine, Andel, et al.'s (2010) mentally ill jail sample had never used outpatient mental health services, which significantly increased the risk of both misdemeanor arrests and felony arrests over those who had used outpatient services. In fact, not receiving outpatient services rendered an individual 23% more likely to be arrested for a misdemeanor, 12% more likely to be arrested for a felony, and 26% more likely to spend additional days in jail in the following quarter (Constantine, Andel et al., 2010). Conversely, receiving outpatient services reduced the risks of subsequent arrest in the Pinellas County sample by 17% one quarter later, by 11% two quarters later, and by 9% three quarters later (Constantine et al., 2012). Similarly, in a recent randomized control study, individuals with serious mental illness who had a history of being repeatedly detained showed a reduction in the number of jail bookings following engagement in an intensive form of outpatient treatment (i.e., forensic assertive community treatment) (Cusack, Morrissey, Cuddeback, Prins, & Williams, 2010). Receiving treatment in an emergency room and/or inpatient psychiatric hospital had the opposite pattern with arrests and jail detention, in that those involved with the criminal justice system are *more* likely to have had an emergency room visit and/or inpatient psychiatric services than those not involved with the criminal justice system. Specifically, 63% of Constantine, Andel, et al.'s (2010) mentally ill jail sample had visited the ER or had been hospitalized during the study period, which statistically increased the risk of a felony arrest. In fact, it increased the risk of arrest and detention by 22% one quarter later, 8% two quarters later, and 11% three quarters later (Constantine et al., 2012).

The least consistent pattern among jail inmates with serious mental illness is in specific diagnoses. Cuellar et al. (2007) found that, in a sample of individuals with serious mental illness, there was a higher percentage of schizophrenia among those who were arrested and jailed (61%) than among those not involved with the criminal justice system (50%). Conversely, there was nearly half the rate of serious depression among those arrested and detained (16%) than among those not involved with the criminal justice system (32%). There was not a significant difference between the groups on bipolar disorder (8.3% CJ-involved vs. 6.7% non-criminal justice involved). Theriot and Segal (2005), Constantine, Andel, et al. (2010) and Swanson et al. (2011), however, found an entirely different pattern of serious mental illnesses. Constantine, Andel, et al. (2010) found that major depression was the most common category among mentally ill jail inmates (31%), followed by bipolar disorder (30%) and psychotic disorders (22%). Theriot and Segal (2005), too, found major depression to be the most common category, but more so among those without criminal justice involvement (67%) than those who had been arrested and jailed (59%). In this study, however, schizophrenia was the next most common disorder (18% of CJ-involved versus 15% of non-CJ involved); and bipolar disorder accounted for only 4% of each of the CJ-involved and non-CJ involved groups. Swanson et al. (2011) found bipolar disorder (63%) to be more common than schizophrenia (37%) among CJ-involved patients, with a more extreme split than Constantine, Andel et al. (2010).

Overall, nearly half of arrests of individuals with serious mental illness are for minor, non-violent crimes (Fisher et al., 2006; Swanson et al., 2011). Of all the previously discussed characteristics, those most significantly related to risk of misdemeanor arrest and additional days in jail were being male, homeless, not having received outpatient mental health treatment, and having an involuntary psychiatric evaluation in the previous quarter (Constantine, Andel, et al., 2010). Those with major depression were less likely than those with psychotic disorders to be arrested and detained for misdemeanors. For felonies, being black, younger than 21 years of age, having a non-psychotic disorder diagnosis, and having a co-occurring substance abuse disorder each predicted arrests and detentions (Constantine, Andel, et al., 2010). Both depression and bipolar disorder elevated the risk of a felony arrest and jailing, as compared to psychosis, as did inpatient treatment.

Reasons for the Overrepresentation of the Mentally Ill in Jails

The overrepresentation of individuals with mental illness in jails cannot be easily explained. As is discussed throughout this book, the criminalization of mental illness is a result of a complex array of historical, societal, institutional, and individual-level factors. With regard to jails, specifically, higher rates of arrest and longer jail stays among those with mental illness (Constantine, Andel, et al., 2010) — i.e., an individual with mental illness is likely to enter jail, but is not released as quickly as someone without mental illness — combine to create a backlog of mentally ill inmates confined within jail walls. In turn, due to limited treatment and discharge services in jail, there are inordinately high rates of recidivism among these individuals. In this way, a self-perpetuating cycle — or "revolving door," as it is so widely referred to in the literature on the intersection of the mental health and criminal justice systems — results. In the following pages, each of these issues will be discussed.

More People with Mental Illness
Are Arrested and Jailed

Without adequate community mental health care available — as has been discussed widely in previous chapters and will be discussed throughout the rest of the book — many individuals with serious mental illness experiencing acute episodes of their illness have nowhere to turn. Family members, if they have any who are involved in their lives, scurry to locate an inpatient bed, which are virtually non-existent and/or to which admission is next to impossible. Even when community mental health resources are available and involved, they too often lack the collateral to secure a bed. As a result, many individuals with mental illness in acute crisis are arrested and incarcerated. It should be no surprise, then, that, as of 2010, there was a sizeable correlation (Spearman's rho = 0.50, $p > 0.001$) between states' expenditures on mental health services and the number of mentally ill inmates in their jails and prisons (Torrey et al., 2010).

Ms. Lynn Hill (2006), a member of the National Alliance on Mental Illness (NAMI), describes problems her son encountered because of lack of community mental health services:

My son is one of those with severe mental illness who is not receiving the care and treatment that he desperately needs because of lack of availability of treatment programs and waiting lists.... In July, my son was found by a Marion County Sheriff's deputy walking up I-75 shirtless and shoeless, with bleeding feet. He was taken to a psychiatric center in Ocala for a psychiatric evaluation and was hospitalized there for 5 weeks. Part of the reason for his prolonged hospitalization was difficulty in achieving stabilization, however there were no treatment programs or secure facilities that had openings for which he met the criteria and he was discharged to a psychiatric Assisted Living Facility (A.L.F). He missed a court date for a misdemeanor charge in Hillsborough County due to circumstances related to his psychiatric instability. In June he had called for a taxi to a job interview at 2:00 a.m. at a Tampa radio station that was nonexistent and for which he was unable to pay. The FACT (Florida Assertive Community Treatment) team contacted the Public Defender's Office in Hillsborough County and arrangements were made to take Michael to court to get the issue resolved.

Unfortunately, before this took place, my son deteriorated to a crisis state which required intervention from crisis intervention trained officers from the Pinellas County Sheriff's Department. The officers were very skilled in their interaction with my son, but because of the outstanding warrant from Hillsborough County, he was taken to jail to await pickup by a Hillsborough County deputy. My son was in the Pinellas County Jail for five days, when he was finally picked up and taken to jail in Hillsborough County, which is where he currently waits. He has currently been in jail a total of 16 days for the misdemeanor charge of inability to pay the $80.00 cab fare and failure to appear for his court date, and at what cost to taxpayers? According to recent statistics citing high numbers of those incarcerated with mental illness, my son's story is sadly just one of thousands, many of whom are much worse. The state is putting money into recovery programs, when people with severe mental illness are suffering and sometimes dying (suicide, etc.) for lack of adequate crisis stabilization, treatment programs, and secured housing where they can get the care that is desperately needed for critical stabilization.

Lynn Hill, National Alliance on Mental Illness (NAMI) Pinellas, Member of Board of Directors, Palm Harbor

Sadly, Ms. Hill's son's story is by no means an isolated incident. Numerous studies have found that up to 40% to 50% of persons with serious mental illness are arrested at some point in their lives (Frankle et al., 2001; Solomon & Draine, 1995; Torrey et al., 2010; Walsh & Bricourt, 1997), and individuals served by the public mental health system appear to be at particularly high risk. Indeed, anywhere from 24% (Cuellar et al., 2007) to 45% (Theriot & Segal, 2005) of persons receiving public mental health services have been arrested, a finding that holds across states and time periods. Those requiring intensive and residential services from the public mental health system are especially at risk (e.g., up to 72% arrest rate in San Francisco; White, Chafetz, Collins-Bride, & Nickens, 2006).

People with Mental Illness Stay in Jail Longer

Next, once individuals with mental illness are arrested and detained, they tend to remain in jail for longer periods of time than those without mental illness who arrested on similar charges (McPherson, 2008; Solomon & Draine, 1995). Mentally ill inmates in New York's Riker's Island Jail, for example, had an average stay of 215 days, compared to the 42-day average stay for all inmates (Butterfield, 1998). Similarly, in the Fairfax County, Virginia, Adult Detention Center, psychotic, male pre-trial defendants who were charged with misdemeanors stayed in jail 6.5 times longer than an average jail inmate (Axelson & Wahl, 1992).

Conditions of Confinement

Individuals with serious mental illness spend longer periods in jail for many reasons, including most obviously, that they do not function well in such settings (Scheyett, Vaughn, & Taylor, 2009). First, the conditions of confinement are difficult for anyone, but especially so for persons with serious mental illness (Appelbaum, Hickey, & Packer, 2001; Human Rights Watch, 2003), and particularly those who enter jail in crisis, after long periods of being off their medications and having abused alcohol and drugs just prior to arrest (Buffington-Vollum, 2011). The chaos of overcrowding, the unsanitary conditions, the lack of privacy, the boredom and stress push anyone's coping mechanisms to the limit. People with severe mental illness, however, are particularly sensitive to excessive sensory stimulation (e.g., lights being on at all times, constant noise) and disruptions in eating and sleeping patterns.

Victimization and Trauma

Next, the very process of arrest, booking, and incarceration can be traumatizing, in and of itself, let alone for individuals who have previously experienced traumas and may have symptoms of post-traumatic stress. The degrading nature of the intake process (e.g., strip search), for example, can re-activate prior traumas and, accordingly, post-traumatic symptoms. Likewise, victimization by other inmates and even staff is heightened among individuals with mental illness (Kondo, 2000). Yet understandably, victimization — and even the ever-present threat of such victimization — depletes one's emotional stamina to cope, further weakening one's ability to defend oneself. Without the ready contact and support of family and friends, all of these stressors can combine to further deteriorate the mentally ill inmate's functioning.

Rule Violations

Inmates with mental illness are known to be major management problems (Torrey et al., 2010). This is evidenced by the fact that jail inmates with mental illness have rates of disciplinary infractions than are 50% (Ditton, 1999) to 100% (Torrey et al., 2010) higher their non-mentally counterparts. Due to impaired thinking, inmates with mental illness often lack the wherewithal to attend to, much less comprehend and comply with, commands issued to them by detention staff (Buffington-Vollum, 2011; Torrey et al., 2010). Mitchell (2009) describes one such inmate, as described by a jail officer:

> He tore up a damn padded cell that's indestructible, and he ate the cover of the damn padded cell. We took his clothes and gave him a paper suit to wear, and he ate that. When they fed him food in a styrofoam container, he ate that. We had his stomach pumped six times, and he's been operated on twice.

In essence, rules are not very important when one is struggling with hearing voices and having impulses to kill oneself (Buffington-Vollum, 2011). Aside from cognitive and emotional symptoms, mental illness can also manifest in difficulty controlling one's behavior, such as in disruptiveness, belligerence, paranoia, and aggression (Human Rights Watch, 2003).

Use of Isolation

In jail, an inability to act as an automaton and follow the rules can — and often, do — result in disciplinary infractions and even new charges for prosecution in the court system (Buffington-Vollum, 2011). Although professional association guidelines discourage use of restraint and/or isolation for punitive purposes, officers frequently justify use of physical interventions on grounds that the inmate was threatening or aggressive.[5] Many jails also place mentally ill inmates in segregation for purposes of convenient administration of treatment, to protect them from assault or exploitation by other inmates, and/or to protect other inmates from mentally ill inmates who

---

5. Of course, it is difficult to determine how much of an officer's assessment of an inmate's threatening or aggressive behavior is merely (mis)perception viewed through the lens, commonly held by a majority of the lay public, that people with mental illness are violent and unpredictable.

might become assaultive. Indeed, use of isolation is such a common practice for this subset of inmates that those with mental illness often comprise the majority of jails' segregated populations.

Inmates in segregation are often stripped and forced to wear a thin paper smock in a cold, barren cell, and experience intense sensory deprivation (Buffington-Vollum, 2011). It is anecdotally known and has been empirically demonstrated that even short periods of isolation can have serious detrimental effects on mental health, ranging from anxiety, headaches, oversensitivity to stimuli, and trouble sleeping to extreme confusion, perceptual distortions (e.g., hallucinations), paranoia, and motor excitement (e.g., "lashing out"). These effects are observed even in individuals without pre-existing mental illness; the effects are exponential for individuals with existing mental health issues (Human Rights Watch, 2003). Ironically, as noted by Haney (2003), although aggression is often the very thing that segregation is intended to eliminate, segregation can often precipitate aggression — toward others and toward oneself — even in a previously non-aggressive mentally ill inmate.

Limited Jail Mental Health Services

The added expense of extra staffing, materials (e.g., medications), and physical space (e.g., offices to confidentially evaluate and treat mentally ill inmates) required to care for inmates with mental illness is immense. To the local levels of government (e.g., counties and cities), who generally bear the entire costs of jail health care,[6] this financial burden is overwhelming. In some areas, it is one of the fastest-growing budget items (Freudenberg, 2001). As such, few jails — and especially smaller county jails — are equipped to provide comprehensive mental health services (Constantine, Andel, et al., 2010; Wilper et al., 2009). In fact, numerous studies have found that fewer than 50 percent of mentally ill jail inmates actually receive mental health services while in custody (Lurigio & Swartz, 2006; Perez, Leifman, & Estrada, 2003; Steadman et al., 1999; Morris, Steadman & Veysey, 1997; Teplin, Abram, & Mc-Clelland, 1997; Veysey et al., 1997; Walsh & Holt, 1999). Even among those jails that do offer mental health services, the inordinate cost leads to often low-quality and infrequent services (Kerle, 1998). However, without treatment, persons with mental illnesses who are jailed are at risk of decompensating and potentially needing more intensive, and even more expensive, treatment, such as inpatient hospitalization (Scheyett et al., 2009).

Another reason why acutely mentally ill inmates have longer jail stays is that they often wait for months for a psychiatric hospital bed to open (Torrey et al., 2010). Although some of these inmates are awaiting hospitalization for emergency treatment of their condition, most are awaiting transfer to a hospital for evaluation of competency to stand trial or for restoration of trial competency after having been found incompetent, as discussed in Chapter 7. In some cases, this process involves multiple trips of "riding the

---

6. Even Medicaid, the largest payer of public mental health services, may not be used to pay for healthcare services in correctional facilities, per federal law (42 U.S.C. § 1905).

bus" back and forth between the jail and the hospital, contributing many months and even years to an inmate's length of stay (Earley, 2006). What's more, some of the most acutely mentally ill — and incompetent — inmates are merely forgotten by defense attorneys2 and left to languish in jail, as they are the least capable of initiating contact with their counsel to request bail or even a psychiatric evaluation (Buffington-Vollum, 2011).

People with Mental Illness Have Higher Rates of Recidivism

Given that there are hardly enough funds to provide mental health services in the jail, discharge planning services are even less likely to be provided (Morris et al., 1997; Teplin et al., 1997; Veysey et al., 1997). This failure to adequately treat in the jail and to provide treatment linkages in the community, however, results in high rates of recidivism (Harris & Koepsell, 1996; Herinckx, Swartz, Ama, Dolezal, & King, 2005; Morrissey et al., 2007; Prince, 2006; Solomon, Draine, & Marcus, 2002). For example, Constantine, Andel, et al.'s (2010) sample of 3,769 individuals detained at a large urban jail had, on average, a mean of 4.6 arrests over the four years of the study. Although no comparison group of non-mentally ill individuals was provided, the raw number of arrests across the entire sample is striking. Likewise, in the Los Angeles County Jail, 90% of mentally ill inmates are repeat offenders, and nearly 10% have been incarcerated 10 times or more (Rivera, 2004). Torrey et al. (2010) cite some notable cases, including a man with schizoaffective disorder who was booked into the Palm Beach County Jail 49 times in 40 months between 2006 and 2009 (Kleinberg, 2010) and a woman in Memphis who was arrested 259 times and detained so many times that she considered the county jail her home (Downing, 1999). Clearly, these "frequent flyers" tax an already overextended jail system.

Jail Inmates' Right to Treatment

Historically, local officials viewed jails as a necessary evil and provided only the most basic needs to inmates in order to enhance the deterrent impact of the jail facility. Since jails are funded by local tax revenues, they are more easily affected by local culture, politics, and attitudes about criminal justice. However, in the last three decades, the federal government has become actively involved in the administration of jails and rights of jail inmates. Supreme Court decisions in *Wyatt v. Stickney* (1972), *Estelle v. Gamble* (1976), *Deshaney v. Winnebago County Department of Social Services* (1989), and *Washington v. Harper* (1990) reflect attempts to balance community protection and the constitutional rights of the mentally disordered offender (Sun, 2005). As a result, jails have become increasingly aware of their responsibility to provide mental health services to their detainees.

U.S. Supreme Court Cases

Estelle v. Gamble (1976)

The general finding of the U.S. Supreme Court across these cases is that inmates in jails and prisons have a legal right to treatment, albeit limited. This right is grounded in the 8th Amendment of the U.S. Constitution, which prohibits the imposition of cruel and unusual punishment. In *Estelle v. Gamble* (1976), the U.S. Supreme Court first held that prisoners have an 8th Amendment right to treatment, and subsequent cases made it clear that this right extends to treatment for mental illnesses as well as physical illnesses (*Bowring v. Godwin*, 1977).

However, this right to treatment is quite narrow. Proof of negligent treatment is not enough to establish a violation of the right to treatment. Rather, individuals seeking to assert their right to treatment must show that they have a serious medical need that correctional officials were aware of but were "deliberatively indifferent" to addressing it (*Estelle v. Gamble*, 1976). These two components will be explained briefly below.

Serious Medical Need

Courts have varied in what they regard as "serious medical need" sufficient to trigger an 8th Amendment right to treatment. However, there is growing consensus that serious mental illnesses, such as schizophrenia, bipolar disorder and major depression, meet the test of "serious medical need" because of their profound impact, particularly when untreated, on the ability of individuals to function (Cohen, 1998).

Deliberate Indifference

To establish deliberate indifference on the part of prison officials, it must be proven that prison officials were aware of an inmate's serious medical need but placed that inmate at serious risk by consciously disregarding that need. The burden is on the inmate to prove that the disregard of his/her medical need was wanton or willful. It is not enough to prove that prison officials should have known of this need (*Farmer v. Brennan*, 1994).

What constitutes serious medical need and deliberate indifference is certainly at issue now in America's jails because of COVID-19. The fact that there is a great deal of turnover in jails on a daily basis ensures that inmates are regularly exposed to, infected with, and in far too many cases, dying from the coronavirus. Jails, however, are ill-equipped to minimize the risk of infections and to treat those with the virus.

Minimally Adequate Treatment

This right to treatment does not require quality mental health care (Wilper et al., 2009), merely that it is "minimally adequate." The next question, then, that must be addressed is what constitutes minimally adequate "treatment" for these individuals. Does "treatment" in this context merely mean the amelioration of acute psychiatric distress or does it require long term treatment with a more rehabilitative, recovery-based purpose?

Ruiz v. Estelle (1980)

The fundamental components of a mental health treatment plan for inmates were set forth in a famous lawsuit in Texas, *Ruiz v. Estelle* (1980). The case was brought by a class of inmates incarcerated in Texas correctional facilities. In their lawsuit, these inmates raised allegations about overcrowding, staff brutality, inhumane conditions of confinement and grossly inadequate medical care in these facilities. With regard to mental health care, the lawsuit cited overall lack of treatment, the administration of inappropriately high dosages of psychotropic medications to control inmates with serious mental disorders, and placement of the most symptomatic, psychotic inmates in a substandard, overcrowded facility under extremely harsh conditions and little treatment. In the case, Judge William Wayne Justice held that the following are key components to minimally adequate correctional mental health treatment for inmates with serious mental illness (*Ruiz v. Estelle*, 1980, p. 1339, italics added):

1. *Screening and evaluation* of inmates in order to identify those who require mental health treatment

2. Treatment, not just segregation and close supervision

3. Trained mental health professionals, in sufficient numbers to identify and treat inmates in an individualized manner

4. Maintenance of accurate, complete, and confidential mental health records

5. Appropriate use of behavior-altering medications (e.g., not in dangerous amounts, by dangerous methods, or without appropriate supervision and periodic evaluation)

6. Suicide prevention and treatment

Although this important decision was issued in 1980, its list of essential components of minimally adequate correctional mental health frequently serves as the framework for evaluation of jails' and prisons' practices today. In addition, two other components have emerged in case law — *access* to mental health services and the existence of *adequate facilities and equipment* to meet prisoners' mental health treatment needs — that must be considered (Cohen, 1998).

The Right to Refuse Treatment

Just as jail inmates have a right *to* treatment, they have a right to *refuse* treatment. This right is grounded in the Due Process Clause of the 5th and 14th Amendments of the U.S. Constitution, based on the fundamental right of individuals to make autonomous medical decisions. The right to refuse treatment has been a source of considerable controversy and disagreement within the mental health and legal fields, with those who believe privacy and bodily integrity to be sacrosanct (i.e., judicial model) clashing with those who believe that involuntary medication is sometimes necessary to protect the well-being of those who may at times be unable to make informed choices about treatment (i.e., medical model). Proponents of the medical model argue that physicians are most knowledgeable and best able to make decisions that are essentially clinical in nature. Proponents of the judicial model argue that physicians will very likely "rubber-stamp" the decisions of colleagues who recommended medications in the first place and therefore cannot be trusted to make objective, unbiased decisions (Levy & Rubenstein, 1996).

As with the right to treatment, the right to refuse treatment is circumscribed. When untreated, inmates who refuse necessary psychotropic medications may create safety and security risks for themselves or others within the jail. The state's interest in administering medication to these individuals centers as much on maintaining security and control within the setting as it does on alleviating the person's symptoms. In 1990, the U.S. Supreme Court directly addressed the issue of involuntary medication in jails and prisons in a case called *Washington v. Harper* (1990).

Walter Harper, an individual with bipolar disorder (manic-depressive illness) had a history of incarceration and hospitalizations. In 1981, his parole was revoked after he assaulted two nurses in a psychiatric hospital. He was returned to prison and sent to a special unit for convicted felons with serious mental illnesses. After initially consenting, he refused to continue taking the medications that had been prescribed to him, and the treating physician sought to administer the medications over his objections. The records of the case clearly demonstrated that Harper deteriorated during periods when he did not take prescribed medications.

The Court began its analysis by acknowledging that inmates such as Harper have a "significant liberty interest in avoiding the unwanted administration of antipsychotic drugs ..." (*Washington v. Harper*, 1990, p. 221). But, it was held, this right must be balanced against the individual's medical needs as well as the interest of the penal institution in maintaining safety and security. The state can meet its burden of justifying the need for involuntary medication by demonstrating (a) that the individual represents a significant danger to him- or herself or others or is gravely disabled, (b) the drugs are administered for treatment and under the supervision of a licensed psychiatrist, and (c) the drugs are in the individual's best medical interests. The Court also upheld the procedure followed by Washington State for determining the need for involuntary medication, stating that an administrative hearing before a committee comprised of a psychiatrist, psychologist and hospital administrator (none of whom were directly involved in the diagnosis or treatment of Harper) comported with minimal constitutional requirements. An adversarial hearing before a judge is not necessary, the Court held.

Discharge Planning

While decisions in cases such as *Ruiz* focus primarily on mental health treatment during periods of incarceration, discharge planning and linkages with services are considered integral to their successful reentry into the community. In the case of mentally ill inmates, discharge planning entails developing a plan for the continuity of services into the community following discharge from an institution, in this case, jail; and it is intended to prevent such individuals from decompensating upon release from jail and recycling needlessly through the criminal justice system (Buffington-Vollum, 2011). Without adequate discharge planning and linkages to services, individuals with serious mental illnesses released from jails are likely to recidivate (Harris & Koepsell, 1996; Herinckx et al., 2005; Morrissey et al., 2007; Prince, 2006; Solomon et al., 2002). Unfortunately, for both the inmate and for the public, most are discharged without adequate planning to address their needs for treatment, supervision, benefits and housing (Haimowitz, 2004). Although no Supreme Court cases have settled on inmates' right to discharge planning, a city-level case and a federal circuit case have addressed the issue. There is entire chapter dedicated to discharge planning later in the book.

Professional Associations' Guidelines

Although *Estelle v. Gamble* and *Ruiz v. Estelle* legally obligated jails and prisons to provide mental health care for inmates, other case law and state statutes have not provided clearer requirements (Steadman et al., 2005). As such, various professional organizations have taken the initiative to devise their own minimum standards to provide guidance to city/county jails and state/federal prisons. Most are largely a re-iteration of *Ruiz* with slight, and in some cases, significant, extension. The American Psychiatric Association (2000) recommended fairly simply that all correctional facilities provide at a minimum mental health screening and referral for further evaluation, crisis intervention and short-term treatment, and pre-release and discharge planning. The American Correctional Association (ACA, 1990) opines that the goal of mental health services is not only "to provide for the detection, diagnosis, treatment, and referral of inmates with mental health problems," which is largely consistent with Ruiz, but "to provide a supportive environment during all stages of an inmate's incarceration" (p. 112). The National Commission on Correctional Healthcare (NCCHC, 1999) provides more specific guidelines — including private interview spaces, written descriptions of inmates' services, and completion of evaluations within 14 days, among others — upon which accreditation of facilities is contingent.

Council of State Government's Recommendations

The Council of State Governments (2002) articulated as part of the Criminal Justice/Mental Health Consensus Project a number of policy statements with specific recommendations to guide improvements in jails with regard to mental health services. In particular, Policy Statement #13 states: "Ensure that the mechanisms are in place to provide for screening and identification of mental illness, crisis intervention and short-term treatment, and discharge planning for defendants with mental illnesses who are held in jail pending the adjudication of their cases" (p. 102). The CSG's specific recommendations for implementation of this policy include the following:

1. Screen all detainees for mental illness upon arrival at the facility.
2. Work with mental health service providers, pretrial service providers, and other partners to identify individuals in jail who may be eligible for diversion

from the criminal justice system. Facilitate the release of information to assist in the identification of need.

3. Ensure that the capability exists to provide immediate crisis intervention and short-term treatment.

4. Facilitate a detainee's continued use of a medication prescribed prior to his/her admission into the jail.

5. Suspend (as opposed to terminate) Medicaid benefits upon the detainee's admission to the facility to ensure swift restoration of the health coverage upon the detainee's release.

6. Commence discharge planning at the time of booking and continue the process throughout the period of detention.

Mental health screening, attempts at diversion, short-term mental health treatment, and discharge planning will be discussed in the coming pages.

Jail Mental Health Services

While it is commendable that correctional professional organizations are giving mental health due consideration, their guidelines are mute regarding how these services can be provided by jails with limited funds, resources, and space (McLearen & Ryba, 2003). While many professional standards are presented as enforceable regulations for the provision of adequate mental health services, widespread complications related to understaffing and financial constraints limit jails' ability to comply with the standards (McLearen & Ryba, 2003). As such, many facilities approach the guidelines as merely aspirational in nature (McLearen & Ryba, 2003). A 2011 survey by AbuDagga et al. (2016) of sheriff department staff/officers found that vast majority of jails *don't* provide individual (38%) or group psychiatric care (90%).

In particular, mental health services provided within jails vary as a function of jails' sizes and funding. Large jails, which tend to enjoy greater funding and larger staffs than small county jails, are more likely to operate like a prison and provide a comprehensive array of medical and mental health services to their inmates (Veysey, 2011). They usually employ their own health care staff and provide direct services. Some even have surgical units and the capability to provide inpatient psychiatric care, as well as specialized housing units and therapeutic communities for persons with mental illness. Smaller jails, on the other hand, have to rely almost exclusively on service providers in the community for provision of medical and mental health care; and in cases requiring emergent care, officers must transport inmates to a local hospital (Veysey, 2011).

In total, these factors impact the degree to which effective jail mental health "triage" (National Institute of Correction and the Urban Institute [NIC & UI], 2007) can be achieved. Effective triage comprises a three-stage process. The first stage consists of routine, systematic mental health *screening* of all inmates, to identify those who may need closer monitoring and referral for a more in-depth mental health *assessment*.

Screening is usually performed by jail staff during the intake or classification process, as close to the point of arrival to the facility as possible. In-depth *assessment*, just mentioned, represents the second stage of jail mental health triage. To successfully manage potential risk, assessment should be performed within 24 hours of a positive screen by trained mental health personnel. As at the prior stage, a positive finding during the assessment suggestive of mental illness, serves as the indicant of need for progression to the final stage, which is full psychiatric *evaluation* by a psychiatrist or otherwise qualified medical professional.

From a jail administrative perspective, these steps of mental health triage serve important functions toward effective management of the facility, avoidance of potential liability lawsuits, and toward the ultimate cost of running the institution (NIC & UI, 2007). Initial mental health screening is relatively inexpensive, as it is performed by jail officers. Yet it is an extremely important — and thus, cost-effective — aspect of managing inmates' risk to self or others, which affects jail management and can lead to liability lawsuits. More in-depth assessment by jail mental health or medical staff is useful to "screen out" those who have been flagged as positive during the intake screening whose apparent symptoms initially might have been a result of substance intoxication or withdrawal, stress, or another transient factor. In this way, this stage conserves valuable resources, avoiding investment of manpower to closely watch inmates who were "positive" for mental illness at screening and avoiding unnecessary progression to the next stage, which is by far the most draining to the jail budget. At the psychiatric evaluation stage, inmates are thoroughly examined by a medical professional, often a specialty medical professional (psychiatrist), for a wide range of symptoms of mental illness. Those who are determined to have a mental illness are prescribed medication, if necessary. Between the evaluation services by the psychiatrist and the provision of medication(s), this is by far the most expensive stage for jails (NIC & UI, 2007).

Mental Health Screening

All sources — e.g., legal holdings, professional organization guidelines, and the Criminal Justice/Mental Health Consensus Project — concur that the first mental health "service" that must be provided is screening for mental illness at booking. The Consensus Project (Council of State Governments, 2002) further recommends, consistent with research and practice, that a standardized screening instrument, which includes questions about suicide risk, should be used by a trained screener. Moreover, positive screens should result in a referral for a more comprehensive assessment by a mental health professional, and information should be shared between the jail and the professional.

However, despite a legal right to mental health treatment, which a wide range of experts agree should include adequate screening, not all jails comply with this obligation. As of 1997 (Morris et al., 1997), only 83% of the 835 U.S. jails surveyed had some form of initial screening. Unfortunately, there is no updated information on a national level, but several studies of individual states have been conducted recently.

For example, a 2000 survey in Texas indicated that only 63% of jails provided initial mental health screenings, with large jails more likely to do so than small jails (Fabelo, 2000). More recent studies, however, suggest that as many as 96% of the 80 jails in North Carolina (Scheyett et al., 2009) and 86% of the 63 jails in Virginia (Virginia State Compensation Board, 2011) screen all inmates for mental illness at booking.

Jail-Specific Mental Health Screens

Screening instruments are highly variable across jails (Scheyett et al., 2009). First, screens may contain anywhere from one or two questions about previous treatment to a detailed, structured mental status examination (Scheyett et al., 2009). Second, most jails merely rely on a set of questions devised by the jail itself, rather than adopting a validated, evidence-based screening tool with established psychometric properties. These booking instruments usually include general questions non-specific to mental illness, such as asking about prior treatment for *any* medical condition, *any* current medications, and *any* recent hospitalizations (Buffington-Vollum, 2009; Scheyett et al., 2009).

Jails screening instruments vary in part based on the jail's intention for the questions included. Some jails have well-constructed screening tools intended for the purpose of gathering specific, detailed information that will be useful to clinicians who might later need to make determinations about mental illness. Screens for which this is the purpose tend to include questions in accordance with symptoms for disorders that appear in the Diagnostic and Statistical Manual of Mental Disorders IV (DSM-IV) (e.g., clinical and personality disorders, substance abuse) (Sun, 2005). Most of the time, however, questions are placed (or not placed) on a jail's specific screen based on the needs of the jail, past practices and/or stagnancy, and, personnel's comfort with mental illness.

The risk of using jail-specific booking screens is that they may fail to detect inmates with very real mental illness (Scheyett et al., 2009), and research bears this out. Indeed, Teplin (1990) found that as many as 63% of inmates who were later identified (through independent psychological testing as part of the research) to be experiencing serious symptoms of mental illness had been missed by routine screenings by booking staff and, thus, were left untreated at the time of the independent evaluation (Teplin, 1990). These "false negatives," as they are called in research, can have grave implications for jails, if these inmates were to, for example, commit suicide because they were not detected at screening and placed under close watch.

Evidence-Based Jail Mental Health Screens

Given the fallibility of jail-specific screening instruments that are not evidence-based, jails are increasingly encouraged — at least, by academic experts on the topic and sometimes by state offices that accredit county and city jails — to use a research-based screening tools. According to Steadman et al. (2005), an effective jail mental health screen should have the following characteristics: First, it should be brief. Booking/intake is a hectic process, of which the mental health screen is but one component.

i

By the time inmates are asked mental health screening questions, they are often over-whelmed, irritated, and/or uncooperative. Mental health screenings are based on inmates' self-report; thus, the validity of the data they provide is dependent upon their honesty and willingness to report such sensitive information as previous treatment, use of psychotropic medicines, and thoughts about suicide (Seiter, 2005). In order to obtain the most accurate information from inmates, it is useful for the screen to be as short as possible, while still including needed information. Second, an effective jail mental health screen should have explicit guidelines for administration and scoring, because the officers who perform the screens have limited, or at least differing levels of, mental health training and experience. Furthermore, correctional officers, while frequently confident in their ability to identify overtly psychotic symptoms, are less adept at detecting less obvious signs of mental illness (Steadman et al., 2005). Third, an effective jail mental health screen should not result in many false nega-tives — or, as discussed previously, it should not miss many inmates who actually have a serious mental illness — or in many false positives, e.g., identifying inmates as having a mental illness when they do not. False positives, obviously, are wasteful, which is especially problematic when resources (e.g., mental health staff to treat, se-curity staff to monitor inmates identified to be at risk, expensive medications) are scarce. Finally, as has been noted, inquiries should focus on current symptoms of mental illness, rather than on a history of mental illness, as the former is most salient to current risk in the jail (Maloney et al., 2003).[7]

Numerous screening tools have been developed specifically for criminal justice professionals to detect serious mental illness, with a focus on symptom severity and level of impairment than on diagnosis per se (Lurigio & Swartz, 2006). A discussion of each of these tools is well beyond the scope of the current chapter. The Referral Decision Scale (RDS), which was adapted into the Brief Jail Mental Health Screen (BJMHS; Steadman et al., 2005) is considered to be the most widely recognized and researched jail mental health screening tool (Goldberg & Higgins, 2006; Lurigio & Swartz, 2006).

---

7. Based on these characteristics, many of the approaches identified in the research literature are impractical and, thus, ineffective. Numerous psychologists and psychiatrists have proposed the use of standardized, validated diagnostic interviews, which have complex directions for administration (e.g., use of skip patterns), making it complicated for jail officers to administer, and/or must be ad-ministered by trained mental health professionals (Lurigio & Swartz, 2006). For example, Nicholls, Roesch, Olley, Ogloff, and Hemphill (2005) developed the Jail Screening Assessment Tool (JSAT), but it is intended to be administered by someone who has graduate training and expertise in mental illness and psychological assessment techniques. Obviously, this is infeasible for the purposes of initial mental health screening at booking into jail. Others have recommended the use of self-report ques-tionnaires, but many of these are long, cumbersome, and require a level of reading ability that many inmates do not have. Finally, each of these approaches is geared toward diagnosing specific mental illnesses, which results in unacceptably high levels of false positives; not all individuals with symptoms of mental illness pose a risk to jail management.

Referral Decision Scale (RDS)

Teplin and Swartz (1989) developed the RDS to serve as a quickly administered and easily scored screening tool for use by jail officers to identify inmates who may serious mental illness (Lurigio & Swartz, 2006). The scale consists of 14 items, distilled from a larger diagnostic interview as the items that most predicted a finding of mental illness based on full evaluation. These items correspond to three subscales — schizophrenia, bipolar disorder, and depression — that have empirically identified cutoff scores, which indicate a need for referral for further mental health assessment. Validation research was mixed, however, in terms of the RDS's utility.

Brief Jail Mental Health Screen (BJMHS)

Veysey and colleagues revised the RDS changing the time frame to recent symptoms of mental illness, rather than lifetime occurrence, revised the scoring to yield a single composite scale, rather than multiple scales that had questionable psychometric properties and eliminated items with questionable face validity. They further reduced it to eight items, six reflecting symptoms of psychosis, mania, and depression, and two inquiring about current psychotropic medications and a history of psychiatric hospitalization (Steadman et al., 2005). The new screen was reported to take two to three minutes to administer by officers without mental health training. The scale was renamed the Brief Jail Mental Health Screen (BJMHS) and is available for free at the Substance Abuse and Mental Health Services Administration (SAMHSA) GAINS Center for Behavioral Health and Justice Transformation (n.d.) website.

At the current time, there is no way of knowing how many jails actually employ evidence-based screening measures; no national survey has been performed. There appears to be wide variation from state to state and even between regions within a state. In fact, regional- or state-level initiatives to improve mental health services in jails appear to be the motivating force to incorporate such evidence-based practices.

Suicide Screening

As included in all of the professional organizations' recommendations and guidelines, as well as the Consensus Project report, a key part of any jail screening should be risk for suicide. It is a widely recognized fact that people in jail, especially those in jail for the first time, are at increased risk for suicide (Scheyett et al., 2009). As of 2005, 32% of all deaths in U.S. jails are by suicide (Mumola, 2005), and this was after a notable decrease in suicides in the past two decades as a result of heightened awareness due to early research (Danto, 1973; Hayes, 1983, 1989) and wrongful death lawsuits (Felthous, 2011). Indeed, as of 1983, when the rate of jail suicide was 129 per 100,000 inmates (Mumola, 2005), this rate was nine times that of the general population (Hayes, 1989). Yet between 1983 and 2002, jail suicides declined by 64% (Mumola, 2005), and by 2006 the rate was only three times greater than in the general population (Hayes, 2010).

Regardless of this decline, suicides in jail remain a salient concern from both mental health and jail management perspectives. Recent studies suggest that anywhere from 38% (Hayes, 2010) to approximately 50% (Torrey et al., 2010) of all jail inmates who commit suicide have a serious mental illness. Moreover, among jail inmates who *attempted* suicide in Washington, 77% had a mental illness, versus the 15% of inmates in the general population (Goss et al., 2002). As such, including questions on suicide risk in the booking screen is essential.

Characteristics of Jail Suicides and Suicide Victims

Most of the information on jail inmates who "successfully" commit suicide was based for over 20 years on the early national studies by Hayes (1983, 1989). However, there has recently been a flourish of research on the topic. In 2005, enabled by the Death in Reporting Custody Act of 2000, Mumola performed an analysis of suicides and homicides in U.S. jails and prisons between 2000 and 2002. In 2008, Mumola and Noonan provided updated statistical tables on such deaths in U.S. jails and prisons between 2000 and 2006. Then, in 2010, Hayes performed a national survey of jail suicides, thereby providing updated information that could be directly compared to her early work. Also, Felthous (2011) reviewed Hayes early work and compared and contrasted it with Mumola (2005), a meta-analysis by Fazel, Cartwright, Norman-Nott, & Hawton (2008) of all controlled studies in Western European, English-speaking countries since 1950, and single local- and state-level studies of jail suicides. Surprisingly, Felthous (2011) did not include Hayes (2010) or Mumola and Noonan (2008), but those findings will be included here. Ultimately, between these recent works, our knowledge of contemporary jail suicides is well-established and is generalizable to most jails in the U.S., and Fazel et al. (2008) provides a useful cross-cultural comparison.

According to Hayes (1983, 1989), the typical profile of someone who committed suicide in a U.S. jail was a white single male, in his late-teens and early- to mid-twenties, who was arrested for a minor offense related to drug or alcohol abuse (e.g., public intoxication), and was usually intoxicated at the time of putting placed in jail. According to Felthous (2011), more than 50% of all U.S. jail suicide victims fit these characteristics. Further, the European studies yielded a similar profile, with the exception that inmates tended to be married, more evenly distributed across age groups, and charged with violent offenses (Felthous, 2011). Hayes (1989) also found that jail suicide victims in the U.S. tended to have no significant history of prior arrests, and they tended to die within 24 hours by hanging (Hayes, 1989). Although Hayes found largely the same results in her 2010 study, there were some notable differences. In particular, the age of those who completed suicides in recent years is slightly older; substance abuse was found to not play as great of a role; and she too found that those who committed suicide were more likely to have been charged with violent or personal crimes, rather than minor drug-related offenses.

In terms of legal variables, as previously noted, Hayes (1989) found that a key correlate of completed jail suicides was being charged with minor (28% of suicides), usually substance-related offenses (27%). In this early study, only 25% of those who committed suicide had been charged with interpersonal violence. Twenty years later, however, Mumola (2005) found that suicide was highest among violent offenders (92 per 100,000) and lowest among drug offenders (18 per 100,000). The results of Fazel et al.'s (2008) international meta-analysis were more consistent with Mumola (2005), with suicide being most common among those charged with non-sexual, violent offenses, murder, and sentences over 18 months. Likewise, in Hayes' 2010 study, she concluded that her original finding had changed, as 43% of contemporary jail inmates who committed suicide had perpetrated a personal and/or violent crime.

As noted, Hayes (1989) found that most jail inmates committed suicide within 24 hours of arrival in detention by method of hanging (Hayes, 1989). In particular, Hayes (1989) had found that 57% of suicides occurred within the first 24 hours, with 29% occurring within the first three hours. Nearly 95% of all suicides were by hanging. In her recent study, however, Hayes (2010) found that suicide is less circumscribed to the time shortly after entrance into jail. Now, only 23% of suicides occur in the first 24 hours; whereas 27% occurred between days 2 and 14, and 20% even occur months into inmates' incarceration (e.g., 1 to 4 months). Clearly, this makes officers' task of monitoring inmates for suicide risk much more complicated; no longer can they rely on watching inmates most closely during only the first 24 to 72 hours of an inmates' detention. Hanging was still the most common method of jail suicide, however, with 93% of suicides occurring in this manner.

At the time of Hayes' (1983, 1989) early studies, the single most consistent correlate of jail suicide was single-cell occupancy. This factor accounted for 67% of completed suicides (Hayes, 1989). Even Fazel et al.'s (2008) relatively recent meta-analysis supported this. However, Hayes (2010) analysis of recent U.S. suicides found that isolation was much less commonly a factor, in only 38% of cases. Only 8% were on suicide watch.

Similarly, Hayes (1989) found substance intoxication at the time of detention to be highly related to jail suicides. In particular, she found that inmates under the influence of substances and who committed suicide within 48 hours of detention accounted for over 88% of the completed suicides. Half of these occurred within the first 3 hours. Fazel et al. (2008), too, found alcohol or drug abuse to be related to completed suicides, particularly when the substance use was related to the offense. In Hayes (2010) recent analysis, though, only 20% of jail inmates who committed suicide were intoxicated at the time.

With regard to mental illness, notably, Hayes (1989) did *not* find prior history of mental health treatment to be related to jail suicides. Fazel et al. (2008), however, found both a history of psychiatric diagnosis and use of psychotropic medications to be related to jail suicide. Hayes (2010) most recently found that 38% of inmates who committed suicide had a history of mental illness, and 20% had a history of psychotropic medication use. Another striking finding with regard to mental illness is that neither Hayes (1989) nor Fazel et al. (2008) found schizophrenia to be significantly related to completed jail suicides. This is confusing, given that (a) suicide *is* elevated among those with schizophrenia in general and (b) several individual studies found schizophrenia to be common among (approximately 30%) among jail suicide victims.

Felthous (2011) explains the counterintuitive findings as likely being related to the reliance of Hayes (1989) and many of the studies in Fazel's et al. meta-analysis (2008) on secondary data, which might not include quality data on diagnosis. Despite this reasoning, Hayes (2010) did find in her recent study that psychosis and depression were related to suicide among inmates with mental illness.

In a similar vein, although Fazel et al. (2008) and numerous single studies found that a history of prior suicide attempts was related to jail suicides, Hayes (1989) did not. This is counterintuitive, given that in one study, at many as 77% of individuals who completed jail suicides had attempted suicide previously, often multiple times (He, Felthous, Holzer, & Nathan, 2001). However, Hayes' 2010 study found a rate of prior suicide attempts (34%) that was half that of He et al. (2001). Again, Felthous (2011) postulated that this was related to jails' tendencies at the time of Hayes' (1989) study to not collect much historical information and/or the tendency to not differentiate legitimate suicide attempts from acts of self-injurious behavior without the intention of death (e.g., cutting behavior).

In summary, Hayes (2010) found significant changes in the characteristics of jail inmates who commit suicide and in the circumstances of the suicidal events, in comparison to her early work more than two decades ago. In particular, jail suicides are no longer most common among those committing minor crimes. Substance abuse, in the form of substance-related charges and substance intoxication upon detention in jail, no longer appears to be as salient of a factor. Furthermore, the jail circumstances are not as predictable: Suicides are no longer circumscribed to the first 24 hours or to individuals in isolation cells. These notable changes highlight the need to regularly update our knowledge about this important topic.

Screens for Suicide Risk

Previous studies indicate that mental health screening is critical to identifying and preventing suicide among jail detainees. Indeed, Hayes (1989) found that 89% of inmates who committed suicide in jail had *not* been screened for suicidal behavior at booking. As such, in the past two decades, jails have put a major focus on improving suicide risk detection, primarily through initial screening. Such efforts have obviously been effective in increasing the use of suicide screens, as 77% of jails in which suicides occurred in 2010 had screening mechanisms in place (Hayes, 2010). Of course, this fact—that suicides are still occurring despite the majority of jails employing screening practices—in and of itself is worthy of pause and further exploration. Nevertheless, screening for suicide risk, whether always effective or not, is essential to saving lives.

Taking an explicit inventory of the above risk factors/characteristics should form the basis for any suicide screen and when trying to determine classification and/ or housing. However, it is important to realize that assessing suicide risk at intake is inherently difficult. First, such screens are based on self-report, and inmates contemplating suicide might deny such thoughts. Furthermore, a thorough suicide risk assessment must include consideration of *changes* in an individual's thoughts, feelings, behaviors, and functioning (e.g., changes in appetite, recent lethargy compared to usual). This requires knowledge of the individual prior to entering jail. Yet, obviously, a pre-screen baseline is not a luxury that booking officers typically have available to them.

Numerous authors have compiled lists of risk factors found to be related to jail suicide, which should be asked and/or considered at booking. First, as noted by the World Health Organization (Pompili et al., 2009), booking officers should obtain detailed information about current and past mental illness, psychiatric treatment, current substance abuse, and suicidal ideation, plans, and attempts. Likewise, per the WHO, officers should gather information about the factors mentioned previously (e.g., lack of social support, sense of hopelessness, absence of future orientation), as well as observations of expressions of shame, embarrassment, or worry about the arrest and/ or incarceration; expressions of hopelessness or fear of the future; signs of depression; and acting in an unusual manner. Hayes (2000) suggested questions about changes in appetite, lethargy, mood or behavior, and having increased difficulty relating to others. She also recommended observing for expressions of guilt over the offense, speaking unrealistically about getting out of jail, preoccupation with the past, and severe agitation or aggressiveness.

Despite almost all jails' focus on screening and monitoring for suicide risk, they vary widely in their actual suicide screens. Scheyett et al. (2009), in their examination of North Carolina jails' suicide risk screens, observed that screening for suicidality was erratic. Each jail had a jail-specific combination of factors it considered, ranging from officer observation to direct questions about current suicidal ideation, past suicide attempts, and/or current mental state. This was noted in jails in northwest Virginia, too (Buffington-Vollum, 2009). Jails varied widely, from two jails asking only two suicide risk questions, all the way to three jails (including two smaller county jails) assessing 20 specific suicide risk factors. Over half of the jails assessed at least 10 risk factors. From most to least common, the following factors were assessed by a majority of the jails:

- Current substance abuse
- Current signs or symptoms of mental illness
- Current signs or symptoms of depression (e.g., tearful, crying, emotional flatness)
- History of substance abuse
- Abnormal or bizarre behavior (e.g., acting or talking strangely)
- Having a family member or significant other who has attempted or committed suicide
- Shame or embarrassment
- History of mental illness
- Anxiety or fear

In summary, the ability to screen inmates before placement in cells is critical to preventing suicide. Yet, it is a significant challenge for jail booking officers during peak periods, when suicide risk is at its highest (Sun, 2005). While most jails have screening policies in place, at this point, there has been no comprehensive study to assess the policy implementation and effectiveness of the screens employed.

Substance Abuse Screening

Although previously discussed within the context of mental health and suicide screening, assessment of substance abuse is worth reiterating, given its widespread prevalence within jail populations in general and among inmates with mental illness specifically. Indeed, as noted at the beginning of the chapter, up to 85% of all jail inmates had a substance abuse disorder in 2006 (National Center on Addiction and Substance Abuse, 2010). Further, approximately 75% of jail inmates with mental illness have a co-occurring substance abuse disorder at intake, a rate which has remained consistent over time (James & Glaze, 2006; Teplin & Abram, 1991; Teplin et al., 1996). When considering lifetime comorbidity, the rate reaches 90% (Roskes, Cooksey, Feldman, Lipford, & Tambree, 2005).

Screening for substance abuse issues is important at intake, given that substance intoxication can make inmates unpredictable and put them at risk for impulsively harming themselves or others. Likewise, certain types of substance withdrawal can be life-threatening. Each of these risks, at the least, complicates jail management for officers and, at most, put jails at risk for liability. As such, aside from suicide risk, assessment of substance intoxication and withdrawal were the most commonly included items in Virginia jails' booking screens, with 95% and 79% of jails assessing each, respectively (Buffington-Vollum, 2009).

Administering Jail Screenings

Historically, jail officers have been responsible for screening all inmates, of which mental health screening is a part, during the booking process. By and large, it appears that this is still the case. In North Carolina, for example, jail officers performed screening for mental illness in 79% of the jails (Scheyett et al., 2009). In some larger jails, however, designated booking officers with specialized training and/or jail medical staff conduct these procedures. Again, in 10% of North Carolina jails, and particularly larger jails, screening was conducted by medical staff employed by the jail; in 8% of North Carolina jails screening were performed by jail staff, which was then reviewed by medical staff (Scheyett et al., 2009).

In Virginia, however, it appears that there is a trend away from having booking staff perform the screenings, toward having mental health professionals, either those who work in the jail or independent practitioners, do them (Virginia State Compensation Board, 2010, 2011). Specifically, the use of booking staff for mental health screenings declined from 55% in 2010 to 46% in 2011, whereas jail mental health staff use increased from 17% (2010) to 23% (2011) and independent practitioners increased from 26% (2010) to 31% (2011) (Virginia State Compensation Board, 2010, 2011). Although it is unclear whether this trend generalizes to other states, it would not be surprising, given the increasing pressure in the past decade for jails to provide more effective mental health services.

Some professional and accrediting organizations, such as the NCCHC (1999) further recommend that mental health screenings should be performed in private settings. The ostensible rationale for this is that mental illness is a stigmatizing condition and, thus, privacy is important in order to encourage honest and valid self-reports from inmates (Scheyett et al., 2009). Scheyett et al. (2009) examined the extent to which North Carolina jails comply with this recommendation and found that only 41% consistently performed screenings in private settings. A third of jails reported never or rarely doing so.

Follow-Up Mental Health Assessments

As discussed by the National Institute of Corrections and the Urban Institute (2007), the second stage of mental health triage in jails is a more in-depth mental health assessment, following a positive finding at the initial mental health screening. It is recommended that these assessments be conducted within 24 hours after the initial screening, and they serve as the indicant of whether a full psychiatric evaluation (and potentially, medication) is needed. Again, no national survey has examined the status of this practice. In Virginia (Virginia State Compensation Board, 2011), however, 54% of jails statewide conduct such assessments of *all* inmates who receive a positive screening for mental illness at booking, 38% perform assessment only on inmates who display acute symptoms of mental illness, and 8% do not conduct in-depth assessments at all. Nearly half (47%) of these assessments are performed by professionals from public community mental health agencies, 29% by other mental health professionals (e.g., in private practice, have contracts to provide services to the jail), and 24% by jail mental health staff. In North Carolina, for example, the length of time between referral for mental health assessment, either via being flagged as positive by the initial screening or as a result of behavior reported in the jail, varied (Scheyett et al., 2009). For non-emergency cases (i.e., no immediate risk of harm to self or others), only 35% of inmates were seen within the recommended window of time, i.e., within one day. Moreover, 18% had to wait one to three days, 15% three to five days, 19% five days to a week, and 13% had to wait more than a week. Even for emergencies, while most inmates (80%) were seen within one day, for 18% the wait was one to seven days after the referral was placed, and 2% waited more than one week (Scheyett et al., 2009). Obviously, this is problematic, not only for inmates in distress, but for the officer hours put into closely monitoring such inmates.

Crisis Intervention and Short-Term Mental Health Treatment

In *Wyatt v. Stickney* (1972), an Alabama district court recognized the right of the mentally ill to receive treatment. This decision acknowledged the deplorable conditions in state mental hospitals and led eventually to the creation of alternatives to this intrusive form of treatment. However, today, persons with mental illnesses once again find themselves lost in large, impersonal, ineffective, self-perpetuating, custodial institutions. This time — or maybe we should say, once again, as in the late 1800s — they find themselves in jails.

Jails were not designed to handle the large numbers of mentally ill offenders. However, they have been forced to make adjustments to accommodate the influx of individuals with mental illness as a result of *Estelle v. Gamble* and *Ruiz v. Estelle*. Furthermore, recent evidence suggests that there has been a change in public attitudes in the direction of supporting mental health and substance abuse treatment in jails (Applegate, Davis, Otto, Surette, & McCarthy, 2003). Therefore, jails are increasingly remodeling mental health treatment, modifying staff training, and connecting with community agencies to provide a more effective continuum of care. It is jail mental health treatment to which we now turn.

The Consensus Project (Council of State Governments, 2002) recommends that, at a minimum, jails should have the capacity to provide immediate crisis intervention and short-term treatment. In jails, short-term treatment typically consists of psychiatric medications. With regard to medication, the Consensus Project recommends that jails must ensure a detainee is able to continue on the medications he/she was prescribed prior to jail. Each of these will be discussed below.

Despite the requirements on jails, research shows that most inmates do not in fact receive mental health treatment within the walls of the jail. As of the late 1990s, only around 10% of all jail inmates received treatment (Morris et al., 1997; Ditton, 1999). Even among inmates with mental illness, less than half receive mental health services (Perez et al., 2003; Steadman et al., 1999; Morris et al., 1997; Teplin et al., 1997; Veysey, Steadman, Morrissey, & Johnsen, 1997; Walsh & Holt, 1999), a trend that continues to the current day (Lurigio & Swartz, 2006). In actuality, mental health services tend to be reactive, rather than proactive, focusing on responding to mental health crises and managing symptoms rather than improving coping skills and quality of life for inmates (Buffington-Vollum, 2011). For example, of inmates with mental illness, 34% received medication and only 16% received therapy or counseling (Ditton, 1999). With limited services available, treatment decisions are influenced not only by treatment history and the type of mental illness the inmate has, but by arbitrary factors unrelated to the inmate's mental illness, such as the type of crime and whether jail intake staff document the symptoms (Kinsler & Saxman, 2007; Teplin, 1990).

These numbers are striking in light of the many treatment needs that jail inmates have. Not only are rates of mental illness higher, but inmates — and especially inmates with mental illness — have heightened rates of substance abuse, prior trauma, and psychosocial problems (e.g., family issues, problems in interpersonal relationships, unemployment, financial difficulties, medical issues) that contribute to stress and hinder coping. Additionally, within the jail walls, inmates are exposed to all of the stressors mentioned earlier in the chapter — e.g., constant noise, lack of privacy, rigid rules and harsh discipline for failing to comply, victimization by other inmates and even staff. Yet, they are simultaneously deprived of the social support and self-soothing mechanisms upon which they rely in the community. This confluence of risk factors constitutes a perfect storm.

Crisis Intervention

Although frequently included in the same phrase in correctional mental health treatment guidelines (American Psychiatric Association, 2000; Council of State Governments, 2002), crisis intervention is different than short-term treatment. While both are short-term in nature, as the name suggests, crisis intervention involves immediate action on the part of the responder while individuals are in crisis. Crises, by definition, occur when individuals are confronted with events or situations that are perceived as intolerable (James & Gilliland, 2005) and irresolvable (Caplan, 1964). Further, a person is said to be "in crisis" when the individual's experiences exceed one's coping mechanisms and available resources (James & Gilliland, 2005), resulting in a state of increased tension, anxiety, confusion, and overall emotional unrest (Caplan, 1964), which is followed by a rapid transition to impulsive actions (Dass-Brailsford, 2007) and/or inability to function (Caplan, 1964). With regard to jail inmates, and mentally ill jail inmates, in particular, one can imagine any number of experiences he/she finds him- or herself in jail that would meet the definition of crisis. Merely being in jail—if it is perceived as intolerable and irresolvable, and one cannot cope with the anxiety and confusion involved—is enough in some cases to result in a crisis. Likewise, any number of other stressors related to incarceration that have been discussed previously (e.g., victimization, separation from one's support system) could precipitate a crisis.

Crisis Intervention "Steps"

Effective crisis intervention, as a method, is present- and action-oriented, focused on helping an individual develop specific short-term goals in response to a given situation (Dass-Brailsford, 2007). Although there are numerous models of crisis intervention, all entail preparing individuals to manage the sequelae of a specific crisis-inducing event by learning to identify and enlisting existing coping skills, resources, and support that is available to them. To be effective, the process of crisis intervention should involve several components or—at the risk of suggesting that there is a "recipe" for intervening with a person in crisis—steps (James & Gilliland, 2005). Ensuring client safety must be infused throughout the process and should always be at the forefront of the responder's mind.

The first stage of effective crisis intervention is assisting the individual to define his/her problem (James, 2008). Sometimes, individuals in crisis are unaware of the issue that is causing them distress; and crisis responders[8] can assist them in uncovering the underlying cause by listening empathically to them. By so doing, responders also gain valuable information enabling them to understand the problem from the client's point of view. Consider, for example, an inmate who went into crisis after speaking

---

8. In the jail context, the crisis responder can be a mental health clinician or a jail officer, whoever is the first responder and/or responsible for managing the crisis. Although discussed as a subsection of mental health treatment, these are techniques that can be learned by anyone in a role in which he/she might need to respond to a crisis. As such, crisis intervention should be a component of any training on mental health or suicide prevention for jail officers. See also Kerle (2018).

with his wife by phone. He made angry threats to hang himself but refused to leave his cell to be taken to the isolation room to be placed on suicide watch. As the officers attempted to extract him from his cell, he became aggressive, focusing his blows and cursing at one officer in particular. Upon engaging the inmate, he angrily reveals that he believes his wife has been unfaithful while he is in jail. With further discussion, it becomes clear that he has paranoid and jealous delusions, having become convinced that the particular officer is the one having a relationship with her, despite the fact that the two have never met. Without listening to the inmate and assisting him in defining his problem, the crisis responder would have lacked critical clinical information, both for diagnostic and crisis intervention purposes.

The next step involves providing support to the individual (James, 2008). At the core, this entails conveying to the individual that the crisis responder cares about his/her well-being. Beyond emotional support, this might also involve instrumental support, as much as possible. In the above example, for instance, a crisis responder might work with jail officers to avoid the officer who forms the basis of the inmate's delusions from being involved in his care until he has experienced some relief from his delusion.

During the action stage of crisis intervention, it is the task of the crisis responder to help the individual identify and consider alternatives (James, 2008). This is an important stage as, by definition, most people in crisis (especially those who are suicidal) believe that the precipitating event or stressor is unbearable and unsolvable; they experience a cognitive narrowing and do not believe they have options. For example, the inmate who becomes suicidal after his delusion of his wife's infidelity is triggered perceives his life to not be worth living without her. His thoughts become "stuck" there; he cannot think of anything else. Assisting an individual to identify alternatives often involves assessing and reminding the individual of his/her support system and/ or typical/past coping mechanisms. Another strategy involves modeling for the individual how to brainstorm realistic alternatives and/or to reframe the situation so as to alter his/her perception of the problem and, thereby, to lessen stress and anxiety.

After considering alternatives, the effective crisis responder helps the individual to settle on specific, discrete steps by which to get through the short-term crisis and to regain the early resumption of emotional stability (James, 2008). This involves identifying other people, resources, and/or positive coping mechanisms that can be enlisted immediately for some degree of relief. It is important that the crisis responder be realistic about the situation, however, as being insincere can damage not only the immediate relationship with the individual but his/her trust in other responders in the future. Indeed, the goal of this stage is to instill a sense of control, self-respect, and hope. Particularly with regard to self-respect, most individuals — including those in crisis, and even individuals in the throes of psychosis — can detect when a crisis responder is being disingenuous and patronizing. Further, the ultimate goal of crisis intervention is to obtain the individual's commitment to the plan. In order to do so, the plan must be realistic to the individual; he/she must be convinced of its effectiveness to follow through.

Crisis Intervention for Suicidal Inmates

Although crisis intervention can be used for a variety of reactions to perceived acute stressors, in the jail setting, it most frequently applies to expressions of suicidal ideation and/or gestures. Pompili et al. (2009) examined research and policy recommendations intended to reduce the incidence of patient suicides at psychiatric hospitals and discussed these ideas in the context of jails. Two of the best practices Pompili et al. (2009) identified pertain to ongoing screening (as opposed to only an initial screening at booking) and provision of mental health services:

1. Systematically screen inmates at booking, as well as throughout their stay, for suicide risk. Do not approach suicide screening as a one-time assessment; instead, consider it a process.

2. Mental health resources, within the jail and/or in the community, should be identified to ensure ready access to evaluation and treatment services.

A major controversy in jails is how to respond to inmates who repeatedly threaten suicide and/or engage in self-injurious behavior (also known as self-mutilation). Not infrequently, jail officers conclude that the individual is just seeking attention or is being manipulative and that the best response is to ignore the behavior so as not to reinforce it (Pompili et al, 2009). Often, this implicitly becomes translated into the belief that the behavior is not serious or dangerous. Even some mental health professionals — who generally recognize that inmates who would go so far as to threaten suicide or actually self-mutilate have some emotional problems that require attention (Pompili et al., 2009) — become frustrated by repeated suicidal threats and gestures and to some degree dismiss the behavior as unimportant. However, regardless of the motivation, individuals who engage in suicidal gestures deserve prompt crisis intervention and assessment as outlined above (Scott, 2010), if nothing else because such gestures can unintentionally result in death (Pompili et al., 2009).

Management of Inmates in Crisis

Although the following interventions are discussed in the context of managing suicidal inmates, they apply to all inmates in crisis. The same considerations must be made in regard to using these management strategies with non-suicidal but mentally ill inmates.

Isolation

While at one time isolation was the preferred protocol in jails in response to suicidal ideation, Hayes (2000) and others have argued against isolation, especially during the first 48 hours, because it tends to increase suicide attempts. Although less than found in her early work (Hayes, 1989), Hayes (2010) recently confirmed that suicides frequently occur when an inmate is placed in isolation (38% of suicides).

Nevertheless, this form of intervention — or, in many cases, punishment — continues to be used frequently in U.S. jails, sometimes merely as a location to house mentally ill inmates. This is despite increasing knowledge that "[i]t is an almost surefire guarantee to lead to a worsening of symptoms," as put by NAMI Director of Policy and Legal Affairs, Ronald Honberg (2012) in testimony to the Senate Judiciary Subcommittee on the Constitution, Civil Rights and Human Rights. Based on research by such experts as Craig Haney, who has studied the effect of solitary and supermax confinement (Haney, 2003), these symptoms can involve extreme anxiety and depression, sleep disturbances, paranoia and hallucinations, self-mutilation, and suicide attempts. Use of restraints is nearly as psychologically destructive (Pompili et al., 2009). Furthermore, such punitive management tools can ultimately discourage a suicidal inmate from seeking assistance and/or mental health services in the future (Pompili et al., 2009). Finally, in an opposite vein, using isolation for non-suicidal but self-injuring inmates may actually exacerbate their acting out behavior by causing them to believe they need to "up the ante" to gain the attention they so desperately seek (Pompili et al., 2009).

Although the American Psychiatric Association (2000) recognized the occasional utility of physical restraints and even isolation, they asserted numerous limits on their use. Among others, the APA strongly urged that the least restrictive alternative should always be used first, strict time limits should be enforced, frequent and regular monitoring should occur, and inmates exposed to these interventions should have ready access to mental health professionals (Pompili et al., 2009). Finally, it is essential that policies and procedures be clearly documented so as to limit staff discretion (at least, in the direction of upward departure) in the use of these interventions (Pompili et al., 2009). Indeed, this represents another best practice identified by Pompili et al. (2009) in their review of psychiatric inpatient facilities' suicide prevention and crisis intervention strategies that is applicable to jails.

With limited use of restraint and seclusion, what options, then, does a jail have to manage its inmates in crisis? Pompili et al. (2009) highlighted such accommodations as physical adjustments to the facility, close staff observation/monitoring of inmates at risk or in crisis, increased social contact with and support from other inmates and staff for such inmates, staff training, and improving workplace conditions for staff. Each will be discussed below.

Physical Adjustments to the Facility

Pompili et al. (2009) summarized basic adjustments that should be made to the physical environment or architecture of the facility in order to make it safer. Essentially, anything that a facility can do to remove possible means by which inmates can commit suicide, the better. For example, given that most inmates and psychiatric inpatients commit suicide by hanging, eliminating as much extra clothing, sheets, and towels, as well as minimizing potential hanging points and unsupervised access to lethal materials, is wise. Such is the premise behind paper "suicide gowns" in jails. Similarly, in what have come to be known as "safer cells," all corners are rounded, pipes are covered, lights fixtures and electrical outlets are modified, and ventilators are used to allow air flow in the absence of windows that open (Pompili et al., 2009). However, given the pervasive financial constraints experienced by jails discussed throughout this chapter, the cost of such accommodations is prohibitive or, at least, limits their widespread use.

Staff Observation/Monitoring

Research suggests that the single best protection against suicide is constant observation by staff (Felthous, 2011). Particularly if an inmate is placed in isolation, and especially during conditions of heightened risk (e.g., at shift changes; during night shifts; when staff are unfamiliar with an area of the jail, due to being new or not being typically assigned to the area), it is critical to keep them under close supervision (Pompili et al., 2009). Of course, these are the times when maintaining close observation is inherently most difficult. Indeed, between understaffing and heightened demands due to overcrowding, truly *constant* observation is rarely feasible.

As a result, most jails resort to, at best, 15-minute checks or, increasingly, camera surveillance (Pompili et al., 2009). However, it only takes a matter of minutes for a determined inmate to complete suicide, plenty of time in between checks. While it may seem optimal to have "constant" camera observation, this technology is limited by physical blind spots in the physical set-up of the isolation room, not to mention camera operators who become bored and/or distracted. Ultimately, level of monitoring should be determined based on a case-by-case analysis of risk, and camera surveillance should never be the sole means of monitoring. During periods in which staff-to-inmate ratios are at their lowest (e.g., midnight to six a.m.), administrators should consider either staffing additional officers or placing other inmates in isolation cells with inmates to deter suicides. These seeming inconveniences far outweigh the nightmare of facing liability lawsuits.

Although it is clearly stated that inmates in isolation should be closely monitored, it is not always clear to staff what they should be monitoring for. As outlined by Pompili et al. (2009), routine checks should watch for indications of exacerbation of psychiatric symptoms and/or increasing suicidal intent. Signs of worsening symptoms of mental illness include increased crying, sudden changes in mood, loss of interest in activities or relationships, insomnia or hypersomnia, changes in eating patterns, and/or lethargy or restlessness. Furthermore, officers and mental health staff should take note of medication refusal or an inmate requesting an increased dose as possible indicants of declining mental state.

Social Contact and Support

Simple social contact has been proven to be an effective deterrent to suicide (Pompili et al., 2009). First, suicide is a private phenomenon, so placing inmates in a dormitory or shared cell with others tends to decrease the likelihood that they will attempt to harm themselves. Pompili et al. (2009), however, warn that housing or social interventions that are not well-planned may actually carry risks or, at least, be fruitless. For example, unemphatic cellmates may merely not bother to alert staff when an inmate harms him/herself. Second, placing highly suicidal inmates into shared cells can provide them with readier access to means by which to commit suicide than if he/she was housed alone. As with camera monitoring above, jail staff should never solely rely on other inmates to safeguard a suicidal inmate; it is not a substitute for monitoring by trained staff (Pompili et al., 2009).

Social support expands upon social contact in reducing the risk of suicide. For example, family visits (or visits from other valued persons) can remind a suicidal inmate of a reason to live, and/or concerned family members can forewarn jail staff of an inmate's potential suicidality (Pompili et al., 2009). On the other hand, problems with family members or friends can heighten inmates' suicide risk; thus, officers should supervise visits to some degree. In turn, positive relationships with staff and officers can definitely serve a protective function against inmate suicide. Indeed, jail staff who are attuned to inmates as individuals and are cognizant of significant events going on in inmates' lives are better prepared to notice when inmates' mood and behavior changes. Likewise, Pompili et al. (2009) encourage officers to hold conversations with inmates as they approach these important dates (e.g., sentencing dates, divorce) in order to monitor suicidal ideation. Some facilities have even begun to implement inmate "buddy" programs to encourage social support and monitoring from other specially trained inmates who can empathize with the individual's situation and feelings (Pompili et al., 2009).

Short-Term Mental Health Treatment

Psychotropic Medications

In many jails, the only form of mental health treatment is psychotropic medications (e.g., antidepressants, antipsychotics, and mood stabilizers for mania). This is problematic for many reasons (Buffington-Vollum, 2011). First, medications are not effective for all individuals with mental illness. Thereby, only offering medications as treatment leaves a certain proportion of inmates untreated. Similarly, they only address the symptoms; they do not teach life or coping skills that most mentally ill inmates need. Additionally, given the hierarchical nature of the relationship between inmates and jail staff — not to mention, the distrust and paranoia inherent to various mental illnesses — inmates with mental illness may be resistant to accepting medications administered by staff, even mental health staff. This can easily lead to inmates becoming non-compliant with medications, which as discussed previously, they have a legal right to do (i.e., right to refuse treatment) under many circumstances. Unfortunately, this then tends to lead to (further) psychiatric deterioration.

Next, psychotropic medications have notorious side effects. These side effects are, at least, unpleasant and, at their worst, can be harmful and even deadly. Some medications require regular blood draws to ensure that the physical side effects do not become lethal. The side effects can be especially dangerous if combined with certain other medications and/or substances of abuse taken prior to arrest that have not cleared the individual's system. As such, jail inmates on any medications must be closely monitored, which jail officers are not prepared — and should not be expected — to do.

Yet another limitation, and one that affects the very availability of this treatment option at all, is the expense. Not only are the services of medical professionals who must prescribe the medications expensive, but the cost of the medications is often the largest item on a jail's budget. As of 2009, a single antipsychotic medication could have an average monthly cost of $1,434 (Consumer Reports, 2009), and some inmates with severe mental illness must take numerous psychotropic medications simultaneously to adequately treat their symptoms.[9] Obviously, such expenditures can overwhelm a jail system, particularly small county jails with limited budgets. Furthermore, such treatment may not be sustainable as individuals with mental illness — many of whom are impoverished (Cook, 2006) — are released into the community.

Drug Formularies and Other Cost-Cutting Measures

Given the costs to jails, they have begun to implement — or rather, state legislatures, have begun to impose on jails — cost-cutting measures, such as restrictive drug formularies (Council of State Governments, 2002). As discussed in Chapter 3, drug formularies are lists of medications — usually generic and/or the cheapest medications available in a given class of drugs — that the system will pay for (Koyanagi, Forquer, & Alfano, 2005). As a result, the medications an inmate was taking in the community, if it is not on the drug formulary list, will need to be changed, often abruptly. In Scheyett et al.'s (2009) analysis of North Carolina's jails, 39% of jails employed a prescription formulary for psychiatric medications. Another 20% indicated that, despite having no official formulary, they did not make substitutions for expensive medications — a practice that has the same repercussions as formularies.

Delays in Receiving Medication

Psychotropic medications can only be prescribed by a medical doctor, and they are not typically available much of the time at jails. Indeed, medical services are usually provided by contract physicians on a part-time or on-call basis (Kinsler, 2007). For example, in northwest Virginia, psychiatric care in smaller county jails was typically provided on a monthly to as needed basis (in 88% of jails), and even 40% of larger regional jails provided psychiatric care on less than a weekly basis (Buffington-Vollum, 2009). As such, receipt of necessary medications is often delayed. In North Carolina, although inmates in 45% of jails were reported to receive their medications either the day of or the day after intake, 19% of jails indicated that it can take five days or longer for inmates to receive medications (Scheyett et al., 2009). Such inconsistency in medication dosage — and accordingly, the unstable levels of the medication in the inmate's blood stream — can be, at least, uncomfortable and, in some cases, dangerous.

---

9. This does not even account for the medications an inmate may be on for other medical conditions, such as diabetes and heart disease, which — as discussed in Chapter 3 — individuals with serious mental illness have at higher rates than those without mental illness (Parks, Svendsen, Singer, & Foti, 2006).

Telepsychiatry

In an effort to provide psychiatric care to inmates in a prompter — and, importantly to administrators, cost-effective — manner, the use of telepsychiatry has increased substantially in the past decade (Scott, 2010). Telepsychiatry involves the use of electronic communication and technology to provide psychiatric care at a distance (American Psychiatric Association, 1998). Most of what is known as telepsychiatry today involves live, interactive two-way audio-video communication (i.e., videoconferencing) between inmates in jails and a psychiatrist in a remote location.

By 2001, 26 states used some form of telemedicine, and the provision of mental health care is one of the most common applications (Larsen, Hudnall, Davis, & Magaletta, 2004). Indeed, as of 2009, 32% of jails in northwest Virginia were using telepsychiatry as its primary mode of psychiatric services (Buffington-Vollum, 2009). Despite concerns about the potential effects of the impersonal nature of such provision of care — particularly, on inmates experiencing difficulties with reality testing (e.g., paranoid delusions about technology) — the existing research suggests that various reactions to telepsychiatry do not differ significantly from in-person services (O'Reilly et al., 2007). This includes no differences between the two forms of treatment on perceptions of the therapeutic relationship, post-session mood, or general satisfaction with services (Morgan, Edwards, & Faulkner, 1993). In actuality, by reducing wait times for treatment, follow-up outcomes appear to be improved (Leonard, 2004). Finally, by limiting inmate movement within the facility and by increasing the availability of specialized psychiatric services, which fosters the mental health of the inmates within the institution, safety of staff and security of the facility is improved (Ax et al., 2007). Nevertheless, as noted by Scott (2010), telepsychiatry is not a substitution for having some mental health staff on site.

Psychotherapeutic Treatment

Some larger jails — with larger budgets — who are able to provide more comprehensive mental health services also provide therapy and/or counseling. Typically, it is provided in a group format because it is more efficient and cost-effective. The most common focus of psychoeducational group therapy is substance abuse, given the heightened prevalence of the issue among inmate populations.

Linhorst, Dirks-Linhorst, Bernsen, and Childrey (2009) described an example of a jail-based substance abuse treatment program. According to the authors, the program is intended to help inmates develop skills to improve their life skills so as to be better able to abstain from substances and criminal behavior. It is intensive and all-encompassing, including activities not only related to substance abuse, criminality, and life skills, but to education, employment, family issues, and parenting. It involves didactic psychoeducation, peer support, and completion of written assignments, as well as guest lectures and individual counseling by mental health, criminal justice/court, and social service professionals from the community. Specifically, with regard to substance abuse, inmates attend 10 hours of psychoeducational groups per week, during which they address their "criminality and its association with substance abuse, addictions and recovery, anger management, personal and interpersonal life management skills, and relapse prevention and aftercare" (Linhorst et al., 2009, p. 100), as well as two hours per week of supportive 12-step programming similar to Alcoholics Anonymous (AA) or Narcotics Anonymous (NA). Pertaining to education and employment, inmate-participants attend eight hours of GED classes weekly, if the inmate lacks his/her high school diploma, and participates in individual counseling with community professionals on education (e.g., preparing for GED testing), preparing a job application and/or resume, finding a job, vocational placement, and financial assistance. Inmates participate in family counseling and receive individual counseling from social service professionals on parenting and meeting the emotional and financial needs of their children. Finally, community agencies meet with inmates individually to enroll them in services they will need upon release.[10]

Therapeutic Communities

A commonly used and evidence-based approach to psychotherapeutic treatment is a group approach known as therapeutic communities (TCs). The therapeutic community model is based on a total milieu therapy approach, in which participants live together in a separate "community" for several months; and, by being primarily peer run rather than therapist-driven, residents of the community help each other to recognize, confront, and change their values and behaviors that have contributed to their difficulties (Taxman & Bouffard, 2002).

Although initially adapted for use in prisons for substance abusing populations, TCs have been adapted to jails, rather than merely longer-term prisons. Also, they have been expanded to other groups of inmates, including mentally ill inmates and dually diagnosed (mental illness and substance abuse) inmates.

Unfortunately, most jails are unable or unwilling to provide such intensive therapeutic programming. Indeed, some jails do not even allow volunteer-run AA or NA meetings (Kinsler, 2007). Rarely are the treatments offered in jails empirically validated (Kinsler, 2007).

Models of Mental Health Care Delivery in Jails

As discussed previously, the expenses involved in providing comprehensive mental health care — e.g., hiring of qualified staff, costly materials, such as medications, and the physical space required to confidentially evaluate and treat mentally ill inmates — make it difficult for jails, particularly smaller county jails, to provide the range of

---

10. Although a full discussion is beyond the scope of the current chapter, it should be noted that the best practice for treatment individuals with co-occurring mental illness and substance abuse disorders is an integrated approach, in which a single program or provider treats both disorders simultaneously, rather than one taking priority over the other (Kubiak, Essenmacher, Hanna, & Zeoli, 2011).

services that are recommended. As such, several models of jail mental health care have been proposed and used with varying degrees of success.

Mental Health Services in the Jail

Historically, jails assumed the responsibility of directly providing medical and mental health services, employing treatment staff and purchasing medical supplies (Veysey, 2011). However, the expense involved tended to limit viability of this model of jail health care; and before long, it only became the luxury of larger urban and/or regional jails. For example, as of 2009, only 15% of North Carolina jails reported having a mental health provider, either employed by the jail or on contact as a private provider (Scheyett et al., 2009).

Informal Reliance on the Community Mental Health System

With few other options, jails increasingly called upon local community mental health staff to fill its mental health service needs. However, with no formalized agreement or compensation, this did not benefit the community mental health agency, which was already overextended, underfunded, and understaffed. As such, community mental health clinicians would provide services when they had the time and availability, but the jail was a lower priority than the agency's patients in the community. Obviously, this inconsistency was troublesome for the jail. Often, this led to tension and strained relationships between jails and the community mental health system.

Nevertheless, this arrangement — and this tension — remains in many parts of the country, especially in small county jails. In North Carolina, once again, only 25% of jails that did not have an existing mental health clinician indicated that the community mental health agency would regularly send staff to the jail for services (Scheyett et al., 2009). In fact, in 52% of the jails the community mental health agency never dispatched a mental health counselor to provide services, and in no jails did the community mental health agency send a psychiatrist. Instead, 42% of the jails relied on transporting inmates to a community provider on an as-needed basis. Unsurprisingly, this unreliable arrangement sometimes results in long waits for inmates to receive treatment.

Privatized Correctional Mental Health Care

In recent years, consistent with the trend in the prison system, moderate to large-sized jails have increasingly privatized their health services (Pollack, Khoshnood, & Altice, 1999). In privatized arrangements, jails contract with a for-profit correctional health care company to provide all medical and mental health services, including staff, laboratory services, pharmacy materials, etc. Functioning on a capitated cost system, the company closely dictates and monitors all services, avoiding expensive treatment options that infringe on the its profit margin (Veysey, 2011). As noted by Pollack et al. (1999), such arrangements "by their very nature build in disincentives for the health care organization to provide comprehensive, state-of-the-art treatment" (Veysey, 2011, p. 7). Instead, privatization tends to result in tightly regulated, erratic, and poor quality services.

Community-Oriented Correctional Mental Health Care

In recent years, however, there has been movement toward a model of community-oriented correctional health care. Similar to the model presented above, the jail signs a contract for another agency to provide its medical and mental health services. However, in this model, the contract is with the area community health center. This is different than the previously discussed informal arrangement between the jail and the community mental health system. The benefits of this arrangement are many. First, from an economic standpoint, it keeps money within the local economy, which benefits the community. Similarly, it can potentially promote more humane and empathic treatment, particularly if the service provider knows the inmate. Furthermore, and most importantly in the context of effective mental health care, by utilizing a local service provider who can treat the individual not only in the jail but upon his/her release in the community, it facilitates continuity of care (Veysey, 2011). This also increases the likelihood that the inmate-patient will follow through on their treatment plan upon release. According to Conklin, Lincoln, and Wilson (2002), the arrangement "avoids common information exchange barriers, increases the breadth and quality of services, and provides financial incentives to provide quality care" (Veysey, 2011, p. 8).

Future Directions in Jail Mental Health Care

In constant pursuit of containing costs, states are searching for ways to pay for the inordinate cost of mental health care in jails. Some states (e.g., Florida, Utah), for example, have or are considering policies requiring detainees who have private insurance to pay for medical care they receive in jail (Veysey, 2011). Legislators and the general public tend to support such initiatives, but the insurance industry, of course, is resistant because of the implications for its profit margin (Shimkus, 2003). Other cities and counties are investigating the option of competitive health insurance plans for jail inmates (Bennett, 2010). Yet other states (e.g., Colorado) are instead searching for ways to control costs by limiting what health care providers can charge. The financial implications, however, of reducing the reimbursement rate from 75% or more to 35% has left some providers to merely refuse to treat jail patients (Shimkus, 2003).

Inpatient Mental Health Services

Jails and prisons are noted to being ill-equipped to serve persons with serious mental illness, particularly when in crisis (Human Rights Watch, 2003; Scheyett et al., 2009). Yet mental health crises occur with fair regularity: Of inmates with mental illness, 32% required acute hospitalization in the jail's inpatient unit and 44% were placed in lockdown for at least 72 hours for part of their jail time; in other words, 76% of inmates with mental illness required inpatient care or its equivalent at some point during their incarceration (Lamb et al., 2007). However, many jails do not have the luxury of an inpatient unit or even more than a cell or two for lockdown. As such, most of these jails must transport inmates to hospitals for acute treatment. In North Carolina, 80% of jails transported inmates to state psychiatric hospitals, 73% at least occasionally transported to the state's central prison medical facility, and 24% utilized local hospitals (Scheyett et al., 2009). Not only are some of these types of hospitalization prohibitively expensive, but the transport and constant supervision at the hospital exert huge drains on officer time, particularly when the state psychiatric or prison hospital is hours away from the jail.

Another factor complicating the care of a mentally ill jail inmate is that they are not transferred to state treatment facilities in a timely manner. In Virginia Beach, for example, it typically takes at least six months before an acutely ill inmate in jail can be transferred to the state hospital or even to the nearby psychiatric center (Hammack, 2007). Judges in Miami, Florida, however, found a way to burst through these waiting lists:

In Florida, county jails are allowed to detain a mentally ill offender up to 15 days by law before transfer to state treatment facilities. In 2006, the Florida Department of Children and Families (FDCF), which runs the state hospitals, faced possible legal action for not transferring mentally ill jail inmates to state facilities. Judges in Miami (Dade County), at the time, even considered legal remedies to require FDCF to comply with the law or face contempt charges. The absurdity is that FDCF had an $8 billion budget surplus at the time (Goodnough, 2006). A Pinellas County judge even held the Director of FDCF in contempt of court, which resulted in her resignation. Attention by the media and state judges produced responses by Governor Jeb Bush and state legislators to provide additional funds to FDCF to reduce time mentally ill offenders spend in jail prior to transfer to a state treatment facility. In a press release on May 9, 2007, the FDCF announced that the waitlist of mentally ill offenders in jail awaiting transfer had been reduced to zero under the leadership of newly elected Governor Crist and Secretary Butterworth. Using $16.6 million in state appropriated funds, 251 new forensic treatment beds were added. An additional $4.6 million was provided by the Florida legislature to improve diversion efforts and enhance community and in-jail mental health services (Florida Department of Children and Family Services, 2007). The tragedy is the needless harm to individuals, families, jail staff, and communities.

The need for more inpatient mental health services for jail inmates is also problematic in the context of those found to be in need of evaluation and/or restoration for competency to stand trial. While many untreated mentally ill are stuck in the revolving door between the street and the jail, others are caught in the revolving door between the jail and the state hospital. In one Florida case, a mentally ill inmate who was unfit to stand trial waited months in jail without treatment before transfer to a state mental hospital. In the state psychiatric hospital he took medications and was eventually found competent. At that point he was returned to the county jail, where he legally refused treatment. Without medicine, the inmate's condition worsened until the court found him incompetent again and in need of placement in the state's mental hospital. With limited availability at the state mental hospital, the inmate languished in jail (Christian, 2005). At the time, there were approximately 300 inmates in Florida awaiting placement in a state mental hospital. Similar situations exist across the United States (Tisch & VanSickle, 2006), a process referred to as "riding the bus" (see also Toch, 1982).

One possible solution to the difficulty of procuring precious hospital beds for jail inmates, which has been proposed in recent years, is the building of new "psychiatric jails." States such as Maine have considered closing some existing jails and transforming them into specialty facilities for people with mental illness ("Edge of crisis", 2007). However, the idea of such specialized jails has been met with mixed reviews.

Miami Public Defender Bennett Brummer commended Judge Leifman's proposal to build a new psychiatric jails but expressed concerns that such plans could further erode efforts to treat mental illness in the community and could "wittingly convey the impression that the best, if not only way, to get needed psychiatric help is to be arrested."

Mental Health Records

A final mental health "service" that jails should provide its inmates, as explicated in *Ruiz* and endorsed by various professional organizations, is maintenance of accurate, complete, and confidential mental health records. Such records are important for treatment purposes, discharge planning, and continuity of care. An efficient database of information about inmates' mental health that can be shared between the jail and the mental health provider avoids duplication of efforts and, thereby, improves response times (Fabelo, 2000), which is critical during mental health crises. It is also important for policy and research purposes. Without adequate data collection, storage, and reporting procedures, it is virtually impossible to ascertain the number or characteristics of mentally ill inmates that a jail serves (Fabelo, 2000). As such, it makes it difficult to formulate effective policies. If jail administrators wish to apply for grant funding, for example, it is becoming increasingly important to justify the application with quantitative evidence.

While this is not typically a significant burden for larger urban or regional jails, it can prove to be a challenge for smaller county and city jails. For example, the majority of jails in Texas are small, rural facilities housing fewer than 50 inmates, and they do not have the capabilities to maintain mental health records in a computerized format (Fabelo, 2000). In light of this fact, it is not possible to know the extent to which quality mental health services are available in jails across the nation. This hinders the development of standards of treatment and oversight of service providers to ensure effective mental health treatment (Fabelo, 2000).

Jail Officers

Officers are integral to the successful management of a jail and to mentally ill inmates in particular. As such, they deserve their own section in the current chapter. It is noteworthy how little research there is on jail officers in general, as well as in the specific context of their attitudes and approaches to mentally ill inmates. Although most discussion in the literature on mentally ill inmates focuses on prison officers, as opposed to jail officers, the majority of the literature is applicable to both. Given that jail inmates tend to be sicker when entering jail than when entering prison — and in many cases, the sick*est* they get in either the community or the institution — it is arguably all the more important to consider jail officers.

Symptomatic mentally ill inmates can (and often do) affect the safe and efficient operation of the facility — the very job of jail staff — and, in turn, the jail environment can (and does) exacerbate symptoms of mental illness (Sowers, Thompson, & Mullins, 1999). Overall, individuals with mental illness cope less well to institutionalization than do inmates without mental illness (Morgan et al., 1993; Toch & Adams, 1987). As a result, they tend to violate rules of the institution more often and, thus, spend more time in isolation (Morgan et al., 1993). This, in turn, exacerbates their mental illness; and the cycle begins again. Overall, disruptions to the institution (and, thus, to their job) caused by inmates with mental illness; the difficulty of responding to inmates who are in great distress and potentially self-mutilating, attempting suicide, or at worst, completing suicide; and the constant need to be hypervigilant for potential violence by inmates all contribute to jail officers' stress (Finn, 2000).

Thus, knowledge and experience that makes jail officers more responsive to mentally ill inmates can promote safety and smoother management of the jail, reduce officer stress, and even improve quality of life of inmates. This underscores the need for training on mental illness, suicide, and appropriate management of inmates with these special needs, which will be discussed below. These benefits are augmented if jail officers and mental health/medical staff can work effectively together. Due to distinct professional cultures and missions, however, there is often tension between jail officers and mental health and/or medical staff. This is largely based in inherent ideological differences, which were present even during the rehabilitative era of corrections (Powelson & Bendix, 1951). For example, jail officers, who are primarily responsible for security of the institution, may view mental health staff (if available) as being "soft" and coddling inmates; they may resent that inmates get free services when others in the community — including they, themselves — do not, particularly when they view inmates to be undeserving with mere character flaws (Appelbaum et al., 2001). Furthermore, as members of the lay public, many jail officers subscribe to the same stereotypes about individuals with mental illness. These beliefs are clearly illustrated in the following excerpt from Pete Earley's book, *Crazy* (2006, p. 242), an expose on the criminal justice system's treatment of people with mental illness in Miami, Florida:

> Earley had been told that a mentally ill inmate had been punched several times in his kidney area, as well as his arm twisted behind his back. One officer explained, "You need to instill fear in these inmates or they won't listen to you ... especially crazy inmates, 'cause if you don't scare them, then they will hurt you ... We don't have any way to control these inmates except with behavior modification, which is a nice way to say: putting our hands on them if they get out of line. I mean, how else can we keep them under control?"

An attorney engaged in the lawsuit *Richard v. Sedgwick County Sheriff* (2009) in Kansas alleges that inmates were knowingly allowed by staff to taunt and harass inmates with mental illnesses (L. Wall, personal communication. July 19, 2012). The attorney also reported that correctional personnel held an art contest among employees and would chant demeaning slogans. One of the teams of correctional officers allegedly referred to itself as Team Short-bus, a derogatory term associated with persons who are disabled and intimates the shorter school buses that are often seen transporting special needs children (Potter, 2012). Pictures were reportedly drawn with words spelled backwards and misspelled words (Potter, 2012). The negative art work, chanting and even singing were all allegedly condoned by various administrators, took place in the watch commander's office, and the contest was created by a Lieutenant (Potter, 2012). Things are not quite as funny anymore since the lawsuit has been filed, Edgar Richard, who called himself "the black Jesus," was reportedly the brunt of ridicule, received a severe beating by a detention officer, was knocked unconscious, received a broken jaw, and ultimately died some two years later in a nursing home from stomach cancer (Potter, 2012). As is often the case in such matters, the legal representatives for Richard are taking the "deep pockets approach" — the higher they can link the responsibility for Richard's injuries up in the administration's hierarchy the greater the possibility for obtaining monetary damages.

Reciprocally, some clinicians, whose focus tends to be on treating individual inmates, view jail staff as unduly harsh and punitive (Appelbaum et al., 2001). Certainly, not all jail officers and clinicians endorse these ascribed beliefs or ideology, but enough do to aggravate relationships between them, and even with mentally ill inmates.[11]

---

11. Interestingly, the limited research on the topic suggests that correctional officers actually tend to view serious mental illnesses, such as schizophrenia, as a serious problem, rather than merely a result of stressors, and to correctly differentiate depression from other problems (Callahan, 2004). In fact, officers were twice as likely as members of the general public to over-diagnose as mentally ill a hypothetical inmate with mere life stressors (with no mental illness) (51% versus 22%), and they were very supportive of treatment of inmates. Although encouraging to the degree that officers do not seem to be as unempathic and unresponsive to troubled inmates as stereotypically believed, Callahan (2004) noted several concerns with their tendency to over-diagnose mental illness. These include

Although neither perspective is without some basis in reality, if a facility is run optimally, jail officers and mental health and/or medical staff, if available, can collaborate effectively to fulfill each other's job responsibilities As noted by Appelbaum et al. (2001, p. 1345),

> Alertness, professionalism, and secure but humane treatment keep institutions safe and help avoid unnecessary applications of force. Skillful correctional officers, of whom there are many, embrace these qualities and appreciate the contributions made by a comprehensive mental health program. Similarly, effective mental health care providers generally regard correctional staff as allies, not adversaries ... Everyone benefits when the environment is characterized by mutual respect and reliance on the expertise of both security professionals and mental health professionals.

Not only do jail officers enable mental health/medical staff to do their jobs, they can contribute to treatment in several important ways (Appelbaum et al., 2001). The first essential function that jail officers can perform for treatment staff is consistent, and ideally, skilled, observation of inmates with mental illness. Through virtually constant interaction with inmates on the housing units, officers are usually the first — after other inmates — to notice significant changes in an inmate. Bizarre behavior, deterioration in self-care, and an increase in aggressive or irritable behavior can all be indicants of the development of and/or escalation of mental illness. Also, inmates — even mentally ill inmates — can suppress (or, on the other hand, in the case of malingerers, produce) psychiatric symptoms when they are in the offices of mental health staff. With this being clinicians' primary point of contact with inmates, "behind the scenes" information from officers can be invaluable.

Next, jail officers are, by definition, "essential staff" for monitoring and maintaining the safety of the institution and its inhabitants. From a mental health perspective, they are also integral for monitoring and maintaining the safety of individual inmates deemed to be at heightened risk to themselves or others (Appelbaum et al., 2001). The most common scenario of special monitoring is when an inmate is on "suicide watch." Although typically implemented after an inmate exhibits overt signs of suicidal intentions (e.g., suicide attempt, expression of suicidal ideation), officers can also be helpful for keeping a watchful eye out for warning signs of suicidality, as outlined in the suicide screen and the crisis management sections earlier, among inmates who mental health staff suspect to be experiencing increasing symptoms of depression. In fact, officers should be provided with adequate training to be able to detect potential risk factors for suicide (e.g., personal or legal setbacks), bring them to the attention

---

the fact that mental health care is not necessary for all inmates and, by over-referring inmates to already overburdened mental health services, it detracts from those who actually need it; that officers might have unrealistic expectations for mental health services, thinking if an inmate is only treated it will make the officers' job easier; and labeling as mentally ill even inmates without mental illness can result in negative consequences (e.g., stigma) for those inmates.

to mental health staff, and then monitor these inmates. Indeed, in Hayes (2010) recent national survey of U.S. jail suicides, 63% of jails in which a suicide had been completed either did not provide training or did not provide it on an annual basis. Moreover, 69% of these jails offered two hours or less of training. Furthermore, jail officers can be particularly useful in identifying when patients become noncompliant with treatment.

Optimally, jail officers can also serve as "treatment extenders." Similar to law enforcement officers in the community, jail officers are first responders in the jail setting. As such, officers serve a vital role in preventing suicide, often more so than clinical staff (Appelbaum et al., 2001). For non-emergency cases, a knowledgeable and concerned officer can support an impaired inmate by providing prompts about the requirements of the jail, encouraging attendance at meetings with mental health clinicians and/or compliance with treatment, and alerting staff when the individual refuses to take his/her medication (Appelbaum et al., 2001). Indeed, officers who show a balance between firmness and sensitivity, who apply fair but firm discipline, who are flexible rather than dominant, can be an invaluable tool for helping mentally ill inmates to learn boundaries and consequences (Appelbaum et al., 2001) — a lesson that is important both inside and outside the jail walls.

Training of Jail Officers

Given the high number of mentally ill inmates they have to supervise, training is essential for officers to effectively do their jobs. Most jail officers recognize that jails are ill-equipped to manage inmates with mental illness, and most realize that they lack the knowledge and experience to effectively fulfill this aspect of their position (Regan, Buffington-Vollum, & Raines, 2012; Scheyett et al., 2009). Yet, the amount and quality of training jail officers receive on mental illness specifically varies widely. While most jails provide regular suicide prevention training, many do not offer training on mental illness more generally. The state of North Carolina requires six hours of training, split between the topics of mental illness and mental retardation, for all jail officers; 35% of jails reported offering continued education on mental illness (Scheyett et al., 2009). However, officers still express concern with their lack of preparation to deal with this population. In fact the training in North Carolina is more training on mental illness than is offered in some states.

Schaefer (2017) asserts that the nature of interactions between correctional officers and inmates can promote desistance and offers 10 recommendations to facilitate such communication. They are:

1. Correctional officers should provide correction. Facilities that train staff in the effective use of authority, prosocial modeling and reinforcement, encouraging problem solving, advocacy and brokerage, and the use of high-quality interpersonal skills can expect positive results from offenders.

2. Correctional officers should communicate with prisoners using cognitive behavioral techniques. Key to this process is the principle of responsivity which

refers to using strategies and styles of service that are responsive to the offenders' mode of learning.

3. Correctional officers should act as crisis counselors. Inevitably officers will encounter inmates in crisis. Their ability to intervene effectively will reduce subsequent crisis issues.

4. Correctional officers should act as frontline diagnosticians and health advocates.

5. Correctional officers should act as corrections counselors.

6. Correctional officers should act as life coaches.

7. Correctional officers should encourage identity substitutions which allow inmates to create prosocial versus procrime identities.

8. Correctional officers should suggest new routine activities steering inmates away from criminogenic behaviors.

9. Correctional officers should solicit crime controllers to assist offenders in establishing new routine activities and prosocial identities.

10. Correctional officers should facilitate transitions which increase an offenders success during the reentry process (p. 47).

Shaefer's recommendations are reflective of a former era in corrections when rehabilitation was the dominate philosophy. Research by Andrews and Bonta, Cullen and Gendreau, Paternoster and Bushway (2009) and others have been useful in establishing evidence base practices that are morally and fiscally responsible.

Jail-Based Crisis Intervention Teams

One recent innovation in jail management of inmates with mental illness is CIT (Crisis Intervention Team) training for jail officers. As discussed at length in Chapter 5, CIT was developed and traditionally used for street law enforcement officers, and it met with great success and interest nationwide. Due to its success and the universal appeal of its principles, jails have begun to adapt the CIT model to better serve the needs of mentally ill inmates both in local jails and later upon reentry into society. As with traditional frontline officer CIT programs, jails adopt a team approach to forge new and collaborative partnerships with community stakeholders, such as corrections agencies, local mental health agencies, family advocacy groups, and others (National Institute of Corrections, 2012). And, as with frontline law enforcement CIT, existing jail-based CIT programs have met with great success in "enhancing correctional staffs' knowledge and skills, aiding administrators in improved management and care for a special population, reducing liability and cost, improving community partnerships for increased access to resources and supports, and increasing safety for all" (National Institute of Corrections, 2010). The ability to increase officers' knowledge, skill, and comfort in jail mental health crises is illustrated in the following report by Deputy Sheriff Michael Zabarsky of Ventura County Jail (personal communication to Joyce Wilde, CIT Program Administrator of the Ventura County Sheriff's Office, California, May 1, 2007):

The main point I want to make is that your training changed the way I handled this event [involving drug-induced psychosis]. It made me a better peace officer ... I firmly believe that the CIT training enabled me to do several things: 1) Quickly assess the situation and determine what needed to be done in order to have a good conclusion. 2) Recognize the symptoms of the psychosis and use the various CIT techniques provided in the training to "mentally control" the subject, not just physically control him. 3) Have the confidence to "step in" and direct resources. 4) Project confidence and expertise in a subject matter no one else present was trained for or able to understand. 5) Assure that no escalation of force was necessary to end this situation; I was able to keep my fellow officers from being over-bearing and applying too much force despite the fierce resistance. 6) Resolve the situation without compromising officer safety.

Such jail-based CIT programs exist in an increasingly number of locales, including in several counties in Maine (Cattabriga, Deprez, Kinner, Louis, & Lumb, 2007), Hancock County Jail in Ohio (NAMI Ohio, 2009), and in several jails in northwest Virginia (Buffington-Vollum, 2009). The state of Utah has developed the statewide CIT Corrections Academy (Crisis Intervention Team Utah, n.d.). These programs have been so well received, in fact, that the National Institute of Corrections offers a training, initially broadcast in March 2012, entitled, "Crisis Intervention Teams: A Frontline Response to Mental Illness in Corrections," designed to build an agency's capacity to implement locally owned and administered jail-based CIT program.

Jail (Correctional) Officer Mental Health

The primary focus on the study of effects of mental illness in criminal justice has been on offenders. There has been scant research on the mental health of those that work in the criminal justice system (Regher, et al., 2019). The work of correctional officers (jail, prison and probation/parole) is stressful. Officers work in overcrowded prisons and are exposed to violence, direct threats, and at times work-related injury. Bourbonnais et al. (2007) reported 38% of correctional officers in their study reported a high degree of psychological distress.

Regher et al.'s (2019) review of research on the effects of mental illness on correctional officers found the prevalence of post-traumatic stress disorder, major depressive disorder and anxiety disorder in correctional officers was strongly associated with exposure to violence and injury in the workplace. Kunst et al. (2009) reported prevalence of PTSD was 15% in a Netherlands sample. Carelton et al. (2018) reported prevalence of PTSD was 29% in a Canadian sample while Spinaris et al. (2012) reported prevalence of PTSD 34% in an American sample. In each case the prevalence rate was over three times the national prevalence. Similar findings were found for rates of anxiety and depression (Regher et al., 2019). Targeted workplace interventions that provide organizational supports, positive professional images and strong work relationships can serve to protect correctional officers from mental distress (Goldberg, 1996; Liu et al., 2013; Regher et al., 2019).

Jail Diversion

As has been discussed throughout this chapter, jailing persons with mental illnesses is expensive. First, jailing inmates with mental illness costs significantly more than jailing those without mental illness. In Broward County, Florida, Sheriff Jenne indicated that it costs his agency $80 a day to house a general population inmate versus $130 a day to detain a person with mental illness, a 63% increase in cost (Miller & Fantz, 2005). Figures from the Polk County Jail in Bartow, Florida, which has a special needs unit staffed by personnel with specialized training, reveal that housing a person with mental illness in jail is more than twice as costly as housing a person without mental illness in jail: $99.61 compared to $40.53 a day (J. Rice, personal communication, August 10, 2007). Miami reports even more extreme differences, costing the city six times more to detain an inmate without mental illness ($18 per day) than to house and treat a mentally ill inmate ($125 per day) (Miller & Fantz, 2005). The extra cost of jailing mentally ill inmates comes from multiple sources as outlined previously: increased staffing needs, evaluations requiring the services of psychiatrists, psychiatric medications, and increasing numbers of lawsuits (Torrey et al., 2010).

Second, housing and treating inmates in jail is more expensive than merely providing community treatment for them in the first place, which might have prevented their decompensation and detention in the first place. According to the Office of National Drug Policy, for every dollar invested in treatment, four to seven dollars are saved in terms of the costs of crime and criminal justice, broadly speaking (Treating Mental Illness Makes Sense, 2008). With regard to jails specifically, providing individuals with mental illness—even high-risk individuals with mental illness—with community treatment consistently costs half that of housing and treating the mentally ill in jail (Greenberg, 2001; Phaneuf, 2012). In Pinellas County, Florida, for example, it only costs $60 per day to divert an individual to community treatment versus $130 to jail them (Miller & Fantz, 2005). Add in the additional reduction in costs from community treatment preventing recidivism and return to the jail,[12] and the cost savings to jails are impressive.

While jail administrators point to cost savings, mental health advocates (and even criminal justice professionals) highlight that provision of community treatment— and the resulting reductions in criminal justice involvement (e.g., arrests, jail time)— is more humane. Regardless of the exact reason an individual endorses, mental health and criminal justice professionals alike have supported the widespread development

---

12. Certainly, not all community mental health treatment is successful for all people. Indeed, its effectiveness hinges on the availability and quality of services in the local area. And as discussed in Chapters 3 and 5 (and throughout the book), the community mental health system in many parts of the country is underfunded and overextended.

of what has come to be referred to as "jail diversion." As will be discussed in more detail in Chapter 10, jail diversion refers to programs that divert individuals with serious mental illness (and often co-occurring substance use disorders) away from jail and provide linkages to community-based treatment and support services (Technical Assistance and Policy Analysis Center for Jail Diversion [TAPA], 2007). The individual thus avoids arrest or spends a significantly reduced time period in jail and/or lockups on the current charge or on violations of probation resulting from previous charges (TAPA, 2007).

The term "jail diversion" has come to be used rather loosely, encompassing everything from pre-booking law enforcement-based diversion programs to post-booking court-based programs (Munetz & Griffin, 2006). Primarily relevant to the current chapter, however, are post-booking programs that divert individuals with mental illness out of the jail to community treatment. The most well-known program of this kind is the Thresholds Jail Project in Cook County, Illinois. Its multifaceted nature — the key to the success of such programs — along with its cost-effectiveness, are described below:

Thresholds staff forge relationships with clients while they are still in jail, sometimes even securing early release into Thresholds custody. Once released from the jail, the members are expected to adhere to treatment regimens, to work with a psychiatrist, and to nominate Thresholds as a payee. Thresholds provides services for substance abuse, vocational training, education, and peer supports. Thresholds has developed relationships with housing providers and the police department to ensure community support and to enlist assistance in monitoring program members. Thresholds provides 24-hour services; if a member is missing, Thresholds staff will go into the streets to locate the member. Thresholds staff do not carry individual caseloads; instead, a multidisciplinary team shares responsibility for each member, with a psychiatrist overseeing the treatment program. Unlike many programs that provide services for a limited time, Thresholds provides services as long as the member needs them (quoted from Consensus Project, n.d.).

The Thresholds Jail Project has proven to be remarkably effective in reducing numbers of jail days and hospital days. In a study of the first 30 individuals enrolled in the first year of the program's existence, outcomes from one year before enrollment to the end of the first year while in the program were examined (Talbott, 2001). The total number of jail days declined by 83% from the year before enrollment (2,741 days) to the end of the year while in the program (469 days), resulting in a savings in costs to the jail of $157,000. Likewise, hospital days declined from 2,153 to 321 in the first year of the program's existence, an 85% decrease worth $917,000 in savings. Through the second year, the cost savings was

$209,000 in jail costs and $1,154,000 in psychiatric hospital costs (Lurigio, Fallon, & Dincin, 2000).

Whatever an individual's reasoning, jail diversion has received significant support. Both the Council of State Governments (2002) and the President's New Freedom Commission on Mental Health (2003) recommended implementing programs for diverting persons with mental illnesses from jails. Similarly, in NAMI's Grading the States Report, the two highest scores, Connecticut and Ohio, were bolstered by their significant use of programs to divert persons with mental illnesses from jail (Daly, 2006). Despite their widespread praise and endorsement, however, research on only 13 comprehensive *jail* diversion programs existed (Lamberti, Weisman, & Faden, 2004). Chapter 10 will provide a more in-depth discussion of diversion programs.

Conclusion

Most jails are local, county or city operations. They are influenced by local politics, funding allocations, available tax revenues, and the quality of staff that operate jails. Jails are not typically viewed as an appropriate setting for the treatment of the mentally ill. Although diversion is still considered preferable, knowledge about mental health screening, services, and effective management of mentally ill inmates is improving and evolving. This is in large part due to efforts by such influential organizations as the National Alliance on Mental Illness, the American Correctional Association, the American Psychiatric Association, and the Council of State Governments.

In consideration of existing conditions in jails, Haneberg et al. (2017) suggest 6 questions that need to be answered by local leaders to reduce the number of people with mental illness in jail. They are:

1. Is our leadership committed?

2. Do we conduct timely screenings and assessments?

3. Do we have baseline data?

4. Have we conducted a comprehensive process analysis and inventory of services?

5. Have we prioritized policy, practice and funding improvements?

6. Do we track progress?

Cities and counties of all sizes can make big differences in the lives of individuals with serious mental illness who find themselves in jails. First and foremost, it takes devoted and caring members of the criminal justice and mental health systems to recognize and draw attention to the issue. While pre-trial diversion offers great promise, sustained attention to treatment while in jail and connection to community-based services is necessary to maintain the continuity of care for the increasing number of individuals living with mental illness that become justice involved. (Sayers et al., 2016).

Cook County Jail, one of the three largest providers of psychiatric services in the U.S., was once known for its deplorable conditions has in recent years implemented a new approach to dealing with the criminalization of mental illness. Cook County has invested over $86 million in a new "jail" which houses approximately 600 offenders living with mental illness. The Cook County Jail has become "a window for people to get treatment while they do their time" and serves as an example of how people can leave correctional institutions better than they came in. (Riley, 2019).

A similar commitment led by Judge Leifman is being made in Miami where a former forensic seven story 80,000-square-foot forensic jail is being converted to facilitate the diversion and treatment of individuals living with mental illness from the justice system. Leifman says it will be a central piece in a comprehensive system and will be the first of its kind in the country, a true diversion facility with all the essential elements (Butin, 2015).

The devolving mental health system has placed sheriffs in a very difficult place. In April, 2018, the Police Executive Research Forum sponsored a conference attended by sheriffs and jail administrators from across the United States. They made the following recommendations: 1) Successful programs have the full backing of the sheriff. 2) Strong and diverse partnerships are essential to combine the efforts of sheriff's offices, other criminal justice agencies, and community-based providers. 3) Diverting low level offenders, especially those with mental health issues, away from the criminal justice system is a win-win approach. 4) Identifying mental illness among inmates as early as possible and beginning treatment immediately are critical to success. 5) New approaches to providing mental health services in jail can reduce costs (especially the costs of medication) and improve outcomes. 6) Preparing inmates for continuity of care after their release is both humane and cost effective (Police Executive Research Forum, 2018).

As a society we have become dependent upon the criminal justice system to provide solutions to many of the woes of modern life that it was not designed or equipped to handle. The use of jails for the seriously mentally ill is inappropriate under current funding, architectural, and operational constraints. Treatment of individuals with mental illness — both inside and outside of jails — must be a community responsibility. The failure to attend to shortfalls in the funding of community mental health initiatives will only continue to haunt those lives that intersect with the jail — offenders, families, and the legal community — and ultimately affect the quality of life for all.

References

42 U.S.C. § 1905.

AbuDagaa, A, Wolfe, S., Carome, M., Phatdouang, A., & Torrey. E. (2016). Individuals with serious mental illness in county jails: A survey of jail staff's perspectives. A research report from the Public Citizen's Health Research Group and The Treatment Advocacy Center. Retrieved from: https://www.treatmentadvocacycenter.org/storage/documents/jail-survey-report-2016.pdf.

American Psychiatric Association. (1998, July). *APA resource document on telepsychiatry.* Washington, D.C.: Author.

American Psychiatric Association. (2000). *Psychiatric services in jails and prisons: A task force report of the American Psychiatric Association (2nd ed.).* Washington, D.C.: Author.

Andrews, D. & Bonta, J. (2010). *The psychology of criminal conduct (5th edition).* New Providence, NJ: LexisNexis.

Appelbaum, K. L., Hickey, J. M., & Packer, I. (2001). The role of correctional officers in multidisciplinary mental health care in prisons. *Psychiatric Services, 52*(10), 1343–1347.

Applegate, B., Davis, R., Otto, C., Surette, R., & McCarthy, B. (2003). The multifunction of jail: Policy makers' views of the goals of local incarceration. *Criminal Justice Policy Review, 14*(2), 155–170.

Armon, R. (2012, February 13). Sheriff closes jail to violent mentally ill. *Akron Beach Journal Online.* Retrieved from http://www.ohio.com/news/local/sheriff-closes-jail-to-violent-mentally-ill-1.264640.

Ax, R., Fagan, T., Magaletta, P., Morgan, R. D., Nussbaum, D., & White, T. W. (2007). Innovations in correctional assessment and treatment. *Criminal Justice and Behavior, 34,* 893–905.

Bourbonnais, R. Jauvin, N., Dussault, J., & Vezina, M. (2007). Psychosocial work environment, interpersonal violence at work and mental health among correctional officers. International *Journal of Law and Psychiatry, 30*(4–5), 244–368.

Bowring v. Godwin, 351 F.2d 44 (4th Cir. 1977).

Brad H. v. City of New York, 712 NYS2d 336 (2000).

Bronson, J, & Berzofsky, M. (2017). *Indicators of mental health problems reported by prisoners and Jail inmates, 2011–12.* U.S. Department of Justice, Office of Justice Programs, Bureau of Justice Statistics. (NCJ 250612).

Buffington-Vollum, J. K. (2011). Mental illness and the criminal justice system. In F. P. Redding & G. Bonham, Jr. (Eds.), *Flawed criminal justice policies: At the intersection of the media, public fear, and legislative response* (pp. 221–256). Durham, N.C.: Carolina Academic Press.

Butin, J. (2015). Miami's model for decriminalizing mental illness in America. Retrieved from https://www.governing.com/topics/public-justice-safety/gov-miami-mental-health-jail.html.

Callahan, L. (2004). Correctional officer attitudes toward inmates with mental disorders. *International Journal of Forensic Mental Health, 3*(1), 37–54.

Caplan, G. (1964). *Principles of preventive psychiatry.* New York, NY: Basic Books.

Carleton, R., Afifi, T., Turner, S., Taillieu, T., Curanceau, S., LeBouthillier, D., & Groll, D. (2018). Mental disorder symptoms among public safety personnel in Canada. *The Canadian Journal of Psychiatry, 63,* 54–64.

Cattabriga, G., Deprez, R., Kinner, A., Louie, M., & Lumb, R. (2007, December). Crisis Intervention Team (CIT) training for correctional officers: An evaluation of NAMI Maine's 2005–2007 Expansion Program. Corrections & Mental Health: An Update of the National Institute of Corrections. Retrieved from http://www.pacenterofexcellence.pitt.edu/documents/Maine%20NAMI%20CIT-3.pdf.

Christian, J. (2005). Riding the bus: Barriers to prison visitation and family management strategies. *Journal of Contemporary Criminal Justice,* 21, 31–48.

Cohen, F. (1998). *The mentally disordered inmate and the law.* Hoboken, NJ: Civic Research Institute.

Committee on Ethical Guidelines for Forensic Psychologists. (1991). Specialty guidelines for forensic psychologists. *Law and Human Behavior, 15,* 655–665.

Committee on Ethical Guidelines for Forensic Psychologists. (2011). Specialty guidelines for forensic psychologists. Retrieved from http://www.apls.org/aboutpsychlaw/SGFP_Final_Approved_2011.pdf.

Conklin, T. J., Lincoln, T., & Wilson, R. (2002). *A public health manual for correctional health care.* Ludlow, MA: Hampden County Sheriff's Department.

Consensus Project. (n.d.). Thresholds Jail Project. Retrieved from http://consensusproject.org/program_examples/thresholds_jail_program.

Constantine, R., Andel, R., Petrila, J., Becker, M., Robst, J., Teague, G., … Howe, A. (2010). Characteristics and experiences of adults with a serious mental illness who were involved in the criminal justice system. *Psychiatric Services, 61*(5), 451–457.

Constantine, R. J., Petrila, J., Andel, R., Givens, E. M., Becker, M., Robst, J., … Howe, A. (2010). Arrest trajectories of adult offenders with a serious mental illness. *Psychology, Public Policy, and Law, 16*(4), 319–339.

Constantine, R. J., Robst, J., Andel, R., & Teague, G. (2012). The impact of mental health services on arrests of offenders with a serious mental illness. *Law and Human Behavior, 36*(3), 170–176.

Consumer Reports. (2009, August). Antipsychotic drugs: Drug comparisons. Retrieved from http://www.consumerreports.org/health/best-buy-drugs/antipsychotics.htm.

Cook, J. (2006). Employment barriers for persons with psychiatric disabilities: Update of a report for the President's Commission. *Psychiatric Services, 57,* 1391–405.

Council of State Governments. (2007). Corrections. Criminal Justice/Mental Health Consensus Project. New York, NY: Author. Retrieved from http://consensusproject.org/issue-areas/corrections/.

Council of State Governments, Police Executive Research Forum, Pretrial Services Resource Center, Association of State Correctional Administrators, Bazelon Center for Mental Health Law, and the Center for Behavioral Health, Justice, and

Public Policy. (2002). *Chapter III: Pretrial issues, adjudication, and sentencing.* Criminal Justice/Mental Health Consensus Project. New York, NY: Council of State Governments. Retrieved from http://consensusproject.org/the_report/toc/ch-III/ps13-intake-detention.

Crisis Intervention Team Utah. (n.d.). Statewide program. Retrieved from http://www.citutah.com/Default.aspx?pageId=1139885.

Cuellar, A. E., Snowden, L. M., & Ewing, T. (2007). Criminal records of persons served in the public mental health system. *Psychiatric Services, 58*(1), 114–120.

Cullen, F. & Gendreau, P. (2000). Assessing correctional rehabilitation: Policy, practice and prospects. In J. Horney (Ed.), *Criminal justice: Policies, processes, and decisions of the criminal justice system* (vol. 3, pp. 109–175). Washington, D.C.: U.S. Department of Justice, National Institute of Justice.

Cusack, K., Morrissey, J., Cuddeback, G., Prins, A., & Williams, D. (2010). Criminal justice involvement, behavioral health service use, and costs of forensic assertive community treatment: A randomized trial. *Community Mental Health Journal, 46,* 356–363.

Daly, R. (2006). States get disappointing marks on MH report card, *Psychiatric News, 41*(8), 8, 71.

Danto, B. (1973). *Jail house blues.* Orchard Lake, MI: Epic Publications.

Dass-Brailsford, P. (2007). *A practical approach to trauma: Empowering interventions.* Los Angeles, CA: Sage.

Deshaney v. Winnebago County Social Services Department, 489 U.S. 189 (1989).

Ditton, P. M. (1999, July). *Special report: Mental health treatment of inmates and probationers (NCJ 174463).* Washington, D.C.: U.S. Department of Justice, Bureau of Justice Statistics.

Downing, S. (1999, March 30). A third of inmates in county jails mentally ill, survey finds. Commercial Appeal.

Earley, P. (2006). *Crazy: A father's search through America's mental health madness.* New York, NY: G.P Putnam and Sons.

"Edge of crisis" for jails, (2007, August 31). *Lewiston-Auburn Sun Journal.* Retrieved from http://www.sunjournal.com/node/679043.

Estelle v. Gamble, 429 U.S. 97 (1976).

Fabelo, T. (2000). *Mentally ill offenders and county jails: Survey results and policy issues.* Austin, TX: Criminal Justice Policy Council.

Farmer v. Brennan, 511 U.S. 825 (1994).

Fazel, S., Cartwright, J., Norman-Nott, A., & Hawton, K. (2008). Suicide in prisoners: A systemic review of risk factors. *Journal of Clinical Psychiatry, 69*(11), 1721–1731.

Felthous, A. R. (2011). Suicide behind bars: Trends, inconsistencies, and practical implications. *Journal of Forensic Science, 56*(6), 1541–1555.

Fields, G. (2006, May 3). No way out: Trapped by rules, the mentally ill languish in prison. *Wall Street Journal Online.* Retrieved from: http://online.wsj.com/article_print/SB114662497280042311.html.

Finn, P. (2000, December). Addressing correctional officer stress: Programs and strategies. Washington, D.C.: National Institute of Justice. Retrieved from www.ncjrs.org/pdffiles1/nij/183474.pdf.

Fisher, W. H., Roy-Bujnowski, K. M., Grudzinskas, A. J., Clayfield, J. C., Banks, S. M., & Wolff, N. (2006). Patterns and prevalence of arrest in a statewide cohort of mental health care consumers. *Psychiatric Services, 57,* 1623–1628.

Freudenberg, N. (2001). Jails, prisons, and the health of urban populations: A review of the impact of the correctional system on community health. *Journal of Urban Health, 78*(2), 214–235.

Goldberg, A. L., & Higgins, B. R. (2006, August). Brief mental health screening for corrections intake. *Corrections Today,* 82–84.

Goldberg, P., Landre, M., Goldberg, M., Dassa, S., & Fuhrer, R. (1996). Work conditions and mental health among prison staff in France. *Scandinavian Journal of Work, Environment and Health, 22,* 45–54.

Goodnough, A. (November 15, 2006). Officials clash over mentally ill in Florida jails. *New York Times.* Retrieved from http://www.nytimes.com/2006/11/15/us/15 inmates.html?pagewanted=print.

Goss, J. R., Peterson, K., Smith, L. W., Kalb, K., & Brodey, B. B. (2002). Characteristics of suicide attempts in a large urban jail system with an established suicide prevention program. *Psychiatric Services, 53,* 574–579.

Greenberg, S. F. (2001). Police response to people with mental illness. In M. Reuland, C. S. Brito, & L. Carroll (Eds.), *Solving crime and disorder problems: Current issues, police strategies and organizational tactics* (pp. 43–58). Washington, D.C.: Police Executive Research Forum.

Guerino, P., Harrison, P. M., & Sabol, W. J. (2012, February 9). *Prisoners in 2010 (NCJ 236096).* Washington, D.C.: U.S. Department of Justice, Office of Justice Programs, Bureau of Justice Statistics. Retrieved from http://bjs.ojp.usdoj.gov/content/pub/pdf/p10.pdf.

Haimowitz, S. (2004). Slowing the revolving door: Community reentry of offenders with mental illness. *Psychiatric Services, 55*(4), 373–375.

Hammack, L. (2007, October 15). Jail can offer temporary refuge for those suffering from mental illness. *Roanoke Times.*

Haney, C. (2003). Mental health issues in long-term solitary and "supermax" confinement. *Crime & Delinquency, 49*(1), 124–156.

Haneberg, R., Fabelo, T., Osher, F., & Thompson, M. (2017). *Reducing the number of people with mental illness in jail: Six questions county leaders need to ask.* A report for The Stepping Up Initiative.

Harris, V., & Koepsell, T. D. (1996). Criminal recidivism in mentally ill offenders: A pilot study. *Bulletin of the American Academy of Psychiatry and Law, 24,* 177–186.

Hausman, K. (2003). Mentally ill inmates win right to discharge planning. *Psychiatric News, 38*(6), 21.

Hayes, L. (1983). And darkness closes in: A national study of jail suicides. *Criminal Justice and Behavior, 10,* 461–484.

Hayes, L. (1989). National study of jail suicides: Seven years later. *Psychiatric Quarterly, 60,* 7–29.

Hayes, L. (2000). Suicide risk despite denial (or when actions speak louder than words). *Jail Suicide/Mental Health Update, 10*(1), 1–6.

Hayes, L. (2010, April). *National study of jail suicide: 20 years later.* Washington, D.C.: U.S. Department of Justice, National Institute of Corrections. Retrieved from http://static.nicic.gov/Library/024308.pdf.

He, X. Y., Felthous, A. R., Holzer, C. E., & Nathan, P. (2001). Factors in prison suicide: One year study in Texas. *Journal of Forensic Science, 46*(4), 896–901.

Herinckx, H. A., Swart, S. C., Ama, S. M., Dolezal, C. D., & King, S. (2005). Re-arrest and linkage to mental health services among clients of the Clark County Mental Health Court Program. *Psychiatric Services, 56,* 853–857.

Haneberg, R., Fabelo, T., Osher, F., & Thompson, M. (2017). *Reducing the number of people with mental illnesses in jail: Six questions leaders need to ask.* The Stepping Up Initiative. Retrieved from https://stepuptogether.org/wp-content/uploads/2017/01/Reducing-the-Number-of-People-with-Mental-Illnesses-in-Jail_Six-Questions.pdf.

Honberg, R. (2012, June 19). "Like gasoline on a fire": NAMI testifies on dangers of solitary confinement and mental illness. *PRNewswire.* Retrieved from http://presswire.einnews.com/article/101522185/like-gasoline-on-a-fire-nami-testifies-on-dangers-of-solitary-confinement-and-mental-illness.

Human Rights Watch. (2003). *Ill-equipped: U.S. prisons and offenders with mental illness.* New York, NY: Author.

International Centre for Prison Studies. (2012, August 28). *Entire world—prison population rates per 100,000 of the national population.* Retrieved from: http://www.prisonstudies.org.

James, R. K. (2008). *Crisis intervention strategies.* City: Cengage Learning.

James, R. K., & Gilliland, B. E. (2005). *Crisis intervention strategies.* Belmont, CA: Thomson.

Kaeble, D., & Glaze, L. (2016). Correctional populations in the United States, 2015. *Bureau of Justice Statistics.* Retrieved from: https://www.bjs.gov/content/pub/pdf/cpus15.pdf.

Kerle, K. E. (1998). *American jails: Looking to the future.* Boston, MA: Butterworth-Heinemann.

Kerle, K. E. (2018) Discovering CIT across the CJS. In K. Frailing and R. Slate (Eds.), *The criminalization of mental illness: A reader* (pp. 107–120). Durham, NC: Carolina Academic Press.

Kessler, R. C., Chiu, W. T., Demler, O, & Walters, E. E. (2005). Prevalence, severity, and comorbidity of twelve-month DSM-IV disorders in the National Comorbidity Survey Replication (NCS-R). *Archives of General Psychiatry, 62,* 617–627.

Kinsler, P. J., & Saxman, A. (2007). Traumatized offenders: Don't look now, but your jail's also your mental health center. *Journal of Trauma & Dissociation, 8*(2), 81–95.

Kleinberg, E. (January 31, 2010). System at loss for solutions to multiple-time, small-time offenders. *Palm Beach Post.*

Kondo, L. L. (2000). Therapeutic jurisprudence: Issues, analysis and applications: Advocacy of the establishment of mental health specialty courts in the provision of therapeutic justice for mentally ill offenders. *Seattle University Law Review, 24,* 373–377.

Kunst, M, Bogaerts, S, & Winkel, F. (2009). Peer and inmate aggression, type D personality and post traumatic stress among Dutch prison workers. *Stress and Health Journal of the International Society for the Investigation of Stress, 25*(5), 387–395.

Koyanagi, C., Forquer, S., & Alfano, E. (2005). Medicaid policies to contain psychiatric drug costs. *Health Affairs, 24*(2), 536–544.

Kubiak, S. P., Essenmacher, L., Hanna, J., & Zeoli, A. (2011). Co-occurring serious mental illness and substance use disorders within a countywide system: Who interfaces with the jail and who does not? *Journal of Offender Rehabilitation, 50,* 1–17.

Lamb, H. R., Weinberger, L. E., & Gross, B. H. (2004). Mentally ill persons in the criminal justice system: Some perspectives. *Psychiatric Quarterly, 75,* 107–126.

Lamb, H. R., Weinberger, L. E., Marsh, J. S., & Gross, B. H. (2007). Treatment prospects for persons with severe mental illness in an urban county jail. *Psychiatric Services, 58*(6), 782–786.

Larsen, D., Hudnall, S. B., Davis, K., & Magaletta, P. R. (2004). Prison telemedicine and telehealth utilization in the United States: State and federal perceptions of benefits and barriers. *Telemedicine Journal and e-Health, 10*(S2), S81–S90.

Leifman, S. (2001, August 16). Mentally ill and in jail. *Washington Post.* Retrieved from http://www.psychlaws.org/GeneralResources/article50.htm.

Leonard, S. (2004). The development and evaluation of a telepsychiatry service for prisoners. *Journal of Psychiatric Mental Health Nursing, 11,* 461–468.

Lerner-Wren, G. (2000). Broward's mental health court: An innovative approach to the mentally disabled in the criminal justice system. *Community Mental Health Report, 1*(1), 5–6, 16.

Levy, R., & Rubenstein, L. (1996). *The rights of people with mental disabilities*. Washington, D.C.: American Civil Liberties Union.

Linhorst, D. M., Dirks-Linhorst, A., Bernsen, H. L., & Childrey, J. (2009). The development and implementation of a jail-based substance abuse treatment program. *Journal of Social Work Practice in the Addictions, 9*(1), 91–112.

Liu, L., Hu, S., Wang, L., Sui, G., & Ma, L (2013). Positive resources for combating depressive symptoms among Chinese male correctional officers: Perceived organizational support and psychological capital. *BMC Psychiatry, 13*(1), 89.

Los Angeles County Sheriff's Office. (2007). *Twin Towers Correctional Facility*. Retrieved from http://www.lasd.org/divisions/custody/twintowers/index.html.

Lurigio, A. J., Fallon, J. & Dincin, J. (2000). Helping the mentally ill in jails adjust to community life: A description of a post-release ACT program and its clients. *International Journal of Offender Therapy and Comparative Criminology, 44*, 450–466.

Lurigio, A. J., & Swartz, J. A. (2006). Mental illness in correctional populations: The use of standardized screening tools for further evaluation of treatment. *Federal Probation, 70*(2), 29–35.

Lutterman, T., Shaw, R., Fisher, W., & Manderscheid, R. (2017). *Trend in psychiatric inpatient capacity, United States and each state, 1970 to 2014*. National Association of State Mental Health Program Directors. Retrieved from: https://www.nri-inc.org/our-work/nri-reports/trends-in-psychiatric-inpatient-capacity-united-states-and-each-state-1970-to-2014/.

Maloney, M. P., Ward, M. P., & Jackson, C. M. (2003, April). Study reveals that more mentally ill offenders are entering jail. *Corrections Today*, 100–103.

McCoy, M. L., Roberts, D. L., Hanrahan, P., Clay, R., & Luchins, D. J. (2004). Jail linkage assertive community treatment services for individuals with mental illnesses. *Psychiatric Rehabilitation Journal, 27*(3), 243–250.

McDonnell, J. (2016). *Custody Division Quarterly Report, Los Angeles County Sheriff's Department*. Retrieved from: http://www.la-sheriff.org/s2/static_content/info/documents/PMB_Q22016.pdfm.

McLearen, A.M., & Ryba, N.L. (2003). Identifying severely mentally ill inmates: Can small jails comply with detection standards? *Journal of Offender Rehabilitation*, 37, 25–40.

McPherson, W. (2008). Managing the mental health population at the Broward Sheriff's Office. *Corrections Today, 70*, 62–67.

Miller, C. M., & Fantz, A. (2005, September 11). Special 'psych' jails planned. Retrieved from: http://www.prisonpotpourri.com/PRISON_NEWS/Mental%20cases/Herald_com%20%2009-11-2005%20%20Special%20'psych'%20jails%20planned.html.

Minton, T. (2012, April 26). *Jail inmates at midyear 2011-Statistical tables (NCJ 237961).* Washington, D.C.: U.S. Department of Justice, Office of Justice Programs, Bureau of Justice Statistics. Retrieved from http://bjs.gov/index.cfm?ty=pbdetail&iid=4293.

Minton, Todd & Zeng, Zhen (2015) *Jail Inmates at Midyear 2014.* U.S. Department of Justice Programs, Bureau of Justice Statistics.

Mitchell, J. (2009, January 25). Treatment, not jail, urged for mentally ill in Mississippi. *Jackson Clarion Ledger.*

Morgan, D. W., Edwards, A. C., & Faulkner, L. R. (1993). The adaptation to prison by individuals with schizophrenia. *Bulletin of the American Academy of Psychiatry and the Law, 21,* 427–433.

Morris, J. J. (2006, June 12). *Survey of jail mental health treatment needs and services, Senate Finance Public Safety Subcommittee, State Compensation Board.* Richmond, VA: Department of Behavioral Health and Disability Services. Retrieved from: http://www.dbhds.virginia.gov/documents/reports/adm-JCHCMorris061206.pdf.

Morris, S. M., Steadman, H. J., & Veysey, B. M. (1997). Mental health services in US jails: A survey of innovative practices. *Criminal Justice Behavior, 24,* 3–19.

Morrissey, J. P., Cuddeback, G. S., Cuellar, A. E., & Steadman, H. J. (2007). The role of Medicaid enrollment and outpatient service use in jail recidivism among persons with severe mental illness. *Psychiatric Services, 58*(6), 794–801.

Morrissey, J. P., Steadman, H. J., Dalton, K. M., Cuellar, A., Stiles, P., & Cuddeback, G. S. (2006). Medicaid enrollment and mental health service use following release of jail detainees with severe mental illness. *Psychiatric Services, 57*(6), 809–815.

Mumola, C. (2005). *Suicide and homicide in state prisons and local jails: Special report.* Washington, DC: U.S. Department of Justice, Office of Justice Programs, Bureau of Justice Statistics.

Mumola, C., & Noonan, M. (2008). *Deaths in custody statistical tables.* Washington, DC: U.S. Department of Justice, Office of Justice Programs, Bureau of Justice Statistics.

National Alliance of Mental Illness Georgia (2017). *Emptying the new asylums: A beds capacity model to reduce mental illness behind bars.* Retrieved from https://namiga.org/report-emptying-new-asylums-beds-capacity-model-reduce-mental-illness-behind-bars/.

National Institute of Corrections. (2010). *Crisis Intervention Teams: An effective response to mental illness in corrections.* Washington, D.C.: Author. Retrieved from http://nicic.gov/Library/024517.

National Institute of Corrections. (2012, March 12). *Crisis Intervention Teams: A frontline response to mental illness in corrections.* Washington, D.C.: Author. Retrieved from http://nicic.gov/Training/12B3203.

National Institute of Corrections and the Urban Institute. (2007). *A triage approach to targeted interventions. Transition from jail to community: Online learning toolkit.* Retrieved from http://www.urban.org/projects/tjc/Toolkit/module5/section1_1.html.

Nicholls, T., Roesch, R., Olley, M., Ogloff, J., & Hemphill, J. (2005). *Jail Screening Assessment Tool (JSAT): Guidelines for mental health screening in jails.* Burnaby, British Columbia, Canada: Mental Health, Law, and Policy Institute, Simon Fraser University.

O'Reilly, R., Bishop, J, Maddox, K., Hutchizon, L., Fisman, M., & Takhar, J. (2007). Is telepsychiatry equivalent to face-to-face psychiatry? Results from a randomized controlled equivalence trial. *Psychiatric Services, 58*, 836-843.

Parish, J.J. (2007, April 30). Testimony: Status of the implementation of the Brad H. Settlement. New York: City Council Hearing. Retrieved from www.urbanjustice.org/pdf/publications/BradHTestimony.pdf.

Parks, J., Svendsen, D., Singer, P., & Foti, M.E. (2006). *Morbidity and mortality in people with serious mental illness.* Alexandria, VA: National Association of State Mental Health Program Directors.

Paternoster, R. & Bushway, S (2009). Desistance and the "feared self": Toward an identity theory of criminal desistance. *Journal of Law and Criminology, 99*, 1103–1156.

Perez, A., Leifman, S., & Estrada, A. (2003). Reversing the criminalization of mental illness. *Crime & Delinquency, 49*(1), 62–78.

Perez, L. M., Ro, M. J., & Treadwell, H. M. (2009). Vulnerable populations, prison, and federal and state Medicaid policies: Avoiding the loss of a right to care. *Journal of Correctional Health Care, 15*(2), 142–149.

Police Executive Research Forum (2018). *Managing mental illness in jails: Sheriffs are finding promising new approaches.* Washington, D.C. ISBN:978-1-934485-47-1.

Pew Center on the States. (2008). *One in 100: Behind bars in America 2008.* Washington, D.C.: Pew Charitable Trusts, Public Safety Performance Project.

Phaneuf, K. M. (2012, January 26). State pays high price for incarcerating mentally ill. *The CT Mirror.* Retrieved from: http://ctmirror.org/story/15199/state-pays-high-price-incarcerating-large-numbers-mentally-ill.

Pollack, H., Khoshnood, K., & Altice, F. (1999). Health care delivery strategies for criminal offenders. *Journal of Health Care Finance, 26*(1), 63–77.

Pompili, M., Lester, D., Innamorati, M., Del Casale, A., Girardi, P., Ferracuti, S., & Tatarelli, R. (2009). Preventing suicide in jails and prisons: Suggestions from experience with psychiatric inpatients. *Journal of Forensic Science, 54*(5), 1155–1162.

Potter, T. (2012, June 10). Court papers allege supervisors aware of abuse at Sedgwick County Jail. *The Wichita Eagle*. Retrieved from: http://www.kansas.com/2012/06/10/2366767/court-papers-allege-supervisors.html.

Powelson, H., & Bendix, R. (1951). Psychiatry in prison. *Psychiatry, 14*, 73–86.

President's New Freedom Commission on Mental Health. (2003). *Achieving the promise: Transforming mental health care in America. Final report*. Retrieved from: www.mentalhealthcommission.gov/reports/finalreport/fullreport-02.htm.

Prince, J. D. (2006). Incarceration and hospital care. *Journal of Nervous and Mental Disease 194*, 34–39.

Public Health Research Institute. (2005). Crisis Intervention Teams in Maine's Androscoggin County Jail: A report on the early stages of implementing a new corrections-based practice working with mentally ill offenders. *Corrections & Mental Health: An Update of the National Institute of Corrections*. Retrieved from: http://community.nicic.gov/blogs/mentalhealth/archive/2011/08/04/crisis-intervention-teams-in-maine-s-androscoggin-county-jail-a-report-on-the-early-stages-of-implementing-a-new-corrections-based-practice-working-with-mentally-ill-offenders.aspx.

Regan, P., Buffington-Vollum, J., & Raines, J. (2012, May 2). *The Bryne Grant Project: Assessing the impact of and responding to the mentally ill in the criminal justice system*. Presentation at the 2012 Virginia Community Services Boards Conference, Williamsburg, VA.

Richard v. Sedgwick County Sheriff (2009), 18th Judicial District, District Court, Sedgwick County, Kansas, Civil Department, Case No. 09CV3377.

Regehr, Carey, M., Wagner, S. Alden, L., ... & White, N. (2019). Prevalence of PTSD, depression, and anxiety disorders in correctional officers: A systematic review. *Corrections: Policy, Research and Practice*. DOI: https://doi.org/10.1080.237746572019.1641765.

Riley, R. (2019). Cook county jail in Chicago known for mental health care despite its hellish past. *The Gazette*. Retrieved from https://gazette.com/news/cook-county-jail-in-chicago-known-for-mental-health-care/article_060a304c-cf36-11e9-b505-73814f80f711.html.

Rivera, R. M. (2004). The mentally ill offender: A brighter tomorrow through the eyes of the Mentally Ill Offender Treatment and Crime Reduction Act of 2004. *Cleveland State University Journal of Law and Health, 19*, 107–139.

Roberts, A. R. (Ed.). (2000). *Crisis intervention handbook: Assessment, treatment and research*. New York, NY: Oxford University Press.

Robins, L., & Reiger, D. (1991). *Psychiatric disorders of America: The epidemiologic catchment area study*. New York, NY: Free Press.

Roskes, E., Cooksey, C, Feldman, R., Lipford, S., & Tambree, J. (2005). Management of offenders with mental illnesses in outpatient settings. In C. L. Scott, & J. B. Gerbasi (Eds.), Handbook of correctional mental health. Arlington, VA: American Psychiatric Publishing, Inc.

Ruiz v. Estelle, 503 F. Supp. 1265 (S.D. Tex. 1980).

Sabol, W. J., & Minton, T. D. (2008). *Jail inmates at midyear 2007 (NCJ 221945)*. Washington, D.C.: U.S. Department of Justice, Office of Justice Programs, Bureau of Justice Statistics.

Sayers, S.K., Domino, M.E., Cuddeback, G.S., Barrett, N.J., Morrissey, J.P. (2016). Connecting mentally ill detainees in large urban jails with community care. *Psychiatric Quarterly, 88*, 323–333.

Schaefer, L. (2017). Correcting the "correctional" component of the corrections officer role: How offender custodians can contribute to rehabilitation and reintegration. *Corrections: Policy, Practice and Research, 3*, DOI: 10.1080/23774657.2017.1304811.

Scheyett, A., Vaughn, J., & Taylor, M. F. (2009). Screening and access to services for individuals with serious mental illnesses in jails. *Community Mental Health Journal, 45*, 439–446.

Schuckit, M. A., Herrman, G., & Schuckit, J. J. (1977). The importance of psychiatric illness in newly arrested prisoners. *Journal of Nervous and Mental Disease, 165*, 118–125.

Scott, C. L. (2010). *Handbook of correctional mental health (2nd edition)*. Washington, D.C.: American Psychiatric Association.

Seiter, R. (2005). Corrections: An introduction. Upper Saddle River, NJ: Pearson/Prentice Hall.

Shimkus, J. (2003, Fall). Community provider fees too steep? There oughta be a law! *Correct Care.*

Shaefer, L. (2018). Correcting the "correctional" component of the corrections officer role: How offender custodians can contribute to rehabilitation and reintegration. *Corrections: Policy, Practice and Research, 3*(1), 38–55.

Sigurdson, C. (2000). The mad, the bad, and the abandoned: The mentally ill in prisons and jails. *Corrections Today, 62*(7), 70–78.

Solomon, P., & Draine, J. (1995). Issues in serving the forensic client. *Social Work, 40*(1), 25–33.

Solomon, P., Draine, J., & Marcus, S. C. (2002). Predicting incarceration of clients of a psychiatric probation and parole service. *Psychiatric Services, 53*, 50–56.

Sowers, W., Thompson, K., & Mullins, S. (1999). *Mental health in corrections: An overview for correctional staff*. Lanham, MD: American Correctional Association.

Steadman, H. J., Osher, F. C., Robbins, P. C., Case, B., & Samuels, S. (2009). Prevalence of serious mental illness among jail inmates. *Psychiatric Services, 60*, 761–765.

Steadman, H. J., Scott, J. E., Osher, F. C., Agnes, T. K., & Robbins, P. C. (2005). Validation of the Brief Jail Mental Health Screen. *Psychiatric Services, 56*, 816–822.

Steadman, H. J., & Veysey, B. (1997, January). *Providing services for jail inmates with mental disorders (Research in brief).* Washington, D.C.: National Institute of Justice.

Substance Abuse and Mental Health Services Administration GAINS Center for Behavioral Health and Justice Transformation. (n.d.). *Brief Jail Mental Health Screen.* Retrieved from http://gains.prainc.com/topical_resources/bjmhs.asp.

Sun, K. (2005). Mentally disordered offenders in corrections. In R. Muraskin (Ed.), *New correctional issues* (pp. 120–127). Upper Saddle River, NJ: Pearson/Prentice Hall.

Spinaris, C., Denhoff, M. & Kellaway, J. (2013). Posttraumatic stress disorder in United States corrections professionals.: Prevalence and impact on health and functioning. Retrieved from: https://desertwaters.com/wp-content/uploads/2016/07/MCO-Paper_FINAL.pdf.

Swank, G., & Winer, D. (1976). Occurrence of psychiatric disorder in a county jail population. *American Journal of Psychiatry, 133*, 1331–1333.

Swanson, J., Swartz, M., Gilbert, A., Frisman, L., Lin, H., Rodis, E., ... Henson, A. (2011, December 28). Costs of criminal justice involvement among persons with severe mental illness in Connecticut. Retrieved from: http://ctmirror.org/sites/default/files/documents/Costs%20of%20Criminal%20Justice%20Involvement%20in%20Connecticut%20%20Final%20Report%20_Dec%2028%202011_.pdf.

Swartz, J. A., & Lurigio, A. J. (2005). Screening for serious mental illness among criminal offenders. *Research in Social Problems and Public Policy, 12*, 137–161.

Swartz, J. A., & Lurigio, A. J. (2007). Serious mental illness and arrest: The generalized mediating effects of substance use. *Crime and Delinquency, 53*(4), 581–604.

Talbott, J. A. (Ed.) (2001). Psychiatric services: Gold award. Helping mentally ill people break the cycle of jail and homelessness. *Psychiatric Services, 52*, 1380–1382.

Technical Assistance and Policy Analysis Center for Jail Diversion. (2007). *Definition: Jail diversion.* Delmar, NY: National GAINS Center. Retrieved from: http://gains center.samhsa.gov/html/tapa/jail%20diversion/definition.asp.

Taxman, F. S., & Bouffard, J. A. (2002). Assessing therapeutic integrity in modified therapeutic communities for drug-involved offenders. *The Prison Journal, 82*(2), 189–212.

Teplin, L. A. (1990). The prevalence of severe mental disorder among male urban jail detainees: Comparison with the Epidemiologic Catchment Area program. *American Journal of Public Health, 80*, 663–669.

Teplin, L. A. (1994). Psychiatric and substance abuse disorders among male urban jail detainees. *American Journal of Public Health, 84*(2), 290–293.

Teplin, L. A., & Abram, K. M. (1991). Co-occurring disorders among mentally ill jail detainees: Implications for public policy. *American Psychologist, 46*(10), 1036–1045.

Teplin, L. A., Abram, K. M., & McClelland, G. M. (1996). Prevalence of psychiatric disorders among incarcerated women. *Archives of General Psychiatry, 53*, 505–512.

Teplin, L. A., Abram, K. M., & McClelland, G. M. (1997). Mentally disordered women in jail: Who receives services? *American Journal of Public Health, 87*(4), 604–609.

Teplin, L. A., & Swartz, J. A. (1989). Screening for severe mental disorder in jails. *Law and Human Behavior, 13*, 1–18.

Theriot, M. T., & Segal, S. P. (2005). Involvement with the criminal justice system among new clients at outpatient mental health agencies. *Psychiatric Services, 56*, 179–185.

Tisch, C., & Vansickle, A. (2006). Mentally ill left to wait in jails: Hundreds of inmates wait months for a bed in a state hospital, county officials blame DCF. *St. Petersburg Times*. Retrieved from: http://www.Sptimes.Com/2006/09/20/News_Pf/Tampabay/Mentally_Ill_Left_To_.Shtml.

Toch, H. (1982). The disturbed and disruptive inmate: Where does the bus stop? *Journal of* Psychiatry and Law, 10, 227–249.

Toch, H., & Adams, K. (1987). The prison as dumping ground: Mainlining disturbed offenders. *Journal of Psychiatry and Law, 15*, 539–553.

Torrey, E. F., Fuller, D. A., Geller, J., Jacobs, C., & Ragosta, K. (2012, July 19). *No room at the inn: Trends and consequences of closing public psychiatric hospitals.* Arlington, VA: Treatment Advocacy Center.

Torrey, E. F., Kennard, A. D., Eslinger, D., Lamb, R., & Pavle, J. (2010, May). *More mentally ill persons are in jails and prisons than hospitals: A survey of the states.* Arlington, VA: Treatment Advocacy Center. Retrieved from: http://www.treatmentadvocacycenter.org/storage/documents/final_jails_v_hospitals_study.pdf.

Torrey, E. F., Stieber, J., Ezekiel, J., Wolfe, S. M., Sharfstein, J., Noble, J. H., & Flynn, L. M. (1992). *Criminalizing the seriously mentally ill: The abuse of jails as mental hospitals.* Washington, D.C.: Public Citizen's Health Research Group and the National Alliance for the Mentally Ill.

Torrey, E. F., Zdanowicz, M., Kennard, A., Lamb, H., Eslinger, D., Biasotti, M., & Fuller, D. (2014). The treatment of persons with mental illness in prisons and jails: A State Survey Treatment Advocacy Center. Retrieved from: https://www.treatmentadvocacycenter.org/storage/documents/treatment-behind-bars/treatment-behind-bars-abridged.pdf.

Treating mental illness makes sense. (2008). Cape Fear, NC: Mental Health Association in North Carolina. Retrieved from: http://www.capefearhealthyminds.org/library. cgi?article=1115919700.

Vesey, B. M. (2011, January). *Issue paper: The intersection of public health and public safety in U.S. jails: Implications and opportunities of federal health care reform.* Exploring Health Reform and Criminal Justice: Rethinking the Connection between Jails and Community Health. Oakland, CA: Community Oriented Correctional Health Services. Retrieved from: http://www.cochs.org/files/Rutgers%20Final.pdf.

Veysey, B. M., Steadman, H. J., Morrissey, J. P., & Johnsen, M. (1997). In search of the missing linkages: Continuity of care in U.S. jails. *Behavioral Sciences and the Law, 15*, 383–397.

Veysey, B. M., Steadman, H. J., Morrissey, J. P., Johnsen, M., & Beckstead, J. W. (1998). Using the Referral Decision Scale to screen mentally ill jail detainees: validity and implementation issues. *Law and Human Behavior, 22*, 305–315.

Wakefield v. Thompson, 177 F. 3d 1160 (9th Cir. 1999).

Walsh, J., & Bricourt, J. (1997). Services for persons with mental illness in jail: Implications for family involvement. *Families in Society: The Journal of Contemporary Human Services, 78*(4), 420–428.

Walsh, J., & Holt, D. (1999). Jail diversion for people with psychiatric disabilities: The sheriffs' perspective. *Psychiatric Rehabilitation Journal, 23*(2), 153–160.

Washington v. Harper, 494 U.S. 210 (1990).

Watson, A., Hanrahan, P., Luchins, D., & Lurigio, A. (2001). Mental health courts and the complex issue of mentally ill offenders. *Psychiatric Services, 52*(4), 477–481.

White, M., Chafetz, L., Collins-Bride, G., & Nickens, J. (2006). History of arrest, incarceration and victimization in community based severely mentally ill. *Journal of Community Health, 31*(2), 123–135.

Wilper, A. P., Woolhandler, S., Boyd, J. W., Lasser, K. E., McCormick, D., Bor, D. H., & Himmelstein, D. U. (2009). The health and health care of US prisoners: Results of a nationwide survey. *American Journal of Public Health, 99*, 666–672.

Winerip, M. (1999, May 23). Bedlam on the streets. *New York Times Magazine, 56*, 42–49, 65–66, 70.

Wyatt v. Stickney, 325 F. Supp. 781 (M.D. Ala. 1971), 334 F. Supp. 1341. (1971), 344 F. Supp. 373, and 344 F. Supp. 385 (1972).

Zeng, Z. (2020). *Jail Inmates in 2018*. U.S. Department of Justice. Office of Justice Programs. Bureau of Justice Statistics. (NCJ 253044).

Chapter 7

Competency & Criminal Responsibility of Criminal Defendants[1]

"While competency and insanity are not the same things and the standards of proof are different, they are undoubtedly first cousins."

— Mark M. Bell[2]

Introduction

Serious mental illness is a problem for many defendants presented in and processed through the criminal courts in the United States every day. These defendants pose practical and immediate issues to themselves and the efficiency, safety, and resources of the public, police, courthouse, and correctional staff, and remain a perplexing challenge to Constitutional concepts of due process and fundamental fairness. The range of problems means greater use of resources in all phases of the criminal justice system (law enforcement, courts, corrections). There is a finite range of resources allocated to cases involving seriously mentally ill individuals. Additional challenges include the poor identification of such cases in the criminal justice system and the inability of all segments of the criminal justice system to address criminal cases with mental illness effectively rather than efficiently.

Stepping into court, the roles seem clear. The prosecutor seeks out issues and facts to strengthen the state's case against a criminal defendant. The defense attorney challenges those facts and brings others to light that bear on the state's ability to prove each element of a crime beyond a reasonable doubt. In each case, the judge is meant to ensure that justice is properly administered, the prosecutor should seek justice for all parties, and the defense attorney advocates to minimize, mitigate, or avoid consequences for the acts alleged. Despite their respective roles, all parties are expected to help ensure a fair and just trial.

---

1. With Paul Gormley, J.D., LP.D. Lynn University.
2. Bello (2021).

The mental health status of the defendant, whether mentally ill, developmentally delayed, or otherwise cognitively impaired, is important information for the judge, prosecutor, and defense attorney. As the mental health of the defendant can impair the defendant's ability to properly interact with the judicial system or to understand the crimes alleged, there is significant risk to the defendant's procedural and substantive constitutional rights and may result in a trial that is not fair, impartial, and cannot be trusted to have achieved a just result.

Attorneys, despite any training or collateral degrees, are not appropriate parties to assess their clients for mental health issues — specifically the criminal responsibility or competency to stand trial of their clients. Additionally, there is no explicit correlation between a specific mental health issue or diagnosis and criminal offending or competency to stand trial. Millions of people in this country cope with mental health issues every day without committing crimes or presenting issues of competency or criminal responsibility. To the contrary, if anything, mental illness is more commonly a predictor that an individual will be a victim than an offender (Stuart, 2003).

Preparing for court, the attorney must consider that the defendant's mental illness may have interfered with the ability to understand social cues or interactions escalating a situation, precluded the ability to understand or process instructions from police (including Miranda warnings), and diminished the ability to act in the defendant's own interests regarding waivers of counsel, arraignment proceedings, jury trial rights, and plea negotiations (Shannon & Benson, 2005).

At some point in the events from arrest to ultimate disposition, someone in the criminal justice system identifies an issue in the defendant's demeanor, behavior, response to stimuli, etc. If this observation is brought to the attention of the court, the next step is likely to be an evaluation of the defendant by a clinician. Every state and court has different resources and the availability of the resources determines the timing, duration, and next step in resolving the concerns that arose mental health issues. In many urban courts, a clinician is co-located in the court or nearby and is able to perform a preliminary screening. For purposes of this chapter, in such cases, the preliminary screening triggers a referral for further evaluation of criminal responsibility, competency to stand trial, or both. This further evaluation can occur on an in-patient/custodial basis at a locked mental health facility, local jail, or, if conditions of release permit, on an out-patient basis.

Competency to Stand Trial

In criminal procedure terms, competence to stand trial examinations determine whether the defendant has the mental capacity to understand the current criminal proceedings and assist the defense attorney in defending the case. This concept is entirely separate and different from criminal responsibility which considers whether the defendant's mental state meets the state's chosen test of insanity and is not criminally responsible for the crime alleged (Samaha, 2017). The determinations of competence to stand trial (commonly shortened to CST) and criminal responsibility (referred to as CR) are independent concepts in every way except their shared foundations of the defendant's mental health and the due process concept that all defendants are entitled to a fair trial. Further, competency is a moving target that may come and go with the effect of medication, stress, education, or other factors. This moving target means that the issue of competence to proceed with court activity may be presented or arise once, many times, during arraignment or motions, not until the time of trial, or only at arrest never again thereafter. Further, issues of competence may be presented by issues of physical trauma. One defendant's injuries from a motor vehicle accident impaired his ability to store and recall names, faces, and places threatened his competence to participate in the criminal justice process until, through repeated education by state hospital staff, he was able to sustain limited forms of competence adequate to resolve his charges.

In contrast, criminal responsibility only applies to the mental status of the defendant at the time of the offense and any other time is legally irrelevant to the legal proceedings. Even after disposition of the criminal charges, competency remains an issue regarding the validity of capital punishment.

There is a substantial body of law surrounding both these issues and much of it is found in decades of Supreme Court decisions. These decisions considered issues of defendant competency to waive or proceed as his own counsel, validity of confessions provided to police or in court, ability to waive trial and plead guilty, and the ultimate question of the defendant's ability to proceed to trial (Perlin, 2003).

Key Supreme Court Decisions

The foundation of and modern standard for defendant competency is set forth in cases starting with *Dusky v. United States*, 362 U.S. 402 (1960). In a brief decision, the Supreme Court found on consideration of the record submitted to the Court, that the trial court must find more than the "defendant [being] oriented to time and place and [having] some recollection of events" and established the binding terms that the test of competence to stand trial "must be whether [the defendant] has present sufficient ability to consult with his lawyer with a reasonable degree of rational understanding [and] and a factual understanding of the proceedings against him" (*Dusky*, 1960). Although the short decision set forth the standard with clarity, the brevity of the opinion left open how to define and test for these criteria. There were no guidelines from the Court to distinguish a rational understanding from a factual understanding, what a sufficient ability meant, and how to define a reasonable degree of any of these concepts.

Six years after the *Dusky* decision, in *Pate v. Robinson*, 383 U.S. 375 (1966), the Supreme Court considered the issue of defendant competence in the context of state-federal court interaction. The underlying case, a murder tried in Illinois, was rushed to trial and verdict and found the defendant guilty despite manifest mental health issues that were summarily rejected by the trial court. Sending the case back to Illinois for further hearings and potential retrial, the Supreme Court stated that conviction of a legally incompetent defendant is a due process violation and imposed a burden on the court to order a competency examination and a hearing thereafter to consider competency (*Dusky*, 1960). The Supreme Court observed that it is "contradictory to argue that a defendant may be incompetent, and yet knowingly or intelligently "waive" his right to have the court determine his capacity to stand trial" (*Pate*, 1966). Thereafter, observing significant evidence questioning the defendant's competence, the court must, on its own motion, conduct a sanity hearing in accord with statutory and Constitutional due process requirements (*Pate*, 1966).

Three years later, factual issues arose warranting further consideration of competency practices by the Supreme Court. In 1975, the Supreme Court examined these issues again and in greater detail in *Drope v. Missouri*, 420 U.S. 162 (1975). In *Drope*, the defendant was prosecuted for rape and, in both pretrial proceedings and witness testimony, details of psychiatric issues were obvious. Despite a number of further factual and intervening issues, the defendant was convicted, and he ultimately appealed to the Supreme Court. The trial court had rejected a suicide attempt by the defendant during trial as evidence of mental health issues, regardless of other evidence and testimony of insanity, and viewed it as indicia that the defendant understood the case and consequences (*Drope*, 1975). The circumstances presented by the suicide attempt and evidence of mental health issues required the trial court to be alert to "circumstances suggesting [that the defendant was] unable to meet the standards of competence to stand trial (*Drope*, 1975).

At various times following these decisions, states took steps to have statutes addressing the concepts and requirements of competency to stand trial and the obligations of the courts to raise the issues on their own motions when warranted by the evidence, procedural aspects, or other circumstances of the cases before them. In some states, competence is defined to include specific aspects of cognition or abilities (Zapf & Roesch, 2008).

Defendants' Competence

The result of these and other cases and the evolution of competency statutes is that the broad terms of competency have grown to recognize that competency to stand trial requires a present level of ability and understanding but not a complete and unimpaired set of abilities and should be compared to the complexity of the case involved and that the adequate state of competence observed at one point may not be present or the same at another point in time (Zapf & Roesch, 2008). The requirement of competence for a shoplifting charge that carries no possibility of incarceration is dramatically different from that required of a capital murder case and the defendant who can calmly discuss and understand the case today is not competent in the middle of a mental health crisis tomorrow and need bear no relation to mental state at the time of the offense alleged. These shifting circumstances and static standard may require close attention by the court and affiliated clinicians.

What of the defendant who chooses to proceed to trial or disposition of the criminal matter without an attorney? The standards of competence to understand the proceedings and assist counsel in one's own defense do not appear to make an adequate foundation to proceed without counsel. Presenting this issue to the Supreme Court, the case of *Godinez v. Moran*, 509 U.S. 389 (1993) resulted in a holding that followed the standards for competence set for in *Dusky v. United States* (see above). The defendant, Moran, was examined by psychiatrists during trial-level proceedings and both opined that he "understood the nature of the criminal charges against him, was able to assist in his defense, that he was knowingly and intelligently waiving his right to the assistance of counsel, and that his guilty pleas were freely and voluntarily given (*Godinez*, 1993).

Upon hearing at the Supreme Court, the justices held that the standards of competency for trial-related decisions were one — whether the defendant has, citing the *Dusky* decision, "sufficient present ability to consult with his lawyer with a reasonable degree of rational understanding and a rational as well as factual understanding of the proceedings against him" (*Godinez*, 1993). There is no greater standard of mental fitness required for any of the defendant's potential decisions to elect trial, waive trial with a plea decision, or waive any other specific Constitutional rights than the other. If the defendant has the mental fitness to make an intelligent and knowing decision in any of these categories, it is adequate competence for a decision in any of these domains; the implication is that if the defendant lacks competency in one of these areas, it stands that such incompetence applies in all trial-related decisions. This creates a question of whether competence to proceed to trial, waive trial, or make other counsel-involved trial-related decisions is adequate to combine these decisions and waive counsel and proceed to trial representing one's self. Further, the Supreme Court has not resolved other questions regarding of competency. Will this standard for competency apply to sentencing decisions and advocacy, appeal rights and pursuit thereof, waivers of Miranda rights, and granting permission to law enforcement for searches without a warrant? While inferences can be drawn from this line of cases, those inferences lack the imprimatur of the Supreme Court and will progress in the coming decades to find specific answers.

These issues outside of trial decisions are critically important to the pretrial status and posture for the defendant — the defendant's competence to make statements or assert Miranda rights, decline or permit a search without a warrant, or, more basic, ask for the assistance of counsel are problems considered daily by trial courts but without the depth or detail that an examination for competency to stand trial provides. As these questions rarely involve the presence of counsel without a defendant's assertion of the right to counsel, the problems are capable of repetition without appellate review until they are raised as a due process issue of fundamental defendant rights. The closest we come to guidance from the Supreme Court on these questions is the concurring opinion in *Dusky* implying a timeline where competency standards attach and end — that the standards of competency control from the time of arraignment until the jury returns a verdict (Perlin, 2003). This timeline explicitly excludes all decisions regarding searches, interrogation, and a failure to invoke counsel rights prior to arraignment and appears to end competency consideration with a trial verdict, excluding all post-trial motions, filings, and appeals. To find any relief for an incom-

petent defendant making statements against a penal interest requires consideration
that the Miranda warnings themselves are premised on the execution by the defendant
of a voluntary, knowing, and intelligent waiver of the right to remain silent and/or
seek the assistance of counsel (Perlin, 2003).

In a case highlighting these very issues, a defendant suffering from an unspecified
psychosis that included command hallucinations traveled across the country to confess
to a murder and did so despite repeated administration of Miranda warnings. The
police took no coercive action, and state courts found that the defendant's confessions
were not a product of his "rational intellect and free will" and excluded their use at
trial (*Colorado v. Connelly*, 1986). On appeal to the Supreme Court, the court held that
Colorado had erred in suppressing these statements and that, in the absence of coercion
by police, there was no coercion occurring to justify treating the defendant's statements
as involuntary and obtained in violation of Constitutional and due process protections
and expressly rejected the Colorado court's view that "notions of free will" should be
considered in the court's assessment of voluntariness (*Colorado v. Connelly*, 1986).

Numerous state and federal courts have considered the defendant's rights regarding
courtroom presence and admissibility of statements but there is no agreement among
the courts of the standards and application of current Supreme Court holdings to
activities occurring before the defendant is presented in the trial courts (Perlin, 2003).
Connelly's circumstances present the clear result. The defendant's inability, through
the command of mental illness or under circumstances of apparent incompetence,
to rationally analyze the consequences of making a statement, permitting a search,
waiving Miranda rights, and a range of other pre-court criminal procedure rights —
fall outside the scope and consideration of competence and Supreme Court jurisprudence and will be admissible against the defendant.

In daily court practice, the standards of competence are minimal and revolve
around a defendant's ability to understand the concepts of crime, identify the roles
of the judge, prosecutor, and defense attorney, and the basic operational concepts of
a trial. Many counsel can provide stories of clients pushed by the court to proceed
with some pretrial or trial decision based on questioning by the judge of the defendant's understanding of these roles and concepts at a grade-school level. At this point,
the states and Supreme Court have not raised the bar for defendant competence to
make such decisions to the spirit of the decisions, if not the words. The defendant's
active delusions, altered mental state, or auditory or visual hallucinations do not slow
the wheels of a criminal justice system that lacks the time, staff, and funds for defendants with such a minimal standard in daily use.

The first problem in such cases is the presumption, regardless of any bizarre circumstances or observations of the underlying case or arrest, that the defendant is
competent in all material respects. Such a presumption is forced by the volume of
cases handled every day. It would be impossible and wasteful to evaluate every defendant for mental health status at the point of arrest or arraignment. This rule of
criminal procedure exists across the nation in forms similar to California's statutes
that provide a presumption that the defendant is competent, and the party claiming

incompetence bears the burden of proving that the defendant is incompetent by a preponderance of the evidence and this burden upon the defendant has survived Supreme Court review (*Medina v. California*, 1992).

Defense Counsel's Competence

Compounding this problem of identifying and proving incompetence to the preponderance standard is ineffective assistance of counsel presents potential due process and malpractice claims, especially as recent Supreme Court decisions expanded the scope of ineffective assistance of counsel for legal malpractice (Richards, 2011). Appellate courts evaluate claims of ineffective assistance of counsel by whether the attorney's defective performance deprived the defendant of a fair trial — but for counsel's poor conduct, the result of the trial would probably be different (*Strickland v. Washington*, 1984). While this is a valid standard of review, it denies the incompetent defendant substantive due process and related harms.

For these reasons, all court participants have a moral duty to consider the mental status of the accused. A moral duty is not enforceable at law. However, defense counsel are required by Constitutional provisions to work on behalf of the defendant and raise these issues. The problem is the defense attorney's ability to do so. The defense attorney has an obligation and duty to provide zealous advocacy to the defendant (Uphoff, 1988). Arriving in court as a criminal defendant with mental illness, a defendant is represented in most cases by an attorney provided at public expense (Saubermann & Spangenberg, 2006). The attorney likely received training in criminal defense but it is likely, as in Massachusetts, that the coverage of mental health issues was a brief lecture (MCLE, 2009) and a single chapter in a textbook (MCLE, 2010). The education and training in mental health matters received in law school is nearly non-existent (Redding, 2004).

The state and federal governments provide attorneys at government expense to indigent defendants in criminal matters as a Constitutional requirement under a sequence of Supreme Court decisions culminating with the *Gideon* ruling in 1963. While the Supreme Court decisions require appointment of counsel, when counsel are not well trained in mental health matters or are inexperienced, it is unclear how effective or efficient these attorneys can be (Feeney & Jackson, 1990–1991). This deficiency of counsel may prompt the attorney to reject signs of mental illness as personality issues, results of substance abuse, or fail to observe them at all. Under these circumstances, issues of both CST and CR are likely to remain unexplored for such defendants.

For such a significant issue, how does the mental health of the defendant come before the court and why? It is the legal and Constitutional duty of defense counsel. Further, between the combination of duty and interaction with the defendant, even the Supreme Court recognizes that defense counsel likely has the "best-informed view of the defendant's ability to participate in his defense" (Morris, Haroun, & Naimark, 2004). Defense counsel fears that testimony by the defendant in any competency hearing that occurs will implicate or waive Fifth Amendment rights against self-incrimination or attorney-client communications will reasonably advise their clients not to testify. Defense counsel are precluded from testimony in their role as counsel but make arguments with factual content to the court. Regardless of the information that could come from the defendant or counsel, the report returned to the court and any testimony from the forensic clinician will carry more weight with the court than the words of an advocate or a defendant whose mental status is the subject of the court's inquiry (Morris, et al., 2004).

The defendant and defense counsel may be placed in a difficult relationship. Defendants with mental health issues rarely possess insight and understanding of their own circumstances but they do know that they want their freedom and may abandon all other case issues in favor of freedom. This may even prompt the defendant to attempt to discharge counsel in favor of self-representation but the courts rarely allow the discharge of counsel in the early steps of criminal proceedings for practical and procedural reasons. The conflict between the defendant and counsel is real and places the attorney in conflicting roles of advocating for the best interests of the defendant over the defendant's own wishes which the attorney is required to advocate for zealously. Massachusetts, like many other states, drafted specific rules to address such a conflict and require counsel to protect both self and the client while serving the interests of the client and the court in an ongoing balancing act guided by the Rules of Professional Conduct Rule 1.14: Client with Diminished Capacity (2008). This conflict and balancing act continues until resolved by the report of examination and any hearing triggered by that report.

Despite the qualities of defense counsel and potential for zealous advocacy, rather than identification by defense counsel, the earlier and more common identification of mental health issues in a newly arrested defendant comes from law enforcement. As was made clear in Chapter 5, people with mental illness have greater contact with law enforcement for a variety of reasons. Aberrant behavior justifying treatment in a psychiatric unit is viewed in public as a disturbance and prompts a police response (Markowitz, 2011). A police report filed thereafter may highlight circumstances of suspicions that mental health was a factor in the circumstances. If not, the observations by prosecutor, judges, or courthouse personnel may be raised in court. The defense attorney, appointed at the time of first appearance in court, is only a few minutes ahead of the judge and courtroom in meeting and assessing the issues that the defendant presents. The realities of large public defender caseloads and fast-food style justice do not consistently afford counsel qualitative opportunities to assess the mental state of the defendant and the circumstances of the arrest, to say nothing of the number of prisoners detained with and near the defendant, and the open nature of the areas where attorneys meet their new clients, both of which inhibit such an assessment.

That said, representing a defendant with mental illness is not casually undertaken by attorneys: the defendant's liberty and life are placed in the hands of defense counsel. There are countless details, deadlines, procedures, legal and factual issues in flux throughout the entire case. Defense attorneys in Massachusetts who represent indigent criminal defendants receive, at their own expense, five days of training in substantive law and procedure on criminal matters and only a small portion of the training concerns mental health issues of defendants (MCLE, 2009). The schedule for the five days of training does not include the coverage of mental health issues and defendant mental health and is only one of sixteen chapters in the training materials provided (MCLE, 2009).

In many cases, attorneys confuse mental health issues for defendant behavioral and personality issues. If defendants act in an aggressive, confrontational, otherwise argumentative manner, counsel may interpret this as an angry and uncooperative client and decline to invest themselves in the case. Failing to build a rapport and relationship with the client precludes an understanding of the client and case and eliminates any opportunity to examine and raise mental health issues as mitigation or defense of the case. Poor attorney-client relations fostered by a failure to visit the client in custody, lack of resources, training, and experience are more likely to predict adverse results when the clients are mentally ill, especially when the existence or extent of the mental illness is not known to counsel (MacLean, 2008–2009).

The next problem involves client competency and whether to raise it with the court. If the defense attorney raises the issue without consent of the client, the attorney usurps the client's basic rights of self-determination and imposes the attorney's judgment on the client, which may anger and alienate the client. A failure to raise the issue risks even greater issues including malpractice and ineffective assistance of counsel (Davoli, 2009–2010). Again, these decisions are evaluated by counsel on the basis of five days of training, a chapter of training materials, and any intervening experience and education (MCLE, 2009).

Once attorneys raise and resolve the competency issues, they must ultimately advise and represent the client through pretrial processes that will result in dismissal, plea, or trial. Mental health issues that bear on defense tactics impose a burden on counsel to raise the issues as an effective advocate on the specifics of mental health and defendant culpability. Improper handling of these issues and decisions leads to potential ineffective assistance of counsel claims (Covarrubias, 2008–2009).

Tactical choices by defense attorneys are based on the relative strengths of the state's case compared to the defendant's, skills of defense counsel, prevailing norms of case disposition of the court, and the ability of defense counsel to evaluate these and other factors. The defendant's mental illness is a key factor in this calculation. The defense attorney has a legal duty to identify and investigate mental health defenses to mitigate or avoid criminal liability. Unfortunately, unidentified mental health issues do not become part of the case investigation or advocacy and that omission constitutes ineffective assistance of counsel (Covarrubias, 2008–2009).

Counsel's failure to identify serious mental illness in defendants results from several common issues. As seen in Chapter 3, these individuals often develop coping and masking skills to overcome the stigma of serious mental illness and cloak their symptoms in a variety of adaptations to their environment. Further, serious mental illness is an issue of variable presentation. It is rarely florid and constantly interfering with the defendant's ability to function in society. Issues of mental illness are concealed by the defendant and hamper the attorney's efforts to investigate mitigating factors to the charges. Even if observed, counsel frequently lack the resources to identify the mental illness, experts to assess the defendant, or understand how to present the issues to the court (Covarrubias, 2008–2009).

Plea Agreements

If any clinician or screening tool identifies mental illness in the client, the defense attorney faces a difficult choice. The mentally ill client, like every other defendant, wants to get out of court and custody as fast as possible with some certainty in the case resolution. However, serving the mentally ill client's immediate wish is likely to conflict with his or her long-term best interests and can thwart therapeutic jurisprudence. Quick disposition of the case through a plea precludes consideration of mental health issues and potential defenses. If the client pleads guilty and is placed on court supervision, the client's immediate wishes are served (Laberge & Morin, 1998). The attorney can plead the client out and wash his hands of the later consequences of the guilty plea.

However, the attorney is legally required to consider client's ability to evaluate the risks and benefits of an immediate plea. The attorney must weigh the client's ability to make choices, communicate choices to counsel, allow counsel to act on those choices, and the client's potential to testify in court with decorum. The conflict between the obligation of counsel to consider the client's wishes and the long and short-term results of those choices arises numerous times during the representation. Every occasion of this conflict and the choices made by the defense attorney results in differing outcomes (Laberge & Morin, 1998).

Over 94 percent of felony cases prosecuted in the United States are resolved through plea agreements (Cohen & Kyckelhahn, 2010). A plea agreement requires that the defendant waive trial rights in exchange for concessions by the prosecution — commonly reductions of charges, penalties, or sentencing. The likelihood of a plea is strong, and factors considered by defense attorneys weighing against a trial involve concerns about how the judge and jury perceive the mental health status of the defendant, evidentiary strength of serious mental illness, severity of charges and penalties, and the ability of the defendant to testify in a coherent manner. Also filtered into the decision and advice to the defendant are the attorney's skill and confidence as an advocate, the ability to skillfully examine expert witnesses in the defendant's case, and cross examine police and other witnesses.

Into this mix comes the case of *Lafler v. Cooper*, 566 U.S. 156 (2012). The Supreme Court ruled that ineffective advice by counsel prompted the defendant to unwisely reject an advantageous plea offer. The decision extends concepts of ineffective assistance into the standard measured by trial outcome. The *Lafler* decision asserted that the prejudice to the defendant was not an unfair trial but of actually going to trial. The court held that, but for the ineffective advice of the attorney, there is a reasonable probability that the plea offer would have been made, presented, and accepted by the court and that the conviction, sentence, or both, under the offer's terms would have been less severe than under the actual judgment and sentence imposed after trial. The decision, written by Justice Kennedy, found counsel ineffective and looked to earlier cases of grossly ineffective counsel and reconsidered the scope of the critical stages of criminal proceedings (*Lafler v. Cooper*, 2012).

This case and issue flow from the premise that the option and opportunity to resolve a criminal case short of trial is both *the* critical stage of a case and at the heart of the criminal justice system. Effective analysis and decision making hinges on the importance of competent counsel (*Lafler v. Cooper*, 2012). This holding reflects the prevailing views of practitioners in the prosecution and defense roles, that there is an ethical and enforceable obligation upon counsel to relay all offers to plead out a case extended by the prosecution to the defendant. This duty of counsel is coupled with an obligation by defense counsel to provide competent and factual legal advice to the defendant whenever such an offer is made.

The leading case cited in the *Lafler* decision is *Strickland v. Washington*, 466 U.S. 668 (2004). The key holdings of the *Strickland* case are that:

- the Sixth Amendment guarantees the right to the effective assistance of counsel;
- this right is measured by whether counsel's conduct sufficiently undermined the functioning of the adversarial process that the trial cannot be relied on as having produced a just result;
- a claim that counsel's assistance was so defective must show that counsel's performance was both deficient and deprived the defendant of a fair trial;
- the deprivation of a fair trial is determined by a two-prong test for evaluating ineffectiveness claims:
  - first, that counsel's representation fell below an objective standard of reasonableness according to prevailing professional norms; the inquiry is case-specific and context driven, taking into account all the circumstances, and;
  - second, the defendant must demonstrate prejudice that there is a reasonable probability that, but for counsel's unprofessional errors, the result of the proceeding would have been different (*Strickland v. Washington*, 1984).

The *Lafler* case presented a different issue — that counsel's deficiencies in the pretrial stages lead to a fair trial, but that the trial would not have occurred but for the incompetent counsel and advice given (*Lafler v. Cooper*, 2012). When the case result's prejudice and deficiency of counsel is measured only by the fairness of the trial, the issue of competent pretrial practice and effective advocacy is lost. The *Lafler* case presented issues that evaded review under *Strickland*, namely, pretrial advocacy and advising when trial is not the anticipated result. In part, much of the problem is that no individual defendant burdens these systems any more than a grain of sand makes a beach. In the aggregate, hundreds of thousands of arrests passing through the criminal justice system daily and the proportional resources that these cases draw is significant. In the 1980s, Los Angeles police officers spent almost 20,000 hours each month responding to calls involving people with mental illness; similarly, people brought into emergency rooms by the police represented more than 30 percent of the psychiatric admissions in New York and Los Angeles (Lurigio & Swartz, 2000).

For the case where competent defense counsel identifies the issues and raises them before the court, it may cause conflict between the defendant and counsel, cause significant delays in case resolution, or cause long-term of the commitment. Counsel is obligated to present the issue to the court at any time that the issue presents itself factually and, depending on local practice and resources, seek evaluation of the defendant for competency through a court clinician designated to serve the court, seek funds for evaluation, or for a limited-term commitment for evaluation in a mental health facility under strict security. In an effort to save costs of independent evaluations and commitments for evaluation, many courts adopted a policy of screening with a court-provided clinician to determine the level of the defendant's need for a more costly and qualitative evaluation. While this may eliminate some cases of malingering of attorney use of the evaluation process to delay the case or seek other advantage, some counsel observe that it only delays when the in-depth evaluation occurs and the court addresses the mental health issues of the defendant regarding both CST and CR. Assuming that the attorney's or court's perception, local clinician screening, or case circumstances warrant further evaluation, a referral or commitment is made for that purpose.

Court-Ordered Evaluations of Competency

This raises issues in misdemeanor cases that the evaluation process takes longer than the defendant would likely serve if sentenced on the underlying offense. Due to limited resources, most evaluations take several weeks of record-gathering, interviews, observations, and testing. In many cases, facilities and clinicians will petition the court to enlarge the time for the evaluation. This creates a further conflict between client and counsel: that the defendant could have taken a plea and been out of custody with fines, fees, or court supervision but not held in a locked mental health facility.

Once the court orders the evaluation, a clinician or facility is designated to perform an examination and respond with a written report to the court. Each jurisdiction has statutory provisions designating forensic clinicians for this purpose and they are credentialed in a manner that recognizes the education, training, and experience to perform the task. The Code of Massachusetts Regulations, for example, provides extensive detail on the specific issues of designating and appointing such clinicians and refers out to related statutory provisions in the Designation and Appointment of Qualified Mental Health Professionals (104 CMR 33.00, n.d.).

In Massachusetts, the Department of Mental Health has several secure facilities for performing mental health evaluations (regardless of whether the evaluation is for CST, CR, or both) and many defendants are ordered by the court for evaluation to State Hospitals with appropriate forensic units. For defendants whose case or behavior presents a threat, Bridgewater State Hospital is a mental health facility that performs forensic mental health evaluations in a complex within a compound shared with the Department of Corrections (Bridgewater State Hospital, n.d.). The number of forensic evaluations performed annually varies by source, jurisdiction, and method of counting. The state of Florida reported over 1,500 evaluations annually in a 2014 report analyzing usage of forensic mental health services around the nation (Forensic Mental Health Services in the United States, 2014). In contrast, in 2019, Massachusetts reported 18,249 outpatient forensic evaluations and 771 inpatient forensic evaluations while having a population half the size of the state of Florida (State Mental Health Plan, 2019). Although reasonable inferences drawn from these two data points demonstrate that tens of thousands of forensic mental health evaluations are done every year across the nation, the number asserted by multiple sources is that 60,000 CST evaluations are done annually (Zapf, Roesch, & Pirelli, 2013). Hoge (2016) adds that defense counsel question the competency of defendants in about 10 to 15 percent of their cases.

The evaluation of competency may draw on several sources of information. The most common are screening instruments and assessment instruments, interview processes and instruments (Zapf, Roesch, & Pirelli, 2013). In addition to these resources are police reports, docket entries, and other materials provided by the court. The result of the evaluation process is potentially twofold. The first is to assess the defendant's ability to consult with counsel with a reasonable degree of rational and factual understanding of the proceedings against him (*Dusky*, 1960). The second, predicated on the outcome of the first evaluation, is whether the defendant can be made competent to that degree and what would be required to achieve that result (Zapf, Roesch, & Pirelli, 2013). Further, the evaluation process is subject to many influences including the participation of counsel in the process. The involvement of counsel through consultation with forensic staff may sway evaluative judgments; this, combined with other assessment and factors of evaluation result in substantial variability in conclusions and recommendations in the CST process (Zapf, Roesch, & Pirelli, 2013).

The forensic CST process is a functional evaluation of the defendant's ability to participate rationally in the criminal justice process. Many misdemeanors are considered to require a lower level of functional ability due to the less complex nature of the case and proceedings; serious felonies with more complex trial processes and harsher penalties are likely to demand a higher ability of the defendant to rationally participate in legal processes (Zapf, Roesch, & Pirelli, 2013). In broad terms, the evaluation determines and the court weighs the extent to which mental illness affects the defendant's ability to consult with and assist his or her lawyer (understand, evaluate, and act in accord with legal advice) and the extent to which the mental illness affects the defendant's ability to testify, or not, on his own behalf (Zapf, Roesch, & Pirelli, 2013).

While the sequence of events will vary with local practices, regulations, best practices, the availability of specific instruments and other resources, and the cooperation of the defendant and other parties, the forensic mental health evaluation commonly involves some combination of clinical interviews by forensic staff, standardized instruments, information contributed by the court, witnesses, victims, and counsel.

Forensic staff have a variety of instruments at their disposal and more are always in development to assess and evaluate mental health functions of the defendant.

Competency screening tests are designed and may be used to weed out malingering and otherwise competent individuals to minimize the time and expense allocated to such individuals. Such instruments are empirical, drawing on the defendant's knowledge of legal processes and terms, but have failures that are skewed to false positive results that rate defendants incompetent who are later evaluated competent (Zapf, Roesch, & Pirelli, 2013).

Competency assessment instruments and fitness interviews are used as mechanisms to structure clinical interviews to assure assessment of specific issues of legal and procedural understanding and capacity. These approaches provide comprehensive coverage of a range of legal and procedural topics and may include psychological features. The structured nature of these instruments or interview processes is designed to probe a range of issues germane to the defendant's fitness for and understanding of different steps of criminal proceedings, court participants, ability to assess the facts and circumstances of the charges, processes, defenses, penalties, and possible outcomes. More comprehensive instruments draw from leading cases on defendant competence and are designed to specifically and directly assess the defendant's ability to consult with and assist counsel, the factual and rational understanding of the criminal court proceedings, and build in psychological assessment features in five subscales: Realistic, Psychotic, Nonpsychotic, Impairment, and Both (Psychotic and Nonpsychotic combined) (Zapf, Roesch, & Pirelli, 2013).

Some jurisdictions have specifically developed tests for various portions of the forensic evaluation process and will involve different psychological factor and legal information assessments (Zapf, Roesch, & Pirelli, 2013). The range of screening and preliminary assessment instruments is broad and are designed for various environments and circumstances (police interviews, emergency room evaluations, etc.). Despite the close tailoring and degrees of interrater reliability and tested validity, there is no single test or instrument that will reliably assess the depth and breadth of the factors of competency. Some of these short screening instruments have been recommended for use in lockups to rapidly assess defendant mental status in preparation for first appearance or arraignment hearings to screen as a form of "wellness" to proceed into the courtroom in a manner that is rational and safe for the court participants (counsel, staff, and defendant).

One weakness of these tests and instruments is that they are likely to be ineffective with intellectually disabled defendants — including both developmental delays and, in some cases, traumatic brain injuries. The population of developmentally delayed will frequently pretend to understand their lawyers and court personnel and may be able to hide their deficits in certain circumstances having developed a cloak of competence that allows these defendants to present the apparent function of competency in this context of assessments (Zapf, Roesch, & Pirelli, 2013). One lawyer, in his 1990s representation of a defendant with a 1970s-era traumatic brain injury, reviewed documentation from prior cases to discover extensive reporting of the degree of injury to the defendant's brain that caused obvious short-term memory deficits. However, his "frequent flier" status in the local police departments and courts gave him this cloak of competence because he could use the terms correctly but his ability to rationally understand the facts of each new case, the specific proceedings and defenses, potential outcomes, and methods to avoid future conduct completely eluded him. For such defendants, legally relevant impairments often only become apparent when the individual also has a severe mental illness or acts in a strange or disruptive manner (Zapf, Roesch, & Pirelli, 2013).

Despite the range of tests and instruments and collateral sources of information, the human and qualitative insights gained through the clinician's interviews and interactions with the defendant provide context to the other forms of information gathering. At some point in the evaluation, the clinician will seek information from counsel. As it was the inability of the defendant to "work" rationally with this attorney, the observations and interactions of counsel are of considerable interest to the CST process. In one case handled by this author, a defendant was consistently evaluated to be competent by a court-based clinician despite claims of irrational interactions between the defendant and counsel. It was only when the clinician sat in on a consultation between counsel and the defendant and observed the irrational inferences and conclusions stated by the defendant that the clinician gained insight into the difficulties of that defendant and reached a new conclusion.

The information gathered in the evaluation process bears directly on the clinician's evaluation of the defendant's mental fitness for court proceedings. The information provided by personal background (education, family, childhood and adolescence, occupation, orientation to the world, prior criminal history, medical and psychiatric history, etc.), police reports, court dockets, information from counsel, and more are weighed against the defendant's perceptions and recitations of those events. In the course of the clinician's interviews with the defendant, the defendant's ability, or lack thereof (absent malingering), provides crucial clues to assessing the defendant's ability to rationally evaluate the facts of the allegations, assist counsel in navigating the proceedings, and understand the interplay of those facts, counsel's questions and answers, and court activity.

Forensic Interviewing

To commence the forensic interview, the clinician starts with a warning of the lack of confidentiality provided by the interview and evaluation process. Each state has its own cases, regulations or guidelines and, in Massachusetts, the notice is a "Lamb Warning" (Guidelines for Notification of the Limits of Confidentiality/Privilege for Court Ordered Evaluations of Adults, 2016). The guidelines provided by the Massachusetts Executive Office of Health and Human Services provides a set of required elements which include the name of the evaluator, discipline, type of evaluation(s), that the evaluation(s) is ordered by the court, the purpose of the evaluation(s), that information is not confidential and can be reported to the court, that the defendant can decline to participate in whole or in part, that the clinician will file a written report regardless of the person's participation and may provide oral testimony, and that the result of the evaluation could be commitment for further evaluation or treatment (Guidelines, 2016). In a manner analogous to Miranda warnings against self-incrimination, the notice provides that the evaluation could be used against the defendant if mental health issues are raised at a hearing or trial (Guidelines, 2016). There are several other required and optional components to the notice but they are not germane to the forensic evaluation process (Guidelines, 2016). Now provided notice, the interview can begin in earnest.

The interviewer gathers background and historical information about the defendant in a process that allows for assessment of this information against externally supplied data and establishes a working relationship between the clinician and defendant. The skilled clinician also uses this process to draw inferences about mood, self-control, thought content, mental organization, and concentration, while providing an understanding of the defendant's relationships, understanding of his own medical and mental status and insight, and ability to recall and accurately report the defendant's experiences in and knowledge of the current and prior criminal proceedings (Mossman, et al., 2007).

The clinician's mental status examination is performed to gather information about the defendant's psychiatric symptoms, mental status, mood, scope of memory, information processing, and ability to concentrate in a manner that is different from the information gathering aspects of the clinician's interview of the defendant. The tests and instruments used in this portion of the evaluation seek specific details that may lead to a diagnostic conclusion as well as insights into the defendant's psychological strengths and weaknesses, which leads to an ultimate conclusion about the defendant's ability to participate rationally in the criminal proceedings (Mossman, et al., 2007).

The clinician may take multiple approaches to a process of gathering information about the facts of the charges alleged. Inquiries may be addressed at a range of times during interviews and other data gathering; the end result should be a sequence of experiencess leading up to the matters alleged, the events themselves, and the circumstances and actions that followed the incident. Clear gathering of this information may be difficult because of objections from counsel, directions to the client, or physical or psychological impairments of recollection by the defendant (Mossman, et al., 2007).

These efforts and exercises of gathering information, interviewing the defendant, performing assessment exercises, and administering tests will ultimately lead to a conclusion that will likely include both a recommendation to the court that the defendant is or is not competent and, may include a range of diagnoses of the psychological issues impairing this defendant (regardless of competence). The diagnosis of psychological malady is not a designation of incompetence and should not be confused for each other (Zapf, Roesch, & Pirelli, 2013).

Assuming the clinician's professional opinion and report conclude that the defendant is not competent to stand trial, the next step is a recommendation, if permitted or required by the jurisdiction or court rules regarding the ability of the defendant to be restored to competency. The recommendation should consider a range of issues, most notably, whether the defendant's incompetence results from a condition that can be remedied (Mossman, et al., 2007). Some defendants cannot be made competent to stand trial because of developmental delays (Anderson & Hewitt, 2002), physical incapacity, or traumatic injury (Hodgkinson, 2009). For those defendants whose incompetence is a deficit subject to education or treatment, the clinician's conclusion will recommend a course of action that may include specific education and training in details of the trial process, a course of medication, and other forms of psychiatric treatment as well as projections of the likelihood that the defendant's competency will be created or restored (Anderson & Hewitt, 2002; Mossman, et al., 2007).

Outcomes of CST Evaluations

When the defendant was ordered to undergo the CST process, the court docket set a return date for further proceedings with an assumption that the defendant and a report evaluating the defendant's CST would be provided. As described above, if the report concludes that the defendant is incompetent, there is a recommendation by the clinician for further action. In some cases, such recommendations will be made even in the circumstances that the defendant is reported to be competent based on diagnostic work by the clinician. In court, the clinician's report is commonly received by the judge, prosecutor, and defense attorney. The report's conclusion presents a tactical choice for the defense attorney to make in consultation with the defendant. If the report asserts that the defendant is incompetent, does the defense agree and argue for a finding of incompetence or disagree and challenge the clinician's conclusion? The same decision tree exists for a recommendation of competence. The decision tree prompts the prosecutor to make a responsive decision. If the defense and prosecution agree that the defendant is incompetent, the court likely accepts the report as it is and orders the defendant committed and any course of treatment recommended by the clinician to follow. If the defense and prosecution agree, based on the report, that the defendant is competent, this step in the process is complete and criminal procedures follow from here unless competency is raised again. If the defense and prosecution disagree, regardless of the positions taken, an evidentiary hearing will follow in which the materials gathered, assessments and test administered, and evaluative process is brought before the court to make a ruling after testimony, direct and cross-examination of any relevant witness, certainly to include the clinician. It is entirely possible for the defendant to assert incompetence and the prosecution to assert competence or the reverse, and there are many tactical reasons for each to do so. After a hearing, the court makes a ruling based on the preponderance of the evidence. As above, if the defendant is ruled incompetent, a commitment assessment and treatment follow. If the defendant is ruled competent, that aspect of the matter is resolved unless it should recur.

Depending on the charges, the success or failure of restoration to competency, legal method of commitment, duration of the process, and interest of the attorneys, witnesses, and victims, the defendant who is agreed, found, or ruled incompetent may be returned to court for trial or disposition of the charges, have the charges dismissed now or in the future, or never be released.

Criminal Responsibility

An event of variable frequency is that a defendant presents issues that prompt the court participants to question the defendant's criminal responsibility, the defendant's mental capacity to be responsible for the criminal acts alleged. As with competence, discussed above, there are many ways that such issues are identified and presented in court. It is common that a police prosecutor, court security staff, or prosecutor will have awareness of the defendant as a "frequent flier" or of the circumstances of the incident, charges, arrest, or behavior in custody ahead of the defense attorney's knowledge. In one such case, a police prosecutor advised defense counsel not to shake hands with the defendant because he had spent overnight in jail painting the cell walls with his own feces. A court clinician was available, and evaluative processes started immediately and ultimately resulted in dismissal of the charges.

As many parties in the courthouse may be aware of such circumstances, it is common that one of these parties will report it to the court officially or unofficially and inquiry will commence on the issue. Unlike the defendant's competence, which is an issue and can be raised at any time in the proceedings, the concept of criminal responsibility is a fixed target. It only applies to the defendant's mental status at the time of the offense alleged. It is common for a defendant to be incompetent to stand trial, not criminally responsible, neither, or both. The defendant's fluctuating competence, particularly for defendants whose competence is restored or assured through medication, does not control that status of the defendant as criminally responsible (or not) at the time of the events alleged. For a defendant in a florid psychotic episode at the time of the incident and later compliant with treatment, competency may return but the mental status at the time of the crime alleged is frozen in time.

A basic definition of criminal responsibility observes that a person is *prima facie* criminally responsible when he or she commits a crime while validating its constitutive elements: the *actus reus* and the *mens rea*. The *actus reus* is the material element of a crime and the mens rea is the mental element, which is to say the state of mind of the accused at the moment of committing that act (Bigenwald & Chambon, 2019).

The United States has four different standards for assessing the lack of criminal responsibility and their application is set forth in a mix of court decisions and statutes; Further, some states have rejected the insanity defense entirely. To be certain of the details of the standard and its application requires research focused on the jurisdiction involved. The four tests in use are:

- M'Naghten Rule — the defendant was unable to distinguish between right and wrong or otherwise did not understand what they did because of a disease of the mind.

- Irresistible Impulse Test — the defendant was unable to control their impulses due to a mental disorder, leading to the commission of a criminal act. [As noted by Fabian (2021), this standard is also known as the policeman at the elbow test, meaning a person could not hold their criminal impulses in check even if a police officer were present].

- Model Penal Code — the defendant was unable to act within legal constraints or failed to understand the criminality of their acts due to a mental defect.

- Durham Rule — the defendant's mental defect led to the commission of a criminal act, regardless of clinical diagnosis [only New Hampshire uses this standard] (Insanity Defense Among the States, 2019).

A minority of states reject the insanity defense. Nevada enacted legislation eliminating the defense, but the state Supreme Court struck down the legislation "holding that it violated due process of both the United States Constitution and the State Constitution" (DiSilvestro, 2021). The states of Kansas, Idaho, Montana, and Utah passed similar legislation eliminating the insanity defense and survived review in their respective state court. Further, other states have cut back or are considering such legislation to limit the insanity defense to considerations of mens rea, which would limit but not eliminate the insanity defense. The Supreme Court, as of March 23, 2020, holds that a state's failure to allow a mentally ill defendant to raise such a defense does not violate the Constitution (Howe, 2020). The underlying case that came to the Supreme Court as *Kahler v. Kansas* held that the 1995 abolishment of the insanity defense that was upheld by the Kansas Supreme Court was affirmed by the United States Supreme Court (*Kahler v. Kansas*, 2020). The Supreme Court further held that a state's refusal to allow an insanity defense is unconstitutional if it offends fundamental principles of justice and whether a mentally ill defendant cannot be held liable for his crimes are questions that the Supreme Court has left to the states, further stating that due process imposes no single canonical formulation of legal insanity (Howe, 2020).

For those states and United States territories where a defense of criminal responsibility can be raised, much like competence to stand trial, when the issue is raised, there will be a referral for an evaluation. However, before any defendant considers pursuit of this defense, the defendant and counsel are advised to consider the demographics of such a defense. While society holds a belief that a criminal responsibility defense is commonly asserted, research estimates indicate that the insanity defense is used in 0.1 percent to 0.5 percent of felony cases, and the defense is successful in approximately 25 percent of such assertions (Schouten & Brendel, 2008). Out of 10,000 felony cases, a defense of a lack of criminal responsibility will be asserted by 1 to 5 defendants and somewhere between 1 and 2 will be successful. The mythology of a psychiatric crime wave remains a myth.

For those 1 to 5 defendants out of 10,000, they will likely be committed, just as with CST claims, to a mental health facility for the evaluation. There, much like the CST process, there is a battery of assessments and tests, collateral information gathered, discussions with witnesses and victims, etc., combined with clinician interviews of the defendant, a report, and if justified by the conclusion, recommendations for treatment and/or commitment. The CST is not a linear process but rather a collation of multiple sources of data that both inform and are informed by clinical observation, interview, and insight (Goldstein & Weiner, 2003).

In the exact same way that the CST requires a warning to the defendant of the lack of confidentiality, use of the information gathered, name and role of the clinician, and potential use of the whole process in later court hearing, the regulatory and due process rules apply in the criminal responsibility (CR) examination. Moreover, the CR is one place that attorneys will sometimes instruct their clients not to talk to clinicians about the events alleged and/or attempt to prohibit the clinicians from inquiring about the facts of the charges.

One aspect that differs from the CST process is that the CR process focuses on different criteria, the mental state of the defendant at the time of the offense, and a different standard, whatever test is used by the jurisdiction to determine criminal responsibility. This combination of a different criteria and different standards means that the assessments and tests employed focus not on the defendant's understanding of procedure and criminal justice concepts but through a broad range of tests to measure intelligence, information processing, personality inventory, reported symptoms, malingering, psychopathology, as well as instruments designed specifically for the evaluation of criminal responsibility and more (Goldstein & Weiner, 2003).

The problem that further differs from the CST is that the CR attempts to evaluate mental state at a time in the past as a static event rather than focusing on current mental health and status. The tests and interviews provide substantial data about mental state at the time of the crime (Goldstein & Weiner, 2003). It is incumbent on the clinician to work backward from the currently gathered information, observation, and insights to assemble a coherent view of the defendant's mental state at the time and circumstances of the incident.

The clinician may be hampered in the evaluation because some disturbed defendants will be receiving psychotropic medications to treat diagnosed mental illness. Despite this, the clinician is compelled to bear in mind that these mental states, although related to that at the time of the incident, are separable, but the process is challenging. A further complication of existing treatment is that it may impair the defendant's ability to recall and relate the facts and mental state during the events that bring the defendant to court and this evaluation (Zapf, Golding, Roesch, & Pirelli, 2013).

Forensic assessment instruments that may assist in this reconstruction of the defendant's mental state at the time of the incident alleged include specifically developed tools including the Mental State at the Time of Offense Screening Evaluation. This evaluation was developed to strongly rule in or out defendants on the issue of criminal responsibility and is well-suited to eliminating defendants who are not insane and identifying other defendants who are "obviously insane and do not require a more comprehensive evaluation" (Zapf, Golding, Roesch, & Pirelli, 2013).

Another focused forensic instrument set is the Rogers Criminal Responsibility Assessment Scales. This toolset was designed to quantify the elements of the test for lack of criminal responsibility but is focused on meeting the test set forth by the Model Penal Code; while it may be applicable to other tests, it is speculated that it may be effectively analogized to the other major tests of insanity due to similarities in the test concepts (Zapf, Golding, Roesch, & Pirelli, 2013). Other applicable tests exist and are in use but are not as closely tailored to the issues of the CR examination as these listed.

Written Reports & Testimony on Issues of CST and/or CR

Many defendants will be referred for a joint evaluation of both CST and CR. While there are substantial differences in the issues, competencies, and mental state required for these two concepts, this author's experience is that many defendants sent for evaluation are returned to court with matching conclusions—both incompetent and not criminally responsible or both competent and criminally responsible. The result of this alignment for defendants is the likelihood of a significant battle in court challenging both CST and CR in circumstances that may be dispositive of the underlying criminal charges. For these reasons, the clinician should be prepared to write a solid report of examination.

The most effective forensic clinician is the one whose efficacy is reflected in both the conduct and result of the evaluation and the report that communicates the information to the parties in court. Effective reports are detailed, support their conclusions with specific observations and findings and prompt action by the judge, prosecutor, and defense attorney. A report that reaches a strong conclusion that the defendant is not CST and/or CR weakens the position of the prosecutor and strengthens that of the defense. Conversely, a strong conclusion that the defendant is CST and/or CR weakens the position of the defense and strengthens that of the prosecutor. Either combination diminishes the likelihood of further evidentiary hearings and trial while prompting a less formal resolution by agreed disposition.

Clinician opinions, like those of attorneys, are valuable only when they are conveyed meaningfully in reports they write. The criminal court is an adversarial system by design and pits the parties against each other in a win or lose competition. The role and practices of a forensic practitioner are hugely different from that of a treating clinician seeking to aid the parties. The evaluating clinician in criminal cases, while taking a scientific and neutral position, takes a position that favors one side or the other merely by asserting that a defendant is or is not CST or CR (Otto & Weiner, 2013).

The prosecutor and defense attorney will make decisions based on the CST and CR reports that will alter the flow of trial strategy or case resolution. Those decisions will lead to freedom or incarceration of the defendant through trial or other disposition and protect or damage the standing, reputation, and malpractice coverage of the attorney. Forensic clinicians need an awareness of these issues as they write clear, detailed, and unbiased evaluation reports that will go to court free of jargon. The clinician should be prepared for the report to be read in open court or used as a source of cross-examination when the clinician is testifying in the hearing or trial about the defendant's mental health status (Otto & Weiner, 2013).

The testimony of a clinician in a hearing or trial on issues of the CST or CR examination is as an expert witness, and this triggers a variety of evidentiary considerations under the Federal Rules of Evidence or, by analogy, state evidentiary rules (Federal Rules of Evidence, Rule 702. Testimony by Expert Witnesses, 2011). For the attorney making use of the clinician's testimony, there are preparations and discovery obligations to consider before calling the clinician to testify.

Experienced clinicians will be ready to testify if called, and experienced attorneys know whether the clinician is a reliable expert. Counsel is required to comply with Discovery Rules regarding disclosure and sharing of reports, resumes, curriculum vitae, and, in the absence of a report, any summary of the expert opinion to be offered in the form required by local Criminal Procedure Rules. As the attorney calling this witness, regardless of the role as prosecutor or defense counsel, the attorney must qualify the witness as an expert and accept the evidence offered. A failure to qualify the witness as an expert and offer the relevance of the witness to these proceedings may result in exclusion of the witness from testifying or rejection of the proffered evidence (Rahman, 2020).

As the attorney offering this evidence, questioning of the witness to establish the status as an expert witness and to admit other testimony requires open-ended questions that cannot be answered with a "yes" or a "no." The opponent of the evidence or conclusions that this expert seeks to offer can ask cross-examination questions which are, when used properly, designed to control a witness, limit damaging testimony, and only be answered with a "yes" or a "no" (Rahman, 2020).

Defense Counsel's Competence

As discussed in earlier pages, the training for defense attorneys representing offenders with mental illness is nearly non-existent. There is a growing body of literature on issues of criminal justice, mental health and the significant overlap between the two populations. Despite this awareness, the training of defense attorneys has not changed in a manner consistent with greater research and awareness of mental health issues in society and the criminal justice population.

Lawyers in criminal cases should be encouraged and trained to consider and address neuroscience in competence to stand trial and criminal responsibility inquiries. There is an ethical obligation to gain familiarity with neuroscience-related literature, and these efforts will help courts to follow suit. To perform defense services ethically and competently, defense attorneys should be able to evaluate neuroscience-related concepts that could explain the defendant's mental state as it bears on CST and CR and to effectively represent a mentally ill client. Unfortunately, only a small number of defense attorneys know of the testing and instrument use of assessment systems and protocols in use by forensic clinicians. They recognize that competency is the most common way that forensic mental health professionals are involved in the criminal justice system but do not adequately understand the concepts and issues involved (Philipsborn, 2019).

The failure of defense attorneys to step up, improve their skills and knowledge in these areas arguably violates their competence and raises issues of ineffective assistance of counsel. It is the attorney's duty and ethical obligation to investigate the defendant's responsibility and competence; the courts have relegated this role to counsel on the assumption that counsel will fill the need and fulfill their duties. The court's limited interaction with the defendant preclude the court's ability to identify and ascertain the defendant's competency impairment (Philipsborn, 2017).

Americans with Disabilities Act

This shared failure of the courts and defense counsel violates the Americans with Disabilities Act. In 1999, the Supreme Court held that the Americans with Disabilities Act (ADA) included mental illness as a disability and that no individual with a disability could be excluded from programs or benefits provided by a public entity on the basis of that disability. Beyond forbidding discrimination in the services provided by a public entity, the Supreme Court further held that the ADA requires public entities to make reasonable modifications when necessary to avoid discrimination as long as these accommodations do not alter the services in a fundamental manner (*Olmstead v. L.C.*, 527 U.S. 581, 1999). Despite this ruling, courts routinely violate the ADA because mental health disabilities are not readily observed compared to physical obstacles.

Following from the *Olmstead* decision, the Supreme Court specifically held that the ADA requires that all judicial facilities and services, including the provision of counsel to the indigent, be accessible to all without regard to disability in accord with the Supreme Court decision in *Tennessee v. Lane*, 541 U.S. 509 (2004). This case, interpreting both the ADA and the 14th Amendment, incorporates provisions of the 1st Amendment and the 6th Amendment (Cress, Grindstaff, & Malloy, 2006). The judicial process meant is to administer justice, not merely determine guilt and punishment. The ADA is part of the legislative environment giving rise to mental health courts and other specialized services for mentally ill defendants. When defendants do not receive equal access to and administration of justice through the court system, an ADA violation occurs (Cress, et al., 2006).

Under the ADA, mental illness falls within the definition of disability and requires accommodation of those brought before the court, detained, or sentenced in criminal cases. The ADA does not require complete accommodation of all disabilities but requires that public entities, including courts and judicial processes, identify and remove barriers that interfere with or preclude provision of and access to public services (Rubin & McCampbell, 1995). While common application of the ADA is that screening processes and criteria cannot bar those entitled to services without ADA-compliant justification, the inverse situation arises: the failure to screen for mental health disabilities in the defendant population means that the appropriately tailored counsel services for indigent defendants with mental illness are not provided by the courts in the administration of justice or appointment of counsel.

The Supreme Court's decision in *Tennessee v. Lane*, 541 U.S. 509 (2004) does not require that all means available be used to resolve access to justice by the disabled. The Court held that the ADA requires courts to make reasonable modifications that do not otherwise fundamentally alter the nature of services provided or incur undue financial or administrative burdens so that judicial services and the benefits thereof are made available to the disabled (Cress, et al., 2006). It is insufficient to merely provide counsel to an indigent defendant identified as having a mental illness. The ADA requires that no one be denied the benefits of the services, programs, or activities of a public entity by reason of the disability. Once a mental health disability is identified in a defendant, the ADA requires that a defense attorney qualified to help deliver accessible judicial and defense services be appointed (Cress, et al., 2006). However, this obligation is only realized through screening practices implemented prior to arraignment and appointment of counsel. In the absence of any screening process, there is no obligation to provide accommodation that would both assure equal access to justice and the services of counsel required under the Constitution (Cress, et al., 2006).

An issue emerges from a conflict between the *Olmstead* decision and earlier decisions of the Supreme Court permitting defendants acquitted by reason of mental illness and held in locked psychiatric facilities for periods beyond the maximum penalty if found guilty of the underlying offense. Olmstead's holding required discharge of institutionalized persons, as a qualified right under the ADA, to community treatment and services rather than ongoing hospitalization in a state hospital. Application of least restrictive alternative principles to these indefinitely detained acquitted defendants held in maximum security psychiatric facilities appears to mandate discharge of those originally charged with misdemeanors and non-violent felonies. Read in conjunction, the *Olmstead* decision appears to invalidate the statutes and court practices that mandate unending detention of non-violent and lower risk defendants. *Olmstead* does not preclude application to acquitted or untried individuals with mental illness committed under the color of criminal law to psychiatric facilities (Perlin, 2000).

Some reasoning of this nature exists and predates *Olmstead*. In *Jackson v. Indiana*, 406 U.S. 715 (1972), the U.S. Supreme Court held that indefinite detention of criminal defendants lacking competence to stand trial violates the equal protection and due process clauses of the 14th Amendment of the Constitution. Comparing civil and criminal commitment statutes, as applied to untried criminal defendants who stood unconvicted of the underlying offense, prompted a finding that a defendant cannot be held more than a reasonable period to determine whether it is likely that he will attain competency. In an attempt to render one competent to stand trial, the U.S.

Supreme Court has held that, as with all involuntary commitment treatment standards a defendant must be a danger to him or herself, and such treatment can only be administered involuntarily if the defendant is facing a serious charge, if the treatment is medically appropriate, is substantially unlikely to have side effects that could undermine the fairness of the trial, and is the least restrictive alternative viable to further important governmental interests (*Sell v. United States,* 2003). If the defendant will not attain competency in that reasonable period, the State must release the defendant or commence civil commitment proceedings (Kaufman, Way, & Suardi, 2013). While this provides some measure of protection and relief for defendants with mental illness who have not been convicted of their underlying offenses — it provides no immediate relief for defendants indefinitely detained after acquittal by reason of insanity.

Moving beyond Competency and Insanity Considerations

The criminal justice process is more involved with competency evaluations and attempts to restore competency than consideration of insanity defenses. Failure to restore competency for a defendant can result in involuntary commitment to a mental health facility until competency is restored. In some jurisdictions across the country, Not Guilty by Reason of Insanity (NGRI) defenses are allowed and such verdicts can result in involuntary confinement to a mental hospital for an undetermined amount of time until the person is considered "rehabilitated." Those found NGRI are typically held after such a determination for longer periods than those found guilty (McClleland, 2017). Other states limit insanity pleas to Guilty But Mentally Ill (GBMI), and Cotrone (2016) reports those determined to be GBMI were serving over 20 percent longer in prison than those found guilty for similar offenses.

Specialty courts have been devised to address other mental health concerns of those who encounter the criminal justice system. We turn in Chapter 8 to an examination of mental health courts.

References

104 CMR 33.00: *Designation and appointment of qualified mental health professionals.* (2016). Boston: Commonwealth of Massachusetts. Retrieved from: https://www.mass.gov/regulations/104-CMR-3300-designation-and-appointment-of-qualified-mental-health-professionals.

Anderson, S. D., & Hewitt, J. (2002). The effect of competency restoration training on defendants with mental retardation found not competent to proceed. *Law and Human Behavior, 26*(3), 343–351.

Bello, M. M. (2021). *Betrayal High.* Retrieved on February 8, 2021 from https://www.goodreads.com/quotes/10368073-while-competency-and-insanity-are-not-the Bridgewater State Hospital. (n.d.) *Boston: Commonwealth of Massachusetts.* Retrieved from: https://www.mass.gov/locations/bridgewater-state-hospital.

Bigenwald, A., & Chambon, V. (2019). Criminal responsibility and neuroscience: No revolution yet. *Frontiers in Psychology, 10*(1406). doi:10.3389/fpsyg.2019.01406.

Cohen, T. H., & Kyckelhahn, T. (2010). *Felony defendants in large urban counties, 2006.* Washington DC: Bureau of Justice Statistics Retrieved from: http://bjs.ojp.usdoj.gov/content/pub/pdf/fdluc06.pdf.

Colorado v. Connelly, 479 U.S. 157 (United States Supreme Court 1986).

Covarrubias, R. J. (2008–2009). Lives in defense counsel's hands: The problems and responsibilities of defense counsel representing mentally ill or mentally retarded capital defendants. *The Scholar: St. Mary's Law Review on Minority Issues, 11*, 413–468.

Cotrone, E. E. (2016). The guilty but mentally ill verdict: Assessing the impact of informing jurors of verdict consequences. *University of South Florida, Doctoral Dissertation.* Retrieved from: https://scholarcommons.usf.edu/cgi/viewcontent.cgi?article=7683&context=etd.

Cress, R., Grindstaff, J. N., & Malloy, S. E. (2006). Mental health courts and Title II of the ADA: Accessibility to state court systems for individuals with mental disabilities and the need for diversion. *Saint Louis University Public Law Review, 25*, 307–350.

Davoli, J. M. (2009–2010). Physically present, yet mentally absent. *University of Louisville Law Review, 48*, 313–350.

DiSilvestro, M. (2021). *Kahler v. Kansas*: The Supreme Court case to decide the Constitutionality of abolishing the traditional insanity defense and reconcile the split among the circuits. *John Marshall Law Review, 53*(3), 634–671.

Drope v. Missouri, 420 U.S. 162 (United States Supreme Court 1975).

Dusky v. United States, 362 U.S. 402 (United States Supreme Court 1960).

Fabian, J. M. (2021). Relevant legal standards: NGRI evaluations. Retrieved from: http://johnmatthewfabian.com/not-guilty-by-reason-of-insanity/.

Federal Rules of Evidence, Rule 702 (2011). *Testimony by expert witnesses.* Washington: Legal Information Institute. Retrieved from: https://www.law.cornell.edu/rules/fre/rule_702.

Feeney, F., & Jackson, P. G. (1990–1991). Public defenders, assigned counsel, retained counsel: Does the type of criminal defense counsel matter? *Rutgers Law Journal, 22*(2), 361–456.

Forensic Mental Health Services in the United States. (2014). *Alexandria, VA.* National Association of State Mental Health Program Directors. Retrieved from: https://nasmhpd.org/sites/default/files/Assessment%203%20-%20Updated%20Forensic%20Mental%20Health%20Services.pdf.

Gideon v. Wainwright, 372 U.S. 335 (United States Supreme Court 1963).

Godinez v. Moran, 509 U.S. 389 (United States Supreme Court 1993).

Goldstein, A. M., & Weiner, I. B. (2003). *Handbook of psychology, Volume 11*. Retrieved from: http://www.123library.org/book_details/?id=5343.

Guidelines for Notification of the Limits of Confidentiality/Privilege for Court Ordered Evaluations of Adults. (2016). *Boston: Executive Office of Health and Human Services*. Retrieved from: https://www.umassmed.edu/globalassets/forensic-training/documents/limits-of-conf-priv-guidelines.pdf.

Hodgkinson, R. (2009). Permanently incompetent to stand trial. Reno County, KS. Retrieved from: https://casetext.com/analysis/permanently-incompetent-to-stand-trial.

Hoge, S. K. (2016). Competence to stand trial: An overview. *Indiana Journal of Psychiatry*. Retrieved from: https://www.ncbi.nlm.nih.gov/pmc/articles/PMC5282614/

Insanity Defense Among the States. (2019). *Insanity defense among the states*. Retrieved from: https://criminal.findlaw.com/criminal-procedure/the-insanity-defense-among-the-states.html.

Jackson v. Indiana, 406 U.S. 715 (United States Supreme Court 1972).

Kahler v. Kansas, 140 S. Ct. 1021 (2020).

Kaufman, A., Way, B., & Suardi, E. (2013). Forty years after *Jackson v. Indiana*: States' compliance with the "reasonable period of time" Ruling. *Journal of the American Academy of Psychiatry and the Law Online, 40*(2), 4.

Laberge, D., & Morin, D. (1998). Evaluating the case, evaluating the cost: Criteria for constructing the defense strategy of persons suffering from mental illness. *Journal of Social Distress and the Homeless*, 7(3), 189–209.

Lafler v. Cooper, 566 U.S. 156 (United States Supreme Court, 2012).

Lurigio, A. J., & Swartz, J. A. (2000). Changing the contours of the criminal justice system to meet the needs of persons with serious mental illness. *Criminal Justice 2000, 3*, 45–108.

MacLean, B. A. (2008–2009). Effective capital representation and the difficult client. *Tennessee Law Review, 76*, 661–676.

Markowitz, F. E. (2011). Mental illness, crime, and violence: Risk, context, and social control. *Aggression and Violent Behavior, 16*(1), 36–44.

McClelland, M. (2017). When 'not guilty' is a life sentence. *New York Times Magazine*. Retrieved from: https://www.nytimes.com/2017/09/27/magazine/when-not-guilty-is-a-life-sentence.html.

MCLE. (2009). *CPCS zealous advocacy in the district & juvenile courts certification training*. Retrieved from: http://www.mcle.org/program-calendar/program-catalog.cfm?product_code=2090018P03.

MCLE. (2010). Table of contents: Massachusetts district court criminal defense manual. In *Massachusetts District Court Criminal Defense Manual*. Boston, MA: Massachusetts Continuing Legal Education.

Medina v. California, 505 U.S. 437 (United States Supreme Court 1992).

Morris, G. H., Haroun, A. M., & Naimark, D. (2004b). Health law in the criminal justice system symposium: Competency to stand trial on trial. *Houston Journal of Health Law and Policy, 4*, 193–238.

Olmstead v. L.C., 527 U.S. 581 (United States Supreme Court 1999).

Otto, R. & Weiner, I. (2013). *Handbook of forensic psychology.* Hoboken NJ: John Wiley & Sons, Inc.

Pate v. Robinson, 383 U.S. 375 (United States Supreme Court 1966).

Perlin, M. L. (2000). "For the misdemeanor outlaw": The impact of the ADA on the institutionalization of criminal defendants with mental disabilities. *Alabama Law Review, 52*, 193–241.

Perlin, M. L. (2003b). Beyond *Dusky* and *Godinez*: Competency before and after trial. *Behavioral Sciences & the Law, 21*(3), 297–310.

Philipsborn, J. T. (2017). Competently lawyering competence. *Criminal Justice, 32*(3), 34–39.

Philipsborn, J. T. (2019). Lawyering competence to stand trial with an eye on neuroscience. *The Champion,* 6. Retrieved from: https://www.nacdl.org/Article/Nov2019-LawyeringCompetencetoStandTrialwithanEyeon.

Rahman, M. (2020). *Preparing your expert witness for trial: A checklist.* Retrieved from: https://www.expertinstitute.com/resources/insights/preparing-expert-witness-trial-testimony/.

Redding, R. E. (2004). Why it is essential to teach about mental health issues in criminal law (And a primer on how to do it). *Villanova School of Law Working Paper Series*(3), 407–440.

Richards, J. (2011). Suing your criminal defense lawyer for malpractice? You better have a good alibi. Retrieved from: http://lawblog.legalmatch.com/2011/01/27/suing-your-criminal-defense-lawyer-for-malpractice-you-better-have-a-good-alibi/.

Rules of Professional Conduct (2008). *Rule 1.14: Client with diminished capacity.* Boston: Massachusetts Supreme Judicial Court. Retrieved from: https://www.mass.gov/supreme-judicial-court-rules/rules-of-professional-conduct-rule-114-client-with-diminished-capacity.

Rubin, P. N., & McCampbell, S. W. (1995). *The Americans With Disabilities Act and criminal justice: Mental disabilities and corrections* (NCJ 155061). Washington DC: US Department of Justice.

Samaha, J. (2017). *Criminal law, 12th ed.* Boston, MA: Cengage.

Saubermann, J. M., & Spangenberg, R. L. (2006). *State and county expenditures for indigent defense services in fiscal year 2005.* West Newton, MA: The Spangenberg Group.

Schouten, R., & Brendel, R. W. (2008). Chapter 85: The role of psychiatrists in the criminal justice system. In T. A. Stern, J. F. Rosenbaum, M. Fava, J. Biederman, & S. L. Rauch (Eds.), *Massachusetts General Hospital Comprehensive Clinical Psychiatry* (pp. 1155–1164). Philadelphia, PA: Mosby.

Sell v. United States 123 S. Ct. 2174 (2003).

Shannon, B., & Benson, D. (2005). *Texas criminal procedure and the offender with mental illness: An analysis and guide, 3rd ed.* Austin TX: National Alliance for Mentally Ill (Texas).

State Mental Health Plan. (2019). *Boston: State Mental Health Planning Council.* Retrieved from: http://www.mass-smhpc.org/wp-content/uploads/2019/04/State-Mental-Health-Plan_First-draft_Posted.pdf.

Strickland v. Washington, 466 U.S. 668 (United States Supreme Court 1984).

Stuart, H. (2003). Violence and mental illness: An Overview. *World Psychiatry, 2*(2), 121–124.

Tennessee v. Lane, 541 U.S. 509 (Supreme Court 2004).

Uphoff, R. J. (1988). The role of the criminal defense lawyer in representing the mentally impaired defendant: Zealous advocate or officer of the court? *Wisconsin Law Review, 65,* 65–109.

Zapf, P., Golding, S., Roesch, R., & Pirelli, G. (2013). Chapter 12: Assessing criminal responsibility. In R. Otto & I Weiner (Eds.), *Handbook of forensic psychology.* Hoboken NJ: John Wiley & Sons, Inc.

Zapf, P., & Roesch, R. (2008). *Evaluation of competence to stand trial.* New York, NY: Oxford University Press.

Zapf, P., Roesch, R., & Pirelli, G. (2013). Chapter 3: Applying psychology to criminal proceedings. In R. Otto & I Weiner (Eds.), *Handbook of forensic psychology.* Hoboken NJ: John Wiley & Sons, Inc.

Chapter 8

Mental Health Courts

"Nothing is more unequal than the equal treatment of unequal people."

— Thomas Jefferson[1]

Why Mental Health Courts?

Specialty or problem-solving courts have evolved in a number of forms across the country to fill a seeming void that traditional courts have missed. Criminal courts in the U.S., as discussed previously, have traditionally considered mental illness in terms of competency and sanity — not focusing the resources of the judiciary on recovery for persons with mental illnesses who have encountered the justice system. There is an estimated annual admission to jails of two million persons with serious mental illnesses in the United States (Redlich, Siyu, Steadman, Callahan, & Robbins, 2012); some advocates believe that with proper intervention at least one-fourth of such persons could be properly treated in the community (Knopf, 2011). This revelation becomes even more troublesome when it is considered that, according to the U.S. Department of Justice, it costs 60% more to incarcerate a person with a serious mental illness than it costs to lock up a typical inmate (Johnson & Johnson, 2012). While mental health courts have proven effective in reducing recidivism (Cummings, 2010), the inadequate approach taken by traditional criminal courts in America has proven costly fiscally and in terms of human suffering as persons with mental illnesses have continued to recycle through the criminal justice system (Council of State Governments, 2008).

High utilizers of mental health and public safety services are being targeted in a number of jurisdictions across the country. For example, Miami-Dade County judge Steve Leifman reports that over a five-year period, 97 persons with a primary diagnosis of schizophrenia were arrested approximately 2,200 times and stayed 27,000 days in jail at a cost of $13 million to taxpayers (National Public Radio, 2011). With the U.S. leading the way with 26.4% of mental disorders over fourteen countries from Europe, the Middle East, Africa, and Asia, it is no wonder that there is a need for mental health courts in America (World Health Organization, 2004).

In an attempt to identify recidivists and prevent their recycling through multiple systems, Andrews, Bonta, and Wormith (2006) identified eight criminogenic risk

---

1. As cited in Zamir (2011, p. 1023).

factors that, when present in varying degrees and combinations, may be predictive of individual criminality. Osher and Taxman (2011) constructed a list of the central needs that correspond to these risk factors, as can be seen in Table 1. As noted by Skeem (2009) and Osher (2012), offenders with mental illnesses tend to have more of the eight risk factors than those without mental illnesses. This, in turn, is more likely to propel persons with mental illnesses to the attention of authorities; and, once under the scrutiny of the criminal justice system, such persons are less likely to comport themselves and are more likely to spend longer periods of time under the control of the justice system. Without proper interventions like mental health courts, such individuals are destined to become high utilizers.

Table 1. "Central Eight" Risk Factors for Criminal Recidivism

Risk Factor	Need
History of Antisocial Behavior	Build alternative behaviors
Antisocial Personality Pattern	Problem solving skills, anger management
Antisocial Cognition	Develop less risky thinking
Antisocial Attitudes	Reduce association with criminal others
Family and/or Marital Discord	Reduce conflict, build positive relationships
Poor school or work performance	Improve performance, rewards
Few leisure or recreation activities	Improve outside involvement
Substance abuse	Reduce use

(Osher and Taxman, 2011)

Traditional criminal courts have fallen short of addressing how to prevent future occurrences of aberrant behavior by persons with mental illnesses and how to enable them to avoid the criminal process (Odegaard, 2007). Specialty or problem-solving courts take a different approach. As offenders appear before such courts, the question is not "'[w]hat is this case about'[, but] '[w]hat brought you here? ... Why are you here?" (A Conversation With The Experts, 2010, p. 137). Judges in such settings seek not only to resolve the case but also the problem that created the issue before the court (Odergaard, 2007). The focus shifts from being solely on the individual standing before the court to consider the circumstances that may have contributed to propelling the person to the attention of the authorities.

Specialty courts have emerged in an attempt to solve problems associated with specific populations. This has resulted in these problem-solving courts being established to address social issues surrounding substance abuse, mental health, domestic violence, prostitution (Quinn, 2009), the elderly (Zamir, 2011), veterans (Castellano, 2017; Cavanaugh, 2011; Walls, 2011), the homeless (Cummings, 2010), those reentering society from incarceration [reentry courts] (Rossman et al., 2012a), and juveniles [including both specialized drug courts (Kozdron, 2009) and mental health courts

(Daniel, Tillery, & Whitehead, 2009)]. These specialty courts do not always have mutually exclusive jurisdictions. While in some jurisdictions veterans courts have been established to handle matters related to military personnel who have returned from service experiencing Post-Traumatic Stress Disorder and symptoms associated with traumatic brain injury resulting in encounters with criminal justice authorities (Cavanaugh, 2011; Walls, 2011), these maladies are not unique to veterans and can also be addressed via mental health courts. Likewise, while courts for the elderly may routinely consider concerns pertaining to dementia and Alzheimer's, these same matters can be addressed in mental health courts when criminal violations are involved. It is crucial that specialized forums be available to address such issues, as it is projected that the number of persons over the age of 65 in the United States will double within the next 25 years (Van Duizend, 2008).

The development of mental health courts was inspired by the nation's first drug court in Dade County, Florida, in 1989 (Denckla & Berman, 2001; Hasselbrack, 2001). Today, there are close to 2,500 drug courts across the country (Quinn, 2009). In some jurisdictions mental health courts emerged under the auspices of a drug court (Goldkamp & Irons-Guynn, 2000; Lurigio, Watson, Luchins, & Hanrahan, 2001). Given the high correlation between substance abuse and mental disorders, which occurs with such regularity that these two conditions have come to be referred to as "co-occurring disorders" or "dual diagnoses," there appears to be a logical relationship between drug and mental health courts (Denckla & Berman, 2001; Osher, Steadman, & Barr, 2003). As will be discussed, both types of courts rely upon the principles of therapeutic jurisprudence (Steadman, Davidson, & Brown, 2001), a perspective that humanizes the law by recognizing the law as a social force that produces behavior and consequences, thereby impacting participants' emotional life and psychological well-being (Wexler & Winick, 1996). Of course, mental health courts can be distinguished from drug courts in that possession and use of drugs constitutes a crime, whereas being mentally ill and not complying with treatment protocols does not (Haimowitz, 2002). Prior to the establishment of what is considered the nation's first mental health court, Lamb, Weinberger, and Reston-Parham (1996) recommended that in certain cases, such as misdemeanors, courts should consult with psychiatrists when considering treatment; and they should subsequently mandate and monitor such treatment, when warranted.

The Emergence of the Nation's First Mental Health Court

Although some claim the first mental health court may have originated as early as 1980 in Marion County, Indiana (Steadman et al. 2001), Broward County, Florida's, Mental Health Court, established in 1997, is recognized by most as the nation's first mental health court (Denckla & Berman, 2001; Binder, 2015; Elwell, 1998; Lurigio et al. 2001; McGaha, Boothroyd, Poythress, Petrila, & Ott, 2002; Mikhail, Akinkunmi, & Poythress, 2001; Poythress, Petrila, McGaha, & Boothroyd, 2002; Ridgely et al.,

2007; Rossman et al., 2012b; Slate, 2000; Wolff 2018). It was not a pure coincidence that Broward County is a neighboring county to the location of the first drug court.

As with the development of police-based diversion programs, tragedy often drives policy, and so it was with the nation's first mental health court.

Broward County's Mental Health Court

Then Chief Public Defender Howard Finkelstein related the following case that resulted in the development of Broward County's Mental Health Court (H. Finkelstein, personal communication, June 25, 1998):

> An individual who had suffered a traumatic head injury, upon hearing voices in a grocery store, ran outside and into a little old lady, knocking her and her bag of groceries to the ground. Witnesses observed him trying to put her groceries back into the bag and believed he was trying to rob her. The lady ultimately died from injuries sustained in the fall, and the fellow with the head injury was indicted for manslaughter. Finkelstein implored the grand jury that, if they were going to indict his client, they should indict the mental health and criminal justice systems for failing the man time and again and putting him in the position for this to happen. The grand jury launched an investigation that resulted in a 153-page report lambasting both the mental health and criminal justice systems. The grand jury's recommendations provided the impetus for the establishment of Broward County's Mental Health Court.

Judge Lerner-Wren, founding judge of the Broward County Mental Health Court, describes in her own words the beginnings and the essence of what is considered the nation's first mental health court (G. Lerner-Wren, personal communication, July 17, 2007). She has also written a book describing the uniqueness of her court (Lerner-Wren, 2018). This court has become an exemplar for a number of different jurisdictions considering implementation of their own mental health courts (Slate, 2000), serving as the model for 1999 federal legislation called the Criminal Reduction and Diversionary Court Legislation.

> In June, 1997, Broward County, Florida, implemented the nation's first criminal court dedicated to addressing the complexities of the mentally ill in the criminal justice system. An extension in theory of drug courts and other specialty treatment-oriented courts, this court-based diversionary strategy was the historic outgrowth of a number of converging perceptions. There was a perception in the community that the jail had become the largest de facto hospital, due to a severely underfunded and highly fragmented community-based system of care. There was also a law enforcement perception that it was easier and quicker to arrest and book individuals that may be psychiatrically acting out than to have them evaluated at a local crisis center or hospital. The lack of a coordi-

nated police friendly central crisis system was cited as contributing to the arrest of those in psychiatric crisis in the Broward County grand jury report in the spring of 1995.

The concept for a specialized mental health diversionary court was conceived by public defender Howard Finkelstein, through the creation of a mental health criminal justice task force, assembled to seek solutions. The task force, a cross-section of mental health advocates, lawyers, judges, community treatment providers, social service administrators and family members, met for years before settling on a course of action. The Court was established in the County Court Criminal Division via administrative order by Chief Circuit Judge Ross (Broward County Circuit Court, 1997). The Court was charged with processing mentally ill misdemeanants, as long as they were not facing driving under the influence, domestic violence, or assault (unless their victim voluntarily consented for the case to be handled in mental health court) charges. Formal referrals to the Court, as specified in the administrative order establishing the Court, could come from sources such as other judges, district attorneys, and defense attorneys, and the Court would decide if the accused meets the necessary criteria. Others, including family members, the police and jail personnel, could informally initiate referrals. County Court Criminal Judge Ginger Lerner-Wren was selected to preside over this voluntary, part time criminal division based on her expertise in mental health disability law and community-based systems of care.

A well-stated shared vision and commitment [were] developed and maintained. For Broward, the judicial construct of therapeutic jurisprudence was adopted as the philosophy of the court which addresses low level non-violent misdemeanor offenses.

Judge Lerner-Wren (personal communication, July 17, 2007) outlined the goals and guiding principles that were developed in line with this philosophy:

The goals of Broward's Mental Health Court are to:

- Create effective interactions between the criminal justice and mental health systems.
- Ensure legal advocacy for the mentally ill defendant
- Ensure that mentally ill defendants do not languish in jail because of their mental illnesses.
- Balance the rights of the defendant and the public safety by recommending the most appropriate, workable disposition using existing community-based resources.
- Increase access for the mentally ill defendant to community-based treatment and services and utilize the court to integrate and help ensure access to care

(including housing, case management, substance abuse treatment, peer services, primary health care, etc.).

- Reduce the contact of the mentally ill defendant with the criminal justice system by creating a bridge between the systems.
- Monitor the delivery and adequacy of community treatment and services.
- Solicit participation from consumers and family members in the court process whenever possible.
- Promote recovery and the reduction of stigma surrounding the illnesses.

Guiding Principles:

- The court process should be trauma-informed, dignified, individualized, consumer-based and recovery-oriented. Participants must be permitted to tell their stories.
- Public safety is always paramount to treatment.
- Court participation should be voluntary, confidentiality protected (e.g., respecting private patient medical records), and constitutional rights and legal rights should never be sacrificed for treatment.
- The Court environment is significant and unique. A judge, for example, should strive to be empathetic, compassionate and therapeutic when possible while clearly and continually restating participant goals and expectations. The Court should make efforts to honor personal treatment choice and create an environment of trust and dignity. Strength-based language should be used, and procedural due process and giving voice to the court participant is extremely vital.

According to Raybon (1997), successful operation of the Court requires extra staff, as well as support and cooperation from all stakeholders. Two contractual employees were provided to help the judge in making assessments within the courtroom and in follow-up. One was the court clinician, a licensed clinical social worker from the Florida Department of Children and Families, who offers clinical expertise to the Court in assessing treatment needs. The other was a court monitor from a local private mental health center, who keeps the court informed of the treatment status and compliance of participants. The Court was supported even by the prosecutor's office, which recognized that public safety is maintained by the Court's ability to examine long-term treatment plans and keep defendants closely monitored and functioning in the community instead of revolving through the door of the criminal justice system (Raybon, 1997).

Figure 1 delineates the typical processing of cases over which Judge Wren presides in the Broward County Mental Health Court.

Figure 1.

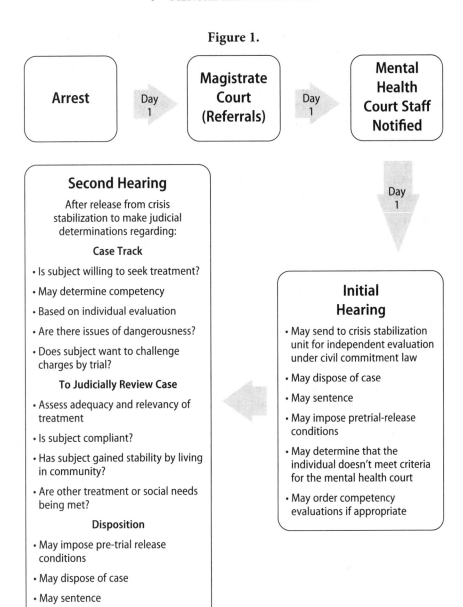

Diagram modified from Slate (2000, p. 442).

The Broward County Court has also implemented other innovative practices that have established it as the gold standard for other mental health courts. First, they have modified the probable cause affidavit required for all arrested individuals within the state of Florida so that officers can check off on a form whether they noticed any sign of mental illness during the arrest process to alert others involved in processing a subject. If a person is taken to jail, such notification is noted at booking so that proper handling will follow. Also, at booking, each arrestee's pertinent information is registered into a computer system and then cross-referenced with mental health care providers in the area to establish any history of mental illness. In addition, Broward County has implemented mobile crisis stabilization units, specially trained clinicians, in the transportation and treatment of the mentally ill. Before these units, the process for civilly committing individuals was often time-consuming, keeping law enforcement officers away from their other duties for hours. Thus, officers found it simpler and time efficient to take the mentally ill to jail as opposed to becoming tied up by the commitment process. With mobile units, the police who meet a mentally disoriented subject on the street can merely call the unit, which responds to the chosen location and transports the subject to a suitable receiving facility, thereby freeing the police to return to their normal duties.[2]

Research on participants' perceptions and outcomes of the Broward County Mental Health Court has been encouraging. Petrila (2002) reported in an initial assessment of the Court that clients perceive the procedures as fair and non-coercive, and clients are able to access treatment services more effectively than misdemeanants processed through the traditional criminal court system. The latter has been corroborated by studies conducted by Boothroyd, Poythress, McGaha, and Petrila (2003), as well as by Levin (2006). Christy, Poythress, Boothroyd, Petrila, and Mehra (2005) found that participants in Broward County's Mental Health Court have significantly shorter stays in jail than those in a comparable group.

Specialized mental health courts are playing a crucial role in reducing the needless suffering of many persons with mental illnesses who encounter the criminal justice system. As such, mental health courts continue to be developed. In a survey of mental health courts, the Council of State Governments (2005b) reports that "in 1997, only four mental health courts existed in the country; by January 2004, 70 courts were known to be in operation; as of June 2005, there [were] approximately 125 operational courts in 36 states[,]" and in 2007 there were roughly 150 mental health courts in operation across the nation (Steadman, 2007). Today, there are more than 300 mental health courts in almost all the states Fisler 2015; Wolff, 2018, with Linhorst and Linhorst (2015) maintaining there are as many as 375 such courts in the U.S. SAMHSA (2021) provides an interactive U.S. map with mental health court locations indicated across the country. Even so, the number falls way short of an estimated 3,000 drug courts across the nation (Office of Justice Programs, 2020; Wolff, et al., 2011). There are also adaptations of mental health courts outside the United States, such as in Canada (Boyle, 1998) and England and Wales (Mikhail et al., 2001).

The majority of mental health courts are reportedly located in southern and western states (Rossman et al., 2012a). Forty-one specialized juvenile mental health courts have been identified in 15 states (Callahan, Cocozza, Steadman, & Tillman, 2012). A few mental health courts have programs focusing exclusively on females, and one of the longest established programs is the Behavioral Health Court in San Francisco, California (see California Realignment, 2011; Cook County Sheriff's Office, 2012;

---

2. R. Slate witnessed the mobile crisis stabilization unit being summoned to the Judge's courtroom to remove a debilitated, jailed individual for civil commitment processing during observation of the court in operation.

Council of State Governments, 2005c). There is even a federal mental health court in Salt Lake City, Utah (Rendo, 2012). Overall, these courts have enjoyed widespread support, including being embraced by national institutions, such as the Conference of Chief Justices and the Conference of State Court Administrators (Gunther, 2005).

What Are Mental Health Courts?

Whereas drug courts typically utilize punishment, some mental health courts are generally reluctant to be punitive. This is primarily due to the understanding that persons with mental illnesses may be prone to relapse, and thus punishment would result in penalizing someone because of their status of being mentally ill (Petrila, 2002). Mason (2005) concurs, "The drug court with coercive sanctions for noncompliance as the model for the mental health court is both problematic and in the long term offers little for persons with mental illness[es] who already walk daily with coercion as a constant companion" (p. 7). Instead, mental health courts are aimed at problem-solving by minimizing punitive approaches and maximizing treatment options (Sublet, 2005; Tonry, 2006).

As mentioned previously, problem-solving courts center on the concept of therapeutic jurisprudence. As discussed in Chapter 1, therapeutic jurisprudence principles avoid looking solely backward, finding fault, assessing blame, and/or imposing punishment with little, if any, consideration for the consequences of decisions rendered by the justice system. Instead, problem-solving courts based on therapeutic jurisprudence seek to "respond ... to crime by seeking to rehabilitate the offender and repair the harm suffered by the victim and community rather than by punishing the offender according to retributive or deterrent principles" (Lanni, 2005, p. 359).

A problem-solving court focused on serving individuals with mental illness, a "mental health court," is characterized by the following:

> [It has] a specialized docket for certain defendants with mental illnesses. These courts vary as to the types of charges and mental illness diagnoses accepted as well as the participants' demographics and plea requirements, but they are united by the common themes of substituting a problem-solving model for traditional criminal court processing and an emphasis on linking defendants to effective treatment and supports. In general, mental health court participants are identified through mental health screening and assessments and voluntarily participate in a judicially supervised treatment plan developed jointly by a team of court staff and mental health professionals. Incentives reward adherence to the treatment plan or other court conditions; non-adherence may be sanctioned, and success or graduation is defined according to predetermined criteria (Almquist & Dodd, 2009, p. 5).

Thompson, Osher, and Tomasini-Joshi (2007) identify ten essential elements of a mental health court. According to them, *planning and administration* of a mental health court is guided by a broad range of stakeholders from the criminal justice, mental health, and substance abuse treatment systems. They also maintain that a *target pop-*

ulation should be identified based on public safety concerns and a community's treatment capabilities with consideration of the connection between a defendant's offense(s) and mental illness. There should also be *timely identification of participants in the court's program and linkage to relevant services*, with clearly delineated *terms of participation* and focus on both public safety and treatment concerns. Participants should be allowed to make *informed choices* with the assurance that these decisions are competently determined. *Confidentiality* for consumers of mental health services should be guaranteed, and information divulged should not be used against those individuals returned for criminal processing. The *team* of criminal justice and mental health professionals should be employed to *monitor individuals and ensure compliance* with court dictates, connecting persons with evidence-based *treatment support and services* engaged in the community when practical. Lastly, data should be collected and assessment should occur to ensure *sustainability* and community support for the mental health court program (see Almquist & Dodd, 2009; Kimber, 2008; Thompson et al., 2007).

The overall purposes of mental health courts are to protect society while applying the tenets of therapeutic jurisprudence and striving for linkages to dignified treatment. Successful implementation of mental health courts requires cooperation between the criminal justice and mental health systems, identification of the most effective and least restrictive treatment interventions, effective legal advocacy for the mentally ill, assessment of mental health service delivery and receipt of services, involvement of consumers and family members in the court process, and diversion to community mental health treatment programs (Cowart, 1997). Mays and Thompson (1991) have referred to the courts as the gatekeepers of America's jails in their ability to directly influence jail populations.

Those who receive treatment via mental health court often do so to avoid jail time. However, as time passes, they often intentionally participate in their recovery and stress the significance of relationships with mental health court staff and judges (Eschbach, Dalgin, & Pantucci (2018). Establishing such relationships is important, as stigma can be an impediment to seeking and receiving mental health treatment (Corrigan, Druss, & Perlick, 2014). Stigma, it is argued, has also thwarted advancement in studying mental illness adequately (Rasenick, 2017). As such, even Fisler (2015), Gruber and Saxbe (2018), and Ennis et al., (2016) point to a limited amount of research on the impact of mental health courts. Fisler (2015) adds what research there is suggests such courts have a positive impact. Similarly, Costopoulous and Wellman (2017) found that mental health court defendants were less likely to be arrested after completing mental health court treatment and enjoyed longer days in the community without re-arrest. Thus, they found recidivism was reduced for mental health court participants after release. With mental health courts reducing jail stays, lower lockup costs are realized; with linkages to treatment, fewer bookings occur, and quality of life is improved for participants resulting in, at the very least, modest savings for jurisdictions (Kelly, 2015).

According to Stone (1997), individuals without adequate community health placements and insurance coverage can find their mental health deteriorating and may as a result exhibit behaviors that land them in jail, often with much longer stays than those encountered by similarly situated non-mentally ill defendants (Finkelstein & Brawley, 1997).[3] However, as discussed in Chapters 6 and 9, individuals with mental illness do not receive adequate treatment in facilities devoted to punishment and "correction." Instead, the overcrowded, loud, and otherwise stressful conditions only serve to exacerbate any existing symptoms and to cause others to emerge. Finally, since most jails, even those with diversion programs, do not have follow-up programs to oversee the therapeutic progress of offenders once they return to the community, the cycle continues (Steadman, Morris, & Dennis, 1995; Walsh & Bricourt, 1997). Judges are dissatisfied with the inordinately high recidivism rates among this population, causing some to push for solutions (Acquaviva, 2006). Indeed, mental health courts have evolved in an effort to address these issues, with the ultimate goal of ending needless recycling of persons with mental illnesses through the criminal justice system.

Mental Health Court Dynamics: A Different Approach with Altered Roles

The approach of mental health courts is vastly different from traditional courts, which, as noted by Judge Lerner-Wren (personal communication, July 17, 2007), "have typically been concerned with mental illness and mental retardation only insofar as the mental disability of the defendant is raised to question competency and sanity. The focus in these instances is on legal issues (i.e., restoration of competency and criminal responsibility) and not on clinical treatment and recovery." Burns (2014) contends that elements of restorative justice can be found in some mental health courts whereby offenders with mental illness and their victims are both treated as victims. Daicoff (2006) compares the traditional court process to that of mental health courts that utilize therapeutic jurisprudence. In the traditional system, adjudication is the primary focus, whereas with therapeutic jurisprudence the main concern is after adjudication and on alternative means to resolve disputes. The judge acts more as an arbiter in the traditional process but more as a coach in the mental health courts guided by therapeutic jurisprudence principles. Reflective of the past versus future focus, the traditional system is based on precedent, whereas

---

3. Judge Janeice Martin of the Collier County, Florida, Mental Health Court states, "It's important to note that the vast majority of our participants are indigent and/or are disabled. This lack of financial resources presents a unique challenge to this population, and to our Court. One of the best tools we've found to work through some of these limitations is community service. Under Florida law, a judge can grant a defendant the option of working off their fines and court costs, and we frequently do so in MHC cases. The benefits are two-fold: (1) these defendants are accountable to society and are not simply getting a "pass" due to their illness, and (2) they receive an obvious therapeutic benefit from doing this work, benefitting others, and paying off a debt. Many participants continue the work even after they finish their obligations, and a few have actually gotten paid employment out of their community service work" (J. Martin, personal communication, July 22, 2012).

under therapeutic jurisprudence principles, the emphasis is on planning. Participants and stakeholders are limited with the traditional process, whereas the therapeutic jurisprudence approach is inclusive and exhaustive with regard to involving stakeholders. Lastly, the traditional system is formal, legalistic, and efficient, while the therapeutic jurisprudence approach is informal, commonsensical, and effective. Indeed, Winick (1997) contends that the criminal defense model is not conducive to addressing the mental health treatment needs of those who pass through the traditional court system, and this approach is anti-therapeutic. "Advocates for treatment courts assume that being processed through traditional courts impedes access to treatment and argue that breaking the cycle of arrest, release from jail, and re-arrest without community treatment warrants a more explicitly therapeutic approach by the courts" (Petrila, 2002, p. 2). The unique therapeutic jurisprudential philosophy is apparent in the following mental health court judge's comparison of her traditional versus problem-solving courts:

Judge Janice Martin of the Collier County, Florida, Mental Health Court (MHC) (personal communication, July 22, 2012) maintains, "[My] philosophy is actually fairly consistent between my MHC and my regular court (and my Adult Felony Drug Court, which I also run). My approach in every court is to endeavor to make the court response meet the needs of the situation.... I know that each of my colleagues on the misdemeanor and felony benches are *very* happy to have a useful place to refer their mental health cases. These cases used to clog and plague regular criminal dockets because these defendants are square pegs in a system that requires stability and consistency, especially when they're not getting the treatment they need. I am confident that when my colleagues come across these defendants on their criminal dockets, they are relieved to know they can refer them to MHC where we'll meet the multiple goals of keeping the system moving forward and ensuring an appropriate response will be fashioned to meet the needs of the state, the defendant and also the victim, if there is one.

... [I]n our treatment courts, there are 3 main advantages over a traditional court: (1) the focus — even from the State — is on treatment, more so than punishment, (2) I will generally have *much* more information upon which to fashion a court response, and (3) most importantly, I have a team working together to fashion that response with me, including representatives of the prosecution, defense, probation and treatment. At the core, our goal is to set our expectations appropriately to the capabilities of the individual defendant, to provide the necessary support to help them maximize their capabilities, and then to hold them accountable to that standard. Along the way, they will make restitution to any victims, as well as pay their debt to society, all the while gaining the treatment and support that they need to (hopefully) avoid re-entering the system down the road....

In order to be successful, a MHC has to have a buy-in from each of the stakeholders. The prosecutors and law enforcement must feel the Court brings real justice because these crimes and their victims are real. Likewise, they must also feel the Court brings a meaningful reduction in repeat offenses, so the benefit is worth the extra cost in time and energy. On the flip side, the defense must find a real benefit to their clients, as many may be asked to consider waiving certain valid defenses in order to gain the benefits of participation in MHC. Plus, MHC is hard, often requiring much more of participants than regular probation. Likewise, fellow judges must feel they can hand over a file with confidence that they won't be criticized by victims or the public for being too soft on crime. All of these concerns are valid, and the Court must be a reflection of its community if it is to succeed.

For these reasons, I have placed a special emphasis on my own neutrality. I have resisted calls from both sides to try to steer certain participants into, or out of, MHC. It has been my firm belief that the adversarial process — the prosecution and the defense — must be allowed to be played out in the preparation of a case for MHC. The State has to push for the penalties it needs, and the defense has to push for the mitigation it needs. When those two sides reach an agreement, I'll bless it and welcome the defendant into MHC. If I meddle in that process, I lose the buy-in of one side or both, and the Court collapses. This has been particularly difficult at times, but the overarching goal of a strong MHC, and a cohesive MHC team, has been a worthwhile result of that effort."

Judges in mental health courts assume a much different role than in traditional courts. Mason (2005) depicts this role as follows:

> Active judicial involvement and the explicit use of judicial authority to motivate individuals to accept needed services and to monitor their compliance and progress characterize the therapeutic jurisprudence of the new problem solving courts. It is a hands-on approach with the judge, no longer merely a detached referee or umpire ruling on evidentiary and procedural issues between the competing parties and interests, but a choreographer, directing the dance of a 'holistic' resolution employing public health concepts to the amelioration of social and behavioral problems that cause individual suffering and deterioration of the quality of community life (p. 4).

The influx of persons with mental illnesses into the criminal justice system has aided public mental health systems by shifting costs from these agencies to local and state correctional facilities (Seltzer, 2005). Sublet (2005) advocates increasing the number of mental health courts and contends that mental health courts can keep mental health providers accountable. Mental health court judges are uniquely positioned to sanction clients, law enforcement, and mental health providers via fines and contempt of court citations when necessary to ensure compliance with court dictates (Wolff & Pogorzelski, 2005).

The courts act as gatekeepers to treatment for the impoverished mentally ill, yet with managed care's emphasis on cost containment and branching out into the public arena, as seen with Medicaid, the government has attempted to place guards at the gate to control expenses (Petrila, 1998). Petrila points out, however, that courts can even hold managed care authorities in contempt of court for failure to comply with treatment orders.

In this new role, strong charismatic judicial leadership is essential, as different complex and independent systems, criminal justice, and mental health and substance abuse must come together in collaboration (G. Lerner-Wren, personal communication, July 17, 2007). Castellano (2017) describes it as the "politics of benchcraft" (p. 398), crafting solutions to fit the circumstances facing those appearing before the court. Judge Lerner-Wren acknowledges that her court has evolved over time. "For the past several years I have broadened my focus on court integration re: elements to establish a trauma informed court, Suicide Prevention, disability rights, trauma, ACE's, recovery, peer support, first episode teams, empowerment, reducing mass incarceration, and social determinants of health, the human rights/social justice mission of the court, and leading cultural change" (G. Lerner-Wren, personal communication, June 7, 2020). Judge Lerner Wren, who shares her vast experience and knowledge with students as an adjunct professor, indicates "[t]here is excellent work being done in so many jurisdictions. My students are interested in the technologies of the bench craft, the role of dignity, the need for early intervention, expanded community resources and advocacy (personal communication, June 7, 2020). Broward County's mental health court has a human rights focus" (G. Lerner-Wren, personal communication, June 7, 2020).

Not all judges are comfortable with — or willing to assume — this position as treatment planners and system navigators, especially in communities struggling with the provision of mental health services to the citizenry (Petrila, 2002). However, if willing to assume this responsibility, judges are clearly and legitimately positioned to ensure accountability in the treatment of persons with mental illnesses who encounter the criminal justice system.

The distinction between the formal role of the judge in traditional courtrooms versus the informal role in the mental health court is evident in some of the examples that follow. As shared by Broward County public defender Howard Finkelstein (personal communication, June 25, 1998; Slate, 2000),

> This case was initially heard in a traditional courtroom, before ultimately making it to the Broward County Mental Health Court. A man had just been released from the hospital; and upon release, he stood on the steps of the hospital waiting for a stretch limousine to come pick him up, as he believed he was to be married to Joan Rivers in New York. The limousine never materialized, however. Hospital attendants called the police, and the subject was arrested. At the initial appearance, the presiding judge did not appreciate the use of profanity by the man and charged the man with contempt of court, ordering him to spend 179 days in jail.

Scenarios such as this, involving individuals misbehaving in the courtroom related to symptoms of mental illness, are all too common in our country's courtrooms. Yet responding by ordering additional time in jail, often without treatment, serves no one. Not only does this case illustrate the rigidness of a traditional courtroom, it highlights the need for continuing legal education. Most judges and lawyers would benefit from training regarding the signs and symptoms of mental illness and appropriate measures for processing persons with mental illnesses who encounter the criminal justice system. Indeed, Judge Lerner-Wren (personal communication, July 17, 2007) goes even further in arguing for the need for training, "More formal education and cross-training on mental health disability law, mental health and substance abuse treatment issues, evidence-based research and systems of care models need to continue to be provided to judges, lawyers, forensic clinicians, case managers and others who work in and support these courts." Some states (e.g., Florida) have gotten mental illness awareness training mandated as part of the state bar's continuing legal education credits (Vickers, 2001).

Moreover, the example above is in stark contrast to the less rigid atmosphere that can be found in most mental health courts. Judge Scott Anders of Vancouver, Washington, for instance, allows consumers in his mental health court to address him by his first name (S. Anders, personal communication, November 29, 2001).

Talesh (2007) has described mental health court judges as risk managers, functioning almost like social workers diagnosing and executing a plan, with a shift in focus toward healing and away from retribution (see also "The Law of Mental Illness," 2008). A team approach tends to permeate the mental health court process, whereby the judge is no longer a referee engaged in an adversarial process but is a team member often working with other government, social service, and non-profit entities to attempt to bring about successful resolutions (Odegaard, 2007). Judge Susan Flood (personal communication, July 27, 2012) describes the establishment and evolution of the Mental Health Court in Polk County, Florida. Note how she describes her court, noting a less stigmatizing name change to "behavioral health court" and a focus on the team approach and treatment:

In October 2007, Polk County, Florida's, Mental Health Court began as a pilot program. It commenced as a voluntary diversion program for persons charged with misdemeanor offenses and who suffer from a mental or developmental illness. Since that time, the program has been renamed the Polk County Behavioral Health Court (BHC) and has been modified to a post adjudication court. Polk County's Behavioral Health Court addresses the unique needs of defendants with a mental health or developmental disability in the criminal justice system.

The BHC, though overseen by the court, has a dedicated team of a clinical coordinator, case managers, and treatment providers. The BHC is sponsored by the Polk County Board of County Commissioners and operates with the commitment of the Prosecutor's Office, the Public Defender's Office and County Probation. The BHC is considered a therapeutic court, but it is anything but soft on crime. Like other therapeutic or "problem solving" courts, the BHC seeks to address the underlying problems which may be contributing to criminal behavior. Our vision is to keep those with mental illnesses from cycling again and again through the criminal justice system and through our county jail. We strive to, on an individual basis, treat each participant's needs through a year of intensive and structured supervision. Though we do expect accountability and responsibility for actions, those expectations are tempered with the understanding that to reduce recidivism, many issues need to be resolved before mental health treatment can be effective. Some of those issues are as basic as stable housing and necessary medication.... Because of the success of Polk County's BHC, we continue to explore the possibility of expanding the program to accept those charged with third degree felonies and perhaps even juvenile cases.

Most mental health court judges realize that "[f]ailing to hold offenders with mental illness accountable for illegal behavior is beneficial to neither individuals nor communities" (Morabito, 2007, p. 1586). For example, Judge Angela Cowden, who was formerly a prosecutor, reflects upon her shift from prosecutor to mental health court judge and the ability to sometimes have extended supervision over mental health court clients (A. Cowden, personal communication, January 30, 2008):

> Transitioning from prosecutor to judge took a little time, but I had great training along the way and hope that in each role I have performed my duties to the best of my ability. As a judge, my role is as 'a neutral and detached magistrate', meaning I cannot advocate for one side or the other and must remain neutral until the case is concluded and I then make a decision based on the law as it applies to the case. In Mental Health Court that responsibility is modified to an extent to try to relate to the participants who come before me, to encourage their continued participation and compliance and to make the ultimate call if diversion is or is not appropriate, depending on the participant's willingness.

Prosecutors must function with a slightly different mentality as well. Traditionally, prosecutors are viewed as punitive in their orientation. However, Assistant State Attorney Lee Cohen of Broward County (personal communication, June 29, 1998) opined, "We should punish when punishment is deserved, but when someone does not possess the mental capacity to form the intent to commit a criminal offense then they should not be punished. The goal is to ensure public safety and bring justice by prosecuting and/or restoring competency. Restoring competency with an aim toward prevention of future deviant acts and reoccurrences of mental aberrations can serve to bring justice." He noted that a benefit of mental health courts, from his perspective as a prosecutor, is that more time and more information are allowed in rendering decisions; and by having all the knowledge and resources managed within one courtroom, it ensures greater efficiency.

State Attorney Brian Haas, in Bartow, Florida, shared his observations regarding mental health courts with the following information.

> Mental health courts have increasingly become a very important component of the criminal justice system. As a prosecutor, it's my primary responsibility to keep our community safe, while appropriately handling thousands of cases per year that are referred to my office from law enforcement. Criminal defendants, who are dealing with mental health issues, present challenges to our system, but also opportunities and incentives to help them with their problems. We often see defendants dealing with mental health issues repeatedly committing minor-low level crimes. Traditionally, those defendants would be sentenced to fines, probation, or short jail sentences. Often, those punishments do nothing to solve the problem and additional criminal offenses will likely occur. Mental health treatment courts allow for the ability to provide services and help to those suffering from mental illness. Having to deal with the pending criminal charges often provides the necessary incentive for the defendant to accept the assistance being offered. If the help is accepted and successful, the hope is that the criminal justice system won't have to deal with that defendant again and at the same time their life has hopefully improved.
>
> Our challenge is meeting the needs of those in need of mental health court because of funding and staffing issues. In the long run, if we can help the defendant, we will save resources by not having to deal with them again. Some cases, even while the defendant is dealing with mental health issues, are not appropriate for mental health court. Sometimes the issues presented by the defendant are too significant for the program to handle or the crimes committed are far too serious. Ultimately, we have to keep the public safe. It's the balance that we work every day to achieve. The trend in the criminal justice system is toward more "problem solving courts." We must do our best to handle each case appropriately, being ever mindful of the important rights of the defendants, the victims and the community. (Personal communication, May 14, 2020)

In fact, prosecutors have been found to be more inclined to make referrals to the mental health court than the defense bar (Slate, 2003). Mark Kammerer with the Cook County State Attorney's Office in Chicago (personal communication, September 26, 2006) reported that, after they implemented a mental health court within their jurisdiction, it was almost like a role reversal with the legal participants, with prosecution seeming to have the defendants' best interests in mind more so than defense attorneys. Defense attorneys are often resistant to diversion, particularly for misdemeanors, because more extensive probation may expose their clients to longer periods under control of the criminal justice system (Murphy, Friedman, & Andriukaitis, 2007). For example, in mental health courts, defendants can be placed into treatment on a misdemeanor for a year and then face potential jail sentences for a year for failures to comply with conditions of release (Fisler, 2005). Even Judge Wren (2010) and Redlich et al. (2012) acknowledge that diversion via the mental health court process is not always swift. Thus, some attorneys believe it is easier with less interference from authorities to serve a short sentence as opposed to having to be compliant with longer term treatment processes and conditions. This might be summed up as the "McJustice" approach — "we sure aren't good for you, but we are fast" (Odegaard, 2007, p. 229).

However, given defense attorneys' typical role, it is not entirely unexpected that they might initially be resistant to mental health courts. Defense attorneys tend to concentrate on their clients' civil liberties and desires in the adversarial process (Miller, 1997), even if their clients' requests are irrational or not in their clients' best interests. Lawyers are not inclined to consider ramifications of their legal decisions and are prone to disregard the long-term outcomes of those decisions (Finkelman & Grisso, 1994). At the extreme, "winning" the case at hand takes priority, even if their legal tactics ultimately bring about tragic results for their client and society (Pawel, 2001). As noted by Mills (1979), who was a defense attorney, in his discussion of the legal process, "The exultation of winning dampens any moral feelings you have.... I'm not concerned with ... the consequences of [my client] going free" (p. 247). However, many would argue that this approach has not served defendants with mental illnesses well. Keele (2002) argues that defense attorneys in the mental health court setting must be willing to shed some of their traditional defense modes and embrace a more holistic approach, considering the consequences of their actions into the future, beyond the current case at hand. Others have described the roles of defense attorneys in such settings as less zealous advocates/adversaries and more advisors to clients and team players with the mental health work group (Yermish, 2009; Zamir, 2011). Perlin and Weinstein (2016) caution that rarely may attorneys circumvent a client's desires, an exception being when a person has been determined to be civilly incompetent. They maintain that if a client is having difficulty making a decision on a pertinent matter, significant others may be consulted to assist. Of course, Perlin and Weinstein (2016) contend that persons with mental illnesses still have civil rights regarding their treatment options. Similarly, Castellano (2011) maintains that the role of treatment providers/monitors under the auspices of mental health courts is different from that of other counseling professionals as they ride the fence between treatment and law; she describes such case managers as double agents who can request leniency or punitiveness from the mental health court.

Case Examples in Mental Health Courts

Below are several examples illustrating successful interventions that have occurred in mental health courts in the country. Note the innovative therapeutic jurisprudence principles the judges embrace as they respond to those under their care, even providing a house call. This is certainly a different type of jurisprudence.

Judge Stephanie Rhoades (personal communication, July 13, 2007) discusses the following two cases handled by her court in Anchorage, Alaska:

John's Story

John is a 52-year-old Caucasian male with diagnoses of schizophrenia, undifferentiated type, cocaine dependence in full sustained remission, antisocial personality disorder, who also has several medical problems (diabetes, hypertension and congestive heart failure). John has an extensive criminal history dating back to the late 1970s — the crimes were mainly misdemeanor crimes, such as criminal trespass, minor drug-related crimes, shoplifting, and malicious destruction of property. John's current charge was a felony, malicious destruction of property which was later reduced to a misdemeanor criminal mischief charge. John was at the bank where he was attempting to cash his weekly check from his payee and became angry with the teller who would not cash the check as it was postdated. John left the bank and smashed the bank window with a trash can sitting next to the bank door. The police were quickly dispatched to the scene and within ten minutes had located a suspect matching the description of John. When John was asked about what happened at the bank he informed the police officer he threw a trash can at the door because he was angry the teller did not cash his check and now he did not have money to buy cigarettes.

John was arrested at the scene. He was initially housed in general population in the Department of Corrections (DOC) until it came to the attention of the mental health staff that John was receiving services from the local mental health center and had a history of multiple psychiatric hospitalizations. John was assessed by the DOC psychiatrist and it was discovered that John had been homeless for much of the past year and had been off his psychiatric medications for several weeks. John was restarted on medications and the DOC began the discharge planning process, obtaining releases of information for the mental health provider to determine where John would be housed upon release from the DOC. John spent several weeks in jail as his case was a felony and he could not afford to bail out of jail; when the charge was reduced to a misdemeanor. John was immediately referred to the mental health court. The mental health court was explained and John agreed to work with the specialty court. He was assigned a case coordinator who helped devise a release plan. Due to John's health problems, history of homelessness, and difficulty caring for himself it was determined an assisted living facility would be an appropriate fit. The mental health court case coordinator worked with the treatment provider to secure funding for the assisted living facility (ALF) and arrange for immediate placement. John was not keen about living in an ALF — the facility specialized in housing persons with mental health disorders and John wanted independence — but agreed to try the ALF.

John got off to a rocky start. Upon release from jail he did not appear for his next court hearing. It was discovered he was seen at the psychiatric emergency room and admitted to the state psychiatric hospital for treatment. To complicate matters, John's health problems began to deteriorate and his risk for stroke increased. John was treated in the hospital and released back to the ALF where he did well for several months. However, John began to refuse to take his medical and mental health medication and refused to come to court. He began to have problems with his roommates which placed him at risk of eviction, his psychiatric symptoms increased, and his blood pressure and diabetes were out of control, resulting in psychiatric hospitalization where both psychiatric and medical needs were again cared for. After this hospitalization John seemed to get much better — he was started on new psychotropic medication with less side effects, lost weight and improved his health enough to discontinue a portion of his diabetes medication. He still needed close monitoring for his health problems and began to settle in at the ALF, where his medications were monitored and he took a more active role in caring for his health. John expressed wanting to have more money for a trip out of state but was unable to afford this on his limited income. He started working with a job coach and got a job cleaning in a warehouse and was able to save funds to make his trip out of state to visit family he had not seen in many years. After doing well for several more months, John was recommended for graduation from mental health court. John expressed his appreciation to the judge upon graduation for the support and encouragement received during participation. Upon graduation John's charges were dismissed.

We now hear from John every couple of months; he comes in the court to say hello, still living in the ALF, works at his job in the warehouse, and visits relatives out of state every year. John had a history of 27 criminal convictions spanning over 20 years. Since his graduation three years ago, he has remained out of the criminal justice system. He is now housed, reengaged with his family, employed, and successfully managing his medical and mental health symptoms.

Violet's Story

Violet is a 22-year-old African-American woman with diagnoses of bipolar disorder, most recent episode manic, with psychotic features, a history of marijuana, cocaine, and amphetamine abuse, and personality disorder. Violet is the youngest of seven siblings and grew up in the foster care system. Violet was physically and sexually abused by an older brother prior to foster care placement and does not have contact now with any of her siblings. She was placed in a foster care setting at the age of 14 with an affluent family who adopted her at age 16; the family is still very much involved with Violet. Violet had her first psychiatric hospitalization at the age of 17. After release from the hospital, Violet spent two months in the youth mental health treatment facility out of state for two assault convictions against her adoptive mother.

Violet has a poor history of medication compliance with her chief complaint that medications make her gain weight. As a result, Violet has had six psychiatric hospitalizations in a four-year period. Violet voluntarily admitted herself at the last admission and left within three days against medical advice. Within 24 hours, Violet was in jail. Violet was charged with a misdemeanor theft charge. She entered a Wal-Mart store, loaded the cart until it was overflowing with snacks from the grocery store and ran from the store into the street causing several cars to swerve to miss hitting her. Police were dispatched and as the officers approached Violet, she began screaming that she did not take anything and threw herself on the road, blocking lanes of traffic. Violet was arrested and taken in to custody. Violet was not able to be arraigned in custody, appeared to be experiencing visual and auditory hallucinations, and made threats to kill herself, other inmates, and correctional staff. Substance use was suspected but Violet was uncooperative and a screening could not be conducted. The court requested a competency evaluation based on the client's erratic behavior. The evaluation included a review of previous hospitalizations, which indicated the client would likely be restored to competency within a 14-day period.

Violet was transferred to the state psychiatric hospital for competency restoration and started on medications. Violet expressed concern about weight gain and was started on newer medications that did not cause weight gain problems. Violet responded well to the medications and was found to be competent to proceed with her legal case. She was arraigned and chose to participate in the mental health court program. With assistance from the court case coordinator, Violet was connected to a case manager and therapist to work on immediate needs. Safe and sober housing, as well as recent suspected substance use were of immediate concern. Violet participated in a substance abuse assessment and was able to enter into a pre-treatment bed immediately upon discharge from jail. Violet was able to participate in pre-treatment activities for several weeks until a residential dual diagnosis bed opened through a Salvation Army program. Violet stayed in the residential program for 90 days. She found a sponsor while in treatment and continued with the aftercare portion of treatment for six months as an outpatient. Violet was referred to a specialized housing program for clients who cycled through institutions. This program was able to set her up with her own apartment and help with funds for furniture and other basic household items. The case manager from the housing program helped Violet with the social security application process and benefits were granted, helping to pay 30% of the income for rent. Violet responded very well to the medication regimen she was prescribed, with very few side effects (and no weight gain). She began working with the state Division of Vocational Rehabilitation program and was able to secure grant funding to go to college, and she began courses. She obtained her driver's license, was able to purchase a car with help from her adoptive parents, completed community work service and paid all fines associated with the criminal charge. She began group and individual therapy to address trauma issues from childhood and successfully completed the group portion and continues with an individual monthly session. Violet was recommended for graduation and her case was dismissed. She has had no new criminal charges in two years.

Probate Judge Mark Heath (personal communication, June 21, 2007) reports on a case he handled in his mental health court in Bennettsville, South Carolina:

David's Story

David had been placed on probation for assaulting his neighbor. Upon his initial interview, his version of the offense was that he had been trying to sleep during the day as he worked at night. The neighbor on several occasions continued to play his radio very loudly. After repeatedly asking the person to turn it down, he lost his composure and assaulted the neighbor. As we got into the interview, he disclosed that his wife had been having an affair and their marriage was already going sour after just a few years. When asked if he had ever thought about hurting himself or killing himself, he became visibly upset and left the office without permission. The next day after visiting him at his home, I explained to him that I thought he should go to the local mental health center and talk to them about depression. He agreed to go see them and after several months on an antidepressant, he was able to return to a normal way of life and salvage his marriage.

Judge Janeice Martin (personal communication, July 22, 2012) shared the following information regarding an individual who appeared before her court in Naples, Florida:[4]

Mark's Story

[Mark] ... was very, very sick when we first met him. He'd been arrested for fleeing from officers at a very high rate of speed, naked. [Mark] quickly accepted the program and took advantage of its resources. He got plugged in with NAMI and participated in many of their programs. He acquired not one, but two paying jobs. Despite his success, we found out [Mark] eventually came to believe he didn't need his meds anymore, and quit taking them without

---

4. For the purposes of this case example, we have assigned the young man the name of "Mark." NAMI refers to the National Alliance on Mental Illness, the mental health advocacy organization noted throughout the book; CIT refers to police crisis intervention training, as highlighted in Chapter 5; MHC stands for mental health court.

telling us. Predictably, he was soon in a psychotic state again. Fortunately, his father knew to get him to NAMI, and once there, an employee knew to call in a CIT officer to get him safely to a crisis unit. Interestingly, [Mark] tested the officer a bit, and an untrained officer might have taken exception to this odd behavior and placed him under arrest. However, the CIT officer practiced well his skills in de-escalation and managed to persuade [Mark] peaceably to come with him to a crisis unit. [Mark] was stabilized and went on successfully to graduate from MHC. He's been a great ambassador in the community for both CIT and for MHC. Even with all of his success, [Mark] provided a stark reminder for all of us that mental illness isn't cured; it doesn't go away once one is stabilized. He will battle his illness for the rest of his life and will never safely be able to let down his guard.

Mental Health Court Models

It has been said, "If you have seen one mental health court, you have seen one mental health court" (Council of State Governments, 2008, p. 7). There is no single model of a mental health court that is suitable to all communities (Goldkamp & Irons-Guynn, 2000; Lurigio et al., 2001; Steadman et al., 2001; Watson, Hanrahan, Luchins, & Lurigio, 2001; Watson, Luchins, Hanrahan, Heyrman, & Lurigio, 2000). The establishment of mental health courts is susceptible to local personalities within the criminal justice and mental health systems (Redlich et al., 2010). While much of the initial funding may come from the federal level, the functioning of mental health courts is dependent upon what services are or are not available locally. Each jurisdiction has to collaboratively assess available resources, personnel, and orientations to determine what is right for a particular area. As such, mental health courts vary widely in terms of eligibility, plea agreements, supervision, incentives, sanctions for noncompliance, and completion standards. No matter the differences, the commonality across such courts is the focus on diversion of persons with mental illnesses from the criminal justice system into treatment (Boothroyd, Mercado, Poythress, Christy, & Petrila, 2005).

In 2005, the Council of State Governments (2005b) reported that 34% of 90 mental health courts under study accepted only misdemeanor cases, 56% indicated that they accepted misdemeanor and felony cases on a case-by-case basis, and 10% handled only felony cases. Most early mental health courts handled misdemeanants (Fields, 2006), but they are increasingly handling felons as well. According to Hafemeister, Garner, and Bath (2012), today only 27% of mental health courts restrict participation to misdemeanant clients, and almost half (46%) allow persons with mental illnesses to participate if they are charged with a felony, particularly if the behavior that lands them before the court is non-violent. Other mental health courts may allow some combination of misdemeanors and felonies before the court. Some mental health courts exclude those charged with certain crimes, such as domestic violence, crimes against children, and driving while impaired or violent felonies (Slate, 2003). Glassberg and Dodd (2008) caution that as mental health courts increasingly handle persons with mental illnesses charged with felonies public scrutiny will be greater as will the need to engage victims in court processes. Luskin and Ray (2015) found that mental health courts tend to primarily exclude clients with active warrants in place for their arrests, those who were depressive, and those abusing substances near the time of arrest.

Mental health courts also differ by the way that cases are resolved. Griffin, Steadman, and Petrila (2002) identified three types of post-booking statuses among mental health courts they studied. Specifically, some jurisdictions withheld adjudication without a plea being entered, and, provided the court's treatment regimen was successfully completed, dismissal of charges would ultimately result.[5] In other judicial districts, after entering a plea and/or adjudication, sentence imposition would be deferred, contingent on satisfying treatment stipulations by the court. Yet other judicial circuits convicted persons with mental illnesses and then placed them under probation supervision, sometimes via a deferred or suspended sentence. Research finds that guilty pleas were required to be entered by participants in 40% of the mental health courts that responded to a Council of State Governments (2005b) survey. Contrary to the standard practice in drug courts, Griffin et al. (2002) found that most of the courts they examined rarely utilized jail as punishment for not complying with treatment requirements imposed by the court, and charges were usually dismissed after successful adherence to treatment regimens. One jurisdiction allowed the retraction of guilty pleas, and another, after dismissal of charges, allowed for the possibility of expungement of arrest records following successful completion of treatment requirements (Griffin et al., 2002).

Typically, mental health court teams are composed of "a judicial officer; a treatment provider or case manager; a prosecutor; a defense attorney; and, in some cases, a court supervision agent such as a probation officer. Many mental health court teams also utilize a court coordinator to be responsible for the overall administration of the court and for encouraging communication and coordination among team members" (Glassberg & Dodd, 2008). Griffin et al. (2002) found court supervision of persons with mental illnesses differed by court. Supervision of persons under the jurisdiction of the mental health court generally takes place via one of three different formats: community mental health treatment providers, probation officers or mental health court staff, or a combination of both mental health treatment professionals and probation officers on teams to monitor and aid in compliance. Supervision agents serve as boundary spanners linking persons with mental illnesses to essential treatment services and other vital needs such as housing, benefits, and vocational/employment options (McCampbell, 2001; Steadman et al., 2001). In turn, supervision agents, whether probation officers and/or mental health professionals, monitor compliance

---

5. Watson et al. (2000) pointed out that state law may need to be examined to determine if individuals not convicted of a crime can legally be placed on probation or supervised release.

to treatment protocols and keep the court apprised of the client's progress at regular status hearings (Lurigio & Swartz, 2000; Petrila, Poythress, McGaha, & Boothroyd, 2001).

There appears to have been distinct stages in the evolution and growth of mental health courts in terms of these variables. Redlich, Steadman, Petrila, Monahan, and Griffin, (2005) recognized two generations of mental health courts, with a general trend toward greater punitiveness, more in line with drug courts. Specifically, first generation mental health courts were reported to be more misdemeanant-focused, avoided convictions, and relied more on mental health clinicians to supervise and monitor treatment compliance of mental health court participants in the community. Second generation mental health courts, on the other hand, tend not to be restricted to non-violent misdemeanors and are more likely to employ a post-adjudicative format whereby guilty pleas must be accepted to allow participation in the courts' processes. These second generation courts tend to utilize supervision affiliated with the criminal justice system, such as probation officers; and in an attempt to ensure compliance participants are more likely to have the sanction of jail imposed. Redlich et al. (2005) advise that, based on the evolution of mental health courts thus far, there may even come a time in the development of third and fourth generation mental health courts when persons with mental illnesses accused of misdemeanors will no longer be processed by these courts. This seems to be a far cry from the initial calls for adherence to the principles of therapeutic jurisprudence associated with the emergence of mental health courts (Miller & Perelman, 2009).

The following two examples of mental health courts—Queens Mental Health Court in New York City (as described by Judge Marcia Hirsch, personal communication, July 16, 2012) and the Collier County Mental Health Court in Naples, Florida (as discussed by Judge Janeice Martin, personal communication, July 22, 2012)—illustrate the individuality of these courts as influenced by local personalities and dynamics:

Queens Mental Health Court — New York City

Queens County is one of the five boroughs (counties) of New York City and has 2.2 million people. [Judge Marcia Hirsch] currently preside[s] over 5 treatment courts: Queens Drug Treatment Court, Queens Mental Health Court, Queens DWI Treatment Court, Queens Drug Diversion Court, and Queens Veterans Court. All are for felony offenders, almost all cases utilize pre-plea diversion, and all benefit from a dismissal or reduction of charges upon successful completion. The Queens Mental Health Court opened in November 2005, staffed with existing members of the Queens Drug Treatment Court team and with no additional financial resources. Training was provided by the New York State Office of Court Administration, the Center for Court Innovation, and local mental health providers. The Queens County District Attorney Richard A. Brown was and is extremely supportive of problem-solving courts and agreed that felony defendants could participate, provided that their crime was non-violent, that they suffered from an Axis I disorder, and the victims agreed. While victim consent is still required, our court has evolved to accept an increasing number of violent crimes including attempted murder, arson, attempted kidnapping, assaults, sexual abuse, and robbery. Many of our participants have co-occurring alcohol and substance abuse issues. They range in age from 17 to 85 and reflect the diversity of our county, which is a virtual "melting pot" of nationalities, ethnicities and cultures. The most common mental illnesses diagnosed in our population are: bipolar disease, schizophrenia, paranoid schizophrenia, major depressive disorder, and post-traumatic stress disorder.

Collier County Mental Health Court — Naples, Florida

According to Judge Janeice Martin, the Collier County Mental Health Court (MHC) in Naples, Florida, has been in existence since the fall of 2007.... For the 1st year or so, we took only misdemeanants, while we built up the program, but have taken felonies as well ever since. We take cases both on a pre-trial diversion basis, and on a post-conviction (plea, then probation) basis.... [T]he diversion cases will end with a dismissal (nolle prosequi) upon successful completion. For the plea/probation cases, the probation will be terminated upon successful completion. For about the past year or so, I've been pleased to see the State Attorney's Office (SAO) accepting some tougher cases (folks with more serious charges and/ or longer records) into MHC. This has been done with either a lengthy suspended sentence, or a term of probation to continue *after* completion of MHC, or both. One person, a female with a very large financial crime, came into MHC on a plea that sent her immediately to prison, with X years of probation and MHC to follow that prison term. We do not require a guilty plea.... A plea of no contest will do. However we *do* adjudicate some folks guilty, as opposed to withholding adjudication. On felony cases this would mean that some of our folks will be convicted felons, *even if* they successfully complete. Obviously, I'm not excited about that fact, but the terms of *all* pleas and diversion agreements are strictly between the attorneys in negotiation — I don't meddle in those affairs. If I do, I risk the SAO excluding these cases, or pulling their support entirely, and then I'm nowhere.

Results from Mental Health Court Programs

A number of studies have assessed the characteristics and results of implementation of mental health court programs across the country. Overall, findings reveal that "[w]hen outpatient treatment is mandated either through mental health courts or outpatient commitment statutes, participating persons tend to do better than non-treatment control samples" (Redlich, 2005, p. 615).

Figure 2. Queens Mental Health Court, New York

Outcome of Screenings

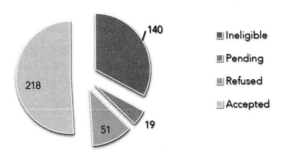

Figure 3. Queens Mental Health Court, New York

Participant Status
(on 6/30/2012)

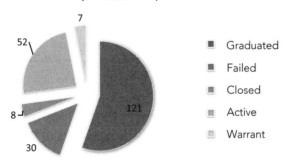

Not every referral is suitable for mental health court participation. For example, according to Judge Hirsch (personal communication, July 16, 2012; data from Dr. Shelly Cohen, SUNY Stonybrook), "Since its inception in November of 2005, the Queens Mental Health Court (QMHC) has screened 428 defendants for inclusion into the program. Of these 428, 140 (33%) were deemed ineligible due to criminal or clinical characteristics, 19 (4%) were pending decisions..., 51 (12%) refused to participate, and 218 (51%) were accepted into the program." See Figure 2.

As illustrated in Figure 3, "Of the 218 defendants that were accepted into the QMHC, 121 (56%) successfully graduated, 30 (14%) were terminated unsuccessfully, 8 (4%) had their cases closed due to death or physical/mental illness that prevented them from continuing, 52 (24%) were active participants..., and 7 (3%) were in warrant status.... Thus, only 14% were terminated for non-compliance and 3% were on warrant status."

Of course, successfully completing a mental health court program does not guarantee that participants will steer clear of the justice system in the future. As such, various studies have examined the outcomes of mental health courts in terms of recidivism.

In a longitudinal study covering courts in San Francisco, Minneapolis, Indianapolis, and Santa Clara County, California, Steadman et al. (2011) concluded that mental health courts lower both post-treatment arrest rates and days incarcerated when compared to prior participants' involvement in the court. Hiday and Ray (2010) found that participants who completed a mental health program were significantly less likely to recidivate, even after two years away from the program, when compared to their pre-court involvement. According to Judge Susan Flood of the Polk County, Florida, Behavioral Health Court (BHC) (personal communication, July 27, 2012), "As of July 2012, only 25% of the graduates have been charged with a new criminal offense. In contrast, 56% of those who were dismissed from the program or otherwise dropped out have been charged with at least one new criminal offense. These statistics don't even begin to address recidivism for those with mental illnesses in the criminal justice system that never even reach BHC." Rossman et al. (2012a), in a study of two mental health courts discovered that mental health court participants in Brooklyn and the Bronx, New York were significantly less likely to be re-arrested than those with mental illnesses processed in traditional, "business-as-usual" courts. They also reported that Brooklyn Mental Health Court participants were significantly less likely to be reconvicted when compared to those exposed to traditional, business-as-usual court processing. Redlich et al. (2010) indicate that there is evidence that mental health courts lower re-arrest rates for mental health court clients in comparison with the clients' pre-mental health court experience or in comparison with control groups. Likewise, Herinckx, Swart, Shane, Dolezal, and King (2005) found that graduation from the mental health court program was a critical factor in preventing individuals from recycling back into the criminal justice system, as graduates of the program in Clark County, Nevada, were almost four times more likely not to recidivate as compared to those individuals who did not successfully complete the program. They also determined that participants one year after enrollment in the program were four times more likely to not be arrested compared to the year prior to their enrollment in the program, resulting in 54% of the participants not being arrested and a 62% reduction in probation violations.

In another study focusing on courts in Oregon and Washington, re-arrests decreased after persons with mental illnesses completed a mental health court program (Levin, 2006). Trupin and Richards (2003) followed Seattle mental health court clients over a nine-month follow-up and found that those who opted to participate in the courts' programs were significantly less likely to be booked after entry into the program compared to bookings prior to beginning the program. Participants also had fewer bookings than those who opted not to engage in the courts' programs. In North Carolina, researchers found that mental health court treatment programs not only decrease the number of re-arrests for participants but also tend to lessen the severity of any subsequent charges. Those individuals who completed mental health court programs were even less likely to be re-arrested than participants who withdrew from the program (Hiday, Moore, Lamoureaux, & Magistris, 2005; Moore & Hiday, 2006).

Finally, in Santa Barbara, California, where mental health court clients were placed in intensive case management in the form of assertive community treatment teams, mental health court participants showed improvements in performance, less involvement in illegal activity, and greater reductions in time spent in jail than those assigned to traditional case management (Cosden, Ellens, Schnell, & Yamini-Diouf, 2005).

Several studies have examined participants' perceptions of their experiences in mental health courts and whether this affects their willingness to comply with court directives. Importantly, "initial mental health court comprehension [i.e., competency] is predictive of future success or failure in the court" (Redlich, 2005, p. 614) and lessens perceptions of coerciveness. In turn, when participants do not perceive their interactions with the court as coercive and instead view the mental health court process as procedurally fair, they are more likely to be cooperative with court-imposed terms and conditions (Poythress et al., 2002) and to be satisfied with the outcomes of their interaction (Miller, 1997). In terms of violating conditions of mental health courts, only 19 of the Brooklyn mental health court's 244 felony clients were returned to jail for violations of their court-imposed conditions over the course of four years (Fields, 2006). Defendants in Washington, too, have shown fewer probation violations (Levin, 2006).

Enrollment in mental health courts seems to also be associated with improved mental health and psychosocial functioning via increasing access to treatment services and engagement of clients in the treatment process (Redlich et al., 2010). In the Oregon study mentioned above, mental health court clients required fewer inpatient treatment days, more outpatient treatment days, and fewer crisis interventions than in the year before they became enrolled in the mental health court's service program (Levin, 2006; Trupin & Richards, 2003). Likewise, Ridgely et al. (2007) found that entry into the mental health court in Brooklyn resulted in improved psychosocial adaptations and significant decreases in abuse of substances and psychiatric hospitalizations. Cosden et al. (2005), too, found decreases in substance abuse among their mental health court participants under the care of assertive community treatment teams.

The most often cited study to date assessing mental health court costs and measuring the influence fiscally of such courts on the social welfare, mental health, and criminal justice systems is the research by Ridgely et al. (2007). In their two-year study of the Allegheny County Mental Health Court, they discovered that a "leveling off of mental health treatment costs and [a] dramatic drop in jail costs yielded a large and statistically significant cost savings at the end of [their] period of observation" (p. 20). They reported a total cost savings of $9,584.00 per mental health court participant (n = 66) over the two-year period of the evaluation for a total savings of over a half million dollars as a result of the implementation of the mental health court in Allegheny County. In practical terms, they found that it costs less to divert persons with mental illnesses from the criminal justice system into treatment via mental health courts than it does to jail them (Ridgely et al., 2007; Rivera, 2004). While start-up costs may outweigh initial savings, over time it was determined that the mental health court can result in governmental savings as a therapeutic environment develops and recidivism and use of expensive treatments, such as hospitalization, decreases. A more recent attempt to conduct a cost-benefit analysis of mental health courts in the Bronx and Brooklyn, New York, however, fell short due in part to the decentralization of multiple agencies, providers, and record keeping systems (Rossman et al., 2012a). More recently, Kubiak, Roddy, Comartin, and Tillander (2015) found a total cost savings for mental health court participants of $1,411,020 over other offender groups one year after mental health court supervision.

Areas of Concern

Mental health courts are not without their critics, however. These criticisms tend to revolve around the need to establish better mental health resources in the community before mental health courts can be successful, funding, patients' rights and competency to participate voluntarily in the court process, potential stigmatization and criminalization of people with mental illnesses, and an insufficient evidence base on which to establish mental health courts. Each will be discussed in detail below.

Need for Adequate Services in the Community

Although mental health courts do appear to increase access to treatment for persons who appear before them, ample and quality treatment services need to be in place for them to be successful. However, this is rarely the case. Moreover, the courts have little control over these factors (Boothroyd et al., 2005; Levin, 2006; Mason, 2005). Likewise, co-occurring treatment resources and services for daily living (e.g., housing options) are inadequate (Lurigio et al., 2001).[6] Mental health court judges can help negotiate and navigate treatment services, but because they must rely on what is available rather than creating new services, they have to learn to prioritize the services (Haimowitz, 2002). In the following discussion, Judge Stephanie Rhoades of the Alaska District Court in Anchorage (personal communication, July 13, 2007) describes her difficulties at locating mental health and substance abuse treatment, as well as services for daily living (e.g., housing):

> The mental health court is reliant upon existing community resources to link a participant to treatment. For example, a person with a mental health diagnosis is eligible for services at the community mental health center. A person with a developmental disability (DD) is typically eligible for DD services through the

---

6. The Council of State Governments (2005a) estimates that three-fourths of offenders with mental illnesses are also experiencing a co-occurring substance abuse disorder; Peters and Osher (2003) address how co-occurring disorders should be considered in specialty courts such as mental health courts.

specialized facilities (ARC, ASSETS, or HOPE Community Resources). A person with a traumatic brain injury may be eligible for services at any of these agencies, depending upon their individual circumstances, and also may benefit from AC-CESS Alaska services which specialize in working with persons with brain injuries. Yet, challenges arise in a person's unique situation at any one of these agencies. With Medicaid refinancing of previously grant-funded services, we see challenges with reduced services for clientele — previous case management, individual and group services are now more limited. Grants which previously assisted indigent clients now are not available. The DD waitlist is years long. Adults with [Fetal Alcohol Spectrum Disorders] FASD are extremely difficult to link to services as very limited services exist in the community.

There are a number of community gaps which contribute to the costly, unnecessary and repeated jail, hospital, and other institutional stays. The number one challenge the mental health court faces is being able to link participants to safe, sober, and affordable housing. Homelessness is very serious. In one Alaska Department of Corrections study, 35% of people with mental illnesses were released from jail to homelessness; too often mentally ill persons are indigent and can not afford housing, food, clothing and other basic necessities on release from jails/institutions. The mental health court does receive funds from the Alaska Mental Health Trust Authority to help with emergent housing, food, transportation and medical needs; but funds are limited and typically are a one time only expenditure for individual participants.

Another challenging area is ensuring that when a mentally ill person is released from jail or a psychiatric hospital that linkages to community mental health services are available. Mentally ill persons may run out of medications before they can see an outpatient psychiatric provider, resulting in erosion of mental stability. The mental health court has case coordinators that aid in setting up expedited intake appointments so that a participant can access services and not run out of medication, and there are special projects that attempt to address some of the problems; but even with more intensive services, we continue to see a reduction in outreach services for beneficiaries.

A huge problem area exists with accessing services for those with co-occurring disorders. There are not enough treatment slots for people with co-occurring substance abuse and behaviorally challenging mental health disorders, including persons with developmental disabilities and traumatic brain injuries. Intake appointments for substance abuse assessments take 3 to 4 months, and treatment placement occurs several months after the initial assessment.

Special needs housing and treatment for the most behaviorally challenged individuals is extremely difficult to access. These are persons who frequent emergency systems (psychiatric emergency room, psychiatric hospital, jail, shelters). These are persons with significant behavior challenges, seriously mentally ill youth in transitions, and seriously mentally ill individuals convicted of sex offenses or certain violent crimes. The bottom line is that many Alaska Mental Health Trust Authority beneficiaries have chronic co-occurring mental health and substance use disorders that will require long-term treatment for both disorders in the community, or they will predictably return to jail.

A continuum of services does exist within the department of corrections and in the outpatient behavioral health community. Over the years these programs/initiatives have resulted in increased collaboration between agencies, which helps beneficiaries, but the reality is there continues to be significant challenges if treatment and housing services do not exist. This continuum helps divert persons from the criminal justice system and provides a level of support to assist beneficiaries to remain in the community; but without adequate and appropriate treatment and housing services for beneficiaries, we will see the inevitable recycling of these individuals into institutions and continued high usage of expensive emergency services.

Another criticism is that consumption of resources by mental health court program participants results in rationing of services when there is already limited availability of treatment resources. Such rationing may delay or even prevent intervention for non-forensic patients, persons who are in need of mental health services but have not been arrested (Clark, 2004; Goldkamp & Iron-Guynn, 2000; Haimowitz, 2002; Steadman et al., 2001; Watson et al., 2001). However, Honberg (2002) reports that there is little to no evidence that mental health courts and their associated programs have taken any monies away from other equally deserving persons. Furthermore, it can be argued that those in mental health courts *are* the ones most in need of treatment, as their inappropriate behavior cannot avoid contact with the criminal justice system. Instead of begrudging those individuals treatment for their mental health problems, perhaps we should be pressuring our lawmakers and policymakers for sensible solutions and improving the availability of sufficient mental health treatment services for all who need them.

Inadequate Funding and Sparse Data

Funding is almost always at the base of a need for more and better services, and this is certainly the case with mental health services. Public mental health services are woefully lacking. Since 2009, states during economic hard times have cut non-Medicaid spending for mental health care across the nation by almost $2 billion (Thomas, 2011).

Funding from federal legislation has been a significant source of financial support in the implementation and continuing operation of mental health courts. Congress authorized $4 million to be dispensed by the U.S. Attorney General to provide funding under President Clinton (America's Law Enforcement and Mental Health Project, 1999). Congress also appropriated $5 million to the Substance Abuse and Mental Health Services Agency (SAMHSA) to aid criminal justice diversion projects specifically for persons with mental illnesses (M. Thompson, personal communication, March 18, 2002). SAMHSA had approximately three quarters of a million dollars available in 2007 to fund two diversion projects (SAMHSA, 2007). President Bush signed the Mentally Ill Offender Treatment and Crime Reduction Act (MIOTCRA) into law in 2004 which authorized federal grant monies for mental health court and other diversion projects, plus made funds available for treatment while incarcerated and upon reentry into the community (Bossolo, 2004). In the first fiscal year of operation, the Bureau of Justice Assistance oversaw funding for thirty-seven mental health courts in twenty-nine different states for a total of $5.5 million in allocations (Sublet, 2005). Most recently, the funding allocated for MIOTCRA for fiscal year 2013 by House and Senate subcommittees, awaiting approval by the full Congress, is $9 million (Council of State Governments, 2012).

Some have marveled at the growing popularity of mental health courts and the appropriation of funds by Congress for the establishment of mental health courts without outcome data being available (Griffin et al., 2002). The emergence and evolution of mental health courts, prior to their establishment as an evidence-based practice, has been significantly impacted by frustration with the overcrowding of jails and prisons by persons with mental illnesses (Petrila, 2002; Wolff & Pogorzelski, 2005).

As illustrated by Judge Rhodes in Anchorage (personal communication, July 13, 2007) in the previous gray box, a concern with external funding sources is that they may dry up after an initially specified period of time. Therefore, it is important to have accurate data keeping mechanisms in place to monitor and report outcomes so that community leaders can clearly see the advantages of investing in worthy programs aimed at addressing the needless recycling of persons with mental illnesses through the criminal justice system. There is a need for more valid outcome data so mental health courts can be established as an evidenced-based best practice which can attract more adequate funding (Council of State Governments, 2005a; Steadman, 2005).

Indeed, crises often drive policies. However, "[t]he exceptional, high profile event, while often a catalyst for political action, usually posits the wrong premise on which to build effective policy and practice" (Steadman, 2008, p. xiv). The variability of mental health courts, susceptible to local influences, has contributed to a lack of standardization of mental health court practices and resulted in a number of researchers lamenting the continued growth of mental health courts based on a paucity of quality research (Almquist & Dodd, 2009; Bozza, 2007; Miller & Perelman, 2009; Redlich et al., 2010). In fact, the evidence base on which the increase in the number of mental health courts across the country has occurred has been described as "speculative, ...

consisting of numerous descriptive accounts, anecdotal assessments, and quasi-ex-perimental-studies" (Wolff, Bekenko, Fabrikant, & Huening, 2011).

Efforts are being made in some jurisdictions to train judges engaged in traditional criminal court processes, not just specialized mental health court judges, in recognizing signs and symptoms of mental illnesses, de-escalation skills, and ready familiarity with resources and linkages to mental health treatment (see Florida Partners in Crisis, 2011; Gunther, 2005). Those considering alternatives to mental health court involve-ment often focus on opportunities for intervention along the various points designated on the Sequential Intercept Model as discussed in Chapter 1 (see Carter, 2009; Fader-Towe & Louison, 2012). This can sometimes avoid a criminal label being imposed. Of course, the key is that justice personnel situated at various intercept points along the model have been trained to recognize signs and symptoms of mental illnesses and to assist with linkages to treatment. Furthermore, some researchers believe it makes more sense to invest in preventative treatment programs and even use pro-bation, which is already in place, instead of employing the expensive judicial process in such matters (see Bozza, 2007; Carter, 2009).

Patients' Rights and Competency

Seltzer (2005) cautions that mental health courts are not a panacea in and of them-selves because, without proper resources, they may function merely as a coercive force. Indeed, a number of scholars have questioned whether mental health courts are coercive (Goldkamp & Irons-Guynn, 2000; Haimowitz, 2002; McCampbell, 2001; see Miller & Perelman, 2009; Munetz et al., 2014). Some question whether a person who is mentally ill can even make a rational or competent decision to voluntarily participate in treatment.

In terms of voluntariness, Boothroyd et al. (2003) found that truly voluntary par-ticipation in the Broward County Mental Health Court was suspect for the majority of participants. Likewise, Redlich, Hoover, Summers, and Steadman (2010) found in a study of 200 newly enrolled mental health court clients that, while most indicated they chose to participate, the majority of those enrolled actually reported they were not told participation in the court was voluntary or made aware of court rules and regulations before signing up. The researchers also reported that a minority of the participants were discovered to have issues impacting their competence to make legally informed decisions.

One aspect of competency to participate in mental health courts is comprehension of the limits to confidentiality (Goldkamp & Irons-Guynn, 2000). However, there are a number of ways in which individuals' rights can be safeguarded, as noted by Judge Ginger Lerner-Wren (personal communication, July 17, 2007). It can be re-quested that competent individuals appearing before the court sign waivers to allow release of mental health assessments and records to the court for consideration in determining the best way to proceed. Mental health court judges can also limit in-quiries so that no Fifth Amendment rights regarding self-incrimination are violated by focusing on the mental health of persons before the court instead of the elements of a potential crime. Family members of persons with mental illnesses, who are not bound by the doctor-patient privilege, can prove to be a good source of information for the court and its officers. Also, mental health clinicians used by the court can facilitate the dispensing of information from one mental health provider to another. Additionally, via interagency computer networks, jailers can apprise mental health providers of those being booked into jail so that cross-checks can be done to determine if they have received mental health treatment in the past, as is done in Broward County, Florida. Murphy et al. (2007) indicate that law enforcement officers as first responders are exempt from the Health Insurance Portability and Accountability Act (HIPAA) requirements and have an obligation to meet the mental and physical health care needs of individuals while in their custody.[7]

Ultimately, many have argued that concerns about coercion and competency to stand trial in mental health courts are overstated. Petrila et al. (2001), in their initial review of the mental health court in Broward County, discovered that the court used several diagnostic tools to determine an individual's competence and allowed the individual to choose whether or not to participate in the mental health court process. Also, Honberg (2002) found no evidence supporting the coerciveness of mental health courts and instead indicated "that judges are bending over backwards to protect the rights of and afford due process to individuals who come through [mental health] courts" (p. 36). Similarly, Rivera (2004) reported that when given the option, nearly 95% of clients in one mental health court opted for treatment in the community. Since participants were allowed to choose, Rivera did not find the mental health court process coercive and asserted that those who opted for processing via the mental health court were more than twice as likely to receive treatment as offenders in counties without mental health courts. Griffin et al. (2002) caution that focusing on the coercive argument may lead to undervaluing the increased benefits of teamwork between mental health and criminal justice agencies.

Balancing public safety and civil liberties in the legal arena is a tenuous task at best. "Some have argued that the informality of the mental health court and the lack of adversarial process results in a diminution of individual rights that need[s] to be preserved in the criminal courts" (Petrila, 2002, p. 2). Hardin (1993), however, counters: "Far from respecting civil liberties, legal obstacles to treating the mentally ill limit or destroy the liberty of the person." Undoubtedly, this debate with regard to mental health courts will continue for some time.

---

7. Sometimes laws on privacy can be more restrictive than HIPAA dictates, however, and may require modification to facilitate the sharing of information from one system to another. In similar fashion to the process used in the mental health court in Broward County, Florida, Texas jailers are able to divert detainees with mental illnesses from the criminal justice system to treatment by cross-referencing new detainees in databases connected with mental health centers across the state and identifying those in need of mental health treatment (Wolf, 2006). Likewise, via a data-link, which required a change in state law, anyone booked into the Cook County Jail in Chicago can be cross-checked with the mental health client list for the state of Illinois to see if he/she has received mental health services in the past three years (Murphy et al., 2007).

Stigmatization and Criminalization

Some express concern that persons who are identified as mentally ill and are processed through a specialized mental health court docket will be stigmatized (Clark, 2004). Moreover, some argue that while all courts under the Americans with Disabilities Act (ADA) have a duty to accommodate persons with mental illnesses, development of specialized mental health courts blatantly segregates persons with mental illnesses (see Wilborn-Malloy, 2006). Thus, some maintain that mental health courts can be doubly stigmatizing, as persons are singled out for having a mental illness and are then labeled via their involvement in the criminal process (see Miller & Perelman, 2009). Proponents of mental health courts counter that compliance with mental health court requirements, attaining suitable treatment, and possibly avoiding a criminal record in the future are less stigmatizing, more hopeful, and more benevolent than the recycling of persons with mental illnesses through the system (Petrila et al., 2001). Indeed, the alternative to mental health court is imprisoning persons with mental illnesses for actions over which they had little control, giving them little to no treatment while their symptoms worsen, with no plans for community follow-up; this process guarantees failure via recidivism and is expensive for taxpayers.

Despite the above argument about the alternative to mental health courts (e.g., the traditional system and recycling through the jails), some insist that mental health courts may actually result in criminalization of people with mental illness and/or widen the net of criminal justice control over the citizenry (Barr, 2001; Clark, 2004; Haimowitz, 2002). First, with mental health courts in place, prosecutors might be more inclined to prosecute individuals with mental illness who would have otherwise been released (e.g., those charged with misdemeanors), considering the courts the opportunity to force treatment (Slate, 2000). Likewise, defendants in mental health courts tend to receive longer sentences and/or be under the court's scrutiny for longer periods of time than those processed through the traditional criminal justice system (Haimowitz, 2002).

Those who argue that mental health courts breed criminalization and net widening offer several solutions. Some mental health advocates argue that misdemeanants should be excluded from mental health court jurisdiction as a matter of course (Levin, 2006). According to the Bazelon Center for Mental Health Law,

> [M]isdemeanants are ill suited for mental health courts because they should be diverted from the criminal justice system entirely [via] prebooking diversion programs.... Mental health courts should close their doors to people charged with misdemeanors[,] as [s]ome ... jails will not accept misdemeanants (primarily because of overcrowding) regardless of mental health status (Redlich et al., 2005, p. 537).

Bernstein and Seltzer (2003) recommend that mental health courts only be utilized when individuals are facing significant jail or prison time. In any case, protection of individual rights and provision of appropriate levels of community mental health services should be ensured at all times.

If mental health courts are going to continue, Haimowitz (2002) advocates models that defer adjudication for an extensive period of time to give treatment an opportunity to work and avoid findings of guilt or guilty pleas. This is based on the premise that reintegration into the community and lowered recidivism rates are more likely to be accomplished by those courts that do not accept guilty pleas, as having a criminal record — even if from pleading guilty in order to be involved in a mental health court instead of a traditional court — hampers obtainment of housing and meaningful employment opportunities (Seltzer, 2005).

Conclusion

It would behoove administrators and benefit taxpayers to explore more fiscally sound and effective alternatives to incarceration through such mechanisms as mental health courts. In a short period of time, mental health courts have enjoyed significant success in reducing recidivism rates of persons with mental illnesses who encounter the criminal justice system, and Acquaviva (2006) recommends that short-sighted policymakers should begin funding these model court projects indefinitely instead of relying on temporary grants.

Bruce Winick, now deceased, is considered one of the pioneers of the therapeutic jurisprudence movement, acknowledges that some alternatives, like assertive community treatment and police diversion programs, may indeed be better interventions than utilizing mental health courts (Stefan & Winick, 2005). However, Winick favored the use of mental health courts over the criminalization of persons with mental illnesses, realizing that the mental health system has a tendency to drop its problems on the courthouse doorsteps (Stefan & Winick, 2005). Haimowitz (2002) does not see mental health courts as the only answer but agrees that they can be part of the solution. Lurigio et al. (2001) contend that the implementation of an integrated, specialized mental health court is a step toward establishing "a unified, accountable, case management system for maintaining the mentally ill in the community" (p. 188).

Certainly, the initial costs associated with mental health courts may seem excessive. The initial outlay of resources and personnel costs of a mental health court may be higher than the current total expenditures for incarceration of persons with mental illnesses. Initially guaranteeing treatment services and access to antipsychotic medications may be more expensive than merely putting persons in jail and having them mentally decompensate. Overall, it may take 18 months or longer from the initiation of a diversionary program, such as a mental health court, before positive returns can be realized (Steadman, 2003), However, the long-range objective must be to prevent people from recycling through the system. We must vigilantly collect outcome data to show the advantages of mental health courts.

In consideration of the consequences of past shortsighted decisions rendered, Goldkamp and Irons-Guynn (2000) contend that the establishment of mental health courts operating on the principles of therapeutic jurisprudence will produce collaborative changes in the mental health and criminal justice systems that will link individuals to appropriate treatment and halt the recidivism of persons with mental illnesses through the criminal justice system. When that occurs, mental health courts will have served their purpose and will no longer be necessary. However, until that time there are not enough mental health court judges that are sufficiently motivated and positioned to require all parties, including mental health providers, to be responsible and avert unnecessary suffering for persons with mental illnesses and society.

Change in bureaucracies is slow and arduous. History indicates that collaboration between the criminal justice and mental health systems has been difficult and infrequent. Sensitivity, awareness, and political activation of judges will force collaborations and determine, to a large extent, the success of alternatives to imprisonment for the mentally ill offender. The next chapter examines persons with mental illnesses in prisons.

References

A conversation with the experts: The future of problem-solving courts. (2010, June 15). Transcript of symposium panel discussion. *University of Maryland Law Journal of Race, Religion, Gender and Class, 10*, 137–160.

Acquaviva, G. L. (2006). Mental health courts: No longer experimental. *Seton Hall Law Review, 36*, 971–1013.

Almquist, L., & Dodd, E. (2009). *Mental health courts: A guide to research-informed policy and practice.* New York, NY: Council of State Governments Justice Center. Retrieved from http://consensusproject.org/jc_publications/mental-health-courts-a-guide-to-research-informed-policy-and-practice/Mental_Health_Court_Research_Guide.pdf.

America's Law Enforcement and Mental Health Project, S. 1865, 106th Cong. (1999).

Andrews, D. A., Bonta, J., & Wormith, J. S. (2006). The recent past and near future of risk and/or need assessment. *Crime & Delinquency, 52*(1), 7–27.

Barr, H. (2001). *Mental health courts: An advocate's perspective.* New York, NY: Urban Justice Center. Retrieved from http://www.urbanjustice.org/publications/pdfs/mentalhealth/Mental HealthCourts.pdf.

Bernstein, R., & Seltzer, T. (2003). The role of mental health courts in system reform. *University of the District of Columbia Law Review, 7*, 143–162.

Binder, R. (2015). Mental health courts: An effective alternative to incarceration. *Psychiatric News*, November 12.

Boothroyd, R. A., Mercado, C. C., Poythress, N. G., Christy, A., & Petrila, J. (2005). Clinical outcomes of defendants in mental health court. *Psychiatric Services, 56*(7), 829–834.

Boothroyd, R. A., Poythress, N. G., McGaha, A., & Petrila, J. (2003). The Broward County mental health court: process, outcomes, and service utilization. *International Journal of Law and Psychiatry, 26*(1), 55–71.

Bossolo, L. (2004, November 4). *Mentally Ill Offender Treatment and Crime Reduction Act becomes law.* Washington, D.C.: American Psychological Association. Retrieved from http://www.apa.org/releases/S1194_law.html.

Boyle, T. (1998, January 22). Special court for mentally ill seen in March: Need recognized for 'awful long time,' judge says. *The Toronto Star*, p. B3.

Broward County Circuit Court. (1997). *Administrative order: Creation of a Mental Health Court Subdivision within the County Criminal Court Division.* Issued by D. Ross, Chief Judge, Seventeenth Judicial Circuit, Broward County, FL.

Bozza, J. A. (2007). Benevolent behavior modification: Understanding the nature and limitations of problem-solving courts. *Widener Law Journal, 17*, 97–143.

California Realignment. (2011). *Mental health: San Francisco Behavioral Health Court.* Retrieved from http://www.calrealignment.org/resource-directory/tools/mental-health.html.

Burns, J. (2014). A restorative justice model for mental health courts. *Southern California Review, Law & Social Justice, 23*, 427–455. Callahan, L., Cocozza, J., Steadman, H. J., & Tillman, S. (2012). A national survey of U.S. juvenile mental health courts. *Psychiatric Services, 63*(2), 130–134.

Carter, A. (2009). Fixing Florida's mental health courts: Addressing the needs of the mentally ill by moving away from criminalization to investing in community mental health. *Journal of Law in Society, 10*(1), 1–32.

Castellano, U. (2011). The politics of benchcraft: The role of judges in mental health courts. *Law & Social Inquiry, 42*(2), 398–422.

Castellano, U. (2011). Courting compliance: Case managers as "double agents" in the mental health court. *Law and Social Inquiry, 36*, 484–511.

Cavanaugh, J. M. (2011). Helping those who serve: Veterans treatment courts foster rehabilitation and reduce recidivism for offending combat veterans. *New England Law Review, 45*, 463–488.

Christy, A., Poythress, N. G., Boothroyd, R. A., Petrila, J., & Mehra, S. (2005). Evaluating the efficiency and community safety goals of the Broward County mental health court. *Behavioral Sciences & the Law, 23*(2), 227–243.

Clark, J. (2004). *Non-specialty first appearance court models for diverting persons with mental illness: Alternatives to mental health courts.* Delmar, NY: GAINS Center, Technical Assistance and Policy Analysis Center for Jail Diversion.

Cook County Sheriff's Office. (2012). *Justice and Mental Health Court.* Chicago, IL: Author. Retrieved from http://www.cookcountysheriff.org/womens_justice_services/wjs_MentalHealth.html.

Corrigan, P.W., Druss, B.G., & Perlick, D.A. (2014). The impact of mental illness stigma on seeking and participating in mental health care. *Psychological Science in the Public Interest, 15*(2), 37–70.

Cosden, M., Ellens, J., Schnell, J., & Yamini-Diouf, Y. (2005). Efficacy of a mental health treatment court with assertive community treatment. *Behavioral Sciences and the Law, 23*(2), 199–214.

Costopoulos, J.S. & Wellman, B.L. (2017). The effectiveness of one mental health court: Overcoming criminal history. *Psychology Injury and Law, 10,* 254–263.

Council of State Governments. (2005a). *A guide to mental health court design and implementation.* New York, NY: Author.

Council of State Governments. (2005b). *Mental health courts: A national snapshot.* Washington, D.C.: Bureau of Justice Assistance, Office of Justice Programs, U.S. Department of Justice. Retrieved from http://www.ojp.usdoj.gov/BJA/pdf/MHC_National_Snapshot.pdf.

Council of State Governments. (2005c, October). *San Francisco Behavioral Health Court to focus on women with mental illness.* New York, NY: Author. Retrieved from http://consensusproject.org/updates/announcements-and-events/Oct-2005/SFBHC-announcement.

Council of State Governments. (2008). *Mental health courts: A primer for policymakers and practitioners.* New York, NY: Author. Retrieved from http://consensusproject.org/mhcp/mhc-primer.pdf.

Council of State Governments. (2012). *$9 million slated for the Mentally Ill Offender Treatment and Crime Reduction Act in 2013.* New York, NY: Author. Retrieved from http://consensusproject.org/announcements/9-dollars-million-slated-for-the-mentally-ill-offender-treatment-and-crime-reduction-act-in-2013.

Cowart, G. R. (1997). Mission statement. *Mental Health Court News, 1*(1), 3.

Cummings, J. E. (2010). The cost of crazy: How therapeutic jurisprudence and mental health courts lower incarceration costs, reduce recidivism, and improve public safety. *Loyola Law Review, 56,* 279–310.

Daicoff, S. (2006). Law as a healing profession: The "comprehensive law movement." *Pepperdine Dispute Resolution Law Journal, 6,* 1–61.

Daniel, J., Tillery, A., & Whitehead, D. (2009). Fresno's behavioral health court: A better way to serve youth. *Clearinghouse Review: Journal of Poverty Law and Policy, 43,* 43–48.

Denckla, D., & Berman, G. (2001). *Rethinking the revolving door: A look at mental illness in the courts.* New York, NY: Center for Court Innovation/State Justice Institute. Retrieved from http://www.courtinnovation.org/pdf/mental_health.pdf.

Elwell, M. F. (1998). *Broward County's mental health court: An emergency response to mentally ill petty offenders.* Rockville, MD: National Institute of Corrections, National Institute of Justice.

Ennis, A.R. et al., (2016). The role of gender in mental health court admission and completion. *Canadian Journal of Criminal Justice, 58*(1), 1–30.

Eschbach, L.A., Dalgin, R.S., & Pantucci, E. (2018). A three stage model for mental health treatment court: A qualitative analysis of graduates' perspectives. *Community Mental Health Journal.*

Fader-Towe, H., & Louison, A. M. (2012, March). *Moving beyond mental health courts: Introduction to the range of court-based initiatives.* Justice and Mental Health Collaboration Program Grantee Orientation Meeting, New York, NY. Retrieved from http://www.cases.org/resources/presentations/Moving%20Beyond%20MH%20Courts.pdf.

Fields, G. (2006, August 21). In Brooklyn court, a route out of jail for the mentally ill. *Wall Street Journal*, p. A1.

Finkelman, D., & Grisso, T. (1994). Therapeutic jurisprudence: From idea to application. *New England Journal on Criminal and Civil Confinement, 20*, 243–257.

Finkelstein, H., & Brawley, D. (1997). The mission of the mental health court is to address the unique needs of the mentally ill in our criminal justice system. *Mental Health Court News, 1*(1), 1–2.

Fisler, C. (2015). Toward a new understanding of mental health courts. *Judges'Journal, 54*(2), 8–13.

Fisler, C. (2005). Building trust and managing risk: A look at a felony mental health court. *Psychology, Public Policy, and Law, 11*, 587–604.

Florida Partners in Crisis. (2011, January 6). *Judicial education project ramps up.* Merritt Island, FL: Author. Retrieved from http://flpic.org/news/judicial-education-project-work-ramps-up.html.

Glassberg, H., & Dodd, E. (2008). *A guide to the role of crime victims in mental health courts.* New York, NY: Council of State Governments Justice Center. Retrieved from http://consensusproject.org/downloads/guidetocvinmhc.pdf.

Goldkamp, J. S., & Irons-Guynn, C. (2000). *Emerging judicial strategies for the mentally ill in the criminal caseload: Mental health courts in Fort Lauderdale, Seattle, San Bernardino, and Anchorage.* Washington, D.C.: U.S. Department of Justice, Office of Justice Programs, Bureau of Justice Assistance.

Griffin, P. A., Steadman, H. J., & Petrila, J. (2002). The use of criminal charges and sanctions in mental health courts. *Psychiatric Services, 53*(10), 1285–1289.

Gruber, J. & Saxbe, D. (February 27, 2018). Five improvements we should make to mental health care. *Slate.*

Gunther, J. B. (2005). Reflections on the challenging proliferation of mental health issues in the district court and the need for judicial education. *Maine Law Review, 57*, 541–552.

Hafemeister, T. L., Garner, S. G., & Bath, V. E. (2012). Forging links and renewing ties: Applying the principles of restorative and procedural justice to better respond to criminal offenders with a mental disorder. *Buffalo Law Review, 60,* 147–223.

Haimowitz, S. (2002). Can mental health courts end the criminalization of persons with mental illness? *Psychiatric Services, 53*(10), 1226–1228.

Hardin, H. (1993, July 22). Uncivil liberties. *Vancouver Sun.* Retrieved from http://www.psychlaws.org/GeneralResources/Article1.htm.

Hasselbrack, A. M. (2001). Opting in to mental health courts. *Corrections Compendium, 26*(10), 4–25.

Herinckx, H. A., Swart, S. C., Shane, M. A., Dolezal, C. D., & King, S. (2005). Rearrest and linkage to mental health services among clients of the Clark County Mental Health Court Program. *Psychiatric Services, 56*(7), 853–857.

Hiday, V. A., Moore, M. E., Lamoureaux, M., & Magistris, J. D. (2005). North Carolina's mental health court. *Popular Government, 70*(3), 24–30.

Hiday, V. A., & Ray, B. (2010). Arrests two years after exiting a well-established mental health court. *Psychiatric Services, 61*(5), 463–468.

Honberg, R. S. (2002, December). Mental health courts: An alternative to criminalization. *Attention @ chadd.org,* 34–39. Retrieved from http://www.chadd.org/webpage.cfm?cat_id'7&subcat_id'38.

Johnson, M., & Johnson, L. A. (2012). Bail: Reforming policies to address overcrowded jails, the impact of race on detention, and community revival in Harris County, Texas. *Northwestern Journal of Law & Social Policy, 7,* 42–85.

Keele, C. E. (2002). Criminalization of the mentally ill: The challenging role of the defense attorney in the mental health court system. *University of Missouri-Kansas City Law Review, 71,* 193–210.

Kelly, M.M. (2015). Rehabilitation through empowerment: Adopting the consumer-participation model for treatment planning in mental health courts. *Case Western Reserve Law Review, 66*(2), 581–607.

Kimber, K. (2008). Mental health courts: Idaho's best kept secret. *Idaho Law Review, 45,* 249–282.

Knopf, A. (2011, November 15). Up to one in four incarcerations should be prevented. *Behavioral Healthcare, 31*(8). Retrieved from http://www.behavioral.net/article/one-four-incarcerations-should-be-prevented.

Kozdron, N. A. (2009). Midwestern juveniles drug courts: Analysis & recommendations. *Indiana Law Journal, 84,* 373–396.

Kubiak, S., Roddy, J., Comartin, E., & Tillander, E. (2015). Cost analysis of long-term outcomes of an urban mental health court. *Evaluation and Program Planning.* Retrieved from https://pubmed.ncbi.nlm.nih.gov/25982871/.

Lamb, H. R., Weinberger, L. E., & Reston-Parham, C. (1996). Court intervention to address the mental health needs of mentally ill offenders. *Psychiatric Services, 47*(3), 275–281.

Lanni, A. (2005). The future of community justice. *Harvard Civil Rights-Civil Liberties Law Review, 40*, 359–405.

Lerner-Wren G. with Eckland, R.A. (2018). *A court of refuge: Stories from the bench of America's first mental health court.* Boston, MA: Beacon Press.

Levin, A. (2006). MH courts garner mostly favorable reviews. *Psychiatric News, 41*(8), 32–37.

Linhorst, D.M. & Dirks-Linhorst, P.A. (2015). Mental health courts development, outcomes, and future challenges. *Judges' Journal, 54*(2), 22–27.

Lurigio, A. J., & Swartz, J. A. (2000). Changing the contours of the criminal justice system to meet the needs of persons with serious mental illness. In J. Horney (Ed.), *Policies, processes, and decisions of the criminal justice system* (pp. 45–108). Washington, D.C.: U.S. Department of Justice, National Institute of Justice.

Lurigio, A. J., Watson, A., Luchins, D. J., & Hanrahan, P. (2001). Therapeutic jurisprudence in action: Specialized courts for the mentally ill. *Judicature, 84*(4), 184–189.

Luskin, M.L. & Ray B. (2015). Selection into mental health court: Distinguishing among eligible defendants. *Criminal Justice and Behavior, 42*(11), 1145–1158.

Mason, B. G. (2005, October). Mental health courts: The newest development in problem-solving courts and therapeutic jurisprudence. *The Nebraska Lawyer*, 4–8.

Mays, G. L., & Thompson, J. A. (1991). The political and organizational context of American jails. In J. A. Thompson & G. L. Mays (Eds.), *American jails: Public policy issues* (pp. 3–21). Chicago, IL: Nelson-Hall.

McCampbell, S. W. (2001). Mental health courts: What sheriffs need to know. *Sheriff, 53*(2), 40–43.

McGaha, A., Boothroyd, R. A., Poythress, N. G., Petrila, J., & Ott, R. G. (2002). Lessons from the Broward County mental health court evaluation. *Evaluation and Program Planning, 25*, 125–135.

Mikhail, S., Akinkunmi, A., & Poythress, N. (2001). Mental health courts: A workable proposition? *Psychiatric Bulletin, 25*, 5–7.

Miller, R. D. (1997). Symposium on coercion: An interdisciplinary examination of coercion, exploitation, and the law: III. Coerced confinement and treatment: The continuum of coercion: Constitutional and clinical considerations in the treatment of mentally disordered persons. *Denver University Law Review, 74*, 1169–1214.

Miller, S. L., & Perelman, A. M. (2009). Mental health courts: An overview and redefinition of tasks and goals. *Law & Psychology Review, 33*, 113–123.

Mills, J. (1979). I have nothing to do with justice. In J. J. Bonsignore, E. Katsh, P. d'Errico, R. Pipkin, & S. Arons (Eds.), *Before the law: An introduction to the legal process* (2nd ed., pp. 239–252). Boston, MA: Houghton Mifflin Company.

Moore, M. E., & Hiday, V. A. (2006). Mental health court outcomes: A comparison of re-arrest and re-arrest severity between mental health court and traditional court participants. *Law and Human Behavior, 30*(6), 659–674.

Morabito, M. S. (2007). Horizons of context: Understanding the police decision to arrest people with mental illness. *Psychiatric Services, 58*(12), 1582–1587.

Murphy, J., Friedman, F., & Andriukaitis, S. (2007, June 22). *How NAMI members can contribute to building CIT in your community*. Paper presented at the National Alliance on Mental Illness Annual Convention, San Diego, CA.

National Public Radio. (2011). *Nation's jails struggle with mentally ill prisoners*. Retrieved from http://www.wbur.org/npr/140167676/nations-jails-struggle-with-mentally-ill-prisoners.

Odergaard, A. M. (2007). Therapeutic jurisprudence: The impact of mental health courts on the criminal justice system. *North Dakota Law Review, 83*, 225–259.

Osher, F. (2012). *Responding to adults with substance abuse and mental health needs under correctional supervision*. Paper presented at the Council of State Governments Justice Center's Making the Most of Second Chances Conference, Washington, D.C. Retrieved from http://www.nationalreentryresourcecenter.org/documents/0000/1465/Respon ding_to_Adults_with_BH_Needs.pdf.

Osher, F., Steadman, H. J., & Barr, H. (2003). A best practice approach to community reentry from jails for inmates with co-occurring disorders: The APIC model. *Crime & Delinquency, 49*(1), 79–96.

Osher, F., & Taxman, F. S. (2011). *Understanding criminogenic needs: Untangling the role of mental health and substance abuse*. Paper presented at the Council of State Governments Justice Center Making the Most of Second Chances Conference, Washington, D.C. Retrieved from http://www.nationalreentryresourcecenter.org/documents/0000/0999/Taxman_Osher.pdf.

Pawel, M. A. (2001). Imprisoning the mentally ill: Does it matter? *Criminal Justice Ethics, 20*(1), 2, 66.

Perlin, M.L. & Weinstein, N.M. (2016). Said I, but you have no choice: Why a lawyer must ethically honor a client's decision about mental health treatment even if it is not what s/he would have chosen. *Cardozo Public Law Policy & Ethics Journal, 15*(73), 73–116.

Peters, R. H., & Osher, F. C. (2003). *Co-occurring disorders and specialty courts*. Delmar, NY: GAINS Center.

Petrila, J. (1998). Courts as gatekeepers in managed care settings. *Health Affairs, 17*(2), 109–117.

Petrila, J. (2002, November). *Policy brief: The effectiveness of the Broward mental health court: An evaluation*. Tampa, FL: University of South Florida, Department of Mental Health Law & Policy, Louis de la Parte Florida Mental Health Institute.

Petrila, J., Poythress, N. G., McGaha, A., & Boothroyd, R. A. (2001). Preliminary observations from an evaluation of the Broward County mental health court. *Court Review, 37*, 14–22.

Poythress, N., Petrila, J., McGaha, A., & Boothroyd, R. (2002). Perceived coercion and procedural justice in the Broward mental health court. *International Journal of Law and Psychiatry, 25*(5), 517–533.

Quinn, M. (2009). The modern problem-solving court movement: Domination of discourse and untold stories of criminal justice. *Washington University Journal of Law & Policy, 31*, 57–82.

Rasenick, M. (January 24, 2017). Mental health research is stagnant: Here's why. *Care for Your Mind.*

Raybon, K. (1997). State attorney perspective. *Mental Health Court News, 1*(1), 2–3.

Redlich, A. D. (2005). Voluntary, but knowing and intelligent? Comprehension in mental health courts. *Psychology, Public Policy, and Law, 11*, 605–621.

Redlich, A. D., Hoover, S., Summers, A., & Steadman, H. J. (2010). Enrollment in mental health courts: Voluntariness, knowingness, and adjudicative competence. *Law and Human Behavior, 34* (2), 91–104.

Redlich, A. D., Siyu, L., Steadman, H. J., Callahan, L., & Robbins, P.C. (2012). Is diversion swift? Comparing mental health court and traditional criminal justice processing. *Criminal Justice and Behavior, 39*(4), 420–433.

Redlich, A. D., Steadman, H. J., Callahan, L., Robbins, P. C., Vessilinov, R., & Ozdogru, A. A. (2010). The use of mental health court appearances in supervision. *International Journal of Law and Psychiatry, 33*, 272–277.

Redlich, A. D., Steadman, H. J., Petrila, J., Monahan, J., & Griffin, P. A. (2005). The second generation of mental health courts. *Psychology, Public Policy, and Law, 11*, 527–538.

Rendo, J. (2012). *Mental health courts.* West Valley City, UT: National Alliance on Mental Illness, Utah. Retrieved from http://www.namiut.org/component/content/article/23/115-mental-health-courts.

Ridgely, M. S., Engberg, J., Greenberg, M. D., Turner, S., DeMartini, C., & Dembosky, J. W. (2007). *Justice, treatment, and cost: An evaluation of the fiscal impact of Allegheny County Mental Health Court.* Santa Monica, CA: Rand Corporation. Retrieved from http://www.rand.org/pubs/technical_reports/2007/RAND_TR439.pdf.

Rivera, R. M. (2004). The mentally ill offender: A brighter tomorrow through the eyes of the Mentally Ill Offender Treatment and Crime Reduction Act of 2004. *Cleveland State University Journal of Law and Health, 19*, 107–139.

Rossman, S. B., Willison, J. B., Mallik-Kane, K., Kim, K., Debus-Sherill, S., & Downey, P. M. (2012a). *Criminal justice interventions for offenders with mental illnesses: Evaluation of mental health courts in Bronx and Brooklyn, New York.* Washington, D.C.: U.S. Department of Justice. Retrieved from http://www.urban.org/UploadedPDF/412603-Criminal-Justice-Interventions-for-Offenders-With-Mental-Illness.pdf.

Rossman, S. B., Willison, J. B., Mallik-Kane, K., Kim, K., Debus-Sherill, S., & Downey, P. M. (2012b). *Criminal justice interventions for offenders with mental illnesses: Evaluation of mental health courts in Bronx and Brooklyn, New York, Executive Summary.* Washington, D.C.: U.S. Department of Justice. Retrieved from https://www.ncjrs.gov/pdffiles1/nij/grants/238265.pdf.

SAMHSA (2021). Adult mental health treatment court locator. *U.S. Department of Health and Human Services.* Retrieved from https://www.samhsa.gov/gains-center/mental-health-treatment-court-locator/adults.

Seltzer, T. (2005). Mental health courts: A misguided attempt to address the criminal justice system's unfair treatment of people with mental illnesses. *Psychology, Public Policy, and Law, 11,* 570–586.

Skeem, J. (2009). *Individuals with mental illnesses in the criminal justice system: Addressing both criminogenic risks and mental health needs.* Washington, D.C.: U.S. Department of Justice, Bureau of Justice Assistance, Justice and Mental Health Collaboration Program Webinar. Retrieved from http://www.slideserve.com/telyn/individuals-with-mental-illnesses-in-the-criminal-justice-system-addressing-both-criminogenic-risks-and-mental-health-n.

Slate, R. N. (2000). Courts for mentally ill offenders: Necessity or abdication of responsibility. In G. L. Mays & P. R. Gregware (Eds.), *Courts and justice* (2nd ed., pp. 432–450). Prospect Heights, IL: Waveland Press.

Slate, R. N. (2003). From the jailhouse to capitol hill: Impacting mental health court legislation and defining what constitutes a mental health court. *Crime & Delinquency, 49*(1), 6–29.

Steadman, H. J. (2003, June 24). Technical Assistance and Policy Analysis Center for Jail Diversion Meeting, Bethesda, MD.

Steadman, H. J. (2005). *A guide to collecting mental health court outcome data.* New York, NY: Council of State Governments.

Steadman, H. J. (2007, June 21). *Treatment not jails: New leadership and promising practices.* Paper presented at the National Alliance on Mental Illness (NAMI) Annual Convention, San Diego, CA.

Steadman, H. J. (2008). Foreword. In R. N. Slate & W. W. Johnson, *Criminalization of mental illness: Crisis and opportunity for the justice system.* Durham, NC: Carolina Academic Press.

Steadman, H. J., Davidson, S., & Brown, C. (2001). Mental health courts: Their promise and unanswered questions. *Psychiatric Services, 52*(4), 457–458.

Steadman, H. J., Morris, S. M., & Dennis, D. L. (1995). The diversion of mentally ill persons from jails to community-based services: A profile of programs. *American Journal of Public Health, 85*(12), 1630–1635.

Stefan, S., & Winick, B. J. (2005). Foreword: A dialogue on mental health courts. *Psychology, Public Policy, and Law, 11,* 507–526.

Stone, T. H. (1997). Therapeutic implications of incarceration for persons with severe mental disorders: Searching for rational health policy. *American Journal of Criminal Law, 24,* 283–358.

Sublet, C. (2005). Has the cold mercy of custodial institutionalization been supplanted by the cold merciless steel of the jailhouse? *Kansas Journal of Law & Public Policy, 15,* 159–183.

Substance Abuse and Mental Health Services Administration [SAMHSA]. (2007). *Grant announcement: Targeted capacity expansion grants for jail diversion programs.* Rockville, MD: Author. Retrieved from http://www.samhsa.gov/Grants/2007/SM_07_004.aspx.

Talesh, S. (2007). Mental health court judges as dynamic risk managers: A new conceptualization of the role of judges. *Depaul Law Review, 57,* 93–132.

The law of mental illness. (2008). Mental health courts and the trend toward a rehabilitative justice system. *Harvard Law Review, 121,* 1168–1179.

Thomas, M. (2011, March 12). States make deep cuts in mental health funding. *Chicago Sun-Times.* Retrieved from http://www.suntimes.com/news/metro/4224421-418/states-make-deep-cuts-in-mental-health-funding.html?print=true.

Thompson, M., Osher, F., & Tomasini-Joshi, D. (2007). *Improving responses to people with mental illnesses: The essential elements of a mental health court.* New York, NY: Council of State Governments Justice Center, Criminal justice/Mental Health Consensus Project, Bureau of Justice Assistance. Retrieved from http://consensusproject.org/mhcp/essential.elements.pdf.

Tonry, M. (2006). Purposes and functions of sentencing. *Crime and Justice, 34,* 1–53.

Trupin, E., & Richards, H. (2003). Seattle's mental health courts: Early indicators of effectiveness. *International Journal of Law and Psychiatry, 26*(1), 33–53.

Van Duizend, R. V. (2008). The implications of an aging population for the state courts. In C. R. Flango, A. M. McDowell, C. F. Campbell, & N. B. Kauder (Eds.), *Future Trends in State Courts, 2008* (pp. 76–80). Williamsburg, VA: National Center for State Courts. Retrieved from http://contentdm.ncsconline.org/cgi-bin/showfile.exe?CISOROOT=/famct&CISOPTR=208.

Vickers, A. D. (2001). Attorney education about mental illnesses. *Catalyst, 3*(4), 2–4.

Walls, S. (2011). The need for special veterans courts. *Denver of International Law & Policy, 39,* 695–729.

Walsh, J., & Bricourt, J. (1997). Services for persons with mental illness in jail: Implications for family involvement. *Families in Society: The Journal of Contemporary Human Services, 78*(4), 420–428.

Watson, A., Hanrahan, P., Luchins, D., & Lurigio, A. (2001). Mental health courts and the complex issue of mentally ill offenders. *Psychiatric Services, 52*(4), 477–481.

Watson, A., Luchins, D., Hanrahan, P., Heyrman, M. J., & Lurigio, A. (2000). Mental health court: Promises and limitations. *Journal of the American Academy of Psychiatry and the Law, 28,* 476–482.

Wexler, D. B., & Winick, B. J. (1996). *Law in therapeutic key: Developments in therapeutic jurisprudence.* Durham, NC: Carolina Academic Press.

Wilborn-Malloy, S. E. (2006). Mental health courts and Title II of the ADA: Accessibility to state court systems for individuals with mental disabilities and the need for diversion. *St. Louis Public Law Review, 25,* 307–349.

Winick, B. J. (1997). The jurisprudence of therapeutic jurisprudence. *Psychology, Public Policy, and Law, 3,* 184–206.

Wolf, S. (2006). Criminal law: Mentally impaired offenders and the criminal justice system. *Texas Bar Journal, 69,* 244–247.

Wolff, N. (2018). Are mental health courts target efficient? *International Journal of Law and Psychiatry, 57,* 67–76.

Wolff, N., & Pogorzelski, W. (2005). Measuring the effectiveness of mental health courts: Challenges and recommendations. *Psychology, Public Policy, and Law, 11*(4), 539–569.

Wolff, N., Bekenko, S., Fabrikant, N., & Huening, J. (2011). Mental health courts and their selection processes: Modeling variation for consistency. *Law & Human Behavior, 35*(5), 402–412.

Wolff, N., Fabrikant, N., Balenko, S. (2011). Mental health courts and their selection processes: Modeling variation for consistency. *Law and Human Behavior, 35*(5), 1–15.

World Health Organization (2004). Prevalence, severity, and unmet need for treatment of mental disorders in the world health organization world mental health surveys. *Journal of the American Medical Association, 291*(21), 2581–2590.

Wren, G. L. (2010). Mental health courts: Serving justice and promoting recovery. *Annals of Health Law, 19,* 577–593.

Yermish, S. N. (2009). An overview of the ethical issues created by problem-solving courts and the mentally ill client: The NACDL task force issues a report and calls for reform. *The Champion, 33,* 14–17.

Zamir, N. (2011). Problem-solving litigation for the elderly: An eventual shift with a cautionary approach. *Journal of Civil Rights & Economic Development, 25,* 1023–1049.

Chapter 9

Mental Illness in the Prison Population: Secure and Treat?

"The degree of civilization in a society can be judged by entering its prisons."

— Fyodor Dostoevsky[1]

"It is deplorable and outrageous that this (TX) state's prisons appear to have become a repository for a great number of its mentally ill citizens. Persons who, with psychiatric care, could fit well into society are instead locked away, to become wards of the state's penal system. Then, in a tragically ironic twist, they may be confined in conditions that nurture, rather than abate, their psychoses."

— Judge William Wayne Justice[2]

Approximately a half million people were treated in state mental hospitals in the 1950s. Between 1960 and 2010 there was a 90% decrease in the number of state hospital beds (Insel, 2010). Between 2010 and 2016 state hospital beds decreased another 17% resulting in an additional loss of more than 6,000 beds. In 2016, there were 7,679 beds remaining in state hospitals. Since the 1950s, there has been a 96.5% drop from peak hospital numbers in the 1950s (Fuller et al. 2016). This continuous decline in state hospital beds has resulted in substantial increases in the incarceration of individuals living with mental illness.

Public policy has been significantly influenced by anecdotes and exceptional news headlines, contributing to increases in the incarceration of persons with mental illnesses (Vitiello, 2010). As has also been discussed previously in this book, this transinstitutionalization from state hospitals to the custody of the criminal justice system is due to a number of reasons including deinstitutionalization and restriction of civil commitment criteria; increased reliance on already overextended and underfunded community mental health services; the relatively high costs of psychiatric hospital-

---

1. Cohen (2012).
2. *Ruiz v. Johnson* (1999, p. 915).

ization, changes in Medicaid policies, and thus a significant decrease in the number of long-term commitments; and the ease of police placement of persons with mental illnesses in jail. This trend is aggravated by the fact that inmates with severe mental disorders spend more time in prison and jails than offenders that are not living with mental illness. This is caused by the stigma of mental illness, the paucity of effective prison mental health treatment, and the inability of community mental health services to provide adequate post-release supervision and care. Prolonged periods of institutionalization in correctional settings has a cyclical effect: Extended confinement tends to sustain and/or exacerbate abnormal and maladaptive behaviors for inmates with mental illness, which leads to more disciplinary infractions and loss of "good time," and ultimately to longer periods of confinement and treatment (Teplin, 1994). All of this combines to have a backlog effect, as discussed in Chapter 1.

In total, there are a substantial number of inmates with mental illness in prisons. Naturally, persons with serious mental illness are three times more likely than those without to be incarcerated (Inglot, 2011). Furthermore, individuals with mental illness are three times more likely to be in the criminal justice system than hospitals (Fellner, 2006; Leifman, 2001; Lerner-Wren, 2000; Torrey, Kennard, Eslinger, Lamb, & Pavle, 2010). In some states, such as Nevada and Arizona, the ratio is closer to ten times more people with mental illness in jails and prisons than in hospitals (Insel, 2010).

While the U.S. is still a global leader in the use of imprisonment, in recent years prison populations have begun to decline. Between 2008 and 2018, prison populations fell by 15%. In 2018, a little over 1.5 million were in prisons (Carson, 2019). While the small drop in the number of prison inmates in the U.S. is somewhat encouraging, the inmates who remain incarcerated are literally trapped with very few means to avoid exposure to, infection with, and in too many cases, death due to the coronavirus.

The management of offender populations requires different resources and different management strategies than those used 30 years ago. One major factor in driving change in correctional management has been the scrutiny by the United States Supreme Court, the American Civil Liberties Union, The Southern Poverty Law Center, and Human Rights Watch of virtually every aspect of corrections. While working to improve the treatment of inmates, correctional executives still struggle to balance the demands of maintaining security with the treatment needs of a growing population of offenders living with mental illness in an institutional setting.

Prisoners with Serious Mental Illness

As discussed in Chapter 1, rates of recent mental health history (i.e., within the past year from the time of analysis) range from 7% to 45% of federal inmates and 16% to 56% of state inmates (Ditton, 1999; James & Glaze, 2006).[3] Wilper et al. (2009)

---

3. The low rates are from Ditton's (1999) BJS study, whereas the high rates are from James and Glaze's (2006) BJS study, which has been criticized for using too liberal of a definition of mental illness.

found rates somewhere in between the two reports, with 14.8% of federal inmates and 25.5% of state inmates reporting a recent history of mental illness.

Not only are the numbers of mentally ill in prison increasing but there is evidence of an increase in the severity of the mental illnesses. Bloom (2010), for example, reported that approximately 15% of persons incarcerated had a serious mental illness. Blevins and Soderstrom (2012) found rates of serious mental illness in the range of 9.5% (in Southern states) to 11% (in non-Southern states).

Another rough indicator of mental illness that is frequently used is the percent of the institutional population that is prescribed psychiatric medications. Estimating current mental illness, Blevins and Soderstrom (2012) found that 14.8% to 21.3% of inmates in Southern and non-Southern states, respectively, are on psychiatric medications. Among previously treated inmates in Wilper et al.'s (2009) study, 26% of federal inmates and 30% of state inmates had been taking medication for their illness at the time of arrest.

Haney (2017) contends that many of the signs of mental illness are not obvious, are difficult to detect and that existing statistics underestimate the prevalence of mental illness among inmates. The lack of training for correctional officers to more accurately detect behaviors indicative of specific mental illnesses, administrative focus on control over treatment, and the host of practices that creates distance between inmates and correctional officers creates a "ecology of cruelty" that results in a "culture of harm" (Haney, 2018). As a result, estimates of mental illness are under reported.

Challenges Posed by Prisoners with Serious Mental Illness

The manner in which mentally ill inmates are (or are not) "treated" impacts the overall atmosphere in prison. While concerted efforts are made to structure and control prison life, they are difficult places to be for both the "kept" and the "keepers." Prisons are stressful environments for even inmates who are not mentally ill to navigate; for those with mental illnesses, prisons can be toxic and brutal environments. They are noisy, often overcrowded, filled with individuals competing for status and limited resources. They lack privacy and offer few opportunities for personal growth. "Prisons fail to adequately screen inmates for mental illness during intake, they fail to offer special programming or housing, they often fail to provide basic treatment, and they fail to address special needs upon release. The result is that mentally ill prisoners get sicker, stay longer, suffer more, and wind up back in prison soon after their release" (Ball, 2010, p. 5). Rich (2009) contends this is because prisons are more concerned about assessing risk and maintaining security than ensuring appropriate treatment for prisoners.

Mentally ill offenders can suffer from a variety of debilitating symptoms, including delusions, hallucinations, and uncontrollable mood swings. Such inmates who are cognitively and emotionally unstable present a threat to the order of prison. First, prisoners with the most severe — and especially, psychotic — mental disorders are least able to understand and abide by strict prison rules of behavior. As such, they often create more disruptions if and when they become delusional, are hallucinating, or are unable to communicate. They might engage in unsanitary and/or painful acts, such as "rub[bing] feces on themselves, stick[ing] pencils in their penises, bit[ing] chunks of flesh from their bodies, slash[ing] themselves" (Human Rights Watch, 2003, p. 30). Moreover, this behavior, fueled by delusions and hallucinations, tends to be unpredictable and, thus, the most difficult to manage in the correctional setting. Even inmates with less serious, but still distressing, disorders such as anxiety disorders (e.g., severe obsessive-compulsive disorder and severe generalized anxiety disorders) and borderline personality disorder can act out irrationally and unpredictably and pose significant management challenges.

The vast majority of Department of Corrections' Mental Health Chief Administrators (CMHCAs) in Blevins and Soderstrom's (2012) study agree that treating offenders with mental illnesses is one of the greatest challenges facing department of corrections today across the country. Furthermore, unfortunately, only 22.2% of the Southern CMHCAs and 31.3% of the CMHCAs from other states either agree or strongly agree that departments of corrections are receiving adequate legislative support regarding the treatment of offenders with mental illnesses.

Disciplinary Infractions

Available data indicate that mentally ill prisoners have higher than average disciplinary rates (Toch & Adams, 2002). Prisoners with mental illness in state and federal prisons are more likely than other inmates to have been charged with breaking prison rules (Adams, 1986; Ditton, 1999). Overall, 62% and 41% of state prisoners and federal prisoners with mental illnesses were formally charged with breaking prison rules, compared to 52% and 33% of state and federal inmates without mental illnesses, respectively (Ditton, 1999). More recently, according to James and Glaze (2006), approximately 58% and 40% of state and federal prisoners with mental illness were formally charged with institutional disciplinary violations, compared to 43% and 28% of state and federal inmates without mental illness. With regard to particular types of infractions, 21% of federal prisoners with mental illnesses were involved in at least one fight compared to only 9% of prisoners without a diagnosed mental illness; and 36% of state prisoners with mental illnesses were involved in fights compared to 25% without a diagnosed mental illness (Ditton, 1999).

Felson, Silver, and Remster (2012) examined the types of mental illness that are most related to disciplinary infractions. They analyzed the results of a survey of over 16,000 state and federal inmates nationwide. They found that psychosis and major depression were strongly related to both aggressive and non-aggressive infractions, which they interpreted to reflect a disinhibitory effect on behavior generally. In particular, consistent with prior research on mental illness and violence, as discussed in Chapter 3, paranoid thinking was the best predictor of acting out behavior in prisons.

Many mentally ill inmates serve their maximum sentence because their mental illness is not considered as a factor in disciplinary proceedings and/or parole hearings.

In 1999, Ditton reported that inmates with mental illnesses serve sentences that are approximately 15 months longer than other state prisoners. In another study, it was found that inmates with serious mental illness in Pennsylvania prisons were three times more likely to serve their maximum sentences than inmates without mental illness (Council of State Governments, 2002). In some cases, inmates with mental illness serve even longer than their original prison sentence. For example, one inmate in Ohio who was profiled in the PBS documentary, *Frontline: The New Asylums* (Navasky & O'Connor, 2005), served 13 years on a 3 year sentence. This may result from having additional criminal charges, to be distinguished from institutional disciplinary infractions, brought against one for crimes committed while incarcerated.

Clark (2018) reported that inmates with a mental illness are more likely to receive a severe punishment (segregation) compared other possible less severe sanctions such as loose privileges, given extra work, and confined to their own cell. One explanation offered was administrators may use solitary confinement to ease strain on the general prison population (Hresko, 2006). Regardless of the justification, there is substantial evidence that solitary confinement exacerbates mental illness and creates a revolving door within the prison between solitary confinement and the general prison population.

Judge Henderson, in *Madrid v. Gomez* (1995), stated that placing inmates with severe mental illnesses in isolated confinement is like putting an asthmatic in a place with little air to breathe. He asserted that the risk to them is high enough [in general population] and the risk of putting them in solitary confinement is plainly "unreasonable."

Victimization

The mental illness stigmas that most inmates and staff bring with them into prison are frequently reinforced and, in many cases, intensified in prison. Exposure to disruptive inmates with mental illness — particularly those with personality disorders, rather than serious mental illness per se — often leads others to conclude that all are merely engaging in nuisance and/or manipulative, attention-seeking behavior. Victor Hassine (1996), for example, a prisoner in Pennsylvania writing on his prison experiences, contended that the increases in mentally ill offenders have "destroyed the stability of the prison system" (p. 29). Many prisoners and staff are unfamiliar with the sometimes bizarre behaviors exhibited by prisoners with untreated mental illness and may be afraid of such individuals (Vitiello, 2010). In response, inmates and correctional officers are often annoyed by, abusive to, and/or avoid inmates with mental illness, which can further exacerbate mentally ill inmates' stigmatization, isolation, and loss of contact with reality.

Some inmates — and even some staff — target inmates with mental illness, seeing them as weak, a primary draw for predators. Blitz, Wolff, and Shi studied both physical victimization (Blitz, Wolff, & Shi, 2008) and sexual victimization (Wolff, Blitz, & Shi, 2007) in prison among more than 7500 inmates, distinguishing between those with and without mental illness. They found that rates of victimization were indeed higher among inmates with serious mental illness. Specifically, 31% of male inmates with schizophrenia or bipolar disorder had been physically victimized by another inmate, and 10% had been sexually assaulted, in comparison to only 18% and 3% of those without mental illness, respectively. This equates to rates of physical victimization twice as high and sexual victimization three times as high for inmates with mental illness as for those without. These inmates were also slightly more likely to be assaulted by staff: 27% of male inmates with mental illness versus 24% of those without mental illness were physically assaulted by a staff member, and 9% of inmates with mental illness versus 7% of those without were sexually assaulted by a staff member.

Given the primary goal of prisons is security, and the primary strategy for maintaining order is routine and obedience to rules, it is important that inmates with serious mental illness be treated and that they comply with their treatment. (More detailed information about prison treatment will be discussed later in the chapter.) Indeed, treatment and compliance with treatment are key variables in determining inmates' classification and housing assignments, as well as in parole considerations. However, receiving treatment can sometimes be a double-edged sword. Like on the "outside," other inmates stigmatize inmates "in treatment" or who are "on meds." In fact, inmates "in treatment" are doubly stigmatized by other inmates: not only are they stigmatized for their mental illness but for being "weak" or "pathetic" in participating in treatment. Furthermore, anti-psychotic medication can slow physical reaction times, making inmates with mental illness especially susceptible to victimization. In essence, as noted by Ball (2007):

> [M]entally ill prisoners can find themselves in a vicious circle. Mental illness leads to discipline or victimization problems, which leads to solitary confinement and decompensation. This worsens mental illness and results in further discipline or victimization with further segregation. Mentally ill prisoners suffer these harms for longer periods of time because they serve [as noted earlier], on average, fifteen months longer for the same crimes than do the non-mentally ill. Since their illnesses often prevent them from engaging in prison programming that results in the acquisition of 'good time' credits, mentally ill prisoners also tend to serve a greater percentage of their sentences (p. 4).

Suicide

Not only are inmates with mental illness at risk of aggression by others, they also are more likely than inmates without mental illness to attempt or "successfully" commit suicide. Baillargeon et al. (2009) studied suicides in the largest prison system in the United States, Texas Department of Criminal Justice, between September 2006 and September 2007. Of 234,031 inmates, there were 41 completed suicides (18 suicides per 100,000 inmates). Reportedly, 51% of these persons who committed suicide had a serious mental illness. In particular, inmates with non-schizophrenia-related psychotic disorders had the highest rate of suicide (144 per 100,000), followed by schizophrenia (91 per 100,000), major depression (61 per 100,000), and bipolar disorder (49 per 100,000). Clearly, rates of suicide in prisons are many times higher for inmates with mental illness than for those without. Blevins and Soderstrom (2012) identify various methods in Table 1 used by departments of corrections in an attempt to prevent suicides from occurring. Many of these overlap with strategies used by jails, as discussed in Chapter 6.

Table 1. Suicide Prevention Methods in Prisons

Which of the following methods does your state DOC use to prevent suicide?	Southern States %	Other States %
Surveillance (suicide watch)	100.0	100.0
Inmate companions/observers	33.3	18.8
Safety smocks/blankets	100.0	100.0
Strip cells	77.8	68.8
Safe cells	77.8	68.8
Protective custody	77.8	62.5
Screening	88.9	87.5
"Flags"	33.3	43.8
Specialized or designated housing	66.7	87.5
Medication	100.0	100.0
Additional staff contact	88.9	87.5
Manualized counseling courses	33.3	6.3
Family involvement	11.1	18.8

Blevins & Soderstrom (2012)

Self-Injurious Behavior

Inmates with mental illness are also at risk for self-injurious behavior, to be distinguished from suicidal behavior. Self-injurious behavior (also known as self-mutilation) involves cutting, burning, hitting, head banging, ingesting or inserting objects into one's body, and even self-amputation, without suicidal intent (Appelbaum et al., 2011). Inmates tend to engage in self-injurious behavior for purposes of self-soothing and/or attempting to establish control over something (e.g., their body) in an environment in which they have very little control (Herpertz, 2007). Given these dynamics and the conditions of imprisonment, it should not be surprising that up to 30% of inmates engage in self-injurious behavior at some point during incarceration (Appelbaum et al., 2011), and half of these incidents occur in restricted housing conditions (e.g., segregation, supermax) (Jones, 1986).

In a recent nationwide survey, state and federal prison mental health directors indicated that although they involve few inmates (i.e., less than 2% of inmates engage in self-injurious behavior), most prisons have to deal with such events on a regular basis (Appelbaum et al., 2011). Specifically, 85% of prisons reported that such instances occur in their system at least weekly, and some indicated that it occurs daily. The survey confirmed the findings of prior research that found that the highest rates of self-injury occur in maximum-security and lockdown units. With regard to diagnosis, the majority of cases of self-mutilation involved personality disorders (52%), versus only 16% involving mood disorders and 8% involving psychosis (Appelbaum et al., 2011).

Although not being overtly suicidal in nature, self-injurious can be extremely difficult behavior for prisons to manage. First, self-injurious behavior can only be distinguished from suicidal behavior based on the intent (i.e., thought) of the individual. As such, the responsibility of determining intent must be undertaken by professionals with extensive mental health training. Yet, correctional officers have the most contact with inmates and are left with the responsibility of "detecting" risk and reporting it to mental health staff (if any is available), ideally before it occurs. Because it happens with such regularity, however, correctional officers often become desensitized and come to view the behavior as manipulative and attention-seeking. This is dangerous, given that, although there is no suicidal intent, self-mutilators can easily die from their injuries if the injuries are severe and left untreated.

It appears that it is not only correctional officers who minimize self-injurious behavior. Instead, it is likely related to the culture of the institution. Of the prisons that responded to Appelbaum et al.'s (2011) survey, only 32% had policies on responding to such events. As a result, there was a great amount of inconsistency in the way prisons respond to such incidents, both within prisons (e.g., officers within a single prison respond differently) and between prisons (e.g., prisons respond very differently). Moreover, very few prisons were collecting data on self-injurious incidents and/or they were categorizing them inappropriately as suicide attempts. Nevertheless, most respondents recognized that self-injury is a challenge to the management of their prison and poses liability issues and thus were motivated to learn more about the issue. This is evident in the high response rate to the survey (77%) and the fact that most mental health directors were interested in participating in follow-up research (Appelbaum et al., 2011).

Management of Prisoners with Serious Mental Illness

Prison Design and Operational Procedures

Prisons are highly structured environments. In most states, prison operations are directed by department and institutional policy. However, current prison design and operational protocols have yet to be sufficiently modified to deal with the plethora of management challenges that mentally ill inmates create. For example, the Human Rights Watch (2003) reported a case in which an inmate at Phillips Correctional Institution in Georgia warned staff that he might snap and attack his cellmate. The guards responded by giving him a new cellmate. When the guards observed continued signs of aggression, instead of isolating the mentally ill prisoner, they brought him another cellmate. In the night, the inmate snapped and stomped his cellmate to death and shoved a pencil through his eye. This particular case illustrates the need to better manage mentally ill inmates. The liability to the agency and risk to inmates and staff will remain as long as lack of protocols and resources remain an issue for correctional executives.

Segregation/Supermax Confinement

Prisons throughout the United States have struggled to deal with the "baddest" of the bad and maddest of the mad. Inmates in crisis, who are persistent management problems or who may pose a danger to themselves or others, are often segregated from the general population. In recent years, prisons have designed high-tech, high-security facilities to deal with the worst inmates. These facilities have a variety of designations to include: high security, administrative segregation (ad seg), supermax, protective custody, and isolation. In 1999, there were over 20,000 inmates housed in supermax facilities.

Haney (2003) and others have argued that lockdown for up to 23 hours a day in such isolation cells/units can produce or aggravate mental health problems. The following case example, highlighted by Cohen (2012a), illustrates the deleterious mental health effects of supermax confinement:

The Case of Jack Powers

When Jack Powers arrived at maximum-security federal prison in Atlanta in 1990 after a bank robbery conviction, he had never displayed symptoms of or been treated for mental illness. Still in custody a few years later, he witnessed three inmates, believed to be members of the Aryan Brotherhood gang, kill another inmate. Powers tried to help the victim get medical attention and was quickly transferred to a segregated unit for his safety, but it didn't stop the gang's members from quickly threatening him.

Not then, and certainly not after Powers testified (not once but twice) for the federal government against the assailants. The threats against him continued and Powers was soon transferred to a federal prison in Pennsylvania, where he was threatened even after he was put into protective custody. By this time, Powers had developed insomnia and anxiety attacks and was diagnosed by a prison psychologist as suffering from Post-Traumatic Stress Disorder.

Instead of giving Powers medicine or proper mental health therapy, officials transferred him yet again, this time to another federal prison in New Jersey. There, Powers was informed by officials that he would be removed from a witness protection program and transferred back into the prison's general population.

Fearing for his life, Powers escaped. When he was recaptured two days later he was sent to ADX-Florence, part of a sprawling prison complex near Florence, Colorado, often referred to as "ADX" or "Supermax," America's most famous and secure federal prison.

From there, things got worse. The Supermax complex, made up of different secure prison units and facilities, is laden with members of the Brotherhood. There Powers was no safer than he had been anywhere else. Time and again he was threatened at the Colorado prison. Over and over again he injured or mutilated himself in response. Over and over again, he was transferred to the federal government's special mental health prison facility in Missouri, diagnosed with PTSD, and given medication. Repeatedly that medication was taken away when he came back to Supermax.

As he sits today in Supermax, Powers had amputated his fingers, a testicle, his scrotum and his earlobes, has cut his Achilles tendon, and had tried several times to kill himself. Powers had no tattoos until 2009, when he started mutilating with a razor and carbon paper. He did much of this—including biting off his pinkie and cutting skin off his face—in the Control Unit at ADX while prison officials consistently refused to treat his diagnosed mental illness. Rules are rules, prison officials told him, and no prisoners in that unit were to be given psychotropic medicine no matter how badly they needed it (para. 1–5).

In *Madrid v. Gomez* (1995), dealing with California's Pelican Bay Security Housing Unit (SHU), it was determined that mentally ill prisoners and those with conditions making them susceptible to mental illness should be banned from placement in the SHU due to its deleterious effects. Other states, such as Massachusetts, have established secure treatment units as an alternative to segregating mentally ill inmates for disciplinary rule violations due to the negative impact such lock-ups can have on self-injurious and suicidal behavior (Spencer & Fallon, 2012).

Practitioners, however, continue to support the use of supermax confinement. In fact, a national survey of wardens (Mears & Castro, 2006) indicated unanimous support for supermax-type facilities. Despite acknowledging that supermax confinement diminishes mental health, increases suicide attempts, and that inmates placed in such isolation receive little to no appropriate treatment or services, they nevertheless support its use on grounds that it increases safety, order, and control and is useful in incapacitating violent and disruptive inmates. Joseph Porte, commissioner of the Maine Department of Correction, for example, contends that he has data to demonstrate that selective segregation does help reduce violence in the general population (Mears & Castro, 2006). This is not an undisputed fact, however. In an interview with Jacob McCleland (2012), Dan Mears, a criminologist at Florida State University, contended that the research base is unclear whether supermax prisons actually reduce violence in the general prison population.

Current State of Supermax Confinement

As a result of litigation, supermax facilities are gradually closing. For example, at one time there were over 1,000 inmates in Mississippi's Unit 32 Supermax facility, including hundreds of mentally ill and death row inmates. Dr. Terry Kupers, a national expert on prison mental health issues, described the prison as a place of "hopelessness and despair" (Mitchell, 2012). In response to a lawsuit by the American Civil Liberties Union (ACLU), a consent decree was issued in 2006 requiring the Mississippi Department of Corrections (MDOC) to make changes in the administration of its supermax facility.

In 2010, working with the ACLU and the U.S. Department of Justice, MDOC Director, Chris Epps, completed changes that pertained to health care, mental health care, the use of force, the development of a new classification instrument, and the reassignment of supermax inmates to other units in Mississippi (Byrd, 2010). This move created substantial savings for the state and made it one of the first states in the nation to close its supermax facility (Byrd, 2010).

Illinois, in 2012, became the most recent state to close its supermax facility (McKinney, 2012). The Supermax Tamms unit housed approximately 200 offenders. It cost about $62,000 per inmate per year or approximately $12.5 million a year, a rate three times that of the state average. Policymakers and correctional executives will be looking to states like Mississippi, Illinois, and California as they reconsider their supermax operations.

Likewise, at the federal level, in June 2012, five prisoners at the ADX-Florence/Supermax unit filed a lawsuit against the Bureau of Prisons (*Bacote v. Federal Bureau of Prisons*, 2012). They alleged that prison officials have failed or refused to adequately diagnose and treat mentally ill prisoners. Below are just a few of the allegations contained in the *Bacote* lawsuit:

Bacote v. Federal Bureau of Prisons

The following describes the case of Michael Bacote, the first named plaintiff in the 2012 class action lawsuit:

Age 37, functionally illiterate, and deemed "mildly mentally retarded" a decade ago by a prison psychologist, Michael Bacote was sent to ADX in 2005 after pleading guilty to murder in a case involving the death of a fellow inmate at the federal prison in Texas. Bacote has been diagnosed as suffering from "major depressive disorder with psychotic features" as well as from "paranoid ideations," and he also may suffer the after-effects of severe closed-head injury.

Bacote refuses to take medicine that has been ground up from pill form by prison officials. And they, in turn, refuse to allow Bacote to take his medicine in pill form. Bacote has repeatedly tried to transfer out of Supermax. Over and over again, his requests have been denied. Despite the prior diagnoses from prison doctors, for example, the complaint alleges that ADX officials in April 2009 told Bacote that "a review of your files does not indicate you are mentally ill or mentally retarded" (Cohen, 2012b, para. 9–10).

Among other dubious practices, the Bacote lawsuit alleges that Federal Bureau of Prison officials typically place incoming prisoners who are on psychotropic medication in the Control Unit where such medication is prohibited, only to discontinue it. As noted in the complaint,

> The BOP justifies this in Orwellian fashion: it discontinues the prisoner's medication, thereby making the now non-medicated prisoner "eligible" for placement in the Control Unit. Then, when this newly "eligible" prisoner requests medication needed to treat his serious mental illness, he is told that BOP policy prohibits the administration of psychotropic medication to him so he should develop "coping skills" as a substitute for the medication being withheld. Instructing a prisoner confined in long-term segregation and who has Schizophrenia or Bipolar Illness to self-treat his disease with coping skills is like demanding that a diabetic prisoner learn to "cope" without insulin. Likewise, the required 30-day "individual evaluations" are in actuality rarely performed on inmates in the Control Unit. Indeed, and as an example, upon information and belief, one obviously and seriously mentally ill inmate in the ADX Control Unit who habitually resides in a cell reserved for the seriously mentally ill which is fitted with, among other things, Plexiglas sheets over the internal barred grill, was not out of his cell at any point between November 2011 and May 2012 and during that time had no substantive communications whatsoever with any BOP mental health professional (*Bacote v. Federal Bureau of Prisons*, 2012, p. 23).

Another allegation in the complaint includes the following disregard for an inmate known to be at risk for suicide:

> In 2010 a severely and chronically depressed prisoner who had attempted to kill himself a few months earlier was escorted to the ADX [Security Housing Unit] after throwing milk at a corrections officer. He was placed in a cell from which the BOP had just removed another chronically and notoriously mentally ill prisoner who had smeared the cell's floors, walls, bed and mattress with feces. The prisoner arriving was given no cleaning supplies, and was not issued a blanket, towel, or sheet. He used the roll of toilet paper in the cell to try to wipe the feces off of a spot on the bare concrete floor that was large enough to enable him to lie down. For two days, he remained lying on that single

"clean" space. When he had not been issued cleaning supplies, a towel, sheet or blanket after two days, he covered the Plexiglas wall in his cell with newspapers to block the view from the hallway and then prepared to hang himself with his shoelaces. Before he succeeded in doing so an "emergency response team" assembled because of the newspaper on his cell windows, forcibly entered the cell, restrained the inmate, and moved him to another cell where he was handcuffed hand and foot to a concrete pedestal for another day, during which he was unable to reach the food left for him on the desk in the cell (*Bacote v. Federal Bureau of Prisons*, 2012, p. 28). Other allegations can be found in the complaint.

Blevins and Soderstrom (2012) found in their study that 66.7% of the Southern Correctional Mental Health Chief Administrators (CMHAs) used a mental/behavioral health classification system, and only 50% of the CMHAs in the other states reported classifying inmates this way. Such classification schemas can enhance identification of persons with mental illnesses. Due to the anti-therapeutic milieu permeating incarceration in general, much less in solitary confinement, the need for residential care has emerged for persons with mental illnesses who require a therapeutic environment separate from the general population. As a result, more and more correctional facilities are going to special needs housing units to provide for such things as residential treatment and supportive living units for anywhere from 30 to 50 inmates per housing unit (Metzner, 2007). Likewise, contrary to public opinion most of the inmates housed in supermax return to our communities (Haney, 2003). Treatment in prison and transitional services that include the implementation of effective discharge plans reduce the possibility that an inmate will reoffend (Cohen, 2012a).

More recently Butler, Steiner, Makarios and Travis (2017) assessed the effects of exposure to supermax confinement on offender post release behaviors. Contrary to popular belief they found that supermax had no significant effect on post release behavior. In other words, time in supermax confinement is not positively correlated with recidivism.

Correctional Officers

Correctional officers play a critical role in the maintenance of order in prison settings. Their job requires them to be in a constant state of vigilance, contributing to job stress. Moreover, repeated exposure to disruptive mentally ill inmates can lead staff, including but not limited to correctional officers, to become desensitized to their behavior and/or jaded, dismissing the behavior as manipulative and/or deceptive.

While there is a more thorough discussion of correctional officer mental health in Chapter 6 (jails), research has demonstrated that the prevalence of Post-Traumatic Stress Disorder (PTSD), anxiety and major depressive disorders are substantial higher than in the general population (Regher et al., 2109). The cumulative effects of stress can be disastrous, given that officers are responsible for making decisions about when to call in mental health professionals, remove someone from their cell, recommend placing them in protective custody, or ignore their behavior. Sometimes, tragedies result, such as in the case of Timothy Souders that follows, as reported by Scott Pelley of *60 Minutes* (Hamlin, Granatstein, Flaum, & Klug, 2007, p. 1):

The Case of Timothy Souders

Timothy Souders had been diagnosed with anxiety and manic depressive disorders and had been treated on several occasions at a mental hospital. "After one hospital stay, he was caught shoplifting two paintball guns. He grabbed a pocketknife, threatened employees, and then begged a cop to shoot him. Instead, he was stunned with a Taser." He pleaded guilty to resisting arrest and assault. He was sentenced to three to five years at the Southern Michigan Correctional Center. During his incarceration, as a result of minor rule-breaking, "Souders was chained down, hands, feet and waist, up to 17 hours at a time. By prison rules, all of it was recorded on a 24-hour surveillance camera and by the guards themselves. The tape records a rapid descent: he started out apparently healthy, but in four days Souders could barely walk. In the shower, he fell over. The guards brought him back in a wheelchair, but then chained him down again. On August 6th, he was released from restraints and fell for the last time. Souders had died of dehydration and only the surveillance camera took notice."

Correctional officers are limited in the resources they can access to deal with inmates who have personality disorders, such as antisocial personality disorder (ASPD), in which individuals disregard others' rights and tend to be impulsive and aggressive. Such disorders are not readily amenable to medications, but these traits can significantly affect an inmate's willingness and/or ability to be compliant with orders and/or treatment. While there are questions regarding the reliability of ASPD diagnoses and the utility of diagnosing a disorder that can be ascribed to most inmates in prisons, the ability to differentiate between the "bad" and the "mad" remains a challenge and is critical to maintaining ethical treatment and punishment (Human Rights Watch, 2003). Contributing to the difficulty is that serious mental illness (e.g., psychosis) and personality disorders are not mutually exclusive; it is not uncommon for a psychotic inmate to also have a personality disorder, such as ASPD. This was likely the case with Richard Street, as detailed by Pfeifer (2007, para. 15):

The Case of Richard Street

On Thanksgiving 2004, a notoriously mad inmate named Richard A. Street hanged himself in a segregation unit at the 800-inmate, maximum-security state prison in Walpole. His death marked the start of a rash of 12 suicides in Massachusetts prisons in 26 months, compared with five in the nearly six years before. A look at Street's prison experience might explain this phenomenon, which is unfortunate but not uncommon in modern prisons.

Street, 53, was [described as] a wretched man who had indiscriminately shot two people one night in Boston in 1980 and then went on to exhaust the patience and resources of the Massachusetts prison system. Suffering from schizoaffective disorder and calling himself "Jesus Christ, Future King of the Vampires," he would rant, self-mutilate, and perform naked pirouettes around a basketball in the prison yard.

Recently the state Department of Correction commissioned a report on suicide prevention in Massachusetts prisons and has promised to put its recommendations into practice. Street's chilling case starkly illustrates the need for changes.

In a six-week period, Street, a thin man with a bushy, reddish-brown beard and long dark hair, was twice found hanging in his cell. He repeatedly gouged his skin, swallowed a 1 1/2-inch piece of metal, and was taken to a local emergency room six times. He smeared feces in his hair and complained that solitary confinement was making him hurt himself.

Photographs show a handcuffed Street displaying a gruesome array of scabbed and mottled wounds on his legs and arms. Nonetheless, his records suggest skepticism, common on the part of overworked prison clinicians, of Street's pathology. After he had been found in an earlier episode to be "unresponsive" and with gauze tied around his neck, a clinician wrote that Street "is not depressed ... nor at risk of harm due to mental illness." He had been known to "feign unconsciousness," the record noted. The last time, at least, he was not feigning.

Training

Rich (2009) indicates that correctional personnel often do not have adequate training to be able to distinguish aberrant acts influenced by mental illness from infractions instigated purposefully by those who are not ill. With proper training and preparation, though, correctional officers can be prisons' greatest assets in managing inmates with mental illness. Correctional officers often spend years with some inmates. They get to know their moods and behaviors. However, according to the National Institute of Corrections (2001), the training of correctional staff on how to respond to offenders with mental illnesses is severely lacking. Only seven states reported providing correctional officers with more than four hours of training on dealing with mental illness issues in correctional settings. Some states appear to be taking steps to rectify these issues, though. For example, the Texas Department of Corrections in 2007 adjusted their training requirements to 20 hours of specialized training for all correctional officers and increased the emphasis in pre-service training on mental illness issues (Doug Dretke, Director of Correctional Management Institute, personal communication, May 1, 2007).

As discussed in Chapter 1, the Council of State Governments et al. (2002), in the Criminal Justice/Mental Health Consensus Project, has provided a number of recommendations for each component of the criminal justice system. One of their policy statements focuses on training correctional staff on recognizing and responding to inmates with mental illness. Specific recommendations for implementation of this policy include:

a. Provide basic training regarding mental health issues to all corrections staff who come into contact with detainees or inmates with mental illness.

b. Incorporate competency-based training in mental health issues in existing academy (pre-service) training programs and in-service programs for corrections staff.

c. Provide advanced training to corrections staff assigned to work specifically with inmates with mental illness.

d. Provide parole board members with training in order to inform them about issues regarding the release of people with mental illness from prison.

e. Provide training for parole officers to improve their ability to supervise parolees with mental illness.

More recently, DeHart and Iachini (2018), in coordination with United States Department of Justice's Bureau of Justice Assistance, implemented a three-stage process in the development of a curriculum for training correctional officers on the mental health needs of prisoners. They developed 14 modules that covered four primary areas. They are:

a. Introduction to mental health issues in the corrections system

b. Characteristics of mental disorders as they relate to rights and experiences of incarcerated persons

c. Screening and response for mental disorders

d. Self-care for corrections staff that come into contact with persons who are incarcerated and living with mental illness.

Further research is needed to test these approaches and fine tune the training process.

Correctional Crisis Intervention Teams

As with law enforcement and jails, prisons have begun to increasingly recognize the utility of specialized mental health response units. Washington State Department of Corrections, for example, implemented a mobile consultation team to work with prison staff to address specific issues related to the management of mentally ill offenders (Adams & Toch, 2002). Also gaining in popularity are Crisis Intervention Teams (CIT) in prisons.

As discussed in Chapter 5, CITs have been used successfully by law enforcement to deescalate potentially violent encounters with individuals living with mental illness. It has been demonstrated to reduce harm to police officers and link offenders living with mental illness to treatment. Though many jails and prisons have individuals that employ crisis intervention techniques effectively, they have historically relied on SWAT-like teams to deal with crisis situations. Several organizations have adapted CIT training programs, aimed primarily at mastering de-escalation techniques and being able to identify signs and symptoms of mental illness, for their correctional personnel (Hodges, 2010). The Oklahoma Department of Corrections, for example, trains both correctional officers and probation officers and calls their modified-CIT training corrections crisis resolution training (CCRT) (Hodges, 2010). A number of jails in Maine and Florida have implemented modified-CIT training programs for their detention personnel as well (Harkinson, 2009; Immarigeon, 2011).

The use of CIT strategies by prison and jail staff in interactions with inmates is a relatively new development, and there has been no comprehensive study on the teams, the training, and/or implementation outcomes. However, it has the potential to change prison management culture. Correctional executives, for the most part, understand that the use of non-violent approaches to dealing with inmate non-compliance is good management, solid fiscal policy, reduces the odds of lawsuits, and is the ethically appropriate manner to deal with such situations.

Treating Prisoners with Mental Illness

Prisoners' Right to Mental Health Treatment

Like jails, as discussed in Chapter 6, most prisons have neither the resources nor the expertise to provide quality mental health treatment. Prisons may have a psychiatrist on call or a psychiatric nurse on staff, but these individuals are frequently overwhelmed by the numbers of people they have to serve as well as the poor conditions in which to serve them. Further, the costs of providing mental health treatment to inmates are borne entirely by states, because, under federal law, Medicaid (the largest payer of public mental health services) may not be used to pay for healthcare services in correctional facilities (Earley, 2006).

As with jail inmates, however, inmates in prisons do have a limited legal right to treatment grounded in the 8th Amendment. The U.S. Supreme Court first recognized this right in *Estelle v. Gamble* (1976). The right is implicated when an inmate has a "serious medical need." Most recent courts have agreed that serious mental illnesses, such as schizophrenia, bipolar disorder, and major depressive disorder, qualify as a "serious medical need" (Cohen, 1998). As noted by Krelstein (2002, p. 489), "Legally convicted prisoners are entitled to psychological or psychiatric care for serious mental or emotional illness. 'There is no underlying distinction between the right to medical care for physical ills and its psychological or psychiatric counterpart.'" Inmates who claim that prison officials violated their rights to treatment must prove that the officials were aware of their medical need; it is not sufficient that prison officials *should* have known (*Farmer v. Brennan*, 1994). Finally, it must be proven that the officials were "deliberately indifferent" to the need and that the neglect was wanton or willful.

While inmates only have a right to minimally adequate treatment, *Ruiz v. Estelle* (1980) established the fundamental components of a mental health treatment plan for inmates, which remain in effect today. These components include screening and evaluation; suicide prevention; availability of trained mental health professionals; treatment, not just segregation or supervision; appropriate use of psychiatric medications; and proper maintenance of confidential records of treatment. More recent decisions have also added access to mental health services, adequate facilities and equipment (Cohen, 1998; Metzner, 2007), and even discharge planning to the list of requirements (e.g., *Brad H. v. City of New York*, 2000; *Wakefield v. Thompson*, 1999). Furthermore, the American Disabilities Act mandates reasonable accommodations for all disabled, including inmates. Likewise, inmates also have a right to refuse treatment. This right has been recognized at all levels of the criminal justice process, from the pre-trial stage to the post-conviction stage.

Current Status of Mental Health Services in Prisons

According to the Pew Center Prison Count 2010, there were 1,404,053 inmates in state prisons (Bosh, 2010). While it is unclear how many of these inmates would benefit from psychiatric treatment, it is suggested that 15% to 20% will require some form of psychiatric intervention during their incarceration (Metzner, Cohen, Grossman, & Wettstein, 1998). Applying these estimates to the 2010 inmate population data, 210,608 (15%) to 280,811 (20%) inmates require some form of psychiatric intervention during their incarceration.

In light of these sheer numbers, it is not surprising that prisons have been ill-equipped to deal with mentally ill offenders and slow to improve their prisons to provide services. As a result, many inmates over the years have gone without much-needed assessment and treatment (Human Rights Watch, 2003). In 2001, for example, Beck and Maruschak performed a national survey of 1,109 state confinement facilities (i.e., prisons) and found that, despite the legal mandates of *Ruiz v. Estelle* (1980), less than 80% screened inmates at intake and/or conducted psychiatric assessments to identify potential mental illness. In terms of treatment, 84% provided therapy/

counseling, 83% distributed psychotropic medications, and only 63% provided 24-hour crisis mental health care. Thus, 20 years after the *Ruiz vs. Estelle* ruling was handed down, 50 prisons (4.6%) still provided no screening or treatment services at all. Moreover, of all inmates in these facilities, only 13% received mental health therapy or counseling, 10% received medications, and less than 2% were housed in a 24-hour mental health unit (Beck & Maruschak, 2001). These percents, too, fall short when compared to Metzner et al.'s (1998) estimates of those in prisons who need psychiatric treatment.

Blevins and Soderstrom (2012) provide a recent, and more optimistic, picture of the types of mental health services offered around the country, albeit in a self-selected group of states. They found that 100% of the MHCAs in Southern States and 87.5% in the other states used standardized mental illness screening instruments to identify inmates with mental illness at the outset. Additionally, among the various treatment interventions, all of the mental health administrators indicated that crisis intervention, stabilization care for acute episodes of mental illness, and psychiatric treatment (i.e., medication) were available in their prisons. Likewise, individual therapy and psycho-educational therapy were available in 90% or more of states, and staff-lead group therapy and peer-lead drug and alcohol treatment (e.g., Alcoholics/Narcotics Anonymous) were close behind.

Due to the anti-therapeutic milieu permeating incarceration in general, the need for residential care has emerged for persons with mental illnesses who require a therapeutic environment separate from the general population. As a result, more and more correctional facilities are creating special needs housing units, in which 30 to 50 inmates live together, provide support to each other, and receive treatment as a group (Metzner, 2007). Moreover, treatment in prison and transitional services that include the implementation of effective discharge plans reduce the possibility that an inmate will reoffend (Cohen, 2012a). It appears that prisons realize this, as nearly 90% of the CMHAs surveyed by Blevins and Soderstrom (2012) indicated they provide pre-release/transitional services.

McKenna et al. (2018) evaluated the impact of an assertive community treatment model of care on the treatment of prisoners with serious mental illness. This prison model of care (PMOC) was based on the principles of assertive engagement, continuity of care, multi-disciplinary service delivery and small caseloads. The PMOC was delivered in five steps — screening, referral assessment, treatment and release planning. They concluded that this approach to the treatment of offenders with serious mental illnesses can improve service delivery without adding new resources.

Challenges of Treating Prisoners with Mental Illness

The care of the mentally ill in prison is a difficult task at best. Most of the jails and prisons in the U.S. were not designed to meet the needs of the increasing numbers of mentally ill inmates, yet they have become the new asylums (Navasky & O'Connor, 2005). While no prison system intentionally sets out to harm mentally ill prisoners, the existence of substandard care limits the ability of mentally ill inmates to function adequately to meet the stringent requirements of the correctional setting, thereby setting them up for failure. The delivery of care to mentally ill offenders is affected by a variety of factors, including whether or not an effective screening and classification system is in place, the availability of treatment, the quality of treatment, the orientation of the custodial and support staff, the design of the institution, and access to medication (Human Rights Watch, 2003). Reduced quality of psychiatric intervention in any of these realms has a direct impact on prison environments, especially concerning the safety of officers, staff, and inmates. Moreover, since almost all prisoners are eventually released, prison psychiatric intervention strategies have far reaching effects on families of inmates and members of local communities.

Despite this knowledge, the goal of most correctional health systems is to merely stabilize the patient and to facilitate the maintenance of the mentally ill inmate in "general population," minimizing the need for limited and specialized services (Human Rights Watch, 2003). Thus, the physical and social environments of most prisons run counter to the promotion of coping skills appropriate to life on the "outside." Issues most commonly found in correctional mental health systems include understaffing, poor screening and tracking of mentally ill prisoners, misdiagnoses, and concerns related to proper medication and adequate access to specialized care for seriously ill prisoners (Human Rights Watch, 2003).

While prisons today increasingly provide a variety of resources to accommodate mentally ill offenders, including psychiatric hospital beds, separate intermediate care housing, therapy, medication, and targeted programming, in many states the waiting list for special services is long (Human Rights Watch, 2003). In some cases, the most significant issue confronting correctional executives is the lack of skilled mental health professionals willing to work in prisons. While protocols and facilities may exist to provide for the care of the mentally ill inmate, it is the professional correctional mental health provider that determines the quality and effectiveness of care that inmates receive. For example, the Human Rights Watch (2003) report found that while medication was readily available, what is needed are the resources and commitment to determine what medication is needed and the staff necessary to monitor its distribution and effect. As indicated by Rich (2009), an increased use of psychotropic medication within prisons is not necessarily a positive sign for treatment of mentally ill inmates, as medication is sometimes used to sedate inmates — acting as chemical restraints. Keltner and Vance (2008) note that inmates are sometimes apprehensive of taking such prison-issued medication, even voicing concerns that they refuse the medication because they don't want to be turned in to a zombie. For perceived reasons of self-preservation and a general lack of trust of correctional personnel, inmates will be reluctant to take medication or refuse to take it altogether (Morgan, Steffan, Shaw, & Wilson, 2007).

The Commission on Safety and Abuse in American's Prisons reported in 2006 that inadequate staffing, high turnover, and burnout hinder many correctional mental health providers. Human Rights Watch (2003) contends that, in part due to provider issues, serious mentally ill inmates often receive no treatment, are accused of malingering, and/or are treated as disciplinary problems. This is disturbing, given that failure to respond in a timely and appropriate manner to mentally ill offenders presenting symptomatic behaviors can be dangerous. It is at least disruptive, affecting virtually every facet of correctional life (Gibbons & Katzenbach, 2006).

Costs of Incarcerating Prisoners with Mental Illness

The costs of health care are considered one of the greatest challenges facing the U.S. Insel (2008) estimated the cost for serious mental illness at $317 billion, not including the cost of incarceration, the costs of homelessness, and financial costs to families with members living with mental illness. In turn, the number of offenders with mental illnesses sentenced to correctional facilities and the costs of treating them has increased dramatically in the last twenty years. Izumi, Schiller and Hayward (1996) estimated over fifteen years ago that California alone was spending between $1–2 billion a year arresting, housing and treating mentally ill inmates. Nearly ten years ago the imprisonment of the mentally ill in the United States cost approximately $9 *billion* a year (National Alliance on Mental Illness, 2004). Undoubtedly, those costs are much higher now.

Blevins and Soderstrom (2012) inquired about the proportion of state departments' of corrections budgets were spent on mental health care for inmates. They found that departments spend between 2.5% (in Southern states) and 6% (in non-Southern states) of their annual budgets on mental health services. Approximately 1.5% to 2% is spent on medications alone. Furthermore, correctional mental health administrators tend to disagree that they receive adequate funding from their legislatures for the treatment of inmates with mental illness. In particular only 22% of Southern and 31% of non-Southern correctional mental health administrators agree to strongly agree that they receive enough funding to perform their responsibilities for inmates with mental illness.

Despite studies demonstrating the long-term fiscal, ethical, and legal benefits of treating inmates, public support for punishment has remained strong for over 30 years (Cullen, 2006). Millions of dollars have been spent to build new prisons to satiate the public's desire to incarcerate and punish, but spending on the treatment and diversion of mentally ill offenders is severely lacking. Can there be a middle ground?

Privatization of Prison Health Care

As discussed in Chapter 6, an alternative being used in correctional health care is outsourcing/privatization of prison medical and mental health services (Leonard, 2012). About 20 states (40%) have transferred all or portions of their health care services to less expensive private firms such as Wexford and Corizon. Such moves to save taxpayers money have not come without criticism, however. Groups like the Florida Nurses Association, Health Care Project at Prisoners Legal Services in Massachusetts, the American Federation of State, County, and Municipal Employees, and the John Howard Society contend that inmates are not receiving adequate care, arguing that private firms focus on profit, not public safety. According to Daniel (2007),

> The profit motive may trump quality and compromise ethics standards and practice. Profit-oriented service providers tend to keep certain key staff positions unfilled or partially filled and encourage less expensive treatment approaches and medications, potentially jeopardizing patient care. Although the experience of private vendors indicates that they are more successful in recruiting professionals, including psychiatrists and psychologists, the correctional system still lags behind other provider systems in attracting qualified personnel (p. 407).

Swanson et al. (2011) recently conducted the first comprehensive study of the costs of criminal justice involvement among adults living with serious mental illness. This study computes costs with and without forensic hospitalization as criminal justice (CJ) system costs. The cost for CJ-involved individuals with mental illness was approximately $49,000 over the two-year period of the study compared to approximately $25,000 for their non-CJ-involved counterparts. Consistent with research described previously, the CJ sample was more likely to be admitted for inpatient psychiatric care but spent fewer days in the hospital than the non-CJ sample. Jail diversion represented a very small proportion of the total CJ system costs, despite the potential to substantially reduce total costs by preventing further CJ involvement.

In addition, Swanson et al. (2011) examined the proportion of costs borne by various agencies in their comparison of the CJ-involved with the non-CJ-involved mentally ill samples. Overall, they determined that the state department of mental health paid for approximately 61% of the expenditures, the state department of social services and Medicaid paid for approximately 25% of the costs, the department of corrections covered 11% of the costs, while the courts and law enforcement paid for approximately 4%. The state department of mental health paid for, in particular, approximately 50% of the costs for the CJ-involved sample and about 70% for the non-CJ involved sample. This translated into the department of mental health spending approximately $8,000 more per person in the CJ-involved sample than in the non-CJ involved sample. The researchers noted that long hospitalizations and periods of incarceration impacted costs in both systems.

Beyond the costs of lack of treatment within prisons, prisoners are beginning to return to our communities under the supervision of overburdened and underfunded parole agencies. Programs such as Assertive Community Treatment (ACT) — one proven, evidence-based approach to working with individuals with mental illness in the community — would allow community treatment teams to make home visits, administer medication, and provide in-home care. According to Satel (2003), ACT teams have been proven to reduce re-hospitalizations by up to 80%. However, the major payer for public mental health services — which most CJ-involved individuals with mental illness use — Medicare and Medicaid regulations limit payment to clinicians for such services (Satel, 2003). Such short-sightedness, and the inability to respond to this growing population of special needs offenders in our communities, will certainly impact life in every community. ACT will be discussed in more detail in the next chapter.

Conclusion

Since 2008 the federal government has continued to decrease funding of mental health care, shifting the burden of care to state and local governments. As a result, there are fewer inpatient facilities for the mentally ill. According to Torrey, Entsminger, Geller, Stanley, and Jaffe (2008), there is a deficit of nearly 100,000 inpatient beds in the United States which results in increased homelessness, emergency room overcrowding, and use of jails and prisons as de-facto psychiatric hospitals. Fellner (2003) contends that only the wealthy have access to mental health services in the community and that many prisoners could have avoided expensive incarceration had publicly funded treatment been available. To reiterate Judge William Wayne Justice's opinion in the landmark case, *Ruiz v. Johnson* (1999), as he summarized it best:

> It is deplorable and outrageous that this (TX) state's prisons appear to have become a repository for a great number of its mentally ill citizens. Persons who, with psychiatric care, could fit well into society, are instead locked away, to become wards of the state's penal system. Then, in a tragically ironic twist, they may be confined in conditions that nurture, rather than abate, their psychoses (p. 915).

The success of correctional intervention in the new millennium is contingent upon the ability of wardens and their staffs to more effectively manage and treat mentally ill offenders. To be sure, the performance of correctional mental health systems is being scrutinized by court systems and a proliferation of prison "watchdog" groups like the Humans Rights Watch, The National Prison Project of the ACLU, the Vera Institute, and the Commission on the Safety and Abuse in America's Prisons. Taking care of the offender living with mental illness enhances not only the order and functioning of the prison environment, reducing officer and inmate assaults, it increases the chance of successful reentry and, thereby, community safety.

Certainly, treating mental illness is expensive. However, failure to treat mental illness is even more expensive. Until state and federal governments expand funding of mental health hospitals and community mental health treatment initiatives, prisons will be forced to do more with limited resources. Perhaps most regrettable is that the failure to treat will result in the loss of lives. There is some hope that in the shadows of three decades of "binging" on imprisonment policymakers are beginning to accept research findings that demonstrate that treatment of the mentally ill offender is a good investment, both good fiscal policy and a good investment in the life of communities. Almost all offenders return to our communities; how they return affects us all.

References

Adams, K. (1986). The disciplinary experiences of mentally disordered inmates. *Criminal Justice and Behavior, 13*(3), 297–316.

Adams, K., & Toch, H. (2002). *Acting out.* Washington, D.C.: American Psychological Association Books.

Andrews, D. A., Bonta, J., & Hoge, R. D. (1990). Classification for effective rehabilitation: Rediscovering psychology. *Criminal Justice and Behavior, 17*, 19–52.

Appelbaum, K. L., Savageau, J. A., Trestman, R. L., Metzner, J. L., & Baillargeon, J. (2011). A national survey of self-injurious behavior in American prisons. *Psychiatric Services, 62*, 285–290.

Bacote vs. Federal Bureau of Prisons. (2012). The United States District Court for the District of Colorado, Case 1:12-cv-01570. Retrieved from: http://www.supermax lawsuit.com/Complaint-and-Exhibits-Bacote-v-Federal-Bureau-of-Prisons.pdf.

Baillargeon, J., Penn, J. V., Thomas, C. R., Temple, J. R., Baillargeon, G., & Murray, O. J. (2009). Psychiatric disorders and suicide in the nation's largest state prison system. *Journal of the American Academy of Psychiatry and the Law, 37*, 188–193.

Ball, W. D. (2007). Mentally ill prisoners in the California Department of Corrections and Rehabilitation: Strategies for improving treatment and reducing recidivism. *Journal of Contemporary Health Law & Policy, 24*(1), 1–42.

Beck, A., & Maruschak, L. (2001, July). *Special report: Mental health treatment in state prisons, 2000* (NCJ 188215). Washington, D.C.: U.S. Department of Justice, Bureau of Justice Statistics. Retrieved from http://bjs.ojp.usdoj.gov/index.cfm? ty=pbdetail&iid=788.

Blevins, K., & Soderstrom, I. (2012, September 28). *Examining regional differences in states' approaches to the treatment of offenders with mental illness.* Paper presented at the Southern Criminal Justice Conference, Atlantic Beach, FL.

Blitz, C. L., Wolff, N., & Shi, J. (2008). Physical victimization in prison: The role of mental illness. *International Journal of Law and Psychiatry, 31*, 385–393.

Bloom, J. D. (2010). "The incarceration revolution": The abandonment of the seriously mentally ill to our jails and prisons. *Journal of Law, Medicine and Ethics, 38*, 727–734.

Brad H. v. City of New York, 712 NYS 2d 336 (2000).

Butler, D., Steiner, B., Maakarios, M. & Travis, L. (2017). Assessing the effects of exposure to supermax confinement on offender post release behaviors. *The Prison Journal.* DOI: https://doi.org/10.1177%2F0032885517703925.

Byrd, S. (2010, June 5). Mississippi shutting down Parchman's notorious Unit 32: Prison conditions had been called inhumane. *The Commercial Appeal: Memphis, Tennessee.* Retrieved from http://www.commercialappeal.com/news/2010/jun/05/miss-shutting-down-notorious-prison-unit/.

Bosh, S. (2010, April). *The Pew Center Prisoner Count 2010: State population declines for the first time in 38 years*. Washington, D.C.: Pew Center Charitable Trusts, Inc.

Carson, E. A. (2019). *Prisoners in 2018*. Washington, D.C.: U.S. Department of Justice, Bureau of Justice Statistics. Retrieved from: https://www.bjs.gov/content/pub/pdf/p18.pdf.

Clark, K. (2018). The effect of mental illness on segregation following institutional misconduct. *Criminal Justice and Behavior, 45*(9), 1363–1382.

Cohen, A. (2012a, June 18). An American gulag: Descending into madness at supermax. *The Atlantic*. Retrieved from: http://www.theatlantic.com/national/archive/2012/06/an-american-gulag-descending-into-madness-at-supermax/258323/.

Cohen, A. (2012b, June 19). The faces of a prison's mentally ill. *The Atlantic*. Retrieved from: http://www.theatlantic.com/national/archive/2012/06/supermax-the-faces-of-a-prisons-mentally-ill/258429/.

Cohen, F. (1998). Legal issues and the mentally disordered inmate and the law. *National Institute of Corrections*, 55–163.

Council of State Governments. (2002). *Fact sheet: People with mental illness in the criminal justice system: About the problem*. New York, NY: Author.

Council of State Governments, Police Executive Research Forum, Pretrial Services Resource Center, Association of State Correctional Administrators, Bazelon Center for Mental Health Law, and the Center for Behavioral Health, Justice, and Public Policy. (2002). *Criminal Justice/Mental Health Consensus Project*. New York, NY: Council of State Governments. Retrieved from consensusproject.org/the_report.

Cullen, F. (2006). It's time to reaffirm rehabilitation. *Crime and Public Policy, 5*(4), 665–672.

Daniel, A. E. (2007), Care of the mentally ill in prisons: Challenges and solutions. *Journal of the American Academy of Psychiatry and the Law, 35*, 406–410.

Ditton, P. M. (1999, July). *Special report: Mental health treatment of inmates and probationers* (NCJ 174463). Washington, D.C.: U.S. Department of Justice, Bureau of Justice Statistics. Retrieved from http://bjs.ojp.usdoj.gov/index.cfm?ty= pbdetail&iid=787.

Earley, P. (2006). *Crazy: A father's search through America's mental health madness*. New York, NY: G.P. Putnam and Sons.

Estelle v. Gamble, 429 U.S. 97(1976).

Farmer v. Brennan, 511 U.S. 825 (1994).

Fellner, J. (2003, October). *United States: Mentally ill mistreated in prison*. Retrieved from http://hrw.org/english/docs/2003/10/22/usdom6472.htm.

Fellner, J. (2006). A corrections quandary: Mental illness and prison rules. *Harvard Civil Rights-Civil Liberties Law Review, 41*, 391–412.

Felson, R. B., Silver, E., & Remster, B. (2012). Mental disorder and offending in prison. *Criminal Justice and Behavior, 39*(2), 125–143.

Fuller, D.A., Sinclair, E., Geller, J., Quanbeck, C., & Snook, J. (2016). Going, going, gone: Trends and consequences of eliminating state psychiatric beds. Treatment Advocacy Center. Retrieved from https://www.treatmentadvocacycenter.org/storage/documents/going-going-gone.pdf

Glaze, L. E. (2011). *Correctional populations in the United States, 2010* (NCJ 236319). Washington, D.C.: U.S. Department of Justice, Bureau of Justice Statistics. Retrieved from: https://www.bjs.gov/content/pub/pdf/cpus10.pdf.

Gibbons, J. J., & Katzenbach, N. B. (2006, June). *Confronting confinement: A report of the commission on safety and abuse in America's prisons.* New York, NY: Vera Institute of Justice. Retrieved from http://www.vera.org/download?file=2845/Confronting_Confinement.pdf.

Guerino, P., Harrison, P. M., & Sabol, W. J. (2012). *Prisoners in 2010.* Washington, D.C.: U.S. Department of Justice, Bureau of Justice Statistics. Retrieved from: http://bjs.ojp.usdoj.gov/content/pub/pdf/p10.pdf.

Hamlin, J. F., Granatstein, S., Flaum, A. T., & Klug, R. (2007, February 11). The death of Timothy Souders [Television series episode]. In J. Fager (Executive Producer), *60 Minutes.* New York, NY: Central Broadcasting Service. Retrieved from http://www.cbsnews.com/2100-18560_162-2448074.html.

Haney, C. (2003). Mental health issues in long-term solitary and "supermax" confinement. *Crime and Delinquency,* 49, 124–156.

Haney, C. (2008). A culture of harm: Taming the dynamics of cruelty in supermax prisons. *Criminal Justice and Behavior.* 35, 956–984.

Haney, C. (2017). "Madness" and penal confinement: Some observations on mental illness and prison pain. *Punishment and Society. 19*(3), 310–326.

Harkinson, R. (2009). CIT training and the mentally ill. *American Jails, 23*(1), 15–16, 18.

Hassine, V. (1996). *Life without parole: Living in prison today.* Los Angeles, CA: Roxbury.

Herpertz, S. (2007). Self-injurious behaviour: Psychopathological and nosological characteristics in subtypes of self-injurers. *Acta Psychiatrica Scandinavica, 91,* 57–68.

Hodges, J. (2010). Crisis intervention teams adapted to correctional populations. *Corrections Today,* 72(5), 106–107.

Human Rights Watch. (2003). *Ill equipped: U.S. prisons and offenders with mental illness.* New York, NY: Author.

Hresko, T. (2006). In the cellars of the hollow men: Use of solitary confinement in U.S. prison and its implications under international laws against torture. *Pace International Law Review,* 18, 1–27.

Immarigeon, R. (2011). Crisis intervention team training for correctional officers: Introduction. *Corrections and Mental Health*, National Institute of Corrections. Retrieved from http://community.nicic.gov/blogs/mentalhealth/archive/2011/08/04/crisis-intervention-team-training-for-correctional-officers-introduction.aspx.

Inglot, S. (2011, October 3). Snyder calls for mental health reform. *Grand Rapids Business Journal*, p. 9.

Insel, T. (2010). *Turning the corner, not the key, in treatment of serious mental illness.* National Institute of Mental Health. Retrieved from http://www.nimh.nih.gov/about/director/2010/turning-the-corner-not-the-key-in-treatment-of-serious-mental-illness.shtml.

Izumi, L. T., Schiller, M., & Hayward, S. (1996). *Corrections, criminal justice, and the mentally ill: Some observations about costs in California: Mental health briefing.* San Francisco, CA: Pacific Research Institute.

James, D. J., & Glaze, L. E. (2006, September). *Special report: Mental health problems of prison and jail inmates* (NCJ 213600). Washington, D.C.: U.S. Department of Justice, Bureau of Justice Statistics. Retrieved from http://bjs.ojp.usdoj.gov/content/pub/pdf/mhppji.pdf.

Jones, A. (1986). Self-mutilation in prison: A comparison of mutilators and nonmutilators. *Criminal Justice and Behavior, 13*, 286–296.

Keltner, N. L., & Vance, D. E. (2008). Biological perspectives: Incarcerated care and Quetiapine abuse. *Perspectives in Psychiatric Care, 44*(3), 202–206.

Krelstein, M. S. (2002). The role of mental health in the inmate disciplinary process: A national survey. *Journal of the American Academy of Psychiatry and the Law, 30*, 488–496.

Leifman, S. (2001, August 16). Mentally ill and in jail. *Washington Post*. Retrieved from http://www.psychlaws.org/GeneralResources/article50.htm.

Lerner-Wren, G. (2000). Broward's mental health court: An innovative approach to the mentally disabled in the criminal justice system. *Community Mental Health Report, 1*(1), 5–6.

Leonard, K. (2012, July 22). State efforts to outsource prison health care come under scrutiny. *Kaiser Health*. Retrieved from http://www.kaiserhealthnews.org/Stories/2012/July/23/prison-health-care.aspx?p=1.

Madrid v. Gomez, 889 F. Supp. 1146 (N.D. Cal. 1995).

McCleland, J. (2012, June 19). *The high costs of high security at supermax prisons.* Washington, D.C.: National Public Radio. Retrieved from: http://www.npr.org/2012/06/19/155359553/the-high-costs-of-high-security-at-supermax-prisons.

McKenna, B., Skipworth, J., Tapsell, R., Pillai, K., Madell, K., Simpson, A., Cavney, J. & Rouse, P. (2018). Impact of an assertive community treatment model of care on the treatment of prisoners with a serious mental illness. *Australasian Psychiatry, 26*(3), 285–289.

McKinney, D. (2012, February 25). Ex-inmate on controversial prison: 'Tamms never leaves my head.' *Sun-Times Springfield Bureau*. Retrieved from: http://www.sun times.com/10862646-417/tamms-never-leaves-my-head.html.

Mears, D., & Castro, J. (2006). Warden's views on the wisdom of supermax facilities. *Crime and Delinquency, 52*(3), 398–431.

Metzner, J. L. (2007, September 1). Evolving issues in correctional psychiatry. *Psychiatric Times, 24*, 10. Retrieved from http://www.psychiatrictimes.com/show Article.jhtml?articleID=201802883.

Metzner, J., Cohen, F., Grossman, L. S., & Wettstein, R. M. (1998). Treatment in jails and prisons. In R. M. Wettstein (Ed.), *Treatment of offenders with mental disorders* (pp. 230–233). New York, NY: Guilford.

Mitchell, J. (2010, June 4). Parchman's Unit 32 to remain closed. *Clarion Ledger*. Retrieved from http://www.clarionledger.com/article/20120718/NEWS/207180334/ Parchman-s-Unit-32-remain-closed.

Morgan, R. D., Steffan, J., Shaw, L. B., & Wilson, S. (2007). Needs for and barriers to correctional mental health services: Inmate perceptions. *Psychiatric Services, 58*(9), 1181–1186.

National Alliance on Mental Illness. (2004, March). *Spending money in all the wrong places: Jails and prisons.* Arlington, VA: Author. Retrieved from http://www. nami.org/Template.cfm?section=Fact_Sheets&Template=/ContentManagement/ ContentDisplay.cfm&ContentID=14593.

National Institute of Corrections. (2001, February). *Special issues in corrections: Provision of mental health care in prisons.* Longmont, CO: U.S. Department of Justice, NIC Information Center. Retrieved from http://static.nicic.gov/Library/016724.pdf.

Navasky, M., & O'Connor, K. (Producers). (2005, May 10). *Frontline: The New Asylums* [Television broadcast]. Boston: PBS/WGBH Educational Foundation.

Pfeifer, M. B. (2007, March 1). Prison: A wasteland for mentally ill. *Boston Globe*. Retrieved from: http://www.boston.com/news/globe/editorial_opinion/oped/ articles/2007/03/01/prison_a_wasteland_for_mentally_ill/.

Reassessing solitary confinement: The human rights, fiscal and public safety consequences. (2012, June 19). Hearings before the Subcommittee on the Constitution, Civil Rights and Human Rights of the Committee on the Judiciary. Washington, D.C.: U.S. Senate. Retrieved from: http://www.judiciary.senate.gov/hearings/ hearing.cfm?id=6517e7d97c06eac4ce9f60b09625ebe8.

Regehr, Carey, M., Wagner, S. Alden, L., … & White, N. (2019). Prevalence of PTSD, depression, and anxiety disorders in correctional officers: A systematic review. *Corrections: Policy, Research and Practice*. DOI: https://doi.org/10.1080.237746 572019.1641765.

Rich, W. J. (2009). The path of mentally ill offenders. *Fordham Urban Law Journal, 36*, 89–119.

Ruiz v. Estelle, 503 F. Supp. 1265 (S.D. Tex. 1980).

Ruiz v. Johnson, 37 F. Supp. 2nd 855 (S.D. Tex. 1999).

Satel, S. (2003, November 1). Out of the asylum, into the cell. *New York Times*, p. A1.

Shaw, L. B., & Morgan, R. D. (2011). Inmate attitudes toward treatment: Mental health service utilization and treatment effects. *Law & Human Behavior, 35*, 249–261.

Spencer, L. S., & Fallon, C. M. (2012, August). Today's special needs call for new approaches. *Corrections Today*, 6–8.

Stone, T. H. (1997). Therapeutic implications of incarceration for persons with severe mental disorders: Searching for rational health policy. *American Journal of Criminal Law, 24*, 283–358.

Swanson, J., Swartz, M., Gilbert, A., Frisman, L., Lin, H., Rodis, E., ... Henson, A. (2011, December 28). *Costs of criminal justice involvement among persons with severe mental illness in Connecticut*. Retrieved from: https://ps.psychiatryonline. org/doi/full/10.1176/appi.ps.002212012.

Teplin, L. A. (1994). Psychiatric and substance abuse disorders among male urban jail detainees. *American Journal of Public Health, 84*, 290–292.

Toch, H., & Adams, K. (2002). *Acting out: Maladaptive behavior in confinement*. Washington, D.C.: American Psychological Association.

Torrey, E. F., Entsminger, K., Geller, J., Stanley, J., & Jaffe, D. J. (2008). *The shortage of public hospital beds for mentally ill persons: A report of the Treatment Advocacy Center*. Arlington, VA: Treatment Advocacy Center. Retrieved from http://www. treatmentadvocacycenter.org/index.php?option=com_content&task=view&id=81.

Torrey, E. F., Kennard, A. D., Eslinger, D., Lamb, R., & Pavle, J. (2010, May). *More mentally ill persons are in jails and prisons than hospitals: A survey of the states*. Arlington, VA: Treatment Advocacy Center. Retrieved from http://www.treatmentadvocacycenter.org/storage/documents/final_jails_v_hospitals_study.pdf.

Vitiello, M. (2010). Addressing the special problems of mentally ill prisoners: A small piece of the solution to our nation's prison crisis. *Denver University Law Review, 88*, 57–71.

Wakefield v. Thompson, 117 F. 3d 1160 (9th Cir. 1999).

Ward, T., Mesler, J., & Yates, P. (2007). Reconstructing the Risk-Need-Responsivity model: A theoretical elaboration and evaluation. *Aggression and Violent Behavior, 12*, 208–228.

Wilper, A. P., Woolhandler, S., Boyd, J. W., Lasser, K. E., McCormick, M. D., Bor, D. H. & Himmelstein, D. U. (2009). The health and health care of U.S. prisoners: Results of a nationwide survey. *American Journal of Public Health, 99*, 666–672.

Wolff, N., Blitz, C. L., & Shi, J. (2007). Rates of sexual victimization in prison for inmates with and without mental disorders. *Psychiatric Services, 58*, 1087–1094.

Chapter 10

Diversion and Reentry: Strategies for Discharging Offenders Living with Mental Illness

"For these are all our children. We will profit by, or pay for whatever they become."

— James Baldwin[1]

This chapter examines the variability of diversion and/or discharge planning around the country and discusses a number of exemplary programs. We will also consider the role that probation, parole, Assertive Community Treatment (ACT), families, and organizations such as the National Alliance on Mental Illness (NAMI) are playing in ensuring adherence to community treatment dictates. Particular attention will be paid to the importance of collaboration in planning and facilitating prisoner reentry, as well as a review of best practices.

Approximately 622,400 people are released from U.S. federal and state prisons each year, and millions more are released from jails (Bronson & Carson, 2019). Prisoners that don't live with mental illness reentering society face serious challenges. During the first 2 weeks after release, former prisoners released back into society have 12 times the rate of death than the general population (Binswanger et al., 2007). For those offenders living with mental illness the challenges are exponential. Individuals with mental illnesses are significantly overrepresented in corrections settings, but for probation and parole officers burdened with large caseloads and the time-consuming needs of this population, their ability to be effective transition agents is limited. As such, it is no wonder that offenders with mental illness are twice as likely to have their community supervision revoked (Prins & Draper, 2009).

The implementation of discharge plans is a key component to reentry of both jail inmates and prisoners. However, only one-third of inmates with mental illness receive

---

1. As cited in Birckhead (2012, p. 1). A more complete discussion is provided later in this chapter.

discharge-planning services (Bazelon Center, 2010). As a result, prisoners with mental illness are more likely to violate their parole and be returned to prison, delaying their recovery, which is an ineffective use of public safety dollars (Bazelon Center, 2010).

There are, though, promising programs for reducing the recidivism of this population. Mauch, Mulligan, and crane (2018) refer to SSI/SSDI, Outreach, Access, and Recovery (SOAR) as one such program that has seen recidivism drop from 70 to 22 percent when those being released from custody have had their benefits restored. Similarly, they report that Multonomah County Mental Health and Addiction Services resulted in over 6 million dollars in savings by reducing hospital and jail stays. Polk County Sheriff Grady Judd, who already has a Special Needs Unit in his jail in Bartow, Florida, has implemented a "Helping Hands" program to assist those being released from jail who have been selected for the program due to mental health needs. People are identified and then prepared for participation while in jail and followed upon release. Peer counselors are used and Emergency Medical Technicians (EMTs) provide a safety net in the community upon release. The EMTs can transport those released to medical appointments and check to make sure meds are taken by clients, as anosognosia often permeates those with mental illness. As such, this writer saw a presentation to the Helping Hands staff by Hamilton Baiden, Chief Managing Officer, of Heritage Health Solutions. He said his company had a contract with the U.S. Marshals Service. One of the services Hamilton said they could offer was the ability to track medication compliance without needless use of manpower. He said that they could include capsules of medication that when swallowed would mix with gastric juices of a participant and then set off a frequency inside a telephonic device, which would then signal headquarters that medication had been consumed (personal communication, February 28, 2019).

According to Willingham and Elkin (2018), almost every U.S. citizen will encounter some type of mental health crisis at some juncture in their lives. They argue this becomes of particular concern in rural areas where two-thirds of non-metropolitan counties do not even have one psychiatrist in residence.

The following describes a classic "frequent flyer," an individual with mental illness who repeatedly cycles between jail and the streets:

The Case of Michael Jung

Mentally ill with bipolar disorder and fearing voices telling him he's the devil, Michael Jung turns up over and over in Ventura County's main jail. He has been booked at least 15 times in the past 10 years, revolving from a cell to temporary lodgings to the street and back. "I've gotten slightly institutionalized," said the Camarillo man with a litany of drug and alcohol convictions, but no violent felonies. "I know this is where I have to be." Until his latest release in September, he was confined for six weeks in G Quad, the unit where psychiatric inmates stay in their cells for all but one hour of the day. Jung said he's been taken to what he calls "lower purgatory" many times, referring to the so-called rubber rooms where suicidal inmates stay until they calm down. Still, he calls his treatment in jail "pretty fair." He saw a psychiatrist, took his medications and a nurse stopped by his cell to help him fend off the voices, he said. But doctors and family members say the challenge is to keep inmates like Jung from coming back (Wilson, 2009).

Discharge protocols that fail to provide a network of support for released offenders with mental illness can only result in the continued recycling of persons with mental illnesses through the criminal justice system and needless suffering for these individuals and society. Without appropriate intervention, failure should be expected and will likely continue.

The purpose of the criminal justice system "is the protection of the order and security of society" (Kittrie, 1978, p. 12). Police often have emblazoned on their cars the motto "protect and serve," and this responsibility is expected of criminal justice professionals. With this responsibility comes the authority to take our freedom away from us. Although it is not always evident, the protect *and* serve credo still applies once an individual is brought under the supervision, custody, and care of the criminal justice system. While policies often involve protocols of care, organizational culture frequently overrides policy. For example, New York City's Department of Correction mission statement as of the year 2000 indicates as follows:

> The Department of Correction provides custody, control and care of misdemeanants and felons sentenced to one year of incarceration or less; detainees awaiting trial or sentence; newly sentenced felons awaiting transportation to State correctional facilities; alleged parole violators awaiting revocation hearings; and State prisoners with court appearances in New York City. Professional care and services, including health and mental health care, opportunities for religious observance, educational instruction, vocational training and substance abuse counseling are provided (Giuliani, 2000, p. 37).

In the above statement, the word "care" is mentioned three times. While the words look nice and resonate well with us on paper, what is horrific and inexcusable is the reality of how the New York City Department of Correction in practice was carrying out the "custody," "control," and "care," and offering "professional ... services" to persons with mental illnesses. Indeed, these policies were in place at the time that the travesties delineated in the class action case known as *Brad H.* occurred.

As referred to in Chapter 6 rather than providing discharge planning, the New York City Department of Corrections would drop off former inmates with mental illness at Queens Plaza with nothing more than $1.50 in cash and a two-fare Metrocard (Barr, 2003a; Parish, 2007). They performed these drop-offs four mornings a week, between 2 and 6 a.m. Why between 2 and 6 a.m.? The citizenry would be much less likely to become aware of such a practice. This practice ultimately led to the *Brad H.* lawsuit (Barr, 2003a). At the time the suit was filed, Brad H. was a 44-year-old homeless man with schizophrenia who had been treated 26 times in jail for mental illness but never received any linkage to treatment in the community or assistance with accessing Medicaid benefits, Social Security disability payments, or shelter upon any of his releases back into the community (Saulny, 2003).

The *Brad H.* complaint referred to a system whereby, at a minimum, 25,000 jail inmates a year were receiving mental health treatment in jail, but almost no one received discharge planning for release. This literally set individuals up to fail and return to the criminal justice system (Barr, 2003a). As noted by Barr (2003a), and as discussed in Chapters 6 and 9, mental health treatment in jails and prisons has been mandated by the U.S. Supreme Court since 1976 with *Estelle v. Gamble*; however, discharge planning has largely been ignored by such institutions. The *Brad H.* attorneys pursued the Department of Correction on the prohibition against cruel and unusual punishment clause of the 8th Amendment to the U.S. Constitution and a New York state law, entitled the Mental Hygiene Law, which dictates that providers of inpatient mental health treatment services must provide discharge planning (Barr, 2003a).

The assistance sought in the *Brad H.* class action suit asked for the following for each of the 15,000 persons with mental illnesses released from jail: an adequate supply of medication, at least a shelter with a bed, access to mental health services, and assurance of immediate benefits like Medicaid and food stamps without a 45-day waiting period (Bernstein, 2000). When one of the attorneys for Brad H. was queried about how much such a plan would cost the city, she replied that based on the repercussions of what they were currently doing, in terms of repeated recycling of individuals through the jail, it should save them a fortune.

"On January 8, 2003, the parties settled the case with an agreement that the City would provide people who have received mental health treatment or have taken medication for a mental health condition while in jail with discharge planning" (Parish, 2007, p. 6). The settlement went into effect in June of 2003. Compliance was to be monitored for an initial five years by attorneys for the plaintiffs and by two special court-appointed monitors, Henry Dlugacz and Erik Roskes (Parish, 2007). This litigation is still being monitored through July 31, 2020 and may be extended further (Erik Roskes, personal communication).

Judge Steve Leifman, a long-time advocate of mental health courts, stated, "We have a criminal justice system which has a very clear purpose: You get arrested. We want justice. We try you, and justice hopefully prevails. It was never built to handle people that were very, very ill, at least with mental illness" (National Public Radio, 2011). While litigation can be long, drawn-out, costly, and protracted, sometimes that is what it takes to right injustices. Without intervention, the New York City system was clearly setting individuals up to fail and recycle through the criminal justice system at great costs, not only financially but in terms of needless human suffering for persons with mental illnesses and sometimes members of society.

It is estimated that at least 80% of all offenders returning to prison have chronic physical, mental, and/or substance abuse issues: 41% of men and 71% of women were likely to have a mental illness. Comparisons of screening and self-report data indicate that approximately 25% of recidivists have an undiagnosed mental illness; 16% of male and 31% of female recidivists reported symptoms consistent with Post-Traumatic Stress Disorder alone (Mallik-Kane & Visher, 2008). These findings are particularly important considering the financial costs of securing and treating offenders with mental illness.

As in the previously discussed case of Michael Jung, the costs associated with such recycling compounds over time. "According to [one] study, more than 70% of the mentally ill offenders who were released from the jail in Lucas County, Ohio, were re-arrested within a three-year period. A second study showed that 90% of the mentally ill inmates in the Los Angeles County Jail were repeat offenders, and nearly 10% of those mentally ill offenders had been incarcerated on ten or more instances" (Rivera, 2004, p. 132). Also noted by Torrey, Kennard, Eslinger, Lamb, and Pavle (2010), mentally ill inmates cost more than non-mentally ill inmates for a variety of reasons, including increased staffing needs. In Broward County, Florida, it costs $80 a day to house a regular inmate but $130 a day for an inmate with mental illness. In Texas prisons 'the average prisoner costs the state about $22,000 a year,' but 'prisoners with mental illness range from $30,000 to $50,000 a year.' Psychiatric medications are a significant part of the increased costs; ... at Ohio's Clark County Jail, prescription drugs costs for inmates [have] exceeded the costs of feeding inmates. Psychiatric examinations are also expensive. In Palm Beach County, each time Jonathan Goode was arrested he was required to have a psychiatric exam, each costing $2,000, producing an expenditure of $98,000 over 40 months. Finally, there is the cost of an increasing number of lawsuits, such as the suit brought in New Jersey ... by the family of a "65-year-old mentally ill stockbroker [who was] stomped to death in the Camden County Jail" (Torrey, Kennard, Eslinger, Lamb, & Pavle, 2010, pp. 9–10).

Community treatment has potential as an effective preventative strategy while providing a cost-saving alternative to incarceration. Assertive Community Treatment (ACT) programs, as discussed in Chapter 3, cost less than incarceration at anywhere from $9,000 to $14,000 per participant per year and less than hospitalization (over a $100,000 a year) or group homes (over $30,000 a year) (Edgar, 1999).[2] More recently, an assessment of Forensic Assertive Community Treatment (FACT) involving high jail utilizers with serious mental illnesses in California took place (Cusack, Morrissey, Cuddeback, Prins, & Williams, 2010). As suggested by the term "forensic," such treatment teams are aimed at assisting justice-involved persons with mental illnesses from breaking the cycle of contact with the criminal justice system. In the California study, researchers found that persons with serious mental illnesses monitored by FACT teams, when compared to a randomized, representative group who received treatment as usual, were more likely to have lower per person inpatient costs ($5,426 vs. $8,852

---

2. A more complete discussion is provided later in this chapter.

in the first 12 months; $4,266 vs. $7,156 in the second year) and lower per person jail costs ($814 vs. $2,226 in the first 12 months; $2,043 vs. $3,019 in the second year) (Cusack, Morrissey, Cuddeback, Prins, & Williams, 2010). Participants monitored by outpatient FACT teams had higher outpatient costs than their treatment as usual counterparts during the study ($13,474 vs. $5,115 in the first 12 months; $8570 vs. $4,722 during the second year); however, the researchers noted that these outpatient costs were somewhat offset by less jail and inpatient costs for FACT participants. Of course, in accordance with the principles of therapeutic jurisprudence, the potential for long-term savings should be considered. More research on the cost-effectiveness of such programs is needed (Ryan, Brown, & Watanabe-Galloway, 2010).

The Thresholds program in Chicago utilizes a version of ACT, linking persons with mental illnesses released from jails to treatment in the community to reduce re-arrests, re-incarcerations, and re-hospitalizations (Lurigio, Fallon & Dincin, 2000). Thresholds' clients can enter the program from pretrial or post-adjudication stages. Those entering the program from the pretrial stage may do so from referral while awaiting trial in the community or via referral while being supervised by pretrial services as they await trial. After adjudication, persons with mental illnesses are re-ferred to Thresholds by judges or probation officers (Lurigio et al., 2000). "In a study of the first 30 patients enrolled in the Thresholds Jail Project, the total number of jail days dropped from 2,741 in the previous year to 469 during the first year of en-rollment. The total number of hospital days dropped from 2,153 to 321 for the group. Total savings in jail costs during the one-year study period was $157,000, and total savings in hospital costs was $917,000" (Lamberti, Weisman, & Faden, 2004, p. 1289). In a comparison of costs associated with the same cohort for 2 years pre- and post-program it was determined that jail days were reduced by 82.5% (with at least $209,000 saved), and psychiatric hospital days were reduced by 84.7% (with at least $1,154,000 saved) (J. Dincin, personal communication, December 11, 2002). Thus, the bulk of cost-savings occurred in the first year. The total estimated savings per person enrolled in the Thresholds program over the two years was $18,873.[3] The program remains in operation and recently reintegrated 250 persons with criminal justice involvement back into the community (Thresholds, 2011).

Discharge Planning, Diversion and Reentry

The distinctions between diversion and reentry and what constitutes discharge planning sometimes overlap and can be somewhat murky. Oftentimes the terms di-version and reentry are used interchangeably, and discharge planning can take place with both diversion and reentry. According to the Substance Abuse and Mental Health Services Administration (SAMHSA)-funded Technical Assistance and Policy

---

3. For more information see http://www.thresholds.org.

Analysis (TAPA) Center, "jail diversion" refers to programs that divert individuals with serious mental illness (and often co-occurring substance use disorders) away from jail and provide linkages to community-based treatment and support services (TAPA, 2007). The individual thus avoids arrest or spends a significantly reduced time period in jail and/or lockups on the current charge or on violations of probation resulting from previous charges (TAPA, 2007). Key jail diversion program activities include: defining a target group for diversion, identifying individuals as early as possible in their processing by the justice system, negotiating community-based treatment alternatives to incarceration, and implementing linkages to comprehensive systems of care and appropriate community supervision consistent with the disposition of the criminal justice contact (TAPA, 2007). While all diversion programs engage in some form of identification and linkage, there is no definitive model for organizing a jail diversion program (TAPA, 2007). Different jail diversion strategies are needed because local criminal justice systems vary so much in size, structural characteristics, levels of perceived need, resources available within the communities' mental health and substance abuse services network, and local politics and economics (TAPA, 2007).

Although Travis (2005) focuses on state prisoners returning to society, he indicates reentry applies to return to the community, regardless of whether supervision or conditional release is imposed, from any type of incarceration, including juvenile institutions, jails, and federal correctional facilities. Travis also notes that approximately 20% of the more than 630,000 prisoners who reenter society each year do so unconditionally and indicates that one-third of prisons fail to link prisoners with mental illnesses with mental health treatment providers upon release into the community. In a National Institute of Corrections study, less than half of the responding corrections departments acknowledged partnering with community mental health providers to facilitate linkages to treatment for persons with mental illnesses returning to the community from prison:

> 'Discharge planning' refers to the practice whereby a provider of mental healthcare develops a plan for the continuation of a patient's treatment after the patient's discharge from the provider's care. It is universally recognized as an essential part of adequate mental health treatment.... Discharge planning includes assistance in obtaining continuing mental health treatment, public benefits, and housing upon release, depending on an individual's diagnosis, level of functioning, and need for social services (Parish, 2007, p. 6).

In other words, if a jail or prison has been providing mental health treatment to one in their custody, upon release, it would logically follow that there is a responsibility to ensure for the provision of care upon leaving the correctional institution's custody.

Extensive information on diversion and reentry of persons with mental illnesses from the criminal justice system can be obtained from the GAINS Center (n.d.-b, n.d.-c). Also, a series of fact sheets are available from the GAINS Center (n.d.-d) addressing matters pertaining to the diversion and reentry of females with mental illnesses from the criminal justice system; information on persons with co-occurring disorders involved with the justice system can be ascertained from the GAINS Center (n.d.-a).

Since discharge planning can apply to both diversion and reentry programs,[4] the essential elements and examples of discharge planning will be discussed. Then, the benefits and specific examples of diversion and reentry programs will be presented and discussed.

Discharge Planning

Although discharge planning has long been considered a necessary component of effective psychiatric treatment in the community, Steadman and Veysey (1997), in an analysis of jail services, found such planning for those who had been jailed to return to the community to be the least often provided mental health service offered by jails, and, the larger the jail, the least likely discharge planning was to occur. "Because of the relatively short incarceration periods in jails and the frequently unpredictable timing of release, transition planners are often limited in their ability to help inmates establish linkages with community services" (Baillargeon, Hoge, & Penn, 2010, p. 369).

Haimowitz (2002) advocates for treatment protocols to address co-occurring disorders, the use of assertive community treatment, peer involvement, and the inclusion of housing and employment services to assist persons with mental illnesses who encounter the criminal justice system. Rivera (2004) recommends that multidisciplinary teams work with inmates with mental illnesses on discharge planning and linkages to treatment in the community. Sultan (2006) argues that reentry efforts for persons with mental illnesses must begin on the first day of incarceration and starts with intake screening. She maintains that reentry counselors are needed as transitional case managers in correctional facilities, as current processes, unfortunately, typically leave it up to the incarcerated individual to plan their own transition from custody to free society, perhaps with a limited supply of medication and often no assurances of linkages to treatment in the community.

Fulwiler (2000) also contends that inmates with mental illnesses should be engaged in release planning early on during their incarceration. He maintains that family members should be involved in the discharge planning process and indicates that NAMI is a valuable resource in communities throughout the country for offering support and advice to consumers of mental health services returning from prison and their family members. With the lack of mental health benefits available, many families serve as the primary caregiver for their mentally ill loved ones. Such education is essential for family member caregivers.

---

4. Hands Across Long Island (HALI) (2007) is a grassroots mental health self-help organization that offers a number of forensic programs to assist persons with mental illnesses that have encounters with the criminal justice system; the programs include both pre-booking diversion and reentry planning. HALI works with the local police to provide mobile outreach and potential diversion from the criminal justice system to persons with mental illnesses. Note this single program can serve both the functions of diversion and reentry.

Two such programs in operation in New York understand the value of work in assisting with recovery and bringing about self-empowerment, the Howie T. Harp Center in New York City was founded in 1995 to prepare consumers of mental health services for human service field careers (Harper, 2002). Since that time the Center, "based on a collaborative model" (Power, 2006), has trained more than 200 consumers and placed more than 150 in jobs. They also train forensic peer specialists, who know what it is like to be incarcerated, to work with others who currently find themselves entangled with the criminal justice system (Harper, 2002). Power (2006) identifies the Howie T. Harp Center as a collaborative model for employment training and placement for consumers of mental health services. Also Hands Across Long Island (2007), in their reentry programs, provides peer support via "bridgers" to work with inmates two months prior to release and up to four months after release to facilitate reentry.

Barr (2003b) argues that to ensure continuity of care linkages must be established between jail personnel and community treatment providers, and clinicians in the community should be instructed on how to track persons with mental illnesses who enter into the criminal justice system. She also maintains that community treatment providers should make contact with their client's jail-based clinician, and such connections should serve to facilitate discharge planning which should link persons with mental illnesses to community treatment services prior to release into the community. Included in this discharge planning should be the provision of housing, a month's supply of medication, expedited reinstatement of benefits, and the establishment of specialized probation and parole caseloads for supervision of persons with mental illnesses that have had encounters with the criminal justice system (Barr, 2003b). For those inmates with mental illnesses released from court as opposed to the jail, Barr (2003b) indicates that offices should be set up in courthouses to allow these individuals to check for linkages to treatment and shelter in the community.

Osher, Steadman, & Barr (2003) contend that persons with mental illnesses who have brief contacts with jails require quick interventions that are somewhat different from individuals with extensive stays in jails and prisons. They maintain that transition planning is bi-directional; thus, partnerships need to be established in the community with key stakeholders such as mental health providers and probation officers, even bringing them into the jail setting to assist with the APIC model, which is described as follows: Once individuals' needs are assessed, plans for identifying necessary community treatment services after release and coordinating the plan to make sure services are delivered in the community must be undertaken (Morrissette, 2017; Osher et al., 2003). Baillargeon et al. (2010) maintain that preferably transition should commence immediately upon the recognition that an inmate has a mental illness. Of course, this is tougher to accomplish in the transient jail setting and typically begins anywhere from 1 week to 6 months before release (Baillargeon et al., 2010).

Forensic transition teams (FTT), comprised of caseworkers and clinicians, have been established by the state department of mental health in Massachusetts to assist with discharge planning and linkages to community treatment for individuals with mental illnesses leaving prisons and jails. With prison releasees with mental illnesses more readily identifiable due to longer stints incarcerated, jails may want to consider ways to expedite evaluations and assessments to ensure adequate release planning (Hartwell & Orr, 2000). The FTT follows individuals selected for the program for three months after release. After the first year of operation of the program, almost 60% of the program's participants were residing in the community and utilizing mental health services, while only 10% were known to have been re-incarcerated; 20% had been hospitalized immediately after arrest (Hartwell & Orr, 1999). Hartwell (2004) also found that offenders with co-occurring disorders, as opposed to mental illness only, on average pose more of a challenge for FTT members upon release from correctional institutions and require more specialized interventions, such as a need for appropriate housing, to prevent potential re-contact with the criminal justice system.

In *Wakefield v. Thompson* (1999), a federal appellate court considered an 8th Amendment claim at a California prison regarding whether the refusal to provide medication upon release to a mentally ill inmate constituted cruel and unusual punishment. The court held that the state must provide an outgoing prisoner who is receiving and continues to require medication with a supply sufficient to ensure that he has that medication available during the period of time reasonably necessary to permit him to consult a doctor and obtain a new supply. A state's failure to provide medication sufficient to cover this transitional period amounts to an abdication of its responsibility to provide medical care to those who by reason of incarceration are unable to provide for their own medical needs.

For all newly discharged offenders, the highest risk of recidivism is in the first six months after release from prison (Council of State Governments, n.d.). It can be challenging for former prisoners to reunite with friends and family and adapt to all of the other aspects of the psychological and physical adjustment to a life outside of prison. Navigating the bureaucratic maze to access benefits and services — e.g., to locate housing and employment, gain access to public assistance, traverse the complicated mental health system, and secure scarce treatment resources — can prove daunting for anyone. Yet, it is much more so for persons with mental illnesses, who may even be symptomatic upon their reentry from prison. Their future in society is frequently uncertain, with the potential inability to meet basic survival needs such as food, shelter and job concerns. Thus, offenders with mental illnesses who do not receive adequate discharge planning or a continuity of treatment upon release are at a particular disadvantage during this crucial readjustment. Individuals with mental illnesses leaving prison without sufficient supplies of medication, connections to mental health and other support services, and housing are almost certain to decompensate (Council of State Governments, 2002). This, in turn, may very well result in behavior that constitutes a technical violation of release conditions or a new crime (Human Rights Watch, 2003).

Department of Correction (DOC) involvement in discharge planning varies from state to state. Most recently, Blevins and Soderstrom (2012) in their study of Department of Corrections' Mental Health Chief Administrators (CMHCAs) found, as reflected in Table 1, that the majority of CMHCAs reported that interagency referrals for aftercare were made for inmates with mental illnesses leaving prison; meanwhile CMHCAS in Southern states were over twice as likely as CMHCAs in the other states to provide a supply of psychotropic medication to inmates upon returning to society. Baillergeon et al. (2010) indicates that in a 1998 study, only 7 of 41 (17%) of the DOCs reported providing discharge planning to inmates, although 23 of the 41DOCS provided medication; in a 2007 study of 43 state DOCs, 44% of the DOCs indicated that they provided a written discharge plan, and 100% of the DOCs reported providing prescription medication to those inmates taking it at the time of their release. Thus, it appears that state prisons are increasingly providing discharge services.

Table 1. Aftercare

	Southern States %	Other States %
Medication Only	77.8	31.3
Counseling Only	0.0	6.3
Medication and Counseling	11.1	31.3
Interagency Referrals	77.8	87.5
No Aftercare	0.0	6.3
Would you like to see aftercare services improved? (Yes)	88.9	87.5

Blevins & Soderstrom (2012)

The following information about DOC engagement in this process is provided by the Human Rights Watch (2003). In Nebraska, for example, inmates released into the community with mental illnesses are usually given a 14-day supply of medication and given names of community mental health providers, but no appointments are made for them. Released prisoners in Arkansas receive a one-week supply of psychotropic medicine and are urged to choose a private mental health provider upon release. Absent that, DOC personnel will try to make an appointment for them with a public provider, but there are no guarantees, as the availability of public services varies widely around the state. Virginia provides a 30-day supply of medication at release, and inmates with mental illnesses have a release plan devised in conjunction with mental health counselors, and the DOC makes an effort to make appointments for after-care for those released. However, there are not enough community resources, and some exit prison with no appointments established. North Carolina purportedly individualizes a treatment plan for persons with mental illnesses being released from prison and provides a 30-day supply of medication, as well as makes an appointment with a mental health provider for the release and provides the contact information for the provider to the inmate (Human Rights Watch, 2003).

Notice, an essential element missing from all of these discharge plans is a follow-up component. In other words, there is no single entity designated as being responsible for ensuring that individuals upon release from custody see mental health providers and engage in treatment. As will be discussed in the last chapter, failure to ensure such follow-up can lead to tragic consequences.

Jurisdictions have used various approaches to divert persons with mental illness from jails. Gill and Murphy (2017) report on one such program coordinated by a prosecutor's office that reduced re-arrest and fewer days incarcerated for this population. Sirotich (2009) in another study concluded jail diversion programs can reduce time in jail for people with mental illness. Likewise, Tartaro (2015) found a substantial reduction (218 days) in time before being incarcerated with a diversion program in New Jersey. Of course, follow-up is an essential ingredient for success in such programs.

Most states, though not required by federal law to do so, strike prisoners from Medicaid rolls and require application for reinstatement of Medicaid benefits upon release (Human Rights Watch, 2003). In fact, according to Baillargeon et al. (2010) the majority of prisoners with mental illnesses upon release have no health insurance, and 60% of them still have no health benefits 8 to 10 months after reentering society. They argue along with Scotti (2017) such benefits should be temporarily suspended, not terminated, since there is no federal law requiring termination; legislation has been passed in Maryland and New York requiring that Medicaid be only suspended for persons who have such benefits upon entering jail or prison.

Supplemental Security Income (SSI) benefits are required to be terminated upon being incarcerated for a year or longer by federal law, and the law mandates that Social Security Disability Insurance (SSDI) benefits be suspended, but not terminated, at the point of incarceration (Human Rights Watch, 2003). Obviously, maintaining access to Medicaid benefits enhances linkages to care and reduces the monetary burden on local and state governments (Veysey, 2011). Jails, where stints in custody are much shorter than in prisons, have been found to sometimes not get around to suspending Medicaid benefits (Veysey, 2011).

According to the Human Rights Watch (2003), it generally runs a month and a half to three months to have benefits reinstated after release from custody, which is hardly conducive to continuity of care. Varying degrees of assistance are rendered by states to inmates in securing benefits upon release; some DOCs establish mechanisms to ensure that benefits are available upon release, with some DOCs assisting in completing applications for reinstatement of benefits (Human Rights Watch, 2003). Advocates have called for legislation restoring such assistance immediately upon release. Kara Salim is an example of what can happen when benefits are not available upon release from jail (NPR, 2016). "At age 26 she got out of the Marion County, Indiana, jail in 2015 with a history of domestic-violence charges, bipolar disorder and alcoholism — and without Medicaid coverage. As a result, she couldn't afford the fees for court-ordered therapy. Without therapy she wasn't allowed to see a psychiatrist for her medications. Without medication she spiraled downward, eventually threatening suicide at a court hearing. When court officers tried to bring her to a psychiatric hospital, she erupted, kicking and scratching them and landing back in jail, with new felony charges: battery against a public safety officer" (p. 9).

Of course, just because benefits are reinstated and even appointments with mental health providers in place upon release there is no assurance that each prisoner with mental illness will receive treatment upon release.

Just because benefits are reinstated, there is no guarantee that the person will be able to get an appointment in a timely manner. The Council of State Governments (2007) in a study of four states (Minnesota, New York, Pennsylvania, and Texas) identified the common elements of success in making sure that prisoners with mental illnesses have access to Medicaid, Supplemental Security Income (SSI), and Social Security Disability Insurance (SSDI) upon leaving prison and returning to the community. Commonalities among the states included interagency involvement, whereby at least two different agencies would coordinate efforts to properly handle enrollments. Inmates ready for release and initial discharge planning were identified anywhere from one to three months prior to their anticipated release. In turn, new programs or agencies were established in each state and/or specialized caseloads were established for staff to focus on acquiring specific benefits. Other promising practices in the four states were clearly specifying which agency was responsible for what; sharing information via technology between agencies to facilitate the process; releasing plans early, with Minnesota beginning three months in advance; and providing DOC-coverage of benefits to releasees up to 45 days after release to ensure access to needed medication and food, as is done in New York State. Communication is key, even among county agencies; and clarifications regarding convoluted federal rules over eligibility requirements should be sought from the Social Security Administration (SSA) and the Centers for Medicare and Medicaid Services (CMS) (Council of State Governments, 2007).

Diversion

While we have discussed police-based diversion and mental health courts in previous chapters, we will attempt to focus this segment of the chapter on diverting persons with mental illnesses from the criminal justice system. However, as we have indicated, the lines between diversion and reentry are blurred.

Criminal justice diversion programs generally can be classified as either pre-booking or post-booking. Pre-booking implies that diversion occurs prior to arrest charges being entered by law enforcement, and post-booking indicates that diversion is transpiring after an individual has been booked into jail with charges entered against him/her (Steadman, Deane, Borum, & Morrissey, 2000). Previously discussed police-based diversion programs, such as CIT, would be illustrative of pre-booking diversion, while mental health courts can be indicative of post-booking diversion.[5]

---

5. It should be noted that it is estimated that about half of all post-booking diversion programs are associated with mental health courts (Case, Steadman, Dupuis, & Morris, 2009).

Other types of diversion programs in existence include: assertive community treatment, residential support, intensive case management, and intensive psychiatric probation and parole (Ryan et al., 2010). Some believe the combination of pre and post booking diversion programs can work in tandem in terms of linking persons with mental illnesses to treatment in the community.

A 1994 survey of jails with a capacity for 50 or more detainees resulted in responses from 760 jails. Of these, only 52 had a formal diversion program for persons with mental illnesses that complied with their research specifications (Steadman, Barbera, & Dennis, 1994). Thus, at that time, approximately 7% of jails examined were determined to have a formal diversion program in place. More recently, it has been estimated that there are over 560 jail diversion programs in operation in 47 states (Case, Steadman, Dupuis, & Morris, 2009). Rogers (2015) provides an overview of diversion programs in 18 states and the federal government; she notes as of 2010, 45 states had diversion laws in place.

Case et al. (2009) report that persons with mental illnesses who are linked to community-based services when diverted from jail are less likely to be arrested and serve fewer days in jail; these researchers caution that the best predictor of future contact with the criminal justice system for diversion participants is prior contact, i.e. criminal history.

There are some commonalities among diversion programs. Steadman et al. (1999) maintain that "two core elements are necessary for diversion programs: aggressive linkage to an array of community services, especially those for co-occurring mental health and substance use disorders, and nontraditional case managers" (p. 1623) ... ..." Major goals for mental health diversion programs include the avoidance or the reduction of jail time..., an overall reduction of recidivism rates, and continuing linkage of ... detainees with comprehensive community-based services" (p. 1623). As noted by Steadman, Morris, & Dennis (1995), jail diversion programs do not operate merely to let persons with mental illnesses out of jail; to be successful they must provide discharge planning, establish linkages to treatment in the community, and ensure follow-up. To ease reintegration into the community, Seltzer (2005) maintains that guilty pleas for persons with mental illnesses should be avoided, as they serve as a hindrance to meaningful employment and to obtaining housing.

Munetz & Griffin (2006) have delineated a model for diversion of persons with serious mental illnesses from the criminal justice system and linkage to treatment in the community. Their model encompasses both pre and post booking diversion with five intercept points identified for intervention in the criminal justice process. The five points in sequential order are (1) police and emergency service providers; (2) after arrest at initial hearings; (3) after first appearance hearings via assessments in jail, by the court, or forensic evaluations and commitments; (4) discharge planning and linkage to appropriate treatment should be ensured for individuals reentering the community from jails, prisons and hospitals; (5) the utilization of community corrections, for example, probation officers, to assist in linking individuals to treatment in the community Munetz & Griffin (2006).

Examples of Diversion Programs

As noted by Clark (2004) there are two critical decision points after arrest: the pre-trial release decision and the decision as to whether or not to defer prosecution. The Bexar County Jail Diversion Program in San Antonio, Texas has been identified as a model program, and, in fact, its successes prompted the Texas legislature to enact legislation requiring all community mental health centers to devise state-approved jail diversion strategies (Bexar County Jail Diversion Program, 2006; see also Pamerleau, 2016; Wang, 2021). This jail diversion program over a two and one-half year time span resulted in $3.8 to $5.0 million in savings to the criminal justice system in Bexar County. The program is arranged in three phases: to initially screen persons with mental illnesses picked up by law enforcement and make alternative recommendations to magistrates prior to booking, to identify persons with mental illnesses who have been booked into the criminal justice system and make recommendations for alternative dispositions such as a mental health bond or relocation to a mental health facility, and to ensure that persons upon release from jail are provided linkages to mental health treatment. The program also includes a Crisis Care Center, which is open around the clock and provides a valuable resource for law enforcement as a one-stop receiving facility, providing psychiatric care, housing, and social work capabilities. Prior to the opening of the Crisis Care Center it was not uncommon for law enforcement officers to have wait times for up to 12 hours when bringing a person with mental illness in to be evaluated. Now wait times on average for such screenings are a little over an hour (Bexar County Jail Diversion Program, 2006).

Harris County, Texas, is an example of another partnership between mental health and criminal justice practitioners. Community mental health personnel literally follow individuals into the jail system to provide continuity of care. CIT is in place, as well as an assertive community treatment team, and a mobile crisis outreach team that can come to and assist persons with mental illnesses released from jail into the community who have difficulty accessing community mental health treatment. Pretrial service personnel are at an individual's first appearance before the court to provide relevant clinical information, and individuals being booked into the jail are cross referenced with a mental health data base system. In stages like those found in Bexar County, persons with mental illness are screened, identified, tracked, diverted when possible, and linked to treatment. Advance notification from the county jail and from the Texas state prison system is made to the Mental Health And Mental Retardation Authority upon the impending release of persons with mental illnesses from custody to assist in linking individuals to treatment in the community. Specialized psychiatric and intensive case management services for persons with mental illnesses on pre-trial release, probation, and parole are available under the New START program in Texas (Harris County, 2021; Harris County Mental Health and Mental Retardation Authority, 2005).

The Nathaniel Project is unique in that it is a two-year alternative to incarceration program established in New York City for persons with mental illnesses who have committed a felony (Barr, 2001; see also Psychiatric Services, 2014). The program targets violent felons, especially when it is believed that the offense committed was the result of previous lack of access to appropriate treatment. Most referrals to the program come from defense attorneys, but referrals have also been made from mental health workers, judges and prosecutors. They refer to their program as "intrusive case management" (Barr, 2001, p. 44) due to the intensive scrutiny that participants receive, as clients can be physically seen up to seven days a week and are seen a minimum of three days a week in the initial phase of the program. Usually a client pleads guilty and is released to the custody of the program. If they successfully complete the program, participants will not be sentenced to incarceration; if they fail, they will receive extensive sentences in state prison.

> In a world with a mental health system comprehensive enough to meet the needs of everyone with a serious mental illness, and where incarceration was used sparingly, the Nathaniel Project would not be necessary. However, given that our mental health system is broken, and incarceration is being used as a solution to many social problems, we believe that the Nathaniel Project is a model that can be used to help some of the most disenfranchised mental health consumers leave the criminal justice system and build new lives (Barr, 2001, p. 44).

In Miami, Judge Steve Leifman has established a mental health program that incorporates, pre-booking diversion via CIT and post-booking diversion whereby mentally ill misdemeanant defendants are identified within 24–48 hours after arrest, assessed by a jail psychiatrist and a determination is made with the court as to whether to divert for mental health treatment to an appropriate mental health facility. The court has in place an integrated comprehensive treatment program, equipped with a court case management specialist and access to adult living facilities and an assertive community treatment team to assist persons with mental illnesses diverted from jail (Perez, Leifman, & Estrada, 2003). Again, the keys to successful diversion of persons with mental illnesses from the criminal justice system is having access to sufficient services, ensuring linkages to treatment, and providing follow-up to ensure compliance with treatment protocols.

Reentry

Prins & Draper (2009) found that former inmates living with mental illness are twice as likely to have their community supervision revoked:

> The usual prejudices that hinder community treatment of the mentally ill may be more severe for mentally ill offenders who may be thought to pose a greater risk to public safety.... [C]ommunity agencies and practitioners sometimes assess mentally ill offenders' risk of violence and overestimate their professional liability risks; thus, they may be reluctant to provide outpatient treatment for mentally ill offenders (Lovell et al., 2002, p. 1291).

"Thomas Murton, on whom the movie Brubaker starring Robert Redford was based, has indicated that putting a person in prison to teach them how to live in society is like putting a person on the moon to teach them how to live on earth. The environments are extremely different" (Anderson & Slate, 2011, p. 377). As such, it is not surprising that Golembeski and Fullilove (2008, p. 185) argue that "[a] more humanistic and community-centered approach to incarceration and rehabilitation may yield more beneficial results for individuals, communities, and, ultimately, society."

The Council of State Governments (2012) emphasizes the importance of focusing on criminogenic risk factors, as was discussed in Chapter 8, so that the relationships between mental health and substance abuse treatment needs can be considered in tandem with the risk for criminal activity (see also Morgan, Fisher, Duan, Mandracchia, & Murray, 2009). This is particularly crucial when it is considered that inmates with mental illness have a substantially higher risk of recidivating, and inmates with bipolar disorders have been found to be over three times more likely to have had four or greater prior incarcerations than prisoners with no major mental illnesses (Baillargeon, Binswanger, Penn, Williams & Owen, 2009).

A number of reentry programs for persons with mental illnesses discharged from incarceration to the community rely on Assertive Community Treatment (ACT) teams or parole officers to monitor those released into the community, sometimes with parole officers actually assigned as members of ACT teams. Again, recalling the interchangeability of reentry and diversion programs, diversion programs also oftentimes rely on probation officers and ACT teams for supervision, with probation officers sometimes a member of ACT teams. We now turn to the examination of ACT teams and the utilization of probation and parole officers in diverting and/or reintegrating persons with mental illnesses to society and linking them to treatment.

Assertive Community Treatment (ACT): An Approach to Diversion, Discharge, and Reentry

As referenced above, though more research is needed, ACT may offer promise as a cost effective alternative to incarceration. Lamberti et al. (2004) discuss the then emerging trend to prevent arrest and incarceration through the use of assertive community treatment (ACT), which they refer to as forensic assertive community treatment (FACT). They note that the effectiveness of diversion "is likely to depend on the availability of appropriate services in the community[, and] many diversion programs lack effective linkages to" treatment (p. 1285). ACT was initially developed to assist persons with severe mental illnesses to function in the community, while attempting to prevent homelessness and hospitalizations. It has been rigorously tested and has scientific support for reducing hospital admissions (Davis, Fallon, Vogel, & Teachout, 2008). However, FACT adds the dimension of trying to prevent incarceration of persons with mental illnesses (Cuddeback, Morrissey, & Cusack, 2008). ACT "engages high-risk individuals in care by using mobile services that are available around the clock and by performing active outreach. Engagement in the program is further promoted through delivery of comprehensive services, including mental health and addiction treatment, transportation, financial services, and vocational support" (Lamberti et al., 2004, p. 1286).

> The ACT team's services include mental health and drug treatment, health education, non-psychiatric medical care, case management, ongoing assessments, employment and housing assistance, family support and education, and client advocacy. Extensive and reliable services are available 24 hours a day, 7 days a week, 365 days a year (Lurigio et al., 2000, p. 540).

Cuddeback et al. (2008) recommend that FACT teams be established to cover roughly 44% of a population of persons with severe mental illnesses within large, urban jurisdictions. Lamberti et al. (2004) in a seminal study examined 16 programs in nine states that utilized FACT in conjunction with persons with mental illnesses with entanglements with the criminal justice system; 13 of these FACT programs' main referral source was from the local jail; and 11 of these FACT models employed probation officers as members of the team. "Eight programs ... had a supervised residential component, with five providing residentially based addiction treatment" (Lamberti et al., 2004, p. 1285).[6] While reductions in hospital utilization and extended stays in the community have been attributed to ACT, according to Lamberti et al. (2004) this treatment approach has not demonstrated convincing results in terms of lowering arrest and incarceration rates. Lamberti et al. (2004) report that 70% of recent studies have indicated no effect by ACT, and 10% have a negative effect on arrest and incarceration rates. However, in examining these FACT teams Lamberti et al. (2004) uncovered positive results. For example, of "the first 18 patients treated in the Arkansas Partnership Program, [s]eventeen patients had remained arrest free and without substance abuse while living in the community an average of 508 days. In a study comparing outcomes among 41 patients during the year before and after enrollment in Project Link, the "average number of days in jail per patient was significantly reduced [and] significant reductions were also noted in the number of arrests and hospitalizations, along with improved community functioning" (Lamberti et al., 2004, p. 1289).

One derivation from ACT is Project Link. It is dissimilar from traditional ACT programs in several significant aspects:

> These differences include its requirement of a history of arrest for admission, its use of jail as the primary referral source, its close partnership with multiple criminal justice agencies to divert clients from further involvement with the criminal justice system, and its incorporation of residentially based addiction treatment. Research has suggested that this program may be effective at reducing rates of arrest, incarceration, and hospitalization as well as improving community adjustment (Lamberti, et al., 2004, p. 1286).

---

6. Of the 16 programs, eight of them were in California. The others were in Birmingham, Alabama (Birmingham Jail Diversion Project); Little Rock, Arkansas (Arkansas Partnership Direct); St. Petersburg, Florida (Suncoast Center Forensic FACT Team); Chicago, Illinois (Thresholds Jail Program); Portland, Maine (Project DOT [Divert Offenders to Treatment]); Rochester, New York (Project Link); Hamilton, Ohio (Substance Abuse and Mental Illness Court Program); and Madison, Wisconsin (Community Treatment Alternatives) (Lamberti et al., 2004).

Lamberti et al. (2004) indicate that publications consistently tout the effectiveness of the adaptability of ACT to effectively reduce arrest and imprisonment rates for persons with mental illnesses, however, such research has lacked methodological rigor.

Project Link is comprised of six community service agencies in Monroe County, New York aimed at preventing recidivism and promoting community reintegration of persons with mental illnesses (Robert Wood Johnson Foundation, 2008). Combining elements of ACT and intensive case management, Project Link has significantly decreased the number of persons with mental illnesses in jail and the number of hospitalizations (Project Link, 1999). Enrollment into Project Link can come from a number of sources, such as the police, public defender's office, or hospitals, with the most referrals coming from prisons and jails. Project Link incorporates a mobile treatment team (taking mental health services to clients when necessary), treatment residences staffed around the clock. A preliminary assessment of the program revealed that as a result of Project Link's (1999) alternatives to incarceration "the average monthly jail costs for the entire group dropped from $30,908 to $7,235 or from $672 to $157 per consumer" (p. 1478–1479). More recently, the consortium reported that after a year of involvement, clients, as a result of reduced direct service and residential costs, realized a yearly savings per client via Project Link of $39,518; average yearly reductions in jail (104 days to 45) and hospital (114 days to 88) stays occurred as well (Robert Wood Johnson Foundation, 2008). Therapeutic leverage is used with those individuals who remain justice involved and have probation or parole officers, as their help is enlisted to reinforce treatment conditions. Lamberti (2007) considers the crucial components for stopping the criminal recidivism of persons with mental illnesses the use of this legal leverage combined with linkage to competent treatment services.

Perceived coercion on the part of recipients to receive mental health services has been associated with longer stays in jail (Cusack, Steadman, & Herring, 2010). Thus, consumer satisfaction with Project Link was 4.6 out of 5, seemingly indicating a lack of coercion. Project Link, unlike most studies involving ACT and intensive case management, resulted in a significant contribution to reducing incarceration among consumers of mental health services (Project Link, 1999). Lamberti et al. (2001) conclude, as did the Project Link (1999) article, that Project Link may actually succeed in reducing jail and hospital recidivism by utilizing service integration. Project Link integrates and spans healthcare, social services and the criminal justice system (Lamberti et al., 2001). Project Link combines a mobile treatment team, a forensic psychiatrist, a dual diagnosis treatment residence, and a culturally competent staff (Lamberti et al., 2001). Via integration, Project Link brings together three complimentary models of service delivery and literally "'makes a whole out of parts'" (Lamberti et al., 2001, p. 73), orchestrating seamless care for the patient.

The main difference in FACT and ACT is the extent to which emphasis is placed on the prevention of arrest and incarceration. With the FACT teams a priority was focusing on mentally ill offenders by requiring a criminal history and relying upon a predominance of referrals from criminal justice agencies, and this is bolstered with the inclusion of probation officers on 69% of the FACT teams included in the study (Lamberti et al., 2004). Engaging probation officers in the process can allow for legal leverage to nudge individuals into treatment thereby avoiding costly and anti-therapeutic incarceration. While some concerns have been expressed that ACT was never to be coercive in nature and the use of probation officers may violate that principle (Solomon & Draine, 1995b), the role of the probation officer may be a little different working with this population compared with the traditional role of probation officers (see Roskes & Feldman, 2000; Slate, Feldman, Roskes, & Baerga, 2004; Slate, Roskes, Feldman, & Baerga, 2003). The emphasis should be on therapeutic outcomes and not so much on an overly zealous focus on revocations of probation. While more outcome data is needed, FACT is perceived as a promising model of prevention and care for persons with severe mental illnesses (Lamberti et al., 2004).

Florida has established a number of ACT teams across the state to enhance services to persons with mental illnesses, and some of those programs have a few members that may be involved in some way with the criminal justice system (Kilroy & Wagner, 2004). The Suncoast Center for Community Mental Health in St. Petersburg represents Florida's first forensic ACT team designed to exclusively handle individuals charged with felonies, albeit nonviolent in nature (Kilroy & Wagner, 2004). The ACT team makes periodic progress reports to the court to ensure that there is compliance with conditions of release (Kilroy & Wagner, 2004). Duval County, Florida has since added a FACT team as well (Winterbauer, Tindell, Diduk, Pierce, & Remo, 2009). FACT teams are becoming more popular and are aimed at reducing exposure to criminogenic risk factors for justice-involved persons with mental illnesses at various intercept points on the sequential intercept model, linking these persons to treatment, and decreasing recidivism (SAMHSA, 2021a).

Although not cited by Lamberti et al. (2004), Conklin (2000) indicates that Detroit-Wayne County, Michigan has a Mental Health-Corrections Outreach Intensive Treatment (M-COIT) program that is based on the ACT approach incorporating a multidisciplinary team of clinicians, probation/parole officers and vocational officers and is aimed at reintegrating parolees and offenders with severe mental illnesses who have maxed out their sentences back into the community. Another example of a program employing ACT principles, not included in the study by Lamberti et al. 2004, is the Connections Program, funded via a competitive grant from the California legislature, that was a partnership between the sheriff's office, the probation department, and clinicians in San Diego and found that participants in the program had significantly less arrests, convictions, and time served in jail than a comparison group of non-participants (see Burke & Keaton, 2004). However, as is often a concern with initiating programs via governmental grants, if there is not buy-in and financial support garnered in local jurisdictions when the state or federal funding cycle ceases the program will also end, as was the case in San Diego for the Connections program.

Community Treatment Alternatives is a forensic ACT program in Madison, Wisconsin, that has achieved significantly positive results in reducing recidivism and jail time among those they serve (Journey, 2017; R. Honberg, personal communication, July 29, 2006). Honberg indicates all clients in this program have either been incarcerated or are facing charges that could lead to incarceration, and, significantly, 85% of those who complete their legal obligation to participate in the program stay in the program voluntarily afterwards. One might surmise that these individuals felt like they were valued and had input into critical treatment decisions — otherwise, why else would they remain (R. Honberg, personal communication, July 29, 2006).

According to NAMI (2007), the implementation of ACT has had measured success across the United States. Oklahoma reports that in the 12 months prior to admission to their ACT program in 2006, 229 consumers had a combined total of 9,583 days of hospital inpatient care and 3,614 days in jail. In the year following implementation of ACT, the number of hospital days fell to 2,612, a 73% decrease. Days in jail dropped to 1,314, a reduction of 64%. Data for 2007 in Virginia indicated that consumers used 76% fewer state hospital days after ACT enrollment than in an equivalent period before enrollment. Of consumers served by ACT teams, 92% had no arrests during the year and 83% experienced stable housing situations. In Georgia, a study of a forensic ACT team revealed a 78% decrease in jail days, 53% reduction in arrests, and 89% drop in hospital days, generating a net cost savings of $1.114 million dollars in one year (NAMI, 2007). Davis et al. (2008) found that ACT was successful in reducing both hospitalizations and arrests as part of a jail aftercare team. More recently, Smith, Jennings, and Cimino (2010) reported that ACT and Intensive Case Management, in terms of non-offending, psychiatric stability, avoidance of substances, alignment with stable housing and involvement in meaningful activities, have shown promise as a continuum of care recovery model.

It is maintained that persons with mental illnesses can be effectively managed by systems with single points of entry, such as ACT, whether those being supervised are encountered pretrial, after trial, or after release from custody (Lurigio et al., 2000). Morrissey, Meyer, and Cuddeback (2007) recommend that FACT models should be adapted to focus on the criminal behavior and tendencies of persons with mental illness who are repeatedly in contact with the criminal justice system; they point to the effectiveness of cognitive behavioral therapy, separate residential-therapeutic units within prisons and jails, and the therapeutic leverage that is available with drug and mental health courts and probation officers to ensure compliance of participants in such programs. Likewise, Erickson et al. (2009) contend that FACT teams should assess criminogenic factors that can impact recidivism for participants, such as prior arrest for violent acts, a history of antisocial behavior, and having been thrown out of residential treatment programs — as these actions are related to arrests while in treatment. Erickson et al. (2009) also note the powerful leverage that judges and probation officers can have with FACT teams. Lurigio et al. (2000) conclude that ACT appears to warrant credibility and should be further explored for managing persons with mental illnesses who encounter the criminal justice system. With this said, as we have seen before in this book, researcher after researcher maintain that more scientific research is needed on the impact, in this case, of FACT on criminal recidivism (Morrissey, et al., 2007; Cuddeback, et al., 2008; Cuddeback, Pettus-Davis, & Scheyett, 2011).

Probation and Parole[7]

Probation

In a national study of mental health directors, Lamberti, Deem, Weisman, and LaDuke (2011) found that the majority of FACT programs reported working with probation officers, and 60% of these FACT teams had a probation officer as a full-time member. The researchers note that involvement of probation officers with FACT teams is common and perceived by most mental health program administrators as beneficial in reducing recidivism.

As of 1984, Solomon and Draine (1995a) indicated that they were not aware of any studies that specified how often probation and parole agencies utilized mental health services. Skeem & Louden (2006) estimate that roughly 15% (at least 500,000 persons) of individuals on probation, supervised release or parole have mental illnesses, and Lurigio and Swartz (2000) reveal that 15% of probation departments nationwide reported having specialized programs for probationers with mental illnesses. Slate et al. (2003) report 18% of the 19,731 individuals under federal probation officer or pretrial officer supervision (parole, supervised release, conditional release or probation) had a special condition of mental health treatment imposed upon them. A federal court has also upheld the imposition of mental health treatment as a legitimate condition for compliance with supervised release (see *USA v. Bull* [2000] and *USA v. Bull* [2001] article in the *Correctional Mental Health Report*).

Generally, most probation officers are not properly skilled to deal with persons with mental illnesses in terms of community supervision (Veysey, 1994). Though they have been criticized for their isolationism and a lack of interagency cooperativeness, probation officers and departments are strategically positioned to operate in the spirit of therapeutic jurisprudence as positive change agents (Slate et al., 2003; 2004). Probation officers have been considered resource brokers or boundary spanners who can operate to identify community resources, such as in the areas of mental health, housing and vocational/employment possibilities, and then properly match those in need of services under their supervision to appropriate services (McCampbell, 2001; Steadman et al., 2001). Solomon and Draine (1995b) discussed the boundary spanning role performed by forensic case managers between criminal justice authorities and the community mental health system. They also discuss the conflicts that can emerge between case managers and probation officers, as there may be mixed loyalties, and they suggest that intensive case management may actually set clients up for re-incarceration, as under such scrutiny noncompliance with treatment dictates are more likely to be uncovered. According to Skeem & Louden (2006), persons with mental illnesses under community corrections control are twice as likely as persons without mental illnesses to have their community supervision revoked.

Rivera (2004) suggested that probation departments develop specialized mental health caseloads supervised by select officers. Some agencies have devised specialized

---

7. See NIC, 2021.

programs to handle persons with mental illnesses under their supervision; for example, in Chicago a specialized program for probationers has been implemented (Lurigio & Swartz, 2000) and for those under federal supervision in the community in Baltimore, the Northern District of Illinois, the Western District of Texas, the Eastern District of Tennessee, and New Jersey (Slate et al., 2004). Probation officers have become members of ACT teams, for example, in Sacramento (Sheppard, Freitas and Hurley, 2002).

Skeem and Petrila (2004) identify the establishment of specialized probation caseloads comprised of persons with mental illnesses as a promising strategy. The traditional role of probation officers as attuned to public safety remains and is combined with a therapeutic role, whereby the officer also focuses on the rehabilitation of the probationer. The balancing of this dual role of monitor and treatment provider is addressed in the research literature by Roskes and Feldman (2000). With this added dimension, emphasis on problem solving and therapeutic approaches to what may have traditionally been more of a focus on revocation occurs when potential violations arise. Skeem and Petrila note that specialized caseloads for persons with mental illnesses emerged a little over 25 years ago and have accelerated in the past five years, and they do not anticipate this trend will slow down anytime soon. They do caution that those agencies with specialized caseloads should consider reduced caseloads, increased probation officer training for those with specialty caseloads, and not merely using probation officers to ratchet up surveillance of persons with mental illnesses in the community but to engage them as therapeutic agents.

Skeem and Manchak (2008) contend that a hybrid model of probation is needed to most effectively supervise probationers with mental disorders (PMD). This synthetic/hybrid model is based on three relationship components: caring-fairness, trust, and toughness-authoritarianism. This is in contrast to the surveillance model which is marked by authoritarianism. Both quasi-experimental designs and qualitative research indicate that there is "powerful support for reintroducing treatment into supervision" (Skeem & Manchak, 2008, p. 237), especially treatment that focuses on high-risk offenders and targets risk factors that leads to reoffending. This model is congruent with the Washington State program which targets dangerous mentally ill offenders (DMIO).

As of 2006, less than 5% of probation agencies had developed specialty mental health caseloads, and among the 5% a "significant number" have increased caseloads to the point where they exceed the prototypical evidence-based model proposed by Skeem and Louden (2006). According to Louden, Skeem, Camp, Vidal, and Peterson (2012), more than 100 probation agencies across the U.S. have now instituted specialty mental health caseloads. Skeem and Louden (2006) compared 66 such specialty agencies to 25 traditional agencies while trying to keep geographic location and population in mind for meaningful comparisons. They were able to specify five key elements that characterized a specialty model focusing on providing correctional supervision to persons with mental illnesses in the community. The five key elements most associated with specialty caseloads were (1) a caseload exclusively devoted to the specialized supervision of persons with mental illnesses; (2) considerably reduced caseloads for officers supervising persons with mental illnesses, thus caseloads approximately two-thirds less than traditional caseloads — 45 persons supervised versus 135 persons; (3) extensive and continued specialized training for officers, typically with anywhere from 20 to 40 extra hours a year of training; (4) officers who do more than monitor, who refer persons with mental illnesses, are actively engaged with teams of treatment providers, and assist individuals in accessing benefits and services such as housing and meaningful employment; (5) officers who operate as problem solvers, not just rule reminders, and involve the participation of offenders in their treatment plan (Skeem & Louden, 2006). While Skeem and Louden (2006) stated that the verdict is still out on whether specialty models lessen the probability of probationers' re-arrest over the long term, they reported that two studies indicate that stakeholders believe specialty caseloads are more successful than traditional ways of handling probation caseloads. Three studies found that specialty models are better at linking persons with mental illnesses to care in the community, enhancing their well-being, and lessening the chances of revocation of their probation. In terms of parole, Skeem and Louden (2006) indicate that there are two studies that suggest specialty models have been successful in lessening the probability of persons with mental illnesses violating parole, at least in the short term. According to Skeem and Manchak (2008), at this time further program evaluation is needed to determine the potential efficacy of special mental health caseloads. More recently, Skeem, Manchak, and Montoya (2017) reported that those on specialty probation were 29 percent more likely to be re-arrested while 52 percent of those on traditional probation were likely to do so.

Skeem and Louden (2006) conclude by saying, "… [E]xisting practices hold promise. Implementing these practices may prevent offenders with mental illness from becoming more deeply entrenched in the criminal justice system, which would better realize the supervision goal of facilitating their reentry to the community" (p. 341).

While probation agencies are moving toward evidence-based models, few agencies have incorporated the hybrid approaches to probation supervision, as proposed by Skeem and Louden (2006). We believe that it will take years to change the culture of probation workers and fully reintroduce treatment into the probation milieu. If prison populations continue to decline, more mentally ill offenders will be placed on probation. It is uncertain how probation agencies will respond and if they will continue to move forward to adopt evidence-based practices.

Certainly, one of the keys to changing the culture of probation work and how they respond to mentally ill offenders is training. Slate et al. (2004) recommended 40 hours of annual training for those entrusted with supervision of persons with mental illnesses in the community. Training components should also address how the criminal justice system has become the de facto mental health system, de-escalation techniques, HIPAA, and the development of and adherence to memorandums of understanding between agencies; a caseload of no more than 35 persons with mental illnesses to ensure optimum supervision and linkages to treatment are recommended (Slate et al., 2004).

With regard to the latter, Skeem and Petrila (2004) maintain that HIPAA concerns can be allayed by the fact that court orders can satisfy HIPAA requirements, and probation conditions can be crafted in such a manner as to obtain consent in writing of the probationer for release of mental health records. Formal agreements (memorandums of understanding for the sharing of information from one agency to the other between probation and various mental health and social service agencies) can be entered into in advance; "[a]lternatively, in the prototypic specialty agency, the probation officer often becomes part of the treatment team, such that as a practical matter 'confidentiality ceases to exist'" (Skeem & Petrila, 2004, p. 15).

While the majority of probation supervision is conducted by probation officers funded by state and local entities, federal probation supervises fewer offenders and is known for lower caseloads. In many ways, federal probation officers are better equipped to address the needs of mentally ill offenders released from federal prisons. Not only are federal probation officers more likely to have higher levels of education but their training incorporates many of the key components of the Memphis Crisis Intervention Team (CIT) training (see Slate et al., 2004). Their training programs typically focus on identifying and augmenting resources and linking individuals to appropriate treatment. Federal probation officers need, for example, to be able to navigate and access multiple entities, (such as the mental health treatment providers, the Federal Bureau of Prisons, courts, law enforcement) and to communicate effectively with offenders living with mental illness (see Slate et al., 2004). A number of probation officers serving as mental health specialists in the federal system have extensive educational credentials in mental health, some as licensed counselors, social workers and even psychologists (Slate et al., 2004).

Parole

As of 1997, Camp and Camp found no specialized programs for parolees with mental illnesses. As of the early 2000s, it was determined in a survey of parole administrators that less than 25% of the respondents offered any specialized programs for individuals with mental illnesses under their supervision (Lurigio, 2001; Petersilia, 2003; Travis, 2005). In *Close v. Weber* (2001), the 8th Circuit upheld the decision that parole could legally be revoked as a result of a parolee agreeing to mental health treatment as a condition of release but refusing to accept the psychotropic medication prescribed for him. Haimowitz (2004) also believes that collaborations are extremely important to success, and he advocates for the use of databases linked across justice and mental health systems, cross training of mental health and criminal justice personnel, and written memorandums of understanding, to include delineation of "who is responsible for what" (p. 374). Haimowitz (2004) also cautions that we should be careful "to guard against mental health services' drifting toward social control functions" (p. 375).[8]

---

8. See similar concerns echoed by Steadman and Honberg in Chapter 5 on law enforcement follow-ups with persons with mental illnesses that they encounter in crises.

Reintegration:
Reentry Courts and Programs

The vast majority of offenders we send to prison return to our communities. It should also be remembered that the majority of those prisoners will return to prisons. The manner in which individuals transition from the jails and prisons to the community varies. It is very difficult for inmates who don't live with mental illness to return to their communities and become productive citizens. For those inmates who live with mental illness, this challenge is even more difficult. Successful transition is dependent most always on some provision of support. For those inmates with functional, supportive families that support can be sufficient. In the vast majority of cases additional support is needed.

Following the wave of success of drug courts and mental health courts, prisoner reentry courts are becoming popular throughout much of the United States. In 2004, there were no federal mental health or reentry courts in the United States. Hamilton (2010) indicated, in his evaluation of Harlem's first reentry court, while there are at least 12 prisoner reentry courts in the United States, little is known about the efficacy of their operations:

> A reentry court can take various forms. Two examples are case-defined and standalone reentry courts. In a case-defined reentry court, a sentencing judge retains jurisdiction over a case during the entire life of the sentence. Alternatively, a reentry court can be established as a standalone court, where it maintains an exclusive docket of reentry cases. In either model, it is expected that the judge would actively engage correctional administrators overseeing the period of imprisonment (Department of Justice, n.d.).

This approach has been previously discussed as a form of therapeutic jurisprudence. In this approach, the duties of the judge extend, like in the highly successful drug courts, beyond the sentencing phase of the justice process.

The Department of Justice's (n.d.) website indicates that of the 20 reentry court programs evaluated 80% "demonstrate promise." There are numerous factors which impact an ex-inmate's transition back into the community; mental illness is just one of those factors. Frisman, Swanson, Marin and Leavitt-Smith (2010) identify the following needs of post incarceral inmates with mental illness: discharge planning, transitional care management by reentry specialists, housing with specialized support services (the Threshold program in Chicago, Illinois and the Transitions Clinic in San Francisco are good examples of such programs), and mental health care services (i.e. FACT, ACT).

Hamilton's (2010, p. 4) evaluation of the Harlem Parole Reentry Court Program provided promising but mixed results:

> The Reentry Court seems to have had a positive effect with regard to preventing new crimes as measured by rearrests and reconvictions. However, participants were found to have higher rates of revocations. In particular, program

participants were more likely to be revoked for technical violations of parole conditions. Given the lower caseload and greater intensity of the program, it is assumed that "supervision effects" are partially responsible for the higher rate of technical violations. In other words, the Harlem Parole Reentry Court may be detecting violations that might otherwise have gone unnoticed. This suggests that reentry courts may want to explore enhancing the use of alternative sanctions in lieu of revocation. Furthermore, reentry courts should explore the possibility of providing greater feedback to parole officers and case managers, making them aware of potential unintended consequences when supervision is increased (see also Harlem Reentry Court, 2021).

These strengths and weaknesses echo the aspects of specialty probation programs highlighted by Skeem and colleagues (Skeem & Louden, 2006; Skeem & Manchak, 2008; Skeem & Petrila, 2004). Ultimately, if prisoner reentry court programs are able to come close to the successes of drug and mental health courts, they will have a bright future and will be of great service to inmates living with mental illness, their family members, our communities, the behavioral health system, and the criminal justice system.

Conclusion

Whether it is diversion or reentry, discharge planning is essential to successful reintegration of former detainees/prisoners with mental illnesses into society. Follow-up and transitional care, which in the treatment community has been called "aftercare" (a term too long missing from our criminal justice vocabulary), is also necessary to ensure that discharge plans are carried out and court-ordered treatments are implemented. The failure to close the gaps in the diversion and community supervision systems, by providing aftercare services that combine treatment with accountability, will result in the continued recycling of offenders. As research has demonstrated, offenders with mental illness, if untreated, will have the most difficult time avoiding reimprisonment. A key to breaking the cycle is treatment. While the move to a public health/treatment model requires investment, research indicates the treatment of mental illness generates long-term savings and is good fiscal strategy. The movement toward evidence-based practices supports these conclusions. As fiscal conservatives process the increasing body of scientific literature that points to the conclusion that rehabilitation does work and can be administered within a system of accountability (Cullen, 2007; Pratt, 2009), greater focus will be given to the "after-life" of ex-inmates.

Since 2010, the number of offenders released from prison has increased; this decrease in the number of prisoners incarcerated is the first in over three decades of prison population growth (Guerino, Harrison, & Sabol, 2011). The future of communities lies in the hands of those developing and implementing discharge plans from jails, prisons, and mental hospitals. With states under the burden of an enormous fiscal crisis, looking to cut corners wherever they can, programs for the mentally ill are especially vulnerable. This is short-sighted because the cost of the mentally ill returning to prison is greater in the long run than the cost of providing them adequate transition counseling and treatment upon release. Without good discharge planning and post-release programs, seriously mentally ill prisoners are likely to cycle endlessly between prison and the community, their illnesses worsening, with chances increasing that they will end up in the high-security units within the prison system. Successful release plans for the mentally ill include partnerships between departments of corrections and other state agencies, the availability of post-release treatment, housing, early enrollment in Medicaid or another form of health care coverage, and pre-release counseling that begins well before a prisoner's release.

The proper funding of discharge planning and post-release programs is a crucial public policy issue. As prisons begin to parole inmates at unprecedented rates, communities need to embrace post-release programming. It serves neither the mentally ill, nor the broader community, to short-change the transitional programs that could serve to break these linkages between mental illness and imprisonment in 21st century America (Human Rights Watch, 2003).

There is a desperate need for more adequate mental health services after arrest, better treatment availability for persons with mental illnesses after release into the community, individualized case management and outreach, appropriate housing arrangements in the community, and some assurance for family members of the ex-inmate that their needs will be addressed and supports put in place to assist them in monitoring their loved one's condition (Lamb, Weinberger, & Gross, 2004).

Failure to close the gaps in transitional services for post-incarceral inmates with mental illness is a prescription for crisis. History has clearly demonstrated, as in the case of Seung Hui Cho, that it is less costly to provide a continuum of sanctions and treatment than to bear the burdens of a system that fails to provide for the needs of communities by ignoring the reintegration of ex-inmates living with mental illness. The task is intimidating but critical to the future of our communities (see also the video entitled The Definition of Insanity, available at: https://www.pbs.org/video/the-definition-of-insanity-7egjih/).

References

Anderson, P. R., & Slate, R. N. (2011). *The decision-making network: An introduction to criminal justice.* Durham, NC: Carolina Academic Press.

Baillargeon, J., Binswanger, I. A., Penn, J. V., Williams, B. A., & Owen, J. (2009). Psychiatric disorders and repeat incarcerations: The revolving prison door. *The American Journal of Psychiatry, 166*(1), 103–109.

Baillargeon, J., Hoge, S. K., & Penn, J. V. (2010). Addressing the challenge of community reentry among released inmates with serious mental illness. *American Journal of Community Psychology, 46,* 361–375.

Barr, H. (2001). The Nathaniel Project: An alternative to incarceration for seriously mentally ill felony offenders. *Community Mental Health Report, 1*(3), 43–44.

Barr, H. (2003a). Transinstitutionalization in the courts: *Brad H. v. City of New York*, and the fight for discharge planning for people with psychiatric disabilities leaving Rikers Island. *Crime & Delinquency, 49*(1), 97–123.

Barr, H. (2003b, November 26). *Prisons and jails: Hospitals of last resort.* New York, NY: Soros Foundation. Retrieved from http://www.prisonpolicy.org/scans/MI Report.pdf.

Bazelon Center. (2010). *Criminal justice experts call for immediate reinstatement of federal benefits for people with serious mental illnesses leaving prisons or jails.* Washington, D.C.: Author. Retrieved from www.bazelon.org/LinkClick.aspx? fileticket=ZE1Ccwk QAio%3D&tabid=275.

Bernstein, N. (2000, July 13). Freed inmates must get care if mentally ill. *New York Times.* Retrieved from http://query.nytimes.com/gst/fullpage.html?sec=health& res=9E0DE1DC1F38F930A25754C0A9669C8B63.

Bexar County Jail Diversion Program. (2006). Providing jail diversion for people with mental illness. *Psychiatric Services, 57*(10), 1521–1523.

Binswanger, I. A., Stern, M. F., Deyo, R. A., Heagerty, P. J., Cheadle, A., Elmore, J. G., & Koepsell, T. D. (2007). Release from prison — A high risk of death for former inmates. *New England Journal of Medicine, 356,* 157–165.

Birckhead, T. R. (2012, September 17). "Children are Different": Culpability and the Mandatory Sentencing of Juveniles after Miller v. Alabama & Jackson v. Hobbs — 2012 Symposium of The University of Minnesota's *Journal of Law & Inequality. Juvenile Justice Blog.* Retrieved from http://juvenilejusticeblog.web.unc.edu/2012/ 09/17/children-are-different-culpability-and-the-mandatory-sentencing-of- juveniles-after-miller-v-alabama-jackson-v-hobbs/.

Bjorklund, R. W. (2000). Linking discharged patients with peers in the community. *Psychiatric Services, 51*(10), 1316.

Blevins, K., & Soderstrom, I. (2012, September 28). *Examining regional differences in states' approaches to the treatment of offenders with mental illness.* Paper presented at the Southern Criminal Justice Conference, Atlantic Beach, FL.

Bronson, J., & Carson, E.A. (2019). *Prisoners in 2017.* Bureau of Justice Statistics. Retrieved from: https://www.bjs.gov/content/pub/pdf/p17.pdf.

Burke, C., & Keaton, S. (2004, June). *San Diego County's Connections Program Board of Corrections final report.* San Diego, CA: San Diego Regional Association of Governments. Retrieved from http://www.sdsheriff.net/library/connections_ grant_final.pdf.

Camp, C., & Camp, G. (1997). *The corrections yearbook.* South Salem, NY: Criminal Justice Institute.

Case, B., Steadman, H. J., Dupuis, S. A., & Morris, L. S. (2009). Who succeeds in jail diversion programs for persons with mental illness? A multi-site study. *Behavioral Sciences and the Law, 27,* 661–674.

Clark, J. (2004). *Non-specialty first appearance court models for diverting persons with mental illness: Alternatives to mental health courts.* Delmar, NY: GAINS Center, Technical Assistance and Policy Analysis Center for Jail Diversion.

Closs v. Weber. (2001, February 9). Mentally ill parolee must take medication. *Corrections Digest, 32*(6), 3.

Conklin, C. (2000, April 26). *M-COIT: An innovative cross-systems approach to assisting seriously mentally ill ex-offenders reintegrate and remain in the community.* Paper presented at the 2000 GAINS Center National Conference, Miami, Florida.

Council of State Governments, Police Executive Research Forum, Pretrial Services Resource Center, Association of State Correctional Administrators, Bazelon Center for Mental Health Law, and the Center for Behavioral Health, Justice, and Public Policy. (2002). *Criminal Justice/Mental Health Consensus Project.* New York, NY: Council of State Governments.

Council of State Governments. (2007). *Ensuring timely access to Medicaid and SSI/SSDI for people with mental illness releases from prison: Four state case studies.* New York, NY: Author. Retrieved from www.reentrypolicy.org/reentry/Document_Viewer.aspx?DocumentID=998.

Council of State Governments. (2012). *Adults with behavioral health needs under correctional supervision: Report summary.* New York, NY: Author. Retrieved from http://consensusproject.org/jc_publications/adults-with-behavioral-health-needs.

Council of State Governments. (n.d.). *Understand why released offenders are reoffending.* New York, NY: Reentry Policy Council. Retrieved from http://reentrypolicy.org/Report/PartI/ChapterI-A/PolicyStatement2/Recommendation2-D.

Cuddeback, G. S., Morrissey, J. P., & Cusack, K. J. (2008). How many forensic assertive community treatment teams do we need? *Psychiatric Services, 59*(2), 205–208.

Cuddeback, G. S., Pettus-Davis, C., & Scheyett, A. (2011). Perceptions of forensic assertive community treatment. *Psychiatric Rehabilitation Journal, 35*(2), 101.

Cusack, K. J., Morrissey, J. P., Cuddeback, G. S., Prins, A., & Williams, D. M. (2010). Criminal justice involvement, behavioral health service use, and costs of forensic assertive community treatment: A randomized trial. *Community Mental Health Journal, 46,* 356–363.

Cusack, K. J., Steadman, H. J., & Herring, A. H. (2010). Perceived coercion among jail diversion participants in a multisite study. *Psychiatric Services, 61*(9), 911–916.

Cullen, F. (2007). Making rehabilitation corrections' guiding paradigm. *Crime and Public Policy, 6*(4), 717–728.

Davis, K., Fallon, J., Vogel, S., & Teachout, A. (2008). Integrating into the mental health system from the criminal justice system: Jail aftercare services for persons with a severe mental illness. *Journal of Offender Rehabilitation, 46,* 217–231.

Department of Justice. (n.d.). *Reentry courts.* Washington, D.C.: Department of Justice, Office of Juvenile Justice and Delinquency Prevention. Retrieved from http://www.ojjdp.gov/mpg/progTypesReentryCourt.aspx.

Edgar, E. (1999). The role of PACT in recovery. *NAMI Advocate, 21*(1), 14–15.

Erickson, S. K., Lamberti, J. S., Weisman, R., Crilly, J., Nihalani, N., Stefanovics, E., & Desai, R. (2009). Predictors of arrest during forensic assertive community treatment. *Psychiatric Services, 60*(6), 834–837.

Estelle v. Gamble, 429 U.S. 97 (1976).

Frisman, L. K., Swanson, J., Marin, M. C., & Leavitt-Smith, E. (2010). Estimating the costs of reentry programs for prisoners with severe mental illnesses. *Correctional Health Care Report, 11*(6), 81–96.

Fulwiler, C. (2000). Release planning for inmates with mental illness. *Correctional Health Care Report, 1*(3), 37–38, 48.

GAINS Center. (n.d.-a). *Co-occurring disorders.* Delmar, NY: Author. Retrieved from: http://gains.prainc.com/topical_resources/cooccurring.asp.

GAINS Center. (n.d.-b). *Jail diversion.* Delmar, NY: Author. Retrieved from: http://gains.prainc.com/topical_resources/jail.asp.

GAINS Center. (n.d.-c). *Reentry.* Delmar, NY: Author. Retrieved from: http://gains.prainc.com/topical_resources/reentry.asp.

GAINS Center. (n.d.-d). *Women's 8 part series.* Delmar, NY: Author. Retrieved from http://gains. prainc.com/topical_resources/women.asp.

Gill, K.J., & Murphy, A.A. (2017). Jail diversion for persons with serious mental illness coordinated by a prosecutor's office. *BioMed Research International.* Retrieved from: https://www.hindawi.com/journals/bmri/2017/7917616/.

Giuliani, R. W. (2000). *The City of New York fiscal 2000 mayor's management report: Volume I — Agency narratives.* New York, NY: Office of the Mayor, Office of Operations. Retrieved from http://www. nyc.gov/html/records/rwg/ops/pdf/2000_mmr/0900_summary.pdf.

Golembeski, C., & Fullilove, R. (2008). Criminal (in)justice in the city and its associated health consequences. *American Journal of Public Health, 98*, 185–190.

Guerino, P., Harrison, P. M., & Sabol, W. J. (2011). *Prisoners in 2010.* Washington, D.C.: U.S. Department of Justice, Bureau of Justice Statistics. Retrieved from: http://bjs.ojp.usdoj.gov/content/pub/pdf/p10.pdf.

Haimowitz, S. (2002). Can mental health courts end the criminalization of persons with mental illness? *Psychiatric Services, 53*(10), 1226–1228.

Haimowitz, S. (2004). Slowing the revolving door: Community reentry of offenders with mental illness. *Psychiatric Services, 55*(4), 373–375.

Hamilton, Z. (2010). *Do reentry courts reduce recidivism?: Results from the Harlem Parole Reentry Court.* New York, NY: Center for Court Innovation.

Hands Across Long Island. (2007). *Forensics program: Reentry and outreach services.* Retrieved from http://www.hali88.org/programs/forensics.htm.

Harlem Reentry Court. (2021). The Harlem Reentry Court helps the parolees make the transition back to the community. *Center for Court Innovation.* Retrieved on May 23, 2021 from https://www.courtinnovation.org/programs/harlem-reentry-court.

Harper, T. (2002, October 28). *Howie T. Harp Advocacy Center.* Paper presented at the National GAINS Center Conference, San Francisco, CA.

Harris County. (2021). Community supervision & corrections department programs. *Field Services.* Retrieved on May 23, 2021 from https://cscd.harriscountytx.gov/Pages/Programs.aspx?Program1=Field+Services.

Harris County Mental Health and Mental Retardation Authority. (2005). *Jail detention and diversion plan.* Houston, TX: Author. Retrieved from www.mhmraharris.org/LocalPlan/documents/8-HarrisCountyJailDiversionPlan2005.pdf.

Hartwell, S. W. (2004). Comparison of offenders with mental illness only and offenders with dual diagnoses. *Psychiatric Services, 55*(2), 145–150.

Hartwell, S. W., & Orr, K. (1999). The Massachusetts forensic transition program for mentally ill offenders re-entering the community. *Psychiatric Services, 50*(9), 1220–1222.

Hartwell, S. W., & Orr, K. (2000, November/December). Release planning: And the distinctions for mentally ill offenders returning to the community from jails versus prisons. *American Jails,* 9–12.

Human Rights Watch. (2003, October). *Failure to provide discharge planning.* New York, NY: Author. Retrieved from http://www.hrw.org/reports/2003/usa1003/24.htm.

Journey. (2017). Community-Based Services. *Journal Mental Health Center.* Retrieved from https://journeymhc.org/community-based-services/.

Kilroy, R., & Wagner, L. (2004). The facts about a forensic F.A.C.T. Team. *NAMI Florida Sun, 6*(6), 10.

Kittrie, N. N. (1978). *The right to be different: Deviance and enforced treatment.* Baltimore, MD: John Hopkins University Press.

Lamb, H. R., Weinberger, L. E., & Gross, B. H. (2004). Mentally ill persons in the criminal justice system: Some perspectives. *Psychiatric Quarterly, 75*(2), 107–126.

Lamberti, J. S. (2007). Understanding and preventing criminal recidivism among adults with psychotic disorders. *Psychiatric Services, 58*(6), 773–781.

Lamberti, J. S., Deem, A., Weisman, R. L., & LaDuke, C. (2011). The role of probation in forensic assertive treatment. *Psychiatric Services, 62*(4), 418–421.

Lamberti, J. S., Weisman, R., & Faden, D. I. (2004). Forensic assertive community treatment: Preventing incarceration of adults with severe mental illness. *Psychiatric Services, 55*(11), 1285–1293.

Lamberti, J. S., Weisman, R. L., Schwartzkopf, S. B., Price, N., Ashton, R. M., & Trompeter, J. (2001). The mentally ill in jails and prisons: Towards an integrated model of prevention. *Psychiatric Quarterly, 72*(1), 63–77.

Louden, J. E., Skeem, J. L., Camp, J., Vidal, S., & Peterson, J. (2012). Supervision practices in specialty mental health probation: What happens in officer-probationer meetings? *Law and Human Behavior 36*(2), 109–119.

Lovell, D., Gagliardi, G. J., & Peterson, P. D. (2002). Recidivism and use of services among persons with mental illness after release from prison. *Psychiatric Services, 53*(10), 1290–1296.

Lurigio, A. J. (2001). Effective services for parolees with mental illnesses. *Crime & Delinquency, 47*(3), 446–461.

Lurigio, A. J., Fallon, J. R., & Dincin, J. (2000). Helping the mentally ill in jails adjust to community life: A description of a postrelease ACT program and its clients. *International Journal of Offender Therapy and Comparative Criminology, 44*(5), 532–548.

Lurigio, A. J., & Swartz, J. A. (2000). Changing the contours of the criminal justice system to meet the needs of persons with serious mental illness. In J. Horney (Ed.), *Policies, processes, and decisions of the criminal justice system* (pp. 45–108). Washington, D.C.: U.S. Department of Justice, National Institute of Justice.

Mallik-Kane, K., & Visher, C. (2008). *How physical, mental, and substance abuse conditions shape the process of re-integration.* Washington, D.C.: Urban Institute.

Mauch, D., Mulligan, G., & Crane, K., (2018) Model jail diversion and reentry services programs updated literature and resource review. *Massachusetts association for mental health.* Retrieved from: https://www.mamh.org/assets/files/Diversion-Services-Literature-and-Resource-Review_MAMH_June-2018.pdf.

McCampbell, S. W. (2001). Mental health courts: What sheriffs need to know. *Sheriff, 53*(2), 40–43.

Morgan, R. D., Fisher, W. H., Duan, N., Mandracchia, J. T., & Murray, D. (2010). Prevalence of criminal thinking among state prison inmates with serious mental illness. *Law and Human Behavior, 34,* 324–326.

Morrissette, D. (2017). Guidelines for successful transition of people with mental or substance use disorders from jail and prison. *Substance Abuse and Mental Health Services Administration (SAMHSA).* Retrieved from: https://nicic.gov/guidelines-successful-transition-people-mental-or-substance-use-disorders-jail-and-prison.

Morrissey, J., Meyer, P., & Cuddeback, G. (2007). Extending community treatment to criminal justice settings: Origins, current evidence, and future directions. *Community Mental Health Journal, 43*(5), 527–544.

Munetz, M. R., & Griffin, P. A. (2006). Use of the sequential intercept model as an approach to decriminalization of people with serious mental illness. *Psychiatric Services, 57*(4), 544–549.

National Public Radio (December 6, 2016). *Signed out of prison but not signed up for health insurance.* Retrieved from: https://www.npr.org/sections/health-shots/2016/12/06/504443879/signed-out-of-prison-but-not-signed-up-for-health-insurance.

National Public Radio. (September 3, 2011). *Nation's jails struggle with mentally ill prisoners.* Retrieved from http://www.npr.org/2011/09/04/140167676/nations-jails-struggle-with-mentally-ill-prisoners.

NIC. (2021). Probation & Parole - Probation - Mentally Ill Offenders. *National Institute of Corrections.* Retrieved on May 23, 2021 from https://nicic.gov/assign-library-item-package-accordion/probation-parole-probation-mentally-ill-offenders.

Osher, F., Steadman, H. J., & Barr, H. (2003). A best practice approach to community reentry from jails for inmates with co-occurring disorders: The APIC model. *Crime & Delinquency, 49*(1), 79–96.

Pamerleau, S. (2016). Jail diversion program a huge success. *My San Antonio Express-News.* Retrieved from https://www.mysanantonio.com/opinion/commentary/article/Jail-diversion-program-a-huge-success-6777745.php

Parish, J. J. (2007, April 30). *Testimony: Status of the implementation of the Brad H. Settlement.* New York, NY: City Council Hearing. Retrieved from www.urban-justice.org/pdf/publications/BradHTestimony.pdf.

Perez, A., Leifman, S., & Estrada, A. (2003). Reversing the criminalization of mental illness. *Crime & Delinquency, 49*(1), 62–78.

Petersilia, J. (2003). *When prisoners come home: Parole and prisoner reentry.* New York, NY: Oxford University Press.

Power, A. K. (2006, April 6). *System transformation at the interface of the criminal justice and mental health systems.* Boston, MA: National GAINS Center Conference.

Pratt, T. (2009). *Addicted to incarceration: Corrections policy and the politics of misinformation in the United States.* Thousand Oaks, CA: Sage.

Prins, S. J., & Draper, L. (2009). *Improving outcomes for people with mental illnesses under community corrections supervision: A guide to research-informed policy and practice.* New York, NY: Council of State Governments Justice Center.

Project Link. (1999). Prevention of jail and hospital recidivism among persons with severe mental illness. *Psychiatric Services, 50*(11), 1477–1480.

Psychiatric Services. (2014). Significant achievement awards: The Nathaniel Project — An effective alternative to incarceration. Retrieved from https://ps.psychiatryonline.org/doi/full/10.1176/appi.ps.53.10.1314.

Rivera, R. M. (2004). The mentally ill offender: A brighter tomorrow through the eyes of the Mentally Ill Offender Treatment and Crime Reduction Act of 2004. *Cleveland State University Journal of Law and Health, 19*, 107–139.

Robert Wood Johnson Foundation. (2008, September). *Model community-based treatment program reduces hospitalization and jail time among people with mental illness and substance abuse.* Princeton, NJ: Author. Retrieved from http://pweb1.rwjf.org/reports/grr/032312.htm.

Rogers, E. (2015). Diversion programs in America's criminal justice system. *Center for Prison Reform.* Retrieved from https://centerforprisonreform.org/wp-content/uploads/2015/09/Jail-Diversion-Programs-in-America.pdf.

Roskes, E., & Feldman, R. (2000). Treat or monitor? Collaboration between mental health providers and probation officers. *Correctional Mental Health Report, 1,* 69–70.

Ryan, S., Brown, C. K., & Watanabe-Galloway, S. (2010). Toward successful post-booking diversion: What are the next steps? *Psychiatric Services, 61*(5), 469–477.

SAMHSA. (2021). Forensic Assertive Community Treatment (FACT). *Substance Abuse and Mental Health Services Administration.* Retrieved on May 23, 2021 from https://store.samhsa.gov/sites/default/files/d7/images/pep19-fact-br-thumbnail.png.

Saulny, S. (2003, January 9). City agrees to help care for mentally ill inmates after release. *New York Times.* Retrieved from http://query.nytimes.com/gst/fullpage.html?sec=health&res=9502EFD9103EF93AA35752C0A9659C8B63.

Scotti, S. (September 2017). Health care in and out of prisons. *State Legislatures Magazine.* Retrieved from: https://www.ncsl.org/bookstore/state-legislatures-magazine/health-care-in-and-out-of-prisons.aspx.

Seltzer, T. (2005). Mental health courts: A misguided attempt to address the criminal justice system's unfair treatment of people with mental illnesses. *Psychology, Public Policy, and Law, 11,* 570–586.

Sheppard, R., Freitas, F., & Hurley, K. (2002, October 28). *Assertive community treatment and the mentally ill offender.* Paper presented at the National GAINS Center Conference, San Francisco, CA.

Sirotich, F. (2009). The criminal justice outcomes of jail diversion programs for persons with mental illness: A review of the evidence. *Journal of the American Academy of Psychiatry and Law, 37*(4), 461–472.

Skeem, J. L., & Louden, J. E. (2006). Toward evidence-based practice for probationers and parolees mandated to mental health treatment. *Psychiatric Services, 57*(3), 333–342.

Skeem, J. L., & Manchak, S. (2008). Back to the future: From Klockar's model of effective supervision to evidence based practice in probation supervision. *Journal of Offender Rehabilitation, 47*(3), 220–247

Skeem, J.L., Manchak. S., & Montoya, L. (2017). Comparing public safety outcomes for traditional probation vs specialty mental health probation. *JAMA Psychiatry 74*(9), 942–948.

Skeem, J. L., & Petrila, J. (2004). Problem-solving supervision: Specialty probation for individuals with mental illnesses. *Court Review, 40,* 8–15.

Slate, R. N., Feldman, R., Roskes, E., & Baerga, M. (2004). Training federal probation officers as mental health specialists. *Federal Probation, 68*(3), 9–15.

Slate, R. N., Roskes, E., Feldman, R., & Baerga, M. (2003). Doing justice for mental illness and society: Federal probation and pretrial service officers as mental health specialists. *Federal Probation, 67*(3), 13–19.

Smith, R. J., Jennings, J. L., & Cimino, A. (2010). Forensic continuum of care with assertive community treatment (ACT) for persons recovering from co-occurring disabilities: Long-term outcomes. *Psychiatric Rehabilitation Journal, 33*(3), 207.

Solomon, P., & Draine, J. (1995a). Issues in serving the forensic client. *Social Work, 40*(1), 25–33.

Solomon, P., & Draine, J. (1995b). Jail recidivism in a forensic case management program. *Health & Social Work, 20*(3), 167–173.

Steadman, H. J., Barbera, S. S., & Dennis, D. L. (1994). A national survey of jail diversion programs for mentally ill detainees. *Hospital and Community Psychiatry, 45*(11), 1109–1113.

Steadman, H. J., Deane, M. W., Borum, R., & Morrissey, J. P. (2000). Comparing outcomes of major models of police responses to mental health emergencies. *Psychiatric Services, 51*(5), 645–649.

Steadman, H. J., Deane, M. W., Morrissey, J. P., Westcott, M. L., Salasin, S., & Shapiro, S. (1999). A SAMHSA research initiative assessing the effectiveness of jail diversion programs for mentally ill persons. *Psychiatric Services, 50*(12), 1620–1623.

Steadman, H. J., Morris, S. M., & Dennis, D. L. (1995). The diversion of mentally ill persons from jails to community-based services: A profile of programs. *American Journal of Public Health, 85*(12), 1630–1635.

Steadman, H. J., Stainbrook, K. A., Griffin, P., Draine, J., Dupont, R., & Horey, C. (2001). A specialized crisis response site as a core element of police-based diversion programs. *Psychiatric Services, 52*(2), 219–222.

Steadman, H. J., & Veysey, B. (1997, January). *Providing services for jail inmates with mental disorders* (Research in brief). Washington, D.C.: National Institute of Justice.

Sultan, B. J. (2006). Policy perspective: The insanity of incarceration and the maddening reentry process: A call for change and justice for males with mental illness in United States prisons. *Georgetown Journal on Poverty Law & Policy, 13,* 357–382.

Technical Assistance and Policy Analysis Center. (2007). *Definition: Jail diversion.* Delmar, New York: National GAINS Center. Retrieved from: http://gainscenter. samhsa.gov/html/tapa/jail%20diversion/definition.asp.

Tartaro, C. (2015). An evaluation of the effects of jail diversion and reentry for mentally ill offenders. *Journal of Offender Rehabilitation, 54,* 85–102.

Thresholds. (2011). *Annual report.* Chicago, IL: Author. Retrieved from: http://www.thresholds.org/images/stories/annualreport2011lowres.

Torrey, E. F., Kennard, A. D., Eslinger, D., Lamb, R., & Pavle, J. (2010). *More mentally ill persons are in jails and prisons than hospitals: A survey of the states.* Arlington, VA: Treatment Advocacy Center. Retrieved from http://coos.or.networkofcare.org/library/final_jails_v_hospitals_study1.pdf.

Travis, J. (2005). *But they all come back: Facing the challenges of prisoner reentry.* Washington, D.C.: Urban Institute Press.

USA v. Bull. (2001, May–June). Mental health treatment as probation condition upheld by eleventh circuit. *Correctional Mental Health Report, 9.*

USA v. Bull, WL 754942 (11th Cir., 2000).

Veysey, B. (1994). Challenges for the future. In *Topics in community corrections* (pp. 3–10). Longmont, CO: U.S. Department of Justice, National Institute of Corrections.

Veysey, B. M. (2011, January). Issue paper: The intersection of public health and public safety in U.S. jails: Implications and opportunities of federal health care reform. *Exploring health reform and criminal justice: Rethinking the connection between jails and community health.* Oakland, CA: Community Oriented Correctional Health Services. Retrieved from http://www.cochs.org/files/Rutgers%20Final.pdf.

Wakefield v. Thompson, 177 F.3d 1160 (9th Cir., 1999).

Wang, J. (2021). Bexar County puts more than $3M toward mental health, substance abuse services. *San Antonio Report.* Retrieved from https://sanantonioreport.org/bexar-county-puts-more-than-3m-toward-mental-health-substance-abuse-services/.

Willingham, A.J., & Elkin, E. (2018). *There's a severe shortage of mental health professionals in rural areas. Here's why that's a serious problem. CNN.* Retrieved from: https://www.cnn.com/2018/06/20/health/mental-health-rural-areas-issues-trnd/index.html.

Wilson, K. (2009, October 11). Recidivism high among mentally ill inmates. *Ventura County Star.* Retrieved from http://www.vcstar.com/news/2009/oct/11/recidivism-high-among-mentally-ill-inmates/?print=1.

Winterbauer, N., Tindell, A., Diduk, R. M., Pierce, K., & Remo, R. (2009). *Duval County Criminal Justice, Mental Health, & Substance Abuse Diversion Strategic Plan.* Retrieved from: http://www.hpcnef.org/files/health-needs-assesments/FINAL_CJMHSA_082709.pdf.

Chapter 11

Conclusion: Striving for Informed Policies

"A wise man should consider that health is the greatest of human blessings, and learn how by his own thought to derive benefit from his illnesses."

— Hippocrates[1]

Punishment and treatment do not occur within a vacuum. The criminal justice and mental health systems are inextricably bound to each other (Johnson, 2011). What happens in one system has an effect on the other system. The increasing number of individuals with mental health and substance use conditions in the criminal justice system has tremendous fiscal, health, and human costs (MHA, 2021). The effects of transinstitutionalization have been under-analyzed and underappreciated (Johnson, 2011; Johnson, 1996). Policies for too long have been developed in silos with bureaucrats protecting their own "fiefdoms" without consideration of the totality of circumstances.

Since the first edition of this book, in 2008, there has been a shift in thinking toward the treatment of offenders living with mental illness. Finding ways to divert such individuals out of criminal justice and into appropriate care — so future incarcerations are reduced or avoided — is vital (Docherty, 2017). Much of the force behind this shift has been led by a combination of factors. These variables include a growing homeless population, an underserved veterans' population, an international fiscal crisis, a number of high-profile public shootings (i.e. Fort Hood, Gabrielle Giffords, Aurora, Colorado, Newtown, Connecticut) that have brought international attention to the role that improperly treated mental illness can play, and a growth in the power and number of agencies advocating for change. These agencies, such as The GAINS Center, The National Alliance on Mental Illness (NAMI), and the University of Memphis Crisis Intervention Team Center, are having a positive effect on the treatment of offenders with mental illness. While these factors, in combination with lawsuits by the ACLU and continuing investigations by the Human Rights Watch and the Department of Justice, have resulted in positive change in the treatment of offenders with mental illness, there is still much work to be done.

---

1. Retrieved from http://www.quotationspage.com/quote/24184.htm.

However, these high-profile shootings have also fueled emotions and, in turn, mental illness stigma. As discussed in Chapter 3 and throughout this book, the pervasiveness of stigma attached to mental illness in our society has perpetuated an "us versus them" mentality. Between mental illness and other disempowered statuses, such as juveniles, females, racial/ethnic minorities and/or immigrants, and veterans — and in too many cases, as "offenders" — members of these groups face multiple layers of stigma. One of if not the main factor that accounts for the disproportionate number of persons with serious mental illnesses in correctional facilities is untreated mental illness (Baldwin, 2018). Such public and institutional stigma hinders the development of effective programs, including those that enhance collaboration between the mental health and criminal justice systems. The history of both systems reflects divisiveness between the punishment and treatment communities. The cumulative effects of previously discussed tragic, high-profile events point to a need to provide effective treatment that dovetails with the criminal justice system. While treatment and/or punishment cannot guarantee such tragedies won't happen, it can reduce their occurrence. Fisher and Drake (2007) offer the following caveat:

> [P]roblems impinging on the most vulnerable persons in society are created and sustained not by the complexity of medical illnesses but rather by the failures of multiple public policies: economic policies, housing policies, urban development policies, drug policies, vocational policies, disability policies, insurance policies, health policies, [and] criminal justice policies.... Mental health treatments, even those adapted to be 'forensic mental health' treatments, may be neither adequate nor effective solutions to these societal problems (pp. 546–47).

However, we believe that there are promising strategies out there, and more research is needed. People often assume that there is a direct connection between mental illness and criminal activity, however scholars and advocacy groups have disagreed with this statement and suggest a more complex set of factors is at play in the correlation between mental illness and crime (Pope, 2016). As groups like NAMI and Florida's Partners in Crisis (2012) work to advocate for changes in behavioral health care and bring down the walls created by stigma, we believe more inclusive policies grounded in evidence-based practices can be put in place. For too long we have failed to face our own mental health issues. While many of the answers may very well lie in government sponsored initiatives, sustainable change can only be affected if there is community involvement and that includes commitments from the private sector, which has a very important role to play.

Since its inception, the criminal justice system has worked to establish and maintain relationships with communities. Variations in the quality of law enforcement across jurisdictions are contingent upon community involvement. The same is true for mental health treatment. Attitudes held by police officers, correctional officials, community leaders, and citizens have shaped responses to mental illness. A largely uninformed, misinformed and apathetic public has contributed to the criminal justice system becoming the de facto mental health system. As Mark Twain once said, "We are all ignorant; just about different things" (Koppel, 2000, p. 33).

News coverage of events involving persons with mental illnesses often brings to the public's attention the complexity of dealing with mental illness. Answers to issues facing individuals living with mental illness lie in the development and sustenance of collaborative relationships. Bureaucracies, by their nature, inhibit communication, collaboration, and the sharing of information. We hope the information in this book will help inform decisions, motivate policymakers and citizens, and provide an opportunity for positive, collaborative change.

Unfortunately, legislation continues to be passed and policies implemented that contribute to the criminalization and recycling of persons with mental illnesses through the criminal justice system. Some believe the effect of the legislation was that persons with mental illnesses were being arrested for behaviors which they previously would have been civilly committed (Linhorst & Dirks-Linhorst, 2015). What is needed is education of everyone: from a citizenry that is bombarded by media sensationalism, to lawmakers that are influenced by an ill-informed citizenry and driven by perceptions of short-term savings that actually have long-term costs, to the legal community, criminal justice practitioners, and mental health providers.

In the long run, providing appropriate mental health care for all will save money. Not only is it the right thing to do, it is worth the investment. We are not merely talking about providing get-out-of-jail-free cards to persons with mental illnesses. In fact, some individuals with mental illness perceive it to be easier and less of an infringement to just do a short stint in jail without the intrusive linkages to community treatment than to go through diversionary programs. We believe that the appropriate response involves providing persons with mental illnesses that come into contact with the criminal justice system with voluntary treatment options; and when possible and appropriate, it should not be connected to the criminal justice system or associated with confinement. In our opinions, when treatment is primarily provided in an institutional setting, within either the mental health or the criminal justice system, we have moved away from the least restrictive environment ideal established by earlier court decisions. State legislatures have enacted policies that make access to healthcare a priority for those with behavioral health issues upon release from prison or jail (Williams, 2015). Indeed, the case examples in this text illustrate the myriad of individuals with mental illnesses who become involved in the criminal justice system and the difficulty the system is having in trying to care for these individuals, particularly in institutions that were never designed to handle offenders with mental illness.

We are also not arguing that having a mental illness automatically exculpates one from criminal liability. Judges, lawyers and expert witnesses struggle on a daily basis throughout America to establish or stretch beyond the limits of credulity causal linkages between the actions of those accused of crimes and their mental health.

It is essential to stop the maddening recycling of mentally ill offenders through the criminal justice system and to develop effective intervention strategies. The loss to individuals, families, and communities from the system's failure to respond to this growing crisis is incalculable. It is imperative that our society go beyond the power of shame so long associated with mental illness and become proactive in the management of our individual and collective mental health.

Accountability can be better ensured when legislators and policymakers make decisions informed by data. To achieve better results for both systems and individuals, legislators are considering and enacting policies to enhance access to mental health services at multiple stages in the criminal justice system and are utilizing multiple sources of data in their quest (Williams, 2015). "Lord Kelvin, a Scottish mathematician of the late 1800s, made this astute observation: 'When you can measure what you are speaking about, and express it in numbers, then you know something about it; but when you cannot measure it, when you cannot express it in numbers, your knowledge is of a meager and unsatisfactory kind'" (Power, 2005). As noted by Kathryn Power (2005), Director of the Center for Mental Health Services of the Substance Abuse and Mental Health Services Administration, we need to do a better job of data-based decision-making. Thus, policymakers need to be provided not only with the reasons for implementing policies but also with the numbers to justify their existence. Experts such as Dr. Henry J. Steadman at the GAINS Center are engaged in assisting agencies in the meaningful compilation and presentation of such data. Despite this recognition, though, as has been discussed throughout this book, crisis — not research — tends to drive policy.

Crisis Drives Policy

The widespread adoption of preventive outpatient treatment legislation following Andrew Goldstein's subway murder of Kendra Webdale, as discussed in Chapter 4, epitomizes the issue of crisis driving policy. Sadly, as previously discussed, Goldstein — and various others like him — repeatedly asked for treatment, yet he was turned away by underfunded and malfunctioning mental health services. Kim Webdale, the sister of Kendra Webdale, testified accurately before members of Congress that the more she and her family delved into Kendra's tragic death, the more Kim found her sister to have been the "unsuspecting victim of a sick man and an equally sick system" (Impact of Mentally Ill Offenders, 2000a, p. 95). Many reports emphasize the core challenges around access to mental health crisis care, which itself is a major issue; 26 percent of people who try to contact support services do not receive the help that they need (MHF, 2018). Unfortunately, however, the implementation of preventive outpatient commitment has not been the panacea that New York legislators hoped it would be. Such policy has flaws, as evidenced by the widely publicized December 2012 pushing death of New York City commuter Sunando Sen by Erika Menendez, a young woman with chronic mental illness (Santora & Hartocollis, 2012).[2] Clearly, as a country, we need to put a priority on arming mental health professionals with resources needed to provide appropriate services (e.g., funds, training, and staffing to provide assertive community treatment).

---

2. Another New York City subway death earlier in December 2012 illustrates the rush of the lay public to label such events as the acts of a "crazy" person. In this incident, Naeem Davis, claimed self-defense after, in the midst of a mutual altercation with the victim Ki-Suck Han, he pushed Han into the tracks of an oncoming subway train. There is no evidence that Davis had a mental illness (Goodman, 2012).

Virginia Tech University

Another instance of crisis driving policy was the mass shooting at Virginia Tech University in April 2007. The incident was preceded, in December 2005, by Seung Hui Cho sending messages to two coeds, resulting in police contact with him and a warning to cease and desist from contacting these women again. Following these events, Cho expressed suicidal ideations to a roommate, and the police re-contacted Cho and escorted him to a mental health facility where he was referred to the court for a commitment hearing (Schulte & Jenkins, 2007). As noted by Schulte and Jenkins (2007), the following day a judge determined Cho to be an imminent danger to himself, due to his mental state, and ordered him into involuntary outpatient commitment. However, there was no follow-up, and the events of April 16, 2007, resulting in the deaths of 32 persons and the gunman, will forever be etched in U.S. history. This incident reawakened the debate on gun violence and led to changes in gun laws, and especially to campus safety (Camera, 2017).

In retrospect, under intense scrutiny, the mental health treatment — or lack thereof — leading up to Seung Hui Cho's massacre at Virginia Tech appears to be a comedy of errors. A Virginia judge maintained that the court's responsibility ceased at the courtroom door following the close of the commitment hearing, as the court had no authority to follow up. In the eyes of judges, Virginia law was clear: mental health agencies "'shall recommend a specific course of treatment and programs' for people, such as Cho, who are ordered to receive outpatient treatment. Since courts are not enforcement bodies and must rely upon other entities, such as the mental health system and law enforcement, to carry out their dictates, Virginia law also said these boards 'shall monitor the person's compliance'" (Schulte & Jenkins, 2007, p. A01). Mental health officials, on the other hand, contended they were never advised that referrals were made to them by the court (Schulte & Jenkins, 2007). When confronted with the wording from the statute following the Virginia Tech incident, an employee of a Virginia mental health agency replied, "That's news to us" (Schulte & Jenkins, 2007, p. A01).

Ultimately, the common belief and practice in Virginia, when the court mandated that someone get treatment, was that the order was essentially to the individual in need of treatment to seek treatment, not to the mental health agency to ensure that the treatment occurred (Schulte & Jenkins, 2007). Of course, reliance on persons with mental illnesses in crisis to seek treatment is extremely suspect considering that many individuals with mental illnesses in crises lack insight into their illnesses (anosognosia). Lack of follow-up was also blamed on a shortage of resources. Typically, Virginia judges found out about problems with their orders for mental health treatment when an individual wound back up before the court after acting out (Schulte & Jenkins, 2007).

In this comedy of errors, no one is laughing. Lack of communication and lack of clearly delineated responsibilities between the mental health system and the courts, as well as a lack of mental health resources, ruled the day and resulted in the deaths of many innocent people.

As discussed in Chapter 4, the Virginia Tech tragedy led to sweeping reforms. First, the events highlighted that courts and the mental health system must, at a minimum, communicate with each other. In response, among other things, the Commonwealth reformed Virginia law to include the specific roles and responsibilities of each member of the outpatient civil commitment process (Virginia Mental Health Law Reform Commission, 2007). This lesson is an important one for all localities. At a minimum, area courts, mental health providers, law enforcement agencies, and any other involved parties should enter into multi-agency memorandums of understanding that ensure comprehensible specification of roles and responsibilities, clearly outlining who is accountable for what actions. Such agreements would go a long way towards overcoming custom and practice, as seen in Virginia, and would seek to ensure accountability. Moreover, due to the apparent confusion and erroneous beliefs by professionals about restrictions on information sharing regarding Cho leading up to the tragedy, the Virginia Tech Review Panel (2007) dedicated an entire chapter in their analysis to privacy laws, such as HIPAA and the Family Educational Rights and Privacy Act (FERPA). Indeed, training on HIPAA requirements — or lack thereof — for mental health providers, courts, and criminal justice professionals should be mandated in all localities.

Second, the Virginia Tech Review Panel addressed gaps in the state's mental health service system as a whole. One tell-tale observation of the panel could apply to almost any area in the United States:

> In the wake of the Virginia Tech tragedy, much of the discussion regarding mental health services ... focused on the commitment process. However, the mental health system has major gaps in its entirety starting from the lack of short-term crisis stabilization units to the outpatient services and the highly important case management function, which strings together the entire care for an individual to ensure success. These gaps prevent individuals from getting the psychiatric help when they are getting ill, during the need for acute stabilization, and when they need therapy and medication management during recovery (Virginia Tech Review Panel, 2007, p. 60).

In response to the tragedy at Virginia Tech, the Virginia Mental Health Law Reform Commission (2007) made recommendations for ways to reduce stigma and empower consumers of mental health services (e.g., endorsing a more empowering, recovery model; legally recognizing psychiatric advanced directives) in order to encourage people to voluntarily seek help in the first place. Further, Virginia appropriated more money to expand a more effective and cohesive network of community mental health services (Virginia Mental Health Law Reform Commission, 2007). Unfortunately, due to the economic downturn of the nation in general, these funds have decelerated and stymied improvements in Virginia's mental health system. Gun violence on campuses still remains a major issue even after the tragic events at Virginia Tech, with a total of 122 people killed and 198 injured by gunfire on campuses in the first 11 years after that tragedy (Jones, 2018).

Another recommendation from the Virginia Tech panel investigating the Cho incident pertained to more rigorous gun restrictions for persons with mental illness

(Virginia Tech Review Panel, 2007). The Virginia Tech campus was designated a gun-free zone, such that even those with concealed weapons permits were not permitted to bring guns onto the university grounds (Barone, 2007). Further, Cho was already legally prohibited by federal law from purchasing a firearm due to having been determined by a judge to be a danger to himself and court-ordered to outpatient mental health treatment prior to the massacre at Virginia Tech (Hammack, 2012; Virginia Tech Review Panel, 2007; Luo, 2007). The loophole in the Virginia law that allowed Cho to slip through the cracks and purchase a gun has now been closed (Hammack, 2012).[3] As noted by Bingham (2012), almost every significant reform to gun legislation has followed mass shootings in the United States. Echoing how crisis drives policy, United States Senator Charles E. Schumer remarked, "We can never know if we could have prevented the shootings at Virginia Tech[.] ... It is a shame that we're again called to act on ... legislation in the face of tragedy, but now it is Congress's moment to take a huge step toward fixing a broken system" (Williamson & Schulte, 2007, p. A12).

Sandy Hook Elementary School

Sadly, numerous other tragedies involving guns and people with mental illness, suspected mental illness, and/or other brain disorders have occurred in the years since Virginia Tech: Jared Loughner, James Holmes, and Adam Lanza are some of the individuals involved. On December 14, 2012, Adam Lanza, age 20, reportedly shot and killed his mother in Newtown, Connecticut, and then proceeded to Sandy Hook Elementary School. There, Lanza, using weapons allegedly legally purchased by his mother, killed 20 innocent children and six adults. According to media reports, it is believed that Lanza had Asperger's Disorder, a high-functioning form of autism affecting primarily interpersonal understanding (Bengali, Hennessy-Fiske, & Murphy, 2012; Halbfinger, 2012).[4] It is a neurodevelopmental disorder first manifested as social awkwardness in childhood (Sue, Sue, Sue & Sue, 2013) but, like most other brain disorders, is not considered a serious mental illness. However, Lanza's father does not believe Asperger's had anything to do with the tragedy (Park, 2014). While not all the signs of bloodshed still exist from the events several years prior, many tangible reminders of the massacre still linger (Rojas & Hussey, 2017).

---

3. Namely, although it was illegal for Cho to purchase a gun, court orders for outpatient mental health treatment in Virginia were not entered into the database used to screen potential gun buyers prior to the Virginia Tech incident — only commitments to mental hospitals were maintained in the database.

4. Cho, too, displayed symptoms of Asperger's (Cullen, 2007), although he was not diagnosed. Instead, he was diagnosed with selective mutism, a condition usually attributed to severe social anxiety, during childhood (Schulte & Craig, 2007); but it is possible that this was a misdiagnosis. Likewise, Loughner (Peele, 2011) and Holmes (Scarborough, 2012) have been suspected to have had aspects of the Asperger's Disorder.

Our hearts and prayers go out to the families, friends, and loved ones of those who died in Newtown. Certainly, they deserve a real effort to solve this problem, so that nothing like this ever happens again. Instead, in the days after the massacre in Newtown, talking heads hit the airwaves, rushing to offer simplistic solutions. Former presidential candidate Mike Huckabee, for example, pointed to the loss of religion. He answered his own question about why we should be so surprised at what took place at Sandy Hook Elementary, concluding that it was related to the systematic removal of God from schools (Your World, 2012). He stated that we don't need any more laws because we already have the law — "thou shalt not kill" — and that is all that is needed (Huckabee, 2012).

Unfortunately, in the aftermath of these tragedies, the tendency is to dehumanize and demonize the individuals who perpetrated them. Wayne LaPierre, executive vice president and CEO of the National Rifle Association, on national television after the Newtown shootings referred to Adam Lanza as a "horrible monster" (*Meet The Press*, 2012). Similarly, Mike Huckabee complimented Governor Mallory of Connecticut for indicating that evil had visited the Newtown community, and Huckabee referred to the incident as "crazed carnage" (Huckabee, 2012). President Obama, too, referred to the act as "unconscionable evil" (Washington Post Staff, 2012). As previously noted by Gusfield in Chapter 3, society rushes to implicate mental illness, to label such behaviors as "sick" and/or "evil", to separate it from ourselves by creating an "us" versus "them" dichotomy, because it allows the citizenry to better cope with such deviance (Williams & McShane, 2004). People seem to find it comforting to be able to point to a dysfunction within these young men, something "wrong" with them, rather than to social factors, as the cause. If we must look to Lanza's (and Cho's, Loughner's, and Holmes', before him) individual inclinations for causes, more significant factors may be that they were fascinated with automatic weapons and, in some of these cases, violent video games, both of which we as a society condone (if only legally). Most likely, though, the cause isn't within individuals, but in society. Undoubtedly, the cause is in complex, multi-faceted, systemic problems, which can only be resolved in wiser and more compassionate social change. Unfortunately, attempts at "fixing [these] broken system[s]," as Senator Schumer alludes to above, often amounts to impulsive, simplistic reductionism (Fedler, 2013).[5]

The rhetoric, the hyperbole, and the media images are vivid, but the reality is that tragedies such as the one in Newtown are infrequent. Even if Lanza's and Cho's conditions were considered to constitute serious mental illnesses, Psychiatrist E. Fuller Torrey emphasizes that only one percent of persons with severe mental illnesses will ever be linked to a violent act (The Takeaway, 2013). Likewise, Xavier Amador, on

---

5. Provost Kyle Fedler, referring to the aftermath of the Sandy Hook Elementary School shooting, made these remarks in his opening presentation to all faculty at the Florida Southern College on January 4, 2013.

CNN, reiterated the admonition offered by Szmukler discussed in Chapter 3, when he stated that the chances of being killed in a mass shooting like the one that occurred at Sandy Hook Elementary is less than the chance of being struck by lightning (*Piers Morgan Tonight*, 2012).

Dr. Torrey adds that the horrific acts at Newtown, Aurora, and Tucson could have been prevented with appropriate treatment (The Takeaway, 2013). Possibly an intact, well-functioning mental health system might have altered the trajectory of these young men's lives. This system should have provided effective prevention, early identification, intervention services, and proper education of the public to overcome stigma and ensure proper care of persons with mental illnesses. Unfortunately, we will never know, and we cannot go back and change these events. All we can do is ensure that this event "awakens [and equally importantly, maintains] the conscience of the country" and catalyzes our legislators to effect "immediate action, urgent action," and sustained action to prevent it from happening again (Biden, 2013).[6] Indeed, in the words of President Obama (Washington Post Staff, 2012) as he spoke to the mourning town of Newtown, and the nation, "We can't tolerate this anymore. These tragedies must end. And to end them, we must change ... Surely we can do better than this ... and surely we have an obligation to try."

In the wake of the Newtown tragedy, President Obama signed 23 executive orders aimed at reductions in gun violence; he urged Congress to act on other related matters (Ungar, 2013). In the series of orders, President Obama specifically addressed mental illness/mental health treatment by calling for a relaxing of HIPPA requirements to facilitate background checks, emphasizing that doctors are not prohibited from asking patients about guns in their homes, ensuring that state health officials are made aware of what mental health treatment services are covered by Medicaid, clarifying parity requirements and regulations, and beginning a national dialogue on mental health (Trotter, 2013). But these actions were not without controversy. For example, Dr. Marc Siegel (2013) questions a policy of doctors asking patients if they have a gun in the home and believes such inquiries may actually serve to discourage persons with mental illnesses from seeking treatment. Similar thoughts are echoed in the passage below.

Ron Honberg (2013), National Director of Policy and Legal Affairs for the National Alliance on Mental Illness, poignantly summarizes the importance of prioritizing mental health treatment in order to bring about real change:

---

6. Undoubtedly, it is striking that on the day that then Vice President Joe Biden announced the plans of the Newtown-inspired gun policy task force was the day in which the prosecution of the Aurora, Colorado, movie theater shootings was scheduled to wrap-up its preliminary hearing and the day after the anniversary of the Tucson, Arizona, shootings of Gabrielle Giffords, her staff, and constituents.

In the aftermath of the tragedy in Newtown, Conn., it's important to consider whether changes to America's gun laws are needed. The focus should be on steps to keep highly lethal weapons out of the hands of dangerous individuals, whether or not they have a mental illness.

One in four Americans experience a mental health problem in any given year. One in 17 lives with a serious mental illness. Most are not violent, and most violent crimes are committed by people who do not have mental illness.

States are supposed to report to the National Instant Criminal Background Check System (NICS) people "committed to any mental institution" or "adjudicated as ... mentally defective." The latter term is both highly offensive and confusing. Some states interpret it as needing to report people committed to a psychiatric hospital for more than 30 days. Others report those brought in for emergency assessments.

Now, some have proposed broadening the law to include anyone who seeks mental health treatment, or all people who have been in psychiatric hospitals, whether voluntarily or involuntarily.

Either approach would be counterproductive. Broadening the criteria would deter people from seeking treatment, the last thing anyone should want.

Clear guidance to states on reporting is a sensible idea. But more concern should be placed on a bigger problem: It's far easier to buy a gun in the U.S. than to access mental health care. We rally around people diagnosed with other conditions, such as diabetes or cancer. We shun people with symptoms of possible mental illness and erect barriers to treatment.

Since 2008, America has cut $4 billion from its already ailing public mental health system. Many community mental health programs have disappeared, and more than 4,000 psychiatric hospital beds have been eliminated. For too many, even basic mental health care is illusory. People can't get help until they go into crisis.

There is some hope. Inclusion of mental health care in the Affordable Care Act, [and the Affordable Care Act's ability to survive the multiple attacks on its existence between 2016 and 2020] are good first steps. More is needed, including mental health screening, early intervention, evidence-based mental health treatment and services, and family education and support.

It is time to make mental health care a continual national priority, not just in the days after tragedies.

But by 2018, little appeared to have changed, and there was another tragedy, this one at Marjory Stoneman Douglas High School in Parkland, Florida. The gunman in that case, who had no history of mental illness to speak of, killed 17 and injured 17 others. After that massacre, it was not politicians, nor voters, but surviving students who took matters into their own hands to enact change, particularly around gun control laws (Bacon, 2019). These students, along with many others, became advocates for change and worked to ensure that these tragedies do not continue. With the student advocacy coming in the wake of Parkland, many organizations such as Moms Demand Action and Everytown were calling loudly for safety in schools. As a result, more than half of the most recent gun restrictions passed were in the year directly following Parkland (Astor & Russell, 2019). But these changes were far from uniform. While some states pushed to impose firearm safety measures, more conservative states passed laws that strengthened gun ownership rights (Wilson, 2019).

It has been said that the Lone Ranger's calling card was a silver bullet because it symbolized purity and justice, but, more importantly, it served as a reminder "of just how heavy a price firing a gun can be" (The Lone Ranger, n.d.). Unfortunately, there are no silver bullets here for purely simple solutions. Multi-faceted collaborations will be required to solve these complex problems. If the Parkland aftermath revealed nothing else, it was the fact that mass shootings seem to further entrench people in their positions on gun control and this remains a major barrier to meaningful change (Silliman, 2018).

Who Wants to Take Responsibility for Ending the Needless Recycling of Persons with Mental Illnesses In and Out of the Criminal Justice System?

There has been a lot of shifting of responsibility for the mentally ill population from one entity to another. The states have been all too happy to shift financial responsibility to the federal government, relying on its provision of benefits to the poor and disabled. They also shift responsibility through such mechanisms as preferred drug lists that serve to restrict access to medication and can send persons with mental illnesses spiraling out of control. In a similar way, gun control responsibilities are always shifting from one group to the other and as a result, there is little lasting change when it comes to gun control reform. Most Americans support gun control but it is not their top priority, whereas those who disagree with gun regulation have it as their top priority, and their beliefs will often outweigh those of others because gun rights are their main priority (Gebelhoff, 2019). The U.S. may be able to learn and hopefully is amenable to lessons from other countries that have successfully implemented gun control laws that benefit the safety of their citizens, including Australia and Brazil (Wogan, 2014), and New Zealand (Hashmi, 2019).

Many mental health providers have been quite content to have someone else handle the job that they are supposed to do. This "someone else" has become emergency rooms and the criminal justice system, whose doors are open 24 hours a day, 7 days a week, 365 days a year. This has resulted in the criminalization of persons with mental illnesses via police encounters, leading to the further status-degrading process of not just being labeled as mentally ill, but of arrest and oftentimes conviction and incarceration in jail or prison. Contrary to many treatment entities, criminal justice facilities do not place any restrictions or stipulate any prerequisites for entry (Abram & Teplin, 1991). Thus, persons with mental illnesses are often locked up simply because more appropriate treatment settings are not accessible or agreeable to providing treatment (Lurigio, Fallon, & Dincin, 2000), because often the community mental health system abdicates its responsibility in treating persons with mental illnesses who encounter the criminal justice system (Solomon & Draine, 1995). For example, while somewhat dated, Torrey et al. (1992) found that 29 percent of jails held people with mental illness *who were not even facing charges* but merely awaiting a hospital bed.

Who can blame the mental health providers, though, particularly if they are designated as accountable yet not equipped with adequate resources to meet such responsibilities? Indeed, as has been discussed throughout the book, the mental health system is notoriously overextended and underfunded. As such, it is not uncommon to find treatment providers opposed to interventions from mental health courts, for example, because such entities seek to hold stakeholders accountable while their resources will likely not be enhanced. Designating accountability without resources and ensuring follow-up is irresponsible. In order for virtually any program to be effective, policymakers must ensure that proper resources are in place to provide appropriate mental health treatment to the citizenry. In addition, people with mental illness are often criminalized in the media, especially after an event like a mass shooting. News media will often portray the perpetrator as someone with a serious mental illness and imply or outright say that serious mental illness can be a driving force for tragedies like mass shootings. As a result, much of society becomes extremely critical of people who have a mental illness and often form very negative views about those individuals (McGinty, Webster, & Barry, 2013).

It is the politicians that fail to adequately fund the public mental health system. While mental health and criminal justice professionals struggle to do their jobs, lawmakers, like the Wizard behind the curtain in Oz, continue with their supposed cost-saving measures, which, instead of helping, only contribute directly to the criminalization and further stigmatization of persons with mental illnesses. Indeed, often their policies drive crises, such as in the case of preferred drug lists, which serve to restrict access to medication and can send persons with mental illness spiraling out of control.[7]

In spite of the apathy or greed of some politicians, informed citizens are beginning to get the message. This is evidenced by the fact that "some innovative mental health program financing has been adopted by [some] states, ... such as California's Propo-

---

7. *Orlando Sentinel* reporter Stephen Hudak investigated a story regarding Keith Howard, a man with schizophrenia, who, after having his medication changed in compliance with preferred drug list requirements implemented by the Florida legislature, killed his mother and is institutionalized having been found not guilty by reason of insanity (S. Hudak, personal communication, September 20, 2007). As R. Slate informed the Florida Senate Committee on Health Care in his 2005 testimony, their policy would be driving crises, but this was to no avail, as the legislature proceeded to implement their pre-

sition 63 initiative in 2004, which provides a stable, significant source of revenue for mental health services through a so-called millionaire's tax" voted in by the citizenry (Daly, 2006, p. 8; see also The Press-Enterprise, 2012).

Multi-System Collaboration Is the Answer

This is not just about making persons with mental illnesses responsible through treatment for their actions. It is also about making actors within the criminal justice and mental health systems responsible for their actions or inactions as well. It is about holding those actors within the criminal justice system, such as the policymakers, accountable for enacting legislation through a public health approach to benefit a multitude of groups (Prevention Institute, n.d.). This is about everyone, every entity, being accountable. As reflected in this book, most of the research publications regarding the interface of the mental health and criminal justice systems are occurring within the psychiatric journals, but presentations are increasing on this topic at professional criminal justice conferences. Perhaps there is promise in the criminal justice system working collaboratively with the mental health system if mental health providers are willing to seek funding for mental health treatment. However, the mental health system, perhaps because it lacks the influence or the will — maybe both — to intervene, has in many respects taken a back seat to efforts to reverse the criminalization of persons with mental illnesses. If mental health providers are not willing to do so, they might as well step aside, as criminal justice authorities have clout and leverage with policymakers and the community to pursue alternatives to the criminal justice system for persons with mental illnesses. In the past decade, sheriffs, police chiefs, judges and the associations they belong to have been quite influential in bringing about meaningful change and influencing lawmakers. In turn, most grants aimed at stopping persons with mental illnesses from recycling through the criminal justice system are spearheaded by criminal justice entities. While the percentage of those individuals with serious mental illness that commit violent crimes are low, there are many societal barriers that prevent them from receiving mental health treatment. There are many complexities to the relationships between serious mental illness and gun violence, but without access to adequate and affordable treatment, these individuals will not be able to get the help they need and reduce violent recidivism (Cornell, et al., 2013).

At least some of the criminal justice professionals who have long been in the dumping grounds for society's ills have begun to stand up collectively, and sometimes in multi-system collaborations, to stop the revolving door of the criminal justice system for them-

---

ferred drug list restrictions. Also, Sgt. Jack Richards of the Ventura Police Department in California fully understands the importance of CIT training and its emphasis on de-escalation techniques. Having been involved in a fatal shooting of a person with mental illness earlier in his police career, while not equipped with such training, Sgt. Richards also points to the failure of the system to provide adequate access to mental health treatment as a significant contributing factor to creating unnecessary situations that lead to hostile confrontations like the one he encountered (J. Richards, personal communication, April 30, 2007).

selves and for persons with mental illnesses. While there are indeed differences between the actors from the various entities involved in the interface of the mental health and criminal justice systems, they share a lot of common ground. It seems that what has worked best in fighting against the criminalization of persons with mental illnesses in jurisdictions across America is collaboration: bringing together law enforcement, judges, prosecutors, public defenders, corrections officials, mental health clinicians, mental health advocates, consumers of mental health services, family members with loved ones with mental illnesses, and victims' advocates to craft workable, meaningful solutions. If additional mental health treatment services are needed, then such multi-system collaborations can be quite successful in lobbying lawmakers to address needs. The challenge — but also the beauty — of multi-system collaborations is finding the issues and approaches that everyone can agree on and putting aside differences (e.g. building consensus). Sterling examples of such collaborations can be found in panels assembled to testify before Congress as spearheaded by the Council of State Governments (CSG), as well as the CSG's (2002) Criminal Justice/Mental Health Consensus Project.

Similar, statewide collaborative initiatives have emerged in an attempt to influence criminal justice/mental health policy at the state and local level in Florida, Oregon, South Carolina, and Washington.[8] For example, Florida's collaborative, particularly with the testimony of Sheriffs, was able to stave off over $100 million in reductions to substance-abuse and mental health services, with no cuts, in a legislative session (Usher, 2012).

Such initiatives, as indicated above, often emerge as the result of crises; whether they want to be or not, judges are uniquely positioned to bring together stakeholders and seek meaningful alternatives to the criminalization of persons with mental illnesses. Judges as well as mental health workers have been positioned to help influence legislators with understanding the complex connections between mental illness and crimes and develop alternative methods for mental health-focused initiatives (Metzl & MacLeish, 2015). As noted by Miami Judge Steven Leifman, Chairman of Florida Partners in Crisis: "When I was a public defender trying to address this problem, I called a meeting of all the key stakeholders, and no one came. When I became a judge I called the same meeting. Everyone was five minutes early" (Council of State Governments, 2007). Seizing upon the pivotal role that judges can play in this process, funding was established for State Supreme Court Chief Justice led task forces in seven states (California, Florida, Georgia, Missouri, Nevada, Texas, and Vermont) across the country to promote partnerships between the criminal justice and mental health systems (Strie & Davey, 2007). In 2009, another solicitation for State Supreme Court Chief Justice led task force applications was offered (Council of State Governments, 2009).

---

8. Websites for Partners in Crisis organizations can be found at: http:// www.flpic.org/ index.php Florida Partners in Crisis; http://www.wapic.org/home/ Washington State Partners in Crisis; http://www.scpartnersincrisis.org/ South Carolina Partners in Crisis; See http://www.lpscc.org/docs/mh_wkgrp_rpt_2005.pdf Oregon Partners in Crisis; http://www.picusa.org/content/view/13/26/Partners in Crisis of America.

Influencing Policy

The use of an "Iron Fist and [a] Velvet Glove" approach may be the best mantra for changing the system (Marx, 1986; Center for Research on Criminal Justice, 1975). During our recent era of "zero tolerance," relationships between criminal justice personnel and the public have become strained, and this is to say nothing of the murder of unarmed citizens, many of them citizens of color, at the hands of law enforcement officers. In attempts to overcome years of "iron fisted" approaches that have not worked, innovative partnerships between key players in the criminal justice and mental health systems such as drug and mental health courts and crisis intervention training for police officers—have been developed, with promising results. These strategies ensure accountability while also emphasizing restoration, a theme that resounds with the notion of tough love. There are a number of additional steps that may help alleviate this strain, including promoting community involvement in prevention efforts, improving trust between law enforcement and people of color, increasing investment on at risk families and communities, and promoting the use of mental health courts and intervention trainings for law enforcement (Paddock, Samuels, Vinik, & Overton, 2017).

Of course, solely diverting someone from the criminal justice system should not be considered a panacea in and of itself. Many of those diverted will require follow-up, either pre- or post-trial, to ensure compliance with conditions, which will serve to ensure that they do not put themselves or anyone else at risk and/or they do not recycle through the system. To assure this, sufficient inpatient and community-based treatment structures need to be in place. Today we often institutionalize persons with mental illnesses in jails and prisons, instead of in hospitals. We can ill afford this de-institutionalization-to-transinstitutionalization movement any longer.

Influencing Policy through Testimony and Legislation

It is our belief that enhanced sensitivity to mental illness would go a long way toward the eradication of stigma which impacts the criminalization of mental illness. As such, it is our hope that the passage of federal parity legislation (see Honberg, 2012; *National Federation of Independent Business v. Sebilius*, 2012), whereby insurance coverage for mental health is on par with that for physical health, will assist in sending the message to the general public that mental illnesses are essentially no different from physical illnesses. We do not, for example, blame someone for being diabetic, which results from a chemical imbalance, nor should we blame someone for having bipolar disorder, which results from a chemical imbalance in another area of the body: the brain. Most importantly, parity should insure greater access to mental health treatment and lessen the burden on the criminal justice system, allowing criminal justice professionals to focus on their roles as crime fighters. We are personally encouraged by calls from the summer of 2020 to defund the police, particularly the aspects that focus on rerouting money to the mental health care system and away from criminal justice. This can serve to free up the police to be the crime fighters they were intended to be for more serious offenses. As we hope is abundantly clear at this point, the criminal justice system is not, nor was it ever meant to the be, the place where people with mental illness should receive care.

The Sentencing Project assessed changes in national health care policy (Phillips, 2012) and contended that federal health care reform legislation could impact offenders living with mental illness in three key ways:

- **Expanded Health Care Coverage** — The Affordable Care Act gives states the option of expanding Medicaid eligibility and makes prevention, early intervention, and treatment of mental health problems and substance use essential health benefits. In the 38 states plus the District of Columbia that chose to expand Medicaid coverage under the ACA, the federal government is covering 90% of those expenditures.

- **Reducing Recidivism** — Because of the role mental health and substance abuse problems play in behaviors that lead to incarceration and recidivism, the Affordable Care Act could help states reduce the number of people cycling through the criminal justice system.

- **Addressing Racial Disparities** — The legislation may contribute to reducing racial disparities in incarceration that arise from disparate access to treatment.

It is uncertain how politics will affect the relationship between those agencies that provide mental health services and the criminal justice system in the future (Hendrickson, 2012). What is certain is that the failure to act and furtherance of existing protocols will be more costly in the long run than the implementation of a proactive public health strategy proposed in the Affordable Care Act. Recently, voters used ballot initiatives to expand Medicaid in Nebraska, Utah, and Idaho (the latter endorsed by the Idaho Sheriffs' Association), thereby boosting criminal justice reform as well (Nichanian, 2018).

Los Angeles Police Department's Approach to Encounters with Persons with Mental Illness

Lt. Rick Wall, mental illness project coordinator of the Los Angeles Police Department (LAPD), elaborates on the agency's efforts at preventing the recycling of persons with mental illnesses through the criminal justice system in testimony before the U.S. House of Representatives Judiciary Committee's Subcommittee on Crime, Terrorism, and Homeland Security (*Criminal justice responses to offenders with mental illness*, 2007). Wall reports on the predictable monthly behavior that began to erupt from a person with mental illness by the name of "Mike" who repeatedly refused to take his medication and would become violently suicidal at approximately the same times each month. During a year and a half period, "Mike" generated 48 calls for police service, with 22 of these calls resulting in mental health holds. Police responses to "Mike" were frequently met by suicide by cop behaviors, as he expressed desires to have the voices in his head silenced. Mike's behaviors could prove quite disruptive, resulting in displacement of as many as 50 nearby residents when evacuations of the area were required (*Criminal justice responses to offenders with mental illness*, 2007).

Several components operate within Los Angeles to try to prevent the recycling of persons with mental illnesses through the criminal justice system. The Mental Evaluation Unit provides a triage desk and is comprised of specially trained officers who respond to questions from dispatchers and patrol officers to assist in identifying incidents involving persons with mental illnesses and providing direction and advice to units engaged with persons with mental illnesses in the field (*Criminal justice responses to offenders with mental illness*, 2007). Wall indicates a confidential database is maintained by the Unit to document pertinent information pertaining to previous police contacts with a particular subject in the field and the circumstances of such contacts; if additional follow-up is required, referrals are made to Systemwide Mental Assessment Response Teams (SMART).

Via a partnership with the county mental health department, the LAPD provides citywide mental health crisis call coverage with 18 SMART teams; Homeless Outreach/Mental Evaluation (HOME) Teams have been added to focus on the "Skid Row" area of the city. The HOME teams are comprised of a sworn police officer and a social worker or registered nurse and operate to assist officers who encounter homeless subjects in linking them to appropriate treatment and preventing them from being victimized (*Criminal justice responses to offenders with mental illness*, 2007).

The LAPD also continues to incorporate CIT training and currently has over 300 officers trained and represented in all of the agency's 19 geographic divisions as first responders to crisis calls involving persons with mental illnesses. In addition, a mobile crisis team is maintained by the mental health department, known as the Psychiatric Mobile Response Team (PMRT), and is available for interventions and evaluations prior to necessitating an emergency response call (*Criminal justice responses to offenders with mental illness*, 2007).

Wall identifies the Case Assessment and Management Program (CAMP) as one of the most innovative of the programs in operation in Los Angeles (*Criminal justice responses to offenders with mental illness*, 2007). This program is operated by the department of mental health and aims to keep minor offenders in the mental health system and out of the criminal justice system. CAMP investigators identify subjects who pose a high risk of danger to themselves or others and have been the subject of repeated police interventions due to their mental illnesses resulting in numerous calls for crisis services. CAMP investigators also provide follow-up and linkages to treatment services and, at the time of Lt. Wall's testimony, had not had a repeat violent incident with any of their clients. In fact,

"Mike," who Lt. Wall began his congressional testimony discussing, became the CAMP program's first client and only required one call for service in 2006, and, via monthly CAMP contact with him and his family, "Mike" has not required a call for police service in over a year (*Criminal justice responses to offenders with mental illness*, 2007). This is how the recycling of persons with mental illnesses is prevented: by putting personnel in place who are appropriately trained and know what they are doing and equipping them with adequate resources to thwart the long term costs and human suffering that occur when such interventions do not take place. The exemplary, comprehensive approach taken by the LAPD to divert persons with mental illnesses from the criminal justice system is to be applauded. Of course, the LAPD has more resources at its disposal than many law enforcement agencies. However, their model provides an example of how collaborations can work effectively.[9]

One of the masterminds of behind the scenes consensus building and impacting criminal justice/mental health legislation is Mike Thompson with the Council of State Governments in New York. He operates much like a director/producer as he orchestrates various organizations in selecting individuals to testify on a particular issue.[10] In addition to the previously discussed congressional testimony of Kim Webdale, what follows is the testimony of Risdon N. Slate (*Impact of Mentally Ill Offenders*, 2000b).

---

9. More recent testimony before the U.S. Senate Judiciary has focused on the negative impact of solitary confinement on inmates with mental illnesses (Reassessing solitary confinement, 2012).

10. Below is an example of a series of panelists Thompson convened for testimony before Congress, which ultimately led to federal funding for mental health courts across the country (Slate, 2003, p. 25). Note the diversity of backgrounds and viewpoints of these people, all in agreement about the need to request interventions to stop the recycling of persons with mental illness through the criminal justice system.

The Honorable Mike DeWine, (R) U.S. Senator, Ohio

The Honorable Ted D. Strickland, (D) U.S. Congressman, Ohio

Dr. Bernard S. Arons, Director, Center for Mental Health Services, Department of Health and Human Services

Chief Bernard Melekian, President, Los Angeles County Police Chiefs Association, and Pasadena Police Department, Pasadena, California

Ms. Kim Webdale, New York, New York

Michael F. Hogan, Ph.D, Director, Ohio Department of Mental Health

Steven Sharfstein, M.D., Medical Director, Sheppard Pratt Health Systems, Baltimore, Maryland

Mr. Donald F. Eslinger, Sheriff, Seminole County, Florida

The Honorable Michael Schrunk, District Attorney, Multonomah County, Portland, Oregon; Risdon N. Slate, Ph.D., Florida Southern College

The Honorable James D. Cayce, Judge, King County Courthouse, Seattle, Washington

Reginald A. Wilkinson, Ed.D, Director, Department of Rehabilitation and Correction, and Vice President, Association of State Correctional Administrators, Columbus, Ohio

The Honorable Robert J. Thompson, State Senator and Chair, Law and Justice Committee, Harrisburg, Pennsylvania

**One-Page Summary Statement of Risdon N. Slate, Ph.D.,
Nami-FL Board Member for Judiciary Committee,
Subcommittee on Crime, September 21, 2000**

In June of 1986, I had earned a master's degree in criminal justice, had two years of experience under my belt as a correctional official, and was just beginning my career as a United States Probation Officer. That promising career soon came to a screeching halt when, within a two week span of time, I was diagnosed with manic-depressive illness, forced to resign my dream job for medical reasons, and I was left while hospitalized and ultimately divorced by my wife. It truly felt like my world had ended.

However, I was encouraged by treatment professionals, and the prescribed medication — lithium (an element on the periodic chart) — worked for me. As a result, I was able to put my life back together, went on to the Claremont Graduate School, earned my Ph.D. in criminal justice, took a job in 1989 as a full-time criminal justice professor in Maine, and then moved to Florida in 1993, where I currently reside and work, taking a job as a criminology professor at Florida Southern College.

Upon my arrival in Lakeland, I located a new physician so I could continue my medical prescription for lithium. Unfortunately, this psychiatrist decided that I was not mentally ill and convinced me to stop taking the medication that I had been taking for eight years. I complied with his advice, and my condition soon deteriorated.

During a visit to South Carolina, I suffered the second manic episode of my life. When police were called, although I was exhibiting bizarre behavior and my wife desperately tried to advise them of my illness and show them the vial containing the medication that I should be taking, they took me to jail and put me in a holding cell with approximately fifteen other detainees. Due to my strange behavior, I was first assaulted by an inmate and then by detention officers who ultimately isolated me in a strip cell.

Finally, a federal probation officer with whom I had once worked, Ronald L. Hudson, intervened. Flashing his badge, he convinced my captors to release me. He has since told me that the jailers were glad to oblige him, as they were admittedly at a loss as to how to deal with my behavior. He transported me to a hospital. Ron probably saved my life, as at no time during my stay in the jail, even after appearance before a magistrate who set my bail at $500, did I see any medical personnel or receive any medical treatment.

If such experiences can happen to me, with a Ph.D. in criminology and my background and knowledge of the criminal justice system, they can happen to anyone. I call upon you to intervene on behalf of those who are unable to do so, because it is the right thing to do! By the grace of God and due to the love, support, and encouragement of my wife, Claudia, and my mother, Virginia, I appear before you today to offer the following suggestions:

In terms of recommendations, persons with mental illness and the practitioners they encounter within the criminal justice system should have more options/choices/alternatives available for successful resolution of problems for the sake of all concerned parties, including the public. Certainly, there will be some mentally ill individuals who will require incarceration, but we must ensure them adequate treatment, not only for their benefit, but also for the well-being of correctional personnel and the potential welfare of society when they are likely released.

The Sequential Intercept Model (SIM) was discussed in Chapter 1. The beauty of the SIM, conceptualized by Munetz and Griffin (2006), is that the model visually presents points for intervention for persons with mental illness who encounter the criminal justice/mental health system. The SIM is intended to present points at which people with mental illness can leave the criminal justice system and re-enter society with linkages to treatment. The points for intervention include police and emergency services, initial detainment and hearings, "[j]ail, courts, forensic evaluations, and forensic commitments, [r]entry from jails, state prisons, and forensic hospitalizations, [and c]ommunity corrections and community support services" (Munetz & Griffin, 2006, p. 545).

More problematic is ensuring that employees at each of the intercept points have training in encountering persons with mental illnesses in crises, recognizing the general signs and symptoms of mental illnesses, and developing skills to link persons with mental illnesses to needed services that are available. For example, as reflected in Slate's congressional testimony presented above (*Impact of Mentally Ill Offenders*, 2000b), although he encountered three intercept points (law enforcement, detainment and initial appearance before a magistrate, and return to jail), at no time did he receive any mental health treatment. In fact, the magistrate who presided over his initial appearance had a real estate background. In essence, though at a critical point for intervention, the magistrate had an apparent lack of understanding of the signs and symptoms of mental illness and/or command of alternatives for intervention.

As noted by psychologist Fred Frese, Ph.D., who lived with schizophrenia, unless individuals have a loved one or friend with mental illness, persons with mental illnesses are often viewed as aliens, creatures from outer space (Compton & Kotwicki, 2007). As we have previously discussed, for criminal justice practitioners their typical familiarity with mental illness is through encounters with persons with mental illnesses in crises. Thus, it is imperative that all criminal justice and mental health professionals who are likely to have interactions with persons with mental illnesses have appropriate training for such encounters — to lessen the possibility for escalation; to remain professional, non-judgmental, and non-stigmatizing; to learn of avenues and resources for linking individuals to suitable treatment. Such personnel should also be exposed to persons with mental illnesses in recovery and be made aware of their significant contributions to society.

In the Florida Supreme Court report, headed by then Florida Chief Supreme Court Justice R. Fred Lewis, funded and convened by the Council of State Governments, included among the numerous recommendations was the involvement of consumers of mental health services in the education and training of judges (Supreme Court of the State of Florida, 2007). Such meaningful involvement of consumers of mental health services is essential for ensuring buy-in and lending credibility to the development of initiatives and policies. Florida's Partners in Crisis (FPIC), with Gail Cordial and Judge Steven Leifman, have actualized this process in Florida by having consumers of mental health services engaged in the actual training of judges regarding the interface of the mental health and criminal justice systems. FPIC has also been involved in creating judicial handbooks on protocol and available services for ready reference when persons with mental illnesses appear before the bench. Likewise, as discussed in Chapter 5, consumers of mental health services play an integral role in training police for such encounters. Risdon Slate has trained and continues to train judges, police, and corrections personnel and wishes that those he encountered when in crisis had also been trained. Collaborations between criminal justice and mental health agencies should always include input from consumers of mental health services and from family members who have loved ones with mental illnesses. These collaborations could also span into preventative measures around gun laws, including mental health screenings as part of the background check (Barry, Webster, Stone, Crifasi, Vernick, & McGinty, 2018).

Influencing Policy through Accountability

One of the powers of the grand jury system across this country is the ability to launch and conduct investigations. Although infrequently used, the grand jury has, as discussed in Chapter 8, served as a mechanism by which the citizenry can investigate and literally indict the mental health and criminal justice systems in an effort to ensure accountability. How many of these systems in jurisdictions throughout America could withstand such scrutiny in their handling of persons with mental illnesses?

In the law, duty follows knowledge (del Carmen, 2006). Joseph Mucenski, a retired Detective from the New York City Police Department, was present when his son was killed in Arizona by police in what was termed a "suicide by cop" incident. Mucenski and his wife filed suit against the law enforcement agency, not because of a desire to obtain money, but to epitomize the spirit of turning crisis into opportunity by seeking assurances that the law enforcement agency would enact more appropriate training standards for their officers. Upon adoption of the CIT training model, the Mucenskis dropped their lawsuit. Now Joseph Mucenski is a leader and proponent of such training internationally. Joseph acknowledges that he is conflicted over what transpired in the incident that resulted in his son's death from his years on the New York City Police force and his role as a father. He admits he is not certain how he would have handled the incident himself if he had been in charge. But, he knows improved training is essential (Mucenski, 2007; J. Mucenski, personal communication, August 30, 2007).

With a similar outcome, Risdon Slate sent a letter to Polk County Sheriff's Colonel Grady Judd after he had announced his candidacy for Sheriff following a tragic shooting of a person with mental illness by an officer in his jurisdiction in Florida. The letter was not meant to cast blame upon the agency, but its contents indicated that we could not know for certain in hindsight if specialized training would have made a difference in this particular matter. The Colonel agreed to meet and made a commitment to implement CIT training as part of his platform for Sheriff. Upon becoming Sheriff, he has stuck by his commitment.

To influence lawmakers you need to contact them, but, Richard Codey, Governor of New Jersey at the time, indicated that most politicians do not realize how big a problem the inadequate treatment of mental illnesses is for their constituents because people are running from the stigma and are ashamed to discuss the topic. Codey knows firsthand, as his wife suffered from postpartum depression (Mulligan, 2005a).

In maverick fashion, as a state senator, Richard Codey went into a state psychiatric hospital to do some undercover work. Having discovered that just about 33% of those employed in the state hospital system had criminal records, some even for homicide, Codey used the name of a deceased felon and got himself hired as an orderly on the midnight shift at New Jersey's Marlboro Psychiatric Hospital. On his first day on the job, he was informed that he was fortunate to be working on the midnight shift because it was easier to have sex with the residents. At the culmination of his undercover work, the president of the hospital and some 35 to 40 other workers were terminated for what Codey uncovered, and now criminal background checks are required on all state hospital employees in New Jersey prior to beginning work (Hennelly, 2004).

Immediately prior to signing an executive order to establish a task force to make recommendations on how to improve mental health service delivery and access to services, Governor Codey stopped by to have breakfast with residents at Greystone Park Psychiatric Hospital in New Jersey (Mulligan, 2005a). Indeed, Codey's first official act as Governor was to sign the aforesaid executive order (Mulligan, 2005b). Governor Codey also signed executive orders and dined with residents of Ancora Psychiatric Hospital, as he wrapped up his tenure as Governor and landmark transformation of the New Jersey mental health system (Heck, 2006).

While it is important to ensure accountability among criminal justice professionals, given the impact of their jobs, it is also essential to recognize — and respond to the fact — that they are operating under increasingly stressful conditions. Criminal justice work is, by nature, dangerous. As discussed in previous chapters, vigilance about one's safety is among the greatest job stressors for law enforcement and correctional officers. Long, erratic work schedules, exacerbated by understaffing and high rates of staff turnover, interfere with an officer's ability to take basic care of him/herself (e.g., working while sleep deprived) and ultimately can impact his or her mental health (Vila, 2006). At the same time, an officer's every move and decision-making is closely scrutinized. All of these factors combine to produce elevated rates of burnout and stress-related depression, anxiety, including Post-Traumatic Stress Disorder (PTSD), substance abuse, and, according to some studies, suicide for police officers (Collins & Gibbs, 2003). Yet, many refuse to seek treatment as a result of a workplace culture that tends to interpret weakness and even incompetence — rather than strength — into an officer's request for psychiatric help. Indeed, it is essential for law enforcement and criminal justice agencies to take steps to modify this mentality, not only for the mental health of its officers but for the individuals they serve, many of whom have mental illness.

Influencing Policy through Knowledge

Some college courses address the issue of the criminalization of mental illnesses and explore means for reversing this trend and honing in on the worth of persons with mental illnesses. For example, Jacqueline Buffington-Vollum, a forensic clinical psychologist and professor, offers a college course entitled Mental Illness in the Criminal Justice System, originally in Virginia and now in Minnesota. Likewise, Risdon N. Slate teaches a Criminalization of Mental Illness course at Florida Southern in Lakeland, Florida. Kelly Frailing teaches a class called Offenders with Mental Illness at Loyola University New Orleans. Wes Johnson offers a course called Criminal Justice and Mental Illness at Southern Mississippi University. Michael Perlin, Professor of Law at New York Law School, has established a mental disability law program and offers such courses as Mental Disability Issues in Jails and Prisons (New York Law School, 2007). However, Mulvey and Larson (2017) note that these offerings are still extremely rare, with just over six percent of institutions offering a bachelor's in criminology and/or criminal justice having a course like those mentioned above in their catalogs.

It would also behoove our criminal justice and mental health systems to consider global perspectives when considering possible strategies for ameliorating the issues surrounding the population of individuals with serious mental illness in the criminal justice system. As Tseng, Matthews, and Elwyn (2004) note about the practice of psychiatry within jails and prisons and for the courts, the same could be said for the overall work to be done with inmates with mental illness:

> Looking beyond our own borders to see how forensic psychiatry is practiced in other societies around the world is both worthwhile and necessary.

Through examining how forensic matters are handled in other societies we learn more about cultural and legal differences between our systems. Further, by acquiring an international perspective, we can obtain insight into our own situation and enrich our understanding about where we might aim for future improvement (p. 307).

Although complete "translation" of programs may not be feasible, it would behoove U.S. criminal justice and mental health professionals to apprise themselves of innovative approaches that could be imported at least in part. For example, the importance of cultural competence in both the mental health system (U.S. Department of Health and Human Services, 2001) and in the criminal justice system (Shearer & King, 2004) has been recognized for quite some time. However, we continue to treat our inmates in a one-size-fits-all manner, with poor results. As such, we might be able to learn something from Australia's indigenous sentencing courts (Marchetti & Daly, 2007), which incorporate elements of therapeutic and restorative justice and aim to make "criminal justice processes more culturally appropriate, to establish better communication and trust between the indigenous community and the judiciary, and to facilitate better understanding of offenders' life stories and situations" (Waye & Marcus, 2010, pp. 395–396; for cultural competence concerns in the U.S., see Eckberg & Dexter, 2018). Educating ourselves and appreciating the varied characteristics and needs of our diverse criminal justice population — not only racial/ethnic minorities and immigrants, but juveniles, females, veterans, and homeless individuals — could go a long way toward improving the mental health of these citizens and the systems of which they are part.

Conclusion

As a country we are once again facing the issues contemplated when Dorothea Dix began her campaign to build mental health hospitals. Americans know that prisons and jails are not the proper place to treat persons with mental illness. We draw an analogy for our societal responsibility from *The Catcher in the Rye*: "The character Holden Caulfield ... envisioned himself standing in a field of rye on the edge of a cliff with the mission of catching all those in danger of falling and saving them from going over the edge of the cliff ... [We] believe that in a civilized society, we are morally responsible for catching those persons with mental illness that we can and saving them from going over the edge of the cliff into the abyss of the criminal justice system" (Salinger, 1991; Slate, 2003, pp. 24–25). Criminal justice practitioners are logically positioned, whether they want to be or not, as the gatekeepers for salvaging persons with mental illnesses.

Beyond the criticisms made by the authors, solutions have been offered when possible. In many instances, appropriate interventions have been in place for some time now, and consequently the care of persons with mental illnesses is improving. However, this is generally the exception rather than the rule. As such, it is imperative that we carefully monitor those essential institutions that have as their primary mission the custody and control of persons with mental illnesses and provide adequate resources and funding to those institutions to ensure viable treatment options. Critical to this success will be measures and processes of accountability.

There are answers to many of the horrific situations recited in this text. Those answers lie in treatment. Untreated mental illness is like untreated cancer. The failure to detect and treat early sends ripple effects throughout families and communities.

While correctional treatment staff can be successful in improving the functioning of many mentally ill offenders, prisons remain an inappropriate environment for treating the seriously mentally ill offender. The cost to "do it right" will be enormous, but the cost of not doing so, both in terms of human suffering and financial resources, is even greater. Innovative funding schemes must continue to be explored locally with long range therapeutic goals in mind. Of course, external reliance on funding sources that may dry up, for example, the federal government, can be problematic. There are only so many slices that can be cut from the "financial pie." Wars are costly to fight (Associated Press, 2008; Kristof, 2008; Tanielian and Jaycox (2008); Mazzetti & Havemann, 2006), and California learned in implementing its Three-Strikes Legislation that getting tough on third-time felons is costly. Schools, hospitals, and communities suffered as monies were diverted from them to pay for our imprisonment binge (Shicor & Sechrest, 1996).

There is no shame in having a mental illness. It knows no socio-economic boundaries. It affects every segment of our society. The shame is in not receiving adequate treatment, and any entity that obfuscates that treatment should be considered criminal. A person should not have to commit a crime to have a chance at some semblance of treatment in America; it should be easier to get mental health treatment than to get a gun. As Beccaria stated in 1764, "The coin of honor is always inexhaustible and fruitful in the hands of one who distributes it wisely" (p. 70). It is time to do the honorable thing, to make judicious funding decisions, to rethink priorities, and to provide appropriate community and institutional care for persons with serious mental illnesses.

References

Abram, K. M., & Teplin, L.A. (1991). Co-occurring disorders among mentally ill jail detainees: Implications for public policy. *American Psychologist, 46*, 1036–1045.

American Psychological Association Communications Staff. (2008, March 27). In the spotlight: Parity achieves historic milestone. *Practice Update, 5*(3). Retrieved from http://www.apapracticecentral.org/update/2008/03-27/index.aspx.

Associated Press. (2008, March 9). *Studies: Iraq a $12 billion-a-month war.* Retrieved from http://www.msnbc.msn.com/id/23551693/print/1displaymode/1098/.

Astor, M., & Russell, K. (2019). After Parkland, a new surge in state gun control laws. *The New York Times.*

Baldwin, M. (2018). Mental illness is not a crime. *Psychology Today*. Retrieved from: https://www.psychologytoday.com/us/blog/beyond-schizophrenia/201810/mental-illness-is-not-crime.

Bacon, J. (2019). 'They have made change:' 1 year after carnage in Parkland, where key figures are now. USA Today. Retrieved from: https://www.usatoday.com/story/news/nation/2019/02/10/parkland-one-year-after-shooting-where-key-figures-are-now/2721798002/.

Barone, M. (2007, April 28). *Feeling safe isn't safe*. Retrieved from http://www.cbsnews.com/stories/2007/05/01/politics/main2747886.shtml.

Barry, C. Webster, D., Stone, E. Crifasi, C., Vernick, J., & McGinty E. (2018). Public support for gun violence policies among gun owners and non-gun owners in 2017. *American Journal of Public Health, 108*, 878–881.

Beccaria, C. E. (1764). *On crimes and punishment*. Indianapolis, IN: Hackett Publishing.

Bengali, S., Hennessy-Fiske, M., & Murphy, K. (2012, December 17). Adam Lanza's family had kept a watchful eye on him. *Los Angeles Times*. Retrieved from http://articles.latimes.com/2012/dec/17/nation/la-na-shooter-profile-20121218.

Biden, J. (2013, January 9). *Press conference on gun policy task force following Newtown shootings*. Atlanta, GA: Cable News Network.

Bingham, A. (2012, July 27). Shootings that shaped gun control laws. *ABC News*. Retrieved from http://abcnews.go.com/Politics/OTUS/shootings-shaped-gun-control/story?id=16863844.

Birckhead, T. R. (2012, September 17). "Children are Different": Culpability and the Mandatory Sentencing of Juveniles after Miller v. Alabama & Jackson v. Hobbs-2012 Symposium of The University of Minnesota's *Journal of Law & Inequality*. *Juvenile Justice Blog*. Retrieved from http://juvenilejusticeblog.web.unc.edu/2012/09/17/children-are-different-culpability-and-the-mandatory-sentencing-of-juveniles-after-miller-v-alabama-jackson-v-hobbs/.

Camera, L. (2017). Virginia Tech 10 years later: When campus safety changed forever. *U.S. News and World Report*. Retrieved from: https://www.usnews.com/news/national-news/articles/2017-04-14/virginia-tech-10-years-later-whats-changed-on-campuses-since-the-2007-shooting.

Center for Research on Criminal Justice. (1975). *The iron fist and the velvet glove: An analysis of the U.S. police*. Berkeley, CA: Author.

Collins, P. A., & Gibbs, A. C. (2003). Stress in police officers: a study of the origins, prevalence and severity of stress-related symptoms within a county police force. *Occupational Medicine, 53*, 256–264.

Compton, M. T., & Kotwicki, R. J. (2007). *Responding to individuals with mental illnesses*. Boston, MA: Jones & Bartlett.

Council of State Governments. (2007). *Why a Judicial Leadership Initiative?* New York, NY: Author. Retrieved from http://consensusproject.org/JLI/info/jli_about/why_jli.

Council of State Governments. (2009, June 28). CSG Launches New Chief Justice-led Task Force Initiative. New York, NY: Author. Retrieved from http://consensusproject.org/features/cjtaskforce11-16.

Council of State Governments, Police Executive Research Forum, Pretrial Services Resource Center, Association of State Correctional Administrators, Bazelon Center for Mental Health Law, and the Center for Behavioral Health, Justice, and Public Policy. (2002). *Criminal Justice/Mental Health Consensus Project.* New York, NY: Council of State Governments. Retrieved from consensusproject.org/the_report.

Cornell, D., Evans, A., Guerra, N., Kinscherff, R. Mankowski, E., Randazzo, M., Scrivner, E., Sorenson, S., Tynan, W. D., & Webster, D. (2013). Gun violence: Prediction, prevention, and policy. *American Psychological Association.* Retrieved from: http://www.apa.org/pubs/info/reports/gun-violence-prevention.aspx.

Criminal justice responses to offenders with mental illness: Hearings before the Subcommittee on Crime, Terrorism, and Homeland Security of the Committee on the Judiciary, House of Representatives, 110th Cong., 1st Sess. 18 (2007, March 27) (testimony of Richard Wall). Retrieved from http://judiciary.house.gov/hearings/printers/110th/34359.PDF.

Cullen, D. (2007, April 27). Talk to the Chos. *New York Times.* Retrieved from http://www.nytimes.com/2007/04/27/opinion/27cullen.html.

Daly, R. (2006). States get disappointing marks on mental health report card. *Psychiatric News, 41*(8), 8, 71.

del Carmen, R. V. (2006). *Criminal procedure: Law and practice* (6th ed.). Belmont, CA: Wadsworth.

Docherty, J. (2017). Creating new hope for mental illness and the criminal justice system. Retrieved from: https://www.nami.org/Blogs/NAMI-Blog/October-2017/Creating-New-Hope-for-Mental-Illness-and-the-Crimi.

Eckberg, D., & Dexter, K. (2018). Cultural factors and mental illness. In K. Frailing and R. Slate (Eds.), *The criminalization of mental illness: A reader* (pp. 3–26). Durham, NC: Carolina Academic Press.

Fedler, K. (2013, January 4). Educating our students. Spring Faculty Forum Presentation: Florida Southern College, Lakeland, FL.

Fisher, W. H. & Drake, R. E. (2007). Forensic illness and other policy misadventures. Commentary on "extending assertive community treatment to criminal justice settings: Origins, current evidence, and future directions." *Community Mental Health Journal, 43*(5), 545–548.

Florida Partners in Crisis. (2012). *Justice, treatment, safety*. Merritt Island, FL: Author. Retrieved from http://flpic.org/.

Gebelhoff, R. (2019). Gun reform doesn't happen because Americans don't want it enough. *Washington Post*. Retrieved from: https://www.washingtonpost.com/opinions/2019/03/04/gun-reform-doesnt-happen-because-americans-dont-want-it-enough/.

Goodman, J. D. (2013, February 5). As victim's family grieves, suspect is charged in subway killing. *New York Times*. Retrieved from http://www.nytimes.com/2012/12/06/nyregion/police-arrest-naeem-davis-in-subway-death.html.

Halbfinger, D. M. (2012, December 14). A gunman, recalled as intelligent and shy, who left few footprints in life. *New York Times*. Retrieved from http://www.nytimes.com/2012/12/15/nyregion/adam-lanza-an-enigma-who-is-now-identified-as-a-mass-killer.html.

Hammack, L. (2012, September 18). Virginia Tech tragedy prompts positive changes. *Roanoke Times*. Retrieved from http://www.roanoke.com/news/roanoke/wb/283546.

Hashmi, S. (2019). How New Zealand's gun laws compare to the States'. Washington Examiner. Retrieved from: https://www.washingtonexaminer.com/opinion/how-new-zealands-gun-laws-compare-to-the-states.

Heck, K. (2006, January 13). Codey visits patients at Ancora Psychiatric Hospital: Governor builds upon achievements improving New Jersey's mental health system. *New Jersey Office of the Governor Press Releases*. Trenton, NJ: New Jersey Office of the Governor. Retrieved from http://www.nj.gov/cgi-bin/governor/njnewsline/view_article.pl?id=2890.

Hendrickson, B. A. (2012). What's at stake in the 2012 elections? *NAMI Advocate, 10*(3), 16–19.

Hennelly, B. (2004, November 14). *Acting New Jersey Governor Dick Codey*. New York, NY: WNYC News. Retrieved from http://www.wnyc.org/articles/wnyc-news/2004/nov/14/acting-nj-governor-dick-codey/.

Honberg, R. (2013, January 2). Another view: More mental health care. *USA Today*. Retrieved from http://www.usatoday.com/story/opinion/2013/01/02/national-alliance-mental-illness/1805471/.

Honberg, R. (2012). Moving forward. *NAMI Advocate, 10*(3), 10–11.

Huckabee, M. (2012, December 15). *Where was God?* New York, NY: Fox News. Retrieved from http://video.foxnews.com/v/2038135300001/huckabee-where-was-god/.

Impact of mentally ill offenders on the criminal justice system: Hearings before the Subcommittee on Crime of the Committee on the Judiciary, House of Representatives, 106th Cong., 2nd Sess. 92 (2000a, September 21) (testimony of Kim Webdale). Retrieved from http://commdocs.house.gov/committees/judiciary/hju67345.000/hju67345_0f.htm.

Impact of mentally ill offenders on the criminal justice system: Hearings before the Subcommittee on Crime of the Committee on the Judiciary, House of Representatives, 106th Cong., 2nd Sess. 138 (2000b, September 21) (testimony of Risdon Slate). Retrieved from http://commdocs.house.gov/committees/judiciary/hju673 45.000/hju67345_0f.htm.

Johnson, W. W. (2011). Rethinking the interface between mental illness, criminal justice and academia. *Justice Quarterly, 28*(1), 15–22.

Johnson, W. W. (1996). Transcarceration and social control policy: The 1980s and beyond. *Crime & Delinquency, 42*(1), 114–126.

Jones, M. (2018). After Virginia Tech shooting, gun violence still claims victims on college campuses. *Collegiate Times.* Retrieved from: http://www.collegiatetimes. com/news/after-virginia-tech-shooting-gun-violence-still-claims-victimson/ article_4c27a5f2-3a98-11e8-9165-4f568030151b.html.

Koppel, T. (2000, Fall). Lulling viewers into a state of complicity. *Nieman Reports, 54*(3), 33.

Kristof, N. D. (2008, March 23). Iraq, $5,000 per second? *New York Times.* Retrieved from http://www.nytimes.com/2008/03/23/opionion/23kristof.html?_r=1&page wanted=printe&ore.

Linhorst, D., & Dirks-Linhorst, P. A. (2015). Mental health courts: Development, outcomes, and future challenges. *American Bar Association.* Retrieved from: https://www.americanbar.org/groups/judicial/publications/judges_journal/2015/ spring/mental_health_courts_development_outcomes_and_future_challenges/.

Luo, M. (2007, April 21). U.S. rules made killer ineligible to purchase gun. *New York Times.* Retrieved from http://www.nytimes.com/2007/04/21/us/21guns.html?_r=1 &oref=slogin.

Lurigio, A. J., Fallon, J. R., & Dincin, J. (2000). Helping the mentally ill in jails adjust to community life: A description of a postrelease ACT program and its clients. *International Journal of Offender Therapy and Comparative Criminology, 44*(5), 532–548.

Marchetti, E., & Daly, K. (2007). Indigenous sentencing courts: Towards a theoretical and jurisprudential model. *Sydney Law Review, 29*, 415–443.

Marx, G. T. (1986). The iron fist and the velvet glove: Totalitarian potentials within democratic structures. In J. Short (Ed.), *The social fabric: Dimensions and issues* (pp. 135–162). Beverly Hills, CA: Sage.

Mazzetti, M., & Havemann, J. (2006, February 3). Iraq War is costing $100,000 per minute. *Seattle Times.* Retrieved from http://seattletimes.nwsource.com/cgi-bin/ PrintStory.pl?document_id= 2002780385&zsectio.

McGinty, E., Webster, D., & Barry, C. (2013). Effects of news media messages about mass shootings on attitudes toward persons with serious mental illness and public support for gun control policies. *American Journal of Psychiatry, 170*, 494–501.

Meet The Press. (2012, December 23). *Transcript.* New York: National Broadcasting Company. Retrieved from http://www.msnbc.msn.com/id/50283245/ns/meet_the_press-transcripts/t/december-wayne-lapierre-chuck-schumer-lindsey-graham-jason-chaffetz-harold-ford-jr-andrea-mitchell-chuck-todd/.

Metzl, J., & MacLeish, K. (2015). Mental illness, mass shootings, and the politics of American firearms. *American Journal of Public Health, 105,* 240–249.

MHA. (2021). Mental health and criminal justice issues. Retrieved from: https://www.mhanational.org/issues/mental-health-and-criminal-justice-issues.

MHF. (2018). The mental health policy landscape: 2017–2018. Retrieved from: https://www.mentalhealth.org.uk/blog/mental-health-policy-landscape-2017-2018.

Mucenski, J. P. (2007, August 30). *Awards banquet.* Presentation at the 3rd Annual Crisis Intervention Team (CIT) Conference, Memphis, TN.

Mulligan, K. (2005a). Firsthand experience spurs Codeys' fight to end stigma. *Psychiatric News, 40*(10), 21.

Mulligan, K. (2005b). New Jersey Governor begins term by naming mental health task force. *Psychiatric News, 40*(10), 1.

Mulvey, P., & Larson, M. (2017). Identifying the prevalence of courses on mental illness in criminal justice education. *Journal of Criminal Justice Education, 28,* 542–558.

Munetz, M. R., & Griffin, P. A. (2006). Use of the Sequential Intercept Model as an approach to decriminalization of people with serious mental illness. *Psychiatric Services, 57*(4), 544–549.

National Federation of Independent Business v. Sebilius, 132 S.Ct. 1618 (2012).

New York Law School. (2007). *Online Mental Disability Law Program: Course descriptions.* Retrieved from http://www.nyls.edu/academics/graduate_and_certificate_programs/mental_disability_law_masters/course_description/course_description1.

Nichanian, D. (2018). How Medicaid expansion and criminal justice reform boosted each other in 2018. *The Appeal-Political Report.* Retrieved from https://theappeal.org/politicalreport/medicaid-in-georgia-nebraska-idaho/.

Office of Justice Programs. (2020). Drug Courts. *Department of Justice.* Retrieved from https://www.ojp.gov/pdffiles1/nij/238527.pdf.

Paddock, E., Samuels, J., Vinik, N., & Overton, S. (2017). Federal actions to engage communities in reducing gun violence. *Urban Institute.* Retrieved from: https://www.urban.org/sites/default/files/2017/02/03/federal_actions_to_engage_communities-in-reducing-gun-violence.pdf.

Park, A. (2014). Don't blame Adam Lanza's violence on Asperger's. *Time.* https://time.com/19957/adam-lanzas-violence-wasnt-typical-of-aspergers/.

Peele, S. (2011, January 11). Can we profile killers like Jared Loughner, Nidal Malik Hasan, and the VA Tech shooter? We can't profile our way out of mass murders.

Psychology Today. Retrieved from http://www.psychologytoday.com/blog/addiction-in-society/201101/can-we-profile-killers-jared-loughner-nidal-malik-hasan-and-the-va-.

Phillips, S. (2012, September). *The Affordable Care Act: Implications for public safety and corrections populations.* Washington, D.C.: The Sentencing Project. Retrieved from http://sentencingproject.org/doc/publications/inc_Affordable_Care_Act.pdf.

Pope, L. (2016). Rethinking mental illness and its path to the criminal justice system. *Vera Institute of Justice.* Retrieved from: https://www.vera.org/blog/rethinking-mental-illness-and-its-path-to-the-criminal-justice-system.

Power, A. K. (2005, June 1). *Transformation: Moving from goals to action.* Paper presented at the Joint National Conference on Mental Health Block Grants and National Conference on Mental Health Statistics, Arlington, VA. Retrieved from http://mentalhealth.samhsa.gov/newsroom/speeches/060105.asp.

Prevention Institute. (n.d.). Gun violence must stop: Here's what we can do to prevent more deaths. Retrieved from: https://www.preventioninstitute.org/focus-areas/preventing-violence-and-reducing-injury/preventing-violence-advocacy.

Reassessing solitary confinement: The human rights, fiscal and public safety consequences. Hearings before the Subcommittee on the Constitution, Civil Rights and Human Rights of the Committee on the Judiciary, (2012, June 19). Retrieved from http://www.judiciary.senate.gov/hearings/hearing.cfm?id=6517e7d97c06eac4ce9f60b09625ebe8.

Rojas, R., & Hussey, K. (2017). Newtown is 'still so raw:' 5 years after Sandy Hook shooting. *The New York Times.* Retrieved from: https://www.nytimes.com/2017/12/13/nyregion/newtown-sandy-hook-five-year-anniversary.html.

Salinger, J. D. (1991). *The catcher in the rye.* Boston, MA: Little Brown & Company.

Santora, M., & Hartocollis, A. (2012, December 30). Troubled past for suspect in fatal subway push. *New York Times.* Retrieved from http://www.nytimes.com/2012/12/31/nyregion/erika-menendez-suspect-in-fatal-subway-push-had-troubled-past.html?pagewanted=1&tntemail1=y&_r=1&emc=tnt.

Scarborough, J. (2012, July 23). James Holmes, suspected Aurora shooter, might have been 'on the autism scale.' *Huffington Post.* Retrieved from http://www.huffingtonpost.com/2012/07/23/joe-scarborough-james-holmes-autism_n_1694599.html.

Schulte, B. & Craig, T. (2007, August 27). Unknown to Va. Tech, Cho had a disorder. *Washington Post.* Retrieved from http://www.washingtonpost.com/wp-dyn/content/article/2007/08/26/AR2007082601410.html.

Schulte, B., & Jenkins, C. L. (2007, May 7). Cho didn't get court-ordered treatment. *Washington Post,* p. A01.

Shearer, R. A., & King, P. A. (2004). Multicultural competencies in probation — issues and challenges. *Federal Probation, 68*(1). Retrieved from http://www.uscourts.gov/fedprob/June_2004/competencies.html.

Shicor, D., & Sechrest, D. (1996). *Three strikes and you're out: Vengeance as public policy*. Thousand Oaks, CA: Sage Publications.

Siegel, M. (2013, January 17). White house enlisting your doctor in gun control push? Cavuto — Fox Business. Retrieved from http://video.foxbusiness.com/v/2101806292001/white-house-enlisting-your-doctor-in-gun-control-push/.

Silliman, R. (2018). Gun control: Who's responsible? *Public Agenda*. Retrieved from: https://www.publicagenda.org/newsroom/gun-control-whos-responsible/.

Sipe, R. V. (1946). Cesare Beccaria, *Indiana Law Journal, 22*(1), 27–42. Retrieved from http://www.repository.law.indiana.edu/ilj/vol22/iss1/4.

Slate, R. N. (2003). From the jailhouse to Capitol Hill: Impacting mental health court legislation and defining what constitutes a mental health court. *Crime & Delinquency, 49*(1), 6–29.

Solomon, P., & Draine, J. (1995). Issues in serving the forensic client. *Social Work, 40*(1), 25–33.

Strie, A. M., & Davey, C. (2007, May 2). National mental illness and courts forum a success. *The Supreme Court of Ohio & the Ohio Judicial System News*. Retrieved from http://www.supremecourt.ohio.gov/PIO/news/2007/mentalIllnessProgram_050207.asp.

Sue, D., Sue, D. W., Sue, D., & Sue, S. (2013). *Understanding abnormal behavior* (10th edition). Belmont, CA: Wadsworth.

Supreme Court of the State of Florida. (2007). *Transforming Florida's mental health system: Constructing a comprehensive and competent criminal justice system/ mental health/substance abuse treatment system: Strategies for planning, leadership, financing, and service development*. Tallahassee, FL: Author. Retrieved from http://www.floridasupremecourt.org/pub_info/documents/11-14-2007_Mental_Health_Report.pdf.

Tanielian, T., & Jaycox, L. H. (2008). *News release: One in five Iraq and Afghanistan veterans suffer from PTSD or Major Depression*. Santa Monica, CA: Rand Corporation. Retrieved from http://rand.org/news/press/2008/04/17/.

The Lone Ranger. (n.d.). *Frequently asked questions*. Retrieved from http://weirdscifi.ratiosemper.com/loneranger/faq.html.

The Press-Enterprise. (2012, July 2). *State: Disjointed budgeting*. Riverside, CA: Author. Retrieved from http://www.pe.com/opinion/editorials-headlines/20120702-state-disjointed-budgeting.ece.

The Takeaway. (2013, January 3). *Expert says laws, not funding, biggest obstacle to effective mental health treatment*. Minneapolis, MN: Public Radio International. Retrieved from http://www.pri.org/stories/health/rethinking-the-approach-to-mental-health-care-in-the-us-12549.html.

Torrey, E. F., Stieber, J., Ezekial, J., Wolfe, S. M., Sharfstein, J., Noble, J. H., & Flynn, L. M. (1992). *Criminalizing the seriously mentally ill: The abuse of jails as mental hospitals.* Washington, D.C.: Public Citizen's Health Research Group and the National Alliance for the Mentally Ill.

Trotter, J. K., (2013, January 16). Here are Obama's 23 actions on gun violence. *The Atlantic Wire.* Retrieved from http://www.theatlanticwire.com/politics/2013/01/obama-executive-actions-gun-list/61075/.

Tseng, W., Matthews, D., & Elwyn, T. S. (2004). *Cultural competence in forensic mental health: A guide for psychiatrists, psychologists, and attorneys.* New York, NY: Routledge.

Ungar, (2013, January 16). Here are the 23 executive orders on gun safety signed by the President. *Forbes.* Retrieved from http://www.forbes.com/sites/rickungar/2013/01/16/here-are-the-23-executive-orders-on-gun-safety-signed-today-by-the-president/.

U.S. Department of Health and Human Services. (2001). *Mental health: Culture, race, and ethnicity — A supplement to Mental health: A report of the Surgeon General.* Rockville, MD: U.S. Department of Health and Human Services, Substance Abuse and Mental Health Services Administration, Center for Mental Health Services.

Usher, L. (2012). Unlikely allies in the fight for mental health services: Criminal justice leaders speak out. *NAMI Advocate, 10*(3), 20–21.

Vila, B. (2006) Impact of long work hours on police officers and the communities they serve. *American Journal of Indian Medicine, 49*(11), 972–980.

Commonwealth of Virginia Commission on Mental Health Law Reform. (2007, December). *A preliminary report and recommendations of the Commonwealth of Virginia Commission on Mental Health Law Reform.* Richmond, VA: Author. Retrieved from www.courts.state.va.us/programs/cmh.

Virginia Tech Review Panel. (2007, August). *Mass shootings at Virginia Tech: April 16, 2007. Report of the Review Panel.* Richmond, VA: Office of the Governor. Retrieved from http://www.governor.virginia.gov/TempContent/techPanelReport-docs/FullReport.pdf.

Washington Post Staff. (2012, December 16). President Obama's speech at prayer vigil for Newtown shooting victims (Full transcript). *Washington Post.* Retrieved from http://articles.washingtonpost.com/2012-12-16/politics/35864241_1_prayer-vigil-first-responders-newtown.

Waye, V., & Marcus, P. (2010). Australia and the United States: Two common criminal justice systems uncommonly at odds, Part 2. *Tulane Journal of International and Comparative Law, 18*(2), 335–401.

Williams, R. (2015). Addressing mental health in the justice system. *NCSL.* Retrieved from: https://www.ncsl.org/research/civil-and-criminal-justice/addressing-mental-health-in-the-justice-system.aspx.

Williams, F. P. & McShane, M. D. (2004). *Criminological theory* (4th ed.). Upper Saddle River, NJ: Prentice Hall.

Williamson, E., & Schulte, B. (2007, December 20). Congress passes bill to stop mentally ill from getting guns. *Washington Post*, p. A12.

Wilson, R. (2019). One year after Parkland, gun debate rages in states. *The Hill*. Retrieved from: https://thehill.com/homenews/state-watch/430071-one-year-after-parkland-gun-debate-rages-in-states/.

Wogan, J. (2014). Lessons in gun control from Australia and Brazil. *Governing*. Retrieved from: https://www.governing.com/archive/gov-gun-control-lessons.html.

Your World. (2012, December 14). *Mike Huckabee responds to the question of 'How could God let this happen?' following Connecticut elementary school attack*. Retrieved from http://foxnewsinsider.com/2012/12/14/mike-huckabee-responds-to-the-question-of-how-god-could-let-this-happen-following-connecticut-elementary-school-attack/.

Epilogue

Prior to this book going to print, law enforcement officers moved Jamal Sutherland from a mental health facility to jail, and on his jail admission form one of the arresting officers checked "No" for any signs of mental illness regarding Mr. Sutherland. At jail, Charleston County, South Carolina, detention officers tried to extract Sutherland, who was mentally ill, from his jail cell so he could go to a bond hearing *he wasn't even required to attend*. Sutherland died in that cell, and an investigation continues. What measures discussed in our text might have been used at various points to prevent this from happening? Here is a link to a video/article of that cell extraction attempt. **Be forewarned, it is incredibly brutal and astonishingly inhumane**. The second link describes the events leading up to the botched extraction:

https://www.thestate.com/news/charleston/article251410728.html

https://www.thestate.com/news/charleston/article252176538.html

What can I do? What can we do? The authors of this book regularly use it as a text in our courses on PWMI who are justice involved and those are inevitably the questions we receive from students at the end of those courses. Some readers may want to work with PWMI who are (or who have been) in the CJS in some capacity. Some readers may have personal or familial experiences with mental illness that would make advocacy a natural fit. But there are two things all readers can do to start to effect the changes that frankly need to be made.

The first of those two things is to educate others on the state of things (how we got here, what here looks like, what we've tried, what we can do better). The second of these is to vote, especially in your local and state elections, for the people whose views on PWMI and reforming the system align with yours.

We firmly believe that it is our obligation as human beings who live in a society to look out for people who don't or who don't always have the capacity to look out for themselves, and importantly, may not have had the opportunities to build that capacity. And a society that is content to subject people with serious and persistent mental health challenges to the CJS where those challenges are only made worse and more deleterious is who we are now, but it does not have to be that way. Yes, we need in system solutions, like CIT, like mental health courts, like mental health care in jails and prisons. There are 500,000 people with serious mental illness who are incarcerated in the U.S. and it seems to us cruel at best and a form of torture at worst for those institutions to make little to no effort to meaningfully and effectively face that reality and be proactive in their approach to changing it; at the very least, they need to make a concerted effort to try to understand PWMI's lived experiences in these institutions and provide relief where and when they can.

But we need so much more than that. We need a well-funded, accessible, high-quality mental health care system. We need that system to be subject to evaluations to ensure it can and does deliver on the things we need it to. We need that system to be able to address co-occurring substance use and dependence, as well as address other challenges that PWMI are known to face, including homelessness, poverty, unemployment, anosognosia, lack of social supports, physical health issues, prior justice system involvement, and the like. And doing everything we can, individually and collectively, to make this a reality is very important at this moment in time. One in five people diagnosed with COVID are subsequently diagnosed with depression or anxiety within three months of the virus diagnosis. So it could be the case that we will have more people with mental illness who run the risk of becoming justice involved *simply for lack of access to treatment and services*. And with the well documented increase in homicides in the US last year and this year and with the country so deeply divided, we are frankly worried that there is an opportunity for tough on crime rhetoric to come back around and once again drive approaches that serve to criminalize PWMI.

That doesn't have to be who we are, the society that simply swapped out the asylum for the prison and threw away the key, the one that made it far easier to get a gun than mental health care. We can be so, so much better than that, so much more humane, and decent, and inclusive, and we can purposefully mount an appeal to "the better angels of our nature." That takes people with vision and knowledge and insight, sure, but the most fundamental, most crucial criterion to participate in the effort to change things is caring about doing so. And if nothing else, we hope what you took away from this book is caring about the need for change.

July 2021

Appendix: Videos

60 Minutes — Journey Into Madness: Russell Weston Jr.
(*What happened to him? Where is he now?*)
https://www.youtube.com/watch?v=qBKiHuFUWZQ (**14:15**)

Anosognosia
https://www.youtube.com/watch?v=uj6ozlzA45o (**4:08**)

The Batman Shootings: James Holmes
(*What happened to him? Where is he now?*)
https://www.youtube.com/watch?v=UeQgz9uDhqY (**57:17**)
Madness at Midnight Aurora CNN (Suspect A)
https://www.youtube.com/watch?v=PJ7F9DvV3x0 (**41:40**)

Competency Hearing Videos:
https://www.youtube.com/watch?v=FwxwbkP-WK0 (**11:47**)
https://www.youtube.com/watch?v=0TPx2W5sD38 (**38:11**)
https://www.youtube.com/watch?v=BmrxHQyIYhY (**3:10**)
https://www.youtube.com/watch?v=HOKGS-XuFqk (**15:19**)
https://www.flmhlaw.com/mock-hearing-videos/ (Includes Sell or involuntary
    medication hearing and a post-restoration competency hearing) (**Various**)

Competency/Insanity: Scott Panetti
(*What happened to him? Where is he now?*)
https://www.youtube.com/watch?v=WAs0-TphqZc (**31:04**)

Crisis Intervention Team Training
https://cahss.d.umn.edu/articles/buffington-crisis-intervention-training (**5:11**)

Emptying the 'new asylums': A model for moving mentally ill inmates out of jail
https://www.youtube.com/watch?v=44SVEooUzOw (**149:09**)

Frontline — The New Asylums
https://www.pbs.org/wgbh/frontline/film/showsasylums/ (**54:32**)

Insanity Defense CourtTV Facebook
 https://www.facebook.com/courttv/videos/347507003318111/ (**19:13**)

Last Week Tonight with John Oliver
 Mental Health
 https://www.youtube.com/watch?v=NGY6DqB1HX8 (**11:54**)
 Prisoner Reentry
 https://www.youtube.com/watch?v=gJtYRxH5G2k (**18:44**)
 Police Accountability
 https://www.youtube.com/watch?v=zaD84DTGULo (**19:54**)
 Police
 https://www.youtube.com/watch?v=Wf4cea5oObY (**33:32**)
 Coronavirus VIII: Prisons and Jails
 https://www.youtube.com/watch?v=MuxnH0VAkAM (**18:32**)
 Prison Heat
 https://www.youtube.com/watch?v=6fiRDJLjL94 (**13:26**)

Minds on the Edge: Facing Mental Illness — A Fred Friendly Seminar
 https://www.youtube.com/watch?v=G6PpSmTlyRY (**56:27**)

NBC News: John Hinckley, Jr.
 (*What happened to him? Where is he now?*) (**Total 44:67**)
 https://www.nbcnews.com/dateline/video/full-episode-hinckley-diary-of-a-dangerous-mind-84086341880 (**6:20**)
 https://www.nbcnews.com/dateline/video/hinckley-diary-of-a-dangerous-mind-part-2-84086853838 (**4:51**)
 https://www.nbcnews.com/dateline/video/hinckley diary-of-a-dangerous-mind-part-3-84085829995 (**5:43**)
 https://www.nbcnews.com/dateline/video/hinckley-diary-of-a-dangerous-mind-part-4-84087877522 (**6:32**)
 https://www.nbcnews.com/dateline/video/hinckley-diary-of-a-dangerous-mind-part-5-84086341933 (**7:02**)
 https://www.nbcnews.com/dateline/video/hinckley-diary-of-a-dangerous-mind-part-6-84087365580 (**6:53**)
 https://www.nbcnews.com/dateline/video/hear-from-the-detective-who-initially-questioned-john-hinckley-jr-67490373662 (**2:19**)
 https://www.nbcnews.com/dateline/video/hinckley-s-descent-into-madness-67490885816 (**2:00**)
 https://www.nbcnews.com/dateline/video/ron-reagan-talks-about-the-day-his-father-was-shot-67467333581 (**2:32**)
 https://www.nbcnews.com/dateline/video/john-hinckley-jr-s-victims-67492421833 (**2:15**)

The State: 'This how you treat the mentally ill?' How Charleston failed Jamal Sutherland
   https://www.thestate.com/news/charleston/article252176538.html (**1:57**)

Terror on the Tracks — Murder and Insanity Defense: Andrew Goldstein
   (*What happened to him? Where is he now?*)
   https://www.youtube.com/watch?v=3sCDL2M56cw (**42:17**)

Treatment Advocacy Center Videos
   https://www.treatmentadvocacycenter.org/about-us/1747 (**Various**)

The Unabomber: Theodore "Ted" Kaczynski
   (*What happened to him? Where is he now?*)
   https://www.youtube.com/watch?v=d8BX_Nd4BPs (**51:15**)

Case Index

Name Index

Rasinski, K., 115
Rawls, J., 181, 187
Ray, B., 388, 389
Raybon, K., 391
Reagan, R., 17
Reddi, P., 243
Redding, F.P., 302
Redlich, A., 188, 391
Regan, P., 295
Regier, D.A., 126
Reichlin, S., 112
Reiger, D., 251
Reinhard, J.S., 184
Reinhart, M., 190
Remo, R., 461
Remster, B., 420
Rendo, J., 391
Reston-Parham, C., 349
Reuland, M., 234, 238, 241–243, 305
Rhoades, S., 365, 376
Rice, J., 298
Rich, W.J., 126, 422
Richard, E., 293
Richards, H., 393
Richards, J., 475
Ricketts, S.K., 55
Ridgely, M.S., 189, 190, 391
Ringel, N.B., 115
Rissmiller, D.J., 61, 126
Rissmiller, J.H., 61, 126
Ritter, C., 234, 242, 244
River, L.P., 115
Rivera, E., 161, 177
Rivera, R.M., 311, 391, 458
Rix, S., 115
Ro, M.J., 310
Robbins, L., 391
Robbins, P.C., 20, 61, 112, 127, 186, 188, 191–193, 312, 391
Roberts, A.R., 311
Roberts, D.L., 308
Robins, L., 251
Robst, J., 114, 303
Roche, B., 191

Rock, R.S., 55
Rodis, E., 313, 423
Roesch, R., 120, 309, 345
Rogers, E.S., 126
Rohland, B.M., 190
Romney, L., 190
Rosenberg, S.D., 117
Rosenberg, S., 117, 126
Rosenfield, S., 190
Rosenhan, D.L., 61
Rosenheck, R., 125, 128, 190
Rosenheck, R.A., 125, 128
Rosenheck, R.R., 125, 128, 190
Roskes, E., 126, 311, 459, 460
Ross, D., 385
Rossman, S.B., 391, 392
Roth, L.H., 185
Roth, L., 122, 185
Rothman, D.J., 20, 190
Rouner, D., 113
Rowan, D., 115
Rowland, L., 61
Rowlands, O.J., 115
Roy-Bujnowski, K.M., 305
Rubenstein, L., 17, 308
Ruiz, J., 242
Ruiz-Grossman, S., 207
Rundell, O.H., 58
Rusch, N., 115
Rush, A.J., 114
Rush, B., 29, 54, 55
Russell, S.A., 244
Russinova, Z., 126
Ryan, S., 459
Ryba, N.L., 267
Rybakova, T., 243

S
Sabbatini, R.M.E., 61
Sabol, W.J., 305, 311, 420, 455
Sack, K., 120
Sadowski, S.R., 117, 186
Saenz, T.J., 242
Saks, E.R., 190

Subject Index